Absorption in No External World
170 Issues in Mind-Only Buddhism

Absorption in No External World

170 Issues in Mind-Only Buddhism

Jeffrey Hopkins

Edited by Kevin Vose

Dynamic Responses to D̄zong-ka-b̄a's
The Essence of Eloquence: III

Snow Lion Publications
Ithaca, New York
Boulder, Colorado

Snow Lion Publications
P.O. Box 6483
Ithaca, NY 14851 USA
(607) 273-8519
www.snowlionpub.com

Printed in USA on acid-free recycled paper.

ISBN-10 1-55939-241-X
ISBN-13 978-1-55939-241-9

Library of Congress Cataloging-in-Publication Data

Hopkins, Jeffrey.
Absorption in no external world : 170 issues in mind-only Buddhism / Jeffrey Hopkins.
p. cm. -- (Dynamic responses to D̄zong-ka-b̄a's The essence of eloquence ; 3)
Includes bibliographical references and index.
ISBN-13: 978-1-55939-241-9 (alk. paper)
ISBN-10: 1-55939-241-X (alk. paper)
1. Tsoṅ-kha-pa Blo-bzaṅ-grags-pa, 1357-1419. Legs bśad sñiṅ po. 2. Dge-lugs-pa (Sect)--Doctrines. 3. Vijñaptimātratā. I. Title. II. Series: Hopkins, Jeffrey. Dynamic responses to D̄zong-ka-b̄a's The essence of eloquence ; 3.
BQ7950.T754L43347 2006
294.3'420423--dc22

2005024769

An Indian *śāstra* first of all frames a special terminology for the concepts with which it operates and establishes clear-cut definitions of these concepts. The Tibetans, being the pupils of Indian tradition, have carried this care of minutely precise definitions to an extreme, almost artistic perfection.

Th. Stcherbatsky, *Madhyānta-Vibhaṅga: Discourse on Discrimination between Middle and Extremes,* iv.

Contents

Detailed Outline

Preface

This book examines a plethora of fascinating points raised in six centuries of Tibetan and Mongolian commentary concerning the first two sections of Ḏzong-ka-ḇa's[a] *The Essence of Eloquence,*[b] the Prologue and the section on the Mind-Only School. In the process of examining 170 issues, this volume

- identifies the teachings in the first wheel of doctrine
- probes the meaning of "own-character" and "established by way of its own character"
- untangles the implications of Ḏzong-ka-ḇa's criticisms of the Korean scholar Wonch'uk
- treats many engaging points on the three natures and the three non-natures, including (1) how to apply these two grids to uncompounded space; (2) whether the selflessness of persons is a thoroughly established nature; (3) how to consider the emptiness of emptiness; and (4) the ways the Great Vehicle schools delineate the three natures and the three non-natures
- and presents the approaches through which the Mind-Only School interprets scriptures.

The aim is to bring to life scholastic controversies in order both to stimulate the metaphysical imagination and to show the non-monolithic plethora of inquiries by the followers of a seminal figure in the Tibetan cultural region.

My annotated translation of these sections in Ḏzong-ka-ḇa's text is to be found in the first volume of this series, *Emptiness in the Mind-Only School of Buddhism.*[1] It is in four parts:

- a historical and doctrinal introduction
- a translation of the General Explanation and the Section on the Mind-Only School in *The Essence of Eloquence* with frequent annotations in brackets, footnotes, and backnotes
- a detailed synopsis of the translation that re-renders the text, with additional information, in more free-flowing English
- a critical edition in Tibetan script of these sections in *The Essence of Eloquence.*

The second volume of this series, *Reflections on Reality: The Three Natures and Non-Natures in the Mind-Only School,* presents an introduction to and analysis of many facets of volume one. In six parts, it

- places reactions to Ḏzong-ka-ḇa's text in historical and social context by

[a] *tsong kha pa blo bzang grags pa,* 1357-1419.

[b] *drang ba dang nges pa'i don rnam par phye ba'i bstan bcos legs bshad snying po;* P6142, vol. 153.

examining the tension between allegiance and rational inquiry in monastic colleges and the inter-relationships between faith, reason, and mystical insight

- presents the religious significance of the central doctrine of the Mind-Only School, the three natures of phenomena
- examines in detail the exchange between the Bodhisattva Paramārthasamudgata and Buddha in the seventh chapter of the *Sūtra Unraveling the Thought* concerning the three wheels of doctrine and the three natures
- documents the markedly different view on the status of reality presented by the fourteenth-century scholar-yogi Shay-rap-gyel-tsen[a] of the Jo-nang-ba[b] order as well as criticisms by Dzong-ka-ba and his Ge-luk-ba[c] followers
- fleshes out Tibetan presentations of the provocative issue of the relationship between two types of emptiness in the Mind-Only School and how the topic of two emptinesses is debated today in America, Europe, and Japan, thereby demonstrating how the two forms of scholarship refine and enhance each other (these discussions continue in the three Appendices)
- demonstrates the types of reasonings establishing mind-only used as means to overcome a basic dread of reality.

Please see the prefaces in volumes one and two for expressions of gratitude to the many Tibetan and Mongolian scholars who have aided me on this project over the last twenty-one years.

Jeffrey Hopkins
Emeritus Professor of Tibetan Studies
University of Virginia

a *dol po pa shes rab rgyal mtshan,* 1292-1361.

b *jo nang pa.*

c *dge lugs pa.*

Technical Notes

It is important to recognize that:

- citations from volume one, *Emptiness in the Mind-Only School of Buddhism,* and volume two, *Reflections on Reality,* are indicated respectively by "*Emptiness in Mind-Only*" and "*Reflections on Reality*" along with a page reference; notes within those citations are not repeated in this volume;
- footnotes are marked "a, b, c"; backnotes are marked "1, 2, 3." References to texts are mostly given in the backnotes, whereas other information, more pertinent to the reading of the material at hand, is given in the footnotes. References to issues in the present volume, *Absorption in No External World,* are often by issue number;
- full bibliographical references are given in the footnotes and backnotes at the first citation in each chapter;
- translations and editions of texts are given in the Bibliography;
- citations of the *Sūtra Unraveling the Thought* include references to the edited Tibetan text and French translation of it in consultation with the Chinese by Étienne Lamotte in *Saṃdhinirmocanasūtra: L'explication des mystères* (Louvain: Université de Louvain, 1935) and to the English translation from the *stog* Palace edition of the Tibetan by C. John Powers, *Wisdom of Buddha: Saṁdhinirmocana Sūtra* (Berkeley, Calif.: Dharma, 1995). There is also a translation from the Chinese by Thomas Cleary in *Buddhist Yoga: A Comprehensive Course* (Boston: Shambhala, 1995), in which the references are easily found, as long as chapter 7 of Lamotte and Powers is equated with chapter 5 of Cleary as per the Chinese edition that he used (see *Emptiness in Mind-Only,* Appendix 2, p. 457ff.). Passages not cited in D̄zong-ka-b̄a's text are usually adaptations of Powers's translation as submitted for his doctoral dissertation under my guidance;
- I have translated the term *drang don* (*neyārtha*) sometimes as "interpretable meaning" and other times as "requiring interpretation," or a variant thereof. There is no significance to the multiple translations other than variety and clarity, the latter being to emphasize that the scripture requires interpretation;
- the names of Indian Buddhist schools of thought are translated into English in an effort to increase accessibility for non-specialists;
- for the names of Indian scholars and systems used in the body of the text, *ch, sh,* and *ṣh* are used instead of the more usual *c, ś,* and *ṣ* for the sake of easy pronunciation by non-specialists; however, *cch* is used for *cch,* not

chchh. In the notes the usual transliteration system for Sanskrit is used;

- transliteration of Tibetan is done in accordance with a system devised by Turrell Wylie; see "A Standard System of Tibetan Transcription," *Harvard Journal of Asiatic Studies,* 22 (1959): 261-267;

- the names of Tibetan authors and orders are given in "essay phonetics" for the sake of easy pronunciation; for a discussion of the system used, see the technical note at the beginning of my *Meditation on Emptiness* (London: Wisdom, 1983; rev. ed., Boston: Wisdom, 1996), 19-22. The system is used consistently, with the result that a few well-known names are rendered in a different way: for example, "Lhasa" is rendered as "Hla-sa," since the letter "h" is pronounced before the letter "l"; and

- an English-Tibetan-Sanskrit glossary is given at the end of this volume.

PART ONE:
BACKGROUND

1. Monastic Inquiry

The Essence of Eloquence[a] by the late-fourteenth- and early-fifteenth-century Tibetan scholar-yogi Ḏzong-ka-ḇa[b] is considered by his followers to be so challenging that it is called his steel bow and steel arrow[c] in that just as it is hard to pull a steel bow to its full extent but when one does, the arrow will course over a great area, so even the words of this text are difficult to understand but, when understood, yield great insight. The martial challenge conveyed by this metaphor was accepted by many brilliant Tibetan and Mongolian scholars over the last six centuries with the result that a plethora of issues in Ḏzong-ka-ḇa's text have received careful analysis, providing an avenue into patterns of thought that came to constitute the environment of the text over this long period of intense interest.

Ḏzong-ka-ḇa was a genius at creating consistency in systems of thought, but sometimes he provided only brief expositions and at other times only suggested his views. Scholars of the Ge-luk-ḇa[d] sect—like others following a founder's words—have been drawn into the complex problems of extending his thought into those areas that he did not clearly explicate and into re-thinking what was clear but did not manifest the presumed consistency. The working premise is that Ḏzong-ka-ḇa's *The Essence of Eloquence,* though carefully crafted, is subject to the highly creative strategy of "positing his thought"[e] as long as consonance with the corpus of his work is maintained. The attempt at resolving apparent contradictions itself fuels increasing interest in the topics, this being a central reason why the Ge-luk-ḇa system of education, centered around scholastic debate, has been so influential throughout Inner Asia.

Although the plethora of issues raised in *The Essence of Eloquence* is susceptible to being laid out in a linear run like a table of contents, the only way a reader can react to the multi-sided style of confronting these points is to be within the perspective of the system being considered. Juxtaposing different parts of a treatise and examining their cross-implications, Tibetan monastic textbooks manifest a basic procedure of bringing the whole treatise to bear on a single part, thereby coaxing the participant into developing the worldview of the system. In this way, the overriding context of exposition involves the ramifications of every part (or at least many parts) of a text; the only way for the reader to adjust to this environment is to form the worldview.

---

a *drang ba dang nges pa'i don rnam par phye ba'i bstan bcos legs bshad snying po;* Peking 6142, vol. 153.

b *tsong kha pa blo bzang grags pa,* 1357-1419.

c *lcags mda' lcags gzhu.*

d *dge lugs pa.*

e *dgongs pa bzhag pa.*

Because the exposition moves from issue to issue in a format of confrontational challenges that are episodic, it can at times seem even disjointed, but monastic students learn to live from within a system by being led—in twice-daily debates—to react inside its viewpoint to a plethora of problems. The center of the process, never communicable in words, is the wholeness of the worldview from within which the student learns to live. Like debaters in a monastic college, we also can experience this only by confronting issue after issue, major and minor, in lively embroilment and with hope that the larger perspective will dawn. With this in mind, I address 170 such focal issues in this book.

Techniques of Analysis

Tibetan and Mongolian commentators employ various strategies for getting at the meaning of a text by:

- dividing the text into sections
- providing a synopsis of the topics through an elaborate outline
- exploring the range of meanings of particular words
- placing an issue in a larger context
- extracting issues for extended analysis
- juxtaposing seemingly conflicting assertions
- finding internal and external evidence to resolve contradictions
- manipulating meanings so as to create coherence
- raising a parallel concern from another context
- exposing terminology hardened over centuries of use to analysis of historical development.

These modes of analysis, like those employed by scholars throughout the world, expose knotty problems and resolve seeming or actual contradictions.

Texts are not viewed in isolation as if they live outside of the situation of their culture; they are related to a body of literature and knowledge in such a way that the study of a text is a study of the world. Also, the context provided is not just that of the culture contemporary to or preceding Dzong-ka-ba's text; often, views of scholars subsequent to the text are similarly juxtaposed because the aim is to provide a worldview relevant to the reader's present situation, a comprehensive perspective that makes use of whatever is available. Beyond this, points peripheral to central topics often take center stage such that they provide a wide cultural context for more important issues—the context imbedding the reader in an all-encompassing worldview. These scholars, even when working on small issues, draw on a reserve of knowledge of larger issues, the basic principles of which are Dzong-ka-ba's. When they unravel his words, the exercise of exegesis imbeds the participants even more in the architecture of a living philosophy.

Issues are treated not just by citing Indian treatises; rather, the dynamics of the architecture of a system suggested by Indian texts takes over. The system is a living phenomenon only suggested by Indian texts. Speculation carrying out its implications is a primary technique. To avoid speculating on such issues merely because clarification is not available in Indian texts would miss the primary intention of these analytic traditions—to stimulate the metaphysical imagination. In the same vein, later terminology from India and Tibet is often used as a device to convey subtleties considered to be embedded in the *Sūtra Unraveling the Thought* and in Asaṅga's works.

Difficult issues are presented in a genre of literature used in monastic colleges called "general meaning,"[a] which are often supplemented with "decisive analyses."[b] These textbooks on seminal Indian or Tibetan texts, such as Ḏzong-ka-ḇa's *The Essence of Eloquence,* stimulate the intellect through juxtaposing assertions that are, or appear to be, contradictory and through making often highly elaborate and esthetically attractive reformulations of assertions in order to reveal, or create, coherence. These textbooks are authored by prominent figures in the monastic colleges, who become so focal that the local leader, modeled on the paradigm of the grand over-all leader—whether Buddha or Ḏzong-ka-ḇa—often comes to assume more importance.

Disagreement with statements by the founder of the sect is promoted within the bounds of not openly criticizing his works but doing so under various polite facades, such as positing the meaning of his thought, that is, creatively adjusting Ḏzong-ka-ḇa's statements so that they do not contradict each other. Through such maneuvers, much room is made for discriminative expansion that is critical but does not assume the outward form of fault-finding. Exegetes, upon exposing seeming discrepancies, seek to explain them away through refinement, creatively adjusting his thought, pretending that his words make perfect sense, even making such bold and creative defenses of the founder that their own ingenuity becomes the focus. Once we recognize the format of exposition as often a mask required in a culture of allegiance to exalted personages, we see that often these scholars really do not think that Ḏzong-ka-ḇa meant what they claim; critical acumen is indeed highly encouraged. If it is not noticed that these scholars are operating within only a facade of non-criticism, their "refinements" often appear to be inexplicably and even ridiculously at odds with what Ḏzong-ka-ḇa said.

What on the surface appears to be apologetic is actually critical analysis—explanation becoming a re-casting of the founder's position. The process causes Ḏzong-ka-ḇa's followers to step into his shoes by using his principles of organization to extend his thought further, such that they come to know his pivotal concepts in an active and creative way, rather than just repeating what he said. Since the principles of his system are put to active use, these come to life in a way otherwise impossible. Examination of problems in debate and in literary

[a] *spyi don.*

[b] *mtha' dpyod.*

composition becomes a method of profound internalization.

For this reason, throughout this book I identify these maneuvers in order to reveal the drama. Otherwise, the tension and conflict of such dramatic re-writing in the guise of explaining the founder's words when they obviously do not say such is dumbfounding—as long as one thinks that all they intend to do is to clarify what is already basically coherent. Sometimes, slippery distinctions are the means by which the exegetical project adapts itself to the seeming rigidity of insistence on consistency, and at other times a perplexing peripheral issue is left with a call for more analysis.

Monastic authors even apply a principle enunciated in their system against another point in their own system. This unabashed honesty raises the level of inquiry far beyond mere explication. Regardless of the format of explaining away, or even covering up, earlier masters' inconsistencies, scholars uncover the flimsiness of the favored position. Such admissions of the tenuousness of their own positions reveal how these scholars use rational inquiry to indicate weaknesses in their own systems despite their allegiance to founding figures.

The sheer variety of invitingly provocative explanations of a single issue sometimes make it seem that a conclusion cannot be reached, enmeshing the reader in a web of intriguing and even bewildering issues of fundamental importance. These scholars' attempts to correct these problems sometimes embroil them in almost unimaginable complexities, the issue becoming so complex that the mind is fractured into unusable bits of information. It is possible to miss the woods for the trees, but when one steps back and surveys the wider scene, basic and undisputed principles of D̄zong-ka-b̄a's outlook emerge with considerable clarity. The style of monastic textbooks—which calls for embroilment in crucial as well as ancillary issues—causes central issues to become the floor of inquiry without our noticing it, resulting in the transformation of it into a topic of vibrant concern in the vast context of a worldview.

I also have become embroiled in a maze of doctrinal considerations, attempting to construct harmony between sūtra sources (here specifically the *Sūtra Unraveling the Thought*), Indian schools, and Tibetans exegesis. Led more deeply into basic issues, I, like Tibetan and Mongolian scholars, have been drawn into a process that begins like being teased by a riddle, then probing a mystery, then finding myself in a maze, and finally the walls of the maze occasionally becoming transparent when the scope of the problem comes into view. Thus, here and there in this book I occasionally present my own "solutions" to conundrums by positing D̄zong-ka-b̄a's thought; still, I cannot claim that my reframing (sometimes offered with a mask of bravado) provides the esthetic delight that even well-crafted apologetic can generate if it has elegant simplicity. Admittedly, sometimes my gambits end up serving merely as means to expose more problems.

The Characters of the Drama

In this book I cite opinions from twenty-two of the twenty-six commentaries on D̄zong-ka-b̄a's *The Essence of Eloquence* that I have located. Preceded by a general category, these are listed below chronologically within their college affiliation—the author's name as cited in the notes, the full name (if different), dates, the title as it is cited in the notes, and the full title (for the Tibetan and other information, see the bibliography).

General

Ke-drup (Ke-drup-ge-lek-b̄el-sang, 1385-1438)

Opening the Eyes of the Fortunate / Opening the Eyes of the Fortunate: Treatise Brilliantly Clarifying the Profound Emptiness

Second Dalai Lama (Gen-dün-gya-tso, 1476-1542)

Lamp Illuminating the Meaning / Commentary on the Difficult Points of "Differentiating the Interpretable and the Definitive" from the Collected Works of the Foremost Holy Omniscient [D̄zong-ka-b̄a]: Lamp Thoroughly Illuminating the Meaning of His Thought

S̄e-ra Jay College

B̄el-jor-hlün-drup (1427-1514)

Lamp for the Teaching / Commentary on the Difficult Points of (D̄zong-ka-b̄a's) "The Essence of Eloquence": Lamp for the Teaching

Jay-d̄zün Chö-ḡyi-gyel-tsen (1469-1546)

General-Meaning Commentary / General Meaning of (D̄zong-ka-b̄a's) "Differentiating the Interpretable and the Definitive": Eradicating Bad Disputation: A Precious Garland

D̄ra-d̄i Ge-s̄hay Rin-chen-dön-drup (fl. mid-seventeenth century)

Ornament for the Thought / Ornament for the Thought of (D̄zong-ka-b̄a's) "Interpretable and Definitive: The Essence of Eloquence"

Tsay-d̄en-hla-ram-b̄a[a]

[a] I have drawn his views from citations by Dön-drup-gyel-tsen, A-ku L̄o-drö-gya-tso, S̄er-s̄hül L̄o-sang-pün-tsok, and Jik-may-dam-chö-gya-tso. Ge-s̄hay Ye-s̄hay-tap-kay (*shar tsong kha pa blo bzang grags pas mdzad pa'i drang ba dang nges pa'i don rnam par phye ba'i bstan bcos legs bshad snying po,* Tā la'i bla ma'i 'phags bod, vol. 22 [Varanasi, India: vāṇa dbus bod kyi ches mtho'i gtsug lag slob gnyer khang, 1997], 327-332), in a list of fifty-eight commentaries on D̄zong-ka-b̄a's *The Essence of Eloquence,* reports (331) that three of his works are listed under the title of *dri lan blo gsal mgul rgyan* by *tshe brtan lha rams pa* in *bod kyi bstan bcos khag gcig gi mtshan byang dri med shel dkar 'phreng ba* (mtsho sngon dpe skrun khang, 1985), 614. The three are:

- *rgyal ba dge 'dun rgya mtsho dang 'jam dbyangs dga' blo 'jam dbyangs chos bshes sogs kyi drang nges gsung rgyun dri med lung rigs gter mdzod*
- *drang nges legs bshad snying po'i spyi don legs pa drang nges rnam 'byed kyi dga' gnad cung zad btus pa*

Ṣer-ṣhül (Ṣer-ṣhül Ge-ṣhay Ḻo-sang-pün-tsok, fl. in early twentieth century)
Notes / Notes on (Ḏzong-ka-b̄a's) "Differentiating the Interpretable and the Definitive": Lamp Illuminating the Profound Meaning
Ḻo-sang-w̄ang-chuk (1901-1979)
Notes / Notes on (Ḏzong-ka-b̄a's) "Interpretable and Definitive, The Essence of Eloquence": Lamp for the Intelligent
Ḏa-drin-rap-d̄en (1920-1986)
Annotations / Annotations for the Difficult Points of (Ḏzong-ka-b̄a's) "The Essence of Eloquence": Festival for the Unbiased Endowed with Clear Intelligence

Ḻo-ṣel-ḻing and Ṣhar-d̄zay Colleges
Paṇ-chen Ṣö-nam-drak-b̄a (1478-1554)
Garland of Blue Lotuses / Distinguishing through Objections and Answers (Ḏzong-ka-b̄a's) "Differentiating the Interpretable and Definitive Meanings of All the Scriptures, The Essence of Eloquence": Garland of Blue Lotuses

Go-mang and Ḏra-ṣhi-kyil Colleges
Gung-ru Chö-jung (Gung-ru Chö-ḡyi-jung-ñay, fl. most likely in the sixteenth century)
Garland of White Lotuses / Decisive Analysis of (Ḏzong-ka-b̄a's) "Differentiating the Interpretable and the Definitive, The Essence of Eloquence": Garland of White Lotuses
Jam-ȳang-shay-b̄a (Jam-ȳang-shay-b̄a Nga-w̄ang-d̄zön-drü, 1648-1722)
Great Exposition of the Interpretable and the Definitive / Decisive Analysis of (Ḏzong-ka-b̄a's) "Differentiating the Interpretable and the Definitive": Storehouse of White Lapis-Lazuli of Scripture and Reasoning Free from Error: Fulfilling the Hopes of the Fortunate
Brief Decisive Analysis of (Ḏzong-ka-b̄a's) "Differentiating the Interpretable and the Definitive"
Notes on (Ḏzong-ka-b̄a's) "Differentiating the Interpretable and the Definitive"
Gung-tang (Gung-tang Ḡön-chok-d̄en-b̄ay-drön-may, 1762-1823)
Annotations / Beginnings of Annotations on (Ḏzong-ka-b̄a's) "The Essence of Eloquence" on the Topic of Mind-Only: Illumination of a Hundred Mind-Only Texts
Difficult Points / Beginnings of a Commentary on the Difficult Points of (Ḏzong-ka-b̄a's) "Differentiating the Interpretable and the Definitive": Quintessence of "The Essence of Eloquence"
Dön-drup-gyel-tsen (fl. late eighteenth and early nineteenth century)

·   legs bshad snying po'i mtha' dpyod mkhas pa'i dbang po 'jam dbyangs chos dpal kyi gsung rgyun.

Four Intertwined Commentaries / Extensive Explanation of (Ḏzong-ka-ḇa's) "Treatise Differentiating the Interpretable and the Definitive, The Essence of Eloquence," Unique to Ge-luk-ḇa: Four Intertwined Commentaries

W̄el-mang Ḡön-chok-gyel-tsen (1764-1853)

Notes on (Ḡön-chok-jik-may-w̄ang-ḇo's) Lectures / Notes on (Ḡön-chok-jik-may-w̄ang-ḇo's) Lectures on (Ḏzong-ka-ḇa's) "The Essence of Eloquence": Stream of the Speech of the Omniscient: Offering for Purification

A-ku Ḻo-drö-gya-tso (Gung-tang Ḻo-drö-gya-tso, 1851-1930)

Precious Lamp / Commentary on the Difficult Points of (Ḏzong-ka-ḇa's) "Treatise Differentiating Interpretable and the Definitive Meanings, The Essence of Eloquence": A Precious Lamp

Pa-bong-ka-ḇa Jam-ḇa-ḏen-dzin-trin-lay-gya-tso[a] (1878-1941)

Brief Notes on Jo-ni Paṇḍita's Lectures / Presentation of the Interpretable and the Definitive, Brief Notes on the Occasion of Receiving Profound [Instruction from Jo-ne Paṇḍita Ḻo-sang-gya-tso in 1927] on (Ḏzong-ka-ḇa's) "The Essence of Eloquence"

Jik-may-dam-chö-gya-tso (1898-1946)

Port of Entry / Treatise Distinguishing All the Meanings of (Ḏzong-ka-ḇa's) "The Essence of Eloquence," Illuminating the Differentiation of the Interpretable and the Definitive: Port of Entry to "The Essence of Eloquence"

S̄e-ra M̄ay College

Ḻo-sang-trin-lay-ye-s̄hay[b]

Summarized Meaning / Summarized Meaning of (Ḏzong-ka-ḇa's) "Differentiation of the Interpretable and the Definitive: The Essence of Eloquence": Ornament for the Necks of Youths with Clear Intelligence

---

[a] Pa-bong-ka himself was affiliated with S̄e-ra Monastic University; Jo-ni Paṇḍita, however, was a follower of Jam-ȳang-shay-ḇa.

[b] His dates are perhaps 1642-1708.

2. The Essence Is Emptiness

Our journey into the metaphysically imaginative realm of the intricate analysis of issues found in Tibetan monastic colleges begins with the title of Ḏzong-ka-ḇa's work *Treatise Differentiating the Interpretable and the Definitive: The Essence of Eloquence* and proceeds through his text issue by issue.

The Title: *The Essence of Eloquence*

Issue #1: What is "eloquence"? What is "the essence"?

One of the more recent commentaries, that by Gung-tang Ḡön-chok-ḏen-ḇay-drön-may,[2] a late eighteenth- and early nineteenth-century scholar of Mongolian descent whose works figure prominently in the syllabus at the Go-mang College of Dre-ḇung Monastic University on the outskirts of Hla-s̄a, at Ḏra-s̄hi-kyil Monastic University and Ḡum-bum Monastic University in Am-do Province, and at many related monasteries, offers a particularly thorough explanation of the title of Ḏzong-ka-ḇa's text. Gung-tang's analysis is valuable since Ḏzong-ka-ḇa does not offer a direct explanation of his title—*Treatise Differentiating Interpretable and Definitive Meanings: The Essence of Eloquence.*

First, Gung-tang[3] points out that in another of Ḏzong-ka-ḇa's texts, *Praise of the Supramundane Victor Buddha from the Approach of His Teaching the Profound Dependent-Arising* which is also titled *The Essence of Eloquence* (sometimes referred to as "*The Lesser Essence of Eloquence*"),[4] Ḏzong-ka-ḇa explicitly speaks of emptiness as the essence of Buddha's teaching. There,[5] he says:

> You [Buddha], the bringer of help, set forth
> The mode of dependent-arising—
> The unparalleled reason for ascertaining **emptiness,**
> **The essence of the teaching**[a]—
>
> As medicine for transmigrating beings.
> How could those who [wrongly] perceive
> That it [proves] the opposite or is non-established
> Understand your system [of the compatibility of emptiness and dependent-arising]![b]

---

[a] *bstan pa'i snying po stong pa nyid.*

[b] Ḏzong-ka-ḇa is explaining that those non-Buddhists who view dependent-arising as not being "established," that is, as not being valid, and those Buddhists who hold that dependent-arising proves, not that phenomena are empty of inherent existence, but the opposite—that phenomena **are** inherently existent—could not possibly understand Buddha's own system, in which dependent-arising itself is the supreme of reasons for proving the emptiness of inherent existence. Ḏra-ḏi Ge-s̄hay Rin-chen-dön-drup (*Ornament for the Thought,* 1.9) cites

Since Buddha's teachings are traditionally called "eloquence,"[a] Gung-tang cogently maintains that since Dzong-ka-ba explicitly identifies the essence of Buddha's teaching as emptiness in this short text also titled *The Essence of Eloquence,* the word "essence" in the title of the long work we are considering—*Treatise Differentiating Interpretable and Definitive Meanings: The Essence of Eloquence*—also must refer to emptiness.[b]

Still, this is evidence external to the text under consideration, and since internal evidence would clinch the point, Gung-tang cites the fact that near the beginning of the longer *The Essence of Eloquence,* when Dzong-ka-ba exhorts his audience to pay attention to his text, he (*Emptiness in Mind-Only,* 68) says:

> Listen intently, O you who wish to be unmatched proponents [of doctrine]
> With discriminating analysis realizing the **suchness of the teaching**.

Dzong-ka-ba himself identifies his subject matter as the "suchness of the teaching," that is to say, emptiness, which is called "suchness" because it remains such, whether it is taught or not or whether it is realized or not. The fact that he himself identifies the subject matter as the suchness of the teaching suggests that "eloquence" in the title refers to Buddha's teachings and that their "essence" is emptiness.

The operative principle is that the title of Dzong-ka-ba's work is based on its subject matter. Jo-ni Paṇḍita[6] speaks of three avenues through which titles are designated: by way of subject matter,[c] the name of the trainee,[d] and the number of chapters.[e] Jo-ni Paṇḍita, agreeing with Gung-tang (though not citing him), says that the title of Dzong-ka-ba's text was given by way of its subject matter, and hence a rough sense of the content can be gained from the title.

Issue #2: Is emptiness the essence of both Sūtra and Mantra?

Since Buddha's teachings are divided into Sūtra and Mantra (also called Tantra), Gung-tang explores whether Dzong-ka-ba intends to include both divisions of Buddha's word when he says that emptiness is the essence of Buddha's teachings. Gung-tang points to the fact that Dzong-ka-ba says at the end of this work:[7]

---

the same passage, thereby indicating that he takes the title the same way as Gung-tang.

[a] *legs bshad, subhāṣita;* literally, "the well-explained."

[b] A somewhat similar explanation is found in Pa-bong-ka-ba's *Brief Notes on Jo-ni Paṇḍita's Lectures* (403.2) where it is said that the essence is the correct view of emptiness, "The meaning of 'the essence' here in the actual [text] is the correct view; moreover, this is described as the essence of eloquence of Sūtra and of Mantra."

[c] *brjod bya.*

[d] *gdul bya.*

[e] *le'u gzhung tshad.*

> You should recognize these modes [of differentiating the interpretable and the definitive] as paths for delineating the suchness of **all of [Buddha's] scriptures, Sūtra and Mantra.**

From this, Gung-tang draws the conclusion that "eloquence" refers to all of Buddha's teachings,[a] and not just the Sūtra teachings.

Based on this identification, Gung-tang cogently explains that for Ḏzong-ka-ḇa both the lesser and greater texts titled *The Essence of Eloquence* settle the suchness of all of Buddha's teachings, both Sūtra and Mantra, even though these two texts do not delineate topics distinctive to Mantra, such as deity yoga, or topics distinctive to Highest Yoga Mantra, such as the structures of channels, winds, and drops of essential fluids. This is because these two texts nevertheless serve to settle the final suchness, emptiness, as presented even in the Mantra Vehicle through delineating the emptiness that is the object realized by the exalted wisdom of clear light, the essence of the Mantra path. For as Gung-tang says, in the Mantra path, in order to abandon the obstructions to liberation from cyclic existence and the obstructions to omniscience it is necessary, as a direct antidote to them, to meditate within taking emptiness—in just the same way as it is explained in the Sūtra system—as the object of one's mode of apprehension even if, in terms of appearance, a deity is appearing. Without such meditation on emptiness, even though one might pretend to be cultivating a high Mantra path, it cannot serve as a path of liberation even from cyclic existence, never mind as a path for attaining the great liberation of Buddhahood. Hence, by explaining emptiness, the two texts titled *The Essence of Eloquence* serve to delineate the final suchness of **both** Great Vehicles—the Sūtra and Mantra forms of the Great Vehicle.

Gung-tang adds that nevertheless the explanation of the view of emptiness is more developed in the Great Vehicle Sūtra system, and thus it is easier to realize emptiness through the descriptions found in it than through those in the Mantra Vehicle alone. At the end of his greater *The Essence of Eloquence* Ḏzong-ka-ḇa—speaking about the two modes of the sūtra system called "chariot-ways" established by the pivotal Indian scholars Nāgārjuna and Asaṅga—says:[8]

> These two chariot-ways—in which suchness is delineated by differentiating the interpretable and the definitive in [Buddha's] scriptures through the ways described earlier—are extensive in the context of the Perfection Vehicle. However, the scholars who made commentaries on the texts of Secret Mantra and those persons who attained [tantric] adepthood do not have a third way of delineating the meaning of suchness other than in accordance with either of those two. Hence, you should recognize that these modes [of differentiating the interpretable and the definitive] are paths for delineating suchness for **all of [Buddha's] scriptures, Sūtra and Mantra**. Consequently, the pursuit

[a] *bstan pa mtha' dag;* Gung-tang's *Difficult Points,* 20.14.

> of suchness without relying on the great chariot-ways of these two modes [of differentiating the interpretable and the definitive by Nāgārjuna and Asaṅga] is like a guideless blind person's rushing in a direction of fright.

It can be understood from this statement by the author himself that the title, *The Essence of Eloquence,* indicates that the text presents emptiness (the essence) of all of Buddha's teachings (called "eloquence") in both Sūtra and Mantra. In this vein, A-ku L̄o-drö-gya-tso,[9] a late nineteenth- and early twentieth-century clarifier of Gung-tang's commentary, speaks of *The Essence of Eloquence* as "a treatise clearly teaching suchness, the essence of the Sūtra and Mantra teachings."

Issue #3: What else could the title mean?

That is Gung-tang's and A-ku L̄o-drö-gya-tso's cogent explanation of D̄zong-ka-b̄a's title. Many other scholars do not address the topic directly, but the textbook by Jam-ȳang-shay-b̄a, which both Gung-tang and A-ku L̄o-drö-gya-tso are ostensibly following, indirectly offers another possibility.

Jam-ȳang-shay-b̄a's text, the brief title of which is *Great Exposition of the Interpretable and the Definitive,*[10] was adopted as a textbook in the Go-mang College of Dre-b̄ung Monastic University, after Jam-ȳang-shay-b̄a's tenure for nine years as abbot of Go-mang and his return to the northeastern province of Tibet, Am-do (put in Gansu Province by the Chinese communist government). There, at L̄a-brang, he founded what is now the largest monastic university in Tibet, called D̄ra-s̄hi-kyil, which also uses Jam-ȳang-shay-b̄a's textbooks.[a]

At the beginning of his commentary, Jam-ȳang-shay-b̄a suggests that the **differentiation** of what requires interpretation and what is definitive among

---

[a] The latest (the sixth) incarnation of Jam-ȳang-shay-b̄a, having been jailed during the Cultural Revolution and freed due to his tutor's assumption of all guilt for his activities by claiming that the current Jam-ȳang-shay-b̄a was then too young to have done anything bad, is an important influence at D̄ra-s̄hi-kyil through serving as liaison with the government, even though he no longer is a monk, having married a Chinese. His tutor was killed in prison.

Gung-tang was a prominent student of Jam-ȳang-shay-b̄a's reincarnation, Ḡön-chok-jik-may-w̄ang-b̄o (*dkon mchog 'jigs med dbang po,* 1728-1791); Gung-tang's line of reincarnations—himself the third incarnation of a Throne-Holder of Gan-den, the head of the Ge-luk-b̄a order*—was recognized as one of the three most important at D̄ra-s̄hi-kyil. The seventh incarnation of Gung-tang, though jailed during the Cultural Revolution, was freed and, remaining a monk, was an important figure in the same monastic university, passing away in 2000.

* E. Gene Smith, *Tibetan Catalogue,* vol. 1, 82, and oral communication from Geshe Thupten Gyatso. According to the latter, Gung-tang is the third in the series (*sku 'phreng gsum pa*), the first being the Throne Holder of Gan-den himself. Gene Smith suggests that he may be the second.

Buddha's scriptures is the essence to which Dzong-ka-ba's title refers. Speaking about that text, he says:[11]

> By way of [treating] difficult points, I will explain this great treatise bestowing—on those endowed with intelligence—independent analytical understanding concerning the meaning of the thought of all [of the Buddha's] scriptures through differentiating which require interpretation and which are definitive among all of the Conqueror's scriptures, [this being] the essence of all eloquence.

It is clear that Jam-ȳang-shay-ba, like his followers Gung-tang and A-ku Lo-drö-gya-tso, identifies "eloquence" as all of Buddha's scriptures, but he seems to be saying that the essence of those teachings is the **differentiation** of what requires interpretation and what is definitive, not emptiness itself.

In a similar vein, regarding the "topic" that Dzong-ka-ba says in his promise of composition he has understood but others have not, Jay-dzün Chö-ḡyi-gyel-tsen[12] identifies it as "the features of the various modes—of differentiating the interpretable and the definitive with respect to the three wheels [of doctrine]—in the systems of the two great chariots," that is, in the Mind-Only School and the Middle Way School founded by Asaṅga and Nāgārjuna respectively. Thus, for Jay-dzün Chö-ḡyi-gyel-tsen, the many features of the **differentiation** of the interpretable and the definitive according to these systems, rather than emptiness itself, is the topic that Dzong-ka-ba realized.

It therefore seems that for him also this is the "essence" of all of Shākya-muni Buddha's teachings, rather than emptiness itself. Despite the seeming difference, I imagine that Jam-ȳang-shay-ba's commentators, Gung-tang and A-ku Lo-drö-gya-tso, could reasonably hold that there is no conflict, since the very meaning of differentiating the interpretable and the definitive is to determine what from among Buddha's teachings present actual reality and what are taught merely for a temporary purpose—the actual reality being emptiness.

Another possibility, not mentioned by these scholars, is that the title refers to the eloquence of Dzong-ka-ba's own text through identifying it as having an essence of eloquence, in which case the title could be translated as *Essence of Eloquence* (meaning "that which has an essence of eloquence") rather than *The Essence of Eloquence*. Indeed, that is the meaning that this frequently used title has in most cases, the convention being to laud one's own work in its title, much as is done on book jackets in the United States. Still, this is not the reading of Dzong-ka-ba's title by any of the commentators who address the issue either directly—Gung-tang, A-ku Lo-drö-gya-tso, Dra-di Ge-shay Rin-chen-dön-drup, and Jo-ni Paṇḍita—or indirectly—such as Jay-dzün Chö-ḡyi-gyel-tsen and Jam-ȳang-shay-ba. Therefore, I have been careful to avoid referring to the book merely as *Essence of Eloquence* and, instead, use *The Essence of Eloquence*.

Promise of Composition and Exhortation to Listen

D̄zong-ka-b̄a (*Emptiness in Mind-Only,* 68) says:

> Many who had much hearing of the great texts,
> Who worked with much weariness also at the path of reasoning,
> And who were not low in accumulation of the good qualities of clear realization
> Worked hard at but did not realize this topic which,
>
> Having perceived it well through the kindness of the smooth protector and guru [Mañjushrī],
> I will explain with an attitude of great mercy.
> Listen intently, O you who wish to be unmatched proponents [of doctrine]
> With discriminating analysis realizing the suchness of the teaching.

Issue #4: Who are those the author indicates he surpassed?

Gung-tang reports that some commentators identify individually the referents of various persons whom D̄zong-ka-b̄a mentions in those two stanzas:

1. Those "who had much hearing of the great texts" are the Translator N̄gok L̄o-den-s̄hay-rap,[a] S̄a-ḡya Paṇḍita Ḡün-ga-gyel-tsen,[b] the great S̄a-ḡya scholar Bu-d̄ön Rin-chen-drup,[c] and so forth
2. Those "who worked with much weariness also at the path of reasoning" are Cha-b̄a Chö-ḡyi-s̄eng-gay[d] and his eight students with the name S̄eng-gay[e]
3. "Those who were not low in accumulation of the good qualities of clear realization" are the Omniscient Döl-b̄o-b̄a S̄hay-rap-gyel-tsen[f] (the chief

---

a *rngog lo tsa ba blo ldan shes rab,* 1059-1109.

b *sa skya paṇḍita kun dga' rgyal mtshan,* 1182-1251.

c *bu ston rin chen grub,* 1290-1364.

d *phya pa chos kyi seng ge,* 1109-1169.

e The eight are:
gtsang nag pa brtson 'grus seng ge (d.1171)
dan bag pa smra ba'i seng ge
bru sha bsod nams seng ge
rma bya rtsod pa'i seng ge (aka *rma bya byang chub brtson 'grus*)
rtsags/brtsegs dbang phyug seng ge (who taught S̄a-ḡya Paṇḍita)
myang bran chos kyi seng ge
ldan ma dkon mchog seng ge
gnyal pa yon tan seng ge.

The list is from George N. Roerich, *The Blue Annals* (Delhi: Motilal Banarsidass, 1949), 333.

f *dol po pa* (or *dol bu ba*) *shes rab rgyal mtshan,* 1292-1361.

promulgator of the Jo-nang-b̄a order), and so forth.

D̄zong-ka-b̄a's main S̄a-ḡya teacher, Ren-da-wa Shön-nu-l̄o-drö, is not mentioned by name, despite the fact that D̄zong-ka-b̄a's commentary on Chandrakīrti's *Supplement to (Nāgārjuna's) "Treatise on the Middle,"* for instance, contradicts a host of Ren-da-wa's opinions in his commentary on the same text.

Whether or not these are D̄zong-ka-b̄a's particular referents, he is indicating that he realized a profound topic that his predecessors had not, thereby making the type of claim to new understanding that can serve to form a new sect.[a] Also, his obeisance in *The Essence of Eloquence* to eleven Indian masters and lack of obeisance to Tibetan teachers suggest that he views his lineage as, in a sense, in a "direct" line from India, by-passing earlier Tibetans, even though he occasionally does refer to his teachers and so forth in other texts.

Gung-tang accepts these identifications but avers that the three clauses also may be taken more fittingly and with more import as applying to all of those scholars in general.[13] Taken that way, the above lines indicate:[14]

> Those excellent beings each possessed many qualities of clear realization of the vast path of compassionate activities; they each engaged in vast hearing of and thinking on the great texts of Sūtra and Mantra in addition to having highly developed intelligence attained from birth [due to high development in past lives]. In particular, each of them, wishing to investigate the essential points of the view of emptiness, worked hard at the path of reasoning without any sense of fatigue. However, they were not able to realize the meaning of suchness, which D̄zong-ka-b̄a, upon engaging in purification of obstructions and accumulation of merit through very strenuous asceticism and upon analyzing the meaning of the texts, found through the kindness of the Protector Mañjushrī's taking care of him as his student.

According to Gung-tang, these points indicate that D̄zong-ka-b̄a possessed all the prerequisites for composing this treatise, *The Essence of Eloquence*, by:

- having the quintessential instructions of earlier masters in that he not only was in an uninterrupted lineage from Buddha through many excellent beings but also was under the tutelage of the deity Mañjushrī

[a] Döl-b̄o-b̄a S̄hay-rap-gyel-tsen similarly expounded a long list of topics that others in Tibet had not realized; see Cyrus R. Stearns, *The Buddha from Dol po: A Study of the Life and Thought of the Tibetan Master Dolpopa Sherab Gyaltsen* (Albany, N.Y.: State University of New York Press, 1999), 33, n. 75. D̄ak-tsang S̄hay-rap-rin-chen reacted to D̄zong-ka-b̄a's claim as being hateful; see Jeffrey Hopkins, *Maps of the Profound: Jam-yang-shay-ba's Great Exposition of Buddhist and Non-Buddhist Views on the Nature of Reality* (Ithaca, N.Y.: Snow Lion Publications, 2003), 546.

- and having inner wisdom realizing their meaning, since he had the fully developed wisdom realizing without error the thought of the scriptures.

Ḏzong-ka-ḇa's reference to the "kindness" of Mañjushrī implicitly indicates that he did not have the capacity alone to realize such and thus is an assumption of humility. His compassionate attitude (indicated by "I will explain with an attitude of great mercy") and the importance of composing the treatise (since there is nothing exceeding this technique for leading trainees to the definite goodness[a] of liberation) also establish the suitability of composing the text.

It might seem out of place for Gung-tang to repeat an identification of those to whom Ḏzong-ka-ḇa is referring since, as Gung-tang himself says,[15] Ḏzong-ka-ḇa often does not mention by name those whom he refutes out of a wish that their teachings about the vast paths of compassionate activities not fade. Identification of those scholars by his followers would seem to defeat his purpose, as perhaps does my repeating them here. Ḏzong-ka-ḇa's followers are interested, however, in finding the meaning of his text, and to do so, it is necessary to establish its historical context—the opinions he is criticizing. Also, the identification of these scholars who, from his viewpoint, did not realize (or at least explicate) properly the view of emptiness also serves sectarian goals of solidifying the difference, the uniqueness, of one's own sect. (My own purpose is different. I consider that it is important to stress Ḏzong-ka-ḇa's claims to exclusivity not only to report the tradition accurately but also to call attention to Ge-luk-ḇas' oft-repeated claim that in their estimation Ḏzong-ka-ḇa's presentation of the view of emptiness is both different and superior. Though the claim **may** find its sole source in a sociological need for distinction from other sects, its philosophical meaning and practical import for the path of liberation and attainment of omniscience should be analyzed closely. I hope that just because I call attention to these claims, no one will assume that I necessarily support them, or that somehow I am perversely seeking to further disharmony among Tibetan sects and their followers; rather, I am seeking to stress Ḏzong-ka-ḇa's own perception that he had found something that others did not. The claim needs to be taken seriously, as well as suspiciously.)

Issue #5: Why exhort the audience to listen?

As Gung-tang says,[16] Ḏzong-ka-ḇa exhorts his audience initially to **listen** to the text with a pure attitude and pure behavior since:

- with regard to the achievement of highest enlightenment in dependence on either Sūtra or Mantra, the essence of Buddha's teachings is none other than the meaning of suchness, emptiness

[a] *nges par legs pa, naiḥśreyasa.* For a discussion of my choice of translation for this term, see Jeffrey Hopkins, *Buddhist Advice for Living and Liberation: Nāgārjuna's Precious Garland* (Ithaca, New York: Snow Lion, 1998), 46.

- and suchness is to be delineated through a serial process of hearing, thinking, and meditating.

He calls on those who aspire to the enlightenment of Buddhahood—in which one can teach others the path in an unparalleled way—to pay attention.

Jay-d̄zün Chö-ḡyi-gyel-tsen,[a] the author of the textbook literature of the Jay College of S̄e-ra Monastic University, says that it is fitting—for those who wish to realize without error the suchness of the teaching and who wish, through their own discriminating realization, to become unmatched propounders of doctrine for other trainees—to listen to D̄zong-ka-b̄a's text, since the transformation into an unmatched propounder of doctrine, a Buddha, can be accomplished only through realization in accordance with what is explained in *The Essence of Eloquence.* He is claiming not that this particular text must be read and understood but that realization that accords with it must be gained. Indeed, Ge-luk-b̄a scholars hold that in Tibet only the texts of D̄zong-ka-b̄a and some of his followers describe reality properly.

Appealing to his listeners' altruistic wishes, D̄zong-ka-b̄a calls them to notice that he has something important to say about the topic of wisdom, required for overcoming the obstructions to omniscience and thereby relevant to their intention to help others. We can understand from the context of the appeal to altruism that, although emptiness (or the differentiation of the interpretable and the definitive) is justifiably called the **essence** of Buddha's teachings, realization of emptiness is not the final goal. Service to others is.

---

[a] Jay-d̄zün Chö-ḡyi-gyel-tsen's *General-Meaning Commentary,* 4a.4-4a.6. He identifies "the suchness of the teaching" not just as emptiness as Gung-tang does, but as "the modes of subsistence" of things, these being "the features of interpretability and definitiveness and so forth" of the scriptures.

3. God of Wisdom and God of Gods

The Homages: Points of Clarification

D̄zong-ka-b̄a (*Emptiness in Mind-Only,* 65-66) first offers homage to Shākya-muni Buddha:

> Homage to the Lord of Subduers, god of gods,
> As soon as whose body was seen by those
> High-and-mighty with presumptions proclaiming
> In the mundane world a great roar of arrogance —
>
> [The gods known as] Bliss-Arising, Cloud Mount, Golden Womb,
> Bodiless Lord, Garlanded Belly, and so on—
> Even they became like fireflies [overwhelmed] by the sun and thereupon
> Paid respect with their beautiful crowns to his lotus feet.

In a manner typical of the genre of his commentary, Gung-tang[17] examines several points that are peripheral to the central topics but, in time (and with a good deal of patience), provide a wide cultural context for more important issues—the context imbedding the reader in an all-encompassing worldview. Texts are not viewed by Tibetan scholars in isolation as if they live outside of the situation of their culture; they are related to a body of literature and knowledge in such a way that the study of a text is a study of the world. The context provided is not just that of the culture contemporary to or preceding D̄zong-ka-b̄a's text; often, commentaries present views of scholars subsequent to the text because the aim is to provide a worldview relevant to the reader's present situation, a comprehensive perspective that makes use of whatever is available.[a]

Issue #6: Is Brahmā egg-born?

The issues raised often stem from juxtaposing a point—mentioned in D̄zong-ka-b̄a's text or in a commentary—with what is known about a related topic from other sources. Frequently, the aim is to avert a possible misunderstanding. In this vein, Gung-tang juxtaposes the epithet "Golden Womb" that is used for Brahmā and the Buddhist depiction of four types of birth—womb-born, egg-born, spontaneously born, and born from heat and moisture. He points out that even though Brahmā might seem to be egg-born because the god is said to have been "born from a golden lotus in the shape of an egg in the midst of a

[a] This being the basic mode of procedure, it takes a scholar of considerable acuity to keep straight what are later accretions and what are not, but there are a small number of such scholars among the Tibetan community just as there are in other communities.

sphere of fire," Brahmā was not born from an actual egg. Rather, gods such as Brahmā as well as hell-beings and beings in the intermediate state between two lives are necessarily spontaneously born. As Vasubandhu's *Treasury of Manifest Knowledge* says:[18]

> Hell-beings, gods, and intermediate state beings
> Are spontaneously born.

Furthermore, gods of the Form Realm, of whom Brahmā is one, are, from birth, complete in size and clothed. Vasubandhu's *Treasury of Manifest Knowledge* says:[19]

> Those of the Form [Realm] are complete
> In all respects [at birth] and just clothed.

Gung-tang then cites the dictum that the four types of birth are mutually exclusive and thus any being is necessarily only one of the four; the consequent problem is that birds are born from eggs that emerge from wombs and would seem to be both egg-born and womb-born. The resolution is a declaration that a bird is egg-born even though the egg comes from a womb. Also, a bird is not born from heat and moisture even though born from the warmth of the mother's body and from the blood of the mother and the semen of the father (both of which are moist).[a]

Issue #7: How could Brahmā appear first when this world system formed?

Using the opportunity provided by D̄zong-ka-b̄a's mention of Brahmā, Gung-tang[20] raises an issue within Buddhist cosmology (see Chart 1, next page). It concerns the seeming contradiction in accounts of the stages of formation in a new eon. Given that when a world-system newly forms, those levels that do not rest on earth form from the higher to the lower, this means that the Third Concentration formed first. However, this conflicts with Buddhists' own accounts that "**initially** the great Brahmā appeared," since Brahmā's land is included within the First and not the Third Concentration.

Gung-tang explains away the seeming contradiction by pointing out that there are different modes of formation after the destruction of the previous eon depending on how that eon ended—whether by wind, in which case the new eon begins with the formation of the Third Concentration; whether by water, in which case the new eon begins with the formation of the Second Concentration; or whether by fire, in which case the new eon begins with the formation of the First Concentration. Therefore, that most texts speak of the formation of

[a] Extrapolating from this, we could say that even from the current scientific point of view in which it is known that a human female has eggs, a human is still not egg-born, but womb-born.

Chart 1: The Three Realms of Cyclic Existence
(from the highest levels to the lowest)

- Formless Realm
  - Peak of Cyclic Existence[a]
  - Nothingness[b]
  - Limitless Consciousness[c]
  - Limitless Space[d]
- Form Realm
  - Fourth Concentration
  - Third Concentration
  - Second Concentration
  - First Concentration
- Desire Realm
  - Gods of the Desire Realm
    - Those Who Make Use of Others' Emanations[e]
    - Those Who Enjoy Emanation[f]
    - Joyous Land[g]
    - Land Without Combat[h]
    - Heaven of Thirty-Three[i]
    - Four Great Royal Lineages[j]
  - Demi-gods
  - Humans
  - Animals
  - Hungry ghosts
  - Hell-beings.[21]

the realms of worldly beings that are established in space as beginning with the world of Brahmā is in terms of the present eon, which formed after the previous eon was destroyed by fire. It had to be formed beginning from the lands of the First Concentration since the Second and Third Concentrations remained from

a *srid rtse, bhavāgra.*
b *ci yang med, ākiṃcaya.*
c *rnam shes mtha' yas, vijñānānantya.*
d *nam mkha' mtha' yas, ākāśānantya.*
e *gzhan 'phrul dbang byed, paranirmitavaśavartin.*
f *'phrul dga', nirmāṇarati.*
g *dga' ldan, tuṣita.*
h *'thab bral, yāma.*
i *sum cu rtsa gsum, trayastriṃśa.*
j *rgyal chen rigs bzhi, cāturmahārājakāyika.*

the previous eon. As Nga-w̄ang-lek-den, abbot of the Tantric College of Lower Hla-s̄a in the 1950's, explained to me, the fact that this eon began with the formation of the First Concentration and its own highest level, called Great Brahmā, explains why Brahmā came mistakenly to think that he created everything. When he saw that other levels formed after him, he erroneously concluded that he created them.

Gung-tang's handling of an apparent contradiction in the Buddhist cosmological explanation suggests that Buddhist accounts can withstand analysis whereas non-Buddhist accounts cannot. Also, his readers are reminded not to be misled into placing confidence in non-Buddhist gods by D̄zong-ka-b̄a's mention of them.

PART TWO:
THE QUESTION

4. Identifying First-Wheel Teachings

The *Sūtra Unraveling the Thought*

According to Dön-drup-gyel-tsen's *Four Intertwined Commentaries,*[22] the *Sūtra Unraveling the Thought*[23] was set forth in Vaishālī, India, by the Supramundane Victor, Shākyamuni Buddha, during the period of his final, third turning of the wheel of doctrine for practitioners of both the Lesser Vehicle and the Great Vehicle. Dön-drup-gyel-tsen reports that:

1. Its **subject matter** is to teach that all phenomena are included in the three natures—imputational, other-powered, and thoroughly established natures.
2. Its **purpose** is to teach that the first and middle wheels of doctrine require interpretation and that the final wheel is of definitive meaning.
3. Its **essential purpose** is the three enlightenments that are attained respectively by the intended trainees of the three vehicles—Hearers, Solitary Realizers, and Bodhisattvas.
4. The **relationship** of these is that the last wheel of the doctrine arises in dependence upon the two earlier wheels.

The *Sūtra Unraveling the Thought* has ten chapters of questions by nine Bodhisattvas and Subhūti and replies by Buddha, except in the first chapter where another Bodhisattva replies. Jay-d̄zün Chö-ḡyi-gyel-tsen[24] and Gung-tang,[25] based on the commentary[26] by Gen-dün-gya-tso,[a] who retrospectively came to be called the Second Dalai Lama when his reincarnation S̄ö-nam-gya-tso received the title "Dalai"[b] from the Mongolian chieftain Altan Khan, identify the principal contents of each chapter:

- The first chapter, the "Questions of Vidhivatpariprcchaka (Proper Questioning)[c] and Answers by Gambhīrārthasaṃdhinirmochana (Unraveling the Thought)"[d] settles the principle of cognition-only.[e]
- The second chapter, the "Questions of Dharmodgata (Elevated

---

[a] 1476-1542.

[b] *tā le.* This is a translation of the last two syllables of his Tibetan name, "gya-tso" (*rgya mtsho*).

[c] *tshul bzhin kun tu dri ba.*

[d] *dgongs pa nges 'grel.*

[e] Since in this initial chapter not Buddha but the Bodhisattva Gambhīrārthasaṃdhinirmochana is questioned by the Bodhisattva Vidhivatpariprcchaka, it may be that the sūtra receives its name from the principal speaker of the initial chapter, Gambhīrārthasaṃdhinirmochana (Unraveling the Thought of the Profound Meaning) as well as from the "unraveling," or explication, of Buddha's thought that occurs in the seventh chapter.

Doctrine),"[a] teaches that the real nature of things[b] is beyond the scope of argumentation[c] or, in other words, is inconceivable by a conceptual consciousness in accordance with exactly how it is.

- The third chapter, the "Questions of Suvishuddhamati (Pure Intelligence),"[d] teaches how, by way of four contradictions each, the two truths—ultimate and conventional—cannot be different entities and cannot be one with no sense of difference at all; in Ge-luk-b̄a vocabulary, this means that the two truths are one entity and different isolates (to be discussed later, 321).
- The fourth chapter, the "Questions of Subhūti (Thorough Application),"[e] teaches the undifferentiability of the ultimate, which is also called "the element of attributes"[f] because meditation within observing it acts as a cause of generating the attributes of Superiors.
- The fifth chapter, the "Questions of Vishālamati (Broad Intelligence),"[g] mainly teaches the mind-basis-of-all.[h]
- The sixth chapter, the "Questions of Guṇākara (Source of Good Qualities),"[i] teaches the three characters—imputational, other-powered, and thoroughly established.
- The seventh chapter, the "Questions of Paramārthasamudgata (Elevated Through the Ultimate),"[j] differentiates the interpretable and the definitive among the Buddha's statements that phenomena have no nature and so forth.
- The eighth chapter, the "Questions of Maitreya (Love),"[k] mainly teaches the presentations of calm abiding and special insight.
- The ninth chapter, the "Questions of Avalokiteshvara (Looking Out of the

---

[a] *chos 'phags.*

[b] *chos nyid, dharmatā.*

[c] *rtog ge, tarka;* this could also be appropriately translated as "logic."

[d] *blo gros rnam dag.*

[e] *rab 'byor.*

[f] *chos kyi dbyings, dharmadhātu.* The translation as "element of attributes" is based on a note by Nga-w̄ang-b̄el-den (*Annotations, dbu,* 8b.8): *khyod la dmigs nas sgom pas 'phags chos kyi rgyu byed pas chos dbyings zhes bya la,* "It is called the element of attributes (*chos dbyings, dharmadhātu*) because meditation within observing it acts as a cause of the attributes (*chos, dharma*) of Superiors (*'phags pa, ārya*)." Emptiness, being uncaused, is not itself a cause (element), but meditation on it causes the development of marvelous attributes; thus, emptiness comes to be *called* a cause, an element producing those attributes.

Gung-tang mentions the import of this chapter, whereas the Second Dalai Lama and Jay-d̄zün Chö-ḡyi-gyel-tsen do not.

[g] *blo gros yangs pa.*

[h] *kun gzhi rnam par shes pa, ālayavijñāna.*

[i] *yon tan 'byung gnas.*

[j] *don dam yang dag 'phags.*

[k] *byams pa.*

Corner of the Eyes),"[a] teaches the layouts of the ten Bodhisattva grounds.
- The tenth chapter, the "Questions of Mañjushrī (Smooth Glory),"[b] mainly teaches the qualities of the Buddha ground.

As Gung-tang adds,[27] the ten chapters set forth presentations of the bases, paths, and fruits of the Mind-Only system in complete form. The first seven chapters present the bases; the eighth and ninth present the path, and the tenth teaches the fruits of the path.

Issue #8: Why does Wonch'uk's version of the sūtra have eight chapters and the Tibetan version have ten?

Jik-may-dam-chö-gya-tso[28] identifies the *Sūtra Unraveling the Thought* described by the Korean scholar Wonch'uk[c] as having eight chapters:

1. Introduction
2. The Character of the Ultimate Truth
3. The Character of Mind, Mentality, and Consciousness
4. The Characters of All Phenomena
5. The Character of Naturelessness
6. Revealing Yoga
7. The Grounds and Perfections
8. Achieving the Activities of a One-Gone-Thus.

The second chapter of Wonch'uk's rendering corresponds to the first four chapters of the Tibetan translation of the sūtra, and the remainder of Wonch'uk's version corresponds to the fifth through tenth chapters of the Tibetan.[d] Thus, the Tibetan version of the text has an introduction and ten chapters.

Issue #9: Why leave out the fourth chapter?

As Gung-tang[29] points out, the Second Dalai Lama's *Commentary on the Difficult Points* does not list the "Questions of Subhūti" (the fourth chapter) as one of the ten chapters and instead counts the introduction as a chapter. The omission is glaring, and Gung-tang works hard to come up with an apologetic that can, even superficially, not look like outright criticism. He finds two "reasons" for the Second Dalai Lama's omission:

1. Ḏzong-ka-ḇa's student Gyel-tsap[30] speaks of ten tenth-ground Bodhisattvas

---

[a] *spyan ras gzigs.*

[b] *'jam dpal.*

[c] Tib. *rdzogs gsal / wen tshig / wen tshegs / wanydzeg,* Ch. *Yüan-ts'e,* 613-696.

[d] For discussion of the Chinese translations and their chapter divisions, see *Emptiness in Mind-Only,* Appendix 2, 457ff.

questioning Buddha, whereas Subhūti is a Hearer, not even a Bodhisattva. Gung-tang's implicit (and far-fetched) point is that the Second Dalai Lama wished to refer only to chapters of the *Sūtra Unraveling the Thought* where tenth-ground Bodhisattvas question Buddha.

2. Subhūti is not mentioned in the introduction to the *Sūtra Unraveling the Thought* even though the ten tenth-ground Bodhisattvas are—the implicit (and again far-fetched) point being that the Second Dalai Lama wished to refer only to chapters of the *Sūtra Unraveling the Thought* in which Buddha is questioned by persons mentioned in the introduction to the sūtra.

Gung-tang politely offers that the Second Dalai Lama could not have failed to notice that the "Questions of Subhūti" is a chapter of the *Sūtra Unraveling the Thought,* since it is obvious in the sūtra itself that it is treated as a chapter and also since Asaṅga's *Compendium of Ascertainments* quotes it (in toto) as a separate chapter.

I would suggest that it is more likely that the Second Dalai Lama mistakenly included the introduction in his list of chapters of the *Sūtra Unraveling the Thought* based on Wonch'uk's and, subsequently, D̄zong-ka-b̄a's mention of the "introductory chapter" (*Emptiness in Mind-Only,* 157). He probably got false confirmation of this deficient list from the abovementioned facts that (1) although the other questioners are mentioned in the introduction, Subhūti is not, and (2) Gyel-tsap speaks of ten tenth-ground Bodhisattvas' questioning Buddha. When Gung-tang puts forward the excuse that the Second Dalai Lama was intending to give a list of chapters in which tenth-ground Bodhisattvas question Buddha and thus did not count the chapter of the "Questions of Subhūti" as one of the chapters of questions **by tenth-ground Bodhisattvas**, what he means is to offer the reasons behind the Second Dalai Lama's mistake and to **pretend** that the Second Dalai Lama was aware of all of this. It is read and appreciated as polite criticism.

In fact, the introduction is not even a chapter of questions but merely sets the scene; thus, it actually is not a chapter in which a tenth-ground Bodhisattva questions Buddha, and thus Gung-tang's apologetic is not elegant—it is weak. Furthermore, Gyel-tsap's statement that ten tenth-ground Bodhisattvas ask questions of Buddha is mistaken, since, as Jik-may-dam-chö-gya-tso[31] points out, in the first chapter questions are put by the tenth-ground Bodhisattva Vidhivatparipṛcchaka to the tenth-ground Bodhisattva Gambhīrārthasaṃdhinirmochana, and not to Buddha.[a]

To recapitulate: Although there are ten tenth-ground Bodhisattvas who are interlocutors in the *Sūtra Unraveling the Thought,* only eight Bodhisattvas ask

---

[a] S̄er-s̄hül (*Notes,* 30a.1-30a.4) says that ten Bodhisattvas do indeed ask questions to the Buddha, since two do so in the first chapter; however, in the first chapter the tenth-ground Bodhisattva Vidhivatparipṛcchaka questions the tenth-ground Bodhisattva Gambhīrārthasaṃdhinirmochana.

questions of Buddha, since Vidhivatparipṛcchaka questions Gambhīrārthasaṃdhinirmochana in the first chapter and Subhūti, a Hearer, is the questioner in the fourth chapter.

Jay-d̄zün Chö-ḡyi-gyel-tsen,[32] L̄o-sang-trin-lay-ye-s̄hay,[33] and D̄a-drin-rap-d̄en[34] similarly omit the "Questions of Subhūti" when listing the ten chapters of the *Sūtra Unraveling the Thought.* It is likely that Jay-d̄zün Chö-ḡyi-gyel-tsen and L̄o-sang-trin-lay-ye-s̄hay simply repeat the Second Dalai Lama's misstatement and that D̄a-drin-rap-d̄en, being a follower of Jay-d̄zün Chö-ḡyi-gyel-tsen, echoes him.

The Question

The question is a source of much analysis by Ge-luk-b̄a scholars. Let us use as our basis the explanations by five scholars associated with the Go-mang tradition:

- the late eighteenth- and early nineteenth-century scholar Gung-tang
- his commentator A-ku L̄o-drö-gya-tso
- the early twentieth-century comparative scholar Jik-may-dam-chö-gya-tso[a]
- their prime source, Jam-ȳang-shay-b̄a, the late seventeenth- and early eighteenth-century author of the textbook literature of the Go-mang College of Dre-b̄ung Monastic University on the western outskirts Hla-s̄a (but now part of the city) and D̄ra-s̄hi-kyil Monastic University in the upper eastern province of Tibet called Am-do, and
- his predecessor Gung-ru Chö-jung.

Their presentations are the most detailed and contain criticisms of other scholars' views, which I will weave into the discussion. The initial step will be to identify first-wheel sūtras, and then to identify how they teach "own-character." Neither the *Sūtra Unraveling the Thought* nor D̄zong-ka-b̄a's *The Essence of Eloquence* identify the sūtras in which Buddha taught the doctrines of the first wheel, and for this reason these commentaries are particularly helpful.

The First Wheel

Issue #10: Just what are first-wheel sūtras?

According to the Go-mang tradition of exegesis, in the first turning of the wheel of doctrine, Buddha taught that all phenomena are established by way of their own character as the referents of their respective conceptual consciousnesses,[b] whereas in the middle wheel he said that no phenomenon is established

---

[a] 1898-1946.

[b] *rang 'dzin rtog pa'i zhen gzhir rang gi mtshan nyid kyis grub pa.*

by way of its own character in the sense of being established from its own side. In the first wheel of the teaching, Buddha gave this teaching with respect to seven topics, called the "seven pronouncements"[a]—the aggregates, the sense-spheres, dependent-arising, the foods, the four noble truths, the constituents, and the harmonies with enlightenment. Strangely enough, the *Sūtra Unraveling the Thought* does not identify particular first-wheel sūtras, nor does D̄zong-ka-b̄a's *The Essence of Eloquence.* Gung-tang and his commentator A-ku L̄o-drö-gya-tso,[35] however, provide this important information with respect to each of the seven topics, the very identifications of which lead to a tangle of issues that they forthrightly face.

Aggregates. Specifically, in the *Sūtra of Advice to King Bimbisāra*[b] in the first turning of the wheel of doctrine, Buddha said:[36]

> Great King, form [that is established by way of its own character as the referent of a conceptual consciousness] has production [that is established by way of its own character as the referent of a conceptual consciousness]; it also has disintegration [that is established by way of its own character as the referent of a conceptual consciousness]. Its production and disintegration [which are established by way of their own character as the referents of conceptual consciousnesses] should be known. Great King, feeling and....

This passage beginning with "Great King, form has production; it also has disintegration," is one of the instances in which Buddha spoke about the entities of the aggregates of forms, feelings, discriminations, compositional factors, and consciousnesses—in which one travels in cyclic existence—as having **own-character**, that is to say, as being **established by way of their own character as the referents of conceptual consciousnesses**. (The absence in such sūtra statements of the phrase "established by way of their own character as the referents of conceptual consciousnesses," or anything remotely resembling this, is striking, but, as is explained in Chapter 8 of *Reflections on Reality,* such is said to be contained even in the **literal** reading. In the indented sūtra citation, I have added "established by way of their own character as the referents of conceptual consciousnesses" in brackets in order to emphasize the absence of such in the actual run of the words.)

---

[a] *bka' stsal bdun.*

[b] Gung-tang (*Difficult Points,* 80.12-80.16) points out that although this passage is not found in a sūtra titled *rgyal po la gdams pa'i mdo,* it is found in *gzugs can snying pos bsu ba,* which is composed of advice to King Bimbisāra (see also Jik-may-dam-chö-gya-tso's *Port of Entry,* 154.3-154.5). In addition, he identifies what is either a mis-translation into Tibetan or a corrupt Indian text (80.16-81.5).

Gung-tang (*Annotations,* 14.2) identifies *dmag ldan gzugs can snying po, bzo sbyangs gzugs can snying po,* and *rgyal po gzugs can snying po* as names of Bimbisāra during various stages of his life; as sources for this he cites *'dul ba lung* and *gleng 'bum.*

In the next sentence, "Its production and disintegration should be known," Buddha also speaks of the aggregates' character or attribute of **production** and **disintegration** through the force of contaminated actions and afflictive emotions—the production and disintegration being established by way of their own character as the referents of conceptual consciousnesses. The first sentence, therefore, teaches that the **entities** of forms are established by way of their own character as the referents of conceptual consciousnesses, and the second teaches that the **attributes** of production and disintegration are so established.

Issue #11: Do passages teaching the entity also teach the attributes?

Since the first sentence of the above citation from the *Sūtra of Advice to King Bimbisāra* speaks of form's production, it seems forced to claim that it speaks of the entity of form and that the second sentence speaks of the attributes. Jik-may-dam-chö-gya-tso[37] cites a hypothetical objection that in fact the first sentence is not to be posited as a first-wheel passage explicitly indicated by Paramārthasamudgata's description of the first wheel as teaching the own-character of **form,** since it is a first-wheel passage teaching the own-character of **form's production** and not of the entity of form itself. He responds that what comes to be communicated[a] by the first sentence is that **both**—factors imputed in the manner of **entity** and factors imputed in the manner of **attribute**—are established as having own-character.

In turn, the hypothetical objector flings the consequence that then any sūtra passage explicitly teaching factors imputed in the manner of attributes would be a sūtra passage explicitly teaching factors imputed in the manner of entities. Jik-may-dam-chö-gya-tso's only response is to suggest that this must be examined, thereby indicating that, for him, the issue is not easily settled;[38] his commentary intentionally exposes the weakness of his own position. There does not seem to be a good answer except perhaps to cite passages where Buddha lays out the five aggregates, as in, "This is form."

Issue #12: Does any passage merely teach the production of form?

Jik-may-dam-chö-gya-tso[39] raises another interesting point by citing Sha-m̄ar Ge-dün-d̄en-dzin-gya-tso's[b] *Notes Concerning Difficult Points in (D̄zong-ka-b̄a's) "Differentiating the Interpretable and the Definitive, The Essence of Eloquence": Victoriously Clearing Away Mental Darkness.*[c] Sha-m̄ar Ge-dün-d̄en-dzin-gya-tso

---

a *brjod don.*

b *zhwa dmar dge 'dun bstan 'dzin rgya mtsho,* 1852-1912.

c *drang nges legs bshad snying po'i dka' gnas las brtsams pa'i zin bris bcom ldan yid kyi mun*

avers that once the mere phrase "form has production" teaches that these phenomena are established by way of their own character as the referents of their respective conceptual consciousnesses, it would be hard to posit **any** teaching to the intended trainees of the first wheel that teaches that production exists without teaching that it is established by way of its own character as the referent of a conceptual consciousness! That Jik-may-dam-chö-gya-tso does not try to solve the conundrum shows how difficult indeed it would be to do so.

In a similar vein, A-ku Lo-drö-gya-tso,[40] feeling the import of Gung-tang's description of first-wheel teachings, speculates that it might have to be said that the statement in the *Sūtra on Dependent-Arising,* "Because this exists, that arises," teaches **on the literal level** that all dependent-arisings (all compounded things) are produced by way of their own character as the referents of conceptual consciousnesses. The problem is left unresolved.

Buddha continues in the *Sūtra of Advice to King Bimbisāra:*[41]

> Great King, Superior Hearers—possessed of hearing [of the doctrine] and who see this way—turn their minds away from forms, feelings, discriminations, compositional factors, and consciousnesses. When [their] minds do so, they become separated from desire. When separated from desire, they become released.

Here, Buddha speaks of the **abandonment** of the aggregates of cyclic existence as established by way of its own character as the referent of a conceptual consciousness.

Buddha continues:

> When released, they perceive the exalted wisdom of release [saying to others], "My births are extinguished. Pure behavior is enacted. What is to be done has been done. Another existence will not be known."

Here, Buddha speaks of thorough knowledge—knowledge that the entities of the aggregates are not established as a self—as itself being established by way of its own character as the referent of a conceptual consciousness. This perhaps may also be taken as the knowledge that the non-establishment of the aggregates as a self is itself established by way of its own character as the referent of a conceptual consciousness.[42] This thorough knowledge is taken as the meaning of Buddha's earlier statement in the *Sūtra of Advice to King Bimbisāra:*[43]

> Great King, in that case, whatsoever forms...should be viewed with right wisdom in this way: "These are not a self. The self is not these. These are not owned[a] by a [substantially existent] self."

In the *Sūtra Unraveling the Thought,* when Paramārthasamudgata questions

---

sel; Jik-may-dam-chö-gya-tso refers to it as *mun sel;* I have not located the text.

[a] Reading *bdag gi ba dag* for *bdag gi bdag.*

Buddha about his teachings in the first wheel, he makes reference to such sūtra passages, saying:

> Supramundane Victor, when I was here alone in a solitary place, my mind generated the following qualm. The Supramundane Victor spoke, in many ways, of the own-character of the aggregates. He also spoke of [their] character of production, character of disintegration, abandonment, and thorough knowledge.

As Gung-tang says, the *Sūtra of Advice to King Bimbisāra* is just one instance of Buddha's many renderings of this type of teaching.

Issue #13: How to take Wonch'uk's two explanations of abandonment and thorough knowledge?

According to Gung-tang,[a] Wonch'uk takes abandonment and thorough knowledge in two ways:

> That which is the thoroughly afflicted form aggregate is what is to be utterly abandoned; that which is the unafflicted form aggregate is what is to be thoroughly known. Or, that which is in the class of objects that are sources [of suffering] is to be utterly abandoned; that which is in the class of true sufferings is to be thoroughly known.

In the first explanation, abandonment refers to the abandonment of the five **contaminated** mental and physical aggregates, and thorough knowledge refers to knowledge of the five **uncontaminated** aggregates. Thus, as A-ku Lo-drö-gya-tso[44] points out, the bases that are abandoned (the contaminated mental and physical aggregates) and the bases that are known (the uncontaminated aggregates) are mutually exclusive. In Wonch'uk's second explanation, abandonment refers to the abandonment of the contaminated causes of the five mental and physical aggregates, contaminated actions and afflictive emotions, and thorough knowledge refers to knowledge of the entities of those five aggregates as like a disease.

Dzong-ka-ba does not refute Wonch'uk's explanation; however, Gung-tang[45] offers his own explanation that "thorough knowledge" is of the non-establishment of the entities, the aggregates, as a self, with this knowledge being

---

[a] Gung-tang's *Difficult Points,* 78.10-79.1. Wonch'uk's second reading is (Peking 5517, vol. 106, chap. 5, 128.5.7; Karma pa sde dge, vol. 118, 546.7):

> "Utter abandonment and thorough knowledge" are characters of suffering and of origins [of suffering] because [contaminated] karma and afflictive emotions which are the true origins [of suffering] are to be utterly abandoned and because the fruits of cyclic existence which are true sufferings are to be thoroughly known.

Wonch'uk (129.1.3) refers to the other reading as being in the third section of the chapter called *khong du chud par gyur nas bka' yang dag par blangs pa'i phyogs.*

established by way of its own character as the referent of a conceptual consciousness. A-ku Lo-drö-gya-tso,[46] trying to ferret out why Gung-tang gives his own explanation, suggests that Gung-tang thought it slightly preferable to Wonch'uk's in that it is applicable to all forms of the aggregates—that is, contaminated and uncontaminated, in that all of these are misapprehended as being established by way of their own character as the referents of conceptual consciousnesses, whereas in Wonch'uk's version the uncontaminated aggregates are not to be abandoned, nor are the contaminated levels of the paths of accumulation and preparation.[47] A-ku Lo-drö-gya-tso describes Wonch'uk's rendering as a general explanation or one in accord with the Hearer Sectarians who are objects of the literal teaching of the *Sūtra Unraveling the Thought,* since it cannot be applied to subtler levels of suffering and the causes of suffering as was done in the previous paragraph;[a] he thereby indicates that Wonch'uk's explanation is not unsuitable.[b]

Sense-spheres, dependent-arising, and foods. In sūtras such as the *Sūtra on Dependent-Arising*[c] and perhaps the *Renunciation Sūtra*[d] in which Buddha gives advice to five hundred yogis with coiled hair, Mahākāshyapa and so forth, this same teaching of establishment by way of the object's own character as the referent of a conceptual consciousness is extended to the twelve sense-spheres—the six objects (forms, sounds, odors, tastes, tangible objects, and other phenomena) and the six senses (eye, ear, nose, tongue, body, and mental sense powers)—the twelve links of dependent-arising (ignorance, action, consciousness, name and form, six sense-spheres, contact, feeling, attachment, grasping, "existence," birth, and aging and death), and the four foods (morsels of food, contact, intention, and consciousness). In the *Sūtra Unraveling the Thought* Paramārthasamudgata refers to these teachings:

> Just as he did with respect to the aggregates, so he also spoke with respect to the sense-spheres, dependent-arising, and also the foods.

Just as Buddha spoke about the **entities** of the aggregates and their **attributes**

---

[a] A-ku Lo-drö-gya-tso (53.3) points out that in the *Sūtra of Manifold Constituents* the meaning of abandonment also cannot be applied to the constituents of learners and non-learners.

[b] Jik-may-dam-chö-gya-tso (*Port of Entry,* 156.3) affirms that it is suitable to assert both of Wonch'uk's explanations.

[c] *rten 'brel gyi mdo* (A-ku Lo-drö-gya-tso's *Precious Lamp,* 52.6).

[d] *mngon par 'byung ba'i mdo.* Gung-tang (*Difficult Points,* 76.16) says that it should be investigated whether these are taught in this sūtra. A-ku Lo-drö-gya-tso (*Precious Lamp,* 53.2), following up on Gung-tang's suggestion, reports that the foods are not mentioned in this sūtra and thus the first-wheel sūtra teaching that these are established by way of their own character as the referents of conceptual consciousnesses must be sought. Gung-tang's questioning the identification indicates that, rather than newly creating identifications of these sūtras, he is reporting a tradition; I give him the credit since, at minimum, he put it to paper.

of production, disintegration, abandonment, and thorough knowledge within the context of these being established by way of their own character as the referents of conceptual consciousnesses, so he spoke about the **entities** of the sense-spheres, dependent-arising, and the foods and their four **attributes** of production, disintegration, abandonment, and thorough knowledge, all within the same context.

Issue #14: Just what are the four foods?

Ser-shül Lo-sang-pün-tsok[48] questions a list of the four foods that is given in Dön-drup-gyel-tsen's *Four Intertwined Commentaries,*[49] these being morsels of food,[a] contact,[b] mind,[c] and meditative stabilization.[d] Ser-shül indicates that he prefers the list found in Asaṅga's *Compendium of Ascertainments,* the commentaries on Maitreya's *Ornament for the Great Vehicle Sūtras,* the commentaries on Asaṅga's *Summary of the Great Vehicle,* and Vasubandhu's *Treasury of Manifest Knowledge.* As given in Gyel-tsap's commentary on Asaṅga's *Summary of Manifest Knowledge,*[e] these are:

1. morsel food,[f] which has a nature of odor, taste, and tangibility (visible form being excluded because it does not function in nutrition)
2. contact food,[g] which is contaminated touch increasing the great elements associated with the sense powers
3. intention food,[h] which is intention (or attention) that involves hope for a desired object
4. consciousness food,[i] which is the six collections of consciousness and mainly the mind-basis-of-all.[50]

Ser-shül cites the third chapter of Vasubandhu's *Treasury of Manifest Knowledge* which indicates that:

- coarse food furthers the body that is the support of this lifetime
- contact furthers the mind that depends on the support of the body
- intention projects future lifetimes (in that it is the main feature of karma)
- consciousness actualizes future lifetimes in the sense that karmas (retained

[a] *kham gyi zas.*

[b] *reg pa.*

[c] *sems.*

[d] *ting nge 'dzin.*

[e] *legs par bshad pa chos mngon rgya mtsho'i snying po;* Collected Works, Labrang ed., vol. ga, 101a.6.

[f] *kham gyi zas, kavaḍaṃkāra-āhāra.*

[g] *reg pa'i zas, sparśa-āhāra.*

[h] *sems pa'i zas, manaḥsaṃcetanāhāra.*

[i] *rnam shes kyi zas, vijñāna-āhāra.*

as potencies in the mind) fill in the details of the lifetime projected by intention.[51]

Ser-shül quotes Vasubandhu's explanation that morsel food exists only in the Desire Realm, whereas the other three exist in all three realms—Desire, Form, and Formless—and are necessarily contaminated. (As Ge-shay Bel-den-drak-ba[52] explained, the foods increase cyclic existence, and thus **uncontaminated** contact, intention, and consciousness are not posited as food.)

Ser-shül paraphrases Asaṅga's *Compendium of Ascertainments* which explains that although meditative absorptions and engaging in pure behavior are means of furthering the body through eliminating unfavorable circumstances, they are not posited as foods, since they do not further the body by way of their own entities. His point must be that meditative stabilization therefore should not be included in the list. However, contrary to this, the late Ge-shay Ge-dün-lo-drö[a] of the Go-mang College of Dre-bung Monastic University and the University of Hamburg includes meditative stabilization and gives mental food as the second:[53]

> The four types of nourishment are (1) coarse food,[b] (2) mental nourishment,[c] (3) nourishment of intention,[d] and (4) nourishment of consciousness.[e] The sense of mental satisfaction that comes when a desire is fulfilled is called mental nourishment. Just as coarse food nourishes the body, so satisfaction nourishes or replenishes the mind upon fulfillment of a desire. The third type, nourishment of intention, is an action[f] that projects the next lifetime. Since it generates or produces the next lifetime, it is called a nourisher, or nourishment; it is the second link of the twelve-linked dependent-arising.[g] Similarly, the third link, which is called consciousness,[h] is known as the food of consciousness. Just as the action that projects, or impels, a future lifetime is called a nourisher, so the consciousness which is imprinted with that action and which will at the time of the effect of that action in the future life be imprinted with other karmas is called a nourisher, or nourishment. Why is [the first link of dependent-arising,] ignorance,[i] not called a nourisher? It is because ignorance is the agent that pervades everything; thus, it is not singled out as a nourisher.

---

a *dge 'dun blo gros,* 1924-1979.

b *kham gyi zas, kavaḍaṃkāra-āhāra.*

c *yid kyi zas.*

d *sems pa'i zas, manaḥsaṃcetanāhāra.*

e *rnam shes kyi zas, vijñāna-āhāra.*

f *las, karma.*

g *rten 'byung, pratītyasamutpāda.*

h *rnam shes, vijñāna.*

i *ma rig pa, avidyā.*

There is still another type of nourishment, that of meditative stabilization.[a] Persons who have achieved calm abiding and special insight and have proceeded to high levels of the path do not need to use coarse food; they have the nourishment of meditative stabilization. If you should wish to investigate this topic, the nourishment of meditative stabilization is discussed in the context of the four developing causes which replenish or increase the body: sleep, meditative stabilization, massage, and coarse food. The sources here are Kamalashīla's *Stages of Meditation* and Maitreya's *Ornament for the Mahāyāna Sūtras* and, in addition, the *Sūtra Unraveling the Thought* and Wonch'uk's commentary on it.

Issue #15: Are these sūtras deceptive?

Four noble truths. In the wheel of doctrine of the four truths, Buddha spoke of the **entities** of the four truths as being established by way of their own character as a referent of a conceptual consciousness. He also spoke of an **attribute** of each the four respectively—**thorough knowledge** of true sufferings as impermanent and miserable, **abandonment** of the sources of suffering (contaminated actions and afflictive emotions), **actualization** of the true cessation of contaminated actions and afflictive emotions and thereby of suffering, and **meditation** cultivating true paths which are the means for attaining true cessation of suffering and its causes. This teaching occurs in the *Sūtra of Renunciation* at the point of turning the wheel of doctrine of the four truths for the five good ascetics.[b] In the *Sūtra Unraveling the Thought* Paramārthasamudgata refers to this teaching, saying:

> The Supramundane Victor also spoke, in many ways, of the own-character of the truths as well as speaking of [their] thorough knowledge, abandonment, actualization, and meditation.

Jik-may-dam-chö-gya-tso[54] raises the interesting question of whether such a sūtra teaching the four noble truths is deceptive with respect to the meaning that it teaches[c] because it teaches that the four truths are established by way of their own character as the referents of their respective conceptual consciousnesses, whereas they are not. Since it would be uncomfortable to hold that a sūtra teaching the four truths is deceptive, he resolves the issue by saying that positing a teaching as being deceptive or not about the meaning that it teaches concerns its **main** topic, which in this case is the four truths. In this way, a

---

[a] *ting nge 'dzin, samādhi.*

[b] Gung-tang (*Difficult Points,* 77.3-77.5) points out that some histories and so forth refer to this teaching as the *Wheel of Doctrine Sūtra* (*chos kyi 'khor lo'i mdo*) but that in fact the latter is only an extract from the *Renunciation Sūtra.*

[c] *rang gi bstan don la slu ba.*

sūtra teaching the four noble truths is non-deceptive about the meaning that it teaches. This distinction preserves the basic validity of the teachings of such sūtras and yet allows that the ontological status being taught with respect to these topics is entirely unfounded.

Constituents. In the *Sūtra of Manifold Constituents*[a] Buddha spoke of the eighteen constituents and six constituents as being established by way of their own character as a referent of a conceptual consciousness. The eighteen constituents are the six sense powers, the six objects, and the six consciousnesses:

Six Sense Powers	*Six Objects*	*Six Consciousnesses*
eye sense power	visible forms	eye consciousness
ear sense power	sounds	ear consciousness
nose sense power	odors	nose consciousness
tongue sense power	tastes	tongue consciousness
body sense power	tangible objects	body consciousness
mental sense power	other phenomena	mental consciousness

The six constituents are earth (hard things), water (fluid), fire (heat), wind (air), space, and consciousness. Like the aggregates, the eighteen and six constituents are those in which one travels in cyclic existence. As with the aggregates, Buddha also spoke of the **abandonment** and **thorough knowledge** of these as being established by way of their own character as a referent of a conceptual consciousness. In the *Sūtra Unraveling the Thought* Paramārthasamudgata mentions these teachings when, in the first part of his question to Buddha about the first turning of the wheel of doctrine, he says:

> The Supramundane Victor also spoke, in many ways, of the own-character of the constituents, as well as speaking of the various constituents, manifold constituents, [their] abandonment, and thorough knowledge.

Issue #16: What are the various and manifold constituents?

In that citation from the *Sūtra Unraveling the Thought* "various constituents"

[a] *khams mang po'i mdo* (Gung-tang's *Difficult Points,* 77.13). Gung-tang (77.9-77.12) indicates that since the type of sūtra to which Paramārthasamudgata is referring must not be disputed by the two Hearer schools—the Great Exposition School and the Sūtra School—the *Collection of Constituents* (*khams kyi tshogs*), for instance, in the Seven Treatises of Manifest Knowledge, which only the Great Exposition School accepts as the word of Buddha, is not suitable as Paramārthasamudgata's reference since some proponents of the Sūtra School say that it was composed not by Buddha but by the Foe Destroyer Pūrṇavardhana (*gang spel/ gang po*) and since others of the Sūtra School say it was composed by a common being with that name and not even a Foe Destroyer.

refers to the eighteen constituents, and "manifold constituents" refers to the six constituents.[55] This is clear from the sūtra itself when later in this chapter Paramārthasamudgata speaks about the three natures in terms the aggregates, sense-spheres, dependent-arising, constituents, and foods **in the same order as his question** and then mentions the six and eighteen constituents. Paramārthasamudgata says:[56]

> Just as this is applied to the form aggregate, so this also should be applied similarly to the remaining aggregates. Just as this is applied to the aggregates, so this also should be applied similarly to each of the sense-spheres that are the twelve sense-spheres. This also should be applied similarly to each of the limbs of existence that are the twelve limbs of existence. This also should be applied similarly to each of the foods that are the four foods. This also should be applied similarly to each of the constituents that are the **six constituents** and the **eighteen constituents**.

That in the same chapter of the *Sūtra Unraveling the Thought* the constituents are listed as the six and the eighteen constituents provides good evidence that "the various constituents and manifold constituents" must be these. Still, the order of six and eighteen must be reversed to accommodate Dzong-ka-ba's statement that these refer to "the eighteen constituents and the six constituents." Indeed, when Gung-tang[57] makes this point, he (or his scribe) edits Dzong-ka-ba's text so that it reads "the six constituents and the eighteen constituents."[a] Still, despite this minor flaw of the order of six and eighteen, the internal evidence that this reference to "the various constituents and manifold constituents" must be to the eighteen and the six is good.

Wonch'uk, however, takes both "various constituents" and "manifold constituents" as referring to the eighteen constituents, the first from the viewpoint of their having internal differences in each of the eighteen and thus being "various," and the second from the viewpoint of their pervading **all** sentient beings in the manner of being their bases of imputation since sentient beings are imputed in dependence upon their constituents. Wonch'uk's *Great Commentary* says:[58]

> The eighteen constituents in the character of the one being different from the others are called the "various constituents." Just those

---

[a] *khams drug dang khams bco brgyad.* Since the Delhi NG dkra shis lhun po (484.3), Guru Deva old *zhol* (448.6), Zi ling sku 'bum (342.17), and Sarnath gtsang (6.4) editions all read *khams bco brgyad dang khams drug,* this is clearly not a variant reading, but I doubt that Gung-tang intended to edit Dzong-ka-ba's text (even though it conveniently makes the sūtra and Dzong-ka-ba agree) since Gung-tang goes to some length to indicate why only the *six* constituents (that is, the manifold) are mentioned after the eighteen (that is, the various). Jik-may-dam-chö-gya-tso (*Port of Entry,* 157.1) points out this discrepancy and calls for examination of it; this means that he finds it troublesome.

eighteen constituents as specifics of limitless sentient beings are called the "manifold constituents."

Gung-tang[59] avers that Wonch'uk's explanation may be based on Asaṅga's *Compendium of Ascertainments* which speaks of the various and manifold constituents in exactly this way:

> What are the various constituents? The eighteen constituents which have mutually different characters. What are the manifold constituents? Just those abiding by way of the divisions of limitlessly various sentient beings.[a]

Gung-tang points out that Asaṅga's explanation in the *Compendium of Ascertainments* is in accord with a description in the *Myrobalan Sūtra*[b] and in Maitreya's *Ornament for the Great Vehicle Sūtras* of the constituents (or constitutions) and interests of sentient beings as being various.[c] Because Asaṅga's *Compendium of Ascertainments* explains the two terms in reliance on the *Myrobalan*

---

[a] Wonch'uk himself (Peking 5517, vol. 106, chap. 5, 129.3.3) refers not to Asaṅga's *Compendium of Ascertainments* but to Asaṅga's *Grounds of Yogic Practice* when he says right after the above explanation, "These should be known in accordance with what is taught in [Asaṅga's] treatise, the *Grounds of Yogic Practice.*"

[b] As cited in Gung-tang's *Difficult Points* (87.15):

> The Supramundane Victor said, "Monastics, for example, if every hundred years someone took a single myrobalan fruit from a pile of myrobalan fruit a hundred yojanas high and a hundred yojanas wide, saying, "This myrobalan fruit is cast away as such and such a constitution [of a sentient being]; this myrobalan fruit is cast away as such and such a constitution," the pile of myrobalan fruit would be reduced only smaller and would be thoroughly exhausted; just so the constitutions [of sentient beings] would be exhausted in that way.

[c] Asvabhāva's commentary on the *Ornament* is Gung-tang's source indicating that Maitreya's explanation is in accordance with the description in the *Myrobalan Sūtra.* As cited in Gung-tang's *Difficult Points* (88.8), Asvabhāva's commentary on the *Ornament* says:

> This is as explained in the *Myrobalan Sūtra*....What is the meaning of "constituents" as it appears in the scripture [that is, the *Sūtra Unraveling the Thought*]? When associated with the teaching of divisions of the constituents—eyes and so forth—and with the *Sūtra of Manifold Constituents,* there are many aspects of divisions of constituents.

Jik-may-dam-chö-gya-tso (*Port of Entry,* 158.1) cites Sha-m̄ar Ge-dün-d̄en-dzin-gya-tso's *Clearing Away Mental Darkness* which challenges Gung-tang's point that the meanings of Asaṅga's *Compendium of Ascertainments,* the *Myrobalan Sūtra,* and Maitreya's *Ornament for the Great Vehicle Sūtras* treat this topic similarly, for the first is in reference to the eighteen constituents, the second is in reference to worldly realms (*'jig rten gyi khams*), and the third is in reference to the constitutions of sentient beings (*sems can gyi khams*). That Jik-may-dam-chö-gya-tso does not answer the objection suggests that he gives it credence.

A more fundamental problem is that Wonch'uk himself refers to Asaṅga's *Grounds of Yogic Practice* and not his *Compendium of Ascertainments.*

Sūtra and not in accordance with this passage in the *Sūtra Unraveling the Thought*, which can be seen to be mainly in reference to the *Sūtra of Manifold Constituents*, Wonch'uk's explanation is rejected as inappropriate. In this vein, Dzong-ka-ba (*Emptiness in Mind-Only*, 80-81), albeit cryptically, says:

> The commentaries [by Wonch'uk and so forth] explain "the various and manifold constituents" [mentioned in the passage from the *Sūtra Unraveling the Thought* cited above] otherwise, but when these are put together with a later occurrence in the *Sūtra* [*Unraveling the Thought*], they are to be taken as the eighteen constituents and the six constituents.

Gung-tang has explained Dzong-ka-ba's cryptic reference to "commentaries" and "a later occurrence in the *Sūtra*" and has identified a possible source for Wonch'uk's reading.

Then, revealing a potential weakness in Dzong-ka-ba's argument, Gung-tang[60] makes the important additional point that Wonch'uk's explanation of the two terms is indeed appropriate in a different chapter of the sūtra, the "Questions of Subhūti," where the two terms are used in the context of applying many attributes to one substratum. However, A-ku Lo-drö-gya-tso[61] saves Dzong-ka-ba's point by making the distinction that although the usage of these two terms **at the point of Paramārthasamudgata's question** does not accord with Wonch'uk's explanation, it is also permissible to explain these terms as they are set forth in the *Sūtra Unraveling the Thought* (in general) as Wonch'uk does, since his explanation is applicable to a certain usage, specifically that in the "Questions of Subhūti Chapter."[a]

The commentators thereby not only reveal the reason behind Dzong-ka-ba's rejection of Wonch'uk's explanation at this point but also, taking the discussion further, indicate the appropriateness of Wonch'uk's explanation in the context of the "Questions of Subhūti Chapter." By citing explanations similar to Wonch'uk's in sūtra (the *Myrobalan Sūtra*), in a treatise (Maitreya's *Ornament for the Great Vehicle Sūtras*), and in a commentary on a treatise (by Asvabhāva), they also give credence to Wonch'uk's exegesis, even if they criticize it for being misplaced.

Issue #17: Why are the eighteen and the six constituents singled out when there are many sets of constituents?

The *Sūtra of Manifold Constituents* speaks of the numerous sets of constituents totaling sixty-two, whereas the *Sūtra Unraveling the Thought* speaks only of the

[a] For identification of the passage, see Jik-may-dam-chö-gya-tso's *Port of Entry*, 157.3. He disputes that the "Questions of Subhūti Chapter" actually treats the constituents this way and says that the fact that it does not is clear in Wonch'uk's commentary (see *Port of Entry*, 157.6).

eighteen and the six. All the other forty-four[62] enumerations can be included in the eighteen, since these contain all phenomena, and thus it is incumbent to indicate why **only** the six constituents are explicitly mentioned in addition to the eighteen. The inventively cogent reason Gung-tang[63] gives is that for delineating selflessness, the six constituents have traditionally been singled out with particular emphasis. Nāgārjuna, for instance, uses the format of six constituents when, in his *Precious Garland,* he speaks of the basis of imputation of a person:[64]

> A person is not earth, not water,
> Not fire, not wind, not space,
> Not consciousness, and not all of them.
> What person is there other than these?
>
> Just as a person is not real
> Due to being a composite of six constituents,
> So each of the constituents also
> Is not real due to being a composite.

As Gung-tang says, in order to ascertain selflessness one must know how persons depend on the six constituents as their basis of imputation.

His point, cogently based on tradition, is that the frequent usage of the six constituents in connection with meditation on selflessness is the context out of which just these are selected in the *Sūtra Unraveling the Thought* for emphasis in addition to the basic eighteen constituents. Gung-tang's attention to contextual detail is impressive.

Harmonies with enlightenment. The last teaching in the first turning of the wheel of doctrine to which Paramārthasamudgata refers in his question is that of the thirty-seven harmonies with enlightenment. They are the antidotes to cyclic existence and to the phenomena associated with it—the aggregates of cyclic existence and so forth. In brief, the thirty-seven harmonies with enlightenment are seven groupings of beneficial phenomena that are concordant with and lead to enlightenment as a Foe Destroyer:[a]

---

[a] With respect to the translation of *arhant* (*dgra bcom pa*) as "Foe Destroyer," I do this to accord with the usual Tibetan translation of the term and to assist in capturing the flavor of oral and written traditions that frequently refer to this etymology. Arhants have overcome the foe which is the afflictive emotions (*nyon mongs, kleśa*), the chief of which is ignorance.

The Indian and Tibetan translators of Sanskrit and other texts into Tibetan were also aware of the etymology of *arhant* as "worthy one," as they translated the name of the "founder" of the Jaina system, Arhat, as *mchod 'od* "Worthy of Worship" (see Jam-ȳang-shay-b̄a's *Great Exposition of Tenets, ka* 62a.3). Also, they were aware of Chandrakīrti's gloss of the term as "Worthy One" in his *Clear Words: sadevamānuṣāsurāl lokāt pūnārhatvād arhannityuchyate* (*Mūlamadhyamakakārikās de Nāgārjuna avec la Prasannapadā Commentaire de Candrakīrti,* Bibliotheca Buddhica, 4 [Osnabrück, Germany: Biblio Verlag, 1970], 486.5), *lha dang mi dang lha ma yin du bcas pa'i 'jig rten gyis mchod par 'os pas dgra bcom pa zhes brjod*

I. FOUR ESTABLISHMENTS THROUGH MINDFULNESS
   1. mindful establishment on body
   2. mindful establishment on feeling
   3. mindful establishment on mind
   4. mindful establishment on phenomena
II. FOUR THOROUGH ABANDONINGS
   5. generating virtuous qualities not yet generated
   6. increasing virtuous qualities already generated
   7. not generating non-virtuous qualities not yet generated
   8. thoroughly abandoning non-virtuous qualities already generated
III. FOUR LEGS OF MANIFESTATION
   9. aspiration
   10. effort
   11. contemplation[a]
   12. analytical meditative stabilization
IV. FIVE FACULTIES
   13. faith

---

la (409.20, Tibetan Cultural Printing Press ed.; also, Peking 5260, vol. 98, 75.2.2), "Because of being worthy of worship by the world of gods, humans, and demi-gods, they are called Arhants."

Also, they were aware of Haribhadra's twofold etymology in his *Illumination of the Eight Thousand Stanza Perfection of Wisdom Sūtra.* In the context of the list of epithets qualifying the retinue of Buddha at the beginning of the sūtra (see Unrai Wogihara, *Abhisamayālaṃkārālokā Prajñā-pāramitā-vyākhyā, The Work of Haribhadra* [Tokyo: Toyo Bunko, 1932-1935; reprint, Tokyo: Sankibo Buddhist Book Store, 1973], 8.18), Haribhadra says:

> They are called *arhant* [Worthy One, from the root *arh* "to be worthy"] since they are worthy of worship, religious donations, and being assembled together in a group, and so forth. (Wogihara, *Abhisamayālaṃkārālokā,* 9.8-9: *sarva evātra pūjā-dakṣiṇā-gaṇa-parikarṣādy-ārhatayarhantaḥ;* Peking 5189, vol. 90, 67.5.7: *'dir thams cad kyang mchod pa dang // yon dang tshogs su 'dub la sogs par 'os pas na dgra bcom pa'o*).

Also:

> They are called *arhant* [Foe Destroyer, *arihan*] because they have destroyed (*hata*) the foe (*ari*). (Wogihara, *Abhisamayālaṃkārālokā,* 10.18: *hatāritvād* ***arhantaḥ;*** Peking 5189, vol. 90, 69.3.6. *dgra rnams bcom pas na dgra bcom pa'o*).

(My thanks to Gareth Sparham for the references to Haribhadra.) Thus, we are dealing with a considered preference in the face of alternative etymologies—"Foe Destroyer" requiring a not unusual *i* infix to make *ari-han,* with *ari* meaning enemy and *han* meaning to kill, and thus "Foe Destroyer." Unfortunately, one word in English cannot convey both this meaning and "Worthy of Worship"; thus I have gone with what clearly has become the predominant meaning in Tibet. (For an excellent discussion of the two etymologies of Arhat in Buddhism and Jainism, see L. M. Joshi, *Facets of Jaina Religiousness in Comparative Light,* L.D. Series, 85 [Ahmedabad, India: L.D. Institute of Indology, 1981], 53-58.)

[a] *sems.*

14. effort
15. mindfulness
16. meditative stabilization
17. wisdom

V. FIVE POWERS

18. faith
19. effort
20. mindfulness
21. meditative stabilization
22. wisdom

VI. SEVEN BRANCHES OF ENLIGHTENMENT

23. correct mindfulness
24. correct discrimination of phenomena
25. correct effort
26. correct joy
27. correct pliancy
28. correct meditative stabilization
29. correct equanimity

VII. EIGHTFOLD PATH

30. correct view
31. correct realization
32. correct speech
33. correct aims of actions
34. correct livelihood
35. correct exertion
36. correct mindfulness
37. correct meditative stabilization

The thirty-seven harmonies with enlightenment are coordinated with the three trainings—in ethics, meditative stabilization, and wisdom.[65] The four establishments through mindfulness are the basis of training; the four thorough abandonings are the training in higher ethics; the four legs of manifestation (an ability gained upon attaining meditative stabilization) are the training in higher meditative stabilization; and the five faculties, five powers, and seven branches of enlightenment are the training in higher wisdom.

As before, Buddha spoke of the **entities** of the thirty-seven as though they were established by way of their own character as the referents of conceptual consciousnesses and also spoke of seven **attributes** of the thirty-seven, all as being established by way of their own character as referents of conceptual consciousnesses. The seven attributes are:

1. their **discordances**, that is, what is to be abandoned by them. In terms of the seven groupings of the thirty-seven harmonies with enlightenment, the discordances are:[66]

four establishments through mindfulness: unknowingness
four thorough abandonings: laziness
four legs of manifestation: distraction
five faculties: non-interest
five powers: little strength of mindfulness and introspection
seven branches of enlightenment: possession of objects of abandonment by the path of seeing
eightfold path: possession of objects of abandonment by the path of meditation.

2. the **antidotes** themselves to those objects of abandonment
3. **production** of virtues or antidotes that have not been produced
4. the **abiding** of those virtues or antidotes that have been produced
5. **non-loss** of antidotes that have been produced
6. their **arising again** when one has familiarized with them again and again
7. **increasing** those antidotes through the power of familiarity **and extending** them limitlessly.

Issue #18: How can redundancy be avoided in the last two attributes?

Wonch'uk explains that the last two attributes mean non-forgetfulness of antidotes that have been produced. Gung-tang[67] cogently rejects this explanation since this would be redundant with the fifth attribute—"non-loss." Rather, he says that the sixth refers to familiarizing with antidotes through actualizing them repeatedly, and the seventh, to increasing them through the power of such familiarity.[68] He explains that in the latter the type of increase being indicated does not have a limit as the action of jumping does or as the heat of water does, but is extendible limitlessly. In this way, these two attributes are, in a general sense, both antidotes but do not repeat the second attribute due to their being more specific.[69]

* * *

In the *Sūtra Unraveling the Thought*, Paramārthasamudgata refers to these teachings on the thirty-seven harmonies with enlightenment, which are set forth in the *Sūtra on Mindful Establishment*[a] and in other sūtras, when he says:

> The Supramundane Victor also spoke, in many ways, of the own-character of the four mindful establishments, as well as speaking of [their] classes of discordances, antidotes, meditation, production of that which has not been produced, the abiding of that which has been

[a] *dran pa nyer bzhag, smṛtyupasthāna.* Gung-tang (*Difficult Points,* 77.16) mentions that one translator into Tibetan considered this text to be a Great Vehicle sūtra, whereas actually it is a Lesser Vehicle sūtra as is evidenced in various lists of sūtras.

> produced, non-loss, [their] arising again, and increasing and extending. Just as he did with respect to the mindful establishments, so he spoke with respect to the thorough abandonings, the legs of magical manifestation, the faculties, the powers, and the branches of enlightenment. The Supramundane Victor also spoke, in many ways, of the own-character of the eightfold path of Superiors, as well as speaking of [their] discordances, antidotes, production of that which has not been produced, the abiding of that which has been produced, recollection, [their] arising again, and increasing and extending.

With this statement, Paramārthasamudgata concludes the first part of his question—describing the mode of Buddha's pronouncement of the first wheel of his teaching.[70] With Gung-tang's fleshing out of the references, the context comes to life, despite the nagging problem of how the sparse words of the sūtras that he has cited teach that these phenomena are "established by way of their own character as the referents of conceptual consciousnesses."

Issue #19: Do all first-wheel sūtras teach the four noble truths?

As can be seen from the seven pronouncements, the topics on which the first wheel of doctrine[a] are based are many. However, Paṇ-chen Sö-nam-drak-b̄a, the textbook author of the L̄o-s̄el-l̄ing College of Dre-b̄ung Monastic University, holds that all first-wheel teachings have as their basis of composition the four noble truths.[b] Though he does not explicitly say so, he undoubtedly bases this on Paramārthasamudgata's summary statement of the meaning of Buddha's answers to his questions, when he describes the first wheel as "teaching the aspects of the four noble truths":

> Initially, in the area of Varaṇāsi in the Deer Park called "Sage's Propounding," the Supramundane Victor thoroughly turned a wheel of doctrine for those engaged in the Hearer Vehicle, fantastic and marvelous which none—god or human—had previously turned in a similar fashion in the world, through teaching the aspects of the **four noble truths**.

The evidence is striking, but Gung-tang[71] disagrees, pointing to the fact that when Paramārthasamudgata lists the teachings, he speaks of the four truths as only one among the seven pronouncements.[72] Gung-tang considers the four

---

[a] Since there are presentations of the wheels of doctrine that do not accord with the *Sūtra Unraveling the Thought*, the reference is to the wheels of doctrines **as described in that sūtra**.

[b] Paṇ-chen S̄ö-nam-drak-b̄a's *Garland of Blue Lotuses*, 12b.3. As Ḡön-chok-tsay-ring (oral teaching) pointed out, once the teaching of the four truths is the **only** basis of composition, one cannot cite other teachings as instances of the first wheel, as Gung-tang did (see the last chapter). This puts Paṇ-chen S̄ö-nam-drak-b̄a's followers in quite a bind.

noble truths to be the **prime** basis of composition, not the only one.

He makes the cogent point that—given the earlier format of the seven pronouncements, of which the four truths are just one category—the purpose of singling out the four noble truths here is to indicate not that the four truths are the basic topic of all first-wheel teachings but that the four truths are the **main** way of settling the meaning of Buddha's scriptures in the first wheel, this being in accordance with the minds of those having the lineage of the two Hearer Schools—the Great Exposition and the Sūtra schools. For instance, in Vasubandhu's *Treasury of Manifest Knowledge*—a principal text expounding in its root stanzas positions of the Great Exposition School and in its commentary positions of what came in Ge-luk-b̄a scholarship to be called the Sūtra School Following Scripture—the chapter structure itself is arranged around the four noble truths—true sufferings, sources, cessations, and paths. The first three chapters teach about true sufferings; the next two, true sources of suffering; and then the next three, true cessations of suffering and true paths. On the other hand, the Mind-Only School mainly delineates the meaning of Buddha's scriptures by way of the three natures—imputational, other-powered, and thoroughly established—in order to demonstrate that there are no external objects, no objects that are different entities from the consciousnesses perceiving them, and that hence there is cognition-only. Also, the Middle Way School mainly settles the meaning of Buddha's scriptures by way of the two truths—conventional and ultimate—in order to establish a union of appearance and emptiness and a union of method and wisdom.

By identifying the principal doctrinal structures of these schools—the four truths, three natures, and the two truths—Gung-tang shows that he is free of the prejudice, often acquired from focusing on the Middle Way School, that the two truths are the most important topic in all four schools. Still, the opposite prejudice, sometimes found in contemporary European, American, and Japanese scholarship—that the four noble truths, the three natures, and the two truths are not important topics in schools other than Middle Way—is also not justified. Rather, the **central theme** in the Great Exposition and Sūtra schools is the four noble truths; in the Mind-Only School, the three natures; and in the Middle Way School, the two truths. (That the two truths dominate so much discussion in Ge-luk-b̄a presentations of tenets is due to their basic Middle Way School orientation, an interest in comparing assertions on the two truths in all systems in order to ascertain more clearly the two truths in the Middle Way School. Despite its pedagogical value, the focus on the two truths naturally introduces distortions of emphasis.)

Showing sensitivity to the use of language in the *Sūtra Unraveling the Thought*, Gung-tang[73] emphasizes that Paramārthasamudgata's repeated usage of the phrase "in many ways," or "in many forms,"[a] when questioning Buddha about the teachings in the seven pronouncements means that he is referring to

[a] *rnam grangs du ma.*

individual sūtras with **different** topics even though all are similar in teaching that phenomena are established by way of their own character as the referents of conceptual consciousnesses. Conversely, when Paramārthasamudgata speaks of the middle wheel, he condenses the teachings into one description, since they all equally speak of all phenomena—ranging from forms through to exalted knowers of all aspects (omniscient consciousnesses)—as natureless, though some passages and sūtras of the middle wheel give more detailed lists of these phenomena than others. Thus, for Gung-tang, the points of reference, called the "bases of composition,"[a] of the teaching in the first wheel of doctrine are the seven categories of objects themselves and not just the four truths.

Issue #20: Do not any and all instances of Buddha's word teach the four noble truths?

Jik-may-dam-chö-gya-tso[74] often offers developments of and counter-opinions to Gung-tang's ideas. He relates an oral tradition that any instance of Buddha's word necessarily teaches the four noble truths, this being because Bhāvaviveka's proof in his *Blaze of Reasoning*[b] that Great Vehicle sūtras are the word of Buddha is founded on the reason that they all unerringly teach the four noble truths. Indeed, if one takes a sūtra's "having the four noble truths as its basis of composition" as meaning that it either directly or indirectly teaches the four truths, then all of Buddha's scriptures would teach the four truths.[c] Jik-may-dam-chö-gya-tso does not explain the difficulty that this raises, but it must be that then even the middle wheel would have the four noble truths as its basis of composition, whereas such clearly would contradict the statement in the *Sūtra Unraveling the Thought* that the middle wheel is "based[d] on just the naturelessness of all phenomena and based on just the absence of production, the absence of cessation, quiescence from the start, and naturally having thoroughly passed beyond sorrow."

Consequently, the meaning of "basis of composition" in the *Sūtra Unraveling the Thought* cannot be that the topic could be taught indirectly but must be that it is taught directly. Otherwise, one would have to hold that a sūtra based on the four truths does not necessarily directly teach the four truths, a position which I think cannot escape the above difficulty that even the middle wheel would have the four noble truths as its basis of composition, since, to accord

a *brtsams gzhi.*

b *rtog ge 'bar ba, tarkajvālā.* The *Blaze of Reasoning* is Bhāvaviveka's commentary on his *Heart of the Middle* (*dbu ma snying po, madhyamakahṛdaya*). Bhāvaviveka's dates are 500-570?; see David Seyfort Ruegg, *The Literature of the Madhyamaka School of Philosophy in India* (Wiesbaden, Germany: Otto Harrassowitz, 1981), 61.

c Jik-may-dam-chö-gya-tso cites Sha-m̄ar Ge-dün-d̄en-dzin-gya-tso's (*zhwa dmar dge 'dun bstan 'dzin rgya mtsho*) *Clearing Away Mental Darkness* as the origin of this qualm.

d *brtsams, ārabhya;* Lamotte, *Saṃdhinirmocana,* 86 [30], n. 18.

with Bhāvaviveka's statement it has to be held that the middle wheel at least indirectly teaches the four noble truths.

These points reveal for me a possible reason for Paṇ-chen Sö-nam-drak-ba's opinion that all first-wheel sūtras are based on the four truths: he may want to hold that first-wheel sūtras either directly or indirectly teach the four truths in order to establish, like Bhāvaviveka, that Great Vehicle sūtras are indeed the word of Buddha. His position is indeed attractive but does not seem to reflect the thrust of the *Sūtra Unraveling the Thought.* I find Gung-tang's position to be more cogent.

5. Probing the Implications

When Dzong-ka-ba summarizes Paramārthasamudgata's description of the middle and first-wheel teachings and his question to Buddha about their seeming contradiction, he says:

> If the statements in some sūtras [that is, in the middle wheel of the teaching] that all phenomena are natureless, and so forth, and the statements in some sūtras [in the first wheel of the teaching] that the aggregates and so forth have an own-character, and so forth, were left as they are verbally, they would be contradictory. However, since [the Supramundane Victor] must be without contradiction, of what were you [Buddha] thinking when [in the middle wheel of the teaching] you spoke of non-nature, and so forth?

Superficially, it seems that we can rephrase Dzong-ka-ba's reading of Paramārthasamudgata's question quite simply:

> In the first wheel you, Buddha, said that all phenomena are established by way of their own character, whereas in the middle wheel you said that no phenomenon is established by way of its own character. What were you thinking?

However, it is not so simple, as the sixteenth-century author of the old textbook literature of Go-mang College, Gung-ru Chö-jung, points out in an early, highly complex commentary on Dzong-ka-ba's text, his *Garland of White Lotuses*, and the late-seventeenth- and early-eighteenth-century scholar Jam-yang-shay-ba repeats with refinements in his *Great Exposition of the Interpretable and the Definitive*.[75] Their critique of other scholars' renditions of Paramārthasamudgata's question serves as a valuable key to the vocabulary and positions of the Buddhist schools involved. Let us probe their points.

Issue #21: What does "aggregates and so forth" mean?

First, Gung-ru Chö-jung and Jam-yang-shay-ba consider the phenomena about which Buddha was speaking in the first wheel. One of the earliest commentators, Bel-jor-hlün-drup, the author of the old textbook literature of the Jay College of Se-ra Monastic University (replaced by the works of Jay-dzün Chö-gyi-gyel-tsen), frames Paramārthasamudgata's question as follows (the portion being contested at this point is in bold print):[76]

> In the first wheel, the Supramundane Victor pronounced that **phenomena ranging from forms through to omniscient consciousnesses** are established by way of their own character; in the middle

> wheel he pronounced that phenomena are natureless, and are unproduced, unceasing, and so forth [that is, are quiescent from the start, and are naturally passed beyond sorrow]. The Bodhisattva Paramārthasamudgata asks, "Since, if taken literally, [these statements] are manifestly contradictory and since the Supramundane Victor must be without contradiction, thinking of what did you teach [in the middle wheel of doctrine that all phenomena are] natureless and so forth?" Having explicitly asked this, [Paramārthasamudgata] also perforce asks, "Thinking of what did you say [in the first wheel of doctrine] that phenomena are established by way of their own character?" For, at the point of the answer both are said to require interpretation by way of indicating the basis in Buddha's thought and by way of indicating the damage to what is explicitly taught [on the literal level] in both of the first two wheels.

Whereas D̄zong-ka-b̄a, as cited above, refers merely to "aggregates and so forth" when he speaks about the first wheel, B̄el-jor-hlün-drup, obviously intending to identify D̄zong-ka-b̄a's reference, expands this to "phenomena ranging from forms through to omniscient consciousnesses," a standard list of one hundred and eight phenomena drawn from the Perfection of Wisdom Sūtras that begins with forms and ends with omniscient consciousnesses.

Without mentioning B̄el-jor-hlün-drup by name, Gung-ru Chö-jung[77] and Jam-ȳang-shay-b̄a[78] object, saying that in the first wheel of doctrine it is inappropriate to identify "aggregates and so forth" here as those ranging from forms through to omniscient consciousnesses because in the first wheel Buddha did not explicitly take the one hundred and eight phenomena—which are the bases of his exposition in middle-wheel sūtras such as the Perfection of Wisdom Sūtras—as his substrata for the teaching that objects are established by way of their own character as the referents of their respective conceptual consciousnesses. Rather, in the explicit rendering of the first wheel it is obvious that he took a smaller number of phenomena (when compared to the one hundred and eight) as his substrata, these being the mental and physical aggregates, the sense-spheres, dependent-arising, the foods, the four noble truths, the constituents, and the harmonies with enlightenment—the seven pronouncements.[a]

[a] Gung-ru Chö-jung (*Garland of White Lotuses,* 5a.4) sees this as the background of D̄zong-ka-b̄a's (*Emptiness in Mind-Only,* 111) saying:

> [Paramārthasamudgata] says that in just the way that [the three natures] are applied to the form aggregate, three natures each are applied also with respect to each of the remaining four aggregates, the twelve sense spheres, the twelve [limbs of] dependent-arising, and the four foods as well as the six and eighteen constituents.

However, D̄zong-ka-b̄a here is not addressing the style of teaching of the first wheel; rather, he is paraphrasing Paramārthasamudgata's presentation to Buddha of the three natures, the explicit context of which is a presentation of the thought behind the teaching in the Perfection of Wisdom Sūtras that all phenomena are natureless. Perhaps it is this inappropriateness

The one hundred and eight phenomena are a division of all objects into two categories—fifty-three in the thoroughly afflicted category and fifty-five in the pure category. These are a Great Vehicle rendition of a table of phenomena,[a] including many (such as the eighteen emptinesses) that the Lesser Vehicle schools—the Great Exposition and the Sūtra schools—do not assert, such as the eighteen and twenty emptinesses and simultaneous knowledge of all phenomena. Implicit in Gung-ru Chö-jung and Jam-ȳang-shay-b̄a's reasoning is that even though the perspective of the present discussion of Paramārthasamudgata's question is that of the Mind-Only School,[b] in which "all phenomena" refer to these one hundred and eight, the first-wheel teachings were for trainees with the inclinations of the Great Exposition and Sūtra schools to whom it could not be said that Buddha spoke within using "all phenomena" **as understood according to the Mind-Only School** as his substrata. Jam-ȳang-shay-b̄a[79] sees D̄zong-ka-b̄a (*Emptiness in Mind-Only,* 242) making just this point when he says:[c]

> Initially, at Varaṇāsi, he spoke of the selflessness of persons; [thus] there is one cycle [of teaching], in which the true establishment of the phenomena of the aggregates and so forth—[these being] **no more than a few** [of the one hundred and eight phenomena]—is not refuted and true existence is mentioned frequently.

When it is said that in the first wheel Buddha takes **all phenomena** as the substrata for his teaching that objects are established by way of their own character as the referents of conceptual consciousnesses, it is necessary to specify "all phenomena" as those renowned to the Lesser Vehicle schools. Otherwise, as Gung-ru Chö-jung and Jam-ȳang-shay-b̄a cogently explain, it would have to be said that in the first wheel the eighteen and twenty emptinesses are taken as substrata for the teaching that phenomena are established this way, in which case it would be necessary to say that the eighteen and twenty emptinesses are

---

of context that caused Jam-ȳang-shay-b̄a to omit this sentence from his cribbing of Gung-ru Chö-jung's text.

It is intriguing that when Paramārthasamudgata presents this material on the three natures, he oddly frames it in the style of teaching of the first wheel—the seven pronouncements—and not of the middle wheel—the one hundred and eight phenomena ranging from forms through to omniscient consciousnesses.

[a] These are listed in Jeffrey Hopkins, *Meditation on Emptiness* (London: Wisdom, 1983; rev. ed., Boston, Ma.: Wisdom, 1996), 201-212.

[b] It will be shown later that "Mind-Only" is indeed a suitable appellation for the position of the early proponents of this "school," that is, Asaṅga, Vasubandhu, and Sthiramati. For the time being, I shall use the term not only for convenience but also because Ge-luk-b̄a traditions, which are our primary concern in this book, use it.

[c] The translation follows Jam-ȳang-shay-b̄a's reading of the sentence; for more discussion of this passage, see 55, 79, 87, and 92.

explicitly[a] taught on the literal level[b] in the first wheel. Absurdly, the emptiness of a self of phenomena would come to be explicitly and extensively taught in the first wheel, whereas this is the province of a Great Vehicle sūtra, not a Lesser Vehicle sūtra, and thus of the middle and final wheels of doctrine, not of the first wheel. As Dzong-ka-ba says,[c] "The Yogic Practitioners and Middle Way Autonomists assert that the selflessness of phenomena is not taught in the scriptural collections of the Lesser Vehicle."[d] Hence, in the first wheel Buddha is not speaking about the one hundred and eight phenomena that are the bases of discussion in the Perfection of Wisdom Sūtras; rather, he is taking only a smaller number of phenomena as the substrata of his teaching—the aggregates and so forth.[80]

Jay-dzün Chö-ğyi-gyel-tsen, in refuting Bel-jor-hlün-drup's position, rubs the point in even more by saying that if the first wheel taught that the one hundred and eight phenomena are established by way of their own character,[e] it would have to teach that the six perfections, a Bodhisattva's aspirational prayers, the ten grounds, omniscience, and a Buddha's qualities such as the ten powers, the four fearlessnesses, the four sciences, great love, great compassion, and the eighteen unique attributes of a Buddha are so established, in which case it would have to teach these. However, since the first wheel is uniquely Lesser Vehicle, it cannot. He cites Nāgārjuna's *Precious Garland* for support:[81]

Bodhisattvas' aspirational wishes, deeds, and dedications [of merit]

---

[a]   *dngos su.*

[b]   *sgras zin la.*

[c]   This is from the beginning of the section on the Consequence School titled "explaining the meaning of the two selflessnesses being set out in dependence on the scriptural collections of the Hearers"; the passage is cited in Jay-dzün Chö-ğyi-gyel-tsen's *General-Meaning Commentary,* 8b.3.

[d]   The term "Lesser Vehicle" (*theg dman, hīnayāna*) has its origin in the writings of Great Vehicle (*theg chen, mahāyāna*) authors and was, of course, not used by those to whom it was ascribed. Substitutes such as "non-Mahāyāna," "Nikāya Buddhism," and "Theravādayāna" have been suggested in order to avoid the pejorative sense of "Lesser." However, translation accuracy is required, and also "Lesser Vehicle" is a convenient term in this particular context for a type of tenet system or practice that is seen, in the tradition being discussed in this book, to be surpassed—but not negated—by a higher system. The "Lesser Vehicle" is not despised, most of it being incorporated into the "Great Vehicle." The monks' and nuns' vows are Lesser Vehicle as is much of the course of study in Ge-luk-ba monastic universities—years of study are put into the topics of Epistemology (*tshad ma, pramāṇa*), Manifest Knowledge (*chos mngon pa, abhidharma*), and Discipline (*'dul ba, vinaya*), all of which are mostly Lesser Vehicle in perspective. ("Lesser Vehicle" and "Low Vehicle" are used interchangeably in this book.)

[e]   I have adapted Jay-dzün Chö-ğyi-gyel-tsen's "established by way of their own character" to read "established by way of their own character as the referents of conceptual consciousnesses" to conform to Gung-ru Chö-jung and Jam-ȳang-shay-ba's explanation. Jay-dzün Chö-ğyi-gyel-tsen's position on this issue will be discussed later in this chapter.

Were not described in the Hearers' Vehicle.
Therefore how could one become
A Bodhisattva through it?

and:[82]

The subjects concerned with the Bodhisattva deeds
Were not mentioned in the [Hearers' Vehicle] sūtras
But were explained in the Great Vehicle.
Hence the wise should accept it [as Buddha's word].[a]

Jam-ȳang-shay-b̄a[83] clinches the point that first-wheel sūtras do not explicitly teach the one hundred and eight phenomena by indicating that this is the significance of Paramārthasamudgata's specifying the seven pronouncements, one by one:

> The Supramundane Victor spoke, in many ways, of the own-character of the **aggregates**.... Just as he did with respect to the aggregates, so he also spoke with respect to the **sense-spheres**, **dependent-arising**, and also the **foods**. The Supramundane Victor also spoke, in many ways, of the own-character of the **truths**.... The Supramundane Victor also spoke, in many ways, of the own-character of the **constituents**, as well as speaking of the various constituents, manifold constituents.... The Supramundane Victor also spoke, in many ways, of the own-character of the **thirty-seven harmonies with enlightenment**....

It is clear that Paramārthasamudgata's specifically mentioning these central topics that are the substrata of the first-wheel teaching excludes, on the negative side, the special phenomena of the Great Vehicle sūtras. Jam-ȳang-shay-b̄a thereby draws out the implications of the vocabulary and style of Paramārthasamudgata's question, settling that the substrata of the first-wheel teachings as described in the *Sūtra Unraveling the Thought* are phenomena ranging from forms through the thirty-seven harmonies with enlightenment—the topics of the seven pronouncements.

Jay-d̄zün Chö-ḡyi-gyel-tsen[84] rubs it in even more by citing D̄zong-ka-b̄a's statement (*Emptiness in Mind-Only,* 112-113) about:

> each of [the phenomena] ranging from the form aggregate through the branches of the path, which were mentioned earlier on the occasion of his question about dispelling contradiction.

It is obvious that D̄zong-ka-b̄a limits the phenomena mentioned in the first wheel to the topics of the seven pronouncements.

---

[a] For D̄zong-ka-b̄a's discussion of these two stanzas, see Tsong-ka-pa, Kensur Lekden, and Jeffrey Hopkins, *Compassion in Tibetan Buddhism,* 173.

Issue #22: Is Paramārthasamudgata concerned with the teaching of just compounded *phenomena in the first wheel?*

The Second Dalai Lama, whose commentary was most likely written after Bel-jor-hlün-drup's, self-consciously uses "aggregates and so forth"[a] instead of "all phenomena" for the first wheel. As is clear later in his commentary,[85] he does this in order not to contradict a cryptic and highly controversial statement later by Dzong-ka-ba (*Emptiness in Mind-Only,* 242) which seems to indicate that not all phenomena in the first wheel were taught to be established by way of their own character or truly established:[b]

> Initially, at Varaṇāsi, he spoke of the selflessness of persons; [thus] there is one cycle [of teaching], in which the true establishment of the phenomena of the aggregates and so forth, except for a few, is not refuted and true existence is mentioned frequently.[c]

Hence, it is the Second Dalai Lama's opinion that, according to Dzong-ka-ba, in the first wheel not all phenomena (including permanent ones such as true cessations) but only all **compounded** phenomena were taught as being truly established and established by way of their own character.[d]

As will be seen below (61), this opinion is problematic since it is clear that in the system of the *Sūtra Unraveling the Thought* and of the Mind-Only School compounded phenomena are indeed established by way of their own character. Also, rather than twisting the meaning of the *Sūtra Unraveling the Thought* to accord with a cryptic statement in Dzong-ka-ba's text, it seems preferable to stick with the language of the sūtra and hold that the substrata of the first-wheel teachings are phenomena ranging from forms through the thirty-

---

[a] *phung sogs:* Second Dalai Lama's *Lamp Illuminating the Meaning of [Dzong-ka-ba's] Thought,* 12.6.

[b] The Second Dalai Lama's citation deviates considerably from Dzong-ka-ba's text, though not in meaning. Second Dalai Lama (15.3):

> ***'khor lo dang por*** *phung sogs* ***kyi*** *chos* ***la*** *nyung shas cig ma gtogs pa* ***shas cher*** *bden par* ***yod*** *pa ma bkag* ***pa dang***

Dzong-ka-ba (*Emptiness in Mind-Only,* 450):

> *phung* ***po la*** *sogs* ***pa'i*** *chos nyung shas gcig ma gtogs pa bden par* ***grub*** *pa ma bkag* ***cing***

[c] This passage was cited just above but with a different translation that accords with Jam-yang-shay-ba's reading:

> Initially, at Varaṇāsi he spoke of the selflessness of persons; [thus] there is one cycle [of teaching] in which the true establishment of the phenomena of the aggregates and so forth—[these being] *no more than a few* [of the one hundred and eight phenomena]—is not refuted and true existence is mentioned frequently.

[d] Paṇ-chen Sö-nam-drak-ba's refutation of the Second Dalai Lama's reading is given in the next chapter, 86.

seven harmonies with enlightenment—the topics of the seven pronouncements, these being what the Lesser Vehicle Buddhist schools consider to be all phenomena, permanent and impermanent.

Issue #23: When the eighteen constituents are taught, are the one hundred eight phenomena taught?

It is the style of monastic textbooks not only to rub in perceived mistakes but also to reveal (or create) complications in what seems obvious. Thus, Jay-d̄zün Chö-ḡyi-gyel-tsen[86] reminds us of the seemingly innocent fact that the eighteen constituents—these being one of the seven pronouncements—include all phenomena, the complication being that the one hundred and eight phenomena are therefore contained within the eighteen constituents. Still, as he says, this does not require that the first wheel's teaching—that all phenomena are established by way of their own character—entails explicitly teaching that the one hundred and eight phenomena are established this way, just as the fact that Proponents of Sūtra **assert** that all phenomena are established this way does not entail that they assert that the one hundred and eight phenomena, including the emptiness of that same status of things, are established this way. Otherwise, they would absurdly be asserting the emptiness of the very status of things that is so central to their system. So far, the point is well taken.

Issue #24: Can this topic be trivialized?

It also is the style of monastic textbooks to make hair-splitting verbal distinctions such that the counter-intuitive comes to be asserted for the sake of its shock-value, not insight. In this fashion Gung-ru Chö-jung[87] and Jam-ȳang-shay-b̄a[88] go on to indicate that they are willing to hold the counter-intuitive position that:

> **Upon the one hundred and eight phenomena being included in the eighteen constituents,** first-wheel sūtras explicitly teach the one hundred and eight as established by way of their own character as the referents of conceptual consciousnesses.[a]

They may mean that **if** for the listener's mind the one hundred and eight phenomena are included in the eighteen constituents, then when the eighteen constituents are taught as being established by way of their own character as the referents of their respective conceptual consciousnesses, the one hundred and eight phenomena are similarly taught to be established this way. However, the one hundred and eight would not be so included for the intended trainees of first wheel of doctrine; hence, there does not seem to be any intended listener

[a] *des de rnams khams bco brgyad du bsdus nas rang 'dzin rtog pa'i zhen gzhir rang gi mtshan nyid kyis grub par dngos su bstan.*

of the first wheel for whom they would be included.

Gung-ru Chö-jung backs up his point by drawing a parallel with two lines from the beginning of Maitreya's *Ornament for Clear Realization*[89]—"The perfection of wisdom/ Is thoroughly explained by the eight categories"—which he says does not explicitly teach the seventy topics (which are the sub-topics of the eight categories)[a] but does explicitly teach them **upon their being included in the eight categories**. However, I do not consider the two to be parallel, since in Maitreya's text the seventy topics are about to be taught as subsections of the eight categories but in the scriptures of the first wheel there is no intention to teach the one hundred and eight phenomena.

Gung-ru Chö-jung and Jam-ȳang-shay-b̄a may merely be making the point that the one hundred and eight phenomena are included in the eighteen constituents and that in the first wheel the eighteen constituents are explicitly taught to be established by way of their own character as the referents of their respective conceptual consciousnesses and hence it must be said that **upon the one hundred and eight phenomena being included in the eighteen constituents**, first-wheel sūtras explicitly teach them as so established. However, this treats the two phrases—(1) "upon the one hundred and eight phenomena being included in the eighteen constituents" and (2) "first-wheel sūtras explicitly teach them as..."—as if they are disconnected, whereas in any meaningful rendering of the grammar they are intimately related. In fact, the shock-value of their presentation rests on the assumption that when in the first phrase it is said that the one hundred and eight phenomena are included in the eighteen constituents, it **seems** that this is being said with respect to the worldview of first-wheel sūtras. Their maneuver trivializes Jay-d̄zün Chö-ḡyi-gyel-tsen's significant point in an attempt to provide a counter-intuitive refinement out of sophistic sport; for me, rather than shock I find frustration.[b]

---

[a] The eight categories are:

1. knowledge of all aspects (*rnam pa thams cad mkhyen pa nyid, sarvākārajñatā*)
2. knowledge of paths (*lam shes nyid, mārgajñatā*)
3. knowledge of bases (*gzhi shes, vastujñāna*)
4. complete training in all the aspects (*rnam rdzogs sbyor ba/rnam kun mngon par rdzogs par rtogs pa, sarvākārābhisaṃbodha*)
5. peak training (*rtse sbyor, mūrdhaprayoga*)
6. serial training (*mthar gyis sbyor ba, anupūrvaprayoga*)
7. momentary training (*skad cig ma'i sbyor ba, kṣaṇikaprayoga*)
8. body of attributes, the effect (*chos sku, dharmakāya*).

[b] For more hair-splitting refinements on this topic, see A-ku L̄o-drö-gya-tso's *Precious Lamp*, 66.1-67.6.

Issue #25: Does the first wheel teach the actual four noble truths?

Gung-ru Chö-jung and Jam-ỹang-shay-b̄a have made the unchallengeable point that the first wheel does not take phenomena ranging from forms through to omniscient consciousnesses as the substrata of its teachings. In the process of proving their point, they use the principle that whatever is taken as a substratum of a teaching is also itself explicitly taught. In this vein, they say that if the first wheel took all phenomena ranging from forms through to omniscient consciousnesses as the substrata of its teachings, then the twenty emptinesses (which are included in this range and are a topic specific to the Great Vehicle) absurdly would have to be taught in the first wheel.

The principle that whatever is taken as a substratum of a teaching is also itself explicitly taught seems well taken; however, consider this problem:

> Since Gung-ru Chö-jung and Jam-ỹang-shay-b̄a themselves hold that the first wheel takes the four noble truths as one of its substrata for the teaching that phenomena are established by way of their own character as the referents of their respective conceptual consciousnesses, they must hold that the first wheel teaches the **actual** four noble truths and not just four noble truths that are established by way of their own character as the referents of their respective conceptual consciousnesses. This is because truths that are established this way are non-existent, and followers of the Lesser Vehicle cannot attain their respective enlightenments through meditating on non-existent objects. Also, if first-wheel sūtras such as the *Turning of the Wheel of the Four Truths* do not teach the actual four truths, then what sūtra does!

As was mentioned earlier (issue #15), Jik-may-dam-chö-gya-tso's solution[90] is:

1. to admit that the first wheel teaches the actual four noble truths both **mainly** and **explicitly**
2. but to hold that **on the literal level** it teaches the four truths to be established by way of their own character as the referents of their respective conceptual consciousnesses.

He uses the tack of splitting the explicit teaching from the literal reading so as to avoid having to hold that anything the first wheel teaches on the literal level can be taken literally and hence would have to be definitive. For if anything on the literal level of the first wheel were definitive, this would contradict the statement in the *Sūtra Unraveling the Thought* that the first wheel is not definitive and requires interpretation.

Issue #26: Does the second wheel explicitly teach the actual twenty emptinesses on the literal level?

Another technique employed by monastic authors is to apply a principle enunciated in their system **against** another point in their own system; the honesty in such self-contestation can even be thrilling. In this vein, A-ku Lo-drö-gya-tso[91] attempts to show how Jam-ÿang-shay-b̄a's principle enunciated with regard to the first wheel that whatever is taken as a substratum of a teaching is also itself explicitly taught **on the literal level** doubles back on his own presentation of the second wheel. Jam-ÿang-shay-b̄a made the point that since B̄el-jor-hlün-drup says that the substratum of the teaching of the first wheel is all phenomena ranging from forms through omniscient consciousnesses, then the actual emptinesses absurdly would explicitly be taught **on the literal level** in the first wheel—with Jam-ÿang-shay-b̄a seemingly unnecessarily adding "on the literal level."

A-ku Lo-drö-gya-tso strikes the absurd consequence that since the second wheel takes the twenty emptinesses as one of the substrata of its teaching that phenomena do not exist from their own side, it would have to explicitly teach the actual twenty emptinesses **on the literal level** despite the fact that the second wheel requires interpretation. However, if the second wheel did teach the twenty emptinesses on the literal level, then it would be literal and thus definitive, something that the *Sūtra Unraveling the Thought* does not allow. A-ku Lo-drö-gya-tso suggests that Jam-ÿang-shay-b̄a may have worded his absurd consequence about the first wheel the way he did because the proponents of Lesser Vehicle tenets do not distinguish between what is explicitly indicated and the literal reading, but he calls for the intelligent to analyze the point. (It is clear that issues raised are not necessarily settled. The genre is aimed at stimulation.)

Own-Character

Issue #27: Does "own-character" mean established by way of its own character?

As we saw above, B̄el-jor-hlün-drup says that Paramārthasamudgata's concern is with an apparent contradiction in Buddha's teaching, namely that in the first wheel of doctrine Buddha taught that phenomena ranging from forms through to and including omniscient consciousnesses (forms being the first and omniscient consciousnesses being the last of the one hundred and eight phenomena) are equally established by way of their own character whereas in the middle wheel he taught that these phenomena are equally not established by way of their own character. Gung-ru Chö-jung (with Jam-ÿang-shay-b̄a following him) finds fault, as detailed above, with B̄el-jor-hlün-drup's mention of "phenomena ranging from forms through to omniscient consciousnesses" as the substrata. Jay-d̄zün Chö-ḡyi-gyel-tsen, whose works replaced B̄el-jor-hlün-drup's as the textbook literature of the Jay College of S̄e-ra, adjusts B̄el-jor-hlün-drup's framing of Paramārthasamudgata's question to take care of this fault:[92]

> "In the first wheel, the Supramundane Victor pronounced that **all phenomena ranging from forms through to the thirty-seven harmonies with enlightenment** are established by way of their own character; in the middle wheel you pronounced that all phenomena ranging from forms through to omniscient consciousnesses are not established by way of their own character. Even if, taken literally, [these statements] are contradictory, the Supramundane Victor must be without contradiction; therefore, thinking of what did you say what you said in the middle wheel of doctrine?" From explicitly asking this, [Paramārthasamudgata] also implicitly asks, "Thinking of what did you say what you did in the first [wheel of doctrine]?"

Besides the correction about the substrata of the teaching of the first wheel, Jay-d̄zün Chö-ḡyi-gyel-tsen also replaces B̄el-jor-hlün-drup's reference to the teaching in the middle wheel that "phenomena are natureless" with "are not established by way of their own character," but this is merely an improvement in clarity.[93] D̄zong-ka-b̄a himself elsewhere in his text (*Emptiness in Mind-Only,* 114) clearly says:

> Thus, in [Buddha's] scriptures, there are three sets of sūtras:
>
> - [A first-wheel] teaching that phenomena **exist by way of their own character**
> - [A middle wheel] teaching that phenomena are not **established by way of their own character**
> - [A final wheel] differentiating well whether phenomena are or are not **established by way of their own character**
>
> Furthermore, these are twofold—(1) that [final set of sūtras] which does and (2) those [first two sets of sūtras] which do not differentiate well the existence and non-existence of nature [with respect to the three natures]. That which does is of definitive meaning since it is not to be interpreted otherwise, and those that do not are of interpretable meaning since they must be interpreted otherwise.

and (*Emptiness in Mind-Only,* 127):

> The bases being posited as interpretable or definitive are the three—the statements [in the first wheel] that phenomena equally[a] have nature in the sense of being **established by way of their own character,**

[a] See issues 44 and 55.

the statements [in the middle wheel] that phenomena equally do not have such, and the good differentiation [in the final wheel] of those [phenomena] that have [such establishment] and those that do not.

Jay-d̄zün Chö-ḡyi-gyel-tsen seems to have framed Ḏzong-ka-b̄a's opinion perfectly:[a] the first-wheel sūtras teach that objects are established by way of their own character, whereas the middle wheel teaches that objects are not established by way of their own character.

However, Gung-ru Chö-jung[94] and Jam-ȳang-shay-b̄a[95] make many objections to this formulation (at least some of which were known to Jay-d̄zün Chö-ḡyi-gyel-tsen). These criticisms, despite being interesting and cogent, complicate the issue to such an incredible degree that at times it seems as if what is left is only a morass of confusion. Such shocking disorientation in which the foundation of one's understanding of important doctrines crumbles is an unstated aim of monastic textbooks and of the daily rounds of debate in monastic colleges. By unflinchingly exploring the implications of positions, the arrogance of thinking that one has command of an issue is confronted with embroilment in self-contradiction, mirroring the meditative process of analysis in which one's most cherished and fundamental postures about the nature of things are undermined. Although on the surface the various systems of exegesis are committed to the posture that there are cogent, reasonable answers to all conceptual problems, the process of training carries the different message that any topic eventually involves self-contradiction.

Gung-ru Chö-jung and Jam-ȳang-shay-b̄a's basic argument is:

1. The Mind-Only School maintains that compounded phenomena are established by way of their own character.
2. If the first-wheel sūtras did explicitly teach that phenomena ranging from forms through the thirty-seven harmonies with enlightenment are established by way of their own character, then since this list of phenomena includes both compounded (or impermanent) phenomena and uncompounded (or permanent) phenomena, the first-wheel sūtras would be sūtras explicitly teaching that **compounded phenomena** ranging from forms through the thirty-seven harmonies with enlightenment are established by way of their own character.
3. Hence, it would absurdly be suitable to assert literally something that the first-wheel sūtras explicitly teach, namely, that compounded phenomena such as forms are established by way of their own character, and thus such

[a] Jik-may-dam-chö-gya-tso (*Port of Entry,* 144.4-144.6) says that it appears that Jay-d̄zün Chö-ḡyi-gyel-tsen's mode of explanation mostly accords with the literal reading of Ḏzong-ka-b̄a's statement as well as of Ke-drup's (to be given later) and the Second Dalai Lama's reading. His implication is that the Gung-ru Chö-jung and Jam-ȳang-shay-b̄a tradition deviates from Ḏzong-ka-b̄a's actual words despite pretending that it does not; I agree, but the question remains as to whether that deviation is preferable.

a first-wheel sūtra would be a sūtra whose explicit teaching is suitable to be accepted literally.

4. However, according to the *Sūtra Unraveling the Thought* the first wheel is supposed to require interpretation, to be unacceptable literally.

Gung-ru Chö-jung and Jam-ȳang-shay-b̄a do not establish here why in the Mind-Only School any impermanent phenomenon must be established by way of its own character, but this point is clearly expressed in the *Sūtra Unraveling the Thought* itself. For in explaining what was behind the teaching in the Perfection of Wisdom Sūtras that phenomena are not produced, Buddha says that imputational natures cannot be produced by causes and conditions because they are not established by way of their own character, whereby it is clearly indicated that establishment by way of the object's own character is a prerequisite for the activity of production. The sūtra says:[96]

> Concerning that, thinking of just character-non-natures [that is, thinking of just imputational factors which are not established by way of their own character], I taught that all phenomena are unproduced, unceasing, quiescent from the start, naturally thoroughly passed beyond sorrow.
>
> Why? Paramārthasamudgata, it is thus: **That which does not exist by way of its own character** is not produced. That which is not produced does not cease. That which is not produced and does not cease is from the start quiescent. That which is quiescent from the start is naturally thoroughly passed beyond sorrow [that is, naturally devoid of the afflictive emotions without depending on an antidote]. That which is naturally thoroughly passed beyond sorrow does not have the least thing to pass beyond sorrow.

This statement is Gung-ru Chö-jung and Jam-ȳang-shay-b̄a's ultimate source for their position that a sūtra explicitly teaching that compounded phenomena are established by way of their own character must be non-deceptive and therefore a literally acceptable sūtra. Consequently, they draw the conclusion that the term "own-character" that Paramārthasamudgata uses when describing the first-wheel teaching about all phenomena cannot refer to establishment by way of their own character but must refer to establishment by way of their own character **as the referents of their respective conceptual consciousnesses**—a status of each and every phenomenon that the Mind-Only School refutes. Their position is cogent indeed, but, as we shall see, there are other cogent possibilities.

Issue #28: Does non-deceptiveness require being literally acceptable?

Contrary to Gung-ru Chö-jung and Jam-ȳang-shay-b̄a, scholars such as B̄el-jor-hlün-drup, Jay-d̄zün Chö-ḡyi-gyel-tsen, and Paṇ-chen S̄ö-nam-drak-b̄a assert that the term "own-character" in Paramārthasamudgata's question refers to establishment of objects by way of their own character. Now, since all Ge-luk-b̄a scholars hold that in the Mind-Only School:

- what is literally unacceptable requires interpretation
- what is literally acceptable is definitive
- and all compounded phenomena are established by way of their own character

these scholars and their followers must struggle to keep from having to admit that a first-wheel sūtra explicitly teaching that compounded phenomena are established by way of their own character is a sūtra whose explicit teaching is suitable to be accepted literally. If they did, they would have to admit that a first-wheel sūtra is definitive, and this flies in the face of the *Sūtra Unraveling the Thought*'s clear statement that first-wheel sūtras require interpretation. Sounds impossible, does it not! (Jay-d̄zün Chö-ḡyi-gyel-tsen's and Paṇ-chen S̄ö-nam-drak-b̄a's opinions are given in the next chapter; the remainder of this chapter sets the stage—larger and larger and larger.)

To make their predicament super-clear, Gung-ru Chö-jung and Jam-ȳang-shay-b̄a make what in other circumstances would be the obvious point that sūtras teaching doctrines that accord with the fact are literally acceptable sūtras. This is how they rub it in, supporting each reason with its own evidence:

> A first-wheel sūtra explicitly teaching that compounded phenomena ranging from forms through the thirty-seven harmonies with enlightenment are established by way of their own character is necessarily a sūtra whose explicit teaching is suitable to be asserted literally,
>
> - because a sūtra that explicitly teaches that compounded phenomena are established by way of their own character is necessarily a sūtra whose explicit teaching is suitable to be asserted literally
> - because a sūtra that explicitly teaches that compounded phenomena are impermanent is necessarily a sūtra whose explicit teaching is suitable to be asserted literally
> - because a sūtra that explicitly teaches the sixteen attributes of the four noble truths is necessarily a sūtra whose explicit teaching is suitable to be asserted literally
> - because a sūtra that explicitly teaches the four noble truths is necessarily a sūtra whose explicit teaching is suitable to be asserted literally

- because a sūtra that explicitly teaches the four noble truths is non-deceptive with respect to the literal reading of its principal topics of explicit teaching[97]
- because a sūtra that explicitly teaches what is to be discarded and what is to be adopted with respect to the four truths (sufferings and their origins are to be discarded, and cessations and paths are to be adopted) is a correct, concordant example that possesses the reason and the predicate in a proof that a sūtra teaching very obscure topics is non-deceptive with respect to what it teaches by reason of the fact that it is a scripture devoid of contradiction
- because Dharmakīrti's *Commentary on (Dignāga's) "Compilation of Prime Cognition"* says:[98]

> Through thorough ascertainment of just these [teachings]
> On adoption [of true cessations] and discarding [true sufferings] as well as [their respective] methods [or causes, that is, true paths and true origins of suffering respectively],
> [It is established by inference through the power of the fact that Buddha's word] is non-deceptive with respect to the principal meaning [the four noble truths].
> Therefore, [due to similarity] it is to be inferred[a] that [Buddha's word is non-deceptive] also with respect to other [very obscure topics as well].

Dharmakīrti is saying that through scriptural inference based on the logical sign, or reason, that a certain passage teaching very obscure objects of comprehension is devoid of contradiction, it can be concluded that the passage is non-deceptive with respect to what it teaches, just as Buddha's teaching on the four truths is non-deceptive. He cites the teaching on the four noble truths in the context of showing that certain of Buddha's teachings on very obscure topics[b] are also non-deceptive with respect to what they teach because of also being purified by way of three analyses in that (1) what they teach about manifest objects is not contradicted by direct perception, (2) what they teach about slightly obscure objects is not contradicted by usual inference (called inference by the power of the fact),[c] and (3) with respect to very obscure objects, inaccessible to either direct perception or usual inference, there are no internal contradictions within Buddha's teachings on those topics.

Because Dharmakīrti uses a sūtra explicitly teaching what is to be adopted and what is to be discarded in terms of the four noble truths as an instance of a

---

[a] This is a scriptural inference (*lung gi rjes dpag*).

[b] That is, very obscure objects of comprehension (*shin tu lkog gyur gyi gzhal bya/ gzhal bya shin tu lkog gyur*).

[c] *dngos stobs rjes dpag.*

sūtra that is **non-deceptive** with respect to what it teaches, it can be concluded that such a sūtra is suitable to be asserted **literally**. And, if non-deceptiveness is the criterion for the suitability of asserting a text literally, one cannot claim that a sūtra that explicitly teaches that compounded phenomena ranging from forms through the thirty-seven harmonies with enlightenment are established by way of their own character is not necessarily a sūtra whose explicit teaching is suitable to be asserted literally. (Using the juxtaposition of seemingly widely separated doctrines, Gung-ru Chö-jung and Jam-ȳang-shay-b̄a have opened up other, barely related topics which, at first reading, divert attention from the principal topic, seemingly fracturing the mind by straying from the issue. However, the excursion imbeds the issue even more within the overall culture, thereby enhancing appreciation of the fabric, the context, of the discussion.)

Still, what is the relevance of Jam-ȳang-shay-b̄a's citing a passage from a work by Dharmakīrti in a discussion that centers around the teachings of the masters of the early Yogic Practice School—Asaṅga and his half-brother Vasubandhu as well as their commentator Sthiramati? The connection is not merely that Ge-luk-b̄a scholars assign Dharmakīrti's views also to the Mind-Only School (also called the Yogic Practice School); rather, the connection is that Dharmakīrti was a follower of Dignāga (though not his direct student), and Dignāga was a student of Vasubandhu, who is said to have converted to the Mind-Only view through the teachings of his half-brother, Asaṅga. However, even more relevant than this historical connection is the appropriateness of showing the general sensibleness of accepting that a non-deceptive scripture is literally acceptable.[a]

Jam-ȳang-shay-b̄a[99] extends the scope of the excursion even further by citing a similar passage from Āryadeva's *Four Hundred:*[100]

Whoever has generated doubt

[a] For Gung-ru Chö-jung and Jam-ȳang-shay-b̄a, even if the teaching of the four truths is literally acceptable, a *first-wheel sūtra* (as described in the *Sūtra Unraveling the Thought*) called the wheel of doctrine of the four truths is not literally acceptable because it teaches on the literal level that these phenomena are established by way of their own character as the referents of their respective conceptual consciousnesses. Paṇ-chen S̄ö-nam-drak-b̄a holds that according to the Mind-Only School a first-wheel sūtra teaching the four truths is not literally acceptable because it is infected with a sense of externality; see issue 35, p. 84. Nevertheless, as Ge-s̄hay Ḡön-chok-tsay-ring explained Paṇ-chen S̄ö-nam-drak-b̄a's position, in the Mind-Only School the teaching of the four truths can be cited as a concordant example of something that is non-deceptive because, even though the literal reading is not literally acceptable, the main topic being basically taught (that is, the four truths) cannot be harmed by valid cognition (and hence is validly established). Thus, although the literal reading is harmed by valid cognition, the basic topic is not. According to followers of Gung-ru Chö-jung and Jam-ȳang-shay-b̄a, however, a first-wheel sūtra as described in the *Sūtra Unraveling the Thought* does not teach the (actual) four truths on the literal level, and thus they do not need to make this particular maneuver; they hold that the first wheel mainly and explicitly teaches the (actual) four truths but not on the literal level.

Toward what is not obvious in Buddha's word
Will believe that only Buddha [is omniscient]
Based on [his profound teaching of] emptiness.

Āryadeva's point is that if Buddha is correct with respect to such a profound topic as emptiness, he must also be correct with respect to less profound but more obscure topics such as minute details of the cause and effects of actions, as long as what he says is not contradicted by any of the three types of analyses listed above.

The main point of these two passages is that the logical verifiability of Buddha's special cognition of the four truths and the verifiability of emptiness become the means of validating his teachings on topics inaccessible to such verification. The principle is that if he is right about such profound topics, he must be right about less profound, even though more inaccessible topics. In this vein, the current Dalai Lama cites these same two passages after saying:[101]

> Thus Buddha, the Blessed One, from his own insight taught this dependent-arising as his slogan[a]—showing that because phenomena are dependent-arisings, they have a nature of emptiness, free of the eight extremes of cessation and so forth. If Buddha is thus seen as a reliable being who without error taught definite goodness [liberation and omniscience] along with its means, one will consequently see that the Blessed One was not mistaken even with respect to teaching high status [the pleasures of lives as humans and gods] along with its means.

If Buddha is found to be right in his teaching about the path to achieve liberation from cyclic existence and to achieve the omniscience of Buddhahood, then, of course, he must be right about other, less profound (even if more obscure) topics such as how to achieve a life of high status within cyclic existence.

Tibetan scholars have used this type of reasoning for centuries as justification for accepting cosmological explanations and so forth that are not subject to usual verification but are devoid of contradiction by direct perception, logical inference, and internal contradictions. The tradition has developed, over centuries, a sense of what, within Buddha's teachings on very obscure topics, can be accepted literally. Among these is the teaching of a flat earth, now obviously contradicted by direct perception from satellites, and this has brought into question the whole scope of teachings on very obscure topics, not only cosmological but also ethical, hitherto considered safely verified. — We also have gone far afield; let us return to the topic.

More evidence. Gung-ru Chö-jung[b] gives another argument why what is

---

[a] The Dalai Lama himself suggested the word "slogan" to translate the Tibetan term *gtam,* which might also be rendered as "principal discourse."

[b] Gung-ru Chö-jung's *Garland of White Lotuses,* 6b.5. Jam-ȳang-shay-b̄a uses this reasoning in his *Brief Decisive Analysis* (490.6-491.4), where, in a move unusual among Ge-luk-b̄a

non-deceptive must be considered to be literally acceptable, namely:

> A sūtra that explicitly teaches the mental and physical aggregates—which are appropriated through afflictive emotions and actions contaminated by them—is necessarily a literally acceptable sūtra,

- because a sūtra that explicitly teaches the selflessness of persons is necessarily a literally acceptable sūtra,
- because a sūtra that explicitly teaches that a self of persons exists is necessarily a sūtra that is not literally acceptable,
- because it is fitting to consider as a sūtra requiring interpretation the sūtra (passage):

> O monks, a burden exists [substantially in the sense of being self-sufficient].[102]
> A bearer of the burden exists [substantially in the sense of being self-sufficient].
> The five aggregates are the burden.
> The bearer of the burden is the person.

It is widely renowned that the teaching in this passage that persons substantially exist in the sense of being self-sufficient is not literally acceptable because it is contradicted by reasoning, and thus this clear instance of a teaching requiring interpretation affirms the principle that what is deceptive is not literally acceptable and that what is non-deceptive is literally acceptable.

Gung-ru Chö-jung[103] then makes the same point from the viewpoint of a sūtra renowned to be literally acceptable and hence definitive. Since Jam-ȳang-shay-b̄a[104] restructures the argument so as to make it more biting, let us cite his rendition first. It need not be repeated that their concern is with Paṇ-chen S̄ö-nam-drak-b̄a's and Jay-d̄zün Chö-ḡyi-gyel-tsen's[a] insistence that the fact that such a first-wheel sūtra explicitly teaches that compounded phenomena ranging from forms through to the thirty-seven harmonies with enlightenment are established by way of their own character does not entail that it is a sūtra whose explicit teaching is suitable to be accepted literally even though the Mind-Only School asserts that compounded phenomena are indeed established this way. From this, Jam-ȳang-shay-b̄a draws the absurd consequence that the "Questions of Paramārthasamudgata Chapter" of the *Sūtra Unraveling the Thought*

scholars with regard to the Mind-Only School, he identifies not just texts but also objects of expression as definitive and as requiring interpretation. He states the principle that if something is definitive (that is, established by valid cognition), a sūtra that explicitly teaches it is a definitive sūtra and that if something requires interpretation, a sūtra that explicitly teaches it is an interpretable sūtra. Usually, Ge-luk-b̄a scholars hold that the usage of "definitive" and "interpretable" for objects is limited to the Middle Way School.

[a] A-ku L̄o-drö-gya-tso (*Precious Lamp*, 66.1) identifies Jam-ȳang-shay-b̄a's concern here as likely being with Jay-d̄zün Chö-ḡyi-gyel-tsen.

could not be a sūtra of definitive meaning. (It is universally accepted that in the Mind-Only School this chapter of the *Sūtra Unraveling the Thought* is definitive because it divides phenomena into what are and are not established by way of their own character, showing that other-powered natures—that is, compounded phenomena—and thoroughly established natures—emptinesses—are established by way of their own character but that imputational natures are not established by way of their own character.) Jam-ȳang-shay-b̄a's point is that once Paṇ-chen S̄ö-nam-drak-b̄a and Jay-d̄zün Chö-ḡyi-gyel-tsen refuse to assert that a sūtra that explicitly teaches that other-powered natures are established by way of their own character is necessarily a sūtra of definitive meaning despite the fact that they admit that in this system other-powered natures are established this way, they must forego the assertion that a sūtra that differentiates between what is and is not established by way of its own character is necessarily a sūtra of definitive meaning, and hence they no longer have any way to determine a sūtra to be definitive, whereby they absurdly have to give up holding that even this chapter of the *Sūtra Unraveling the Thought* is definitive!

Worded in Gung-ru Chö-jung's more positive manner:[105]

> A sūtra that explicitly teaches that compounded phenomena ranging from forms through the thirty-seven harmonies with enlightenment are established by way of their own character is necessarily a sūtra whose explicit teaching is suitable to be asserted literally,
>
> - because a sūtra that explicitly teaches that other-powered natures are established by way of their own character is necessarily a literally acceptable sūtra
> - because a sūtra that explicitly teaches that other-powered natures and thoroughly established natures are established by way of their own character is necessarily a literally acceptable sūtra
> - because a sūtra that explicitly teaches that other-powered natures and thoroughly established natures are established by way of their own character and that imputational natures are not established by way of their own character is necessarily a literally acceptable sūtra
> - because a sūtra that differentiates well the three natures with respect to whether they are truly established or not is necessarily a literally acceptable sūtra
> - because the "Questions of Paramārthasamudgata Chapter" is posited as a sūtra of definitive meaning from the viewpoint of its being a sūtra that explicitly teaches within differentiating well whether the three natures are truly established or not.

Once the *Sūtra Unraveling the Thought* is considered to be definitive because it explains that other-powered natures and thoroughly established natures are established by way of their own character and that imputational natures are not, it is indeed natural to consider that a sūtra that teaches that compounded phenomena (other-powered natures) are established by way of their own character is also definitive. Again, the principle is that what is non-deceptive is literally acceptable and hence definitive.

The next reasoning that Gung-ru Chö-jung and Jam-ȳang-shay-b̄a use is faced squarely by Jay-d̄zün Chö-ḡyi-gyel-tsen in his *General-Meaning Commentary*. First, their reasoning:

> Asaṅga gives reasoning to refute the acceptability of the literal rendering of the first-wheel sūtras, and if a meaning of the literal rendering of the first-wheel sūtras were that compounded phenomena ranging from forms through the thirty-seven harmonies with enlightenment are established by way of their own character, Asaṅga absurdly would be refuting that compounded phenomena are established by way of their own character, in which case it would absurdly have to be said that in the Mind-Only School compounded phenomena are not established by way of their own character.

Jay-d̄zün Chö-ḡyi-gyel-tsen's answer[106] is (1) to agree that Asaṅga's reasoning does indeed explicitly damage, that is, contradict, the literal rendering of the first wheel and that indeed the first wheel explicitly teaches that forms and so forth are equally established by way of their own character, but (2) to refuse to accept that these facts entail that Asaṅga is refuting that forms and so forth are established by way of their own character. The traditions of explanation that follow Jay-d̄zün Chö-ḡyi-gyel-tsen and Paṇ-chen S̄ö-nam-drak-b̄a (insistently) hold that if just because the first wheel teaches something that is so in fact, it had to be literally acceptable, then since the first wheel teaches the four noble truths, the first wheel would absurdly have to be literal. Jay-d̄zün Chö-ḡyi-gyel-tsen could add that then Asaṅga's reasoning would absurdly refute the four truths!

The tradition following Gung-ru Chö-jung and Jam-ȳang-shay-b̄a answers this attempt to reduce their argument to absurdity by stating (or insistently holding) that the first wheel (as described in the *Sūtra Unraveling the Thought*) teaches the four truths mainly and explicitly—after all, Paramārthasamudgata calls it "the wheel of doctrine of the four truths"—but that it does not do so on the literal level, where it teaches only that phenomena, including the four truths, are established by way of their own character as the referents of conceptual consciousnesses. This is all that it teaches on the literal level; the four noble truths are the principal of seven **bases of composition,** or points of reference being taught to be established in this way, and thus since whatever is taken as a substratum of a teaching is also itself explicitly taught, the actual four truths (without the qualification of being established by way of their own character as the referents of their respective conceptual consciousnesses) are mainly and explicitly taught.

Gung-ru Chö-jung's[107] and Jam-ȳang-shay-b̄a's[108] next reasoning is literary in nature. In answering Paramārthasamudgata's question, Buddha (*Emptiness in Mind-Only,* 86) asks a rhetorical question and answers it:

> Paramārthasamudgata, concerning that, what are character-non-natures of phenomena? [That is, what are natureless in terms of being established by way of their own character?] Those which are imputational characters.
>
> Why? It is thus: Those [imputational characters] are characters posited by names and terminology and do not subsist by way of their own character. Therefore, they are said to be "character-non-natures."

If in the first wheel, when Buddha speaks of the "own-character" of the five aggregates, he were speaking of the aggregates as being established by way of their own character as Jay-d̄zün Chö-ḡyi-gyel-tsen and Paṇ-chen S̄ö-nam-drak-b̄a claim he is, then it would absurdly come to be that here in his answer the establishment of the mental and physical aggregates by way of their own character would be the character-nature that is non-existent!

Gung-ru Chö-jung and Jam-ȳang-shay-b̄a's point is that this passage speaking of the character-non-nature demonstrates damage to the acceptability of the literal rendering of the first-wheel sūtras mentioned earlier by Paramārthasamudgata, and thus the literal meanings of the two passages must be contradictory. For the latter to damage the former, the "character-nature" of the latter (Buddha's answer) and the "own-character" of the former (Paramārthasamudgata's question) must be referring to the same thing. However, "character-non-nature" cannot refer to the five aggregates' not being established by way of their own character simply because there is no argument that in the Mind-Only School they **are** established by way of their own character. Rather, according to Gung-ru Chö-jung and Jam-ȳang-shay-b̄a, the "character-nature" that is said to be non-existent in the latter passage is the establishment of objects by way of their own character as the referents of conceptual consciousnesses,[a] and hence, the "own-character" mentioned in Paramārthasamudgata's question must also be the same.

Gung-ru Chö-jung and Jam-ȳang-shay-b̄a's reasoning is quite convincing even though it eventually embroils their tradition in a nexus of distinctions, almost beyond belief, when, as we shall see later (61), they try to show how their reading does not deviate from D̄zong-ka-b̄a's opinion. For the time being,

---

[a] In an aside, Jam-ȳang-shay-b̄a (*Great Exposition of the Interpretable and the Definitive,* 32.4) says that the *Sūtra Unraveling the Thought* at the point at which it is **reporting** this teaching in sūtras of the first wheel is (of course!) not itself **teaching** (*bstan*) that objects are established by way of their own character as the referents of their respective conceptual consciousnesses, for the *Sūtra Unraveling the Thought* itself teaches exactly the opposite.

let us turn to Gung-tang's defense of a seeming slip-up by them.

Issue #29: Can Gung-ru Chö-jung and Jam-ȳang-shay-b̄a's faux pas of citing a passage that proves the opposite point be explained away?

As further but strange evidence for why "own-character" must refer to establishment of objects by way of their own character as the referents of conceptual consciousnesses, Gung-ru Chö-jung[109] (with Jam-ȳang-shay-b̄a[110] following) goes on to say that this is affirmed by D̄zong-ka-b̄a's (*Emptiness in Mind-Only,* 86) statement:

> The nature of character that imputational factors do not have is to be taken as establishment, or subsisting, by way of their own character.

However, the citation is patently irrelevant because, as Jam-ȳang-shay-b̄a himself later[111] says and Gung-tang[112] confirms, D̄zong-ka-b̄a obviously is speaking, not about establishment of objects by way of their own character as the referents of conceptual consciousnesses, but merely about establishment of objects by way of their own character. This is borne out by what D̄zong-ka-b̄a says in the immediately following sentence:

> Here, the measure indicated[a] with respect to existing or not existing by way of [an object's] own character is: not to be posited or to be posited in dependence upon names and terminology.

Since D̄zong-ka-b̄a's context is indeed entirely confined to establishment of objects by way of their own character and does not mention **as the referents of conceptual consciousnesses**, the citation that they quote to seal their point actually does just the opposite.

Gung-tang,[b] loyal to Jam-ȳang-shay-b̄a (and hence here to his source, Gung-ru Chö-jung,) is more than willing to use his considerable talents to rescue questionable points by completely turning them around. He explains away their seemingly irrelevant citation of the same passage in another context[113] by indicating how closely connected **imputational natures'** being established by way of their own character and **imputational natures'** being established by way of their own character as the referents of conceptual consciousnesses are. For although it is true that mere establishment of objects such as pots by way of their own character does not necessitate that they be established by way of their own character as the referents of conceptual consciousnesses, if **imputational natures** are established by way of their own character, they must be established by way of their own character as the referents of conceptual consciousnesses.

---

a *bstan tshod;* see issue 96.

b Gung-tang's *Difficult Points,* 92.13-93.12. This topic is also addressed later, 127.

This is because in the *Sūtra Unraveling the Thought* other-powered natures' emptiness of the imputational nature is taken to be the thoroughly established nature, and, for this reason, if even imputational natures were not just conceptual superimpositions but were truly established like other-powered natures, the character-nature of imputational natures would have to exist right with other-powered natures. This is because the mode of appearance and the mode of subsistence of a form as being the referent of a conceptual consciousness apprehending the form would have to be established by way of their own character.

Gung-tang's defense of Gung-ru Chö-jung and Jam-ȳang-shay-b̄a's irrelevant citation demonstrates the ingenious lengths to which a commentator will go. Indeed, if their citation makes any sense consistent with their assertions, Gung-tang has hit upon it, but it is more likely that they merely slipped up. Still, the value of the point being made shows how even apologetic can communicate insight even if it does not succeed at its appointed task.

Issue #30: Does the middle wheel teach that phenomena are not *established by way of their own character?*

As a final piece of evidence that "own-character" cannot be taken as meaning "established by way of its own character" Gung-ru Chö-jung[114] explains that even with respect to the middle wheel of doctrine, "own-character" cannot mean "established by way of its own character." For if the middle wheel explicitly teaches that phenomena ranging from forms through to omniscient consciousnesses are **not** established by way of their own character, then it must explicitly teach that imputational phenomena (such as uncompounded space) are not established by way of their own character. In that case, the explicit teaching of a middle-wheel teaching that imputational natures are not established by way of their own character would have to be literally acceptable, since imputational phenomena are indeed not established by way of their own character according to the Mind-Only School. However, this is unsuitable because, as we know from Paramārthasamudgata's summation of Buddha's meaning, the second wheel requires interpretation:

> Based on just the naturelessness of all phenomena and based on just the absence of production, the absence of cessation, quiescence from the start, and naturally passed beyond sorrow, the Supramundane Victor turned a second wheel of doctrine, for those engaged in the Great Vehicle, very fantastic and marvelous, through the aspect of speaking on emptiness. Furthermore, that wheel of doctrine turned by the Supramundane Victor is surpassable, affords an occasion [for refutation], requires interpretation, and serves as a basis for controversy.

This is the last piece of evidence in Gung-ru Chö-jung and Jam-ȳang-shay-b̄a's argument refuting that "own-character" in the first wheel refers to establishment of objects by way of their own character. Let us now turn to Jay-d̄zün Chö-ḡyi-gyel-tsen's and Paṇ-chen S̄ö-nam-drak-b̄a's opinions.

6. Other Views on Own-Character

Jay-d̄zün Chö-ḡyi-gyel-tsen's Position

We have seen how Gung-ru Chö-jung and Jam-ȳang-shay-b̄a attempt to damage Jay-d̄zün Chö-ḡyi-gyel-tsen's assertion that the first-wheel teaching—about which Paramārthasamudgata questions Buddha—is that "all phenomena ranging from forms through to the thirty-seven harmonies with enlightenment are established by way of their own character," even though Jay-d̄zün Chö-ḡyi-gyel-tsen seems to be following D̄zong-ka-b̄a to the letter. We know from Jay-d̄zün Chö-ḡyi-gyel-tsen's consideration of a similar argument that he would not challenge the point that in the Mind-Only School impermanent phenomena are established by way of their own character. What he would challenge is the reasoning that a first-wheel sūtra's teaching something that the Mind-Only School also holds to be true necessitates that the sūtra is literally acceptable and thus definitive.[115] Jay-d̄zün Chö-ḡyi-gyel-tsen is willing to admit that:

1. The first wheel, as described here in the *Sūtra Unraveling the Thought,* explicitly teaches that all phenomena are established by way of their own character.[116]
2. Such a first-wheel sūtra is a sūtra that explicitly teaches that all **compounded** phenomena—forms and so forth—are established by way of their own character.[117]

However, he insists that this does not make a first-wheel sūtra that explicitly teaches that all compounded phenomena are established by way of their own character into one that is literally acceptable. He cites the parallel point that since the first wheel mainly and explicitly teaches the four truths, it mainly and explicitly teaches the selflessness of persons, but this does not make the first wheel literally acceptable.[118]

It is clear that Jay-d̄zün Chö-ḡyi-gyel-tsen is trying to avoid admitting that such a first-wheel sūtra (or sūtra passage, the term "sūtra" being used for both an entire text and a passage within such a text) is literally acceptable, it being axiomatic that in the Mind-Only School whatever is literally acceptable is necessarily definitive. The axiom is based on Paramārthasamudgata's associating non-literality with requiring interpretation and associating literality with definitiveness when he presents back to Buddha the import of Buddha's response to his question. As cited above, when Paramārthasamudgata presents to Buddha what he has understood about the first and middle wheels, he (*Emptiness in Mind-Only,* 116) says:

> Furthermore, that wheel of doctrine thoroughly turned by the Supramundane Victor is surpassable, affords an occasion [for refutation], requires interpretation, and serves as a basis for controversy.

About the third wheel of doctrine, he (*Emptiness in Mind-Only,* 116-117) says:

> This wheel of doctrine turned by the Supramundane Victor is unsurpassable, does not afford an occasion [for refutation], is of definitive meaning, and does not serve as a basis for controversy.

Dzong-ka-ba (*Emptiness in Mind-Only,* 126) makes clear the connection between non-literality and requiring interpretation when he explains the meaning of "affording an occasion [for refutation]":

> The reason why the literal meaning of the two former sets of sūtras affords an occasion for fault but this does not is that the literal meaning [of the former two sets] must be interpreted otherwise whereas this does not need to be.

Thus, for Jay-dzün Chö-gyi-gyel-tsen to avoid being forced to accept that a first-wheel sūtra (or sūtra passage) that explicitly teaches that all compounded phenomena are established by way of their own character is definitive, he must hold that it is not a literally acceptable sūtra. He must somehow split a hair.

A-ku Lo-drö-gya-tso[119] teases Jay-dzün Chö-gyi-gyel-tsen's followers with two ways that they could split the hair:

- They could hold that the explicit teaching of the first wheel is non-existent but that **whatever is** an explicit teaching of the first wheel is not necessarily non-existent (that is to say, does not necessarily teach something that is non-existent).
- Or they could differentiate between the explicit teaching and the literal reading—the suggestion being that the explicit teaching could be existent while the literal reading is not.

A-ku Lo-drö-gya-tso says no more, and thus he leaves this question in pregnant hiatus.

Jay-dzün Chö-gyi-gyel-tsen cryptically does not offer a direct treatment of the issue of what teaching makes the first wheel non-literal, but he does say[120] that first-wheel sūtras teach that all phenomena are established by way of their own character as the referents of their respective conceptual consciousnesses. The sparseness and mystery of his position is typical to his text, which sometimes requires almost divination to penetrate. At times it can seem that his insistence is mere stubbornness; however, later traditions of explanation venture to give his meaning.

Issue #31: Can the teaching of establishment by way of its own character also teach something else?

Jik-may-dam-chö-gya-tso,[121] himself a follower but also a critic of Jam-ȳang-shay-b̄a, explains that "others" (who most likely include followers of Jay-d̄zün Chö-ḡyi-gyel-tsen) hold that the words "established by way of their own character" do not merely express what they seem to but **also** express "established by way of their own character as the referents of their respective conceptual consciousnesses." This is held to be feasible since what terms express depends on the intention of the speaker and the mind-set of the listener (this type of explanation being how Gung-tang limits the meaning of "established by way of their own character" **only** to "established by way of its own character as the referent of a conceptual consciousness"). As the contemporary scholar Ge-s̄hay Ḡön-chok-tsay-ring[a] of the L̄o-s̄el-l̄ing College, a follower of Paṇ-chen S̄ö-nam-drak-b̄a, clearly frames the issue:[122]

> Even though it is suitable to assert that forms are established by way of their own character in accordance with the first-wheel teaching that forms are established by way of their own character, such a first-wheel passage is not asserted to be literally acceptable since it also teaches that forms are established by way of their own character as the referents of their respective conceptual consciousnesses.

This explanation of a double message conveyed by the teaching of "own-character" allows us to make sense of Jay-d̄zün Chö-ḡyi-gyel-tsen's clearly enunciated opinions that:

1. the "own-character" of Paramārthasamudgata's question means "established by way of its own character"
2. the first wheel teaches that compounded phenomena are established by way of their own character
3. what the first wheel teaches is not definitive.

The dual explanation is attractive in that it leaves D̄zong-ka-b̄a's identification of "own-character" as "established by way of its own character" untouched while, by adding to its meaning, it avoids difficulties that his apparent identification entails. This reading seems enviably benign, since it shies away from anything that looks like direct criticism of the founder of the sect; however, it has its own difficulties as we shall now explore.

---

[a] *dge bshes dkon mchog tshe ring;* oral communication.

Issue #32: Do the schools following the first wheel assert that uncompounded phenomena are established by way of their own character?

The maneuver of positing a double teaching allows the followers of Jay-d̄zün Chö-ḡyi-gyel-tsen (and Paṇ-chen S̄ö-nam-drak-b̄a) to hold that there is no first-wheel passage that is literally acceptable and hence none that is definitive. However, as Jik-may-dam-chö-gya-tso[123] points out, if the first wheel teaches that all phenomena are established by way of their own character, it thereby teaches that permanent phenomena are established by way of their own character, and thus those schools that follow the first wheel (the Great Exposition School and the Sūtra School) would have to assert that permanent phenomena such as uncompounded space are established by way of their own character. The problem is that texts such as Dharmakīrti's *Commentary on (Dignāga's) "Compilation of Prime Cognition,"* on which the Sūtra School[a] depends, do not assert that generally characterized phenomena such as uncompounded space are established by way of their own character. For it is clear that they do not assert that such phenomena exist without depending on imputation by terms and conceptions—this being the meaning of establishment by way of its own character.

Gung-ru Chö-jung[124] states the problem clearly: If the first wheel teaches that phenomena ranging from forms through the thirty-seven harmonies with enlightenment are established by way of their own character, then the Sūtra School (which follows the first wheel) would have to assert that all phenomena—including even imputational natures such as uncompounded space—are established by way of their own character; however, this is contradicted by the fact that D̄zong-ka-b̄a's student Ke-drup clearly indicates that in the Sūtra School generally characterized phenomena (such as uncompounded space) are not established by way of their own character despite being established from their own side. Ke-drup's *Opening the Eyes of the Fortunate* says,[125] "In the system of the Sūtra School, something does not become established by way of its own character merely due to its being established from its own side." Ke-drup distinguishes between a minimal level of existence called "establishment from its own side" and a more palpable level called "establishment by way of its own character"; thus, something's being established from its own side does not necessitate that it is established by way of its own character.

Ke-drup also indicates that the meaning of something's being established by way of its own character is that it is established from the side of its own uncommon mode of abiding without being merely imputed by conceptuality and is not to be confused with simple establishment from its own side: "If something is established from its own side without depending upon being posited by

---

[a] That is, the Sūtra School Following Reasoning.

conceptuality, it comes to be established by way of its own character." Conversely if something is established from its own side within depending upon being posited by conceptuality, it is not established by way of its own character but does exist.

Hence, according even to the Sūtra School a distinction is to be made between what exists and what exists by way of its own character. Otherwise, imputational phenomena such as uncompounded space would be established by way of their own character, in which case they would be specifically characterized phenomena,[a] since the definition of a specifically characterized phenomenon is that which is established from the side of its own uncommon mode of abiding without being merely imputed by conceptuality. In that case, uncompounded space absurdly would be truly established and hence able to perform the function of generating an effect, since in the Sūtra School specifically characterized phenomenon, that which is able to perform a function, that which is truly established, and ultimate truth are equivalent. However, all Ge-luk-ba scholars (including Jay-dzün Chö-gyi-gyel-tsen) agree that in all Buddhist schools of tenets uncompounded space does not **produce** effects (even if the Great Exposition School accepts that uncompounded space functions to allow the presence of material objects).

Ke-drup indicates that we indeed know that the Proponents of Sūtra assert such, because the Consequentialists object to this very assertion. When the Proponents of Sūtra assert that generally characterized phenomena[b] are not established by way of their own character and that the factor of difference between sound's impermanence and sound's productness is not established by way of its own character, the Consequentialists fling the consequence at them that generally characterized phenomena and so forth would have to be established by way of their own character because of being established from their own side. According to the Consequentialists, being established from their own side requires that these phenomena be established by way of their own character because, for them, there is no difference between these two. Ke-drup says:[126]

> Even though [the Proponents of Sūtra] propound that generally characterized phenomena and the factor of difference between sound's impermanence and sound's productness are not established by way of their own character, according to the Consequentialists they are forced by reasoning into having to assert that they have the meaning of being specifically characterized phenomena by the mere fact that they are established from their own side.

Based on this clear statement of a lack of equivalence in the Sūtra School between being established from its own side and being established by way of its own character, Gung-ru Chö-jung finds it patently absurd for anyone (for

a *rang mtshan, svalakṣaṇa.*

b *spyi mtshan, sāmānyalakṣaṇa*

example, Jay-d̄zün Chö-ḡyi-gyel-tsen) to claim that in the Sūtra School whatever exists is necessarily established by way of its own character. This is powerful evidence against taking at face value Ḏzong-ka-ḇa's frequent statement that the first wheel teaches that **all** phenomena (including generally characterized phenomena, that is, permanent objects such as uncompounded space) are established by way of their own character, since the Sūtra School which follows the first wheel clearly (at least according to Gung-ru Chö-jung) does not assert such.

Ke-drup's opinion carries great weight because of his favored position as one of Ḏzong-ka-ḇa's two most important direct disciples. Nevertheless, Jay-d̄zün Chö-ḡyi-gyel-tsen finds Ke-drup's presentation to be unconvincing.[127] Rather, taking Ḏzong-ka-ḇa at face value, he holds that the first wheel does indeed teach that all phenomena are established by way of their own character. Recognizing the problem and wanting to avoid the consequent fault that then uncompounded space and so forth would produce effects, he holds that in the Sūtra School that which is established by way of its own character is not equivalent to that which is able to perform a function and that which is truly established.[a] He weakens the meaning of establishment by way of its own character such that it is equivalent to established from its own side, and hence, for him, in the Sūtra School all phenomena are established by way of their own character and established from their own side. By holding true establishment to be a stronger level of existence, he is still able to differentiate between those phenomena that can and cannot produce effects. This maneuver allows him to make excellent sense of Ḏzong-ka-ḇa's many statements that in the first wheel Buddha taught that all phenomena are equally established by way of their own character and of Ḏzong-ka-ḇa's otherwise cryptic statement (*Emptiness in Mind-Only,* 242) mentioned in the previous chapter (52 and 55):[b]

> Initially, at Varaṇāsi, he spoke of the selflessness of persons; [thus] there is one cycle [of teaching], in which the **true establishment** of the phenomena of the aggregates and so forth, **except for a few**, is not refuted and true existence is mentioned frequently.

Jay-d̄zün Chö-ḡyi-gyel-tsen holds that Ḏzong-ka-ḇa is here referring to Buddha's refutation in the first wheel of the teaching that imputational phenomena such as uncompounded space are truly established even though he taught that **all** phenomena are established by way of their own character. Finding such good evidence, he discounts Ke-drup's opinion.

---

[a] It is also clear that he does not hold that established by way of its own character (*rang gi mtshan nyid kyis grub pa, svalakṣaṇasiddha*) and specifically characterized phenomenon (*rang mtshan, svalakṣaṇa*) are equivalent.

[b] For further discussion of this passage, see 87 and 92.

Jam-ȳang-shay-b̄a, on the other hand, re-writes the grammar of this passage so that it reads:[a]

> Initially, at Varaṇāsi, he spoke of the selflessness of persons; [thus] there is one cycle [of teaching], in which the true establishment of the phenomena of the aggregates and so forth—[these being] **no more than a few** [of the one hundred and eight phenomena]—is not refuted and true existence is mentioned frequently.

For Jam-ȳang-shay-b̄a, when D̄zong-ka-b̄a speaks of Buddha's teaching in the first wheel that all phenomena are established by way of their own character, D̄zong-ka-b̄a means (or should mean) that Buddha taught that all phenomena are established by way of their own character **as the referents of their respective conceptual consciousnesses**, and hence here also when D̄zong-ka-b̄a describes the first wheel as teaching "true establishment," this also means the same. For this reason, in the first wheel Buddha could not possibly omit even a few phenomena from those taught to be so established, and thus Jam-ȳang-shay-b̄a must make D̄zong-ka-b̄a say something else by re-working the grammar.

To repeat: Jay-d̄zün Chö-ḡyi-gyel-tsen holds that even in the Sūtra School all phenomena, including permanent ones, are indeed asserted to be established by way of their own character. Instead of holding that "established by way of their own character" and "truly established" are synonymous in the Sūtra School, he avers that this school equates the former with "exists" and consider only "truly established" to mean that the object in question exists without depending on imputation by terms and conceptions. He considers it simply to be wrong to hold that "established by way of their own character" and "truly established" are equivalent in the Sūtra School.

Through this move, Jay-d̄zün Chö-ḡyi-gyel-tsen not only avoids the chief fault against taking "own-character" as meaning "established by way of its own character" but also can take D̄zong-ka-b̄a's above-quoted cryptic statement at face value. He has the double benefit of twice not having to twist D̄zong-ka-b̄a's words into meaning something else. His only cost is to have to refuse to accept a set of statements by Ke-drup that in the Sūtra School permanent phenomena are not established by way of their own character—these being so clear that he cannot explain them away and thus he calls them mistakes.

---

[a] Jam-ȳang-shay-b̄a has to twist the Tibetan considerably to get this meaning. The Tibetan reads:

> *dang por wa ra ṇā sir gang zag gi bdag med gsungs shing phung po la sogs pa'i chos nyung shas gcig ma gtogs pa bden par grub pa ma bkag cing bden par yod pa mang du gsungs pa'i skor gcig go/*

As the late Ye-s̄hay-tup-d̄en pointed out, in Jam-ȳang-shay-b̄a's reading the term *ma gtogs pa* is superfluous and inexplicable.

Issue #33: How about fiddling with the subject rather than the predicate?

As attractive as his explanation might seem, Jay-dzün Chö-ḡyi-gyel-tsen's followers have not been content with it (or, as they might say after putting on the mask of pretending to posit his thought, with the **clarity** of his explanation). Tsay-den-hla-ram-ba,[a] a Mongolian follower of Jay-dzün Chö-ḡyi-gyel-tsen, who specifically sought to counter Gung-tang's criticisms, offers a refinement of Jay-dzün Chö-ḡyi-gyel-tsen's explanation that allows him to keep the latter's identification of "own-character" as "established by way of its own character" but modifies just what it is that has such establishment. He does this by identifying the teaching that the aggregates have "own-character" as meaning that the aggregates' **being** the referents of their respective conceptual consciousnesses is established by way of its own character, that is to say, is established in the uncommon mode of abiding of the respective phenomenon.[b] Thus, when in the first wheel Buddha teaches that the aggregates have "own-character," he is teaching not that the aggregates are established by way of their own character but that the aggregates' **being** the referents of their respective conceptual consciousnesses is established by way of its own character.

This is not the above-mentioned explanation that the teaching of "own-character" has two meanings that are conveyed together. Rather, Tsay-den-hla-ram-ba's claim is that while "own-character" simply means established by way of its own character, the term "aggregates" refers here to the aggregates' **being** the referents of their respective conceptual consciousnesses. Instead of inventively reading the predicate—"have own-character"—in the statement, "The aggregates have own-character," he inventively reads the subject—"the aggregates." (We can begin to see that all of these scholars are saying just about the same thing.)

This is an attractive solution in that being the referent of a conceptual

---

[a]   As cited in A-ku Lo-drö-gya-tso's *Precious Lamp*, 64.6-65.3. Ge-šhay Ye-šhay-tap-kay (*shar tsong kha pa blo bzang grags pas mdzad pa'i drang ba dang nges pa'i don rnam par phye ba'i bstan bcos legs bshad snying po*, Tā la'i bla ma'i 'phags bod, vol. 22 [Varanasi, India: vāna dbus bod kyi ches mtho'i gtsug lag slob gnyer khang, 1997], 327-332), in a list of fifty-eight commentaries on Dzong-ka-ba's *The Essence of Eloquence*, reports (331) that three of these are listed under the title of *dri lan blo gsal mgul rgyan* by *tshe brtan lha rams pa* in *bod kyi bstan bcos khag gcig gi mtshan byang dri med shel dkar 'phreng ba* (mtsho sngon dpe skrun khang, 1985), 614. The three are:

- *rgyal ba dge 'dun rgya mtsho dang 'jam dbyangs dga' blo 'jam dbyangs chos bshes sogs kyi drang nges gsung rgyun dri med lung rigs gter mdzod*
- *drang nges legs bshad snying po'i spyi don legs pa drang nges rnam 'byed kyi dga' gnad cung zad btus pa*
- *legs bshad snying po'i mtha' dpyod mkhas pa'i dbang po 'jam dbyangs chos dpal kyi gsung rgyun.*

[b]   *phung po rang 'dzin rtog pa'i zhen gzhir yin pa.*

consciousness is an existent imputational nature, which all Ge-luk-b̄a scholars agree does not exist by way of its own character in any phenomenon, and thus Tsay-d̄en-hla-ram-b̄a's explanation allows him to take D̄zong-ka-b̄a's and Jay-d̄zün Chö-ḡyi-gyel-tsen's identification of "own-character" as "established by way of its own character" without having to twist it into something else. Indeed, another way of saying that phenomena are misconceived to be established by way of their own character as the referents of their respective conceptual consciousnesses is to say that their being the referents of their respective conceptual consciousnesses is misconceived to be established by way of its own character in those objects.

This solution is founded in numerous statements in D̄zong-ka-b̄a's own words,[a] but it is faulted by some for being built around, not the **entities** of the aggregates, but an **attribute** that is an imputational nature associated with them—their **being** the referents of words and conceptual consciousnesses, whereas the concern in the *Sūtra Unraveling the Thought* is with misconception of entities and attributes.

Issue #34: Can the words and the meaning be split?

Perhaps this criticism that Tsay-d̄en-hla-ram-b̄a's reading speaks not to the entity of objects but to an imputational nature associated with them stimulated an early twentieth-century follower of Jay-d̄zün Chö-ḡyi-gyel-tsen, S̄er-s̄hül L̄o-sang-pün-tsok,[128] to tackle the issue from a different angle. In what is for me a movingly unbiased commentary of annotations on difficult points in D̄zong-ka-b̄a's text, he distinguishes between the words and the meaning of those words—a distinction like that used by Gung-ru Chö-jung, Jam-ȳang-shay-b̄a, and their followers. He proposes that in terms of what is explicitly stated in first-wheel sūtras, Paramārthasamudgata is asking about the **statements** in the first wheel that phenomena ranging from forms through the thirty-seven harmonies with enlightenment are established by way of their own character but in terms of the **meaning** of those words he is asking about the teaching that those phenomena are established by way of their own character as the referents of their respective conceptual consciousnesses. Like Gung-tang, he says that this comes to be so from the context of the listeners' mind-set and the speaker's wish to communicate. He says no more, but it may be that, like Gung-tang, he would hold that the meaning is communicated on the literal level and that therefore the literal level is to be distinguished from the mere words.

S̄er-s̄hül L̄o-sang-pün-tsok claims that this is what D̄zong-ka-b̄a, Ke-drup, and Jay-d̄zün Chö-ḡyi-gyel-tsen mean when they all say that the first wheel teaches that all phenomena are equally established by way of their own character. As he puts it, they merely intend to eliminate that Paramārthasamudgata was asking about **words** in the first wheel that phenomena are established by

[a] For a list of nineteen instances, see *Reflections on Reality,* 199ff.

way of their own character as the referents of their respective conceptual consciousnesses. He says that if this were not the case, those scholars' renditions of the first-wheel teaching would be senseless, for if "established by way of its own character" is taken as meaning that the first wheel teaches that all phenomena are established from their own side,[a] there would not be any need to question such a teaching, since the Proponents of Mind-Only themselves assert that all phenomena are established from their own side. Also, he says that if "established by way of its own character" is taken as meaning that all phenomena are ultimately established,[b] there also would not be any need to question such a teaching, since the Proponents of Mind-Only do not claim that the first wheel teaches such (since they recognize that followers of the first wheel do not hold that existent imputational natures such as uncompounded space are ultimately established). Therefore, S̄er-s̄hül L̄o-sang-pün-tsok proposes that the **meaning** of the words in the first wheel that all phenomena are established by way of their own character is that all phenomena are established by way of their own character as the referents of their respective conceptual consciousnesses.

His exegesis suggests that he has felt the force of Gung-ru Chö-jung's, Jam-ȳang-shay-b̄a's, and Gung-tang's criticisms.[c] It represents independent thinking that is not bound to his college's standard positions. His argument strikes me as also aware of faults perceived in Tsay-d̄en-hla-ram-b̄a's explanation even though he does not mention the latter by name. For if the non-factual teaching of the first wheel is that the aggregates' **being** the referents of their respective conceptual consciousnesses is established by way of its own character, then what does "established by way of its own character" mean? If it means that being the referent is ultimately established, then since the Sūtra School does not hold that imputational natures such as being the referent are ultimately established, the Mind-Only School's presentation of emptiness would not be distinctive and hence superior to the Sūtra School. If, on the other hand, it means that being the referent is established from its own side, there would not be any need to question such a teaching since the Proponents of Mind-Only themselves assert that all phenomena, including being the referent of words and conceptual consciousnesses, are established from their own side. These entanglements (which arise because these scholars have assumed the gargantuan task of devising a seamless system for D̄zong-ka-b̄a's reading of the *Sūtra Unraveling the Thought*

[a] This accords with Jay-d̄zün Chö-ḡyi-gyel-tsen's weaker reading of "established by way of its own character" as "established from its own side" in the Sūtra School. That S̄er-s̄hül uses this meaning shows that he agrees with Jay-d̄zün Chö-ḡyi-gyel-tsen that in the Sūtra School all phenomena are held to be established by way of their own character; unlike him, however, he does not use this tenet to leave D̄zong-ka-b̄a's identification of "own-character" as "established by way of its own character" without twisting it into something else.

[b] This accords with the standard Ge-luk-b̄a position that "established by way of its own character" is equivalent to "ultimately established" in the Mind-Only School.

[c] S̄er-s̄hül frequently indicates his acquaintance with Gung-tang's works.

and the schools of tenets that are associated with it) are probably the reason why Šer-šhül does not repeat Tsay-d̄en-hla-ram-b̄a's explanation but offers his own.

Paṇ-chen Šö-nam-drak-b̄a's Position

As is obvious from this plethora of opinions on such a central topic, neither the Ge-luk-b̄a order nor its main monastic universities have monolithic stances on philosophical issues. Also, the colleges that are the sub-units of those universities contain within each of them different streams of oral explanations, and individual debaters, seeking to win in twice-daily contests, often develop divergent opinions. This diversity of stance is the milieu out of which textbooks such as these on D̄zong-ka-b̄a's *The Essence of Eloquence* were composed.

Because the positions presented in these texts reflect traditions of exegesis, the dating of commentaries written by contemporaneous authors is particularly difficult when the year of composition is not given in the colophons to their texts. The mere fact that Paṇ-chen Šö-nam-drak-b̄a, for instance, attacks a position held by Gung-ru Chö-jung does not indicate that his text was later. Also, that Paṇ-chen Šö-nam-drak-b̄a was nine years younger than Jay-d̄zün Chö-ḡyi-gyel-tsen may suggest that his commentary was later, but since these two scholars criticize each others' positions, confirmation is difficult to gain.

Issue #35: Can the teaching of establishment by way of its own character also teach externality?

Paṇ-chen Šö-nam-drak-b̄a[129] begins his commentary on Paramārthasamudgata's question by challenging an opinion fundamental to Gung-ru Chö-jung's presentation (and that of the latter's successor as textbook author of the Go-mang tradition, Jam-ȳang-shay-b̄a), namely, that if the first wheel explicitly taught that other-powered natures and thoroughly established natures are established by way of their own character or truly established, the first wheel would be literally acceptable and thus definitive. Paṇ-chen Šö-nam-drak-b̄a asserts that according to the Mind-Only School other-powered natures and thoroughly established natures are truly established (and hence established by way of their own character), and he asserts that what is literally acceptable is definitive, but he holds that when in the first wheel it is taught that forms, for instance, are truly established, it is being taught that **external** forms—forms that are different substantial entities from the consciousnesses apprehending them—are truly established. Since such external forms do not exist according to the Mind-Only School, the first wheel that teaches that forms are truly established is not literally acceptable and hence not definitive.

Paṇ-chen Šö-nam-drak-b̄a's stance leads to the question of whether one could break first-wheel sūtras into parts, those that are literally acceptable and those that are not. After all, the first wheel is called the wheel of doctrine of the four truths and thus it explicitly teaches the four truths, but if everything taught in the first wheel must be non-literal just because the first wheel is non-literal, then the teaching of the four truths would be non-literal. However, Paṇ-chen S̄ö-nam-drak-b̄a[130] warns that there are not even phrases of first-wheel sūtras—these necessarily being instances of the wheel of doctrine of the four truths—that are definitive because when Buddha speaks about the entities of the four truths he explicitly teaches, for instance, that true sufferings such as the **external** world of the environment are truly established. His point is that the teaching of externality infects the entire first wheel.

Issue #36: Could the first wheel teach that true cessations are truly established?

As a further indication of the non-literality of the first wheel, Paṇ-chen S̄ö-nam-drak-b̄a[131] adds, without comment, that in the first wheel Buddha also explicitly teaches that true cessations are truly established. For Paṇ-chen S̄ö-nam-drak-b̄a, according to the Mind-Only School true cessations are not truly established,[a] but the problem that his laconic statement poses is to explain how the Lesser Vehicle schools assert, in accordance with the first wheel of doctrine, that true cessations are truly established.

Unfortunately, unlike the Go-mang tradition, Paṇ-chen S̄ö-nam-drak-b̄a's works have not spawned a large body of written commentary,[b] but there is a lively tradition of speculation among contemporary scholars who follow him. During a long attempt to make sense out of this passage, the late abbot emeritus of L̄o-s̄el-l̄ing College Ye-s̄hay-tup-d̄en[c] averred that Paṇ-chen S̄ö-nam-drak-b̄a may have meant that the first wheel teaches that true cessations are truly established **within not being of the entity of mind.**[d] However, this attempt still does not answer the question of why Buddha would teach in the first wheel that true cessations are truly established, for Paṇ-chen S̄ö-nam-drak-b̄a

---

a For the Jam-ȳang-shay-b̄a tradition, in the Mind-Only School true cessations are the emptiness of the mind in the continuum of someone who has overcome a portion of the obstructions and thus true cessations are indeed truly established.

b I have seen mention (in Dön-drup-gyel-tsen's *Four Intertwined Commentaries*) of only one sub-commentary, that of Tsül-kang Lek-b̄a-dön-drup, but I have not been able to locate the text.

c *mkhan zur ye shes thub bstan,* died 1988.

d Kensur Ye-s̄hay-tup-d̄en carefully avoided the terminology of external objects because Paṇ-chen S̄ö-nam-drak-b̄a reserves the term "external object" for material objects and true cessations are not material. This is why he substitutes "within not being of the entity of mind" (*sems kyi bdag nyid du ma grub pa*). Other scholars such as Gung-ru Chö-jung and Jam-ȳang-shay-b̄a use the term "external object" for both the material and the non-material, as will be detailed later (367ff.)

holds that truly established and established by way of its own character are equivalent, and he also holds that the Sūtra School Following Reasoning, which follows the first wheel, does not assert that existent imputational natures such as true cessations are truly established, since they are do not create effects.[a] (I will give another slant on Ye-s̄hay-tup-d̄en's refinement at the end of this section.)

Jay-d̄zün Chö-ḡyi-gyel-tsen[132] draws out the absurdities of the notion that existent imputational natures are truly established by making the unchallengeable points that in the Sūtra School Following Reasoning:

1. truly established is equivalent to ultimately established
2. it is clear from Dharmakīrti's statement,

   Whatever is able ultimately to perform a function
   Is ultimately existent here,

   that what is ultimately established is ultimately able to perform the function of generating effects, and
3. therefore, true cessations and so forth absurdly would be able to create effects.

Paṇ-chen S̄ö-nam-drak-b̄a clearly does not want to say that existent imputational natures generate effects, but he holds that the first wheel teaches that existent imputational natures such as true cessations are truly established. Also, he indirectly criticizes the Second Dalai Lama (two years his senior) for asserting that in the first wheel a small number of phenomena are not taught to be truly established.

Although Paṇ-chen S̄ö-nam-drak-b̄a[133] does not mention the Second Dalai Lama by name, he criticizes the corrupt passage—that the Second Dalai Lama uses in support of his argument—as not even being in D̄zong-ka-b̄a's text, and thus the exposition criticized is obviously that of the Second Dalai Lama. Though the citation by the Second Dalai Lama does indeed deviate from D̄zong-ka-b̄a's text,[b] the meaning is the same as that found in the controversial

---

[a] There is some question about the Great Exposition School since, as Ḡön-chok-jik-may-w̄ang-b̄o says in his *Precious Garland of Tenets*, in the Great Exposition School uncompounded space (and thus all imputational phenomena) are ultimate truths and thus truly existent. He also says that in this system all phenomena, permanent and impermanent, are truly established. See Geshe Lhundup Sopa and Jeffrey Hopkins, *Cutting Through Appearances: The Practice and Theory of Tibetan Buddhism* (Ithaca, N.Y.: Snow Lion, 1990), 186-187. This is why the discussion revolves around the Sūtra School and specifically the Sūtra School Following Reasoning, since the Sūtra School Following Scripture asserts a presentation of the two truths like that of the Great Exposition School.

[b] The Second Dalai Lama's citation deviates considerably from D̄zong-ka-b̄a's text, though not in meaning: (differences in bold print)

Second Dalai Lama (15.3):

> ***'khor lo dang por*** *phung sogs* ***kyi*** *chos* ***la*** *nyung shas cig ma gtogs pa* ***shas cher*** *bden par* ***yod*** *pa ma bkag* ***pa dang***

passage mentioned earlier[a] (*Emptiness in Mind-Only,* 242):

> Initially, at Varaṇāsi, he spoke of the selflessness of persons; [thus] there is one cycle [of teaching], in which the true establishment of the phenomena of the aggregates and so forth, except for a few, is not refuted and true existence is mentioned frequently.[b]

Paṇ-chen S̄ö-nam-drak-b̄a cryptically leaves the topic saying,[134] "Whatever the case, this should be analyzed in detail." However, earlier[135] he explains that a Consequence School perspective slipped[c] into D̄zong-ka-b̄a's exposition. Thus, the passage to which the Second Dalai Lama must have been referring does not, according to Paṇ-chen S̄ö-nam-drak-b̄a, afford support for the position that in the first wheel existent imputational natures such as true cessations are not truly established, since he claims that it represents a Consequence School perspective and does not indicate D̄zong-ka-b̄a's opinion about the first wheel as explained according to the Mind-Only School.[d] His reading[136] of the above controversial passage is that according to the Consequence School's own presentation of the first wheel (as opposed to what is taught in the *Sūtra Unraveling the Thought*) the first wheel of doctrine **in a few places** contains a teaching that all phenomena are not truly established, whereby the Consequence School holds that Hearers and Solitary Realizers (though not those following Lesser Vehicle schools of tenets) do indeed realize the most subtle emptiness, as did the good ascetics when they heard the doctrine of the four truths. In this way, Paṇ-chen S̄ö-nam-drak-b̄a reads the above statement as:

> Initially, at Varaṇāsi, he spoke of the selflessness of persons; [thus] there is one cycle [of teaching], in which, except for a few [places], the true establishment of the phenomena of the aggregates and so forth is not refuted and true existence is mentioned frequently.

Jay-d̄zün Chö-ḡyi-gyel-tsen, on the other hand, takes D̄zong-ka-b̄a's statement at face value, concluding that according to the first wheel and thus also

---

D̄zong-ka-b̄a (*Emptiness in Mind-Only,* 450):

> *phung **po la** sogs **pa'i** chos nyung shas gcig ma gtogs pa bden par **grub** pa ma bkag **cing***

[a] See 79 and also 52, 55, and 92.

[b] According to Jam-ȳang-shay-b̄a (*Great Exposition of the Interpretable and the Definitive,* 27.3), the last sentence should be rendered as:

> Initially, at Varaṇāsi, he spoke of the selflessness of persons; [thus] there is one cycle [of teaching], in which the true establishment of the phenomena of the aggregates and so forth—[these being] **no more than a few** [of the one hundred and eight phenomena]—is not refuted and true existence is mentioned frequently.

[c] *thal 'gyur ba'i grub mtha' shor ba:* 4b.5.

[d] It is indeed refreshing that Paṇ-chen S̄ö-nam-drak-b̄a here (and a few other times) openly declares that D̄zong-ka-b̄a mixed perspectives.

according to the Sūtra School Following Reasoning all phenomena are established by way of their own character but existent imputational natures such as true cessations are not truly established. For Jay-d̄zün Chö-ḡyi-gyel-tsen "established by way of its own character" and "truly established" are not equivalent.[137]

To repeat: We can see from Paṇ-chen S̄ö-nam-drak-b̄a's frequent usage of the term "truly established" instead of "established by way of their own character" that for him the two terms are equivalent. Also, his refutation of the Second Dalai Lama's not taking the two to be equivalent indicates that he does not accept the distinction—made by Jay-d̄zün Chö-ḡyi-gyel-tsen—between truly established and established by way of its own character. However, given that Paṇ-chen S̄ö-nam-drak-b̄a accepts the principle that root teachings of the four schools of Indian Buddhism are seamlessly represented in the depiction of the three wheels in the *Sūtra Unraveling the Thought*, he is left with the unanswerable problem of why the first wheel teaches that existent imputational natures such as true cessations or uncompounded space are taught to be truly established. By using the term "truly established," which is the equivalent of "ultimately established," he has precluded himself from Jay-d̄zün Chö-ḡyi-gyel-tsen's escape of weakening the meaning of "established by way of its own character" such that it is not equivalent to "truly established." It seems that Paṇ-chen S̄ö-nam-drak-b̄a's only recourse would be to claim that "truly established" **here** solely refers to not being of the entity of consciousness; this would be analogous to Gung-ru Chö-jung and Jam-ȳang-shay-b̄a's limitation of the meaning of "established by way of its own character" solely to "established by way of its own character as the referent of a conceptual consciousness." Perhaps this is what Ye-s̄hay-tup-d̄en meant—namely, that in the first wheel Buddha taught that existent imputational natures are truly established **in the sense of** (rather than **within**) their not being of the entity of the mind. In this context, "truly established" itself would mean not being of the entity of the mind.

Issue #37: What to do with the middle wheel?

Paṇ-chen S̄ö-nam-drak-b̄a[138] is in a similar bind with respect to the middle wheel when he questions the dictum (enunciated in Gung-ru Chö-jung and Jam-ȳang-shay-b̄a's analysis) that if the middle wheel explicitly teaches on the literal level that imputational natures are not truly established, this would be literally acceptable and thus definitive. Even though he accepts that according to the Mind-Only School existent imputational natures such as true cessations are not truly established, he denies the linkage that a sūtra teaching that true cessations are not truly established would be definitive.

Unfortunately, Paṇ-chen S̄ö-nam-drak-b̄a's commitment to brevity does not allow him to expand on his denial. So, let us speculate: He cannot say (as he did with respect to the first wheel) that when the absence of true establishment is taught on the literal level, an absence of being a different entity from consciousness is also communicated on the literal level, for the latter is validly established in the Mind-Only School, and thus the teaching on the literal level would absurdly be acceptable. Finding it impossible to posit his thought this way with respect to **not** being truly established, we might have to reconsider how, just above, we posited his thought with regard to the first wheel that all phenomena are truly established. However, I have found it awfully hard to posit Paṇ-chen Sö-nam-drak-ba's thought on this topic even when I drop any demand for elegance and symmetry. (The Go-mang tradition—Gung-ru Chö-jung *et al.*—have not let elegance and symmetry keep them from positing that when Dzong-ka-ba speaks of the first wheel as teaching that all phenomena are established by way of their own character, he really means "established by way of their own character as the referents of their respective conceptual consciousnesses" but that when Dzong-ka-ba speaks of the middle wheel as teaching that all phenomena are **not** established by way of their own character, he really means "not established from their own side.")

Issue #38: Are the literal level and the explicit teaching to be distinguished?

Despite being unclear—with respect to the middle wheel—about what "not truly established" means, Paṇ-chen Sö-nam-drak-ba[139] draws in no uncertain terms the important distinction that it is only on the literal level that the middle wheel teaches that all phenomena are not truly established. His point, well-founded in the *Sūtra Unraveling the Thought* (see citation below), is that since **sharp** Bodhisattvas understand—from hearing the middle wheel—that other-powered natures and thoroughly established natures are truly established and that imputational natures are not, the thought of the middle and final wheels is the same, and hence the middle wheel cannot be said **explicitly** to teach that all phenomena are not truly established. Rather, this is done only on the literal level. As Paṇ-chen Sö-nam-drak-ba puts it, to hold that the literal reading of the Perfection of Wisdom Sūtras constitutes the thought of those sūtras is a bad explanation that contradicts all of the sūtras and treatises of the Mind-Only School.

Indeed, the *Sūtra Unraveling the Thought* says:

> Paramārthasamudgata, with respect to this, thinking of just these three types of non-nature, the One-Gone-Thus, by way of the aspect of setting forth sūtras of interpretable meaning, taught the doctrine [of the middle wheel] in this way, "All phenomena are natureless; all phenomena are not produced, not ceasing, quiescent from the start, and naturally thoroughly passed beyond sorrow." Regarding that, [when] sentient beings who have generated roots of virtue, have purified the obstructions, have ripened their continuums, have great faith, and have

> accumulated great collections of merit and wisdom hear this doctrine, they understand—just as it is—this which I explained with a thought behind it, and they develop faith in that doctrine. They also realize, by means of their exalted wisdom, the meaning just as it is. Also, through cultivating their realization they very quickly attain the very final state.

Hearing the Perfection of Wisdom Sūtras, sharp listeners understand the three natures and three non-natures, without having to rely on an explanation such as is found in the *Sūtra Unraveling the Thought.* It is from this perspective that the late Go-mang scholar Ge-s̄hay Ge-dün-l̄o-drö[140] was fond of repeating Gung-tang's statement[141] that, not just for the Proponents of the Middle but also for the Proponents of Mind-Only, the Perfection of Wisdom Sūtras are the supreme of all sūtras. Since the Proponents of Mind-Only are intent on showing how the literal reading of the Perfection of Wisdom Sūtras requires interpretation, there is certain shock value in making the point that they find these sūtras to be even greater than the *Sūtra Unraveling the Thought.* However, sharp Bodhisattvas understand the explicit teaching of the middle wheel—the three natures and their corresponding non-natures—just from hearing the literal rendering that all phenomena are not truly established; for the rest of us, the *Sūtra Unraveling the Thought* provides a key to understanding how to understand the middle wheel, the explicit teaching of which, as understood by such sharp Bodhisattvas, accords exactly with the explicit teaching of the third wheel.

Review

All three of these groups of scholars—(1) Gung-ru Chö-jung and Jam-ȳang-shay-b̄a and their followers, Gung-tang and A-ku L̄o-drö-gya-tso, (2) Jay-d̄zün Chö-ḡyi-gyel-tsen and his followers, Tsay-d̄en-hla-ram-b̄a and S̄er-s̄hül L̄o-sang-pün-tsok, and (3) Paṇ-chen S̄ö-nam-drak-b̄a and his followers, Ken-sur Ye-s̄hay-tup-d̄en and Ge-s̄hay Ḡön-chok-tsay-ring—all[a] read the meaning of "own-character" so that it at least includes either the establishment of objects by way of their own character as the referents of conceptual consciousnesses or externality (or both). Despite considerable differences in how these scholars understand certain phrases in the *Sūtra Unraveling the Thought* and in D̄zong-ka-b̄a's text, there is agreement on just what type of teaching causes the first wheel not to be definitive—the teaching that forms and so forth are established by way of their own character as the referents of their respective terms and conceptual consciousnesses (and the teaching that forms and so forth are external objects). Still, the entanglements spun by their explanations of particular words in the *Sūtra Unraveling the Thought* and D̄zong-ka-b̄a's text become so severe that one can forget this central point.

[a] Tsay-d̄en-hla-ram-b̄a accomplishes this by interpreting "aggregates and so forth" as their being the referents of conceptual consciousnesses; see above.

All are wrestling with the fundamental issue that Paramārthasamudgata's question indicates that there is something wrong with the first-wheel teaching and that it is difficult to make this jibe with Dzong-ka-ba's explanation of the term "own-character" as "established by way of its own character" since most of the phenomena mentioned in the first are indeed so established. To get out of this problem:

- Gung-ru Chö-jung and Jam-yang-shay-ba strictly limit the meaning of "own-character" to the establishment of objects by way of their own character as the referents of conceptual consciousnesses and claim that this is what Dzong-ka-ba meant by "established by way of its own character."
- Jay-dzün Chö-gyi-gyel-tsen leaves Dzong-ka-ba's identification as is and only cryptically suggests that the first wheel also teaches that phenomena are established by way of their own character as the referents of their respective conceptual consciousnesses.
- Paṇ-chen Sö-nam-drak-ba likewise leaves Dzong-ka-ba's identification as is but adds that a difference of entity between subject and object is also taught, and at least some of his followers (for example, Ken-sur Ye-shay-tup-den and Ge-shay Gön-chok-tsay-ring) add that the establishment of objects by way of their own character as the referents of conceptual consciousnesses is also communicated.

It seems to me that Jay-dzün Chö-gyi-gyel-tsen's and Paṇ-chen Sö-nam-drak-ba's followers, feeling the bite of Gung-ru Chö-jung and Jam-yang-shay-ba's analysis, have seen the need to re-state the meaning of their textbooks. Nevertheless, they have not converted to the Go-mang viewpoint because they view it as having deviated too far from what Dzong-ka-ba actually said, and thus they have opted for creative readings of "own-character" as communicating not just establishment of objects by way of their own character but also:

1. establishment of objects by way of their own character as the referents of conceptual consciousnesses and words
2. externality (or being a different entity from the respective consciousness).

The inadequacy of all these attempts to make Dzong-ka-ba's statements sensible promotes the suspicion that the basic problem may be with his text itself. One even wonders whether he slipped up in rejecting Wonch'uk's assertion that the "own-character" of Paramārthasamudgata's question refers to the unique character of an object. We will return to this point in the next chapter when I try to revive Wonch'uk's explanation. First, let us place the discussion of "own-character" in a wider context.

Overview of "Own-Character"

In all Ge-luk-ba systems of exegesis the three wheels of doctrine as described in the *Sūtra Unraveling the Thought* are not general classes into which all of Buddha's teaching can be placed; rather, they are three sets of specific teachings on the nature of objects. Ḍzong-ka-ḇa himself (*Emptiness in Mind-Only,* 242-243) makes this point clearly:

> The three stages of wheels of doctrine mentioned in the *Sūtra Unraveling the Thought* are posited, not by way of the assemblies of [Buddha's] circle or by way of periods in the Teacher's life and so forth but by way of topics of expression. Furthermore, those are in terms of delineating the meaning of selflessness:
>
> - Initially, at Varaṇāsi, he spoke of the selflessness of persons; [thus] there is one cycle [of teaching], in which the true establishment of the phenomena of the aggregates and so forth, except for a few, is not refuted and true existence is mentioned frequently.[a]
> - Then, there is one cycle in which, without [clearly] making distinctions, true establishment is refuted [on the literal level] with respect to all of the phenomena of the aggregates and so forth.[b]
> - Then, there arose one cycle in which, with respect to those, he individually differentiated the mode of the first nature [that is, the imputational nature] as not established by way of its own character and the other two [that is, other-powered natures and thoroughly established natures] as established by way of their own character.
>
> Therefore, [the wheels of doctrine that are the bases for differentiation—in the "Questions of Paramārthasamudgata Chapter" of the *Sūtra Unraveling the Thought* and in the texts commenting on its thought—of what requires interpretation and what is definitive] are taken in terms of these [modes of teaching subject matter]. Other sūtras that teach in a way other than these modes of teaching are not in any sensible way bases of this analysis of the interpretable and the definitive.

As the last sentence says, only passages teaching in certain ways are included in the three wheels; others are simply not any of the three.

With respect to the first wheel, we have seen that Ge-luk-ḇa scholars agree

[a] According to Jam-ȳang-shay-ḇa (*Great Exposition of the Interpretable and the Definitive,* 27.3), the last sentence should be rendered as:

> Initially, at Varaṇāsi, he spoke of the selflessness of persons; [thus] there is one cycle [of teaching], in which the true establishment of the phenomena of the aggregates and so forth—[these being] *no more than a few* [of the one hundred and eight phenomena]—is not refuted and true existence is mentioned frequently.

See issues #21, 32, 36, 38.

[b] See issues #37 and 38.

that the teaching that requires interpretation is that all phenomena are established by way of their own character as the referents of their respective conceptual consciousnesses and are established as different entities from the consciousnesses apprehending them. However, based on varying characterizations of this teaching in Ḏzong-ka-ḇa's writings, they differ on just what the term "own-character" in Paramārthasamudgata's question in the seventh chapter of the *Sūtra Unraveling the Thought* means. Since they agree on the basic point, a value of the controversy lies in revealing the permutations of Mind-Only positions. Since their arguments about "own-character" constantly refer to the tenets of the system, the controversy grounds the participants more and more in the Mind-Only worldview.

In his brief summary of the controversy, Jik-may-dam-chö-gya-tso lists five possible meanings of "own-character" that need to be considered to determine which is appropriate in this context:[142]

1. the unique defining character of an object[a]
2. the capacity to perform a function[b]
3. objective establishment[c]
4. establishment without depending on imputation by terms and conceptual consciousnesses[d]
5. establishment by way of the object's own character as the referent of a conceptual consciousness apprehending it.[e]

These are five meanings of the term that appear in various contexts in Buddhist philosophical literature; the principles that Jik-may-dam-chö-gya-tso uses to determine which is appropriate here are twofold—internal coherence and agreement with Ḏzong-ka-ḇa's pronouncements on the topic. As we have seen, the dictum that these two criteria are in perfect harmony seems destined to stifle creative thought, but, opposite to that, provides a format for promoting inventive reframing of Ḏzong-ka-ḇa's words. We must remain suspicious, however, that these scholars' considerable talents could be used, due to the demands of allegiance, to avoid having to admit to a downright error.

Let us consider Jik-may-dam-chö-gya-tso's brief treatment of the five.

Issue #39: Could "own-character" mean the unique defining character of an object?

About the first position—that "own-character" refers to the unique defining

---

a *thun mong min pa'i mtshan nyid.*

b *don byed nus pa.*

c *yul steng nas grub pa.*

d *sgra rtog gis btags pa la ma ltos par grub pa.*

e *rang 'dzin rtog pa'i zhen gzhir rang gi mtshan nyid kyis grub pa.*

character or nature of an object—Jik-may-dam-chö-gya-tso simply mentions that Dzong-ka-ba himself refutes this. Let us flesh this out.

The Korean scholar Wonch'uk in his *Great Commentary on the "Sūtra Unraveling the Thought"* says:[143]

> "Own-character" is the specific character as in, for instance, the explanation, "Form is obstructive. ... Consciousness is the knower."

Dzong-ka-ba (*Emptiness in Mind-Only,* 78-79) refutes this identification of "own-character" as inappropriate in this context:

> In the Chinese *Great Commentary*[a] [on the *Sūtra Unraveling the Thought* by the Korean scholar Wonch'uk], and so forth, (259) {370} "own-character" here [in this passage in the *Sūtra Unraveling the Thought*] is explained as the unique character [of the aggregates and so forth], but this is not right.[b] For the sūtra itself at the point of [speaking about] imputational factors[c] clearly speaks of establishment by way of [the object's] own character [and does not speak of the unique character], and since even imputational factors have a unique characterization, there would be the fallacy that the character-non-nature could not be explained with respect to imputational factors.[d]

As Jam-yang-shay-ba[144] explains, if "own-character" in Paramārthasamudgata's question referred to the unique character of a phenomenon, then when Buddha (*Emptiness in Mind-Only,* 82) gives his answer speaking about character-non-nature:

> Paramārthasamudgata, thinking of three non-natures of phenomena—character-non-nature, production-non-nature, and ultimate-non-nature—I taught [in the middle wheel of the teaching], "All phenomena are natureless."

the term "character" also would have to refer to the unique character of phenomena simply because of the relatedness of the answer to the question. However, the sūtra itself (*Emptiness in Mind-Only,* 86), at the point of speaking about imputational natures, speaks not of their lacking a unique character but of their not subsisting by way of their own character:[e]

> Those [imputational characters] are characters posited by names and

---

[a] See issue #8.

[b] See issue #48.

[c] See issue #50.

[d] See issue #48.

[e] *rang gi mtshan nyid gyis gnas pa ma yin.*

terminology[a] and do not subsist by way of their own character. Therefore, they are said to be "character-non-natures."

Because imputational natures do not subsist by way of their own character, they are said to be "character-non-natures." Thus, "character" in "character-non-nature" clearly means to subsist, or to be established, by way of its own character. This passage is Ḏzong-ka-ḇa's referent when he says in the citation just above, "The sūtra itself at the point of [speaking about] imputational natures clearly speaks of establishment by way of [the object's] own character."

Ḏzong-ka-ḇa's other point is that although non-existent imputational natures—such as the horns of a rabbit or objects that are established by way of their own character as the referents of conceptual consciousnesses—do not exist and thus do not have a unique character, existent imputational natures—such as uncompounded space, analytical cessations, non-analytical cessations, and so forth—are phenomena[b] and thus exist and hence must have their own unique character distinguishing them from other phenomena.[c] Ḏzong-ka-ḇa concludes that since in Buddha's answer the *Sūtra Unraveling the Thought* indisputably indicates that imputational natures are character-non-natures, the term "character" in that phrase cannot refer to the unique defining character of an object because existent imputational natures have their own unique defining character. From this, Ḏzong-ka-ḇa draws the conclusion that the term "own-character" in Paramārthasamudgata's question also cannot refer to the unique defining character of an object.

Let us merely note here that Ḏzong-ka-ḇa's argument (1) assumes that the *Sūtra Unraveling the Thought* is concerned about existent imputational natures such as uncompounded space or being a referent of thoughts and terminology and is not just speaking about non-existent imputational natures such as the establishment of objects by way of their own character as the referents of thoughts and terminology and (2) assumes that the "own-character" of the question and the "character" in "character-non-nature" are the same. Since, as will be discussed in the next chapter, I find both of these assumptions to be questionable, I am left with the qualm that this issue might just be a case where Ḏzong-ka-ḇa has slipped up but his opinion is so clear that no one can pretend that he did not say what he did. In any case, it is clear that in Ge-luk-ḇa exegesis the term "own-character" in this context cannot refer to the unique, defining nature of an object.

---

[a] See issue #104.

[b] *chos, dharma.*

[c] It is extremely hard to posit the definitions of some phenomena; thus, Ḏzong-ka-ḇa may be referring only to imputational nature itself and not the phenomena that are imputational natures.

Issue #40: Could "own-character" mean the capacity to perform a function?

Another possible meaning of "own-character" is the capacity to perform the function of generating effects. In this case, Paramārthasamudgata would be saying that in the first wheel Buddha taught that all phenomena, even uncompounded space and so forth, have the capacity to generate effects. However, since uncompounded phenomena are not asserted in any Buddhist school to have such a capacity, Jik-may-dam-chö-gya-tso rejects this possibility on the basis that Buddha would have no purpose in teaching such, that is to say, there is no one who needed to hear it.

This refutation is right on the mark, since even though the Great Exposition School asserts that all phenomena, including the uncompounded, are things[a] and thus have the capacity to perform functions,[b] they do not hold that "function" means the generation, or production, of effects; for them uncompounded space performs the function of allowing, but not generating, movement.[c] Also, the other Hearer school, the Sūtra School,[d] clearly asserts that the capacity to perform a function is limited to the function of producing effects.

Issue #41: Could "own-character" mean objective establishment?

If "own-character" meant objective establishment,[e] then in the first wheel Buddha would have been teaching that all phenomena are objectively established. However, the standard Ge-luk-b̄a position is that in the Mind-Only School all phenomena, even existent imputational natures, are objectively established, and thus this reading of "own-character" would absurdly make the first-wheel teaching of "own-character" literally acceptable and thus definitive, whereas the *Sūtra Unraveling the Thought* clearly says that it is not. Rather, given Ge-luk-b̄a scholars' equation of the "own-character" of the question and the "character" of the answer, "own-character" has to be something that imputational natures do not have, since Buddha, in his answer, says that imputational natures are character-non-natures.

Ge-luk-b̄a scholars hold the at-first-blush astonishing position that the Proponents of Mind-Only, despite holding that imputational natures are not established by way of their own character, accept that even imputational natures

---

a *dngos po, bhāva.*

b *don byed nus pa.*

c See Ḡön-chok-jik-may-w̄ang-b̄o's brief explanation of this in Sopa and Hopkins, *Cutting Through Appearances,* 182-183.

d More specifically, the Sūtra School Following Reasoning.

e *yul steng nas grub pa.*

are objectively established and established from their own side. The reason for this is that if the Proponents of Mind-Only understood that imputational natures are not objectively established, they would understand what the Consequence School considers to be the most subtle emptiness and would be able to extend this realization to all phenomena, not just imputational natures. This is impossible, not only because the Consequentialists argue this point against the Proponents of Mind-Only but also because it is clear that the latter assert that other-powered natures are established by way of their own character, thus revealing that they do not realize that other-powered natures are not objectively established, this in turn revealing that they do understand that even imputational natures are not objectively established, for if they did, they would be able to extend the realization to any and all phenomena. The very fact that the Mind-Only School, following the *Sūtra Unraveling the Thought*, holds that imputational natures are not established by way of their own character but other-powered natures are means that even with respect to existent imputational natures they do not refute the status that the Consequentialists deny with respect to all phenomena. For it is cogently held that someone who can understand emptiness with respect to one object can realize it with respect to all phenomena.[a]

Issue #42: Could "own-character" mean establishment without depending on imputation by terms and conceptual consciousnesses?

If "own-character" meant the establishment of objects without depending on imputation by terms and conceptual consciousnesses, then, as Jik-may-dam-chö-gya-tso says, in the first wheel of doctrine Buddha would be teaching the special trainees of the first wheel—the two Hearer schools, the Great Exposition and Sūtra schools—that all phenomena are established this way. He does not unpack the problem, but it is clear that the Sūtra School Following Reasoning, for instance, asserts that the establishment of uncompounded space, for instance, depends on imputation by terms and conceptual consciousnesses, and thus Buddha could not have taught that it has "own-character."

Nevertheless, D̄zong-ka-b̄a more than once says that "character" means establishment by way of its own character and that this, in turn, means establishment without depending on imputation by terms and conceptual consciousnesses. Therefore, Jik-may-dam-chö-gya-tso rescues this meaning of "own-character," **in combination with the next**. However, he does not tell us how Lesser Vehicle schools could possibly assert that imputational natures such as uncompounded space are established without depending on imputation by terms and conceptual consciousnesses. (Seeing that he is violating his own

[a] See *Reflections on Reality*, 228.

principle of internal consistency which requires the maintenance of four schools of tenets, I again am drawn into suspecting that he is making a last-ditch effort to rescue Ḏzong-ka-ḇa's opinion. More on this in the next chapter.) Thus, here Jik-may-dam-chö-gya-tso is refuting that this is the **only** meaning of "own-character" in this context.

Issue #43: Could "own-character" mean establishment by way of its own character as the referent of a conceptual consciousness?

If "own-character" in Paramārthasamudgata's question only[145] means establishment by way of its own character as the referent of a conceptual consciousness (as Gung-ru Chö-jung, Jam-ȳang-shay-ḇa, Gung-tang, and A-ku Ḻo-drö-gya-tso say it does), then since the Mind-Only School refutes this with respect to all phenomena, it would be pointless for Ḏzong-ka-ḇa, in refuting Wonch'uk, to indicate that "own-character" here must be something that the aggregates have but imputational natures do not:

> since even imputational factors have a unique characterization, there would be the fallacy that the character-non-nature could not be explained with respect to imputational factors.

(Gung-tang's valiant attempt to explain away this problem is considered in the next chapter; see issue #49)

For these reasons, Jik-may-dam-chö-gya-tso[a] holds that "own-character" here in Paramārthasamudgata's question refers to both of the latter two meanings, this being despite the fact that he is mainly a follower of Jam-ȳang-shay-ḇa whom he admits[146] Gung-tang is representing when the latter holds that "own-character" here only refers to this last meaning. The dual position (also employed by Jay-ḏzün Chö-ḡyi-gyel-tsen's and Paṇ-chen S̄ö-nam-drak-ḇa's followers) allows them room (1) to explain how the "own-character" of Paramārthasamudgata's question refers to an over-reified status that the first wheel teaches with respect to all phenomena—this being the establishment of objects by way of their own character as the referents of conceptual consciousnesses—and (2) to explain why "own-character" is singled out as something that imputational natures do not have but other-powered natures and thoroughly established natures do. However, the dual position is no cure-all since, as Jik-may-dam-chö-gya-tso himself questions with respect to the fourth meaning, the Sūtra School Following Reasoning, which follows the first wheel of the

---

[a] Jik-may-dam-chö-gya-tso's *Port of Entry,* 145.6 and 149.5. In the latter, he indicates that there are those who assert such; I see this, combined with his earlier statement, as suggesting that he himself prefers this position despite the fact that it does not agree with Gung-tang.

teaching, does not assert that existent imputational natures are established by way of their own character![a]

The dual identification has the advantage of making it so that these scholars do not to have to explain away many statements by Ḏzong-ka-ḇa and Ke-drup that clearly speak about establishment by way of its own character as simply meaning establishment without depending on imputation by terms and conceptual consciousnesses. In such contexts, Jik-may-dam-chö-gya-tso[147] (and the followers of Paṇ-chen S̄ö-nam-drak-ḇa and Jay-ḏzün Chö-ḡyi-gyel-tsen) hold that the reference is only to one part of the dual meaning, that is, establishment by way of its own character. The dual explanation employs the slipperiness of claiming that sometimes "own-character" has both meanings and sometimes only one.

Forging Consistency

Issue #44: How to make Ḏzong-ka-ḇa say something else?

Gung-ru Chö-jung and Jam-ȳang-shay-ḇa have the virtue of employing a single identification, but they must show how to reconcile their explanation with several statements by Ḏzong-ka-ḇa that seem to represent exactly what they are refuting. We have seen how Gung-ru Chö-jung and Jam-ȳang-shay-ḇa hold that in Paramārthasamudgata's question in the *Sūtra Unraveling the Thought*, "The Supramundane Victor [initially] spoke, in many ways, of the own-character of the aggregates," the term "own-character" means the establishment of objects by way of their own character as the referents of conceptual consciousnesses, and we have seen that, for them, the term "character" in Buddha's answer, "Concerning that, what are **character**-non-natures of phenomena? Those which are imputational characters,"[b] means the same (even if, as we will see later, p. 204, there is considerable fudging on this point). But what about Ḏzong-ka-ḇa's description (*Emptiness in Mind-Only*, 127), cited above, that in the first wheel Buddha stated that phenomena are equally established by way of their own character?[c]

---

[a] It will be recalled that Jay-ḏzün Chö-ḡyi-gyel-tsen tries to answer this problem by claiming that in the Sūtra School Following Reasoning all phenomena, including existent imputational natures, *are* held to be established by way of their own character. As detailed above (p. 79), to do this he must simply assert that Ḏzong-ka-ḇa's student Ke-drup is wrong when he indicates that the Sūtra School Following Reasoning does not assert this.

[b] "Imputational character" (*kun btags kyi mtshan nyid, parikalpitalakṣaṇa*) and "imputational nature" (*kun btags kyi rang bzhin, parikalpitasvabhāva*) are synonymous.

[c] The Tibetan (*Emptiness in Mind-Only*, 389) is: *drang nges su 'jog pa'i gzhi ni chos rnams la rang gi mtshan nyid kyis grub pa'i ngo bo nyid yod mnyam du gsungs pa dang med mnyam du gsungs pa dang yod med legs par phye ba gsum yin pa.*

> The bases being posited as interpretable or definitive are the three—the statements [in the first wheel] that phenomena equally have nature in the sense of being established by way of their own character, the statements [in the middle wheel] that phenomena equally do not have such, and the good differentiation [in the final wheel] of those [phenomena] that have [such establishment] and those that do not.

Gung-ru Chö-jung[148] and Jam-ȳang-shay-b̄a[149] answer by insisting that D̄zong-ka-b̄a's statement does not say what it seems to; rather, D̄zong-ka-b̄a is (or should be) saying:

> The first wheel[a] **equally has statements of the words**, "Phenomena ranging from forms through to the harmonies with enlightenment have the nature[b] of being established by way of their own character," and the middle wheel **equally has statements of the words**, "Phenomena ranging from forms through to exalted knowers of all aspects [that is, omniscient consciousnesses] do not have the nature of being established by way of their own character."[c]

My own reading of the grammar (as well as the reading by all of the major commentators except Gung-ru Chö-jung, Jam-ȳang-shay-b̄a, and their followers) is that D̄zong-ka-b̄a is saying that in the first wheel Buddha said that phenomena **equally have** nature in the sense of being established by way of their own character and that in the middle wheel he said that phenomena **equally do not have** such, but, according to Gung-ru Chö-jung and Jam-ȳang-shay-b̄a, that is simply a mis-reading because of the absurdities that such a reading would entail, as were detailed in the last chapter (61). To follow them, the above citation should be translated into English as:

> The bases being posited as interpretable or definitive are the three—the statements **equally [present throughout the sūtras of the first wheel]** that phenomena have nature in the sense of being established by way of their own character, the statements **equally [present throughout the sūtras of the middle wheel]** that phenomena do not have such, and the good differentiation [in the final wheel] of those

---

[a] As always in this context, the reference is to the first wheel "as indicated in the *Sūtra Unraveling the Thought*"; therefore, Jam-ȳang-shay-b̄a (33.5) corrects Gung-ru Chö-jung's *'khor lo dang po* (8a.6) to ***'dir bstan*** *'khor lo dang po.*

[b] Gung-ru Chö-jung (8a.6) reads *ngo bo* ***nyid*** whereas Jam-ȳang-shay-b̄a (33.5/13a.5) reads *ngo bo.*

[c] Jam-ȳang-shay-b̄a's *Great Exposition of the Interpretable and the Definitive,* 33.5: *'dir bstan 'khor lo dang por gzugs nas byang phyogs kyi bar gyi chos rnams la rang gi mtshan nyid kyis grub pa'i ngo bo yod ces pa'i tshig yod mnyam dang/ bar par gzugs nas rnam mkhyen gyi bar gyi chos rnams la rang gi mtshan nyid kyis grub pa'i ngo bo nyid med ces pa'i tshig yod mnyam du gsungs zhes pa'i don yin.* See issue #108.

[phenomena] that have [such establishment] and those that do not.

The grammar does not easily yield what Gung-ru Chö-jung and Jam-ȳang-shay-b̄a see, but it is an inventive, creative way of making sense out of what D̄zong-ka-b̄a says in the light of their decision that "own-character" has to mean the establishment of objects by way of own character **as the referents of conceptual consciousnesses.**" Since they view the rules of allegiance to the founder of their sect such that they cannot refute D̄zong-ka-b̄a's own words, they must make them say something that they do not seem to say. By claiming that what D̄zong-ka-b̄a means is that only the **words** "Phenomena ranging from forms through to the harmonies with enlightenment have the nature of being established by way of their own character," are equally present throughout the first wheel,[a] they can make the further claim that what those words mean is that the first wheel teaches that these phenomena are established by way of their own character as the referents of conceptual consciousnesses. This division into words and meaning allows them to leave D̄zong-ka-b̄a's statement as is and yet read a different meaning into it.

The maneuver, taken at face value, is lame, but when it is seen that it is part of a grand scenario to correct what Gung-ru Chö-jung and Jam-ȳang-shay-b̄a perceive to be a misstatement by the founder of the sect without explicitly adopting the posture of criticism, it becomes a display of their deftness at pretending that the coherent system that they themselves perceive is to be found in D̄zong-ka-b̄a's own words. As one of Jam-ȳang-shay-b̄a's followers told me, "D̄zong-ka-b̄a's writings did much to establish a proper presentation of Indian Buddhist philosophy, but Jam-ȳang-shay-b̄a had to make many adjustments to make everything fit together." In other words, Jam-ȳang-shay-b̄a is seen by his followers as superseding D̄zong-ka-b̄a in many respects despite his adopting the posture of merely explaining the founder. The local leader, modeled on the paradigm of the grand over-all leader, comes to assume more importance than his predecessor. Being local and more recent, he is more relevant, and he also provides an avenue for parochial loyalty to form in a society where political authority was not greatly centralized. This unmasking of Gung-ru Chö-jung and Jam-ȳang-shay-b̄a's **explanation** of D̄zong-ka-b̄a on this point as a basic **re-casting** of the founder's position in order to establish internal consistency is essential to being able to follow their argument. Otherwise, the tension and conflict of such dramatic re-writing in the guise of explaining the founder's words when they obviously do not say such is unbearable—as long as one thinks that all they intend to do is to clarify what is already basically coherent.

The re-writing is not limited to D̄zong-ka-b̄a. Ke-drup, one of D̄zong-ka-b̄a's two main disciples, lends support to the view that the first-wheel passages

[a] I find it particularly interesting that none of these scholars mentions that the words "established by way of its own character" are very hard to find in the first wheel. This problem may be so sensitive that it cannot even be raised.

in question are those in which Buddha teaches that the aggregates and so forth are established by way of their own character. His *Opening the Eyes of the Fortunate* says:[150]

> In the first [wheel Buddha] said that the aggregates and so forth equally exist by way of their own character, and in the middle [wheel] he said that all [phenomena] equally do not exist inherently; since he did not speak within explicitly differentiating what does and does not inherently exist [that is, exist by way of its own character or not], these require interpretation.

Nevertheless, as Gung-tang says,[151] we are again to understand that what Ke-drup had in mind was that the **words,** "Phenomena have a nature of being established by way of their own character," are **equally present** throughout the first-wheel teachings. Ke-drup thereby is held to have understood that the term "own-character" in Paramārthasamudgata's question about the first wheel refers to the establishment of phenomena by way of their own character **as the referents of conceptual consciousnesses,** even though Ke-drup obviously did not use this vocabulary. What is claimed by these commentators to be a revelation of his intention is actually a masking of what is considered to be a misstatement.[a]

Implications

Issue #45: What does the first wheel say and teach?

The implications of such rephrasing spread out in many directions. Many subtle distinctions about what was **said** in the first wheel must be made. According to Gung-ru Chö-jung,[152] Jam-ȳang-shay-b̄a,[153] and A-ku L̄o-drö-gya-tso,[154] when Paramārthasamudgata says, "The Supramundane Victor spoke, in many ways, of the own-character of the aggregates," Paramārthasamudgata is saying only that Buddha **spoke the words of sūtra,**[b] "The aggregates are established by way of their own character." However, Buddha did not **say**[c] that the aggregates are established by way of their own character; nor did he **teach**[d] that the aggregates

[a] Gung-ru Chö-jung (*Garland of White Lotuses,* 8b.1-9a.3) goes on to give a hair-splitting analysis of the difference between saying that this and that exists and saying that there is something that is this and that; for instance, something that is permanent exists and something that is impermanent exists, but something that is (both) permanent and impermanent does not exist. He applies this (in what is to me a mystery) to sūtras of the first and middle wheels. Jam-ȳang-shay-b̄a (*Great Exposition of the Interpretable and the Definitive,* 33.6) omits the entire interlude.

[b] *ces pa'i mdo tshig bka' stsal pa.*

[c] *gsungs pa.*

[d] *bstan pa.*

are established by way of their own character; nor did he even say (in quotes), "The aggregates are established by way of their own character," since that would constitute his saying and teaching such. For, as explained above, if Buddha pronounced in the first wheel that the aggregates are established by way of their own character, such would be literally acceptable. He merely spoke, or uttered, or pronounced **the words of sūtra**, "The aggregates are established by way of their own character."

Jam-ȳang-shay-b̄a[155] addresses the issue through raising a parallel concern from another context: If the mere pronouncement of sūtra words entails the pronouncement of sūtra words **teaching** such, then the *Heart of Wisdom Sūtra* would absurdly teach that forms and so forth do not exist since it contains the sūtra words, "Form does not exist," and so forth. Jam-ȳang-shay-b̄a's cogent point is that although the *Heart of Wisdom Sūtra* has such words, it does not pronounce, say, or teach that forms do not exist because there simply is no purpose in teaching that forms do not exist. As the late Ge-s̄hay Ge-dün-l̄o-drö of Go-mang College said, there is no trainee for the teaching that forms do not exist, and hence Buddha never taught such, even though those words are present in sūtras. The context must be taken into account, either as provided by other passages that specify a status of objects—such as inherent existence—as not existing or as provided by considering Buddha's intent and his listeners' mind-set. Early in the *Heart of Wisdom Sūtra* itself, Avalokiteshvara says, "Forms are to be viewed as empty of **inherent** existence," and hence the qualification "inherently" must be carried over to all the other negations.

The conclusion is that in the first wheel Buddha taught and said, relative to certain trainees, that phenomena are established by way of their own character as the referents of conceptual consciousnesses despite the admitted fact that those very words, or anything resembling them, appear nowhere in such sūtras. A-ku L̄o-drö-gya-tso[156] makes the further distinction that Buddha even **spoke** the words of sūtra, "Phenomena are established by way of their own character as the referents of conceptual consciousnesses," his point undoubtedly being that if Buddha explicitly teaches such on the literal level, he must say it. Indeed, this must be understood within the context of Gung-tang's brilliant discussion of Buddha's intention to teach such and the mind-set of his listeners, since, as A-ku L̄o-drö-gya-tso himself admits, such "does not emerge [that is, appear] in words."[a] It indeed makes sense that since such is held to be communicated on the literal level, it is also spoken.

It might seem that one could just as easily assert that although such is explicitly taught,[b] it is not taught on the literal level,[c] but then the words of sūtra of the first wheel, "Forms are established by way of their own character," would

---

a *Precious Lamp,* 55.6: *'dir dngos su bstan pa'i 'khor lo dang po rnams kyi tshig la rang 'dzin rtog pa'i zhen gzhir rang mtshan gyis grub pa ma thon kyang.*

b *dngos su bstan.*

c *sgras zin la ma bstan.*

be literally acceptable, whereas Dzong-ka-ba holds that Paramārthasamudgata's concern with the first two wheels of doctrine is over their literal reading. This is the driving force behind Gung-tang's insistence that the first wheel teaches **on the literal level** that phenomena are established by way of their own character as the referents of their respective conceptual consciousnesses, despite the obvious fact that such does not appear in the run of the words.

Issue #46: Is Buddha's speech correct when teaching a non-existent?

Buddha's sūtras are supposed to be completely correct means of expression[a] and hence concordant with the fact.[b] Thus, when Buddha, for a temporary purpose, teaches something that is untrue, his speech must still be completely correct. As the late Lo-sel-ling scholar and abbot Ye-shay-tup-den put it, Buddha speaks knowingly, and thus there is a big difference between ordinary speech and sūtra. In ordinary speech if what is expressed is actually non-existent, then the words that express it are not concordant with the fact, but this does not hold for sūtras because of the special cognition from which they are spoken. Sūtra passages, therefore, can be concordant with the fact even though what they express may be non-existent. Through this distinction sūtras are preserved as completely correct means of expression.

Issue #47: How to make a mess out of what were, up until now, evocative distinctions?

A-ku Lo-drö-gya-tso, on the other hand, maintains the factual nature of Buddha's teaching but does not resort to the extraordinary nature of a Buddha's cognition as justification. Essentially, he holds that Buddha gave that teaching **only temporarily** to lead trainees to hold the view (that phenomena are established by way of their own character as the referents of their respective conceptual consciousnesses)—the goal being to lead them to the selflessness of persons—and thus did not teach it. As the Inner Mongolian scholar Gen Den-dzin said,[c] such is taught **relative to the thought of certain trainees** but such is not taught. This is how to preserve that Buddha's teaching is factual: just say he did not teach whatever is non-factual, since he taught it only temporarily relative to certain trainees!

This maneuver reeks of fishiness, and it is most satisfying that A-ku Lo-drö-gya-tso amusingly makes the consequent startling observation that there are no words of sūtra **teaching**, "Phenomena are established by way of their own

[a] *rjod byed rnam dag.*

[b] *don dang mthun pa.*

[c] In a session in Hla-sa at Dre-bung Monastic University during the summer of 1987.

character as the referents of conceptual consciousnesses," his point being that such is taught only **relative to the thought of certain trainees**. Displaying the intellectual honesty that is at the heart of the sport of making such distinctions, A-ku L̄o-drö-gya-tso perforce admits that, because he has to maintain that Buddha spoke words of sūtra teaching that objects are established in this false way, he is left with the seeming double-talk of having to hold that there are no words of sūtra teaching such! In his own words:[a]

> Although in the first wheel [Buddha] spoke words of sūtra teaching that the aggregates and so forth are established by way of their own character as the referents of their respective conceptual consciousnesses and spoke the words of sūtra, "The aggregates and so forth are established by way of their own character as the referents of their respective conceptual consciousnesses," there are no words of sūtra teaching, "The aggregates are established by way of their own character as the referents of conceptual consciousnesses."

How Buddha could speak words of sūtra teaching this when there are no words of sūtra teaching such is mind-boggling to say the least.

It is clear that A-ku L̄o-drö-gya-tso is amused by the ramifications of Gung-tang's presentation of the context of the first-wheel teaching—Buddha's intention and the listeners' mind-set on the one hand and this teaching's being merely provisional on the other hand—juxtaposed to the dictum that Buddha's sūtras are pure means of expression and hence concordant with the fact. As Ye-s̄hay-tup-d̄en put it, if A-ku L̄o-drö-gya-tso had clarified the difference between ordinary speech and a Buddha's speech, he would not have been led into making these questionable distinctions, but I admire A-ku L̄o-drö-gya-tso for not resorting to that device.

Comment

The reasons for and implications of the variety of explanations of D̄zong-ka-b̄a's rendition of the first-wheel teaching are so invitingly provocative that it seems a conclusion cannot be reached. At times, when pursuing the opinions of these scholars, one is caught in a web of intriguing but eventually bewildering issues of fundamental importance, but the bewilderment is at least partially relieved when one sees through the facade of these authors' pretension of explicating D̄zong-ka-b̄a's thought as if it were consistent in every phrase. No matter how complicated these issues and their ramifications become, on the positive side these same arguments bring all the more force to the uniformly accepted

[a] A-ku L̄o-drö-gya-tso's *Precious Lamp,* 62.4:

'khor lo dang por phung sogs rang 'dzin rtog pa'i zhen gzhir rang mtshan gyis grub par ston pa'i mdo tshig dang/ de ltar du grub ces pa'i mdo tshig bka' stsal kyang/ phung sogs rang 'dzin rtog pa'i zhen gzhir rang mtshan gyis grub ces ston pa'i mdo tshig med//

assertion in Ge-luk-b̄a circles that the Mind-Only School is refuting the teaching in the first wheel that mental and physical aggregates, the sense-spheres, dependent-arising, the foods, the four noble truths, the constituents, and the harmonies with enlightenment—that is to say, all phenomena—are established by way of their own character as the referents of words and thoughts. There is no quarrel about this point; the debates are over peripheral issues. The style of the monastic textbooks—focusing on ancillary issues—causes the central issue to become the floor of inquiry without our noticing it (though it is indeed possible to lose all sense of place). When the foundational issue is recalled, it can be seen that the style has embedded the main point in a nexus of implications that transform it from a topic of mere verbalization to an issue of vibrant concern in the vast context of a worldview. This phase is left to the individual; the texts remain with the points of controversy.

7. Wonch'uk: Refutation and Revival

We have seen that the term "own-character" in Paramārthasamudgata's description of Buddha's teaching in the first wheel of doctrine refers to:

Tradition	*Identification of "own-character"*
Gung-ru Chö-jung and Jam-ȳang-shay-b̄a	established by way of its own character as the referent of terms and conceptual consciousnesses
Paṇ-chen S̄ö-nam-drak-b̄a	establishment by way of its own character as well as externality
Jay-d̄zün Chö-ḡyi-gyel-tsen	establishment by way of its own character[a]

There is another explanation, however, that seems—more than just on the surface—to be plausible.

Wonch'uk's Identification

Issue #48: Could "own-character" mean an object's unique character?

As was briefly mentioned in the previous chapter (91), "own-character" is read by the Korean scholar Wonch'uk in his *Great Commentary on the "Sūtra Unraveling the Thought"* (which was written in Chinese and translated into Tibetan) as referring to the unique character or definition of a phenomenon as when Buddha speaks of a phenomenon and then of its unique character that distinguishes it from other phenomena. In the case of form, for instance, this is obstructiveness. Paramārthasamudgata (*Emptiness in Mind-Only,* 76) describes how Buddha taught the five aggregates in the first wheel of doctrine:

> The Supramundane Victor spoke, in many ways, of the own-character of the aggregates. He also spoke of [their] character of production, character of disintegration, abandonment, and thorough knowledge.

In commentary on this, Wonch'uk says:[157]

> "Own-character" is the specific character as in, for instance, the explanation, "Form is obstructive.... Consciousness is the knower." "Character of production, character of disintegration" are general characters because forms and so forth are entities[b] that have the character of production and disintegration. "Utter abandonment and thorough knowledge" are characters of suffering and of origins [of suffering]

---

a As explained earlier (76ff.), some of his followers have felt it necessary to modify this identification.

b *mtshan nyid.*

> because [contaminated] karma and afflictive emotions which are the true origins [of suffering] are to be utterly abandoned and because the fruits of cyclic existence which are true sufferings are to be thoroughly known. Or, "own-character" is the character of self-entity or specific character; the production and disintegration of those two characters pervade all [compounded phenomena and hence are general characters].

Wonch'uk depicts Buddha as speaking first about the character or nature of an object that is specific to it alone, as when he teaches about the obstructiveness of form, which is not shared with other phenomena such as consciousness, and then about characters of form that are shared with other compounded phenomena, such as production and disintegration, and hence are general characters.

Similarly, the *Explanation of the "Sūtra Unraveling the Thought,"*[a] in commentary on the fourth chapter of the *Sūtra Unraveling the Thought,* identifies "observation of the signs of the aggregates"[b] as being "from the point of view of thoroughly analyzing **their own signs**"[c] and "observation of the production of the aggregates"[d] and "observation of the disintegration of the aggregates"[e] as being "from the point of view of **general characteristics** and thorough investigation."[f]

In 1988 while I was studying at Go-mang College on Mount Increasing Virtue above the western Hla-s̄a Valley, a scholar from Inner Mongolia, who momentarily had forgotten Dzong-ka-ba's reading of "own-character" as "establishment by way of its own character," said:

> Own-character is the entity, and the characters of production, disintegration, abandonment, and thorough knowledge are attributes of form. The *Sūtra Unraveling the Thought* puts emphasis on imputation in the manner of entity and attribute.

I was so delighted with his spontaneous explanation of "own-character," which, aided by his memory lapse, concurred with my own suspicion, that I exclaimed, "Except for contradicting Dzong-ka-ba's refutation of Wonch'uk, your explanation is really good because it reflects a format found in the sūtra itself." His jaw dropped slightly, and he gave me a weird glance, never returning to the topic! I knew I must be on to something—now even more suspicious that Dzong-ka-ba

---

[a] (Delhi: Karmapae Choedhey, 1985), *cho,* vol. 205, 109.4. For discussion of the authorship of this commentary, see *Emptiness in Mind-Only,* 454.

[b] *phung po'i mtshan ma dmigs pa, skandhanimittopalambha.*

[c] *rang gi mtshan ma yongs su brtags pa'i sgo nas.*

[d] *phung po'i skye ba dmigs pa, skandhotpādopalambha.*

[e] *phung po'i 'jig pa dmigs pa, skandha-vināśopalambha.*

[f] *spyi'i mtshan nyid dang yongs su brtags pa'i sgo nas.*

was over-anxious to read "own-character" as "established by way of its own character."

Indeed, the format of entity and attribute is important to the discussion of the three natures in the *Sūtra Unraveling the Thought*. The theme is introduced in the sixth chapter when Buddha first describes the imputational nature:

> Guṇākara, if you ask, "What is the imputational character of phenomena," [I reply,] "It is that which is posited by names and terminology as the entities and attributes of phenomena due to imputing whatsoever conventions."

This twofold depiction of conceptuality as being in the manner of entities and attributes is repeated in the seventh chapter when Paramārthasamudgata presents back to Buddha what he has understood about the three natures and the three non-natures:

> That which is posited by names and terminology—with respect to [other-powered natures which are] (1) the objects of activity of conceptuality, (2) the foundations of imputational characters, and (3) those which have the signs of compositional phenomena—in the character of entities or particulars [such as, "This is] a form aggregate," and that which is posited by names and terminology in the character of entities or the character of particulars [that is, attributes, such as] "the production of the form aggregate," "the cessation of the form aggregate," "the abandonment and thorough knowledge of the form aggregate" are imputational characters. In dependence upon those, the Supramundane Victor designated the character-non-nature of phenomena.

Using the format of the first-wheel teachings, Paramārthasamudgata divides the teaching on the imputational nature of the form aggregate into two parts—a teaching from the viewpoint of the entity of form and a teaching from the viewpoint of the attributes of form.[a] When in these chapters he re-formulates

[a] The theme of entity and attribute is central also to Gung-tang's description of Buddha's teaching on the aggregates in the first wheel as having five features—one to do with the entities of the aggregates and four with their attributes:

1. own-character
2. production
3. disintegration
4. abandonment
5. thorough knowledge.

(Abandonment and thorough knowledge are attributes of the aggregates in the loose sense that the contaminated aggregates are the bases to be abandoned and to be known.) The difference between D̄zong-ka-b̄a and Gung-tang on the one hand and Wonch'uk on the other is that the former treat "own-character" not as the entity of the object itself but as referring

Buddha's teachings, Paramārthasamudgata does not even use the vocabulary of the "own-character" of form but speaks of its entity; therefore, I, like Wonch'uk, assume that in the seventh chapter Paramārthasamudgata's mention of the teaching of the "own-character" of form—in his question about the first wheel—refers to the teaching of the entity of form itself. If this is so, it damages Ḏzong-ka-ḇa's position that "own-character" refers to form's being established by way of its own character and not to the teaching of the entity, the distinguishing nature, of form.

Moreover, particularly damaging to the readings by Ḏzong-ka-ḇa and his followers is the fact that in the first wheel it is extremely difficult to find the words "established by way of its own character," never mind "established by way of its own character as the referent of a conceptual consciousness." Also damaging is the fact that Sthiramati, in commenting on Vasubandhu's *The Thirty,* explicitly identifies "character" in the character-non-nature as the defining character of an object:[158]

> The first [of the three natures] is the imputational nature; it is a character-non-nature because its character is imputed. The character of form is: that which exists as form. The character of feeling is: that which experiences. And so on. Since those [imputational natures] are without their own entities, their entities are non-existent, like a sky-flower.

Sthiramati uses the defining characters of form, feeling, and so forth as examples of what "character" in "character-non-nature" means; he then says that since imputational natures do not have such defining characters, they are character-non-natures. Since it can be assumed that Sthiramati is familiar with the statement in the *Sūtra Unraveling the Thought* (*Emptiness in Mind-Only,* 86):

> Those [imputational characters] are characters posited by names and terminology[a] and do not subsist by way of their own character. Therefore, they are said to be "character-non-natures."

it seems that for him to "subsist by way of its own character" merely means to be established by way of **having** its own character, and, by extension, since imputational natures do not have their own character, they are character-non-natures.

Not mentioning this counter-evidence from Sthiramati, Ḏzong-ka-ḇa (*Emptiness in Mind-Only,* 78-79) rejects Wonch'uk's explanation:

---

to the status of the entity, that is to say, its being established by way of its own character (which Gung-tang takes to mean its being established by way of its own character as the referent of a conceptual consciousness) whereas Wonch'uk takes "own-character" as referring to the entity, that is, the specific defining character, of an object.

[a] See issue #104.

> In the Chinese *Great Commentary*[a] [on the *Sūtra Unraveling the Thought* by the Korean scholar Wonch'uk], and so forth, (259) {370} "own-character"[b] here [in this passage in the *Sūtra Unraveling the Thought*] is explained as the unique character [of the aggregates and so forth], but this is not right.[c] For the sūtra itself at the point of [speaking about] imputational factors[d] clearly speaks of establishment by way of [the object's] own character [and does not speak of the unique character], and since even imputational factors have a unique characterization, there would be the fallacy that the character-non-nature could not be explained with respect to imputational factors.

Ḏzong-ka-ḇa's point is that if "own-character" in Paramārthasamudgata's question referred to the unique character of a phenomenon, then when in Buddha's answer (*Emptiness in Mind-Only,* 82-83) he speaks about character-non-nature:

> Paramārthasamudgata, thinking of three non-natures of phenomena—character-non-nature, production-non-nature, and ultimate-non-nature—I taught [in the middle wheel of the teaching], "All phenomena are natureless."

the term "character" also would have to refer to the unique character of phenomena simply because of the relatedness of the answer to the question. Ḏzong-ka-ḇa (*Emptiness in Mind-Only,* 86) points out that the sūtra itself says not that imputational natures do not have their own unique character but that they do not **subsist by way of their own character**:

> Those [imputational characters] are characters posited by names and terminology[e] and do not subsist by way of their own character. Therefore, they are said to be "character-non-natures."

Hence, Ḏzong-ka-ḇa cogently holds that "character" in "character-non-nature" has to mean to subsist, or to be established, by way of its own character.

Ḏzong-ka-ḇa abruptly changes the topic with no further explanation of this important point. Also, none of his commentators unpacks the issue, but we can speculate that his reasoning is this:

> The construction in the *Sūtra Unraveling the Thought* itself, "does not subsist by way of its own character"[f] as opposed to "its own-character [that is, unique character] does not exist,"[g] indicates a certain mode or

[a] See issue #8.

[b] See issues #27-55, 94.

[c] See issue #39.

[d] See issue #50.

[e] See issue #104.

[f] *rang gi mtshan nyid gyis gnas pa ma yin.*

[g] *rang gi mtshan nyid yod pa ma yin.*

> status of existence that imputational natures do not have, rather than that they lack a character that defines them. For a mode of being is indicated through the adverbial instrumental "by way of its own character,"[a] whereas if the sūtra meant to indicate merely that imputational natures do not exist, it would have done so directly.

We have seen, however, that for Sthiramati there seems to be no difference between an object's having a defining character and its being established by way of its own character. Let us imagine, therefore, that Sthiramati and Wonch'uk could object to Ḏzong-ka-ḇa's refutation, pointing out that the phrase could be read, "Imputational natures do not subsist by way of **having** a unique character," thereby retaining the adverbial flavor and yet seeing the passage as indicating that imputational natures do not exist at all. Even in Ḏzong-ka-ḇa's system, among the two types of imputational natures—existent and non-existent (the former being, for instance, uncompounded space and the latter being, for instance, the horns of a rabbit)—the non-existent are called "imputational natures whose character is thoroughly nihil";[b] thus, it makes sense to speak of at least some imputational natures as not subsisting by way of **having** their own character.

We are left, however, with the problem of existent imputational natures such as uncompounded space or an object's being the referent of its respective conceptual consciousness; these exist and have their own defining characters, but imputational natures are clearly said in the *Sūtra Unraveling the Thought* not to be established by way of their own character. A possible solution is to make the case that the *Sūtra Unraveling the Thought* is not concerned with existent imputational natures and thus the three-nature theory does not take them into account. However, this would be inelegant because then the three-nature theory would not apply to permanent phenomena. If these must be included within the three natures, then Sthiramati's and Wonch'uk's explanation cannot be used, since Buddha teaches in the first wheel an "own-character," or defining character, with regard to all phenomena, and it must be held that uncompounded space and so forth do indeed have defining characters, due to which existent imputational natures would not be character-non-natures. A possible solution to this problem is to hold that although defining characters can be posited for uncompounded space,[c] and so forth, these permanent phenomena do not **subsist by way of** their own defining characters because their existence is only imputed in dependence upon conceptuality and so they are not established **by way of** their own character.

In this explanation, even though existent imputational natures have "own-character" in the sense that they have their own entities or defining natures,

---

[a] *rang gi mtshan nyid gyis.*

[b] *mtshan nyid yongs su chad pa'i kun btags.*

[c] The standard defining character of space is a mere elimination of obstructive contact.

they are not established **by way of** their own character due to being conceptually imputed. In this way, the "own-character" of Paramārthasamudgata's question (a defining character) and the "character" of "do not subsist by way of their own character" (a defining character) in Buddha's answer are the same. Both, however, differ from the reference of the word "character" in "character-non-nature" in Buddha's answer which means "to subsist (or be established) by way of its own character." This is a possible solution, requiring inelegant twists and turns but no more than any other solution.

In any case, according to D̄zong-ka-b̄a, Wonch'uk's explanation of "own-character" as the unique character of an object has to be rejected on the grounds that the adverbial construction in Buddha's answer ("It [the imputational character] is a character posited by names and terminology and does not subsist **by way of** its own character") is pointless if it does not refer to a mode of being. The reference is to a status of objects, not to whether they have uncommon characteristics and thus can be defined. For D̄zong-ka-b̄a, this mode of being cannot refer to an object's **having** its own unique character because imputational nature (in general) and existent imputational natures have a character differentiating them from other phenomena; thus an absence of "own-character," if it means unique character, absurdly could not be posited with respect to existent imputational natures.

To repeat D̄zong-ka-b̄a's position: There are existent and non-existent varieties of imputational natures, and if the former had no unique character, they would not exist at all, much like the horns of a rabbit which have no unique character. An imputational nature (in general) has its own unique character, or definition, since the definition of an imputational nature is:[a]

> that which is imputed by conceptuality and does not exist by way of its own character.

Therefore, if the absence of "own-character" merely referred to the non-existence of a unique characterization, such an absence absurdly could not be posited with respect to imputational natures (specifically, existent imputational natures) since they indeed do have a unique character or definition distinguishing them from other phenomena. Because it is obvious that one of the main points of the "Questions of Paramārthasamudgata Chapter" of the *Sūtra Unraveling the Thought* is that imputational natures are character-non-natures, the "own-character" mentioned in Paramārthasamudgata's question cannot refer to a unique characterization (once it is equated in D̄zong-ka-b̄a's reading with the "character" of "character-non-nature" in the answer). This is D̄zong-ka-b̄a's

[a] This definition is standard; see, for instance, Geshe Lhundup Sopa and Jeffrey Hopkins, *Cutting Through Appearances: The Practice and Theory of Tibetan Buddhism* (Ithaca, N.Y.: Snow Lion, 1989), 262. Gung-ru Chö-jung (*Garland of White Lotuses,* 12b.5) gives "that which is a mere superimposition by the consciousness apprehending it" (*rang 'dzin rtog pas sgro btags tsam*).

meaning when he says:

> since even imputational factors have a unique characterization, there would be the fallacy that the character-non-nature could not be explained with respect to imputational factors.

When Buddha declares that imputational natures do not have a nature of character, he is not merely saying that they do not exist—this being how Wonch'uk reads his meaning; rather, Buddha is saying that they lack a certain type of ontological status, a certain type of existence, called subsistence by way of their character[a] or establishment by way of their own character.[b] According to D̄zong-ka-b̄a, there is a class of phenomena that, though existent and having its own unique characterization, does not exist by way of its own character—these being imputational phenomena such as uncompounded space and an object's being the referent of a word or of a conceptual consciousness.

To rephrase: Non-existent imputational natures—such as the horns of a rabbit or objects that are established by way of their own character as the referents of conceptual consciousnesses—do not exist and thus do not have a unique character; however, existent imputational natures—such as uncompounded space, analytical cessations, non-analytical cessations, and so forth—are phenomena[c] and thus exist, having their own unique character distinguishing them from other phenomena but not being established by way of their own character. Though they have their own definition or unique character (*rang gi mtshan nyid, svalakṣaṇa*), they are not specifically characterized phenomena (*rang mtshan, svalakṣaṇa*) in the sense of having their own unique characteristics that can serve as appearing objects to directly perceiving consciousnesses.[d] These phenomena appear in a general way to conceptual consciousnesses; they do not have unique characteristics that can serve as appearing objects to non-conceptual consciousnesses. Also, they are not established by way of their own character (*rang gi mtshan nyid kyis grub pa, svalakṣaṇasiddha*)[e] because they are imputed by conceptuality.

This distinction of four meanings[f] of "own-character"—(1) unique character in the sense of definition, (2) establishment of the object by way of its own character, (3) establishment of the object by way of its own character as

---

[a] *rang gi mtshan nyid kyis gnas pa.*

[b] *rang gi mtshan nyid kyis grub pa.*

[c] *chos, dharma.*

[d] For the qualities of a specifically characterized phenomenon, see Hopkins, *Maps of the Profound,* 247, and Anne C. Klein, *Knowing, Naming, and Negation* (Ithaca, N.Y.: Snow Lion, 1988), 46-53.

[e] As was explained earlier (p. 60), Jay-d̄zün Chö-ḡyi-gyel-tsen takes exception to this with regard to the Sūtra School, which he says asserts that all phenomena are established by way of their own character.

[f] For a similar list of five meanings see p. 93.

the referent of a conceptual consciousness, and (4) specifically characterized phenomenon—is a pivotal technique of Ge-luk-ba attempts to bring clarity and consistency to Indian texts. In the Mind-Only School, impermanent phenomena and emptinesses—called other-powered natures and thoroughly established natures—are established by way of their own character and are specifically characterized phenomena but are not established by way of their own character as the referents of conceptual consciousnesses.

Still, it may be possible to fault Ḏzong-ka-ḇa's identification of "own-character" even within accepting these central Ge-luk-ḇa distinctions, for the "own-character" of Paramārthasamudgata's description of the first wheel ("The Supramundane Victor spoke, in many ways, of the own-character of the aggregates,") can be taken as merely referring to the unique character of objects without harming the rest of Ḏzong-ka-ḇa's presentation. Identifying "own-character" as the unique character of objects also would have the virtue of relieving the tradition of the huge burden of having to fabricate creative readings to disburden Ḏzong-ka-ḇa of contradiction.

It seems to me that Ḏzong-ka-ḇa was thinking of the first wheel in the format that it teaches that all phenomena, including imputational natures, are established by way of their own character, rather than the format that it teaches that all phenomena are established by way of their own character as the referents of their respective conceptual consciousnesses, the latter being more accurate to the style of Paramārthasamudgata's depiction of the first-wheel teaching. Ḏzong-ka-ḇa was emphasizing that the problem with the first wheel is that Buddha taught that factors imputed in the manner of entity and attribute are established by way of their own character, and he chose to express this as Buddha's teaching that all phenomena—including such imputational natures—are established by way of their own character. He did this so as to contrast the teaching of the first wheel with that of the third wheel which is known as the wheel of good **differentiation**—the first wheel does not differentiate between what is and is not established by way of its own character, univocally teaching that all phenomena are established this way. However, his mode of expression has the problem of having to explain how it could be that Buddha taught for first-wheel trainees that other imputational natures such as uncompounded space are established by way of their own character; in addition, this format does not accord with the style of Paramārthasamudgata's question. When Ḏzong-ka-ḇa applied the above-mentioned format to the actual words of Paramārthasamudgata's question, he was drawn into identifying "own-character" as "established by way of its own character."

Apologetic

Perhaps I should claim, like Gung-ru Chö-jung, Jam-ȳang-shay-ḇa, and their followers, that I am merely "positing Ḏzong-ka-ḇa's thought" with the further claim that I do this with considerably more economy of expression! However, my reframing of what was behind what Dzong-ka-ba says seems too openly critical and hence might exceed the bounds of what is acceptable in Ge-luk-ba scholastic circles. Still, let me, for the moment, adopt the format (that is, put on the mask) of less reconstruction and play according to the rules of the debating courtyard that dictate that Dzong-ka-ba cannot be openly criticized. My opponent would start by challenging me:

> It absurdly follows that Dzong-ka-ba was wrong in refuting Wonch'uk's identification of "own-character" in Paramārthasamudgata's question as the unique character of objects because, according to you, "own-character" in Paramārthasamudgata's question means the unique character of objects.

Given the mask that I would be wearing, I would have to say:

> That the "own-character" in Paramārthasamudgata's question means the unique character of objects does not entail that Dzong-ka-ba was wrong to refute Wonch'uk's identification of "own-character" in Paramārthasamudgata's question as the unique character of objects because Dzong-ka-ba did this in consideration that Wonch'uk did not specify that the unique character taught in the first wheel is qualified with the object of negation—a unique character that is established by way of its own character as the referent of a conceptual consciousness.

As always with such apologetic, I would not get off easily, for immediately I would be challenged with:

> Then it absurdly follows that there is no purpose in Dzong-ka-ba's specifying that this sort of "own-character" is something that imputational natures do not have but other-powered natures and thoroughly established natures do have because **nothing** has a unique character that is established by way of its own character as the referent of a conceptual consciousness.

My back to the wall, I would have to change tack:

> That nothing has a unique character established by way of its own character as the referent of a conceptual consciousness does not entail that there is no purpose in Dzong-ka-ba's indicating that this sort of "own-character" is something that imputational natures do not have but other-powered natures and thoroughly established natures do have because, whereas "own-character" in Paramārthasamudgata's question refers to the unique character of objects, Dzong-ka-ba said that it does not mean the unique character of objects in consideration of the fact

> that "character" in "character-non-nature" refers to establishment by way of its own character.

My attempt would not escape the further challenge:

> Then it follows that Ḏzong-ka-ḇa's mode of procedure in refuting Wonch'uk here is wrong because it depends upon his equating the "own-character" of the question with the "character" in "character-non-nature" in the answer, whereas, according to you, such is not the case.

I would have to respond:

> Ḏzong-ka-ḇa's equating the "own-character" of the question with the "character" in "character-non-nature" in the answer does not entail that his mode of procedure in refuting Wonch'uk here is wrong because his mention of the "character" in "character-non-nature" is (actually) in reference to the "character" of "does not subsist by way of its own character."

This, of course, is just convoluted apologetic masking my opinion that Ḏzong-ka-ḇa's way of refuting Wonch'uk here is faulty because he equates the "own-character" of the question with the "character" in "character-non-nature" in the answer, identifying both as meaning "established by way of its own character." As I have suggested above, I think that the "own-character" of the question and the "character" in "character-non-nature" in the answer are not the same—the former is the unique character of objects and the latter is establishment of objects by way of their own character.

8. Creating Consistency

Issue #49: How to make Ḏzong-ka-ḇa say what you want him to say?

It is abundantly clear that Ḏzong-ka-ḇa's reading created havoc for his followers, requiring them (as we saw in the last chapter) to create elaborate explanations, each of which is so bound by difficulties that no single reading emerges with a completely defensible solution. Let us examine how Gung-tang, in a brilliant analysis of central statements on this topic (1) in the sūtra, (2) in Ḏzong-ka-ḇa's *The Essence of Eloquence,* and (3) in Wonch'uk's commentary, raises penetrating hypothetical objections and, in answer, attempts to show how the Gung-ru Chö-jung and Jam-ȳang-shay-ḇa tradition does not warp Ḏzong-ka-ḇa's statements in its creation of coherence.[159] The basis of his discussion is four passages which are by now familiar:

1. the statement in the *Sūtra Unraveling the Thought* (*Emptiness in Mind-Only,* 76) that in the first wheel Buddha taught that the aggregates have "own-character." Paramārthasamudgata says:

    > The Supramundane Victor spoke, in many ways, of the own-character of the aggregates. He also spoke of [their] character of production, character of disintegration, abandonment, and thorough knowledge.

2. Wonch'uk's identification of "own-character" as the unique character of the aggregates:

    > "Own-character" is the specific character as in, for instance, the explanation, "Form is obstructive.... Consciousness is the knower."

3. Ḏzong-ka-ḇa's refutation of Wonch'uk in which he says that "own-character" could not possibly refer to unique character because "own-character" is denied of imputational natures, whereas imputational natures (that is to say, existent ones or the general category) obviously have a unique character. Also, on the positive side, Ḏzong-ka-ḇa says that, instead of the unique character of objects, "own-character" refers to establishment by way of the object's own character as in the statement, "It [the imputational character] is a character posited by names and terminology and does not subsist by way of its own character." He (*Emptiness in Mind-Only,* 78-79) says:

> In the Chinese *Great Commentary*[a] [on the *Sūtra Unraveling the Thought* by the Korean scholar Wonch'uk], and so forth, (259) {370} "own-character"[b] here [in this passage in the *Sūtra Unraveling the Thought*] is explained as the unique character [of the aggregates and so forth], but this is not right.[c] For the sūtra itself at the point of [speaking about] imputational factors[d] clearly speaks of establishment by way of [the object's] own character [and does not speak of the unique character], and since even imputational factors have a unique characterization, there would be the fallacy that the character-non-nature could not be explained with respect to imputational factors.

4. the passage in the *Sūtra Unraveling the Thought* (*Emptiness in Mind-Only,* 86) to which Ḏzong-ka-ḇa must be referring:

> Those [imputational characters] are characters posited by names and terminology[e] and do not subsist by way of their own character. Therefore, they are said to be "character-non-natures."

An objection. Gung-tang formulates a hypothetical objection to Gung-ru Chö-jung's, Jam-ȳang-shay-ḇa's, and his own explanation of Ḏzong-ka-ḇa's identification of the meaning of "own-character." This objection, centering around the passages just given, is (in paraphrase):

> Ḏzong-ka-ḇa did not say in so many words that "own-character" refers to the establishment of objects by way of their own character **as the referents of conceptual consciousnesses** but merely said that it refers to establishment of objects by way of their own character. And, this, in fact, is all he meant because that it refers to the establishment of objects by way of their own character is clear from the passage to which he refers, since it refutes "own-character" with respect to imputational natures and not with respect to the aggregates. That passage (number four above) says:
>
>> Those [imputational characters] are characters posited by names and terminology[f] and do not subsist by way of their

---

[a] See issue #8.

[b] See issues #27-55, 94.

[c] See issue #39.

[d] See issue #50.

[e] See issue #104.

[f] Ibid.

> own character. Therefore, they are said to be "character-non-natures."

The "own-character" refuted in this passage must be something that the mental and physical aggregates have but imputational natures do not. This cannot be the establishment of objects by way of their own character **as the referents of conceptual consciousnesses** because in the Mind-Only School this is denied with respect to **all** phenomena, impermanent and permanent, the mental and physical aggregates, as well as imputational natures.

That objects are established by way of their own character as the referents of conceptual consciousnesses is the main object of negation in the *Sūtra Unraveling the Thought* in terms of all phenomena, not just imputational natures; thus, there would be no purpose in the sūtra's singling out imputational natures as not subsisting by way of their own character. Instead of positing something else—namely, objects' establishment by way of their own character as the referents of conceptual consciousnesses—as what Ḏzong-ka-ḇa meant when he identifies here that "own-character" refers to objects' establishment by way of their own character, why not leave what he said just as it is?

Gung-tang's answer. The answer to this weighty objection is in two stages, the second coming upon a refinement of the objection. First, Gung-tang says that, if "own-character" meant merely the establishment of objects by way of their own character, then, as mentioned earlier, the literal reading of the sūtra passages of the first wheel about which Paramārthasamudgata was speaking when he said, "The Supramundane Victor spoke, in many ways, of the own-character of the aggregates," would be acceptable in its literal form, since, in the Mind-Only School, the mental and physical aggregates are indeed established by way of their own character. However, that the first wheel of doctrine is literally acceptable is clearly inadmissible since the *Sūtra Unraveling the Thought* itself says that those passages are not definitive but require interpretation. Ḏzong-ka-ḇa would be reduced to self-contradiction, and since he could not be self-contradictory, he must have meant something else.

The objector's response. At this point, Gung-tang[160] considers a well-formulated response to his answer:

> *Objection:* Just because the term "own-character" in the passage, "The Supramundane Victor spoke, in many ways, of the own-character of the aggregates," refers to establishment of objects by way of their own character, it is not entailed that the passage, "The Supramundane Victor spoke, in many ways, of the own-character of the aggregates," would have to be literally acceptable. For the mode of pronouncement in the first wheel is to indicate that whatever topic is

> under discussion is established by way of its own character as the referent of a conceptual consciousness, even though the words for this are not present. Thus, even the term "own-character" does not indicate this; it just indicates establishment of objects by way of their own character. Hence, when the *Sūtra Unraveling the Thought* speaks of the own-character of the aggregates, we should take not just aggregates but aggregates **established by way of their own character** as the topic under discussion which, due to the mode of pronouncement, come to be communicated as established by way of their own character as the referent of a conceptual consciousness. For instance, all of the attributes of the four truths—production, disintegration, thorough knowledge, abandonment, and so forth—right through to the seven attributes of the thirty-seven harmonies with enlightenment are, in their literal reading, not to be taken as what is negated—which actually is their establishment by way of their own character as the referents of conceptual consciousnesses. Rather, they [the attributes of the four truths through to the thirty-seven harmonies with enlightenment] are those phenomena in their actuality; nevertheless, their mode of pronouncement is that these are established by way of their own character as the referents of conceptual consciousnesses.
>
> Thus, just as production is taken to be actual production that, due to context, is pronounced as being established by way of its own character as the referent of a conceptual consciousness, so aggregates established by way of their own character are actual aggregates established by way of their own character that, due to context, are pronounced as being established by way of their own character as the referents of conceptual consciousnesses. In this way, "own-character" in Paramārthasamudgata's statement, "The Supramundane Victor spoke, in many ways, of the own-character of the aggregates," can be just establishment by way of its own character, but the mode of pronouncement is that the establishment of the aggregates by way of their own character is established by way of its own character as the referent of a conceptual consciousness."

In framing this objection, Gung-tang's hypothetical opponent uses the same principles of argument that Gung-tang used earlier[a] when showing that Buddha taught on the literal level of the first wheel that objects are established by way of their own character as the referents of conceptual consciousnesses, despite the fact that such words are not to be found in the sūtras of the first wheel. Here, he has the objector using this same principle, holding that although the words are lacking, the mode of pronouncement of the first wheel provides the context from which it can be said that, when in the first wheel Buddha speaks of

---

[a] See *Reflections on Reality*, chap. 8.

production, the problem is not with production itself but with its being established by way of its own character as the referent of a conceptual consciousness. Thus, by extension, when Buddha speaks of "own-character" (which the objector takes to mean just establishment of objects by way of their own character), the problem is not with establishment of objects by way of their own character but with establishment of objects by way of their own character itself being established by way of its own character as the referent of a conceptual consciousness.

The objector's position, despite its suspicious awkwardness, is philosophically attractive and even elegant in that it employs an earlier mode of procedure against its advocate. The tack is also most convenient in Ge-luk-b̄a scholastic circles in that it allows one to take D̄zong-ka-b̄a's statements that "own-character" means the establishment of objects by way of their own character, without having to turn those words into something else—the level of apologetic is more subtle.

The answer. Gung-tang objects that the establishment of the aggregates by way of their own character is an **attribute** of the aggregates, not the **entity** of the aggregates, and thus the teaching that the establishment of the aggregates by way of their own character is itself established by way of its own character as the referent of a conceptual consciousness would not constitute a teaching about the **entity** of the aggregates but would be a teaching about an **attribute** of the aggregates.

As we saw above, fundamental to the *Sūtra Unraveling the Thought* is the point that beings conceive objects in terms of entity and attribute to be established by way of their own character as the referents of thoughts and terminology. Beings apprehend a house, for instance, to be established by way of its own character as the referent of a term for its entity, such as "house" in English, and also apprehend it as similarly established as the referent of terms for the attributes of that house—its size, sturdiness, attractiveness, and so forth.[a] Gung-tang's response is contextual, maintaining an important aspect of the teaching in the *Sūtra Unraveling the Thought*—the discussion of imputational natures in terms of entities and attributes. As he says, it is not suitable only to teach attributes; the substratum, the entity, must be taught.[b]

There is no question that the conceptual mind often (always?) operates this

---

[a] Robert Thurman, in his translation of D̄zong-ka-b̄a's *The Essence of Eloquence*, refers to these two types of imputation as ascriptional and descriptional; for instance, see *Tsong Khapa's Speech of Gold in the Essence of True Eloquence*, 243.

[b] It might seem that Gung-tang's refutation revolves around merely mistaking the opponent's reading of the literal meaning of the "own-character of the aggregates" as being the *establishment* of the aggregates by way of their own character rather than *aggregates* which are established by way of their own character. However, I do not think that he is making this mistake, for, in either case, in "own-character of the aggregates," "own-character" must refer to the *attribute* of their being established by way of their own character.

way. We take an entity to mind and consider its attributes. Furthermore, we consider objects to be, by way of their own nature, the referents of our conceptions of entities and attributes even when we have realized that objects are not necessarily the referents of the **particular** terms of only one language. We consider the object of expression of the term "house" as subsisting out there right with the nature of the actual house, and we consider the object of expression of "the beauty of the house" as subsisting out there right with the nature of the actual house.

Gung-tang's response retrieves this important critique of perception and conception, but he does not face the issue that if, like Wonch'uk, we consider "own-character" to be the entity or unique defining nature, or entity, of an object, his objection—which revolves around the fault that "own-character" if it means "establishment by way of its own character" refers to an attribute and not to the entity—no longer holds. In fact, Gung-tang has shown us how to revive Wonch'uk's identification of "own-character" as the entity or unique defining nature of an object without contravening D̄zong-ka-b̄a's point that an imputational nature has a unique defining character. For we can hold that everything taught in the first wheel is within the context of its being established by way of its own character as the referent of terms and conceptual consciousnesses, and thus the entity or unique nature of an object, which is Wonch'uk's reading of "own-character," is also taught this way. As in D̄zong-ka-b̄a's explanation, this false status of objects constitutes the object of negation, but, unlike D̄zong-ka-b̄a's explanation, it is not indicated by the term "own-character" in Paramārthasamudgata's question; rather, this false status of objects is the context in which everything in the first wheel is taught.

Indeed, this seems to be just what the *Sūtra Unraveling the Thought* is saying, for the failing of the first wheel is not that it teaches a plethora of phenomena but that it does not teach that all phenomena have the same taste in the ultimate character—the thoroughly established nature that is the imputational nature's emptiness of being established by way of its own character. In the third chapter of the sūtra, Buddha tells the Bodhisattva Suvishuddhamati that the ultimate is the general character of all phenomena:[161]

> Suvishuddhamati, if the character of the compounded and the character of the ultimate were different, then the ultimate character in all characters [that is, entities] of compounded things would not be suitable to be [their] general character.[a] Suvishuddhamati, it is the case that the character of the ultimate is not included in the thoroughly afflicted character, and the ultimate character is the general character of the characters [that is, entities] of [all] compounded things; therefore, it is not suitable to say, "The character of the compounded and the character of the ultimate are not different," [and] it is not suitable to

a *spyi'i mtshan nyid, sāmānya-lakṣaṇa.*

> say, "[The character of the compounded] is different from the character of the ultimate."

The first wheel lacks this teaching of the ultimate as the general character of all phenomena.

Dzong-ka-ba, operating under the framework of considering the fault of the first wheel as being that it teaches indiscriminately that all phenomena, including imputational natures, are established by way of their own character, over-extended this perspective to his consideration of the words "own-character" in Paramārthasamudgata's question and took this term as referring to "established by way of its own character." He did this so pointedly that his followers have had to struggle with how to re-write his words to forge consistent sense.

Gung-tang's solution. Gung-tang's tack has been to show that, despite Dzong-ka-ba's clear statement that "own-character" means establishment by way of its own character, he could not have meant so because of a series of faults that would be incurred. Now he is left with having to posit Dzong-ka-ba's "actual" meaning when he used those words. He[162] avers that when Dzong-ka-ba, having criticized Wonch'uk for taking "own-character" as meaning the unique character of an object, says that instead of this the term refers to establishment by way of its own character, he is speaking within the framework of referring to the object of negation—that is, establishment of objects by way of their own character as the referents of conceptual consciousnesses—not actual establishment of objects by way of their own character. Thus, **in this situation** "established by way of its own character" is actually shorthand for "established by way of its own character as the referent of a conceptual consciousness."

Above, when I put on the mask of positing Dzong-ka-ba's thought, I was forced to insist that this is what Dzong-ka-ba must have meant just because he could not be mistaken. One would hope that Gung-tang, on the other hand, could come up with good evidence from within Dzong-ka-ba's own text that at minimum hints that Gung-tang's exposition is warranted. If his solution and its accompanying evidence do not appear to be strained, his explanation will take on an aura of elegance. However, as we will see, Gung-tang can find no such convincing evidence, and thus his proposed solution lacks the esthetic delight that well-crafted apologetic can generate. Gung-tang's "evidence" is that just before that passage, when Dzong-ka-ba restates Paramārthasamudgata's question, he (*Emptiness in Mind-Only,* 78) says:

> This asks the following question:
>
>> If the statements in some sūtras [that is, in the middle wheel of the teaching] that all phenomena are natureless, and so forth, and the statements in some sūtras [in the first wheel of the teaching] that the aggregates and so forth have an

> own-character, and so forth, were left as they are verbally, they would be contradictory. However, since [the Supramundane Victor] must be without contradiction, of what were you [Buddha] thinking when [in the middle wheel of the teaching] you spoke of non-nature, and so forth?

> Through that, [Paramārthasamudgata] implicitly[a] asks of what [Buddha] was thinking when [in the first wheel of the teaching] he spoke of the existence of own-character and so forth.[b]

Gung-tang holds that if "own-character" meant merely establishment of objects by way of their own character, then since the mental and physical aggregates are indeed established by way of their own character, it would be inappropriate for Paramārthasamudgata to ask about the basis in Buddha's thought when he taught such. Thus, Gung-tang insists that it is **clear** that when Ḏzong-ka-ḇa says, "Through that, [Paramārthasamudgata] implicitly asks of what [Buddha] was thinking when [in the first wheel of the teaching] he spoke of the existence of the own-character [of the aggregates] and so forth," the term "own-character" refers to something that does not exist, specifically, the establishment of objects by way of their own character as the referents of conceptual consciousnesses. Hence, he insists that it is clear that when Ḏzong-ka-ḇa goes on to refute Wonch'uk's identification of "own-character" and thereupon concludes that it means establishment by way of its own character, his frame of reference is still something that was said to exist in the first wheel but actually does not exist—establishment of objects by way of their own character as the referents of conceptual consciousnesses.

He seems to be reduced to saying, "Ḏzong-ka-ḇa could not have made such an egregious mistake about the reason for Paramārthasamudgata's questioning the teaching in the first wheel and thus he could not have meant that." However, it is more likely that Gung-tang is indicating that this is what Ḏzong-ka-ḇa **should** have meant. Gung-tang's apologetic appears to be no more elegant than mine.

Issue #50: Why single out imputational natures?

Gung-tang[163] himself raises the objection that if his explanation is right, then what is the point of **singling out** imputational natures as not being established by way of their own character as the referents of conceptual consciousnesses? No phenomenon, according to the Mind-Only School, is established that way. Why does Ḏzong-ka-ḇa say, "For the sūtra itself **at the point of [speaking about] imputational natures** clearly speaks of establishment by way of [the object's] own character" if the latter means "established by way of its own

a See issue #56.

b See issues #21-24.

character as the referent of a conceptual consciousness"? Gung-tang's strained answer, resorting to circumlocution and the vagueness of hinted but unexplained profundity, is that the purpose of the *Sūtra Unraveling the Thought's* teaching that imputational natures are natureless in the sense of character is for the sake of refuting the "own-character" mentioned in the first wheel, and if the "own-character" mentioned in the first wheel did exist, the character-non-nature could not be posited. Thus, it is meaningful to single out imputational natures as not being established by way of their own character as the referents of conceptual consciousnesses. You see what I mean by circumlocution and a hint of unexplained profundity. His back is to the wall!

Such covert admissions of the tenuousness of favored explanations make monastic textbooks provocatively stimulating in that they indicate how these scholars use rational inquiry to reveal weaknesses in their own systems despite their allegiance to founding figures. Regardless of the format of explaining away, or even covering up, earlier masters' inconsistencies, scholars such as Gung-tang reveal with considerable humor the flimsiness of the supposedly favored position. The intellectual honesty, within being bounded by a tradition,[a] is impressive.

Gung-tang is claiming that when Paramārthasamudgata says, "The Supramundane Victor spoke, in many ways, of the own-character of the aggregates," the term "own-character" means "establishment by way of their own character as the referents of conceptual consciousnesses." Similarly, when D̄zong-ka-b̄a says, "For the sūtra itself at the point of [speaking about] imputational natures clearly speaks of establishment by way of [the object's] own character," this also means "establishment by way of its own character as the referent of a conceptual consciousness." Now Gung-tang must face the music, for he himself admits that when the passage in the *Sūtra Unraveling the Thought* to which D̄zong-ka-b̄a refers as his justification says, "Those [imputational characters] are characters posited by names and terminology and do not subsist by way of their own character," the phrase "subsist by way of their own character" means only "establishment by way of their own character"! He cannot claim that the sūtra here means "established by way of their own character as the referents of their respective conceptual consciousnesses" because D̄zong-ka-b̄a himself (*Emptiness in Mind-Only,* 86) clearly explains that in this particular passage the term "own-character" means only establishment of objects by way of their own character:

Here, the measure indicated[b] with respect to existing or not existing by

[a] I do not mean to suggest that rational inquiry that is not bound by tradition exits somewhere, such as in academies in Europe and America. The supposedly "objective criticism" of much current scholarship is bound by traditions of nihilistic relativism and the like.

[b] *bstan tshod;* see issue #96.

way of [an object's] own character is: not to be posited or to be posited in dependence upon names and terminology.[a]

Since Ḏzong-ka-ḇa specifies that in the sūtra the phrase "subsist by way of its own character" means not to be posited in dependence upon names and terminology, this clearly eliminates that the sūtra here is speaking about objects' being established by way of their own character as the referents of conceptual consciousnesses. Gung-tang is self-consciously left in the unenviable position of having to claim that Ḏzong-ka-ḇa cites this sūtra passage to prove that "own-character" in Paramārthasamudgata's question means "established by way of its own character as the referent of a conceptual consciousness." Gung-tang has to hold that despite the fact that the phrase "subsist by way of its own character" means only "established by way of its own character," it is appropriate for Ḏzong-ka-ḇa to cite it to prove that the "own-character" mentioned in Paramārthasamudgata's question and the "character" in "character-non-nature" in the answer mean "established by way of its own character as the referent of a conceptual consciousness"!

Whereas Gung-ru Chö-jung[b] and Jam-ȳang-shay-ḇa[164] either did not notice the problem or, as is more likely, merely wanted to bluff their way around it, Gung-tang[165] and A-ku Ḻo-drö-gya-tso[166] attempt a justification, which (in paraphrase) is:

> ***The problem.*** According to Ḏzong-ka-ḇa, the "own-character" mentioned in Paramārthasamudgata's question ("The Supramundane Victor spoke, in many ways, of the own-character of the aggregates,") must be refuted by the absence of own-character mentioned in Buddha's answer ("Those [imputational characters] are characters posited by names and terminology and do not subsist by way of their own character,") and thus it might seem that there is a lack of parallelism between the question and the answer. For in the Go-mang tradition (Gung-ru Chö-jung, Jam-ȳang-shay-ḇa, Gung-tang, A-ku Ḻo-drö-gya-tso, *et al.*) the "own-character" mentioned in the question means "established by way of its own character as the referent of a conceptual consciousness," whereas "does not subsist by way of its own character" means only "is not established by way of its own character."
>
> ***The solution.*** If imputational natures were established by way of their own character, they would have to be truly established and not just imputed by conceptuality. In that case, that other-powered natures are established by way of their own character as the referents of conceptual consciousnesses would be itself established by way of its

a See issues #105-109.

b Gung-ru Chö-jung's *Garland of White Lotuses,* 12a.6-12b.4. The mind-boggling lack of justification here and in Jam-ȳang-shay-ḇa's text undoubtedly led to Gung-tang's facing the issue head on.

> own character. Hence, other-powered natures would not be empty of the imputational nature, and thus their emptiness of the imputational nature would not be the thoroughly established nature. Through this route, the statement in the *Sūtra Unraveling the Thought*, "Those [imputational characters] are characters posited by names and terminology and do not subsist by way of their own character," despite referring only to the absence of imputational natures' being established by way of their own character, serves to damage the first-wheel teaching that objects are established by way of their own character as the referents of conceptual consciousnesses.

Indeed, since it is imputational natures that are being declared not to exist by way of their own character, the answer clearly refutes the first-wheel teaching that phenomena are established by way of their own character as the referents of their respective conceptual consciousnesses. In this light, the Gung-ru Chö-jung and Jam-ȳang-shay-b̄a tradition's identification of the "own-character" of the question as "establishment by way of their own character as the referents of their respective conceptual consciousnesses" makes sense; the problem for them lies in trying to twist D̄zong-ka-b̄a's clear identification of "subsist by way of its own character" as "established by way of its own character" into supporting this more sensible option, and Gung-tang and A-ku L̄o-drö-gya-tso have provided a scenario that fits with the overall view of the system, even if the manipulation is forced, to say the least.

Issue #51: Does anyone assert such own-character?

Gung-ru Chö-jung[167] and Jam-ȳang-shay-b̄a[168] have made the distinction that the literal level of the first wheel of the teaching (as described here by Paramārthasamudgata in the *Sūtra Unraveling the Thought*) explicitly teaches that phenomena ranging from forms through the thirty-seven harmonies with enlightenment are established by way of their own character as the referents of conceptual consciousnesses. This means that the intended trainees of the first wheel must assert such, in which case the Great Exposition School and the Sūtra School must do so. However, there is a problem: According to these scholars, it is clear that at least the Sūtra School Following Reasoning does not assert that permanent phenomena are established by way of their own character, and if permanent phenomena, such as uncompounded space and nirvana, are not asserted to be established by way of their own character, there does not seem to be any way that this school could assert them to be **established by way of their own character** as the referents of conceptual consciousnesses.

In answer to this, Gung-ru Chö-jung and Jam-ȳang-shay-b̄a make the distinction that the Sūtra School Following Reasoning asserts that such non-disintegrating permanent phenomena are established **through the force of**

their own measure of subsistence[a] as the referents of conceptual consciousnesses. This is because for this school if any phenomenon minimally is not established through the force of its own mode of subsistence, they cannot posit it as even existing. Thus, although the Sūtra School Following Reasoning does not use the term "established by way of its own character" to depict existent imputational natures, in the eyes of the Mind-Only School the Sūtra School Following Reasoning **comes to assert** that all phenomena are **established by way of their own character** as the referents of conceptual consciousnesses. In this vein Dzong-ka-ba (*Emptiness in Mind-Only,* 210) says:

> The two Proponents of [Truly Existent External] Objects [that is, the Great Exposition and the Sūtra schools] do not know how to posit forms and so forth as existing if their being established by way of their own character as the referents of conceptual consciousnesses and as the foundations of imputing terminology is negated. This is not the own-character that is renowned to the Epistemologists.[b]

This is clearly also the reading of this passage by Dzong-ka-ba's student Kedrup whose *Opening the Eyes of the Fortunate* says:[169]

> The Proponents of Sūtra themselves do not use the name "own-character" [that is, "established by way of their own character"] in their assertion that space, nirvana, and so forth are established through the force of space's, nirvana's, and so forth's own measure of subsistence as the foundations of reference of the names for space, the extinguishment of contamination, and so forth. However, according to the Proponents of Mind-Only, the Proponents of Sūtra have come to assert the meaning of own-character. This is the meaning [of Dzong-ka-ba's statement]. Realizing this has very great import.

Therefore, even though Proponents of the Great Exposition and Proponents of

---

a *rang gi gnas tshod kyi dbang gis grub pa.*

b *tshad ma pa, prāmāṇika.* According to A-ku Lo-drö-gya-tso (*Precious Lamp,* 259.2), Dzong-ka-ba is making the point that this sort of own-character is not limited to those objects that perform functions (a category that excludes permanent phenomena) since—according to the Mind-Only School—in the Great Exposition School and the Sūtra School all phenomena, both the permanent (which are **not** able to produce effects) and the impermanent, come to be established by way of their own character as the referents of conceptual consciousnesses and as the foundations of the imputation of terminology. Therefore, in this context "own-character" refers to establishment through the force of objects' own status (*rang gi gnas tshod kyi dbang gis grub pa*) and not to the ability to perform the function of creating an effect, as it does in the system of the "Epistemologists," which here connotes the Proponents of Sūtra, who assert that the definition of own-character is that which is ultimately able to perform a function (*don dam par don byed nus pa*). In other contexts, "Epistemologists" refers also to the Proponents of Mind-Only that follow Dignāga and Dharmakīrti). See issues #40, 121-124.

Sūtra who are the intended trainees of the first wheel **assert** that permanent phenomena are not established by way of their own character as the referents of conceptual consciousnesses, according to the Mind-Only School they have not realized such and thus still need to be taught it.[a]

To make this distinction in a different way: Despite the fact that Proponents of Sūtra realize that permanent phenomena are not established by way of their own character, this does not entail that they have realized that permanent phenomena are not established by way of their own character as the referents of conceptual consciousnesses. One might think that just the opposite would be true since "established by way of its own character as the referent of a conceptual consciousness" seems to be a sub-set of "established by way of its own character," and when, for instance, one ascertains that products are devoid of permanent sounds in general (there being no such thing as a permanent sound), one necessarily ascertains that products are devoid of specific permanent sounds such as of a guitar.[b] According to these scholars, however, that principle does not apply in this case. They do not spell out their reasoning, but it must be that "established by way of its own character as the referent of a conceptual consciousness" is simply not a sub-set of "established by way of its own character" because the former is more subtle.

Conclusion on "Own-Character"

To me, it seems better not to identify the "own-character" of Paramārthasamudgata's question as "established by way of its own character" but to identify it merely as the unique character of objects. This would relieve the Go-mang tradition of having to make sense out of Dzong-ka-ba's identification

[a] This is the position of the Go-mang tradition. Jay-dzün Chö-gyi-gyel-tsen holds that the Proponents of Sūtra assert that all phenomena are indeed established by way of their own character and thus they can hold that all phenomena are established by way of their own character as the referents of their respective conceptual consciousnesses. He also makes the point (*General-Meaning Commentary,* 9b.3 and 10a.2-10a.5) that a sūtra explicitly teaching that phenomena are established by way of their own character is a sūtra explicitly teaching that phenomena are established by way of their own character as the referents of their respective conceptual consciousnesses. (It is apparent that the Paṇ-chen Sö-nam-drak-ba tradition also holds this latter point.) Since terms (*sgra*) and conceptual consciousnesses (*rtog pa*) are held to operate in the same way, this position raises the question of whether a conceptual consciousness apprehending forms as established by way of their own character as the referents of their respective conceptual consciousnesses apprehends forms as established by way of their own character. However, as Jay-dzün Chö-gyi-gyel-tsen says, this cannot be admitted because then one conceptual consciousness would be both incorrect and correct.

[b] Gung-ru Chö-jung (15a.1) and Jam-yang-shay-ba (40.2) cite the dictum from Gyeltsap's *Illumination of the Path to Liberation* (*thar lam sel byed*), "It is established that any ascertainment of [something] as empty of a generality is necessarily an ascertainment that it is empty of a particular" (*spyis stong par nges na/ bye brag gis stong par nges pas khyab pa 'grub bo*).

by claiming that it really means "established by way of its own character as the referent of a conceptual consciousness"; they are then also relieved of having to identify the "character" of the "character-non-nature" as "established by way of its own character as the referent of a conceptual consciousness" despite the sūtra's clear identification of it as meaning "subsisting by way of its own character."

Those like Jay-d̄zün Chö-ḡyi-gyel-tsen and Paṇ-chen S̄ö-nam-drak-b̄a who leave D̄zong-ka-b̄a's identification as it is have the equally unenviable task of having to explain that despite the fact that the first wheel teaches that the aggregates are established by way of their own character and that this accords with the fact, such a teaching is not literally acceptable; as will be remembered, some of their followers claim that this is because such a teaching also communicates that the aggregates are established by way of their own character as the referents of their respective conceptual consciousnesses. Again, my own inclination is to take the first wheel's teaching of "own-character" as a teaching of the unique character of objects **but within the context of its being established by way of its own character as the referent of a conceptual consciousness.**

It seems to me that D̄zong-ka-b̄a's preference for describing the first wheel as teaching that all phenomena, including imputational natures, are established by way of their own character rather than as teaching that all phenomena are established by way of their own character as the referents of their respective conceptual consciousnesses led to his inappropriate rejection of Wonch'uk's identifying the "own-character" of Paramārthasamudgata's question as the unique character of phenomena. His preference for this mode of describing the first wheel may have stemmed from a wish to emphasize the contrast with his own Consequence School, the basic tenet of which is that no phenomenon is established by way of its own character. This perspective may have made him over-anxious to find evidence of the Mind-Only School's assertion of establishment of objects by way of their own character even where it did not exist, that is, in the term "own-character" in Paramārthasamudgata's question. Nevertheless, D̄zong-ka-b̄a's main point that the *Sūtra Unraveling the Thought* and hence the Mind-Only School asserts that other-powered natures (and thoroughly established natures) are established by way of their own character and that imputational natures are not is irrefutable.[a] Still, despite my deep respect for D̄zong-ka-b̄a's work I do not wish to don the mask of the traditional Ge-luk-b̄a exegete and claim that my explication, more radical than those by Tibetan scholars, is merely a positing of his thought, even though the maneuvers that I would use to do so are no more slippery than theirs.

An impressive host of scholars following D̄zong-ka-b̄a have obviously strained to make sense out of his statements; they have creatively posited his thought, pretending that his words make perfect sense. An intent of this variety

[a] It will be remembered that the sūtra says, "That which does not exist by way of its own character is not produced."

of apologetic is to make such a bold and creative defense of the founder of the sect that one's own ingenuity becomes the focus. Once we recognize the format as a mask required in a culture of allegiance to exalted persons, we can see that critical acumen is not dulled. To appreciate their inventiveness we must see that they really do not think that Ḏzong-ka-ḇa meant what they claim.

These scholars, by working on the microscopic issue of the meaning of Ḏzong-ka-ḇa's words, draw on a reserve of knowledge of larger issues; the basic principles by which they unravel Ḏzong-ka-ḇa's words are his own. The exercise of exegesis—even when the odds of success are low—imbeds the participants even more in the architecture of a living philosophy. In the same way we also, by having become embroiled in a maze of doctrinal considerations in these scholars' attempts to construct harmony between the *Sūtra Unraveling the Thought*, Indian schools, and favored Tibetans' exegesis, have been led more deeply into basic issues. This educational system that—over the two-thousand-mile stretch of Tibet and out into its vast cultural region, especially in Mongolian areas—stimulated the metaphysical imagination into creative play with profound principles is one of the great triumphs of the human spirit.

9. Finishing the Question

In a long excursion stemming from the topic of Paramārthasamudgata's question to Buddha about apparent contradictions between his teachings in the first and second wheels of doctrine, we have considered central issues that constitute the context of the exchange between Paramārthasamudgata and Buddha as seen by Tibetan traditions. The diversion, by addressing implications of what it means for an object to be established by way of its own character as the referent of terms and conceptual consciousnesses, has allowed us an occasion to become re-oriented so as to appreciate the crucial import of the drama that is unfolding. Now let us treat a few remaining points concerning Paramārthasamudgata's question and, in the next chapter, Buddha's answer.

Issue #52: Does the Sūtra *explicitly teach both types of emptiness?*

Since the Mind-Only School speaks of two kinds of emptiness (non-establishment of apprehended-object and apprehending-subject as different entities and non-establishment of phenomena by way of their own character as referents of terms and conceptual consciousnesses), the question arises whether the *Sūtra Unraveling the Thought* also speaks of both and, correspondingly, whether it describes the first wheel of doctrine as teaching the opposite of both kinds of emptiness. The sūtra certainly speaks of a thoroughly established nature that is the other-powered natures' emptiness of factors imputed in the manner of entity and attribute, but does it address the emptiness of externality? Also, it is clear that the first wheel of doctrine as described by Paramārthasamudgata teaches that objects are established by way of their own character as the referents of words and conceptual consciousnesses, but does it teach that forms, for instance, are entities external to the consciousnesses apprehending them?

As Gung-ru Chö-jung surmises,[170] one might mistakenly be led to think that D̄zong-ka-b̄a holds that the first wheel of doctrine as described by Paramārthasamudgata even **explicitly** teaches that forms and so forth are external objects[a] because in *The Essence of Eloquence* when explaining how the first wheel

[a] Jik-may-dam-chö-gya-tso (*Port of Entry,* 150.1) reports that this is the position of the L̄o-s̄el-l̄ing College. Indeed, their textbook author, Paṇ-chen S̄ö-nam-drak-b̄a (*Garland of Blue Lotuses,* 11b.6), at first says only that the first wheel teaches externality but later clearly says that the first wheel *explicitly* teaches externality (12b.6 and 13a.2). Since it is taken for granted that the first wheel explicitly teaches that phenomena are established by way of their own character as the referents of their respective conceptual consciousnesses, Jik-may-dam-chö-gya-tso's characterization seems to be accurate. Ye-s̄hay-tup-d̄en, despite being a follower of Paṇ-chen S̄ö-nam-drak-b̄a, uses the distinction that a passage that teaches the one explicitly teaches the other implicitly.

requires interpretation, he speaks about the first-wheel teaching of externality (thus indicating that the first wheel teaches external objects) and then about the teaching of imputation in the manner of entity and attribute. Ḏzong-ka-ḇa (*Emptiness in Mind-Only,* 234-235) initially shows that the teaching of externality requires interpretation:

> When the mode of commentary on the suchness of things by the masters, the brothers [Asaṅga and Vasubandhu], is taken as given above, the description—in the first wheel—of the two, apprehended-object and apprehending-subject, in terms of externality is elucidated as requiring interpretation. The [**factual**] **basis [in Buddha's] thought** is [the appearance of the six types of objects—forms and so forth—to the six types of consciousness as if they were external objects, as is] stated in Vasubandhu's *The Twenty:*
>
> > The Subduer spoke about these—
> > The seeds from which cognitions respectively arise
> > And the appearances [of forms]—
> > In a dualistic way as [internal and external] sense-spheres of those [cognitions].
>
> Also, the **purpose** [of his teaching such] is as the same text says:
>
> > That form-sense-spheres and so forth exist [as external objects]
> > Was said through the force of a thought (*dgongs pa*) behind it
> > With regard to beings tamed by that,
> > Like [the teaching of] spontaneously arisen sentient beings [as substantially established or permanent].
>
> When it is taught that a consciousness viewing forms and so forth arises from external and internal sense-spheres, it is for the sake of realizing that there is no viewer and so forth except for those. The **damage to the literal reading** is the reasonings refuting external objects.

And right after that, Ḏzong-ka-ḇa (*Emptiness in Mind-Only,* 235) goes on to say:

> Since an imputational factor imputed to phenomena in the manner of entity and attribute is a phenomenon-constituent and a phenomenon-sense-sphere, statements that those two [that is, phenomenon-constituent and phenomenon-sense-sphere][a] are established by way of

[a] Since these two, as categories, contain instances (such as uncompounded space) that are permanent, the categories themselves are considered to be permanent and hence not established by way of their own character. Ḏzong-ka-ḇa's more specific reference is to imputational natures that are factors imputed in the manner of entity and attribute, and when it is taught in the first wheel that all phenomena, without differentiation, are established by way of their own character, these imputational natures, being existent, also are included as being

their own character without differentiating [from among phenomena what does and does not exist by way of its own character] also require interpretation.

Since Dzong-ka-ba **first** speaks about the fact that first-wheel teachings of externality require interpretation, it would seem that the first wheel that Paramārthasamudgata describes in his question would explicitly teach external objects.

However, Gung-ru Chö-jung,[171] while admitting that there are first-wheel passages teaching externality, holds that the term "own-character" in Paramārthasamudgata's description refers only to the teaching that objects are established by way of their own character as the referents of their respective conceptual consciousnesses. He holds that the passages teaching these two types of over-reified status of phenomena are separate.[172] This is because in the last line of the passage just cited, Dzong-ka-ba, by using the word "also," separates the two topics, giving the impression that there are separate teachings in the first wheel about external objects and about establishment of objects by way of their own character as the referents of conceptual consciousnesses as well as separate refutations of these teachings in the third wheel. Gung-ru Chö-jung therefore holds that the first wheel is more than what Paramārthasamudgata explicitly describes.

One immediately wonders why Dzong-ka-ba chose first to discuss—as requiring interpretation—the type of reification that Paramārthasamudgata does not explicitly describe and, only after that and as an addendum, mentions the type explicitly set forth in Paramārthasamudgata's description of the first wheel. Gung-ru Chö-jung answers this qualm by claiming that Dzong-ka-ba uses the format of how the teaching of externality requires interpretation as a **model** for showing how the teaching of imputation in the manner of entities and attributes requires interpretation. Gung-ru Chö-jung is attempting to suggest that, even though Dzong-ka-ba's treatment of the teaching of externality is both first and more detailed, he intended it as a model for how the teaching of factors imputed in the manner of entity and attribute requires interpretation.

Gung-ru Chö-jung's point is forced, but he uses it as an opportunity to

---

established by way of their own character. Since they exist but actually do not exist by way of their own character, such scriptures also (that is, in addition to those teaching external objects) require interpretation.

Jik-may-dam-chö-gya-tso (*Port of Entry*, 699.6) says that, with respect to the teaching that all phenomena are established by way of their own character, the **factual basis in Buddha's thought** is that other-powered natures and thoroughly established natures are established by way of their own character; the **purpose** is to prevent the annihilationist view of holding that imputational natures do not exist at all; and the **damage to the literal reading** is the reasonings proving that imputational natures are not established by way of their own character.

About the following word "also," see the remainder of the current issue and issue #53.

show how the latter teaching fits into the threefold schema of showing (1) what was behind it in Buddha's thought, (2) the purpose of Buddha's teaching something that does not accord with the fact, and (3) the refutations showing that such a teaching does not accord with the fact. Thus, according to Gung-ru Chö-jung, Dzong-ka-ba cites Vasubandhu's *The Twenty* in order that one might understand these three factors:

1. **The basis in Buddha's thought:** Just as the factually true basis behind Buddha's non-factual teaching in the first wheel that external objects exist is that awarenesses are generated to which external objects falsely appear, so the factually true basis behind Buddha's non-factual teaching in the first wheel, as described by Paramārthasamudgata, that objects are established by way of their own character as the referents of their respective conceptual consciousnesses is that awarenesses are generated to which forms and so forth falsely appear to be established.
2. **The purpose:** Just as the first-wheel teaching that external objects exist is for the sake of trainees with the outlook of the Great Exposition and Sūtra schools, so the first-wheel teaching, as described by Paramārthasamudgata, that forms and so forth are established by way of their own character as the referents of their respective conceptual consciousnesses is for the sake of trainees with the outlook of the Great Exposition and Sūtra schools.
3. **The refutations of the explicit teaching:** Just as the first wheel that teaches external objects is damaged by the reasonings refuting external objects, so the first-wheel teaching, as described by Paramārthasamudgata, that forms and so forth are established by way of their own character as the referents of their respective conceptual consciousnesses is damaged by the reasonings refuting this.[a]

Gung-ru Chö-jung concludes his argument—that the first wheel, as described by Paramārthasamudgata, explicitly teaches that factors imputed in the manner of entity and attribute are established by way of their own character and does not explicitly teach externality—by using the principle of the hypothetical opponent's objection against him. The opponent claims that Dzong-ka-ba must have considered the teaching of externality to be what Paramārthasamudgata explicitly describes as the first-wheel teaching because Dzong-ka-ba mentions it in a **primary** way when he speaks about how the first wheel requires interpretation. In response, Gung-ru Chö-jung, employing the same principle, points to the fact that when in *The Essence of Eloquence* Dzong-ka-ba gives the reasonings damaging the explicit teaching of the first wheel and proving that other-powered natures are empty of the imputational nature, he **first** cites the reasoning showing that objects are not established by way of their own character as

[a] Gung-ru Chö-jung does not give this third item; it is implicit to his argument, and thus I have supplied it, even though he may have meant to avoid bringing up the matter since he may have considered each of the sets of reasonings as refuting both types of reification.

the referents of their respective names and conceptual consciousnesses. Ḏzong-ka-ḇa (*Emptiness in Mind-Only,* 208) quotes Asaṅga's *Summary of the Great Vehicle*:[173]

> Because an awareness does not exist prior to name,
> Because manifold, and because unrestricted,
> There are the contradictions of being in the essence of that, of many entities,
> And of the mixture of entities. Therefore, it is proven.

From the fact that Ḏzong-ka-ḇa cites this type of reasoning and not one proving the lack of externality, Gung-ru Chö-jung can cogently claim that, for Ḏzong-ka-ḇa, the type of non-factual teaching that Paramārthasamudgata describes as constituting the first wheel is that factors imputed in the manner of entity and attribute are established by way of their own character.

Once the first wheel **as described by Paramārthasamudgata** is explicitly concerned with imputation in the manner of entity and attribute, it cannot explicitly be concerned with externality, since "own-character" can explicitly connote only one meaning. Gung-ru Chö-jung therefore concludes that Paramārthasamudgata does not describe the first-wheel teaching of externality and that these two types of first-wheel teachings are to be found in separate sūtra passages.

I would add that when, in chapter 12 of *The Essence of Eloquence,* Ḏzong-ka-ḇa addresses the issue of the three aspects of sūtra passages that require interpretation—he speaks initially and primarily of the teaching of externality because:

- There is no Indian source that clearly speaks of the three aspects for the teaching of imputation in the manner of entity and attribute and thus it was not convenient to Ḏzong-ka-ḇa's main point.
- In India the emphasis switched to the teaching on externality.

Unfortunately, Gung-ru Chö-jung does not give an example of a separate first-wheel sūtra passage that explicitly teaches externality, and it is likely that the search for one led Jam-ȳang-shay-ḇa,[a] his successor as textbook author for Go-mang, to assert two centuries later that the first wheel that Paramārthasamudgata describes as explicitly teaching that forms and so forth are established by way of their own character as the referents of conceptual consciousnesses also **implicitly** teaches externality. He agrees with Gung-ru Chö-jung that the terms expressing that forms and so forth are established by way of

[a] Jam-ȳang-shay-ḇa's *Great Exposition of the Interpretable and the Definitive,* 34.4-36.1. Jam-ȳang-shay-ḇa rearranges but retains the meaning of the first part of Gung-ru Chö-jung's explanation (*Garland of White Lotuses,* 9b.3-10a.6) about the fact that such a first-wheel passage cannot explicitly teach externality; however, he drops the second part (10a.6-11b.5) about there being separate sūtra passages since he disagrees with it.

their own character as the referents of conceptual consciousnesses do not explicitly express that forms and so forth are established as external objects, but he holds that such is implicitly expressed. Similarly, he agrees that a conceptual consciousness conceiving that forms and so forth are established by way of their own character as the referents of conceptual consciousnesses does not explicitly conceive that these are established as external objects, but he asserts that such is implicitly conceived. The two scholars agree that terms and conceptual consciousnesses operate in an eliminative manner with respect to their referents, zeroing in on only one aspect, and hence cannot **explicitly** express or conceive two things at once. However, Gung-ru Chö-jung draws the conclusion that there must be separate sūtra passages teaching these two topics, whereas Jam-ȳang-shay-b̄a uses the distinction of explicit and implicit teachings to assert that one passage does both.[a]

Jam-ȳang-shay-b̄a agrees with Gung-ru Chö-jung that what is **explicitly** refuted here in this chapter of the *Sūtra Unraveling the Thought* when it speaks of the character-non-nature is that objects are not established by way of their own character as the referents of conceptual consciousnesses. He also agrees that through the force of that refutation one understands cognition-only, the absence of external objects. Since one must enter into, or understand, cognition-only, which means the absence of external objects, in dependence upon explicitly refuting that forms and so forth are established by way of their own character as the referents of their respective terms and conceptual consciousnesses, the realization of the emptiness of such establishment is a method (and hence a precursor) for realizing the emptiness of external objects.[b] For Gung-ru Chö-jung and Jam-ȳang-shay-b̄a, the realization of the former does not constitute realization of the latter but leads to it, and thus it is impossible for the first wheel **explicitly** to teach the opposite of both kinds of emptiness, since the reasoning refuting the one would have to **explicitly** refute the other.[174]

[a] These scholars are forced into their respective positions by D̄zong-ka-b̄a's identification of "own-character" as not referring to the unique character of objects but to establishment by way of its own character, which Gung-ru Chö-jung and Jam-ȳang-shay-b̄a take to mean a misperceived status of phenomena. My own opinion, as explained earlier, is that "own-character" does indeed mean the unique character of objects within the *context* of the teaching that objects are established by way of their own character as the referents of their respective conceptual consciousnesses. The implicit context is that forms and so forth are entities external to the consciousnesses perceiving them.

[b] This sentence is drawn from Gung-ru Chö-jung's *Garland of White Lotuses,* 10a.4-10a.6. Not all Ge-luk-b̄a scholars agree that the two realizations are serial; see *Reflections on Reality,* chapter 19.

Issue #53: How to pretend that the two textbook authors of Go-mang are saying the same thing?

Gung-ru Chö-jung's reason, as detailed above, for holding that there are separate first-wheel sūtra passages that explicitly teach external objects and that explicitly teach that objects are established by way of their own character as the referents of conceptual consciousnesses is that Dzong-ka-ba seems to indicate that the modes of commenting on those two as requiring interpretation are separate, thereby suggesting that there are also separate passages teaching these. However, Gung-tang,[175] following out the principles of Jam-ȳang-shay-b̄a's opinion,[a] answers Gung-ru Chö-jung by averring that it is unsuitable to draw the conclusion that these two types of first-wheel teachings are constituted by separate sūtra passages, for—without the qualification "explicitly"—it is true

---

[a]   Jik-may-dam-chö-gya-tso (*Port of Entry*, 150.6-151.4) shows that Gung-tang also is clearing up some confusion in Jam-ȳang-shay-b̄a's own position. In the first chapter of his *Decisive Analysis of (Maitreya's) "Ornament for Clear Realization,"* Jam-ȳang-shay-b̄a himself describes as separate the first wheel of doctrine that teaches external objects and the first wheel of doctrine that teaches that objects are established by way of their own character as the referents of their respective conceptual consciousnesses. Also, in his *Great Exposition of the Interpretable and the Definitive* Jam-ȳang-shay-b̄a indicates that a first wheel teaching external objects is not a first wheel described in Paramārthasamudgata's question and that any sūtra teaching external objects is necessarily not a sūtra teaching that objects are established by way of their own character as the referents of their respective conceptual consciousnesses. These statements militate against Jam-ȳang-shay-b̄a's own position here that the one implicitly teaches the other. Jik-may-dam-chö-gya-tso (152.1) cites the *Distinctions Concerning the Textbook on the Perfection of Wisdom* (*phar phyin zhib cha*) as explaining that, through the distinction of what are explicitly and implicitly indicated, it can be seen that what Jam-ȳang-shay-b̄a should have said is that whatever is a sūtra *explicitly* teaching external objects is necessarily not a first-wheel sūtra *explicitly* indicated in Paramārthasamudgata's question. Also, the same text explains that a passage such as "In dependence upon an eye and form, an eye consciousness is generated" is a first-wheel sūtra explicitly teaching external objects and is a first-wheel sūtra indicated here in Paramārthasamudgata's question, but is not a first-wheel sūtra *explicitly* indicated here in Paramārthasamudgata's question; it is indicated only implicitly. (A-ku Lo-drö-gya-tso makes the same points in his *Precious Lamp*, 67.6-69.2.)

Despite the obvious advantages of these distinctions, it seems to me that a problem remains. Namely, it seems that the passage, "In dependence upon an eye and form, an eye consciousness is generated," must be considered as *explicitly* teaching that these phenomena are established by way of their own character as the referents of their respective conceptual consciousnesses because otherwise one could not find a passage that explicitly teaches that the twelve sense-spheres and eighteen constituents are so established! In that case, since it can explicitly teach only one thing, it could only **implicitly** teach external objects; and, in that case, one could not find a first-wheel passage that explicitly teaches external objects. This difficulty may be a reason why Paṇ-chen Sö-nam-drak-b̄a asserts that the first-wheel explicitly teaches both; Ye-shay-tup-den (oral teaching) described the two teachings as being synonymous (*ming gi rnam grangs*), and thus the terms expressing one of them also express the other (although the one is expressed explicitly and the other is expressed implicitly).

that whatever is a sūtra passage of the first wheel teaching external objects is necessarily a sūtra passage of the first-wheel teaching that objects are established by way of their own character as the referents of conceptual consciousnesses, and vice versa. In other words, without the qualification "explicitly," the two are equivalent: a sūtra passage of the first wheel, as described by Paramārthasamudgata, necessarily teaches both of these but not necessarily explicitly.[a] In the citation from Ḏzong-ka-ḇa that Gung-ru Chö-jung uses as evidence for the separation of these two teachings:

> statements that those two [that is, phenomenon-constituent and phenomenon-sense-sphere] are established by way of their own character without differentiating [from among phenomena what does and does not exist by way of its own character] **also** require interpretation.

Gung-tang takes the word "also" as meaning that **not only** is the teaching of external objects commented upon as requiring interpretation **but also** the teaching that objects are established by way of their own character as the referents of conceptual consciousnesses is commented upon as requiring interpretation. The same passages do both.

According to Gung-tang, the sūtra passage, "In dependence upon an eye and form, an eye consciousness is generated," must be posited as teaching external objects, for if such a passage is not posited as a first-wheel passage teaching external objects, one could not find any that did! Thus, although this passage also teaches "own-character" (that is, that these phenomena are established by way of their own character as the referents of conceptual consciousnesses), it teaches that these phenomena are external objects.

Despite his direct contradiction of Gung-ru Chö-jung, Gung-tang magnanimously pretends that he is merely positing his thought. He claims that Gung-ru Chö-jung means that although only one sūtra passage indicates that such passages require interpretation, there are two approaches for commenting

---

[a] In Hla-ṡa in the summer of 1987, Gen L̄o-sang-ḏen-dzin asked me whether this meant that any passage teaching external objects necessarily teaches that phenomena are established by way of their own character as the referents of their respective conceptual consciousnesses. I answered in the affirmative, and he immediately asked whether, according to the Mind-Only School, a sūtra passage teaching external objects to Consequentialists also teaches that objects are established by way of their own character as the referents of their respective conceptual consciousnesses. This is impossible since the Consequentialists are persons who need to be taught that there are external objects but also that phenomena are *not* established by way of their own character. It seemed that he had me trapped, but months later it occurred to me that Gung-tang's point is that the equivalence of teaching is true in terms of the first wheel only, whereas the teachings for the Consequentialists are in the second wheel. Thus, I should have answered that it is not the case that any passage teaching external objects necessarily teaches that phenomena are established by way of their own character as the referents of their respective conceptual consciousnesses but that any passage *of the first wheel* teaching external objects necessarily teaches such.

on that single sūtra passage as requiring interpretation—one by way of showing the non-existence of objects established by way of their own character as the referents of conceptual consciousnesses and the other by way of showing the non-existence of external objects. Through such magnanimous commentary, he corrects what for him is a downright error. The pretension of merely revealing Gung-ru Chö-jung's intention serves as a technique to maintain continuity with the past tradition of Go-mang, made possible by the fact that Jam-ȳang-shay-b̄a, though obviously disagreeing with Gung-ru Chö-jung, does not openly say he is.

Despite this difference, Gung-ru Chö-jung and Jam-ȳang-shay-b̄a agree that external objects are only implicitly refuted in the "Questions of Paramārthasamudgata Chapter" of the *Sūtra Unraveling the Thought.* All Ge-luk-b̄a scholars, however, hold that there is an explicit refutation of externality in the "Questions of Maitreya Chapter"[a] of the same sūtra. Thus, even if external objects are openly refuted in the "Questions of Maitreya Chapter," they are not openly refuted in the "Questions of Paramārthasamudgata Chapter," where the refutation of external objects is merely implicit to the refutation of objects as being established by way of their own character as the referents of conceptual consciousnesses.

Thus, Go-mang scholars agree that when Paramārthasamudgata says:

> The Supramundane Victor spoke, in many ways, of the **own-character** of the aggregates.... The Supramundane Victor also spoke, in many ways, of the **own-character** of the truths.... The Supramundane Victor also spoke, in many ways, of the **own-character** of the constituents.... The Supramundane Victor also spoke, in many ways, of the **own-character** of the four mindful establishments.... The Supramundane Victor also spoke, in many ways, of the **own-character** of the eightfold path of Superiors...

the term "own-character" cannot **explicitly** refer to externality, that is, objects being different entities from subjects and subjects being different entities from objects. Jam-ȳang-shay-b̄a and Gung-tang hold that it does so implicitly, whereas Gung-ru Chö-jung does not raise the possibility of such an implicit teaching and only states that there are separate teachings of external objects without giving an illustration of such a passage.

---

[a] See, for instance, Gung-ru Chö-jung's *Garland of White Lotuses,* 10b.4, and Jam-ȳang-shay-b̄a's *Great Exposition of the Interpretable and the Definitive,* 35.4. For an extensive presentation of this topic, see *Reflections on Reality,* chapter 20.

The Middle Wheel

Issue #54: What does the denial of establishment by way of its own character mean in the middle wheel?

Since, according to the Mind-Only School, imputational phenomena are not established by way of their own character, if the Perfection of Wisdom Sūtras taught on the literal level that such phenomena are not established by way of their own character, those sūtras would, in those particular sections, be literally acceptable. Thus, for Jam-ÿang-shay-b̄a and his followers, even though "establishment of objects by way of their own character" in the first wheel means "establishment of objects by way of their own character **as the referents of conceptual consciousnesses**," in the middle wheel it means just "establishment of objects by way of their own character" and also "establishment of objects from their own side" or "inherent establishment."

Issue #55: How can D̄zong-ka-b̄a be made to say this?

Because the meanings of "established by way of its own character" in the first and middle wheels of doctrine are different, the Go-mang school holds that when D̄zong-ka-b̄a (*Emptiness in Mind-Only,* 127) speaks of:

> the statements [in the first wheel] that phenomena equally[a] have nature in the sense of being established by way of their own character, the statements [in the middle wheel] that phenomena equally do not have such, and the good differentiation [in the final wheel] of those [phenomena] that have [such establishment] and those that do not.

his actual meaning is:

> The first wheel **equally has statements of the words**, "Phenomena ranging from forms through to the harmonies with enlightenment have the nature of being established by way of their own character," and the middle wheel **equally has statements of the words**, "Phenomena ranging from forms through to exalted knowers of all aspects [that is, omniscient consciousnesses] do not have the nature of being established by way of their own character."

Jam-ÿang-shay-b̄a's re-presentation, in which he separates word and meaning, is an artful attempt to improve on D̄zong-ka-b̄a's description. Still, as I see it, his assigning different meanings to the same term does not necessitate that Paramārthasamudgata's question arises only from a concern that there is a seeming contradiction in Buddha's using the same **words** (affirmed and denied) in

[a] See also issue #44.

the first two wheels of doctrine. From Jam-ȳang-shay-b̄a's perspective, the meaning of "own-character" in the first wheel—which D̄zong-ka-b̄a describes as "establishment by way of its own character" but is more accurately that objects are established by way of their own character as the referents of conceptual consciousnesses—is contradictory with the declaration of universal naturelessness in the middle wheel, which D̄zong-ka-b̄a describes as "non-establishment by way of its own character" but is more accurately that all phenomena are not established from their own side. If all phenomena were established by way of their own character as the referents of conceptual consciousnesses, they certainly would be established from their own side, and thus for Buddha to teach in the first wheel that they are the former and then in the second wheel that they are not the latter certainly is contradictory.

Thus, it seems to me that Jam-ȳang-shay-b̄a's emphasis on the "equal statement of the words..." is merely because he is seeking to maintain the facade of making D̄zong-ka-b̄a's explication compatible with what he perceives Paramārthasamudgata to be saying. His identification, while being a defense of D̄zong-ka-b̄a, is a bold re-structuring that can be appreciated only when one sees how much it deviates from D̄zong-ka-b̄a's words. As mentioned above, the style of such creatively new explanations is to pretend that it is merely a repetition of the founder's view. Just as much as we miss D̄zong-ka-b̄a's genius if we accept the view, commonly propounded by Ge-luk-b̄as, that he is merely repeating Indian Buddhism, so we miss Jam-ȳang-shay-b̄a's genius if we accept his insistence that he is just presenting D̄zong-ka-b̄a's opinions. The culture, by pretending allegiance while employing analytical ingenuity, has found a way to encourage both—ingenuity being put in the service of reformulating the founder's views in the guise of ferreting out the actual meaning of his words.

Issue #56: Why does Paramārthasamudgata explicitly ask only about the middle wheel?

In summary, according to Gung-ru Chö-jung[176] and Jam-ȳang-shay-b̄a,[177] as well as their followers Gung-tang and A-ku L̄o-drö-gya-tso, Paramārthasamudgata is asking:

> Supramundane Victor, in the first wheel of the teaching, as specified here in my question, you pronounced many times the words of sūtra, "The entities of phenomena[a] ranging from forms through the

[a] Gung-ru Chö-jung and Jam-ȳang-shay-b̄a (also in his *Brief Decisive Analysis*, 493.4) make what seems to be an unnecessary specification of "compounded phenomena," which A-ku L̄o-drö-gya-tso's *Precious Lamp* (59.6) changes to "phenomena"; I have rendered it in accordance with the latter. They are most likely repeating the Second Dalai Lama's specification of "aggregates and so forth" (*Lamp Illuminating the Meaning of [D̄zong-ka-b̄a's] Thought*, 12.6); for a short discussion of the Second Dalai Lama's position, see p. 55. Gung-ru

> thirty-seven harmonies with enlightenment as well as [their attributes of] production, cessation, and so forth that are established by way of their own character exist, exist." In the middle wheel of the teaching, as specified here in my question, you pronounced many times the words of sūtra, "Production, cessation, and so forth that are established by way of their own character do not exist, do not exist, in phenomena ranging from forms through omniscient consciousnesses." If those two were left literally as they are, they would be contradictory, but since the Teacher does not have contradiction, of what where you thinking when you said such in the middle wheel?

Paramārthasamudgata's explicitly asking this question about the middle wheel, implicitly asks, "Of what where you thinking when you said what you did in the first wheel?"

As Gung-tang says,[178] through explicitly asking about the middle wheel, Paramārthasamudgata implicitly comes to ask about the first wheel, for when he states both modes of pronouncement—in the first wheel Buddha's pronouncement of the words of sūtra, "All, without differentiation, are established by way of their own character," and in the middle wheel Buddha's pronouncement of the words of sūtra, "All, without differentiation, are not established by way of their own character,"—and then explicitly asks, "Of what were you thinking when in the middle wheel you spoke such without making any differentiation?" through the force of his words Buddha's speaking without making differentiation comes to be the reason why the pronouncement in the middle wheel requires interpretation. Thereby, one understands that a differentiation is to be made, in which case the same must be so for Buddha's mode of speaking in the first wheel, which Paramārthasamudgata had just stated. Hence, his question comes to concern it also. Gung-tang's analysis is indeed cogent.

D̄ra-d̄i Ge-s̄hay Rin-chen-dön-drup, a follower of Jay-d̄zün Chö-ḡyi-gyel-tsen,[179] cogently explains that the reason for Paramārthasamudgata's explicitly questioning Buddha only about the middle wheel is that he wants to provide an occasion for Buddha to delineate the view of reality in accordance with trainees having the lineage of the Proponents of Mind-Only and thus is mainly concerned with the middle wheel. The trainees being addressed are followers of the Great Vehicle, and thus the question provides an opportunity for Buddha to set forth the true thought of the supreme of all Great Vehicle sūtras, the Perfection of Wisdom Sūtras.

Paramārthasamudgata does not ask this out of his **actually** having the qualm that the literal renderings of the first two wheels are discordant. Rather,

Chö-jung makes the same specification for the middle wheel, but Jam-ȳang-shay-b̄a does not.

he asks the question in order that such a qualm—which will arise in later trainees—might be cleared away.[a]

According to Gung-ru Chö-jung, Jam-ȳang-shay-b̄a, Gung-tang, and A-ku L̄o-drö-gya-tso, the above presentation of Paramārthasamudgata's question is what D̄zong-ka-b̄a (*Emptiness in Mind-Only,* 78) had in mind when he says:

> If the statements in some sūtras [that is, in the middle wheel of the teaching] that all phenomena are natureless, and so forth, and the statements in some sūtras [in the first wheel of the teaching] that the aggregates and so forth have an own-character, and so forth, were left as they are verbally, they would be contradictory. However, since [the Supramundane Victor] must be without contradiction, of what were

---

[a] Jik-may-dam-chö-gya-tso (*Port of Entry,* 152-153.4) lists five assertions on what the entity or nature of a question is:

1. Some say a question is words (*tshig*).
2. Some view questions as being of three varieties—verbal, physical, and mental, or, literally, sounds of speech (*ngag gi sgra*), physical manifestations (*lus kyi rnam 'gyur*), and mental consciousnesses (*yid kyi shes pa*).
3. Some say that words, aside from being the means of questioning (*dri ba zhu byed*), are not the question, and hence Paramārthasamudgata's question is the appearance of the literal readings of the two sets of scriptures as contradictory.
4. Some say that the question here is the qualm in Paramārthasamudgata's mental continuum wondering about the contradiction of the literal reading of the two sets of scriptures.
5. Some say that the question is the topics expressed (*brjod bya*) in the first and middle wheels of doctrine.

Gung-tang (*Difficult Points,* 93.14-94.18) objects to the notion that a question is just words because in that case Paramārthasamudgata's words would question both wheels and hence would explicitly question about the first wheel, since the words that are the means of asking appear explicitly in the sūtra. He says that this is not feasible because the first wheel is questioned only implicitly. Gung-tang adds that questions cannot be limited to mere words because in a *Perfection of Wisdom Sūtra* Indra questions Subhūti mentally.

Jik-may-dam-chö-gya-tso says that "others" (most likely including himself) question the entailments that Gung-tang uses in his argument, and he tries to resolve two seemingly contrary opinions—(1) D̄zong-ka-b̄a's statement "Through that, [Paramārthasamudgata] **implicitly** asks of what [Buddha] was thinking when [in the first wheel of the teaching] he spoke of the existence of the own-character [of the aggregates] and so forth," and (2) Jam-ȳang-shay-b̄a's statement in his *Decisive Analysis of the Perfection of Wisdom* (*phar phyin mtha' dpyod*), "Questions about the first and middle wheels are **explicitly** indicated [by this passage of Paramārthasamudgata's question]." Jik-may-dam-chö-gya-tso's resolution splits a hair: "Although questions about the first and middle wheels **explicitly arose** (*dngos su byung*) [in Paramārthasamudgata, he] **does not explicitly ask a question** (*dngos su ma zhus*) about the first wheel but explicitly asks a question about only the middle wheel, and although he **implicitly asks a question** (*don gyis zhus*) about the first wheel, he does not **implicitly ask a question** about the middle wheel."

> you [Buddha] thinking when [in the middle wheel of the teaching] you spoke of non-nature, and so forth?
>
> Through that, [Paramārthasamudgata] implicitly asks of what [Buddha] was thinking when [in the first wheel of the teaching] he spoke of the existence of own-character and so forth.[a]

The commentators have explicated Paramārthasamudgata's question within the context of a wide variety of implications. In the next chapter, we will consider their rendition of Buddha's answer.

[a] See issues #21-24.

PART THREE:
BUDDHA'S ANSWER

10. Interpretation

The Answer

Buddha's answer[a] to Paramārthasamudgata's question is seen as basically being in two parts—a brief indication[b] and an extensive explanation.[c] In the brief indication—the topic sentence—Buddha (*Emptiness in Mind-Only,* 82-83) says:

> Paramārthasamudgata, thinking of three non-natures of phenomena—character-non-nature, production-non-nature, and ultimate-non-nature—I taught [in the middle wheel of the teaching], "All phenomena are natureless."

After this citation, Ḏzong-ka-ḇa concludes:

---

[a] The discussion of the brief indication and of the structure of the extensive explanation is drawn from:

Wonch'uk's *Extensive Commentary,* Peking 5517, vol. 116, 130.2.3-131.1.5.
Second Dalai Lama's *Lamp Illuminating the Meaning,* 13.4-15.6.

Go-mang and Ḏra-s̄hi-kyil

Gung-ru Chö-jung's *Garland of White Lotuses,* 16b.1-19a.3.
Jam-ȳang-shay-ḇa's *Great Exposition of the Interpretable and the Definitive,* 41.2-48.6.
Jam-ȳang-shay-ḇa's *Brief Decisive Analysis,* 494.3-497.6.
W̄el-mang Ḡön-chok-gyel-tsen's *Notes on (Ḡön-chok-jik-may-w̄ang-ḇo's) Lectures,* 397.4-400.6.
Gung-tang's *Annotations,* 16.1-21.6 (*ma-tsha*).
Gung-tang's *Difficult Points,* 96(second of two 96).8-101.12.
Dön-drup-gyel-tsen's *Four Intertwined Commentaries,* 44.5-47.4.
A-ku L̄o-drö-gya-tso's *Precious Lamp,* 69.3-73.1.
Jik-may-dam-chö-gya-tso's *Port of Entry,* 158.5-170.5.
Pa-bong-ka-ḇa's *Brief Notes on Jo-ni Paṇḍita's Lectures,* 409.5-411.4.

L̄o-s̄el-l̄ing and S̄har-ḏzay

Paṇ-chen S̄ö-nam-drak-ḇa's *Garland of Blue Lotuses,* 13a.6-14a.6 (Hla-s̄a 1987, 10a.4-10b.7).

S̄e-ra Jay

B̄el-jor-hlün-drup's *Lamp for the Teaching,* 12.4-13.6.
Jay-ḏzün Chö-ḡyi-gyel-tsen's *General-Meaning Commentary,* 10a.7-11a.2.
Ḏra-ḏi Ge-s̄hay Rin-chen-dön-drup's *Ornament for the Thought,* 18.2-21.4.
S̄er-s̄hül's *Notes,* 14b.1-15a.3.
Ḏa-drin-rap-ḏen's *Annotations,* 11.4-14.2.

S̄e-ra M̄ay

L̄o-sang-trin-lay-ye-s̄hay's *Summarized Meaning,* 156.6-156.8.

[b] *mdor bstan.*

[c] *rgyas bshad.*

> In consideration of all three non-natures, [Buddha] spoke of non-nature [in the middle wheel of the teaching].[a]

Then he cites Asaṅga's *Compendium of Ascertainments:*

> *Question:* Thinking of what did the Supramundane Victor say [in the middle wheel] that all phenomena are natureless?
>
> *Answer:* Here and there he said such through the force of taming [trainees], thinking of three types of non-nature.

and Vasubandhu's *The Thirty* (stanza 23):

> Thinking of three types of non-nature
> Of the three types of natures [respectively],
> He taught [in the Perfection of Wisdom Sūtras]
> That all phenomena are natureless.

Issue #57: Does the brief indication explicitly team the three natures with the three non-natures?

As Gung-ru Chö-jung[180] and Jam-ȳang-shay-b̄a[181] point out, the brief indication, or topic sentence, that begins this discussion does not **explicitly** indicate that imputational natures are non-natures in the sense that they are not established by way of their own character, or that other-powered natures are non-natures in the sense that they lack self-production, or that thoroughly established natures—emptinesses—are ultimate-non-natures. For if it did so **explicitly**, it would be senseless for Buddha, immediately after it, to ask the rhetorical question, "Paramārthasamudgata, concerning that, what are character-non-natures of phenomena?" and to answer, "Those which are imputational characters," since he already would have said such explicitly.

Gung-ru Chö-jung[182] (with Jam-ȳang-shay-b̄a[183] following him) makes the subtle verbal distinction that the topic sentence explicitly teaches, for instance, a character-non-nature **that is related with substrata** that are imputational natures, even if it does not explicitly indicate that imputational natures are non-natures of character. It similarly indicates a character-non-nature **that is related with correct proofs**, even if it does not explicitly indicate those proofs. For if it did not indicate a character-non-nature **that is related with correct proofs**, there would be no proofs for the character-non-nature. For example, when Buddha speaks of just selflessness without explicitly mentioning the things that are selfless, he nevertheless explicitly speaks of selflessness **that is related with substrata such as forms**, even if he does not explicitly speak of forms. Still, as he says, it would be absurd to say that the expression "selflessness" explicitly indicates that form is selfless; it obviously does not.

---

[a] See also issues #57, 58, 61, 62.

Hence, the brief topic sentence does not **explicitly** indicate illustrations of the three non-natures. It explicitly indicates merely the three modes of nature-lessness—character-non-nature, production-non-nature, and ultimate-non-nature—in consideration of which Buddha said in the middle wheel of doctrine that all phenomena are natureless.

Issue #58: What was the basis in Buddha's thought for the first-wheel teaching of own-character?

Although in Buddha's reply to Paramārthasamudgata he explicitly indicates what was behind his teaching in the Perfection of Wisdom Sūtras that all phenomena are natureless—this being the three non-natures in terms of the selflessness of phenomena—he does not explicitly indicate what was behind his saying in the first wheel that the phenomena of the aggregates and so forth have "own-character." That he **must** implicitly indicate this is clear from the fact that when Paramārthasamudgata summarizes the import of Buddha's answer, he says that both the first and second wheels of doctrine require interpretation.

A-ku L̄o-drö-gya-tso[184] cogently avers that the three non-natures that Buddha indicates as being behind the middle-wheel teaching are explicitly drawn in terms of the selflessness of phenomena, and, correspondingly, it is implicitly to be understood that the three non-natures in terms of the selflessness of persons are what is behind the first-wheel teaching that all phenomena have "own-character." Thus, although Paramārthasamudgata does not **explicitly** question about the first wheel and although Buddha does not **explicitly** answer about it, the question and answer concern both wheels.

Other opinions on what was behind the first wheel. B̄el-jor-hlün-drup[a] holds that Buddha's teaching in the first wheel that phenomena are established by way of their own character has behind it the thought that other-powered natures are established by way of their own character. However, the Second Dalai Lama[185] criticizes the position of "a follower of D̄zong-ka-b̄a" (likely B̄el-jor-hlün-drup) that Buddha taught in the first wheel that **all** phenomena are established by way of their own character; rather, the Second Dalai Lama holds that in the first wheel Buddha taught only that **compounded** phenomena are taught to be established this way—a seemingly astounding notion since the Second Dalai Lama himself holds that in the Mind-Only School compounded phenomena **are** so established. As evidence for this, he cites a statement in

[a] His *Lamp for the Teaching* (16.6-17.2) says:

> Therefore, this passage [from the *Sūtra Unraveling the Thought*], "Those [other-powered natures] arise through the force of other conditions...," explicitly indicates a basis in [Buddha's] thought when he taught in the middle wheel that phenomena are natureless and implicitly indicates that the teaching in the first wheel that phenomena are established by way of their own character has [behind it] the thought that other-powered natures are established by way of their own character.

D̄zong-ka-b̄a's *The Essence of Eloquence* itself that in the first wheel true existence is not refuted except with respect to a few phenomena, that is to say, in the first wheel Buddha taught that most but not all phenomena are truly established.[a]

The Second Dalai Lama also objects to the assertion by the same scholar that what is behind the teaching of the first wheel is only that other-powered natures are truly established. As counter-evidence, he draws the parallel absurd consequence that in the middle wheel in the Perfection of Wisdom Sūtras Buddha's teaching on the literal level that **all phenomena** are not truly existent would have been given in consideration only of the fact that imputational natures are not truly existent, whereas D̄zong-ka-b̄a and the other scholar himself hold that the middle-wheel teaching was given in consideration of all three non-natures.[b]

Issue #59: What is the structure of the extensive explanation?

Buddha's reply[c] begins with his praising Paramārthasamudgata's question and an indication that he will answer and then proceeds to the answer itself, the first part of which can be divided into a brief indication, an extensive explanation, a giving of examples, and a summary sentence. In order to introduce the next issue, let us first cite the sūtra:

> Having been asked that, the Supramundane Victor said to the Bodhisattva Paramārthasamudgata:
>
> > **Praising the question and indicating that he will explain:**[186] "Paramārthasamudgata, the thought in your mind, properly generated virtue, is good, good. Paramārthasamudgata, you are involved in [asking] this in order to help many beings, to [bring] happiness to many beings, out of compassionate kindness toward the world, and for the sake of the aims, help, and happiness of all beings, including gods and humans. You are good to think to ask the One-Gone-Thus about this meaning. Therefore, Paramārthasamudgata, listen, and I will explain that in consideration of

---

[a] Unlike Jay-d̄zün Chö-ḡyi-gyel-tsen, the Second Dalai Lama holds "truly established" and "established by way of their own character" to be equivalent; thus his quarrel is not with an unwarranted switch in terms from "established by way of their own character" to "truly established." For more discussion of this passage as well as the Second Dalai Lama's corrupt citation of it, see pp. 55 and 87.

[b] Paṇ-chen S̄ö-nam-drak-b̄a (*Garland of Blue Lotuses*, 19b.2-19b.6) refutes the same position this way.

[c] The material in this issue is repeated from *Reflections on Reality*, 150ff., as background for the following issues.

which I said, 'All phenomena are natureless; all phenomena are unproduced, unceasing, quiescent from the start, and naturally thoroughly passed beyond sorrow.'

The Answer

Brief indication: "Paramārthasamudgata, thinking of three non-natures of phenomena—character-non-nature, production-non-nature, and ultimate-non-nature—I taught [in the middle wheel of the teaching], 'All phenomena are natureless.'

Extensive explanation: "Paramārthasamudgata, concerning that, what are character-non-natures of phenomena? Those which are imputational characters.

"Why? It is thus: Those [imputational characters] are characters posited by names and terminology[a] and do not subsist by way of their own character. Therefore, they are said to be 'character-non-natures.'

"What are production-non-natures of phenomena?[b] Those which are the other-powered characters of phenomena.

"Why? It is thus: Those [other-powered characters] arise through the force of other conditions and not by themselves.[c] Therefore, they are said to be 'production-non-natures.'

"What are ultimate-non-natures? Those dependently arisen phenomena—which are natureless due to being natureless in terms of production—are also natureless due to being natureless in terms of the ultimate.

"Why? Paramārthasamudgata, that which is an object of observation of purification in phenomena I teach to be the ultimate, and other-powered characters are not the object of observation of purification. Therefore, they are said to be 'ultimate-non-natures.'

"Moreover, that which is the thoroughly established character of phenomena is also called 'the ultimate-non-nature.' Why? Paramārthasamudgata, that which in phenomena is the selflessness of phenomena is called their 'non-nature.' It is the ultimate, and the ultimate is distinguished by just the naturelessness of all phenomena; therefore, it is called the 'ultimate-non-nature.'

Examples: "Paramārthasamudgata, it is thus: for example, character-non-natures [that is, imputational natures] are to be

---

a See issue #104.

b Roughly, this means, "What phenomena are without the nature of self-production?" See issues #76, 77. About "phenomena," see issue #71.

c See issue #67.

> viewed as like a flower in the sky. Paramārthasamudgata, it is thus: for example, production-non-natures [that is, other-powered natures] are to be viewed as like magical creations. From between the [two] ultimate-non-natures, one [that is, other-powered natures] is also to be viewed that way. Paramārthasamudgata, it is thus: just as, for example, space is distinguished by the mere naturelessness of form [that is, as a mere absence of forms] and pervades everywhere, so from between those [two] ultimate-non-natures, one [that is, the thoroughly established nature] is to be viewed as distinguished by the selflessness of phenomena and as pervading everything."
>
> **Summary:** "Paramārthasamudgata, thinking of those three types of naturelessness, I taught, "All phenomena are natureless.""

According to Gung-ru Chö-jung[187] and Jam-ȳang-shay-b̄a,[188] the structure of Buddha's extensive reply is in three sections corresponding to the three non-natures, each of which is in five parts:

1. An explicit, rhetorical[a] question asking for illustrations of the character-non-nature:

   > "Paramārthasamudgata, concerning that, what are character-non-natures of phenomena?"

2. An explicit explanation that factors imputed in the manner of entity and attribute are character-non-natures:

   > "Those which are imputational characters."

3. A rhetorical inquiry into the reasons for that:

   > "Why?"

4. A reply to that inquiry:

   > "It is thus: Those [imputational characters] are characters posited by names and terminology and do not subsist by way of their own character."

5. Summation:

   > "Therefore, they are said to be 'character-non-natures.'"

[a] I have added the word "rhetorical" in items one and three, since Buddha speaks all the lines.

Issue #60: What does Dzong-ka-ba mean by "clear delineation"?

This five-part structure is taken by Gung-ru Chö-jung and Jam-ȳang-shay-b̄a to be D̄zong-ka-b̄a's referent when he (*Emptiness in Mind-Only,* 86) cryptically says:

> Through this clear delineation, the latter two [descriptions of non-nature in the sūtra with respect to other-powered natures and thoroughly established natures] also should be understood.

Just before that, he (*Emptiness in Mind-Only,* 86) says:

> The question and answer in the first two sentences explain that imputational factors are character-non-natures. Then, "Why?" questions the reason for that. In answer to that question, a reason from the negative side—their not being posited by way of their own character—and a reason from the positive side—their being posited by names and terminology—are stated.

Contrary to Gung-ru Chö-jung and Jam-ȳang-shay-b̄a's explanation, it might seem that the "clear delineation"[a] to which D̄zong-ka-b̄a is referring is the fact that there is a reason from the negative side and a reason from the positive side. However, the problem with taking D̄zong-ka-b̄a's meaning this way is that, although the sūtra gives positive and negative reasons for imputational natures' being character-non-natures and for other-powered natures being production-non-natures, it does not give a negative reason for other-powered natures being ultimate-non-natures or for thoroughly established natures being ultimate-non-natures.

Gung-ru Chö-jung and Jam-ȳang-shay-b̄a's explanation of D̄zong-ka-b̄a's reference as being to the above fivefold format is more cogent, for D̄zong-ka-b̄a's explanation appears to be an adaptation of a fivefold format employed by Wonch'uk in his *Extensive Commentary*[189] which we know from his many comments he was reading closely. Wonch'uk's five are question,[b] answer,[c] inquiry,[d] explanation,[e] and summation.[f] Except for omitting the last, these parallel D̄zong-ka-b̄a's explanation cited just above—question, answer, questioning the reason, and answer to that question.[190]

[a] In W̄el-mang Ḡön-chok-gyel-tsen's *Notes on (Ḡön-chok-jik-may-w̄ang-b̄o's) Lectures* (400.5), *dmigs 'byed pa* is glossed by *'tshams byed pa;* I take *'tshams* to be an alternative form of *mtshams.*

[b] *dris pa.*

[c] *lan.*

[d] *brtag pa.*

[e] *rnam par bshad pa.*

[f] *'jug bsdu ba.*

Issue #61: How to handle an untimely citation?

As Gung-ru Chö-jung[191] and Jam-ȳang-shay-b̄a[192] say, just this which the extensive indication teaches is what the following passage from Vasubandhu's *The Thirty* (stanza 23) also explicitly indicates:

> Thinking of three types of non-nature
> Of the three types of natures [respectively],
> He taught [in the Perfection of Wisdom Sūtras]
> That all phenomena are natureless.

In the second line, the phrase, "the three types of natures," explicitly indicates the three natures—imputational natures, other-powered natures, and thoroughly established natures. In the first line, the phrase, "three types of non-nature" explicitly indicates that those three natures are illustrations respectively of character-non-nature, production-non-nature, and ultimate-non-nature. Thus, the passage says that, thinking of the three natures and three modes of naturelessness, Buddha said in the Perfection of Wisdom Sūtras that all phenomena are natureless.

D̄zong-ka-b̄a[a] (*Emptiness in Mind-Only,* 83) cites this passage at the point of speaking about the **brief** indication in the *Sūtra Unraveling the Thought* that, according to Gung-ru Chö-jung and Jam-ȳang-shay-b̄a, does not explicitly associate the three natures and the three non-natures, and thus one might think that, for D̄zong-ka-b̄a, the brief indication in the *Sūtra Unraveling the Thought* does indeed explicitly link the three natures and the three non-natures, since the Indian text that he cites at this point obviously does so. Since a consequence of this would be that the upcoming extensive explanation in the *Sūtra Unraveling the Thought* would be redundant, to get around this fault Gung-ru Chö-jung and Jam-ȳang-shay-b̄a aver that even though the Indian treatise that D̄zong-ka-b̄a cites at the point of speaking about the **brief** indication explicitly says a good deal more than the brief indication in the *Sūtra Unraveling the Thought* itself says, this can be explained by understanding D̄zong-ka-b̄a's purpose in citing it. For D̄zong-ka-b̄a intends to show that both the sūtra and these Indian treatises are similar in indicating that the basis in Buddha's own thought for his statements in the Perfection of Wisdom Sūtras that all phenomena are natureless is the three non-natures—character-non-nature, production-non-nature, and ultimate-non-nature. This is how Gung-ru Chö-jung and Jam-ȳang-shay-b̄a somewhat lamely attempt to explain away D̄zong-ka-b̄a's seemingly untimely citation.

In the same way, Gung-tang[b] excuses as merely a statement "for easy

---

[a] He may have been drawn into citing Vasubandhu at this point simply because Wonch'uk did (*Extensive Commentary,* Peking 5517, vol. 116, 130.4.8).

[b] Gung-tang's *Difficult Points,* 97.17. Jik-may-dam-chö-gya-tso (*Port of Entry,* 163.6-164.2) extends the apologetic to Ke-drup who says:

understanding" the Second Dalai Lama's explanation[a] that the brief indication says that the basis in Buddha's thought is that imputational natures are character-non-natures, other-powered natures are (self-)production-non-natures, and

---

Moreover, with respect to the way in which the *Sūtra Unraveling the Thought* explains the thought of the middle wheel sūtras, it explains that the statements in the Perfection of Wisdom Sūtras and so forth that all phenomena are natureless were made in consideration that imputational natures are character-non-natures, other-powered natures are production-non-natures, and thoroughly established natures are ultimate-non-natures. For, the Bodhisattva Paramārthasamudgata asks the question [in paraphrase]:

> In certain sūtras, the Supramundane Victor said that the aggregates and so forth inherently exist and in some said that they are without inherent existence. In these, in consideration of what does he speak of their being natureless?

And in answer to that question, the *Sūtra Unraveling the Thought* (*Emptiness in Mind-Only,* 82-83) says:

> Paramārthasamudgata, thinking of three non-natures of phenomena—character-non-nature, production-non-nature, and ultimate-non-nature—I taught [in the middle wheel of the teaching], "All phenomena are natureless."

Ke-drup seems to be specifically tying his explanation to the brief indication since the brief indications is all that he cites. As Jik-may-dam-chö-gya-tso says, his explanation should be viewed as not limited to the brief indication.

[a] Second Dalai Lama's *Lamp Illuminating the Meaning of [D̄zong-ka-b̄a's] Thought,* 14.1. Gung-tang does not mention that Jam-ȳang-shay-b̄a in his *Brief Decisive Analysis* (495.1) gives the same rendition of the meaning of Buddha's brief indication but later (496.5) specifies that such is not explicitly indicated for the reason given below. L̄o-sang-trin-lay-ye-s̄hay (*Summarized Meaning,* 3a.1) also includes the three illustrations (imputational, other-powered, and thoroughly established natures) in the brief indication. Similarly, D̄a-drin-rap-d̄en (*Annotations,* 12.1) adds—to the brief indication—the three natures in parentheses. Paṇ-chen S̄ö-nam-drak-b̄a (*Garland of Blue Lotuses,* 14a.2-14a.6) gives a general exposition that does not consider the issue of whether the three natures are explicitly indicated in the brief indication; however, he (13b.2-13b.5) makes the distinction that the brief indication implicitly (*don gyis*) indicates the reasons for the three non-natures (for example, that imputational natures are characters posited by names and terminology and do not subsist by way of their own character) and thus it does indicate them even if not explicitly. He makes the cogent point that the extensive explanation extensively explains just what the brief indication implicitly indicates. Based on his own reasoning, it would have been consistent for him to make the similar distinction that the brief indication does not explicitly indicate illustrations (that is, the three natures) of the three non-natures. Perhaps he did not do so in order to defend D̄zong-ka-b̄a's citation of the passages from Asaṅga and Vasubandhu at this seemingly inappropriate juncture. For the same reason, he may be saying that what the extensive explanation explicitly indicates that was not explicitly indicated in the brief indication is not illustrations of the three non-natures but the reasons for the three non-natures; however, such a move would be lame since it is obvious that the brief indication does not explicitly indicate either illustrations of or reasons for the three non-natures.

thoroughly established natures are ultimate-non-natures. As stated above, if in the brief indication the three natures were explicitly associated with the three non-natures, there would absurdly be no need in the following extensive explanation rhetorically to inquire for illustrations, since they already would have been given. Framed in a less polite way, Gung-tang's point is simply that the Second Dalai Lama mis-spoke; apologetic here is actually deferential criticism.

Issue #62: But why *does Ḏzong-ka-ḇa associate the three natures and the three non-natures here?*

That is all Gung-tang could do for the Second Dalai Lama, but he evidently felt that Gung-ru Chö-jung and Jam-ȳang-shay-ḇa had not done enough to explain Ḏzong-ka-ḇa's untimely citation of Vasubandhu which, as Jam-ȳang-shay-ḇa left it, would amount to mere apologetic. Rather, why would Ḏzong-ka-ḇa want to emphasize **at this point** that both the *Sūtra Unraveling the Thought* and Indian treatises clearly say that the basis in Buddha's thought—when he said in the Perfection of Wisdom Sūtras that all phenomena are natureless—is the three non-natures? Gung-tang[193] makes the case that Ḏzong-ka-ḇa's back-to-back citations of Asaṅga's *Compendium of Ascertainments* and Vasubandhu's *The Thirty* connects forward to his criticism of the Jo-nang-ḇas that immediately follows those citations.

Gung-tang counters the ascription of the fault of redundancy, a literary faux pas, with a literary analysis through pointing to the connectedness of those two citations, not with the brief indication that precedes them but with the material that **follows** the citations—criticism of the Jo-nang-ḇas. Gung-tang aptly exposes the context of Ḏzong-ka-ḇa's citations of the two Indian texts: Ḏzong-ka-ḇa is intent on exposing what he saw as a fallacy in the Jo-nang-ḇa system. Let us turn to that.

Issue #63: What is the Jo-nang-ḇa view that Ḏzong-ka-ḇa is opposing?

The Jo-nang-ḇas, following Döl-ḇo-ḇa Shay-rap-gyel-tsen,[a] hold that the final meaning of the Perfection of Wisdom Sūtras is the Great Middle Way. Thus, according to them:

---

[a] *dol po pa shes rab rgyal mtshan*, 1292-1361. See *Blue Annals*, 775ff. Ḡön-chok-jik-may-ẉang-ḇo says that the Indian source of the Jo-nang-ḇa view is the *Conquest Over Objections about the Three Mother Scriptures* (*'phags pa shes rab kyi pha rol tu phyin pa 'bum pa dang nyi khri lnga stong pa dang khri brgyad stong pa'i rgya cher bshad pa, āryaśatasāhasrikāpañcaviṃśatisāhasrikā-aṣṭadaśasāhasrikāprajñāpāramitābṛhaṭṭīkā*; Peking 5206, vol. 93) which is said to be by Vasubandhu but Ḏzong-ka-ḇa (*Emptiness in Mind-Only*, 232-233) holds is by Damṣhṭasena. For more on the Jo-nang-ḇa view, see *Reflections on Reality*, chapters 16-17d.

- the ultimate is indeed taught in the Perfection of Wisdom Sūtras for those who can see it (much as D̄zong-ka-b̄a holds that, according to the Mind-Only School, sharp Bodhisattvas understand the three natures and three non-natures from the literal statement in the Perfection of Wisdom Sūtras that all phenomena are natureless)
- but the non-empty, the thoroughly established nature, is, on the surface, taught to be self-empty.

Döl-b̄o-b̄a's view is that the statements in the Perfection of Wisdom Sūtras that all phenomena are natureless are in consideration of all **conventional** phenomena and not in consideration also of the ultimate, which does have nature, that is, does ultimately exist.

This position seems to fly in the face of what is clearly said in the *Sūtra Unraveling the Thought*, for, when Paramārthasamudgata (*Emptiness in Mind-Only*, 77-78) asks his question, he says:

> Therefore, I am wondering of what the Supramundane Victor was thinking when he said [in the middle wheel of the teaching], "**All phenomena** are natureless; **all phenomena** are unproduced, unceasing, quiescent from the start, and naturally thoroughly passed beyond sorrow." I [explicitly] ask the Supramundane Victor about the meaning of his saying [in the middle wheel of the teaching], "**All phenomena** are natureless; **all phenomena** are unproduced, unceasing, quiescent from the start, and naturally thoroughly passed beyond sorrow."

Also, when Buddha (*Emptiness in Mind-Only*, 82-83) answers, he says:

> Paramārthasamudgata, thinking of three non-natures of phenomena—character-non-nature, production-non-nature, and ultimate-non-nature—I taught [in the middle wheel of the teaching], "**All phenomena** are natureless."

Although the Jo-nang-b̄as would admit that the Perfection of Wisdom Sūtras merely have the words "all phenomena," they hold that such must be interpreted as referring to "all **conventional** phenomena."[a] According to the Jo-nang-b̄as, the entities of conventional phenomena are empty of ultimate establishment and thus are **self**-empty, but the ultimate is **other**-empty in that its own ultimately established entity is empty of conventional phenomena, in the sense that it is not any conventional phenomenon (which are **other** than it).

Gung-tang says that in order to indicate that the Jo-nang-b̄as' system of explanation is unjustified, D̄zong-ka-b̄a cites these passages from Asaṅga and

[a] Thereby, according to Jam-ȳang-shay-b̄a (*Great Exposition of the Interpretable and the Definitive*, 45.6-46.3; also W̄el-mang Ḡön-chok-gyel-tsen's *Notes on [Ḡön-chok-jik-may-w̄ang-b̄o's] Lectures*, 399.1-399.3), the Jo-nang-b̄as could be accused of taking the basis in Buddha's thought to be conventional phenomena, not the three non-natures.

Vasubandhu in which it is clear that these Indian scholars, who are prime sources for the assertions of the Mind-Only School, did not put forward such a system but left the words of sūtra as they are. Gung-tang's commentary is profoundly contextual, going far beyond apologetic. As Ḏzong-ka-ḇa (*Emptiness in Mind-Only,* 83) says immediately after those two citations:

> Hence [it is contradictory for some, namely, Döl-ḇo-ḇa and others] to explain that the statements in the Perfection of Wisdom Sūtras, and so forth, that all phenomena are natureless are in consideration [only] of all conventional phenomena [which, according to them, are self-empty in the sense of being empty of their own true establishment] but do not refer to the ultimate [which, they say, is itself truly established and empty of being any conventional phenomenon]. They thereby contradict the *Sūtra Unraveling the Thought* as well as the texts of Asaṅga and his brother [Vasubandhu] and are also outside the system of the Superior father [Nāgārjuna], his spiritual sons, and so forth.

Ḇel-jor-hlün-drup[194] reframes Ḏzong-ka-ḇa's statement (including a section to be cited below) in syllogistic form:

> Someone's [that is, the Jo-nang-ḇas'] saying, "The teaching in the Perfection of Wisdom Sūtras that all phenomena are natureless [was given by Buddha] thinking of all conventional phenomena and not thinking of ultimate phenomena, because ultimate truths are truly established," is not reasonable because:
>
> - it is outside of the systems of the *Sūtra Unraveling the Thought,* of Asaṅga and his brother [Vasubandhu], and of Nāgārjuna and his [spiritual] sons
> - the Perfection of Wisdom Sūtras teach that each and every phenomenon, from forms through to omniscient consciousnesses, is natureless
> - the Perfection of Wisdom Sūtras, in particular, teach individually that the sixteen emptinesses, thusness, and so forth do not exist ultimately
> - and emptiness and thusness are ultimate truths.

That the Jo-nang-ḇas have passed outside of Nāgārjuna's system refers to Nāgārjuna's statements that apprehending emptiness to be truly established is an irredeemable view and the like. As Nāgārjuna's *Fundamental Text Called "Wisdom"* says:[195]

> Since the compounded are thoroughly not established [inherently],
> How could the uncompounded be established [inherently]?

Also:

Whoever view emptiness [as inherently existent]
Are said to be impossible to help.

Also, Nāgārjuna's *Supramundane Praise*[196] says:

Because of abandoning all [false] conceptuality
Emptiness is taught as the ambrosia.
Therefore, whoever adheres to it [as inherently existent]
You [Buddha] thoroughly deride.

It is axiomatic for D̄zong-ka-b̄a that whoever is a proponent of Great Vehicle tenets must accord with either of two great openers of the chariot-ways of the Great Vehicle, Nāgārjuna or Asaṅga, and it has already been established that the Jo-nang-b̄as do not, on this point, accord with Asaṅga and his half-brother Vasubandhu, and when they also do not accord with Nāgārjuna, they are shown to be outside the sphere of Great Vehicle schools. Thus, according to Gung-tang,[197] although the Jo-nang-b̄as are attempting a synthesis of the thought of all Great Vehicle Schools in a Great Middle Way, they have turned away from all of them.[a]

---

[a] Jik-may-dam-chö-gya-tso (*Port of Entry,* 169.3-169.5) points out that according to the Jo-nang-b̄as:

- Asaṅga in his *Compendium of Ascertainments* and Vasubandhu in his *The Thirty* set forth the view of the Mind-Only School,
- whereas Asaṅga in his *Commentary on (Maitreya's) "Sublime Continuum"* and Vasubandhu in his *Conquest Over Objections about the Three Mother Scriptures* teach their own actual view of the Great Middle Way, the view of other-emptiness.

(It will be remembered that D̄zong-ka-b̄a holds that Damṣhṭasena, not Vasubandhu, composed the *Conquest Over Objections about the Three Mother Scriptures* (see *Emptiness in Mind-Only,* 225ff.). Also, it is a standard Ge-luk-b̄a position that in his *Commentary on (Maitreya's) "Sublime Continuum"* Asaṅga does indeed present his own actual view which is different from that of the Mind-Only School but is consistent with what D̄zong-ka-b̄a considers to be the view of the Consequence School.) Jik-may-dam-chö-gya-tso draws his readers' attention to the fact that much reflection is required to delineate just how the Jo-nang-b̄as contradict the thought of these texts. Unfortunately, he says no more.

Nevertheless, Jik-may-dam-chö-gya-tso seems unaware that the prime Jo-nang-b̄a, Döl-b̄o-b̄a S̄hay-rap-gyel-tsen, holds that Asaṅga in his *Compendium of Ascertainments,* which is included in the *Grounds of Yogic Practice,* and Vasubandhu in his *The Thirty* evince the view of the Great Middle Way. Döl-b̄o-b̄a's *Ocean of Definitive Meaning* (222.5/110a.6) says:

Although the profound sūtras of the third wheel such as the *Sūtra Unraveling the Thought* and so forth, Maitreya's *Ornament for the Great Vehicle Sūtras, Differentiation of the Middle and the Extremes,* and so forth, and Asaṅga's *Grounds of Yogic Practice, Summary of the Great Vehicle, Summary of Manifest Knowledge,* and so forth temporarily teach mind-only, you should not deprecate their final teachings of the Great Middle that pass far beyond this and are one in meaning with Secret Mantra.

Objection: Through the very name "*Grounds of Yogic Practice*" itself, it is

D̄zong-ka-b̄a himself (*Emptiness in Mind-Only,* 84-85) says:

It is thus: [When Paramārthasamudgata] asks about that in consideration of which [Buddha] spoke of non-nature, he is asking (1) about what [Buddha] was thinking when he taught non-nature and (2) about the modes of non-nature. Also, the answer indicates those two respectively. From between those two, let us explain the first [that is, what Buddha had as the basis in his thought when in the Perfection of Wisdom Sūtras he taught that all phenomena are natureless. There, Buddha] said that the limitless divisions of instances of phenomena ranging from forms through to exalted knowers-of-all-aspects have no nature or inherent nature. These phenomena are included in the three non-natures [that is, three natures[a]—imputational, other-powered,

established as mind-only.

Answer: In that case, it would [absurdly] follow that Āryadeva's *Four Hundred Stanzas on Yogic Practice* also would be a text of mind-only.

See and realize that in Asaṅga's *Compendium of Bases* he again and again speaks of the middle devoid of extremes:

> the middle path of the selflessness of persons, and the selflessness of phenomena, and the middle path that has thoroughly abandoned the two extremes—having abandoned the extreme of superimposition and having abandoned the extreme of deprecation.

and so forth.

Also, although Vasubandhu's *The Thirty* is renowned to be a text of mind-only, in the end it speaks of what has passed beyond cognition-only. Right after saying:

> When apprehensions of consciousness
> Are not apprehended, then
> One abides in cognition-only.

it says:

> Due to the non-existence of the apprehended, the apprehender does not exist.
> That is no-mind, non-apprehension.
> This supramundane exalted wisdom
> Has been transformed
> Through having abandoned the two assumptions of bad states.
>
> Just that is the uncontaminated element of attributes,
> Inconceivable element of attributes, virtue, and stability.
> This is bliss, the body of release,
> The attributes of a great subduer.

Here also the statement of "no-mind, non-apprehension" contradicts the assertion by Proponents of Mind-Only that mind, consciousness, ultimately exists.

[a] It is noteworthy that D̄zong-ka-b̄a uses the term "three non-natures" (*ngo bo nyid med pa gsum*) when the term "three natures" (*ngo bo nyid gsum*) would have been more appropriate; indeed this is how D̄a-drin-rap-d̄en (*Annotations,* 13.4) glosses the term. D̄zong-ka-b̄a's

> and thoroughly established natures].[a] Thinking that when it is explained how those are natureless, it is easy to understand [the individual modes of thought that were behind his statement in the Perfection of Wisdom Sūtras], he included [all phenomena] into the three non-natures [that is, three natures. For] all ultimate and conventional phenomena are included within those three. Also, with respect to the need for [Buddha's] doing thus, in the Mother Sūtras [that is, the Perfection of Wisdom Sūtras] and so forth, all phenomena—the five aggregates, the eighteen constituents, and the twelve sense-spheres—are described as without thingness, without an inherent nature, and natureless. In particular, mentioning all the terminological variants of the ultimate—emptiness, the element of attributes, thusness, and so forth—he said that these are natureless. Therefore, who with a mind would propound that the ultimate is not among the phenomena about which it is said that phenomena are natureless!

Gung-tang[198] rephrases D̄zong-ka-b̄a's argument against the Jo-nang-b̄as on this topic such that the points are made more clearly:

> Thus, on this occasion of a question and answer in the *Sūtra Unraveling the Thought*, the basis in [Buddha's] thought [when he said in the Perfection of Wisdom Sūtras that all phenomena are natureless] is interpreted within including **all phenomena of the two truths** [that is, conventional and ultimate truths] in the three natures. Also, in the root texts, the Perfection of Wisdom Sūtras themselves, the one hundred and eight bases of exposition [which include the eighteen emptinesses] are individually mentioned as being natureless, and in particular all synonyms of emptiness [such as signlessness, wishlessness, suchness, and so forth][199] are mentioned and said to be natureless. This being the case, it is not possible that even one with ears that hear words—never mind one with a mind analyzing the meaning—could say that the ultimate is not among the phenomena that those [Perfection of Wisdom Sūtras] say are natureless!

Gung-tang's commentary is brilliant, elegantly showing that D̄zong-ka-b̄a's citation of these two texts is to be understood within the context of his immediate criticism of the Jo-nang-b̄as.

---

usage of "non-natures" suggests that for him the individual three non-natures and the three natures are equivalent (see issue #101), as long as the **actual** ultimate-non-nature is restricted to thoroughly established natures (see issues #147, 148). To me, it indeed is the case.

[a] See issues #73, 72, 101.

Issue #64: Do the Jo-nang-b̄as hold that the middle wheel teaches the actual ultimate?

Still, D̄zong-ka-b̄a's point cannot be simply that the Jo-nang-b̄as failed to notice that in the Perfection of Wisdom Sūtras emptiness is said to be natureless, that is to say, without ultimate establishment, for such is indeed said over and over again. A-ku L̄o-drö-gya-tso's *Precious Lamp,* therefore, takes the explication a step further, spelling out the situation in creatively illuminating detail:[200]

> The middle wheel of the teaching—the Perfection of Wisdom Sūtras—explains that all phenomena, without any distinction, do not truly exist and hence explains that the mere negation of true establishment in conventional phenomena is the ultimate truth. For the Jo-nang-b̄as, those sūtras require interpretation because, according to them, the basis in Buddha's thought is a mere non-affirming negative, an annihilatory emptiness of true establishment in conventional phenomena. This annihilatory emptiness, they say, is not the actual ultimate [and thus although the Perfection of Wisdom Sūtras speak of an ultimate, it is not the ultimate]. As the ultimate, they posit the Buddha nature, which is called "the matrix-of-one-gone-thus"[a] and which is taught in the ten renowned sūtras[b] on that topic and so forth in the

[a] *de bzhin gshegs pa'i snying po, tathāgatagarbha.*

[b] The ten sūtras on the matrix-of-one-gone-thus are:

1. *Matrix-of-One-Gone-Thus Sūtra*
2. *Questions of King Dhāraṇīshvara Sūtra,* also known as *Teaching the Great Compassion of a One-Gone-Thus Sūtra*
3. *Mahāparinirvāṇa Sūtra*
4. *Angulimāla Sūtra*
5. *Lion's Roar of Shrīmālādevī Sūtra*
6. *Ornament Illuminating Exalted Wisdom Sūtra*
7. *Sūtra Teaching Non-Diminishment and Non-Increase*
8. *Great Drum Sūtra*
9. *Retention for Entering into the Non-Conceptual*
10. *Sūtra Unraveling the Thought*

See Ferdinand D. Lessing and Alex Wayman, *Mkhas Grub Rje's Fundamentals of the Buddhist Tantras* (The Hague: Mouton, 1968; reprint, Delhi: Motilal Banarsidass, 1978), 48-51. Döl-b̄o-b̄a's *Ocean of Definitive Meaning* quotes many other sūtras and does not mention a list of ten.

Ge-luk-b̄a scholars hold that there is a difference between the ten sūtras of the matrix-of-one-gone-thus and the *Sūtra of the Matrix-of-One-Gone-Thus* that Buddha himself cites in the *Descent into Laṅkā Sūtra* as requiring interpretation, since the latter speaks of a matrix endowed with ultimate Buddha qualities of exalted body, speech, and mind already present in the continuums of sentient beings. According to Ge-luk-b̄a scholars' presentation of the Consequence School, the ten sūtras are actually sūtras concordant with the middle wheel of doctrine and hence definitive because these sūtras teach one final vehicle and teach that all

final, third wheel of doctrine, not the second. The matrix-of-one-gone-thus has many qualities:

> It is the great other-emptiness, a Buddha having the essence of the Form Bodies of the five Conquerors, and so forth. It is a body of empty form, which an exalted uncontaminated wisdom—existing intrinsically in the continuums of all sentient beings—takes as the object of its mode of apprehension. It is both permanent and an effective thing. It is an other-emptiness in that it is empty of all conventional phenomena, these being other than the ultimate. It is truly established, and it is autonomous, positive.

This positive matrix-of-one-gone-thus, present in all sentient beings, is what the Jo-nang-b̄as take to be the ultimate truth, and thus from this viewpoint they say that the ultimate is not explicitly taught in the middle wheel of doctrine, even if emptiness and so forth are mentioned extensively and even called the ultimate. Hence, D̄zong-ka-b̄a's criticism of the Jo-nang-b̄as for contradicting the *Sūtra Unraveling the Thought* and the great Indian masters depends upon his own identification that (1) none of these sūtras or masters teach any other ultimate than an emptiness that is a mere negation and (2) the doctrine of emptiness is not surpassed by another doctrine in the third wheel of the teaching.

I find A-ku L̄o-drö-gya-tso's presentation to be remarkably straightforward, penetrating to the heart of what D̄zong-ka-b̄a likely meant (or should have meant) when he said that, for the Jo-nang-b̄as, the ultimate is not among the phenomena said in the Perfection of Wisdom Sūtras to be natureless, that is, without true establishment.

A-ku L̄o-drö-gya-tso[201] refutes the Jo-nang-b̄a position as Gung-tang did above and concludes that it is not even the secondary thought of any Great Vehicle text. He says that the Jo-nang-b̄a ultimate resembles the non-Buddhist assertion of a permanent, unitary, and autonomous self and is a deceptive doctrine that misleads trainees who have faith in the Great Vehicle but whose

---

phenomena are without true establishment. Thus, they also assert that the thought of the ten sūtras is Consequentialist and that Asaṅga's commentary on Maitreya's *Great Vehicle Treatise on the Sublime Continuum* is Consequentialist, not Mind-Only.

As A-ku L̄o-drö-gya-tso (*Precious Lamp*, 169.1, 170.2) puts it, both the Jo-nang-b̄as and Bu-d̄ön have as the source of their confusion the notion that the matrix-of-one-gone-thus and the matrix endowed with ultimate Buddha qualities—called the permanent, stable matrix-of-one-gone-thus (*rtag brtan snying po*)—are the same. For Ge-luk-b̄a scholars, the ten sūtras of the matrix-of-one-gone-thus do not teach this latter type of Buddha-nature which is taught in a separate sūtra that is known in Tibet only through the mention of it in the *Descent into Laṅkā Sūtra.*

mental continuums have not yet matured. He admits that Jo-nang Döl-b̄o-b̄a S̄hay-rap-gyel-tsen's *Mountain Doctrine, Ocean of Definitive Meaning*[a] "establishes" the qualities of the ultimate through citing many sūtras and treatises but says that, like the eighty sūtra sources that the eighth-century Chinese Hva-shang cited to prove that nothing is to be taken to mind, "None of these is seen as something that causes one to think that it approaches the class of a proof." He chillingly warns that since there are many Jo-nang-b̄a transmissions of initiations and permission rites, his readers need to know that they are not allowed to use them in accordance with the Jo-nang-b̄a commentaries. It is clear that, after the Fifth Dalai Lama's destruction of the central Jo-nang-b̄a establishment, many Ge-luk-b̄as sought to eradicate its influence.[b]

Issue #65: Do the Jo-nang-b̄as actually hold that the primordial wisdom consciousness is both permanent and an effective thing?

A basic Ge-luk-b̄a complaint against the assertion of such an ultimate is that since the matrix-of-one-gone-thus, as the Jo-nang-b̄as assert it, is a wisdom, it must be an effective thing that is produced by causes, whereas the Jo-nang-b̄as assert it to be permanent and thus, for Ge-luk-b̄as, unable to perform functions such as creating effects.[c] As Gung-tang[202] points out, similar assertions by the Sāṃkhyas and Mīmāṃsakas are refuted by Dharmakīrti and Dignāga, and since the Jo-nang-b̄as hold that the view of Dharmakīrti's *Commentary on (Dignāga's) "Compilation of Prime Cognition"* is that of the Great Middle Way of Asaṅga and Vasubandhu, they are caught in self-contradiction when they assert just what Dharmakīrti refutes.

Although no one questions whether Döl-b̄o-b̄a S̄hay-rap-gyel-tsen asserts uncompounded exalted wisdom for indeed he repeatedly does so, it needs to be asked whether he holds primordial, uncompounded exalted wisdom—which is the thoroughly established nature and the matrix-of-one-gone-thus—to be both permanent and an effective thing or whether this is a position forced on him from a Ge-luk-b̄a perspective. Gung-tang clearly holds that it is the former, for he[203] feels it necessary to explain away a statement by D̄zong-ka-b̄a's student Ke-drup that seems to depict the Jo-nang-b̄as as holding that the matrix-of-one-

a *ri chos nges don rgya mtsho.*

b The survival of many Jo-nang-b̄a monasteries in eastern Tibet including one in Labrang near Jam-ȳang-shay-b̄a's D̄ra-s̄hi-kyil Monastic University are notable exceptions.

c W̄el-mang Ḡön-chok-gyel-tsen's *Notes on (Ḡön-chok-jik-may-w̄ang-b̄o's) Lectures* (400.1-400.2) reports that Ke-drup in his commentary on Dharmakīrti's *Commentary on (Dignāga's) "Compilation of Prime Cognition"* refutes S̄hay-rap-gyel-tsen's assertion of a truly established, **permanent** non-dualistic exalted wisdom through questioning whether it performs the activity of apprehending an object, whether it has the capacity to do so, and so forth, since if it performs such activities, it must be impermanent.

gone-thus is a non-effective entity. Ke-drup's *Opening the Eyes of the Fortunate* says:

> They hold that these texts teach an other-emptiness in which just the matrix-of-one-gone-to-bliss—**a non-effective entity**—is empty of the collections of compounded, other-powered, effective things.

Gung-tang explains that Ke-drup is thinking either that:

- In general—that is, in fact—the matrix-of-one-gone-thus is a non-effective entity.
- Or, although the Jo-nang-b̄as assert it to be an effective thing, they assert it to be uncompounded, in which case it does not have the meaning of being an effective thing.

However, Jik-may-dam-chö-gya-tso[204] cogently argues that, even though the Jo-nang-b̄as assert that the thoroughly established nature is an uncontaminated primordial wisdom, it is not necessary that they **explicitly**[a] assert that it is an effective thing. For the Jo-nang-b̄as maintain that:[205]

1. The thoroughly established nature is an uncompounded primordial wisdom that is the basis-of-all in that it serves as the basis of all the qualities of a Buddha.
2. It is an actual uncompounded mind and an actual permanent exalted wisdom and not established as an effective thing (that is to say, is not produced by causes and conditions and does not produce effects).
3. Although it is not an effective thing, it is endowed with color and shape, and although it is a wisdom, it is established as the meditatively appearing forms of smoke and so forth (described in the Kālachakra system).[b]
4. These facts would be contradictory in compounded conventionalities, but are not contradictory in an uncompounded ultimate.

Jik-may-dam-chö-gya-tso calls for more analysis of the Jo-nang-b̄as' own texts.

Indeed, analysis of Döl-b̄o-b̄a S̄hay-rap-gyel-tsen's *Ocean of Definitive Meaning* shows that even though he uses the term *dngos po* (*bhāva*), often translated as "effective thing" or "functioning thing," with respect to the ultimate, the matrix-of-one-gone-thus, uncompounded exalted wisdom (as

---

[a] His depiction of the Jo-nang-b̄as as not openly asserting that the primordial exalted wisdom, or matrix-of-one-gone-thus, is an effective thing rings true to similar presentations by the N̄ying-ma-b̄a scholar Mi-pam-gya-tso (1846-1912) in his *Three Cycles on Fundamental Mind,* in which he repeatedly says that fundamental mind is uncompounded.

[b] These are the ten signs of smoke, mirage, fireflies, butter lamp, blazing, moon, sun, rāhu, lightning, and drop. As the Fourteenth Dalai Lama says, "Gradually, the empty forms become more and more subtle to the point where finally a Buddha's Complete Enjoyment Body dawns." See H.H. the Dalai Lama, Tenzin Gyatso, and Jeffrey Hopkins, *The Kālachakra Tantra: Rite of Initiation* (London: Wisdom, 1985; 2d rev. ed. 1989), 278.

opposed to other-arisen, compounded exalted wisdom that arises from cultivating the path), nowhere does he suggest that the term in this context connotes being produced by causes and conditions or producing effects. Rather, it appears to mean "actuality" much like the Ge-luk-b̄a distinction that when the term *dngos po* (*bhāva*) is used loosely, as it sometimes is in Perfection of Wisdom Sūtras, it refers to what exists and hence merely means "actuality" and not effective thing. As Döl-b̄o-b̄a says:[206]

> *Objection:* The basic element of selfhood, the great self, the pure self, and so forth do not at all exist, because self does not at all exist.
>
> *Answer:* In that case, the self of thusness, the pure self also would not exist. Likewise, these also would not exist: the vajra-self born from the vajra; the sole, obstructive,[a] solid[b] vajra self; the supreme self of knowledge and objects of knowledge; the unfluctuating very pure self; the supreme **actuality**[c] that is the self of all buddhas; the self of transmigrating beings as soon as born; spatial over-self[d] displaying variously; self of all the worldly lords; pervasive self supreme of all jewels; pervasive self with committed mind and committed word; great pervasive self jeweled umbrella; supreme over-self of all continua; awakened self very awakened; and pure self of the afflicted constituents.

In another instance, Döl-b̄o-b̄a uses the term for a status of objects that is not asserted:

> The import of Nāgārjuna's *Refutation of Objections:*[207]
>
> If I had any thesis,
> Then I would have that fault [of contradicting my own thesis
> that there is no inherent existence].
> Because I have no thesis,
> I am only faultless.
>
> and of Āryadeva's *Four Hundred:*[208]
>
> Even over a long period of time
> Censure cannot be expressed
> For one who has no position of existence,
> Non-existence, or existence and non-existence.
>
> also is non-conceptual freedom from proliferations in meditative equipoise and the absence of assertions subsequent to meditative equipoise that do not accord with the fact, such as asserting **actualities**.[e]

---

a *sra.*

b *mkhregs.*

c *dngos po mchog.*

d *nam mkha'i bdag po.*

e *dngos po.*

The state of meditative equipoise is totally free from assertion, whereas the state outside of meditative equipoise, despite calling for assertions, does not allow for positions contrary to the fact, such as truly existent compounded phenomena.

In other cases, the term has other common meanings; he cites Kalki Puṇḍarīka's *Stainless Light,* where it means "topic" or simply "thing":[209]

> Yogis do not act in nominal conceptions with regard to the teaching of one **actuality**[a] through a variety of names. This comes from just depending on reliance on the meaning, upon having thoroughly analyzed well by means of the quintessential instructions of a holy guru, as one would do with gold.

He cites the *Mahāparinirvāṇa Sūtra* where it means "features":[210]

> In this way, the buddha-nature has seven **actualities**[b]: permanence, self, bliss, thorough purity, reality, truth, and virtue.

Therefore, it is clear to me that Döl-b̄o-b̄a S̄hay-rap-gyel-tsen does not openly assert that the matrix-of-one-gone-thus or any of its synonyms is an effective thing. Rather, the Ge-luk-b̄a accusation that the Jo-nang-b̄as do so is based on an extrapolation that these Buddha qualities such as physical marks and wisdom that subsist in the matrix-of-one-gone-thus would have to be impermanent, and thus the ultimate truth, as described by S̄hay-rap-gyel-tsen, has to be able to impinge on, not just appear to, consciousness, producing awarenesses the way blue or yellow contribute to the engendering of an eye consciousness. In that case, the permanent matrix-of-one-gone-thus would be an effective thing that produces effects.[c]

---

a *dngos po.*

b *dngos po rnam pa bdun.*

c For an extended discussion, see *Reflections on Reality,* 316-323.

11. Other-Powered Natures

Overview of Other-Powered Natures

Definition of an other-powered nature:[211] that which arises through the power of other causes and conditions.[a]

Divisions: Pure other-powered natures and impure other-powered natures.

Etymology: They are called other-powered because of being produced from their own respective predispositions or being produced through the power of other causes and conditions. And they are called other-powered because they do not have the power to remain more than an instant upon having been produced.[b]

Production-Non-Nature

Issue #66: What is the nature of production that other-powered natures lack?

The *Sūtra Unraveling the Thought* (*Emptiness in Mind-Only,* 87) says:[212]

> What are production-non-natures of phenomena?[c] Those which are the other-powered characters of phenomena.
>
> Why? It is thus: Those [other-powered characters] arise through the force of other conditions and not by themselves.[d] Therefore, they are said to be "production-non-natures."

Dzong-ka-ba's *The Essence of Eloquence* (*Emptiness in Mind-Only,* 87-88) says:[e]

---

[a] *rgyu rkyen gzhan gyi dbang gis byung ba de.*

[b] *rang rang gi bag chags las skyes pa'am rgyu rkyen gzhan gyi dbang gis skyes pas na gzhan dbang dang skyes nas skad cig las lhag par rang nyid gnas pa'i dbang med pas na bzhag dbang.*

[c] See issues #76, 77. About "phenomena," see issue #71.

[d] See issue #67.

[e] Jik-may-dam-chö-gya-tso (*Port of Entry,* 179.2) cites Wonch'uk's *Extensive Commentary* (Peking 5517, vol. 116, 131.2.1) to support the point that Dzong-ka-ba is making. Wonch'uk says:

> [That other-powered natures arise] "not by themselves" indicates [their] naturelessness. They are said to be produced due to causes and conditions that depend on other phenomena.

Later, Jik-may-dam-chö-gya-tso (181.5) points out that (in the next sentence) Wonch'uk identifies the production that other-powered natures lack as being their arising from Īshvara

The nature of production, or intrinsic production, that other-powered natures do not have is production by themselves, since it says, "not by themselves." That is production under their own power; it is as Asaṅga's *Compendium of Ascertainments* says:

> Because compositional phenomena are dependent-arisings, they are produced through the power of conditions and not by themselves. This is called "production-non-nature."

Jam-ȳang-shay-b̄a[213] structures Asaṅga's statement in syllogistic form:

> The subjects, compositional phenomena, are without a nature of [self-] production because of not being produced through their own power and being produced through the power of their own causes and conditions, for they are dependent-arisings.

It is in this sense that other-powered natures are said to be production-non-natures.

Issue #67: Why would anyone think that the nature in terms of production that other-powered natures lack is "production from other-powered natures"?

Gung-tang[214] points out that the misunderstanding that the nature in terms of production that other-powered natures lack is "production from other-powered natures" is based on the *Sūtra Unraveling the Thought* itself where it says, "not by **themselves.** Therefore, they are said to be 'production-non-natures.'" It does indeed seem that "themselves" cannot mean anything but "other-powered natures," and thus the production that other-powered natures lack would seem to be production from other-powered natures. Also, Asaṅga's *Compendium of Ascertainments* similarly speaks of other-powered natures being produced "not by themselves." What could "themselves" mean except other-powered natures? Also, even D̄zong-ka-b̄a says, "The nature of production, or intrinsic production, that other-powered natures do not have is production by **themselves**, since [the sūtra] says, 'not by **themselves**.'"

---

and so forth (*dbang phyug la sogs pa las byung ba ma yin pas skye ba med pa zhes bya'o*), this being production from a discordant cause. He says that this is indeed difficult to assert, his reason no doubt being that D̄zong-ka-b̄a clearly does not explain that the type of production that other-powered natures do not have is production from a god such as Īshvara. Rather, D̄zong-ka-b̄a's followers explain D̄zong-ka-b̄a's meaning two ways—that other-powered natures lack causeless production or that they lack production from causes that are the same entities as themselves. Given the discrepancy between Wonch'uk's and D̄zong-ka-b̄a's readings, which Jik-may-dam-chö-gya-tso himself recognizes, it seems unsuitable for him to cite Wonch'uk here out of context, even if the bare words do accord with D̄zong-ka-b̄a's opinion.

Gung-tang[215] explains that the point of these passages is not at all that other-powered natures are not produced from other-powered natures. When the grammar is properly understood, these passages do not speak of "non-production **from** themselves"[a] or "non-production **from** self";[b] rather, they speak of "non-production **by** themselves"[c] and "non-self-production."[d] These terms refer to production of something under its own power within not relying on whether its causes and conditions are present; this is also called arbitrary, or capricious, production[e] and self-production (but not meaning "production from self"). Gung-tang[216] gives an example: If it is the case that one should be led by another to a king's palace, but, instead, one enters without being led by another, this is called "entering under one's own power" or "self-entry." "Self-production," similarly, does not mean production of something from itself but production under its own power.

Thus, the self-production that other-powered natures lack is causeless production, like that asserted by the Nihilists. In the presentation of four alternative types of production—production from self, production from other, production from both self and other, and causeless production—this is the last.

Issue #68: Could the nature of production that other-powered natures lack be production from self?

Certain Tibetan scholars, however, have taken "self-production" or "intrinsic production" (or, more literally, "production by way of its own entity"[f]) to be "production from self," as is asserted by the non-Buddhist Sāṃkhyas, this being the first of the four alternative types of production, but, according to Gung-tang, they have not even understood what production from self means. For they feel that "production from self" means the production of other-powered

a *bdag nyid las mi skye ba.* The Sanskrit for "production *from* themselves" (*bdag nyid las skye ba*) and for "production *by* themselves" (*bdag nyid kyis skye ba*) would seem to be the same, that is, *na svatas.* Lamotte's rendition of the Sanskrit (p. 68.5, n. 1) is: *idaṃ pratyaya-balād utpannaṃ na svatas.* The choice of terms in Tibetan indicates the understanding of the translators, which does indeed seem to be as Gung-tang says. However, Jik-may-dam-chö-gya-tso (*Port of Entry,* 180.3) points out that the distinction should not be made just on linguistic grounds, for then Ke-drup would be at fault in his *Opening the Eyes of the Fortunate* for saying, "Other-powered natures are called 'production-non-natures' because they must be produced within reliance on other causes and conditions and are not produced **from** their own natures or are not produced **from** their own essence" (*rang gi ngo bo nyid* ***las*** *skye ba'am/ rang gi bdag nyid* ***las*** *skye ba med pa'i phyir...*). The other choice would be to criticize Ke-drup for using *las* instead of *kyis.*

b *rang las mi skye ba.*

c *bdag nyid* ***kyis*** *ma yin.*

d *rang mi skye ba.*

e *'dod rgyal du skye ba,* literally "production in the manner of wish being dominant."

f *ngo bo nyid kyis skye ba.*

natures from other-powered natures, and this, if taken in its strictest reading, would mean that an other-powered nature is produced from that very same other-powered nature, such as a pot being produced from that very pot—a totally absurd position not asserted by any system. Rather, the Sāṃkhyas take "production from self" to be a type of caused production in which an effect is produced from, or manifested from, a cause that is of the same entity as itself.[a]

Like this more refined meaning of production of self, Paṇ-chen S̄ö-nam-drak-b̄a[b] takes the type of production—that other-powered natures are said here to lack—as being production from self, in the way that such is asserted by the Sāṃkhyas. His position is undoubtedly based on the fact that the *Sūtra Unraveling the Thought* says, "Those [other-powered natures] arise through the force

[a] Gung-tang (*Difficult Points,* 125.17; *Annotations,* 24.5-25.2) points out that the Proponents of the Great Exposition assert production of effects from causes that are of the same entity but that this is only in regard to simultaneous cause and effect (as in the case with minds and mental factors). The upper schools do not accept simultaneous cause and effect, but, in a pregnant aside, he says that it is nevertheless established that at the time of its causes an effect exists as the entity of its causes and that, otherwise, there would be no time when any sentient being could be established as a Buddha-entity. Even though Buddhists must assert this, he says, they do not come to have a position like that of the Sāṃkhyas, since Buddhists hold such in consideration of the fact that the effect merely is the entity of its causes at the time of its causes, whereas Sāṃkhyas hold that the very nature of the sprout that exists at the time of the sprout exists even at the time of its causes. Sāṃkhyas hold that otherwise cause and effect would be unrelated; see Hopkins, *Maps of the Profound,* 116-117.

[b] Paṇ-chen S̄ö-nam-drak-b̄a's *Garland of Blue Lotuses,* 33a.3; his position is also presented in Pa-bong-ka-b̄a's *Brief Notes on Jo-ni Paṇḍita's Lectures,* 412.2. Paṇ-chen S̄ö-nam-drak-b̄a makes the distinction that in the Mind-Only system other-powered natures are inherently produced (*rang bzhin gyis skye*) and are produced from their own side (*rang ngos nas skye ba*) but are not autonomously inherently produced (*rang dbang du rang bzhin gyis mi skye*) and are not autonomously produced (*rang dbang gis mi skye*)—the latter also being translated as "not produced through their own power." Indeed, it would be odd to hold that **other-powered** natures are produced through their **own power** (*rang dbang gis skye ba*); however, in one way it is equally odd to hold that according to the Mind-Only School other-powered natures are produced from their own side. The latter concession is made in order to maintain the Consequence School's accusation that the Proponents of Mind-Only hold that whatever exists exists from its own side, this being a distinction that is implicit in the Mind-Only School's refutation of the Consequence School's position that things are produced only conventionally.

Jay-d̄zün Chö-ḡyi-gyel-tsen (*General-Meaning Commentary,* 14b.3) takes the production that is being refuted as "autonomous production without depending upon causes and conditions," as does his predecessor B̄el-jor-hlün-drup (*Lamp for the Teaching,* 16.4) and his follower, S̄er-s̄hül L̄o-sang-pün-tsok (*Notes,* 19a.1), who specifies that the reference is to causeless production and not to production from self, even though, as he says, there are some who have taken it that way. D̄a-drin-rap-d̄en (*Annotations,* 16.6), despite being in Jay-d̄zün Chö-ḡyi-gyel-tsen's college tradition, explains that production from causes that are the same entity as the effect is being refuted; D̄a-drin-rap-d̄en probably just slipped up—I doubt that he intended to refute the author of his college's textbooks.

of **other** conditions and not by **themselves.**"[a] However, Gung-tang[217] makes the incisive point that "production from self" (which is the first of the four extreme types of production) is a type of production in reliance on causes and conditions and hence could not be the production that other-powered natures are said here to lack,[b] since this section of the *Sūtra Unraveling the Thought* emphasizes that things are not produced causelessly but rely on specific causes and conditions. The sūtra passage, cited at the beginning of the last chapter to show the purpose of teaching the other-powered nature, is particularly relevant:[218]

> Paramārthasamudgata, regarding that, I teach doctrines concerning production-non-natures to those beings who from the start have not generated roots of virtue, who have not purified the obstructions, who have not ripened their continuums, who do not have much belief, and who have not achieved the collections of merit and wisdom. These beings, having heard these doctrines, discriminate compositional phenomena which are dependent-arisings as impermanent and discriminate them as just unstable, unworthy of confidence, and as having a nature of change, whereupon they develop fear and discouragement with respect to all compositional phenomena.
>
> Having developed fear and discouragement, they turn away from ill deeds. They do not commit any ill deeds, and they resort to virtue. Due to resorting to virtue, they generate roots of virtue that were not [previously] generated, purify obstructions that were not purified, and also ripen their continuums which were not ripened. On that basis, they have much belief, and they achieve the collections of merit and wisdom.

Buddha speaks of these beginning practitioners' realization that compounded phenomena are dependent-arisings—that they are impermanent. To be compounded means to be made upon the aggregation of causes and conditions. To be a dependent-arising means to have arisen in dependence upon causes and conditions. Therefore, it is unlikely that Buddha, in teaching that other-powered natures are without a nature in terms of production explicitly seeks to counter the notion of a specific type of causation; rather, he is countering the

---

[a] *bdag nyid kyis ma yin pa, na svatas* (Lamotte 68.5, n. 1). The fact that the Tibetan is *bdag nyid kyis* ("by [their] entities") assists in the impression that the reference is to production of an effect from causes that are the same *entity* as themselves. The Sanskrit, if Lamotte is right, is more neutral.

[b] Since Gung-tang follows Jam-ȳang-shay-b̄a on this point, it is amusing that Jam-ȳang-shay-b̄a's reincarnation (who was Gung-tang's teacher), Ḡön-chok-jik-may-w̄ang-b̄o, merely indicates (without any sign of disapproval) that there are those who consider which type of production is being refuted to be a matter of choice—causeless production or production from self (*'di'i med rgyu'i skye ba la rgyu med dang/ bdag skye 'dam kha mdzad mkhan yod:* W̄el-mang Ḡön-chok-gyel-tsen's *Notes on (Ḡön-chok-jik-may-w̄ang-b̄o's) Lectures,* 401.3.

notion of just natural or self-production, causeless production, so that his listeners will pay attention to causation in the conduct of their lives.

Therefore, Gung-tang's point that Buddha is countering causeless production, like that asserted by the Nihilists, and not a specific type of caused production—that is, production from self, like what is asserted by the Sāṃkhyas—is well founded and of dramatic import. It also appears to reflect the thought of Asaṅga's *Compendium of Ascertainments* which deletes the sūtra's reference to "other" conditions and speaks only of production by conditions:

> Because compositional phenomena are dependent-arisings, they are produced through the power of conditions and not by themselves. This is called "production-non-nature."

If Asaṅga had perceived the sūtra as mainly seeking to refute production from self, he surely would have repeated the sūtra's usage of "**other** conditions."

Issue #69: Is the nature of production that other-powered natures lack production that is inherently existent?

As the Second Dalai Lama says,[219] in the Mind-Only School the nature of production that other-powered natures lack cannot be inherently existent production (as it is in the Consequence School), because Proponents of Mind-Only do not know how to posit production if it is not inherently established. Therefore, what is being refuted is the production of things under their own power without relying on causes and conditions.

It needs to be remembered that, according to the Mind-Only School,[220] the *Sūtra Unraveling the Thought* is explaining the final thought of the Perfection of Wisdom Sūtras themselves, and, therefore, when the Perfection of Wisdom Sūtras say in their literal reading that forms and so forth are not inherently produced, the meaning is that forms and so forth are not produced under their own power without relying on causes and conditions.

Issue #70: Is the nature of production that other-powered natures lack production that is established by way of its own character?

W̄el-mang Ḡön-chok-gyel-tsen[221] avers that the Jo-nang-b̄as mistakenly take the *Sūtra Unraveling the Thought* as teaching that other-powered natures are without production that is established by way of its own character. Such a notion would be mistaken because, as was cited earlier, the sūtra itself says, "That which does not **exist by way of its own character** is not produced."

Issue #71: What does "phenomena" mean?

When in the *Sūtra Unraveling the Thought*, Buddha asks the rhetorical question, "What are production-non-natures of phenomena?" is he suggesting that a production-non-nature—which he himself subsequently describes as "Those arise through the force of other conditions and not by themselves"—can be posited with respect to **each and every** phenomenon, including permanent phenomena which are **not** arisen from causes and conditions? Or is he using the word "phenomena" loosely within having divided all phenomena into three classes—imputational, other-powered, and thoroughly established natures—and thus means, "**From among** phenomena what are production-non-natures?"

The first opinion is presented in the textbook literature of the J̄ang-d̄zay College.[222] There, the nature of production that other-powered natures lack is identified, as it was above, as autonomous production without depending on other causes and conditions, but that college goes on to hold that, since such does not exist in *any* phenomenon—impermanent or permanent—all phenomena are posited as production-non-natures. This is because the impermanent are not produced this way, and the permanent are not even produced.

However, Jay-d̄zün Chö-ḡyi-gyel-tsen cogently says that something is called a production-non-nature because of **both** (1) arising in dependence upon its causes and conditions and (2) not arising autonomously without depending on causes and conditions, as is clearly said in the *Sūtra Unraveling the Thought* itself. Thus permanent phenomena are not to be posited as production-non-natures, since they do not fulfill the first criterion.

Jay-d̄zün Chö-ḡyi-gyel-tsen's predecessor as textbook author of the Jay College of S̄e-ra Monastic University B̄el-jor-hlün-drup does not word his statement so carefully, stating only that something is called a production-non-nature due to not being produced autonomously without depending on its conditions. This formulation, therefore, incurs the unwanted extension that the *Sūtra Unraveling the Thought* would be saying that all permanent phenomena are production-non-natures, since, being permanent, they are not produced autonomously without depending on their conditions. This also would militate against the equivalence of other-powered nature and production-non-nature.

Issue #72: Could the other-powered nature of a permanent phenomenon be the valid consciousness apprehending it?

A-ku L̄o-drö-gya-tso[223] reports that the other authors of monastic textbooks—this usually means Jay-d̄zün Chö-ḡyi-gyel-tsen and Paṇ-chen S̄ö-nam-drak-b̄a, even though they are not all-inclusive of Ge-luk-b̄a textbook authors—hold that the discussion is about **all** phenomena without differentiation. For them, Paramārthasamudgata's question is concerned with the production-non-nature that is with all objects, both permanent and impermanent.[a]

They feel that when an other-powered nature is posited even with respect to uncompounded phenomena such as space, it must be an **actual** other-powered nature and thus must be made by causes and conditions and hence impermanent, and this is why they do not say that uncompounded space is the other-powered nature of uncompounded space,[b] even though a table is the other-powered nature of a table, for instance. They say that uncompounded space cannot be the other-powered nature of space because it does not arise from causes and conditions. Rather, they make the unusual step, to be discussed in detail later,[c] of holding that a consciousness validly cognizing uncompounded space is the other-powered nature of uncompounded space. The impetus for making this seemingly extraordinary assertion comes from the difficult spot in which they find themselves upon having asserted that the production-non-nature and the other-powered nature, which are strictly limited to phenomena that arise from causes and conditions, are to be posited **in actuality**

---

[a] A-ku L̄o-drö-gya-tso's presentation is corroborated by Jay-d̄zün Chö-ḡyi-gyel-tsen's (*General-Meaning Commentary,* 14b.3) saying that his exposition of why the other-powered nature of form is called a production-non-nature is to be extended to all other phenomena.

[b] See Jay-d̄zün Chö-ḡyi-gyel-tsen's *General-Meaning Commentary,* 14b.4. He says that this is so despite the fact that uncompounded space's not being established by way of its own character as the referent of a conceptual consciousness is the thoroughly established nature of uncompounded space.

According to Ge-s̄hay Yeshi Thabkhe of the Central Institute of Higher Tibetan Studies in Sarnath, the tradition following Paṇ-chen S̄ö-nam-drak-b̄a does not agree with this latter point, despite agreeing with Jay-d̄zün Chö-ḡyi-gyel-tsen that uncompounded space is not the other-powered nature of uncompounded space, for by merely realizing that uncompounded space is not established by way of its own character, one realizes that uncompounded space is not established by way of its own character as the referent of a conceptual consciousness, and since even Proponents of Sūtra can do this, such non-establishment cannot constitute the subtle selflessness of phenomena in the Mind-Only School. From this, one can see why Jay-d̄zün Chö-ḡyi-gyel-tsen holds the (at first blush startling) position that in the Sūtra School *all* phenomena (including existent imputational natures such as uncompounded space) **are** established by way of their own character. As was explained earlier (p. 79), according to Jay-d̄zün Chö-ḡyi-gyel-tsen, the distinction is to be made that in the Sūtra School Following Reasoning uncompounded space, despite being established by way of its own character, is not truly established; hence, a Proponent of Sūtra can realize that uncompounded space is not truly established but cannot realize that uncompounded space is not established by way of its own character. (For Paṇ-chen S̄ö-nam-drak-b̄a "truly established" and "established by way of its own character" are equivalent.) The Go-mang tradition of Gung-ru Chö-jung and Jam-ȳang-shay-b̄a holds that "established by way of its own character" here means "established through the force of its own mode of subsistence," and thus although the Proponents of Sūtra hold that permanent phenomena are not established by way of their own character, they do not realize that permanent phenomena are not established by way of their own character as the referents of their respective conceptual consciousnesses.

[c] See issue #140, p. 354.

with respect to all phenomena, and thus they cannot take a permanent, uncaused phenomenon itself as that phenomenon's other-powered nature but must come up with something associated with it that is produced from causes and conditions, this being a consciousness validly apprehending it.

It is clear that they do this partly from being boxed in by their own assertions, but the position also makes considerable sense in that a prime tenet of the Mind-Only School is that an object and a consciousness apprehending it are the same entity, due to which these scholars hold that the emptiness of the subject, the consciousness, is the emptiness of the object, and vice versa. (Perhaps because of the difficulty that then the emptiness of a Buddha's consciousness perceiving a sentient being's afflicted consciousness would be the emptiness of that afflicted consciousness and the emptiness of the afflicted consciousness would be the emptiness of a Buddha's omniscient consciousness, Gung-ru Chö-jung, Jam-ȳang-shay-b̄a, Gung-tang, and A-ku L̄o-drö-gya-tso do not accept that the emptiness of the subject, the consciousness, is the emptiness of the object although, of course, they assert that in the Mind-Only School an object and a consciousness apprehending it are the same entity.)

A-ku L̄o-drö-gya-tso objects to taking all phenomena as the field of reference of the production-non-nature, saying that phenomena must be divided into three classes to be applied, respectively, to the three non-natures, for this is the meaning of calling the third wheel of doctrine "the wheel of good differentiation." He makes the following distinction:

- **In general**, the third wheel is called such because it makes a good differentiation between what does and does not truly exist—differentiating that other-powered natures and thoroughly established natures truly exist (or are established by way of their own character) and that imputational natures do not.
- However, the **main** reason why the third wheel of the teaching is called "the wheel of good differentiation" is that it **individually** takes the three non-natures as the bases in Buddha's thought when he said that the three natures (all phenomena) are natureless.

Even though A-ku L̄o-drö-gya-tso does not cite it at this point, a statement by D̄zong-ka-b̄a (*Emptiness in Mind-Only,* 125-126) supports his point:

> With respect to its good differentiation, it, as [explained] earlier, presents three characters each with respect to each phenomenon—forms and so forth—and **differentiates three modes of naturelessness with respect to those**.

In the third wheel (that is, especially in the seventh chapter of the *Sūtra Unraveling the Thought*), Buddha teaches that there were thoughts behind his statements on the literal level in the Perfection of Wisdom Sūtras that all phenomena, without differentiation, are natureless. Making a differentiation among phenomena, he points out that the character-non-nature is behind his saying that imputational phenomena are natureless, because imputational natures are not established by way of their own character. He points out that the production-non-nature is behind his saying that other-powered natures are natureless, because other-powered natures are without production under their own power. He points out that the ultimate-non-nature is behind his saying that thoroughly established natures are natureless, because they are the non-establishment of phenomena as the entity of the self of phenomena. Thus, by the very name of the third wheel of doctrine—"the wheel of good differentiation"—it can be known that when Buddha speaks of "production-non-natures of phenomena," this is to be applied in actuality only to other-powered natures.

A-ku L̄o-drö-gya-tso cogently backs up his reading by pointing out that Buddha proceeds to speak of production "through the force of other conditions," thereby eliminating that his reference also includes permanent phenomena. Also, Asaṅga applies Buddha's explanation only to compounded phenomena; his *Compendium of Ascertainments* (*Emptiness in Mind-Only,* 88) says:[224]

> Because compositional phenomena are dependent-arisings, they are produced through the power of conditions and not by themselves. This is called "production-non-nature."

Asaṅga limits the discussion to compositional (or compounded) phenomena, even though Buddha (*Emptiness in Mind-Only,* 87) used the wider term "phenomena" in his rhetorical lead-in to his explanation:

> What are production-non-natures of phenomena?[a] Those which are the other-powered characters of phenomena.
>
> Why? It is thus: Those [other-powered characters] arise through the force of other conditions and not by themselves. Therefore, they are said to be "production-non-natures."

Were the production-non-nature to be applied even to permanent phenomena, Asaṅga would have used language that allowed for such, but he did not.

Thus, according to A-ku L̄o-drö-gya-tso,[225] this is a case of using a wide term, "phenomena," in a restricted sense. He gives an analogue: When Buddha says that the paths of Hearers are five, all Hearers are posited as those Hearers, but still it is not necessary that all Hearers have all five paths, since there are Hearers who have attained only the first path, and so forth. Likewise, even though all phenomena are posited as the "phenomena" in Buddha's mention of the "production-non-natures of phenomena," the production-non-natures that are explicitly indicated in that passage do not have to include all phenomena.[b]

---

[a] Roughly, this means, "What phenomena are without the nature of self-production?" See issues #76, 77. About "phenomena," see issue #71.

[b] In Pa-bong-ka-b̄a's *Brief Notes on J̄o-ni Paṇḍita's Lectures* (412.1), "phenomena" similarly is said to refer only to other-powered natures.

A-ku Lo-drö-gya-tso adds that such a differentiation of phenomena into three classes that, respectively, are the referents of the three non-natures is seen to be the thought of Vasubandhu's *The Thirty* (stanza 23) where it (*Emptiness in Mind-Only,* 83) says:

> Thinking of three types of non-nature
> Of the three types of natures [respectively],
> He taught [in the Perfection of Wisdom Sūtras]
> That all phenomena are natureless.

As Vasubandhu says, the statements in the Perfection of Wisdom Sūtras that all phenomena are natureless have, as Buddha's own thought behind them, three modes of naturelessness that are unique, respectively, to the individual three natures. Also, Vinītadeva's *Explanation of (Vasubandhu's) [Auto] Commentary on "The Thirty"* says,[226] "In consideration of three types of naturelessness of the three types of natures—other-powered, and so forth...." A-ku Lo-drö-gya-tso[227] cites Jam-ȳang-shay-b̄a[228] who points out that in this passage "the three types of natures" explicitly indicates the three natures—imputational, other-powered, and thoroughly established natures, and "three types of naturelessness" explicitly indicates that those three natures are illustrations respectively of character-non-nature, production-non-nature, and ultimate-non-nature. Thus, the passage in Vasubandhu's *The Thirty* says that, thinking of three natures and three modes of naturelessness, Buddha said in the Perfection of Wisdom Sūtras that all phenomena are natureless.

A-ku Lo-drö-gya-tso extends his already decisive case by pointing out that D̄zong-ka-b̄a himself (*Emptiness in Mind-Only,* 84-85) supports this view when he says:

> [When Paramārthasamudgata] asks about that in consideration of which [Buddha] spoke of non-nature, he is asking (1) about what [Buddha] was thinking when he taught non-nature and (2) about the modes of non-nature. Also, the answer indicates those two respectively. From between those two, let us explain the first [that is, what Buddha had as the basis in his thought when in the Perfection of Wisdom Sūtras he taught that all phenomena are natureless. There, Buddha] said that the limitless divisions of instances of phenomena ranging from forms through to exalted knowers-of-all-aspects have no nature or inherent nature. These phenomena are included in the three non-natures [that is, three natures[a]—imputational, other-powered, and thoroughly established natures].[b] Thinking that when it is

---

[a] For the equivalency of the three non-natures and the respective three natures, see issue #101, as long as the **actual** ultimate-non-nature is restricted to thoroughly established natures (see issues #147, 148).

[b] See also issue #101.

> explained how those are natureless, it is easy to understand [the individual modes of thought that were behind his statement in the Perfection of Wisdom Sūtras], he included [all phenomena] into the three non-natures [that is, three natures. For] all ultimate and conventional phenomena are included within those three.

When Buddha was questioned about the individual modes of naturelessness, he—thinking that his individual modes of thought would be easily understood—included all phenomena ranging from forms through omniscient consciousnesses into three classes, imputational natures, other-powered natures, and thoroughly established natures, and thereupon associated the bases in his own thought, three types of naturelessness, with those three individually.

A-ku Lo-drö-gya-tso[229] concludes that this passage in the *Sūtra Unraveling the Thought* does not set forth with respect to **uncompounded** phenomena either the production-non-nature or the mode of its non-existence. Worded another way, this passage on the production-non-nature sets forth the mode of naturelessness of other-powered natures and not the mode of naturelessness of imputational natures or thoroughly established natures simply because, in speaking about the three non-natures, Buddha divides phenomena into three classes. A-ku Lo-drö-gya-tso's cogently argued point is built on and preserves an important, basic perspective of the *Sūtra Unraveling the Thought*—the explication of the middle wheel teaching of naturelessness within the framework of three classes of phenomena.[a]

Issue #73: Are all phenomena included in the three natures?

In the course of their esthetically stimulating intellectual sport, Tibetan scholars subject topics to unstinting analysis sometimes with profound probing but at other times with superficial quibbling. These levels of inquiry—sublime and trivial—are juxtaposed without warning; the student is expected to shift level with agility. For instance, the division of phenomena into the permanent and the impermanent is said to be all-inclusive, but what about the combined subject, permanent phenomenon and impermanent phenomenon? It seemingly cannot be permanent, since impermanent phenomenon is not permanent; similarly, it cannot be impermanent, since permanent phenomenon is not impermanent. Also, it cannot be both permanent and impermanent, since permanent phenomenon is not impermanent, and impermanent phenomenon is not permanent. In other words, Dick and Jane are not Dick and Jane because Dick is not Jane, and Jane is not Dick.

In this way, analysis of a seemingly common but, in time, strange

[a] Still, as is explained in *Reflections on Reality,* 180-183, A-ku Lo-drö-gya-tso shows, in a brilliant move, how the etymology for "other-powered nature" can be creatively extended to permanent phenomena.

phenomenon seems to indicate that the dictum that each and every phenomenon is necessarily either permanent or impermanent does not hold. However, Tibetan scholars do not want to give up the basic dictum; so, they have manufactured another dictum: in cases of such a combined subject (that is, a set), permanence predominates. **Why** it predominates is not explained.

In a similar fashion, Gön-chok-jik-may-wang-bo,[230] approvingly cites notes taken from remarks by Tri Rin-bo-chay Nga-wang-dra-shi[a] that even though it is asserted that whatever exists is necessarily one of the three natures, if the challenge is put to determine what the combined subject, other-powered nature and thoroughly established nature, is, one must answer that the mode of structuring the statement is faulty.[b] Gön-chok-jik-may-wang-bo cogently justifies this answer by the fact that Indian scholars did not get into such topics—that is to say, such abstract, verbal issues.

The problem is that the combined subject, other-powered nature and thoroughly established nature, (1) cannot be a thoroughly established nature because other-powered natures are not thoroughly established natures, (2) cannot be an other-powered nature because thoroughly established natures are not other-powered natures, and (3) cannot be an imputational nature because neither other-powered natures nor thoroughly established natures are imputational natures. Also, the subject, other-powered nature and thoroughly established nature, is (or are) not other-powered nature and thoroughly established nature because each is not both. Pillar and pot are not pillar and pot, and Dick and Jane are not Dick and Jane. The issue is that although it said that **all** phenomena are divided into the three natures, there are unusual phenomena such as the combined subject, other-powered nature and thoroughly established nature, that are none of the three natures—this fact seemingly destroying the claim that the three natures include all phenomena.

To avoid having to abandon the position that all phenomena are included in the three natures, Gön-chok-jik-may-wang-bo makes a technical objection to the posing of the problem, disallowing consideration of such unusual subjects by saying that the mode of structuring the statement is faulty. He does not explain **why** it is faulty, but we can see that this is a worthy attempt to avoid sophistry.[c] Gön-chok-jik-may-wang-bo's statement that Indian scholars did not bother themselves with such issues and yet his giving an answer suggest that, in Tibet, scholars must come up with an answer to each and every quibble even if the answer is merely a move to skirt the issue.

---

a *khri rin po che ngag dbang bkra shis.*

b *sbyor lugs skyon can.*

c As is well known, the term "sophistry" is an unwarranted smear of the Greek Sophists.

Issue #74: How do other tenet systems identify the production-non-nature?

The Autonomy School, in dependence upon its own reading of the *Sūtra Unraveling the Thought*, holds that the production-non-nature refers to the non-existence of production that is **ultimately** established by way of its own character.

The Consequence School holds that the meaning of the *Sūtra Unraveling the Thought* accords with how the Mind-Only School takes it, but it has its own explanation of the production-non-nature separate from the *Sūtra Unraveling the Thought;* it asserts that the production-non-nature means the non-existence of production established by way of its own character.[231]

The Mind-Only School asserts that other-powered natures ultimately have production established by way of their own character. This is because other-powered natures are produced in a manner not just imputed by conceptuality, since if their production were just imputed by conceptuality, the production of other-powered natures would be just posited in the face of a mistaken awareness. In this fashion, Dzong-ka-ba (*Emptiness in Mind-Only,* 210) says, "Still, this system asserts that once something is only posited by names and terminology, cause and effect are not suitable to occur in it," and (*Emptiness in Mind-Only,* 88), "This [Mind-Only School] is a system that says that other-powered natures are natureless since they are without the nature of such inherent[a] production; it does not say that other-powered natures are natureless because of not being established by way of their own character [as the Consequence School holds]."

Gung-tang[232] says that a distinction must be made between the Consequence School's assertion on the three non-natures **in their own system** and their assertion of what the *Sūtra Unraveling the Thought* says about the three non-natures. This is because Consequentialists accept the *Sūtra Unraveling the Thought* as being a text of the Mind-Only School, and thus they accept that the Mind-Only School's explanation of what the sūtra says about the three natures is indeed what the sūtra says, even if their own position disagrees with that of the sūtra, which they say requires interpretation. The Consequentialists' own presentation of the three natures is made in dependence upon other sūtras with differing meaning, particularly the *Teachings of Akṣhayamati Sūtra* and the *King of Meditative Stabilizations Sūtra.*[b] As Chandrakīrti says:[233]

---

[a] See issue #75.

[b] For Chandrakīrti's presentation of the three natures, see his *Autocommentary to the Supplement to (Nāgārjuna's) Treatise on the Middle Way,* commenting on stanza VI.97 (Louis de la Vallée Poussin, *Madhyamakāvatāra par Candrakīrti* [Osnabrück, Germany: Biblio Verlag, 1970], 201.7). Just before the citation in that book, Chandrakīrti says, "The extensive teaching in sūtras such as the *Teachings of Akṣhayamati Sūtra* should be considered." See Gung-tang's *Difficult Points,* 127.8.

> Thus, one has understood the arrangement of scriptures [of definitive meaning and requiring interpretation]. Any sūtra setting forth non-suchness, teaching that which requires interpretation, is to be interpreted. Through realizing [this, these provisional teachings become a cause of entering into the realization that phenomena do not exist inherently]. Also, know that [any sūtra] that bears the meaning of emptiness is definitive.

In commentary on this, Jam-ȳang-shay-b̄a says:[234]

> Through such passages it is explained that the *Sūtra Unraveling the Thought* requires interpretation where it teaches the differentiation of [true] existence and absence of [true] existence of the first two of the three natures of the Mind-Only School [respectively, other-powered natures and imputational natures]:
>
> - because the teaching in the *Sūtra Unraveling the Thought* that effective things truly exist and so forth [which needs to be interpreted as having their conventional existence as the basis in Buddha's thought] is explained by the *Teaching of Akṣhayamati Sūtra* and so forth to require interpretation, and
> - because [Consequentialists] distinguish the existence and non-existence of the three natures in accordance with the "Questions of Maitreya" [chapter] of the *Twenty-five Thousand Stanza Perfection of Wisdom Sūtra,* [saying that] all phenomena from forms through to omniscient consciousnesses do not ultimately exist but exist only in the terminology and conventions of the world. For there it is said in answer to a question about the way that forms and so forth exist,[235] "They exist according to the terminology and conventions of the world but not ultimately," and thus it is said that all phenomena from forms through to omniscient consciousnesses [only nominally exist].

Jam-ȳang-shay-b̄a cites Chandrakīrti's commentary on his *Supplement:*[236]

> I will say a little bit [about our own system's presentation of the three natures]. For instance, a snake is [only] superimposed on a coiled rope which is a dependent-arising, for there is no snake in the rope. However, a snake is thoroughly established in an actual snake because it is not superimposed. Similarly, that the final nature is in other-powered natures, which are products, is a superimposition [because] the final nature is not a product, for [Nāgārjuna] says:[237]
>
> > Natures are unfabricated
> > And without reliance on others.
>
> This final nature that is superimposed on presently apprehended

products, which are dependent-arisings and like reflections [in that the way they appear and the way they exist do not agree], is the actual final nature as the object of a Buddha. For [as the object of a Buddha's realization] it is not superimposed. Not contacting [or being obstructed by] things that are products, [a Buddha's wisdom knowing the mode of subsistence] actualizes only the final nature. Since they understand suchness, they are called "Buddha."

Hence, one has thus understood the presentation of the three natures—imputational, other-powered, and thoroughly established. [In this way] the thought of the *Sūtra [Unraveling the Thought]* is to be explained [as requiring interpretation].

[The Proponents of Mind-Only treat a difference of entity of] the two, apprehending subjects and apprehended objects [imputed in dependence on other-powered natures] as a [non-existent] imputational nature. This should be considered [that is to say, analyzed], because apprehending subjects and apprehended objects [are other-powered natures and] other-powered natures [that are not subjects or objects] do not exist as effective things.

Jam-ȳang-shay-b̄a explains Chandrakīrti's meaning:

Let us illumine a little the meaning of his words. The way of superimposition is that whereas the final mode of subsistence does not exist as perceived in an other-powered nature, it is perceived there through superimposition. For the perception that other-powered natures exist as their own mode of abiding despite their not actually so existing is an imaginary superimposition, since it is like, for example, the superimposition by a consciousness apprehending a rope as a snake despite the snake's not existing in the rope. This is because other-powered natures do not fulfill the sense of a non-fabricated nature, and so forth.

Other-powered natures presently being seen or apprehended are like mirror reflections in that there is no agreement between the way they appear and the way they are. Their nature or mode of being is an actual thoroughly established nature [that is, an emptiness] according to the sight of Buddhas because they perceive without superimposing existence on what nevertheless does not exist. This is because it is like, for example, a snake's not being superimposed on an actual snake, and thus the object apprehended is thoroughly established.

This establishes a definition and an etymology of "thoroughly established"[a] and also explains that other-powered natures are the bases of the superimposition of imputational natures as well as the bases of emptinesses—thoroughly established natures.

---

[a] *yongs grub, pariniṣpanna.*

Therefore, even if the Consequentialists accept that the meaning of the production-non-nature that is taught in the *Sūtra Unraveling the Thought* is—as the Proponents of Mind-Only say—the non-existence of the production of other-powered natures under their own power, their own meaning of the production-non-nature in general is taken to be the non-existence of inherently established production.

The Consequentialists find this latter type of explanation in several other sūtras. For instance, the *Questions of Anavatapta, the King of Nāgas, Sūtra* says:[238]

> Those which are produced from conditions are not produced.
> They do not have an inherent nature of production.
> Those which depend on conditions are said to be empty.
> Those who know emptiness are aware.

As J̄ang-ḡya's *Presentation of Tenets* says about this stanza:[239]

> In that, production from conditions is the reason. No production is the probandum. The meaning of not being produced is indicated by the second line. It is not that mere production is being eliminated; inherently established production is being eliminated.

Just as in the Mind-Only School's presentation a specific type of production is refuted, so in the Consequence School, inherently existent production is refuted, not production in general. Similarly, the *Descent into Laṅkā Sūtra* says,[240] "O Mahāmati, thinking of no inherently existent production, I said that all phenomena are not produced," and the *One Hundred Fifty Stanza Perfection of Wisdom Sūtra* says:[241]

> All phenomena are empty
> In the manner of no inherent existence.

These passages are sources for the Consequence School, but it should be noted that from the viewpoint of the Mind-Only School "no inherent existence," and so forth, could be taken as referring to "no production under their own power" and not as production that is findable under analysis; indeed, D̄zong-ka-b̄a's reference, just above, to "inherent production" is taken this way. Thus, the point is not one of mere terminology but how that terminology is read.

Another reason why, according to the Consequence School, the *Sūtra Unraveling the Thought* cannot be teaching that other-powered natures lack production established by way of its own character is that, if it did, then the Consequentialists would have to accept the sūtra as being definitive—as mainly and explicitly teaching their version of emptiness; however, they cannot because the *Sūtra Unraveling the Thought* clearly says that whatever is produced necessarily is established by way of its own character. For this reason, Consequentialists, such as Chandrakīrti, do not accept the *Sūtra Unraveling the Thought* as definitive.[a] As Jam-ȳang-shay-b̄a's *Great Exposition of Tenets* says about the Consequence School:[b]

> The first and last wheels require interpretation.
> The middle are definitive sūtras.

For the Consequence School, the third wheel of doctrine, as it is presented in the *Sūtra Unraveling the Thought,* requires interpretation and is not definitive.

The situation is more complicated in the Autonomy School, since it takes the *Sūtra Unraveling the Thought* to be one of its own texts, and hence it takes the production-non-nature that is set forth in the *Sūtra Unraveling the Thought* as indicating the non-existence of truly established production without refuting that production is established by way of its own character.

Issue #75: How to take D̄zong-ka-b̄a's own loose usage of terminology in the midst of his strict distinctions?

As Gung-tang[242] points out, in many texts of the Autonomy School, "true establishment"[c] is frequently referred to as "inherent establishment"[d] or "establishment by way of its own character," and thus even Jam-ȳang-shay-b̄a[243] speaks of the Autonomists as asserting that the meaning of the production-non-nature is the non-existence of production that is established by way of its own character, whereas, in the strict usage of the vocabulary that evolved in Ge-luk-b̄a texts based on D̄zong-ka-b̄a's *The Essence of Eloquence,* he should have said "the non-existence of production that **ultimately** is established by way of its own character."

Despite forging a new, strict usage of vocabulary for the status of phenomena, D̄zong-ka-b̄a uses the same vocabulary in a loose way.[244] For instance, in the section on the Sūtra Middle Way Autonomy School in *The Essence of Eloquence,* he says:[245]

> If other-powered natures were truly established, they would have to be established in accordance with how they appear, and therefore, the statement in the *Sūtra [Unraveling the Thought]* that [other-powered natures] are like illusions would be incorrect. Therefore, they explain that the meaning of the sūtra is that [other-powered natures] are empty of **inherent existence**.

According to his own strict usage of such terminology, D̄zong-ka-b̄a should

[a] For extensive discussion of this, see Jam-ȳang-shay-b̄a's *Great Exposition of Tenets* as translated in Hopkins, *Meditation on Emptiness,* 595-623, and Hopkins, *Maps of the Profound,* 805ff.

[b] See the previous footnote.

[c] *bden grub.*

[d] *rang bzhin gyis grub pa.*

have said that the Sūtra Autonomists explain that when the *Sūtra Unraveling the Thought* says that other-powered natures are like illusions, this means that they are empty of true existence, ultimate existence, or **inherent existence ultimately**. For the only school that refutes inherent existence both conventionally and ultimately is the Consequence School—that is to say, the only school that asserts that existent phenomena are not found when analytically sought among their bases of designation is the Consequence School.

Similarly, in the section on the Yogic Autonomy School Dzong-ka-ba says:[246]

> The wise assert that the explanation [in the *Sūtra Unraveling the Thought*] that since other-powered natures are produced by the power of other conditions and are not produced just by themselves, they are production-non-natures [means] that whatever arises dependently is empty of **inherent existence**.

Again, he should have said that the Yogic Autonomists assert that whatever arises dependently is empty of ultimate existence, or empty of inherent existence ultimately, and so forth. However, as Gung-tang[247] says, these passages are not cases of sloppy writing—not cases of a Consequentialist perspective unwarrantedly slipping into a discussion of another system. Rather, Dzong-ka-ba himself explicitly recognizes that in Indian texts there is no such clear-cut usage of terminology, and he purposely uses the vocabulary loosely to cause readers to determine the specific meaning applicable in a particular context.

This **sounds** like apologetic, but it is not; Gung-tang has perceived a consciously employed technique. Dzong-ka-ba himself points out that, for instance, Chandrakīrti (the chief Consequentialist) and Bhāvaviveka (the chief Autonomist) use similar terminology with respect to both what is negated in emptiness and what remains to exist conventionally; thus, the differentiation of their views of emptiness cannot be made merely by way of the vocabulary they use when they speak of the conventional existence of phenomena or when they speak of the object of negation in the view of emptiness. In the section on the Autonomy School in *The Essence of Eloquence* Dzong-ka-ba says:[248]

> In Consequentialist texts, even existing conventionally is frequently described as a nature[a] of that [object], inherent nature,[b] its own character,[c] and so forth, and also in the texts of this master [Bhāvaviveka][249] there are many cases of [his speaking of an object as being] not established by way of its own nature,[d] not produced by way of [its own]

---

a *ngo bo nyid, svabhāvatā.*

b *rang bzhin, svabhāva.*

c *rang gi mtshan nyid, svalakṣaṇa.*

d *rang gi ngo bo nyid kyis ma grub pa.*

nature,[a] not being substantially established,[b] and so forth. Therefore, it appears to be difficult to differentiate them.

Ḏzong-ka-ḇa does not claim that through tabulating the usage of terminology one could determine that the Autonomy School asserts inherent existence conventionally and that the Consequence School does not. Rather, given that in the terminology there is no clear-cut difference on the topics of what is negated and the status of what exists, detailed contextual analysis is needed to determine the difference between these schools on the status of phenomena.

The hardening of terminology such that in Ge-luk-ḇa texts it is said that the Mind-Only School and Autonomy School assert inherent existence, whereas the Consequence School does not, is built not on finding explicit exclusive use of such terminology in those ways in Indian texts but on textual, philosophical analysis of the implications of statements. Those implications were then communicated in Ge-luk-ḇa scholarship through standard sets of terminology that were never used in that way in India.

To repeat: Gung-tang concludes that it is not the case that, when Ḏzong-ka-ḇa and Jam-ȳang-shay-ḇa do not use the terminology strictly, another school's perspective has slipped in; rather, such loose usage is in reliance on the fact that these schools employ the terminology this way. Ḏzong-ka-ḇa's and Jam-ȳang-shay-ḇa's loose usage is deliberate in that these scholars want readers to learn to probe what is behind the terminology. On the surface, Gung-tang's explanation may indeed look like apologetic, especially given the extraordinary lengths to which he goes—on other occasions of true apologetic—in order to make sense out of what are, at minimum, loose statements in Ḏzong-ka-ḇa's writings. However, I find his explanation to be insightful, for Ḏzong-ka-ḇa's main intent is, through contextual analysis, to forge a new, strict vocabulary that conveys the implicit meaning of these schools' views on the status of phenomena, and, in order to bring this about, it is of prime advantage to cause readers themselves, once he has supplied the principles of exegesis, to determine when the vocabulary is and is not being used strictly. This can sometimes result in a degree of confusion and ambiguity, not only for the uninitiated but also even for the initiated; in these cases (but not here in the one we are considering) Ḏzong-ka-ḇa unintentionally makes his followers retrieve his meaning inventively.

Issue #76: Does "production-non-nature" mean non-nature of *production?*

The nature that other-powered natures lack is self-production and not production; therefore, it cannot be said that other-powered natures are without a

[a] *ngo bo nyid kyis ma skyes pa.*

[b] *rdzas su ma grub pa.*

nature **of** production. Rather, they are without a nature **in terms of** production. Jam-ȳang-shay-b̄a[250] makes this important grammatical point at the end of his section on the production-non-nature. He says that, although a pot is without a nature **in terms of** production,[a] it is not without a nature **of** production,[b] simply because it is an other-powered nature and has production.

The Sanskrit compound *utpattiniḥsvabhāvatā* is a genitive *tatpuruṣa* and the genitive itself can be treated in these two ways, but there is no evidence that Indian scholars sought to make this distinction. It, like most of the points being documented here, is a Tibetan development.

Issue #77: Can this grammatical distinction be extended to the other two non-natures?

Despite the relevance of Jam-ȳang-shay-b̄a's distinction with respect to the production-non-nature, it is not applicable to the other two non-natures. For when it is said that imputational natures are character-non-natures, the nature that they lack is "character" itself, that is, establishment by way of their own character. Therefore, it is feasible to speak of the non-nature **of** character.

Also, as will be explained in Chapter 18, when it is said that other-powered natures are ultimate-non-natures, the nature that other-powered natures lack is the ultimate itself—they are not ultimates. Hence, it is feasible to speak of the non-nature **of** the ultimate when "ultimate-non-nature" is applied to other-powered natures.

---

[a] *skye **ba** ngo bo nyid med pa,* which I also translate as "production-non-nature."

[b] *skye **ba'i** ngo bo nyid med pa.*

12. Imputational Natures

Overview of Imputational Natures

Definition of an imputational nature: a factor superimposed with respect to any object by either terms and conceptual consciousnesses, or names and terminology, that is not the mode of abiding of the object.[a] All generally characterized phenomena except thoroughly established natures are illustrations of imputational natures.

Terminological divisions: enumerated, or existent, imputational natures,[b] such as generally characterized phenomenon (as a category) and uncompounded space; and imputational natures whose character is completely nihil, or non-existent imputational natures,[c] such as the horns of a rabbit, a self of persons, or a self of phenomena.

Definition of an imputational nature relevant on this occasion: that which is merely imputed by conceptuality and is posited from the viewpoint of being a superimposed factor of either a self of persons or a self of phenomena.[d]

Character-Non-Nature: The Subject

Issue #78: Do proponents of the Sūtra School realize that being the referent of a conceptual consciousness is not established by way of its own character?

About imputational natures the *Sūtra Unraveling the Thought* (*Emptiness in Mind-Only,* 86) says:[e]

---

[a] Jik-may-dam-chö-gya-tso's *Port of Entry,* 235.4: *gzhi gang la sgra rtog gam ming brda ci rigs kyis gnas tshul ma yin par sgro btags pa'i cha de/ kun btags kyi mtshan nyid.*

[b] Ibid., 235.6: *rnam grangs pa'i kun btags/ yod rgyu'i kun btags.*

[c] Ibid., 236.1: *mtshan nyid yongs chad kyi kun btags/ med rgyu'i kun btags.*

[d] Ibid., 235.6: *bdag gnyis gang rung du sgro btags pa'i cha nas bzhag pa'i rtog pas btags tsam de/ skabs su mkho ba'i kun btags kyi mtshan nyid.*

[e] The discussion of the character-non-nature in chapters 12-17 is drawn from:

Wonch'uk's *Extensive Commentary,* Peking 5517, vol. 116, 130.3.4-131.1.5.

Second Dalai Lama's *Lamp Illuminating the Meaning,* 15.6-18.3.

<u>Go-mang and Dra-shi-kyil</u>

Gung-ru Chö-jung's *Garland of White Lotuses,* 19a.3-29b.4.

Jam-yang-shay-ba's *Great Exposition of the Interpretable and the Definitive,* 49.2-68.6.

> Those [imputational characters] are characters posited by names and terminology[a] and do not subsist by way of their own character. Therefore, they are said to be "character-non-natures."

Some Tibetan scholars, finding ample justification in Ďzong-ka-b̄a's own words,[b] re-cast this statement syllogistically as:

> With respect to the subject, forms and so forth **being the referents of conceptual consciousnesses**, there are reasons for calling this a "character-non-nature" because the reasons are that (1) from the positive side such is only posited by names and terminology and (2) from the negative side such is not established by way of its own character.

I find this formulation, which is made most clearly by Tsay-d̄en-hla-ram-b̄a,[251] to be highly evocative, but it is not without problems that need to be handled.

Specifically, A-ku L̄o-drö-gya-tso (who it should be remembered is a follower of Gung-tang who made several criticisms of Jay-d̄zün Chö-ḡyi-gyel-tsen, who, in turn, was defended by Tsay-d̄en-hla-ram-b̄a) says that the problem with identifying forms' **being the referents of conceptual consciousnesses** as what is not established by way of its own character is that Proponents of Sūtra, a lower school, realize that forms' being the referents of conceptual consciousnesses is not established by way of its own character, and thus realization of this cannot constitute realization of the selflessness of phenomena in the Mind-Only School. The emptiness described in the Mind-Only School would absurdly be realized by proponents of a lower school, and thus emptiness as it is presented in the Mind-Only School would absurdly not be more subtle than it is in the Sūtra School. However, it must be more subtle since the four schools

---

Jam-ȳang-shay-b̄a's *Brief Decisive Analysis*, 497.6-504.4.
W̄el-mang Ḡön-chok-gyel-tsen's *Notes on (Ḡön-chok-jik-may-w̄ang-b̄o's) Lectures*, 400.6-401.3.
Gung-tang's *Annotations*, 21.6-23.7 (*dza-wa*).
Gung-tang's *Difficult Points*, 99.15-124.15.
Dön-drup-gyel-tsen's *Four Intertwined Commentaries*, 47.4-52.4.
A-ku L̄o-drö-gya-tso's *Precious Lamp*, 73.1-86.5.
Jik-may-dam-chö-gya-tso's *Port of Entry*, 170.5-178.4.
Pa-bong-ka-b̄a's *Brief Notes on J̄o-ni Paṇḍita's Lectures*, 411.4-412.1.

L̄o-s̄el-l̄ing and S̄har-d̄zay

Paṇ-chen S̄ö-nam-drak-b̄a's *Garland of Blue Lotuses*, 27b.5-33a.3.

S̄e-ra Jay

B̄el-jor-hlün-drup's *Lamp for the Teaching*, 14.2-16.1.
Jay-d̄zün Chö-ḡyi-gyel-tsen's *General-Meaning Commentary*, 11a.2-13b.2.
D̄ra-d̄i Ge-s̄hay Rin-chen-dön-drup's *Ornament for the Thought*, 21.4-24.16.
S̄er-s̄hül's *Notes*, 15a.3-18b.6.
D̄a-drin-rap-d̄en's *Annotations*, 16.4-17.4.

a See issue #104.

b See *Reflections on Reality*, 190, 199-202.

are posited in ascending order due to increasing subtlety in their views of emptiness, that is, selflessness, and the Mind-Only School is higher than the Sūtra School.

A-ku Lo-drö-gya-tso holds that the Proponents of Sūtra[a] do indeed realize that forms' being the referents of conceptual consciousnesses is a non-effective, abstract phenomenon, and thus even they realize that it is not established by way of its own character. The background to his position is the common assertion among Ge-luk-ba scholars that in the Sūtra School although form is impermanent and hence established by way of its own character, form's **being** impermanent[b] or even form's **being** form is an abstraction, appearing only to a conceptual consciousness, and thus a non-disintegrative phenomenon.[c] Hence, according to A-ku Lo-drö-gya-tso, form's **being** the referent of a conceptual consciousness is, even for a Proponent of Sūtra, an abstraction and a non-disintegrative phenomenon. It is a non-effective thing and not established by way of its own character even in the Sūtra School.[d]

---

a The reference throughout this discussion is the Sūtra School Following Reasoning.

b *gzugs mi rtag pa yin pa.*

c See Daniel E. Perdue, *Debate in Tibetan Buddhism* (Ithaca, N.Y.: Snow Lion, 1992), 485-486.

d A-ku Lo-drö-gya-tso reports that Tsay-den-hla-ram-ba tries to get around this problem by asserting that although Proponents of Sūtra realize that the referent of a conceptual consciousness apprehending form is not an effective thing (and hence not established by way of its own character), they do not realize that the object **being** the referent of a conceptual consciousness apprehending form is not an effective thing (*gzugs 'dzin rtog pa'i zhen gzhi dngos med du rtogs kyang gzugs 'dzin rtog pa'i zhen gzhi yin pa'i don dngos med du ma rtogs: Precious Lamp,* 75.6-76.1) and hence not established by way of its own character. A-ku Lo-drö-gya-tso (*Precious Lamp,* 76.1) criticizes Tsay-den-hla-ram-ba for making this distinction on the grounds that the object **that is** the referent of a conceptual consciousness (*rtog pa'i zhen gzhi yin pa'i don*) is the object **that is** the conceived object of a conceptual consciousness (*rtog pa'i zhen yul yin pa'i don*), and there are Proponents of the Sūtra School who realize that the conceived object of a conceptual consciousness is a non-effective thing and thus not established by way of its own character. A-ku Lo-drö-gya-tso may mean that in the Sūtra School the general category of "conceived object of a conceptual consciousness" is understood to be an abstraction, and thus there is no way that the Sūtra School could hold that **what is** the conceived object of a conceptual consciousness or **what is** the referent of a conceptual consciousness is not established by way of its own character.

A-ku Lo-drö-gya-tso (76.2) makes a head-spinning point: (in paraphrase)

> Tsay-den-hla-ram-ba holds that being the referent of a conceptual consciousness is to be posited as the character-non-nature and its being established by way of its own character is to be posited as the nature that is non-existent, whereby he holds that the two—the character-non-nature and the nature that is non-existent—are mutually exclusive. Tsay-den-hla-ram-ba flings the absurd consequence that if the establishment of objects by way of their own character as the referents of conceptual consciousnesses were the nature in terms of character at this point in the sūtra, then it would absurdly be both what is refuted and what is proven. A-ku

Issue #79: How to claim that, when Ḏzong-ka-ḇa says "being the referent," he means "superimposed factor"?

In a move typical to his straightforward style, A-ku Lo-drö-gya-tso[252] supplies the source of Tsay-ḏen-hla-ram-ḇa's "mistake" in Ḏzong-ka-ḇa's own writing (*Emptiness in Mind-Only,* 210):

> Thus, form and so forth **being the referents of conceptual consciousnesses** is an imputational factor posited by name and terminology, but, since it is established by valid cognition, it cannot be refuted.[a] However, that it is established by way of the thing's own character is an imputational factor posited only nominally that does not occur among objects of knowledge [that is, does not exist]. Hence, among what are posited by names and terminology there are two [types], those established by valid cognition and those not established by valid cognition.[b] Still, this system asserts that once something is only posited by names and terminology, cause and effect are not suitable to occur in it.[c]

Despite his straightforwardness in bringing to the fore the source of Tsay-ḏen-hla-ram-ḇa's opinion, it strikes me that A-ku Lo-drö-gya-tso's even trying to explain away Ḏzong-ka-ḇa's usage of the vocabulary of "being the referent" is excessively stubborn, given the great number of times he uses this formulation.[d] Indeed, A-ku Lo-drö-gya-tso makes his task easier by treating only this one instance—a not so straightforward maneuver! Let us consider how he tries to handle this citation.

In the context of speaking about the two types of imputational natures, existent and non-existent, Ḏzong-ka-ḇa clearly refers in the first sentence to form and so forth's being the referents of conceptual consciousnesses[e] as the existent variety. A-ku Lo-drö-gya-tso, based on the explanations by Gung-ru Chö-jung and Jam-ÿang-shay-ḇa that will be given below, holds that even though Ḏzong-ka-ḇa did indeed say such, he must be taken as referring to the **superimposed factor** of forms and so forth as established by way of their own

---

Lo-drö-gya-tso faults him for not having understood that there are both existents and non-existents to be posited as the character-non-nature that is explicitly indicated at this point in the sūtra. As support for his criticism, he cites Ḏzong-ka-ḇa's statement (*Emptiness in Mind-Only,* 210), "Among what are posited by name and terminology there are two [types], those established by valid cognition and those not established by valid cognition."

a See issue #108.

b See issue #88.

c See issue #74.

d For nineteen such instances, see *Reflections on Reality,* 199-202.

e *gzugs sogs rtog pa'i zhen gzhi yin pa.*

character as the referents of conceptual consciousnesses[a] simply because on another occasion Dzong-ka-ba (*Emptiness in Mind-Only,* 195) says:

> Therefore, if you do not know what this imputational factor that is a **superimposed factor**[b] of a self of phenomena on other-powered natures is, you will not know in a decisive way the conception of a self of phenomena and the selflessness of phenomena in this [Mind-Only] system.

The term "superimposed factor" in its broadest sense can refer to (1) non-existents such as the establishment of objects by way of their own character as the referents of conceptual consciousnesses and (2) existents such as the **appearance** of objects as established by way of their own character as the referents of their respective conceptual consciousnesses or even a form's **being** the object of a conceptual consciousness. Here, it seems to me to refer to the self of phenomena under discussion, that is to say, the establishment of objects by way of their own character as the referents of conceptual consciousnesses. A-ku Lo-drö-gya-tso, however, desperate to find a source for his reading of Dzong-ka-ba's mention of **being** the referent of a conceptual consciousness as the **appearance** of objects as established by way of their own character as the referents of their respective conceptual consciousnesses twists this mention of a superimposed factor into meaning such an appearance.[c] Then, he views this supposed meaning of Dzong-ka-ba's usage of "superimposed factor" as overriding the usage of "being the referents of conceptual consciousnesses" several pages later (as well as, by extension, the other eighteen occurrences). Indeed, if Dzong-ka-ba had used the vocabulary of "being the referent" only once, A-ku Lo-drö-gya-tso might have been able to twist that one usage by juxtaposing it with another explanation (if it were clear), but the frequency with which Dzong-ka-ba frames the issue in this manner and the lack of support in the evidence that A-ku Lo-drö-gya-tso cites demand that A-ku Lo-drö-gya-tso's re-framing be seen as a criticism of a basic error by Dzong-ka-ba. Thus, despite the openness of A-ku Lo-drö-gya-tso's citing Tsay-den-hla-ram-ba's probable source, he does not own up to the frequency of such statements in *The Essence of Eloquence;* Dzong-ka-ba uses the same phraseology so frequently that it is clear it is not just a slip!

Jik-may-dam-chö-gya-tso[253] takes a tack more to my liking. He holds that although Proponents of Sūtra do not **assert** that a form's being the referent of a conceptual consciousness is established by way of its own character, they do not **realize** that it is not so established. This is because, despite what they assert,

---

[a] *gzugs sogs rtog pa'i zhen gzhir rang mtshan gyis grub par sgro btags pa.*

[b] See issues #96-98 and 100.

[c] Jik-may-dam-chö-gya-tso (*Port of Entry,* 174) reports that the *Clearing Away Mental Darkness* says that it is difficult to find a source in Dzong-ka-ba's writings for the identification of the imputational nature as the superimposed factor of being established by way of its own character as the referent of a conceptual consciousness. I agree.

form's being the referent of a conceptual consciousness is, for them, established by the power of the object itself without depending on terms and conceptual consciousnesses.

Issue #80: Is being the referent itself an imputational nature?

A-ku Lo-drö-gya-tso[254] also attacks Tsay-den-hla-ram-ba's position with reasoning. His objection revolves around the central doctrine that the three natures must be posited with respect to every phenomenon. For instance:

- a form itself is its other-powered nature
- its establishment by way of its own character as the referent of a conceptual consciousness is its imputational nature, and
- its emptiness of being established that way is its thoroughly established nature.

A-ku Lo-drö-gya-tso points out that, therefore, the establishment by way of its own character that is falsely seen as a quality of form's **being** the referent of a conceptual consciousness is a nature of character that is non-existent not with respect to **form** but with respect to form's **being** the referent of a conceptual consciousness, which itself is an imputational nature of form.

His reasoning strikes me as sound, but his own identification of "imputational nature" as a superimposed factor seems to me to be subject to the same fault. For since Gung-tang clearly identifies the "superimposed factor" as the **appearance** of forms and so forth being established by way of their own character as the referents of their respective conceptual consciousnesses, A-ku Lo-drö-gya-tso's reasoning militates against his own view since the appearance of such is not the other-powered nature of form but an imputational nature of form. Even if he took "superimposed factor" as referring to the establishment of objects by way of their own character as the referents of conceptual consciousnesses, this is also an imputational nature of objects!

It seems to me that A-ku Lo-drö-gya-tso faults Tsay-den-hla-ram-ba's discussion of imputational natures as being character-non-natures for not being a discussion of other-powered natures as not established by way of their own character as the imputational nature—a fault that he himself cannot escape.

Issue #81: How to avoid the fault that Proponents of Sūtra could realize that the relevant imputational nature is not established by way of its own character?

The original formulator of the textbook literature of the Go-mang tradition, Gung-ru Chö-jung,[255] attempts to avoid the possible fault that even Proponents of Sūtra Following Reasoning could realize that being the referents of conceptual consciousnesses is not established by way of its own character by substituting the notion of the **appearance** of being established by way of its own character as the referent of a conceptual consciousness. Indeed, Gung-ru Chö-jung's reformulation leads his followers into myriad distinctions that at times become so intense that the topic seems to shrivel under the dry light of so much attention. (Indeed, the reader may want to turn to chapters 18-20 on the thoroughly established nature and return to these issues later.)

Gung-ru Chö-jung reformulates the sūtra statement using a dual subject, one existent and one non-existent:

> With respect to the subject, **the establishment of forms and so forth by way of their own character as the referents of conceptual consciousnesses** and **the superimposed factor [or appearance] of forms and so forth as established by way of their own character as the referents of conceptual consciousnesses**, there are reasons for calling these "non-natures of character" because the reasons are that (1) from the positive side they are only posited by names and terminology and (2) from the negative side they are not established by way of their own character.

He identifies the imputational natures that are relevant on this occasion of the *Sūtra Unraveling the Thought* as twofold:

1. the establishment of forms and so forth by way of their own character as the referents of conceptual consciousnesses
2. the superimposed factor [or appearance] of forms and so forth as established by way of their own character as the referents of conceptual consciousnesses.

Gung-ru Chö-jung chooses a dual subject, the first existent and the second non-existent, because Ḏzong-ka-ḇa emphasizes that among imputational natures there are two varieties—those that exist, such as (to use Ḏzong-ka-ḇa's own words) a form's being a referent of a conceptual consciousness, and those that do not exist, such as a form's establishment by way of its own character as the referent of a conceptual consciousness.

Gung-ru Chö-jung switches from Ḏzong-ka-ḇa's vocabulary of **being the referent of a conceptual consciousness** to a **superimposed factor**, which he implicitly indicates and Gung-tang explicitly identifies to be the **appearance** of forms and so forth as established by way of their own character as the referents of conceptual consciousnesses. Furthermore, he includes in his identification of imputational natures the phrase "established by way of its own character," whereas the intuitive reading of the sūtra statement that imputational natures are without "nature in terms of character" is that non-establishment by way of its own character goes not with the subject (imputational natures), but with the predicate ("are character-non-natures").

Issue #82: How to read Jam-ȳang-shay-b̄a's reducing Gung-ru Chö-jung's dual subject to a single one?

Gung-ru Chö-jung's followers are left with much to unpack. First, Jam-ȳang-shay-b̄a,[256] who cribbed much of his commentary from Gung-ru Chö-jung, repeatedly indicates the importance of this dual identification, but in reformulating the meaning of the sūtra he strangely keeps only the second meaning:

> With respect to the subject, **the superimposed factor [or appearance] of forms and so forth as established by way of their own character as the referents of conceptual consciousnesses**, there are reasons for calling this a "character-non-nature" because the reasons are that (1) from the positive side it is only posited by names and terminology and (2) from the negative side it is not established by way of its own character.

My guess on why he uses only the second meaning is that he wishes to emphasize that the imputational nature relevant on this occasion is not just the first, non-existent one but also is the one that exists. It is also possible that he may just have made an error copying Gung-ru Chö-jung's text at this point, for in his *Brief Decisive Analysis*[257] he gives both. In any case, it is clear from his own and his followers' statements that both are included even though, as will be explained below, Gung-tang expounds on the impact of choosing only the existent subject. Before treating this, let us turn to other issues.

Issue #83: How many relevant imputational natures are there?

As a reason why imputational natures in general cannot be the referent of Buddha's statement, Gung-tang[258] states that the import of the character-non-nature explicitly indicated at this point in the *Sūtra Unraveling the Thought* must be posited as "arriving at the subtle selflessness of phenomena," and, as has been shown, that imputational natures (in general, rather than a specific type of imputational nature) are not established by way of their own character cannot be the subtle selflessness of phenomena in the Mind-Only School (since otherwise uncompounded space's non-establishment by way of its own character would be an emptiness, and it would absurdly have to be said that Proponents of Sūtra realize emptiness). Hence, when the *Sūtra Unraveling the Thought* speaks of imputational natures as not being established by way of their own character, it cannot be referring to imputational natures in general.

Still, Gung-tang holds that the imputational natures relevant here must be of **two** varieties in terms of the selflessness of phenomena and the selflessness of persons, for even though on the explicit level, when the *Sūtra Unraveling the Thought* teaches that imputational natures lack character-nature, it is speaking in terms of the selflessness of phenomena, on the implicit or subsidiary level it is speaking in terms of the selflessness of persons. The reason for this is that in the *Sūtra Unraveling the Thought* (*Emptiness in Mind-Only,* 82-83) the two parts of Buddha's answer to Paramārthasamudgata's question, the brief indication:

> Paramārthasamudgata, thinking of three non-natures of phenomena—character-non-nature, production-non-nature, and ultimate-non-nature—I taught [in the middle wheel of the teaching], "All phenomena are natureless."

and extensive explanation (*Emptiness in Mind-Only,* 86, 87, 88, 90):

> Concerning that, what are character-non-natures of phenomena? Those which are imputational characters.
>
> Why? It is thus: Those [imputational characters] are characters posited by names and terminology[a] and do not subsist by way of their own character. Therefore, they are said to be "character-non-natures."
>
> What are production-non-natures of phenomena?[b] Those which are the other-powered characters of phenomena.
>
> Why? It is thus: Those [other-powered characters] arise through the force of other conditions and not by themselves.[c] Therefore, they are said to be "production-non-natures."
>
> What are ultimate-non-natures? Those dependently arisen phenomena—which are natureless due to being natureless in terms of production—are also natureless due to being natureless in terms of the ultimate.
>
> Why? Paramārthasamudgata, that which is an object of observation of purification in phenomena I teach to be the ultimate, and other-powered characters are not the object of observation of purification. Therefore, they are said to be "ultimate-non-natures."
>
> Moreover, that which is the thoroughly established character of phenomena is also called "the ultimate-non-nature." Why? Paramārthasamudgata, that which in phenomena is the selflessness of phenomena is called their "non-nature." It is the ultimate, and the ultimate is distinguished by just the naturelessness of all phenomena; therefore, it is called the "ultimate-non-nature."

both comment on the Perfection of Wisdom Sūtras explicitly in terms of the selflessness of phenomena and implicitly in terms of the selflessness of persons. This is done by explicitly indicating that, with respect to the middle wheel, the basis in Buddha's thought was the three non-natures in terms of the selflessness

a See issue #104.

b Roughly, this means, "What phenomena are without the nature of self-production?" See issues #76, 77. About "phenomena," see #71.

c See issue #67.

of phenomena and by implicitly indicating that, with respect to the first wheel, the basis in Buddha's thought was the three non-natures in terms of the selflessness of persons. This is done by way of explaining that those having the lineage of the Great Vehicle attain their enlightenment through meditating on the subtle selflessness of phenomena and by way of subsidiarily explaining that those having the lineage of the Lesser Vehicle attain their enlightenment through meditating on the selflessness of persons. Thus, those having the lineage of the Great Vehicle meditate on the thoroughly established nature in terms of the selflessness of phenomena, whereas those having the lineage of the Lesser Vehicle meditate on the thoroughly established nature in terms of the selflessness of persons.

If we skirt, for the time being, a controversy about identifying the selflessness of persons and use a fairly standard formula, the imputational natures relevant at this point in the *Sūtra Unraveling the Thought*—when we take into account both what is explicitly indicated and what is implicitly indicated—are taken in the Go-mang tradition as being:

In terms of the selflessness of phenomena

1. the establishment of forms and so forth by way of their own character as the referents of conceptual consciousnesses
2. the superimposed factor [or appearance] of forms and so forth as established by way of their own character as the referents of conceptual consciousnesses.

In terms of the selflessness of person

1. the establishment of persons as substantially existent in the sense of being self-sufficient
2. the superimposed factor [or appearance] of persons as substantially existent in the sense of being self-sufficient.

Extending this to include the differentiation of the imputation of entities and of attributes, the imputational natures relevant here are twofold in two ways each:

1a. the establishment of forms and so forth by way of their own character as the referents of conceptual consciousnesses **imputing entities**

1b. the establishment of forms and so forth by way of their own character as the referents of conceptual consciousnesses **imputing attributes**

2a. the superimposed factor [or appearance] of forms and so forth as established by way of their own character as the referents of conceptual consciousnesses **imputing entities**

2b. the superimposed factor [or appearance] of forms and so forth as established by way of their own character as the referents of conceptual consciousnesses **imputing attributes**.

In addition, as Jam-ȳang-shay-b̄a[259] says, a distinction must be made between factors imputed in the manner of entity and attribute **in terms of the selflessness of phenomena** and **in terms of the selflessness of persons**. The three natures are to be considered in two lights, one in terms of the selflessness of phenomena—this being the main meaning taught[a] in the middle wheel—and one in terms of the selflessness of persons.

The latter is said to be the secondary meaning taught[b] in the middle wheel of doctrine. The intended trainees of the **explicit** teaching in the middle wheel are (sharp) Proponents of Mind-Only[c] and the intended trainees of the **implicit** teaching of the middle wheel are the two Hearer schools, the Great Exposition and the Sūtra schools.

Issue #84: How can the path of purification be one if practitioners of the Low and Great Vehicles meditate on different thoroughly established natures?

The *Sūtra Unraveling the Thought* says that practitioners of all three lineages—Bodhisattva, Hearer, and Solitary Realizer—attain their respective enlightenments through meditating on other-powered natures as empty of the imputational nature. The "imputational nature," however, is understood differently by those practitioners. For Bodhisattvas, it refers to the self of phenomena, whereas for Hearers and Solitary Realizers it refers to a self of persons.

D̄zong-ka-b̄a (*Emptiness in Mind-Only*, 220-221), paraphrasing the *Sūtra Unraveling the Thought*, says:[d]

> The *Sūtra Unraveling the Thought* says that through manifestly conceiving the imputational nature in other-powered natures, [all] afflictive emotions are produced and, due to that, karmas are accumulated whereby one revolves in cyclic existence. Also, it says that if one sees other-powered natures as without the nature of character that is the imputational character, those are overcome in that order. It then says that the three—Hearers, Solitary Realizers, and Bodhisattvas—through just this path and just this practice attain nirvana, due to which the paths of purification of those [three vehicles] and also their purification are one, there being no second.[e]

---

a *bstan don gtso bo.*

b *bstan don phal pa.*

c The intended trainees of the literal reading of the middle wheel are the Consequentialists.

d This presentation is put forth by an objector, but D̄zong-ka-b̄a has no quarrel with these points.

e See also issue #86.

His first reference to the *Sūtra Unraveling the Thought*—about the process of affliction—is:[260]

> Superimposing the imputational nature onto other-powered natures and thoroughly established natures, sentient beings designate the convention that other-powered natures and thoroughly established natures are of the character of the imputational nature. In just the way that they designate such conventions, [their] minds are thoroughly infused with such designations of conventions, and due to relation with the designation of conventions or due to the dormancies of designations, they manifestly conceive other-powered natures and thoroughly established natures to be of the character of the imputational nature. In just the way that they manifestly conceive this, in that same way—due to the causes and conditions of manifestly conceiving other-powered natures as being of the imputational nature—in the future other-powered natures are thoroughly generated.
>
> On that basis, they become thoroughly afflicted by the afflictions that are the afflictive emotions. Also, they are thoroughly afflicted by the afflictions that are actions and the afflictions that are the production of a lifetime. For a long time, they transmigrate as hell-beings, animals, gods, demi-gods, or humans, and travel about within these transmigrations, not passing beyond cyclic existence.

The second reference—about the process of liberation—is:[261]

> Because, hearing these doctrines, they do not conceive other-powered natures in the manner of the imputational character, they believe, thoroughly differentiate, and realize properly that [other-powered natures] are natureless in terms of production, natureless in terms of character, and natureless in terms of the ultimate.... Moreover, on this basis, they thoroughly develop aversion toward all compositional phenomena, become completely free from desire, become completely released, and become thoroughly released from the afflictions that are the afflictive emotions, the afflictions that are actions, and the afflictions that are births.

The third reference—about the similarity of the paths of the various practitioners—occurs shortly after the passage cited at the beginning of this chapter:[262]

> Paramārthasamudgata, concerning that, even sentient beings having the lineage of those of the Hearer Vehicle attain a nirvana of unsurpassed achievement and bliss through just this path and just this procedure. Also, sentient beings having the lineage of those of the Solitary Realizer Vehicle and those having the lineage of Ones Gone Thus attain a nirvana of unsurpassed achievement and bliss through just this

path and just this procedure. Therefore, this is the sole path of purification of Hearers, Solitary Realizers, and Bodhisattvas, and the purification is also one; there is no second. Thinking of this, I teach one vehicle, but it is not that there are not varieties of sentient beings—the naturally dull, middling, and sharp—among the types of sentient beings.

This passage more than suggests that all three types of practitioners meditate on the same thoroughly established nature and achieve the same state of release, but this is contradicted in the sūtra itself where it indicates that some Hearers achieve merely a solitary state of release. Immediately after the previous passage, Buddha says:

> Paramārthasamudgata, even though all the Buddhas exert themselves [on their behalf], persons who have the lineage of Hearers who proceed solely to peacefulness are unable to attain the unsurpassed, perfect enlightenment upon being set in the essence of enlightenments. Why is this? It is thus: due to very limited compassion and great fear of suffering, they are naturally of an inferior lineage. Just as their compassion is very limited, so they have turned away from the welfare of sentient beings. Just as they are very afraid of suffering, so they have turned away from the thorough compoundedness of all compounded phenomena.
>
> I do not describe those who have turned away from others' welfare and have turned away from the thorough compoundedness of compounded phenomena as unsurpassably, perfectly enlightened. Therefore, they are called "those who seek peace for themselves alone."

Since the sūtra itself describes the attainments of practitioners of the vehicles so differently, Ḏzong-ka-ḇa takes its declaration that the states of purification of the three vehicles are one as meaning merely that all three deliver beings from cyclic existence (even though the path of Bodhisattvas additionally accomplishes Buddhahood). Also, the paths of purification of the three vehicles are the same only in the sense that the path to accomplish this level of nirvāṇa is meditation on the selflessness of persons, even if Bodhisattvas also meditate on the selflessness of phenomena. It is noteworthy that although the selflessness of persons is mentioned once in Chapter Three and three times in Chapter Eight of the *Sūtra Unraveling the Thought*,[a] the fact that Hearers and Solitary

[a] For instance, in the "Questions of Maitreya Chapter," Buddha says:

> ...when one thoroughly knows the objects of the suchness of character, then the signs of selflessness of persons, the signs of selflessness of phenomena, the signs of cognition-only, and the signs of the ultimate are eliminated by the emptiness of what has passed beyond the extremes, by the emptiness of non-things, by the emptiness of inherent existence of non-things, and by the emptiness of the ultimate....

Realizers meditate on the selflessness of persons is never addressed explicitly. However, Ḏzong-ka-ḇa (*Emptiness in Mind-Only,* 224) holds that when it **explicitly** lays out the three natures in terms of the selflessness of phenomena, it **implicitly** indicates that the emptiness of the imputational factor of a self of persons in other-powered natures—the mental and physical aggregates—is posited as the thoroughly established nature that is the selflessness of persons. Therefore, it is implicit to the exposition in the *Sūtra Unraveling the Thought* that Hearers and Solitary Realizers, for whom the first wheel was taught, are suitable as vessels for realizing the thoroughly established nature in terms of the selflessness of persons but not the thoroughly established nature in terms of the selflessness of phenomena. He says that it is in this sense that the *Sūtra Unraveling the Thought* is for the sake of those engaged in **all** vehicles.

For these reasons, imputational natures at this point need to be framed in terms of both the selflessness of phenomena and the selflessness of persons.

Issue #85: How to get around Ḏzong-ka-ḇa's speaking of imputational phenomena as if they were the imputational natures relevant here?

As Gung-ru Chö-jung and Jam-ȳang-shay-ḇa say, the *Sūtra Unraveling the Thought*—when it speaks of imputational natures as not being established by way of their own character—cannot be referring just to any imputational natures:

- because the Proponents of Sūtra realize that imputational natures are not established by way of their own character, since they realize that imputational natures are just imputed by conceptuality,[263] for they are persons who realize imputational natures to be imputational natures.
- A person who, with valid cognition, ascertains imputational natures as imputational natures necessarily is a person who ascertains imputational natures as just imputed by conceptuality because that which is just imputed by conceptuality is the definition of an imputational nature. To realize something, one must know its meaning, its definition, the nature that defines it.

Gung-ru Chö-jung[264] and Jam-ȳang-shay-ḇa[265] add that, furthermore, imputational phenomena such as uncompounded space could not be the "imputational natures" explicitly indicated in the *Sūtra Unraveling the Thought* at the point when in answer to the rhetorical question, "Paramārthasamudgata, concerning that, what are character-non-natures of phenomena?" Buddha says, "Those which are imputational characters." For, such imputational phenomena

See C. John Powers, *Wisdom of Buddha: Saṁdhinirmocana Sūtra* (Berkeley, Calif.: Dharma, 1995), 191.

are not the imputational factor, the emptiness of which is posited as the thoroughly established nature, and thus are not the imputational nature that is relevant on the occasion of positing the thoroughly established nature. As Ḏzong-ka-ḇa (*Emptiness in Mind-Only,* 85) says:

> Although among imputational factors in general there are many, such as all generally characterized phenomena and space, and so forth, the reason why these are not [explicitly] mentioned in the *Sūtra Unraveling the Thought*[a] is that they are not relevant on the occasion of the imputational factor, the emptiness of which is posited as the thoroughly established nature.[b]

Here Ḏzong-ka-ḇa clearly says that imputational natures in this context are not just any imputational phenomena but have to be relevant to the positing of emptiness, the thoroughly established nature.

However, on another occasion (*Emptiness in Mind-Only,* 239) he seems to imply elsewise:[c]

> Since **imputational phenomena** are not established by way of their own character, they are non-natures ultimately [that is, are without the nature of existing ultimately or by way of their own character].

On the surface, it seems that Ḏzong-ka-ḇa is saying that imputational phenomena (which include uncompounded space and so forth) are the imputational natures explicitly indicated at this point and that their not being established by way of their own character is the meaning of the character-non-nature. Gung-ru Chö-jung[266] and Jam-ȳang-shay-ḇa,[d] however, adjust Ḏzong-ka-ḇa's statement so that it reads "Since **the phenomena that are the basis of imputing the imputational nature** are not established by way of their own character as the referents of conceptual consciousnesses...." They creatively adjust

---

[a] Ḏzong-ka-ḇa says that space is "not mentioned in the *Sūtra Unraveling the Thought,*" but Jik-may-dam-chö-gya-tso (*Port of Entry,* 620.6, 625.4-625.6) points out that space is indeed mentioned in the *Sūtra Unraveling the Thought* (see issue #139, for six occurrences in the sūtra) as an example for the thoroughly established nature. Thus he cogently interprets Ḏzong-ka-ḇa as meaning that the sūtra at the point of the extensive indication identifying imputational natures does not explicitly say that space, and so forth, are imputational natures since, except for imputational natures in the manner of entity and attribute, space and so forth are not relevant on the occasion of identifying the thoroughly established nature.

[b] See issues #89-92.

[c] The Tibetan (*Emptiness in Mind-Only,* 447) is: *kun btags kyi chos rnams rang gi mtshan nyid kyis ma grub pas don dam par ngo bo med pa dang.* Both Gung-ru Chö-jung (20b.5) and Jam-ȳang-shay-ḇa (52.5) misquote the passage as *kun btags kyi chos rnams rang gi mtshan nyid kyis ma grub pas* ***mtshan nyid*** *ngo bo med pa dang.*

[d] Jam-ȳang-shay-ḇa's *Great Exposition of the Interpretable and the Definitive,* 53.1: *kun btags 'dogs gzhir gyur pa'i chos rnam rang 'dzin rtog pa'i zhen gzhir rang gi mtshan nyid kyis grub pa...*; he is following Gung-ru Chö-jung's *Garland of White Lotuses,* 21a.1.

Ḏzong-ka-ḇa's statement so that it does not contradict the earlier one.

Thus, according to Gung-ru Chö-jung and Jam-ȳang-shay-ḇa, on this occasion the imputational natures explicitly indicated are not imputational phenomena in general but:

1. establishment of phenomena by way of their own character as the referents of a conceptual consciousness, those phenomena being the bases of imputation of that imputational nature
2. the superimposed factor—that is, the image—of such that appears to the mind.

Hence, the meaning of the **character-non-nature** explicitly indicated on this occasion comes to involve the emptiness of objects' being established by way of their own character as the referents of conceptual consciousnesses and the emptiness of being established in accordance with such a superimposed factor. Gung-ru Chö-jung and Jam-ȳang-shay-ḇa claim that this is what Ḏzong-ka-ḇa's latter statement means even if it blatantly seems to say otherwise. (More likely, Ḏzong-ka-ḇa just slipped up.)

Their re-reading is appropriate in the context of Ḏzong-ka-ḇa's general system because it fits with another statement (*Emptiness in Mind-Only,* 110):

> With respect to the imputational factor of which [other-powered natures] are empty, on both occasions of identifying the imputational factor in the sūtra it does not speak of any other imputational factor than just factors imputed in the manner of entities and attributes. I will explain the reason for this later.

Ḏzong-ka-ḇa later (*Emptiness in Mind-Only,* 217) explains:

> Although among imputational factors in general there are many, such as all generally characterized phenomena, space, and so forth, the reason why these are not [explicitly] mentioned in the *Sūtra Unraveling the Thought* is that they are not relevant on the occasion of the imputational factor, the emptiness of which is posited as the thoroughly established nature.

Again, according to Gung-ru Chö-jung and Jam-ȳang-shay-ḇa, the imputational natures relevant to the positing of emptiness are not uncompounded space and so forth but (1) establishment of objects by way of their own character as the referents of conceptual consciousnesses and (2) the appearance of such.

Issue #86: What do the lower schools realize about the three natures?

What do the intended trainees of the implicit teaching of the *Sūtra Unraveling the Thought*, the Great Exposition School and the Sūtra School, understand about the three natures? Though the sūtra itself does not address the issue, it must be addressed for the differences of the path structures of the Lesser and Great Vehicles to make sense. Most Ge-luk-b̄a commentators say that Lesser Vehicle understanding of the three natures in terms of the selflessness of persons means that they realize that:

1. other-powered natures are things produced, not by themselves, but by causes and conditions
2. imputational natures are the falsely ascribed sense of a substantially existent, self-sufficient person or objects of use of such a person
3. the thoroughly established nature is the absence of such a substantially existent, self-sufficient person or objects of use of such a person.

Taking the three natures this way, practitioners of Lesser Vehicle tenets cultivate the path and achieve their respective enlightenments.

Jam-ȳang-shay-b̄a,[267] however, takes imputational natures (in terms of the selflessness of persons) in a way parallel to that presented for Great Vehicle practitioners. Just as imputational natures in terms of the selflessness of phenomena are the twofold superimposed factors of an object, such as a bulbous-bellied, flat-bottomed thing able to hold fluid, as **established by way of its own character** as the referent of the term for its entity "pot" and as the referent of the term for its attribute "beautiful," so imputational natures in terms of the selflessness of persons are the twofold superimposition of an object, such as a bulbous-bellied, flat-bottomed thing able to hold water, as **established substantially** or **self-sufficiently** as the referent of the term "pot" and as the referent of the term "beautiful." Thus, in terms of the selflessness of persons, the imputational natures to which the *Sūtra Unraveling the Thought* refers are establishment of objects **substantially** or **self-sufficiently** as the referents of terms or conceptual consciousnesses and the superimposed factor (that is, appearance) of objects as established **substantially** or **self-sufficiently** as the referents of terms or conceptual consciousnesses. Jam-ȳang-shay-b̄a considers an awareness that conceives objects to be established this way as a consciousness conceiving a self of persons, even though it does not necessarily have a person as its object of observation. Hence, he also considers the emptiness of being established in this way to be a thoroughly established nature in terms of the subtle selflessness of persons.

Jam-ȳang-shay-b̄a claims that between the selflessness of persons and the selflessness of phenomena there is a great difference in terms of the subtlety of the object of negation because establishment of objects **substantially** or **self-sufficiently** as the referents of conceptual consciousnesses and establishment of objects **by way of their own character** as the referents of conceptual consciousnesses differ considerably in subtlety. However, he does not explicate this difference which, frankly, seems difficult to make! The fact that he merely puts forth such an insistent claim without explicating the difference suggests the difficult spot he finds himself in.

Issue #87: How to quibble against identifying the explicitly indicated imputational nature as "factor imputed in the manner of entity and attribute"?

Once Jam-ȳang-shay-b̄a has given his own different version of the relevant imputational nature, it is incumbent for him to criticize other formulations, during which interesting points become clear. Arguing against Paṇ-chen S̄ö-nam-drak-b̄a's and Jay-d̄zün Chö-ḡyi-gyel-tsen's identification of the imputational nature relevant here as "factors imputed in the manner of entity and attribute," he complains that since this identification does not specify whether the reference is to what is **explicitly** or **implicitly** indicated in the *Sūtra Unraveling the Thought,* it is mistaken to hold that "factors imputed in the manner of entity and attribute" is the imputational nature to which the *Sūtra Unraveling the Thought* **explicitly** refers. For "factors imputed in the manner of entity and attribute" could be either the selflessness of persons or the selflessness of phenomena or both, and the only type of selflessness that is **explicitly** indicated here is that in terms of the self of phenomena.

Jam-ȳang-shay-b̄a's criticism is that the term is too broad to describe what Buddha **explicitly** indicates since "factors imputed in the manner of entities and attributes" include imputational natures in the imputation of entity and attribute **in terms of the selflessness of persons**. However, D̄zong-ka-b̄a himself never qualifies the phrase with either the self of persons or the self of phenomena, such as when he (*Emptiness in Mind-Only,* 110) says:

> With respect to the imputational factor of which [other-powered natures] are empty, on both occasions of identifying the imputational factor in the sūtra it does not speak of any other imputational factor than just **factors imputed in the manner of entities and attributes.**

For all of these scholars, the two selflessnesses are mutually exclusive—whatever is a selflessness of persons is not a selflessness of phenomena and whatever is a selflessness of phenomena is not a selflessness of persons (although whatever is without a self of persons is without a self of phenomena and vice versa). Hence, the thoroughly established nature in terms of the selflessness of persons and the thoroughly established nature in terms of the selflessness of phenomena are also mutually exclusive, the latter being what is explicitly indicated in the *Sūtra Unraveling the Thought* at this point of discussing the middle wheel.

Issue #88: Do the imputational natures indicated here only exist or only not exist?

As we have seen, for Gung-ru Chö-jung and Jam-ȳang-shay-b̄a, the explicit reference of "imputational natures" is (1) to the establishment of a bulbous thing, for instance, by way of its own character as the referent of a conceptual consciousness apprehending it as "pot" or as the referent of the term "pot" or (2) to the superimposed factor (that is, the appearance) of a bulbous thing as established by way of its own character as the referent of a conceptual consciousness apprehending it as "pot" or as the referent of the term "pot."

Gung-ru Chö-jung[268] and Jam-ȳang-shay-b̄a[269] make the point that since the first of those two is non-existent but the second exists, it cannot be said that the imputational natures explicitly indicated at this point in the *Sūtra Unraveling the Thought* either necessarily exist or necessarily do not exist. Although the general category—imputational natures explicitly indicated at this point in the *Sūtra Unraveling the Thought*—exists, whatever is an imputational nature explicitly indicated at this point in the *Sūtra Unraveling the Thought* does not either necessarily exist or necessarily not exist, since one class does and the other class does not. Jam-ȳang-shay-b̄a says that this is what D̄zong-ka-b̄a (*Emptiness in Mind-Only,* 195) has in mind when, later, he says:

> Therefore, if you do not know what this imputational factor that is a **superimposed factor**[a] of a self of phenomena on other-powered natures is, you will not know in a decisive way the conception of a self of phenomena and the selflessness of phenomena in this [Mind-Only] system.

According to Gung-ru Chö-jung and Jam-ȳang-shay-b̄a, in order to make sense of D̄zong-ka-b̄a's referring to "superimposed factor,"[b] an existent imputational nature—specifically the superimposed factor (that is, appearance) of an object as established by way of its own character as the referent of its respective conceptual consciousness—must be posited. (Thus, when Buddha, in answer to his rhetorical question, says, "Those which are imputational characters," they hold that he is explicitly referring to two types of imputational natures, one existent and the other non-existent). Jam-ȳang-shay-b̄a sees D̄zong-ka-b̄a as saying that if one does not know the **mode of superimposition**[c] of the self of phenomena on other-powered natures, one will not have a decisive understanding of the selflessness of phenomena in this system.[d] In order to make this point

[a] See issues #96-98 and 100.

[b] *gzhan dbang la chos bdag* ***sgro btags pa'i*** *kun brtags.*

[c] Jam-ȳang-shay-b̄a's *Great Exposition of the Interpretable and the Definitive,* 55.1: *gzhan dbang la chos bdag* ***sgro btags pa'i sgro 'dogs tshul.*** Gung-ru Chö-jung (*Garland of White Lotuses,* 21b.6) does not include *tshul.*

[d] For a different reading of this passage, see 195.

Jam-ȳang-shay-b̄a switches from "superimposed factor" to "mode of superimposition," whereas his predecessor Gung-ru Chö-jung gives a different, but similarly slippery, reading—according to him D̄zong-ka-b̄a's point is that one will not have a decisive understanding of the **apprehension of a self of phenomena**—this meaning a consciousness apprehending a self of phenomena—and of the selflessness of phenomena in the Mind-Only School.

They point to the further evidence that when D̄zong-ka-b̄a describes the usage—in the *Sūtra Unraveling the Thought*—of a flower in the sky as an example for imputational natures, he makes it clear that imputational natures are of two types. The sūtra (*Emptiness in Mind-Only,* 93) says:

> It is thus: for example, character-non-natures [that is, imputational natures] are to be viewed as like a flower in the sky.

D̄zong-ka-b̄a explains that the example of a flower in the sky (which, like a pie in the sky, is totally non-existent) is used to indicate not that just as a flower in the sky is non-existent so are imputational natures, but that just as a flower in the sky is only imputed by conceptuality, so imputational natures are only imputed by conceptuality. He (*Emptiness in Mind-Only,* 93) says:

> The similarity of imputational factors with a flower in the sky is an example of their merely being imputed by conceptuality and is not an example of their not occurring among objects of knowledge [that is, existents].

Jam-ȳang-shay-b̄a cogently assumes that D̄zong-ka-b̄a in this passage is using the term "imputational factors" in its strict sense, which is limited to those relevant on the occasion of positing emptiness and thus does not include uncompounded space, and so forth; hence, he draws the conclusion that for D̄zong-ka-b̄a the imputational natures mentioned in the *Sūtra Unraveling the Thought*—when Buddha says that imputational natures are character-non-natures—include both existent and non-existent varieties. (Another not so likely possibility is that D̄zong-ka-b̄a moves back and forth between speaking about the imputational natures specifically discussed in the sūtra and imputational natures in general.)

Also, Jam-ȳang-shay-b̄a cogently holds that it is clear that with regard to Buddha's statement, "Those [imputational characters] are characters posited by names and terminology and do not subsist by way of their own character," D̄zong-ka-b̄a makes the distinction that there are two types, those established and those not established by valid cognition. For he (*Emptiness in Mind-Only,* 210) says:

> Thus, form and so forth being the referents of conceptual consciousnesses[a] is an imputational factor posited by name and terminology,

[a] See issues #78-82.

> but, since it is established by valid cognition, it cannot be refuted.[a] However, that it is established **by way of the thing's own character** is an imputational factor posited only nominally that does not occur among objects of knowledge [that is, does not exist]. Hence, among what are posited by names and terminology there are two [types], those established by valid cognition and those not established by valid cognition.

From this, Jam-ȳang-shay-b̄a concludes that the distinction of there being both existent and non-existent imputational natures must be made even with respect to the limited meaning of imputational natures on the occasion of this discussion in the *Sūtra Unraveling the Thought*. It should be noted that Jam-ȳang-shay-b̄a repeatedly takes the existent one as the **superimposed factor** (or appearance) of objects as established by way of their own character as the referents of their respective conceptual consciousnesses, whereas D̄zong-ka-b̄a here and elsewhere speaks of "form and so forth **being** the referents of a conceptual consciousness." As detailed above, Jam-ȳang-shay-b̄a is trying to avoid the fault that proponents of a lower view, the Sūtra School, would absurdly be able to realize emptiness as it is described in the Mind-Only School if D̄zong-ka-b̄a's identification were left as it is.

Issue #89: How is an appearance relevant to positing emptiness?

Since such imputational natures refer to those relevant to positing emptiness, those relevant to positing emptiness must include an existent variety, and since Gung-ru Chö-jung and Jam-ȳang-shay-b̄a want to avoid accepting (despite bountiful evidence to the contrary in D̄zong-ka-b̄a's words) that this is "form and so forth **being** the referents of a conceptual consciousness," they say that the existent variety is the superimposed factor, the appearance, of an object's being established by way of its own character as the referent of a conceptual consciousness or term. In showing **how** this is relevant, they rely on the generally accepted notion that to ascertain the selflessness of phenomena it is necessary for the generic image—technically, the meaning-generality[b]—of such establishment to appear as an object to the mind, for such establishment is the object of negation. To do this, it is necessary for the mode of superimposition of such a self of phenomena to appear to the mind. Thus, Gung-ru Chö-jung and Jam-ȳang-shay-b̄a conclude that both the self of phenomena that is the object of negation (specifically, the establishment of objects by way of their own character as the referents of conceptual consciousnesses and of terms) and the

---

[a] See issue #108.

[b] *don spyi, arthasāmānya.*

superimposed factor (or appearance) of such are relevant on the occasion of positing the thoroughly established nature.[a]

Their attempt to show the relevancy of this appearance to the process of meditating on emptiness is elegant, in the sense that it is founded in standard Ge-luk-b̄a doctrines, for without the appearance of the image—the meaning-generality—of the object of negation, the mere absence that is the negation of it cannot appear to the mind. As an Indian source quote, Ge-luk-b̄a scholars frequently point to Shāntideva's *Engaging in the Bodhisattva Deeds* which says:[270]

> Without contacting the imagined existent
> Its non-existence is not apprehended.

The point that a conceptual image must appear hinges on the fact that since the self of phenomena does not exist, it cannot appear to the mind except through the appearance of an image of it. For example, the **image** of the horns of a rabbit can appear to the mind despite their non-existence.

Gung-ru Chö-jung and Jam-ȳang-shay-b̄a thereby make sense out of not just D̄zong-ka-b̄a's references to the self of phenomena but also to his reference to the **superimposed factor** of such. For even though a superimposed factor could be a non-existent, they feel that D̄zong-ka-b̄a must have had a special meaning in mind to add this term here—that special meaning being the existent appearance of such a non-existent. Still, it needs to be noted that D̄zong-ka-b̄a never identifies the superimposed factor as such an appearance and thus never makes the case that such an appearance is relevant to positing emptiness due to the fact that it must be identified in the process of meditating on emptiness. Gung-ru Chö-jung and Jam-ȳang-shay-b̄a creatively make sense out of a number of D̄zong-ka-b̄a's positions that their founder did not explicitly tie together.

Issue #90: How to twist D̄zong-ka-b̄a's clear suggestion that the relevant imputational nature is non-existent into allowing for an existent appearance?

Gung-ru Chö-jung and Jam-ȳang-shay-b̄a's explanation appears to be forced when we notice that D̄zong-ka-b̄a (*Emptiness in Mind-Only,* 85) does not appear to allow that there are two such varieties when he says:

[a] Although I have identified the "superimposed factor" all along as an appearance or image, it is only in this discussion that we learn this from Gung-ru Chö-jung and Jam-ȳang-shay-b̄a. They first treat the existent imputational nature (*kun btags*) here as being a superimposed factor (*sgro btags*); they then transform this into "mode of superimposition" (Gung-ru Chö-jung, 23a.6, *sgro btags tshul;* Jam-ȳang-shay-b̄a, 57.4, *sgro 'dogs tshul*), which they—with considerable freedom—take to be the "meaning-generality" (*don spyi*) of the object of negation, which must appear to the mind so that the non-existence of this status can be meditated. The circuit of evidence is thin.

> Although among imputational factors in general there are many, such as all generally characterized phenomena and space, and so forth, the reason why these are not [explicitly] mentioned in the *Sūtra Unraveling the Thought* is that they are not relevant on the occasion of the imputational factor, the **emptiness of which is posited as the thoroughly established nature.**

Even Gung-ru Chö-jung[271] and Jam-ȳang-shay-b̄a[272] admit that the imputational nature the emptiness of which is posited as the thoroughly established nature must be just establishment of objects by way of their own character as the referents of conceptual consciousnesses[a] and not the **appearance** of such. That of which phenomena are empty when it is said that they are empty of a self of phenomena is necessarily non-existent, whereas the **appearance** of establishment of objects by way of their own character as the referents of conceptual consciousnesses exists. D̄zong-ka-b̄a's seemingly clear statement poses a problem for Gung-ru Chö-jung and Jam-ȳang-shay-b̄a since they are forced by their own assertions into holding that the imputational natures **relevant** here do not have to be the imputational factor the emptiness of which is posited as the thoroughly established nature.

To undo the problem they make a distinction between (1) the imputational nature the emptiness of which is posited as the thoroughly established nature and (2) the imputational natures relevant **on the occasion** of positing the emptiness of a particular imputational nature as the thoroughly established nature. They drastically re-read D̄zong-ka-b̄a's pivotal statement as:

> Although among imputational factors in general there are many, such as all generally characterized phenomena and space, and so forth, the reason why these are not [explicitly] mentioned in the *Sūtra Unraveling the Thought* is that they are not relevant on the occasion of **positing the emptiness of whatsoever [that is, a particular] imputational nature as the thoroughly established [nature]**.

They admit that the imputational nature the emptiness of which is posited as the thoroughly established nature is just the establishment of objects by way of their own character as the referents of conceptual consciousnesses, but they hold that the imputational natures relevant on the occasion of positing such are not restricted to this.

Still, in D̄zong-ka-b̄a's statement the distinct impression is conveyed that the relevant imputational nature is just the imputational nature of which other-powered natures are empty, namely, the imputational nature the emptiness of which is posited as the thoroughly established nature. That is just the object of

[a] The discussion here is restricted to what is **explicitly** presented in the *Sūtra Unraveling the Thought.* Otherwise, it is necessary to include the difference of entity between subject and object as well as the object of negation in the selflessness of persons.

negation in selflessness. Gung-ru Chö-jung and Jam-ȳang-shay-b̄a's reading is a strained, creative effort to achieve consistency among D̄zong-ka-b̄a's statements that:

1. Other imputational natures are not mentioned in the *Sūtra Unraveling the Thought* at this point.
2. Only those relevant to the positing of emptiness as the thoroughly established nature are mentioned.
3. Among the imputational natures that are mentioned there are existent and non-existent types.

Once they identified the existent type as being the superimposed factor, that is, appearance, of the establishment of objects by way of their own character as the referents of conceptual consciousnesses, they had to show how this is relevant. Their commentary can be considered to be what they think D̄zong-ka-b̄a meant to say or, more bluntly, what he should have meant.

Issue #91: Does the relevant have to exist?

Gung-ru Chö-jung[273] and Jam-ȳang-shay-b̄a[274] examine the far-fetched notion that what is **relevant** to positing emptiness would have to exist. The qualm they are countering is that something non-existent could not be relevant to anything, in which case the imputational natures explicitly indicated at this point would have to exist, simply because they have to be relevant to the positing of the thoroughly established nature. When D̄zong-ka-b̄a (*Emptiness in Mind-Only,* 85) says:

> Although among imputational factors in general there are many, such as all generally characterized phenomena and space, and so forth, the reason why these are not [explicitly] mentioned in the *Sūtra Unraveling the Thought* is that they are not relevant on the occasion of the imputational factor, the emptiness of which is posited as the thoroughly established nature.

one (who did not know that an emptiness is the non-existence of something that never did or will exist) might become confused due to thinking that to be relevant something must exist, since it might seem that relevance and irrelevance could not be posited with respect to the non-existent.

Gung-ru Chö-jung and Jam-ȳang-shay-b̄a answer that although the non-existent cannot be comprehended[a]—the unstated reason being that object of comprehension[b] and existent[c] are equivalent—this does not entail that the vocabulary of relevance cannot be used with respect to the non-existent. Thus the

---

[a] *ma gzhal ba.*

[b] *gzhal bya.*

[c] *yod pa.*

non-existent (specifically, the establishment of objects by way of their own character as the referents of conceptual consciousnesses) can be relevant with respect to positing the thoroughly established nature, for the thoroughly established nature is the emptiness of that.

Issue #92: Is it being refuted that a conceptual appearance is established by way of its own character?

As Gung-ru Chö-jung[275] and Jam-ȳang-shay-b̄a[276] say, it is necessary to understand that what is being refuted is that objects are established by way of their own character as the referents of conceptual consciousnesses and not just that an **appearance to a conceptual consciousness** that objects are established this way is itself established by way of its own character. For to conceive that such an **appearance to a conceptual consciousness** is established by way of its own character is not the subtle apprehension of a self of phenomena. This is because even Proponents of Sūtra ascertain with valid cognition that a conceptual consciousness apprehending that a form, for instance, is established this way is mistaken with respect to such an appearance but in an entirely different way:

> Proponents of Sūtra understand that a conceptual consciousness is mistaken with respect to its appearing object since they realize that even a correct inferential consciousness realizing subtle impermanence, for instance, has a mistaken factor in that its appearing object—an image, or meaning-generality, of subtle impermanence—appears to be subtle impermanence itself whereas it is not.

The consciousness is not wrong in the sense of **conceiving** the image to be the actual thing, but it does have the mistaken factor of the image's **seeming** to be the actual thing, like the image of a face in a mirror seeming to be a face. Since Proponents of Sūtra realize that this sort of image is a superimposed factor that is not established by way of its own character, they realize that the image—of a form's being established by way of its own character as the referent of a conceptual consciousness—which appears to such a conceptual consciousness to be a form established by way of its own character as the referent of a conceptual consciousness is a mere superimposed factor not established by way of its own character. In this vein, Ke-drup's *Opening the Eyes of the Fortunate* says:

> Concerning that, even Proponents of Sūtra have established that the mere appearance that is the appearance to a conceptual consciousness that form and so forth are established by way of their own character as referents of the conventions of entity and attribute is a superimposed factor[a] that is not established by way of its own character.

[a] Superimposed factors (*sgro btags*), in general, are either non-existent, as is the case with the horns of a rabbit, or existent, as is the case with uncompounded space. The mere

> Furthermore, they have already established that such a conceptual consciousness is a consciousness mistaken with respect to that appearance.[a] Hence, there is no way that realization that this conceptual appearance is empty of being established by way of its own character in accordance with how it appears to a conceptual consciousness could constitute realization of the selflessness of phenomena [in the Mind-Only School].

Through citing Ke-drup, Gung-ru Chö-jung and Jam-ȳang-shay-b̄a back up their points (1) that the imputational natures relevant here are of **two** varieties, the object of negation in selflessness and the appearance of such, since why else would Ke-drup bother to mention the latter; (2) neither of these is established by way of its own character; (3) but the fact that the latter is not established by way of its own character does not constitute a subtle selflessness of phenomena, since a lower school, the Proponents of Sūtra, can realize that such an appearance is not established by way of its own character.

From these facts, they make the terminological point that even though at first blush one might think that the subtle selflessness of phenomena is constituted by the non-establishment—by way of their own character—of imputational factors in the imputation of entities and attributes, such is not the case, since imputational factors in the imputation of entities and attributes are of two varieties—(1) the establishment of objects by way of their own character as the referents of conceptual consciousnesses and (2) the appearance of such. The subtle selflessness of phenomena is constituted by the non-establishment only of the first of these.

Issue #93: Does thinking "This is a pot" involve error?

Just what is the imputational nature whose emptiness of being established by way of its own character is posited as the thoroughly established nature? The *Sūtra Unraveling the Thought* itself speaks of factors imputed in the manner of entities and attributes, but what does this mean? Gung-ru Chö-jung[277] cites a possibly misleading statement by D̄zong-ka-b̄a (*Emptiness in Mind-Only,* 195) and then clarifies it:

> Those imputational factors—which are such that a consciousness conceiving imputational factors to be established by way of their own character is asserted to be a consciousness conceiving a self of phenomena—are the nominally and terminologically imputed factors [in the imputation of] the aggregates and so forth as entities, "This is form,"

appearance that is being discussed here is an existent superimposed factor.

[a] It is mistaken in the sense that the appearing object (*snang yul*) of any conceptual consciousness, such as the image of a house that appears to a conceptual consciousness thinking of a house, appears to be a house, much as the image of a face in a mirror *appears* to be a face even if one does not assent to that appearance.

> and as attributes, "This is the production of form," and so forth.

From this statement, it might seem that the imputational factors in question are constituted by merely saying or thinking, "This is a pot,"[a] and, "This is the production of a pot," the first concerning an entity and the second concerning an attribute. However, Gung-ru Chö-jung makes the important point that the mere imputation of such with respect to that which is bulbous, flat-based, and able to hold fluid does not fulfill the import of the imputational nature the emptiness of which is posited as the thoroughly established nature. Rather, the issue revolves around whether that which is bulbous, and so forth, is **established by way of its own character** as an entity that is the referent of the term "pot" and is **established by way of its own character** as an entity that is the referent of the attributional term "production of pot" (or "beautiful"). He sees this as the import of Dzong-ka-ba's immediately subsequent statement:

> Since the aggregates and so forth do exist as just those [entities of such nominal and terminological imputation], the [mere] conception that they exist as those [entities of nominal and terminological imputation] is not a superimposition; rather, the conception that the aggregates and so forth **exist by way of their own character** as those entities [of nominal and terminological imputation] is a superimposition.

Flexibility

To acquire a general picture of what constitute the imputational natures relevant at this point and to appreciate how Dzong-ka-ba's presentation is read by these scholars, it may help to take a more flexible approach. To me, it seems that the imputational natures generally relevant on this occasion of positing the emptiness of certain imputational natures as the thoroughly established nature are of four varieties (not just two as posited above):

1. The establishment of objects by way of their own character as the referents of conceptual consciousnesses and of terms. This is the imputational nature the emptiness of which is the thoroughly established nature in terms of the selflessness of phenomena. It is non-existent but is tenaciously imagined to exist; assent to this reified status of objects serves as the basis of all afflictive emotions and thus all involvement in cyclic existence and also constitutes the obstructions to omniscience, the inability to realize all phenomena simultaneously and hence the inability to be of supreme help to others.
2. The meaning-generality, or generic image, of establishment of objects by way of their own character as the referents of conceptual consciousnesses

[a] I am switching from "form" to "pot" since the definition of the latter is much more evocative than the definition of form, that is, that which is suitable as form (*gzugs su rung ba*).

and of terms. In meditation, this must be brought into clear focus, for although such establishment does not exist, the image of it does, and through this image it is understood what such establishment would be if it did exist. Except through the route of this image, there is no way to understand what the self of phenomena is, and without that, there is no way to realize the selflessness of phenomena.

3. Being the referent of conceptual consciousnesses and of terms. Although objects are indeed referents of conceptual consciousnesses and of words, they are not established so by way of their own character; thus it is vital to understand that objects are indeed referents of conceptual consciousnesses and of words; otherwise, language becomes impossible. How could "Pass the bread" have the wanted effect?
4. The appearance of objects even to sense consciousnesses as established by way of their own character as the referents of words and of conceptual consciousnesses. Even though the mind meditating on emptiness is the mental consciousness and even though it ascertains the object of negation by way of a conceptual image, it is important to realize that even in raw sensation objects appear to sense consciousnesses as if they are established by way of their own character as the referents of terms and of conceptual consciousnesses. It is crucial to understand that along with the appearance of an object to a sense consciousness there is also an appearance—to that sense consciousness—of an abstracted image which we take to be the referent of our thoughts about it and our terms expressing it. When we think about objects or talk about them, we quite naturally but wrongly view the referents of our thoughts and terms as subsisting right with those objects by way of their inner character. Such is "natural" because our previous verbalizations have left impressions on our minds that give rise to this appearance right with the appearance of the object. This appearance is not an overlay from current conceptuality but a result of past conceptuality, manipulating what we see even in raw sensation. Since it seems to come from the object itself, it is no wonder that we believe that it inheres in the object by way of the object's own character.

Since I find the explanation by D̄zong-ka-b̄a, Paṇ-chen S̄ö-nam-drak-b̄a, Jay-d̄zün Chö-ḡyi-gyel-tsen, and Tsay-d̄en-hla-ram-b̄a—that being the referent of a conceptual consciousness is what is being shown to lack establishment by way of its own character when Buddha says that imputational natures are character-non-natures—to be evocative, I prefer to try to find a way to support their view. Perhaps this can be done by asserting that:

1. Although the Proponents of Sūtra realize that **being** a form, for instance, is not established by way of its own character, they are unable to distinguish between the appearance of a form and the appearance (even in direct perception) of a form's being the referent of terms and thoughts.

2. Hence, since they hold that forms are established by way of their own character, they come to hold that forms' being the referents of terms and thoughts is established by way of its own character.

In this way I can hold that meditating on the fact that objects' being the referents of conceptual consciousnesses is not established by way of its own character is the same as meditating on the fact that objects are not established by way of their own character as the referents of their respective conceptual consciousnesses.

The difficulties that these scholars have unearthed in trying to identify in a consistent way the imputational natures that are the subject of the predicate, not being established by way of their own character, highlight a central point of the sūtra—that the main meditation being advocated is on **other-powered natures** as not being established by way of their own character as the referents of conceptual consciousnesses and not on imputational natures as not being established by way of their own character, even if we can see that the latter means the same thing. The entanglements of explaining that imputational natures are character-non-natures lead one to see that the only solution is to fall back on the sūtra's own description of the main meditative procedure.

13. Entering the Maze

In the sentence:

> Imputational natures are called "character-non-natures" because (1) from the positive side they are only posited by names and terminology and (2) from the negative side they are not established by way of their own character.

we have discussed the subject ("imputational natures"). Now let us enter the maze of considering the predicate ("are called character-non-natures").

Issue #94: Do the "own-character" of the question and the "character-nature" of the answer have the same meaning?

Most of the textbook traditions clearly hold that "character-non-nature" means "something lacking the nature of being established by way of its own character." Their reason is simply that the *Sūtra Unraveling the Thought* says that they are called "character-non-natures" because they are "posited by names and terminology and **do not subsist by way of their own character**," and everyone agrees that "do not subsist by way of their own character" means "are not established by way of their own character" and that in the Mind-Only School this is equivalent to "not truly established" and "not ultimately established." Thus, once it is said in the sūtra that imputational natures are called "character-non-natures" because they are not established by way of their own character, the character-nature that imputational natures lack must mean establishment by way of their own character.

This is the way the meaning of the term "character-nature" is taken by most of the colleges. However, the Go-mang tradition holds the at first mind-boggling position that the "character-nature" that imputational natures lack is establishment by way of their own character as the referents of conceptual consciousnesses and establishment in accordance with the superimposition or appearance that objects are established by way of their own character as the referents of their respective conceptual consciousnesses. As was discussed earlier, the foremost scholars of this tradition—Gung-ru Chö-jung, Jam-ȳang-shay-b̄a, Gung-tang, and A-ku L̄o-drö-gya-tso—hold this position so that there is symmetry between (1) the "own-character" of Paramārthasamudgata's question when he (*Emptiness in Mind-Only,* 76-77) describes Buddha's first turning of the wheel of doctrine:

> The Supramundane Victor spoke, in many ways, of the **own-character** of the aggregates. He also spoke of their character of production, character of disintegration, abandonment, and thorough

> knowledge. Just as he did with respect to the aggregates, so he also spoke with respect to the sense-spheres, dependent-arising, and the foods. The Supramundane Victor also spoke, in many ways, of the **own-character** of the truths.... The Supramundane Victor also spoke, in many ways, of the **own-character** of the constituents, as well as speaking of the various constituents, manifold constituents.... The Supramundane Victor also spoke, in many ways, of the **own-character** of the thirty-seven harmonies with enlightenment....

and (2) the "character-non-natures" of Buddha's reply (*Emptiness in Mind-Only,* 86) when he says:

> It is thus: Those [imputational characters] are characters posited by names and terminology and do not subsist by way of their own character. Therefore, they are said to be "**character-non-natures**."

Despite calling for symmetry here, Gung-tang[278] admits that the reason that the sūtra gives for why imputational natures are called "character-non-natures," namely, that they are "posited by names and terminology and do not subsist by way of their own character" means just that imputational natures are not established by way of their own character and does **not** mean that they are not established by way of their own character **as the referents of conceptual consciousnesses.** In other words, this tradition calls for consistency in explaining two uses of "character" but not the third; two mean "established by way of its own character as the referent of a conceptual consciousness," but one means "established by way of its own character."

They make this shift because the *Sūtra Unraveling the Thought* frames this part of the reason clearly as "do not subsist by way of their own character," and Dzong-ka-ba (*Emptiness in Mind-Only,* 86) clearly says:

> The nature of character that imputational factors do not have is to be taken as establishment, or subsisting, by way of their own character.[a] Here, the measure indicated[b] with respect to existing or not existing by way of [an object's] own character is: not to be posited or to be posited in dependence upon names and terminology.[c]

Here in the reason clause, the absence of own-character is not to be taken as referring to the object of negation in the Mind-Only view of selflessness—establishment of objects by way of their own character as the referents of conceptual consciousnesses and of terms—but as referring to establishment by way of its own character, or true establishment. These latter two terms mean that an

a See issue #29.

b *bstan tshod;* see issue #96.

c See issues #105-109.

object is established from its own side **and** is not posited in dependence upon names and terminology.

The non-Go-mang traditions within Ge-luk-ba hold that all three usages of "character" in the above citation mean "established by way of its own character," complications resulting from which have been discussed in chapter 11. In addition, it is evident that in order to have their cake and eat it too, at least part of the Go-mang tradition (namely, A-ku Lo-drö-gya-tso) has recognized the problems with their college's position and has opted for the slippery position that the **meaning** of the character-nature is establishment by way of its own character but that establishment by way of its own character as the referent of a conceptual consciousness is an **illustration** of the character-nature. Let us probe this device through the roundabout course of considering a related question—whether a character-non-nature is an emptiness. The inquiry yields many provocative points, even if the conclusion is not entirely satisfying.

Issue #95: Is a character-non-nature an emptiness?

Gung-tang's teacher, Gön-chok-jik-may-wang-bo,[a] raises a qualm central to the three natures and three non-natures that Gung-tang[279] goes to some length to answer. Gön-chok-jik-may-wang-bo points out that Gung-ru Chö-jung identifies the non-existent character-nature as the imputational nature that is relevant on the occasion of positing its emptiness as the thoroughly established nature—this being establishment of objects by way of their own character as the referents of their respective conceptual consciousnesses.[280] He adds that, for Gung-ru Chö-jung, a consequence of this is that the meaning[b] of the character-non-nature that is explicitly mentioned in the brief indication is the thoroughly established nature.[c] Gung-tang reports that Jam-yang-shay-ba[281] cribbed the same from Gung-ru Chö-jung and that such also is held in an oral transmission of Go-mang positions. However, he raises the qualm that if the character-non-nature mentioned in the brief indication is the subtle selflessness of phenomena, it would have to be the ultimate-non-nature, in which case here in the brief indication of the three non-natures, the ultimate-non-nature would be given twice, and the character-non-nature would not at all be described.

Gung-tang cogently explains that this portion (in bold print) of Buddha's brief answer, "Paramārthasamudgata, thinking of three non-natures of

[a] Wel-mang Gön-chok-gyel-tsen's *Notes on (Gön-chok-jik-may-wang-bo's) Lectures,* 397.4-399.1; also cited in Dön-drup-gyel-tsen's *Four Intertwined Commentaries,* 46.4-47.3. Jik-may-dam-chö-gya-tso (*Port of Entry,* 164.6-167.6) first gives three problematic statements (which I treat in the next section), then cites Gön-chok-jik-may-wang-bo's qualm, and finally Gung-tang's analysis.

[b] *don.*

[c] Gung-ru Chö-jung (*Garland of White Lotuses,* 26b.5) openly accepts that the character-non-nature is the subtle selflessness of phenomena.

phenomena—**character-non-nature**, production-non-nature, and ultimate-non-nature—I taught [in the middle wheel of the teaching], 'All phenomena are natureless,'" should be setting forth the imputational nature, not the ultimate-non-nature that negates it. Also, in Buddha's extensive explanation, it would absurdly be inappropriate when he poses the rhetorical question, "Concerning that, what are character-non-natures of phenomena?" for him to answer, "Those which are imputational characters," since he, according to this mis-reading, should have said, "Those which are thoroughly established characters." Moreover, it would absurdly be inappropriate for Buddha, when giving an example (or analogue) of character-non-natures, to say that they are like a flower in the sky, in the sense that they are just imputed by conceptuality, since the ultimate-non-nature, or thoroughly established nature, is established by way of its own character and is not just imputed by conceptuality.

Ḡön-chok-jik-may-w̄ang-b̄o asks his audience to analyze whether it would be more concordant with the thought of both the *Sūtra Unraveling the Thought* and of D̄zong-ka-b̄a's *The Essence of Eloquence* to consider that what is indicated to be non-existent in the character-non-nature is establishment by way of its own character. Feeling the pinch of going against his own college's tradition of exegesis, he defensively says that he raises this qualm out of concern that the Go-mang tradition's explanation of the topic does not sit comfortably in his mind and is difficult to understand. Thereby, he blames his own inadequacy for appearing to contradict his tradition. He stresses that he is not refuting the college's textbook literature and does not want his audience to decide, based on his explanation, that the textbook is wrong. Rather, using a double negative, he emphasizes that it is not that one is not permitted to state qualms regarding the textbook, since it is permissible to state qualms even about what D̄zong-ka-b̄a has said and even about what Buddha said. He asks his audience to analyze and eliminate the qualm. His touching deference to the tradition is actually a way to mask criticism—at once to preserve allegiance to a tradition and to maintain the prerogative of critical analysis.

Ḡön-chok-jik-may-w̄ang-b̄o's qualm—that in Gung-ru Chö-jung and Jam-ȳang-shay-b̄a's explanation the character-non-nature is the subtle selflessness of phenomena and thus is the ultimate-non-nature—certainly seems to be on the mark, for the Go-mang tradition holds that objects' establishment by way of their own character as the referents of conceptual consciousnesses is the character-nature, and a negation of that is an emptiness in the Mind-Only School.[a] Indeed, D̄zong-ka-b̄a and his close disciple Ke-drup make clear

[a] Also, according to the other traditions, the imputational nature's character-non-nature would seem to be an emptiness, because they hold that the imputational nature that is negated—as being established by way of its own character—is factors imputed in the imputation of entities and attributes and they identify the nature of character as meaning "established by way of their own character," and we know that for them also one type of the selflessness of phenomena is constituted by imputational natures' non-establishment by way of

statements to this effect; Gön-chok-jik-may-wang-bo does not cite them, but they bring even more drama to the argument since not just Gung-ru Chö-jung and Jam-yang-shay-ba but also Dzong-ka-ba and Ke-drup are being challenged. First, Dzong-ka-ba (*Emptiness in Mind-Only,* 194-195):

> the *Sūtra Unraveling the Thought* explains that other-powered natures are not established by way of their own character as factors imputed in the manner of entity and of attribute and that, **therefore, the absence of [such] a nature of character is the selflessness of phenomena.**[a]

He clearly says that a character-non-nature is a selflessness of phenomena. Ke-drup says the same:[282]

> Moreover, the *Sūtra Unraveling the Thought* explains that since other-powered natures are not established by way of their own character as entities of imputation as entity and attribute, **the character-non-nature is the selflessness of phenomena.**

In a similar vein Dzong-ka-ba (*Emptiness in Mind-Only,* 224) says that Hearers and Solitary Realizers realize the character-non-nature in terms of the selflessness of persons; he speaks as if "realizing the character-non-nature" can be substituted for saying that they realize the thoroughly established nature in terms of the selflessness of persons:

> the trainees for whom the first wheel was spoken are suitable as vessels for realizing the character-non-nature in terms of the selflessness of persons and are not suitable as vessels for realizing the character-non-nature[b] in terms of the selflessness of phenomena.

If, as these foremost leaders of the Ge-luk-ba sect say, the character-non-nature is the selflessness of phenomena, it is certainly emptiness, the thoroughly established nature. But, as Gön-chok-jik-may-wang-bo queries, why should two of the three natures mean emptiness?

Gung-tang, prior to taking up his teacher's challenge, rephrases the qualm so that its logical steps are clearer. In his rendition, the words "character-non-nature" in the brief indication would then explicitly indicate emptiness, in which case the sūtra passage about the character-non-nature would explicitly indicate not only this non-nature but also the third non-nature, the ultimate-non-nature, and if that were so, there would absurdly be no need for the *Sūtra Unraveling the Thought* (*Emptiness in Mind-Only,* 82-83) to go on to mention the ultimate-non-nature, whereas it does:

> Paramārthasamudgata, thinking of three non-natures of phenomena—

their own character.

[a] See issues #98, 99, 102, and 103.

[b] See issue #95.

character-non-nature, production-non-nature, and ultimate-non-nature—I taught [in the middle wheel of the teaching], "All phenomena are natureless."

Gung-tang rephrases the other two permutations of this position:

1. If the character-non-nature, explicitly indicated in the topic sentence, were emptiness and that emptiness is other than a true cessation,[a] then its object of negation would necessarily have to be the object of negation on the occasion of positing its emptiness as the thoroughly established nature.[b]
2. Also, if the character-non-nature were emptiness, it would pervade all phenomena and be distinguished by being a mere absence of the self that is its object of negation and hence would be fit for comparison with the example of space—just as the ultimate-non-nature is—since it would be the subtle selflessness of phenomena. However, the *Sūtra Unraveling the Thought* compares the character-non-nature not with space but with a flower in the sky in that, except for being only imputed by conceptuality, a flower in the sky is not established by way of its own character. As the *Sūtra Unraveling the Thought* (*Emptiness in Mind-Only,* 93) says:

   > It is thus: for example, character-non-natures [that is, imputational natures] are to be viewed as like a flower in the sky.

   and D̄zong-ka-b̄a (*Emptiness in Mind-Only,* 94) says:

   > The similarity of imputational factors with a flower in the sky is an example of their merely being imputed by conceptuality and is not an example of their not occurring among objects of knowledge [that is, existents].

---

[a] In the Go-mang tradition of Gung-ru Chö-jung and Jam-ȳang-shay-b̄a that Gung-tang is following, a true cessation is an emptiness but among its objects of negation are the obstructions (which exist), since a true cessation is also an absence of an obstruction in the continuum of someone who has attained conquest over a level of the obstructions. Thus, a true cessation is an emptiness, but its objects of negation include existents. This is why Gung-tang specifies that the emptiness in question is "other than a true cessation."

[b] Gung-tang (102.17-103.3) goes on to say that if that were the case, then not only would the character-non-nature be the ultimate-non-nature, but also it would absurdly be appropriate to turn this around and hold that the ultimate-non-nature is the character-non-nature. As the reason for this, he points out that in the sūtra's first treatment of the ultimate-non-nature it says that other-powered natures are non-natures of the ultimate in the sense that they are not the ultimate, since they are not final objects of observation of the path. Thus, he says that in the ultimate-non-nature the nature of the ultimate that is non-existent is also explained as being the final object of observation by a path of purification, this being the way the ultimate is taken on the occasion of the first explanation of the ultimate-non-nature in the *Sūtra Unraveling the Thought.* (I have not understood why Gung-tang draws the conclusion that this would require that the ultimate-non-nature be the character-non-nature.)

A question fundamental to the difference between the three natures (other-powered, imputational, and thoroughly established) and fundamental to the difference between the three non-natures (production-non-nature, character-non-nature, and ultimate-non-nature) is being posed.

Gung-tang concludes that for the above reasons, the character-non-nature explicitly indicated in the topic sentence cannot explicitly indicate emptiness. As A-ku Lo-drö-gya-tso[283] cogently adds, in the *Sūtra Unraveling the Thought* the character-non-nature is clearly said, on the positive side, to be only posited by names and terminology and, on the negative side, not to be established by way of its own character, but we know that emptiness is established by way of its own character.[a] Indeed, this has to be the reason why Buddha posited only imputational natures, and not also thoroughly established natures, as illustrations of the character-non-nature. Therefore, although the character-non-nature may look dangerously like emptiness, it cannot be.[284]

Issue #96: What extra understanding is gained by taking a superimposed factor or appearance as the subject?

Still, the issue of whether a character-non-nature is an emptiness cannot be left merely at that, for great scholars put forth what at least seems to be the opposite opinion. Gung-tang tackles this touchy issue by examining the ramifications of Jam-ȳang-shay-ba's[285] framing of Buddha's (*Emptiness in Mind-Only,* 86) statement:

> Those [imputational characters] are characters posited by names and terminology[b] and do not subsist by way of their own character. Therefore, they are said to be "character-non-natures."

as:

> With respect to the subject, the superimposed factor [or appearance] of forms and so forth as established by way of their own character as the referents of conceptual consciousnesses, there are reasons for calling this a "character-non-nature" because the reasons are that (1) from the positive side it is only posited by names and terminology and (2) from the negative side it is not established by way of its own character.

The final sentence in Buddha's statement ("Therefore, they are said to be

[a] The *Sūtra Unraveling the Thought* clearly indicates that other-powered natures are established by way of their own character when it says that whatever is not so established cannot be produced, but it never openly says that thoroughly established natures are established by way of their own character. The extrapolation made in Ge-luk-ba scholarship is that if other-powered natures are so established, then surely their final nature must also be. Their position makes excellent sense.

[b] See issue #104.

'character-non-natures,'") becomes the first clause in Jam-ȳang-shay-b̄a's syllogistic rendering ("With respect to the subject, the superimposed factor [or appearance] of forms and so forth as established by way of their own character as the referents of conceptual consciousnesses, there are reasons for calling this a 'character-non-nature'"). Jam-ȳang-shay-b̄a takes the word "they" in Buddha's statement, the antecedent of which is "imputational characters," and renders it not as factors imputed in the manner of entity and attribute but as "the superimposed factor [or appearance] of forms and so forth as established by way of their own character as the referents of conceptual consciousnesses." He then uses the first part of Buddha's statement ("Those [imputational characters] are characters posited by names and terminology and do not subsist by way of their own character,") as the reason clause of the syllogism ("because the reasons are that from the positive side it is only posited by names and terminology and from the negative side it is not established by way of its own character"). The only inventive part of Jam-ȳang-shay-b̄a's rendition is his identification of "they," or "imputational characters," as "the superimposed factor [or appearance] of forms and so forth as established by way of their own character as the referents of conceptual consciousnesses."

Gung-tang[286] explains that a special understanding arises when this superimposed factor, or false appearance, is taken as the subject and the reason is left as non-establishment by way of its own character. He says:

> If the superimposed factor or appearance of the establishment [of objects] by way of their own character as the referents of conceptual consciousnesses were established by way of its own character, then it would not be merely imputed to there [that is, from the subject's side to the object] by conceptuality but would be truly established right with the object. If it were so established, then when one analyzes whether or not it is established in accordance with its mode of appearance, it would come to be a final object found under such analysis, able to bear such analysis. However, in this Mind-Only system, something that is established as able to bear analysis at the end of analyzing whether it is established by way of its own character as the referent of a conceptual consciousness is posited as a self of phenomena, and non-establishment as such is posited as the selflessness of phenomena.
>
> Therefore, when just this relevant imputational nature—and not just imputational natures in general—is taken as the basis [for understanding an absence of being established by way of its own character], the character-non-nature that is merely on the level of literal indication does not come to be emptiness, but the **meaning** of the mode of naturelessness established through the pressure of reasoning goes as [or involves] emptiness.[a] This is why D̄zong-ka-b̄a's *The Essence of*

[a] 109.9: *rigs pas 'phul gyis sgrubs pa'i don de stong nyid du 'gro ba.*

Eloquence says that there is a measure [that is, level] indicated by the words[a] and a measure [that is, level] of meaning gotten at,[b] [this distinction being the intent of Ḏzong-ka-ḇa's (*Emptiness in Mind-Only,* 86) saying]:

> Here, the measure indicated[c] with respect to existing or not existing by way of [an object's] own character is: not to be posited or to be posited in dependence upon names and terminology.[d]

This is also why in the textbook [that is, the *Great Exposition of the Interpretable and the Definitive,* Jam-ȳang-shay-ḇa] again and again says, "The **meaning** of the character-non-nature...."

Gung-tang justifies his explanation not only in terms of Jam-ȳang-shay-ḇa's usage of the word "meaning" but also in terms of Ḏzong-ka-ḇa's unusual usage of the term "measure indicated" when speaking of establishment of the object by way of its own character. For him, this suggests that Ḏzong-ka-ḇa was conceiving of two levels with regard to the meaning of something's being established by way of its own character—one level indicated by the words and another level of the meaning gotten at—even though Ḏzong-ka-ḇa never lays out what the latter would be. Gung-tang's perspective with regard to Ḏzong-ka-ḇa's text is clearly that of dealing with the work of a genius whose every syllable is pregnant with meaning that, despite its importance, is not necessarily spelled out overtly. (That he also views the work as requiring considerable adjustment is obvious from the numerous "clarifications" that he makes.)

According to A-ku Ḻo-drö-gya-tso,[287] what Gung-tang sees as indicated on the level of meaning gotten at is this:

- When this superimposed factor, or appearance, of forms and so forth as established by way of their own character as the referents of conceptual consciousnesses is realized, it must (of course) be realized to be a superimposed factor.
- When one realizes this, one must realize that a consciousness conceiving forms and so forth to be established by way of their own character as the referents of conceptual consciousnesses is a wrong consciousness, for one is realizing that this appearance is a superimposed factor.
- To realize that such a consciousness is a wrong consciousness, one has to realize emptiness, that is, that objects are **not** established by way of their own character as the referents of their respective conceptual consciousnesses as they are conceived to be by such a consciousness.

---

a *tshig gis bstan tshod.*

b *don gyi thob tshod.*

c *bstan tshod.*

d See issues #105-109.

- If a consciousness conceiving forms and so forth to be established by way of their own character as the referents of conceptual consciousnesses were not a superimposition (that is to say, a consciousness that superimposes as existent something that does not exist), what appears to such an awareness would have to be truly established in accordance with how it appears, but it is not, and, hence, establishment in that way is the subtle self of phenomena, and the emptiness of such establishment is the subtle selflessness of phenomena.

This is how the **meaning**, or import, of the character-non-nature explicitly indicated at this point **comes to be**, or involves, emptiness but the character-non-nature itself is not emptiness. A-ku Lo-drö-gya-tso's explication is indeed clear. Through this maneuver, both he and Gung-tang are able to hold the cogent position that a character-non-nature is not an emptiness and yet to support their predecessors' seeming assertion that it is.

Issue #97: Is there a source in the Sūtra Unraveling the Thought *for this?*

Gung-tang[288] adds that taking the subject not just to be imputational natures in general but to be the superimposed factor or appearance of objects as established by way of their own character as the referents of conceptual consciousnesses is both very meaningful (as shown above) and the final thought of the *Sūtra Unraveling the Thought* itself. For Chapter 6, the "Questions of Guṇākara," says that imputational natures are to be identified in terms of a factor of appearance wrongly superimposed by a mistaken awareness:

> The imputational character is to be viewed as like the flaws of dark spots that form in the eye[-sight] of one with the disease of dim-sightedness.

and:

> Apprehending the imputational character in other-powered characters should be viewed as like wrongly apprehending a very clear crystal as a precious jewel—sapphire, the blue gem, ruby, emerald, or gold.[a]

---

[a] The entire passage is:

Guṇākara, it is like this: For example, the imputational character is to be viewed as being like the faults of clouded vision that exist in the eye of a person who has clouded vision. It is like this: For example, the other-powered character is to be viewed as being like the appearance of signs of clouded vision of that very being—the signs of a hair-net, or flies, or sesame seeds; or an appearance of either a sign of blue, a sign of yellow, a sign of red, or a sign of white. Guṇākara, it is like this: For example, when the eyes of just that very being become thoroughly purified and faults of clouded vision that have formed in the eyes do not exist, the thoroughly

Since imputational natures in this context are to be identified in terms of a factor of appearance **wrongly** superimposed by a mistaken awareness, the imputational natures in the clause, "Therefore, **they** are said to be 'character-non-natures'" cannot be objects' merely **being** the referents of conceptual consciousnesses, for such exists. Without the qualification of such being established by way of its own character, no factor of wrong appearance is involved. Hence, from Gung-tang's viewpoint, it is mistaken to hold that, when the *Sūtra Unraveling the Thought* says that imputational natures are not established by way of their own character, it is saying that being the referent of a conceptual consciousness is not established by way of its own character. (It is important to remember that Ḏzong-ka-ḇa, as detailed in *Reflections on Reality,* Chapter 13, puts forth just this identification many times.)

---

established character is to be viewed as being like the object of operation which is the natural object of operation of that person's eyes.

Guṇākara, it is like this: For example, when a very clear crystal is in contact with the color blue, it appears at that time to be a precious jewel such as a sapphire or an *indranīla.* Moreover, because it is wrongly apprehended as a precious jewel, such as a sapphire or an *indranīla,* sentient beings are thoroughly deluded. When it is in contact with the color red, it appears at that time to be a precious jewel such as a ruby. Furthermore, because it is wrongly apprehended as a precious jewel such as a ruby, sentient beings are thoroughly deluded. When it is in contact with the color green, it appears at that time to be a precious jewel such as an emerald. Moreover, because it is wrongly apprehended as a precious jewel such as an emerald, sentient beings are thoroughly deluded. When it is in contact with the color gold, it appears at that time as gold. Furthermore, because it is also wrongly apprehended as gold, sentient beings are thoroughly deluded.

Guṇākara, it is like this: For example, the other-powered character should be viewed as being [under the influence of] the predispositions for conventions that are the imputational nature, like a very clear crystal that is in contact with a color. It is like this: For example, the other-powered character that is apprehended as the imputational character should be viewed as being like the mistaken apprehension of the very clear crystal as a sapphire, an *indranīla,* a ruby, an emerald, or gold. Guṇākara, it is like this: For example, the very clear crystal should be viewed as the other-powered character. Guṇākara, it is like this: For example, just as the very clear crystal is thoroughly not established as [having] the character of a sapphire, an *indranīla,* a ruby, an emerald, or gold, and is without those natures in permanent, permanent time and in everlasting, everlasting time, so other-powered [natures] are thoroughly not established in permanent, permanent time and in everlasting, everlasting time as the imputational character, and are without that nature; just that non-establishment or naturelessness is to be viewed as the thoroughly established character.

See also Powers, *Wisdom of Buddha,* 83-87.

Issue #98: If a pot's establishment by way of its own character is not to be refuted, why should a superimposed factor's establishment by way of its own character be refuted? Or, is it amazing if a bird can fly?

Gung-tang[289] concludes that a Proponent of Sūtra could not realize that such a superimposed factor is a non-effective thing and thus not established by way of its own character.[a] Still, it might be objected that even if the superimposed factor or appearance of objects as established by way of their own character as the referents of conceptual consciousnesses were established by way of its own character, the meaning of such could not be logically forced into being a self of phenomena because the parallel of this is not true for a pot. Specifically, despite a pot's being established by way of its own character, no amount of reasoning can force its establishment this way into becoming a self of phenomena, since a pot **is** indeed established by way of its own character.

Gung-tang[290] answers that the two cases are not parallel. For if the superimposed factor or appearance that objects are established by way of their own character as the referents of conceptual consciousnesses is established by way of its own character, it involves a self of phenomena as explained above, whereas if it is not established by way of its own character, it does not have to be utterly non-existent, since in fact it is only imputed by conceptuality and is not established by way of its own character but does exist. However, if an other-powered phenomenon such as a pot is not established by way of its own character, it must be utterly non-existent,[291] but its being established by way of its own character does not entail its being a self of phenomena,[292] that is, it does not have to be established by way of its own character as the referent of a conceptual consciousness. Gung-tang gives the example of its being amazing if a human can fly in the sky but not a flaw if a human cannot, whereas if a bird cannot fly in the sky, it is a flaw, but if it can, it is not amazing.

As corroboration, Gung-tang points to the fact that D̄zong-ka-b̄a identifies the imputational nature—which, when conceived to be established by way of

[a] It seems to me that he is speaking only of the false appearance to a *conceptual* consciousness of an object's being established by way of its own character as the referent of a conceptual consciousness, even though the Mind-Only School holds that objects appear to have this false status to both sense consciousnesses and the mental consciousness. For there is no qualm that a Proponent of Sūtra could realize that such an appearance to a sense consciousness is a superimposed factor; it is clear that a Proponent of Sūtra could not.

As was mentioned earlier, a Proponent of Sūtra can realize that the appearing object of a conceptual consciousness is a superimposed factor in that it appears to be the object but is only an image of it. However, a Proponent of Sūtra cannot realize that the false appearance of objects as being established by way of their own character as the referents of conceptual consciousnesses is a superimposed factor, since such involves realizing that it indeed is a superimposed factor and for this, realization of emptiness is required.

its own character, it by that fact goes as the self of phenomena—not just as imputational natures in general but a specific one. Dzong-ka-ba (*Emptiness in Mind-Only,* 195) says:

> Those imputational factors—which are such that a consciousness conceiving imputational factors to be established by way of their own character is asserted to be a consciousness conceiving a self of phenomena—are the nominally and terminologically imputed factors [in the imputation of] the aggregates and so forth as entities, "This is form," and as attributes, "This is the production of form," and so forth.[a]

Thus, for the Go-mang tradition "imputational factors" in this context refer to the superimposed factor or appearance of objects as established by way of their own character as the referents of conceptual consciousnesses or the establishment of objects this way. Gung-tang's conclusion is that although the character-non-nature at this point is not emptiness, its meaning, its import, arrives at emptiness.

Issue #99: How to explain away Jam-ȳang-shay-ba's inconsistencies?

Although Gung-tang is mainly carrying out the implications of Jam-ȳang-shay-ba's elaborate presentation, both he and A-ku Lo-drö-gya-tso must also posit Jam-ȳang-shay-ba's thought by explaining away seemingly contradictory statements in his commentary.[293] Some seem simple at first but then become more complex and even intriguing.

For instance, about the character-non-nature, Jam-ȳang-shay-ba says (in paraphrase):[b]

---

a See issues #79 and 93.

b *Great Exposition of the Interpretable and the Definitive* (49.6-50.1), which is a re-casting of a similar presentation by Gung-ru Chö-jung (*Garland of White Lotuses,* 26b.5ff). Literally, Jam-ȳang-shay-ba says:

> It follows with respect to the subject, the imputational nature's non-establishment by way of its own character, that it is the subtle selflessness of phenomena because of being the meaning/import of the character-non-nature explicitly indicated on this occasion. [Being the meaning/import of the character-non-nature explicitly indicated on this occasion] entails [being a subtle selflessness of phenomena] because the meaning/import of the character-non-nature explicitly indicated on this occasion is posited as the subtle selflessness of phenomena and the meaning/import of the character-non-nature in terms of the selflessness of persons that is implicitly indicated is posited as the subtle selflessness of persons.

Jik-may-dam-chö-gya-tso (*Port of Entry,* 167.2) reports that in Sha-mar Ge-dün-den-dzin-gya-tso's (*zhwa dmar dge 'dun bstan 'dzin rgya mtsho*) *Clearing Away Mental Darkness* Gung-tang's apologetic is not accepted.

> Whatever is the meaning of the character-non-nature explicitly indicated on this occasion necessarily is a subtle selflessness of phenomena.

This statement seems to indicate that the character-non-nature is emptiness. Indeed, this is just what gives rise to Gön-chok-jik-may-wang-bo's qualm with which we began this excursion. Gung-tang,[294] responding to his teacher's call to find a way to undo his qualm, claims that Jam-yang-shay-ba's reference is to the **meaning** of the character-non-nature explicitly indicated on this occasion[a] and not just to the character-non-nature explicitly indicated on this occasion, since the former arrives at emptiness, whereas the latter is not emptiness. By making this distinction Gung-tang avoids (1) the unwanted consequence that the character-non-nature is the ultimate-non-nature and hence the thoroughly established nature and (2) the resultant redundancy of one of the three non-natures. Gung-tang's explanation is brilliant apologetic in that his justification for this maneuver is founded in the fact that Jam-yang-shay-ba uses "meaning" (*don*) not only in this clause but also throughout this section.

However, is the meaning of the character-non-nature at this point emptiness? Given Gung-tang's commentary thus far, we certainly would have thought that those in his tradition would hold such, but A-ku Lo-drö-gya-tso, repeating Gung-tang's own choice of words, makes the distinction that the meaning of the character-non-nature at this point **goes as** or (perhaps this would be rendered better in English as) **arrives at** or **involves** emptiness,[b] but that "being only posited by names and terminology and not being established by way of own character"[c] must be posited as the meaning of the character-non-nature at this point. A-ku Lo-drö-gya-tso holds that, therefore, a distinction is to be made between an illustration of—that is, something that is—the character-non-nature at this point (primarily the superimposed factor or appearance of objects as being established by way of their own character as the referents of conceptual consciousnesses and secondarily such establishment) and **that which is posited as the meaning** of the character-non-nature at this point (that is, being only posited by names and terminology and not being established by way of own character).

A-ku Lo-drö-gya-tso's point is well taken since the *Sūtra Unraveling the Thought* itself says that imputational natures are called character-non-nature because they "are characters posited by names and terminology and do not subsist by way of their own character." (It seems to me that A-ku Lo-drö-gya-tso thereby brings the topic back to the sūtra and that, even though he does not openly say so, he is suggesting that Gung-ru Chö-jung and Jam-yang-shay-ba have confused the meaning of the character-non-nature with something that is

---

a *skabs 'dir dngos su bstan pa'i mtshan nyid ngo bo nyid med pa'i don.*

b *don stong nyid du 'gro ba*: *Precious Lamp*, 80.1.

c Jik-may-dam-chö-gya-tso (*Port of Entry*, 170.5-171.2, 172.3) identifies the non-existent nature in terms of character this way.

an illustration of it—they have substituted a discussion of imputational natures for a discussion of the character-non-nature.)

In these ways, Gung-tang and A-ku L̄o-drö-gya-tso handle, so to speak, Jam-ȳang-shay-b̄a's seeming indiscretion, which was founded on a similar one by Gung-ru Chö-jung. However, both Gung-ru Chö-jung[295] and Jam-ȳang-shay-b̄a[296] complicate the issue by making the faux pas of saying that the non-existent nature in Buddha's statement, "Therefore, they are said to be 'character-non-natures,'" does not occur among objects of knowledge, that is, is just non-existent. On the surface, this excludes their own explanation of that nature as being of two varieties—(1) the establishment of objects by way of their own character as the referents of conceptual consciousnesses (which indeed does not exist) and (2) the superimposed factor or appearance of such (which exists). Worse, in seeming confirmation of this self-contradiction, Jam-ȳang-shay-b̄a[297] says even more clearly, "Whatever is the nature of character explicitly indicated is necessarily establishment by way of its own character as a referent of conceptual consciousness and establishment from its own side as a referent of conceptual consciousness." He leaves out the existent variety!

Gung-tang[298] explains away the apparent self-contradiction by pointing out that since Jam-ȳang-shay-b̄a at this point is drawing from the earlier textbook literature of the Go-mang College by the omniscient Gung-ru Chö-jung, we can—by turning to Gung-ru Chö-jung's text—determine what Jam-ȳang-shay-b̄a meant to say. Since Gung-ru Chö-jung[299] also speaks of "non-establishment in accordance with a superimposed factor as being established by way of its own character as the referent of a conceptual consciousness," Gung-tang concludes that since the earlier textbook from which Jam-ȳang-shay-b̄a was cribbing at this point speaks of a superimposed factor, Jam-ȳang-shay-b̄a also must have meant that the character-non-natures include such an (existent) superimposed factor.

Here, the technique of "positing Jam-ȳang-shay-b̄a's thought" in order to make sense out of his exposition is to suggest that when he cribbed from Gung-ru Chö-jung, he left out a phrase. It indeed is possible that once Jam-ȳang-shay-b̄a's principal source takes this stance, his own self-contradictory statements can be resolved through consulting that source, even though on other occasions such discrepancies are taken as the result of critical analysis. In other words, Jam-ȳang-shay-b̄a suffered a slip of the pen when copying.

Gung-tang's point is that the superimposed factor is to be included in the nature of character and that establishment in accordance with such a superimposed factor does not occur among existents and is necessarily a self of phenomena that is refuted in the selflessness of phenomena. Still, it seems to me that since Gung-ru Chö-jung speaks of the **establishment** of objects in accordance with such a superimposed factor and not the mere superimposed factor, it also does not exist. For "establishment in accordance with a superimposed factor as being established by way of its own character as the referent of a conceptual consciousness" and "established by way of its own character as the referent of a conceptual consciousness" essentially mean the same thing. Hence, even if Jam-ÿang-shay-b̄a meant to include establishment in accordance with such a superimposed factor, the superimposed factor itself, though mentioned **within** the phrase, still has been omitted.

Gung-tang[300] does consider the flip side of my qualm. First, he suggests that one would naturally think that since the superimposed factor, or appearance, of objects as established by way of their own character as the referents of their respective conceptual consciousnesses is identified as a nature of character **that does not exist**, then such a superimposed factor or appearance would not exist. However, he insists that although in the words, "character-non-nature," it might seem that such a superimposed factor or appearance is negated, the meaning must be explained as being that existence **in accordance with** such a superimposed factor or appearance is what does not exist. It is in this way that the meaning involves, or arrives at, emptiness. The technique here is to add the phrase "in accordance with," whereas just above with Gung-ru Chö-jung's statement it was to subtract the same phrase. Such slipperiness is how the exegetical project adapts itself to the seeming rigidity of insistence on consistency.

Issue #100: Could the imputational factor be both the nature of character and the character-non-nature?

The number of distinctions that have been made is so great that drawing conclusions seems risky, but some semblance of order is required in preparation for a pithy point Gung-tang is about to make. It seems to me that according to Gung-ru Chö-jung and Jam-ÿang-shay-b̄a, in Buddha's statement, "Therefore, they are said to be 'character-non-natures' ":

1. "They" refers to imputational natures—mainly the superimposed factor (or appearance) of forms and so on as the referents of conceptual consciousnesses and secondarily the establishment of objects by way of their own character as the referents of conceptual consciousnesses
2. "Nature" and "character" are the same—the establishment of objects by way of their own character as the referents of conceptual consciousnesses, and
3. "Non" negates their being so established.

This may seem simple enough, but when put into a sentence, it reads, "Imputational natures—mainly the superimposed factor (or appearance) of forms and so on as the referents of conceptual consciousnesses and secondarily the establishment of objects by way of their own character as the referents of conceptual consciousnesses—are not established by way of their own character as the referents of their respective conceptual consciousnesses." It is downright weird to be making the point that the establishment of objects by way of their own character as the referents of conceptual consciousnesses is not established by way of its own character as the referent of a conceptual consciousness!

Why not just say that the establishment of objects by way of their own character as the referents of conceptual consciousnesses does not exist? If it is because the **appearance** of such does exist but does not exist by way of its own character, why not just say that the imputational natures relevant here are not established by way of their own character! Even more so, how much simpler it would be to use D̄zong-ka-b̄a's language and say that being the referent of a conceptual consciousness is not established by way of its own character! D̄zong-ka-b̄a's rendition has been nit-picked and replaced with what can only charitably be called circumlocution.

It is amusing that such a seemingly simple topic has become so complicated that making any statement seems risky. One can imagine the anxiety of students as they prepare to debate these topics, as well as the intellectual courage that is needed to continue without becoming discouraged or without falling into the escapism of allowing debate to become sterile.

Taken according to the primary meaning of "imputational nature," Buddha's answer is that the superimposed factor (or appearance) of forms and so on as the referents of conceptual consciousnesses is called **that which lacks the nature of character**, for such a superimposed factor is posited by names and terminology and is not established by way of its own character. With this reading as our context, an objection that Gung-tang raises and his answer are illuminating. Gung-tang says (in paraphrase):[301]

> Someone might feel:
>
> > The establishment of objects by way of their own character as the referents of conceptual consciousnesses could not be the **nature** of character explicitly indicated in the topic sentence when Buddha says, "Paramārthasamudgata, thinking of three non-natures of phenomena—**character-non-nature**, production-non-nature, and ultimate-non-nature—I taught, 'All phenomena are natureless.'" For it is the **character-non-nature** in that!
>
> However, my [that is, Gung-tang's] response is that it is not the case that whatever is the **character-non-nature** [that is, that which lacks the nature of character] explicitly indicated in the topic sentence is necessarily not the **nature** of character explicitly indicated in the topic sentence [because the establishment of objects by way of their own character as the referents of conceptual consciousnesses is both].
>
> The establishment of objects by way of their own character as the referents of conceptual consciousnesses is the character-non-nature in the topic sentence because the *Sūtra Unraveling the Thought* says,

"Paramārthasamudgata, concerning that, what are character-non-natures of phenomena? Those which are imputational characters." The sūtra's saying this entails that such establishment is the character-non-nature in the topic sentence because the question is concerned with an **illustration** of character-non-nature [that is, that which is without the nature of character and is not concerned with the character-non-nature itself].

A-ku L̄o-drö-gya-tso[302] sees Gung-tang as saying that the **nature** of character and **character-non-nature** explicitly indicated at this point in the *Sūtra Unraveling the Thought* are mutually inclusive—whatever is the one is the other. He explains that, therefore, the rhetorical question (which I have translated as "What are character-non-natures of phenomena?" but could be rendered as "What is the naturelessness of phenomena in terms of character?") is not asking, "What is the **emptiness** of nature of character at this point?" or "What is the **non-existence** of nature of character at this point?" Rather, the question is, "What is the nature of character that is non-existent?" For it is asking about the object of negation—that of which other-powered natures are empty. The point is crucial.[a]

A-ku L̄o-drö-gya-tso[303] makes the—what would have been startling but now is sensible—conclusion that:

- at this point (1) the establishment of objects by way of their own character as the referents of conceptual consciousnesses and (2) the superimposed factor or appearance of such are taught to be both the **nature** of character that is non-existent and the **character-non-nature**,
- but an emptiness of objects' being established by way of their own

[a] Gung-tang (*Difficult Points,* 107.5) says that further verbal distinctions are needed but does not spell them out. According to A-ku L̄o-drö-gya-tso (*Precious Lamp,* 80.2) what Gung-tang had in mind was that even though whatever exists necessarily appears to be established by way of its own character as the referent of a conceptual consciousness and thus the nature of character explicitly indicated in the topic sentence (that is, such false appearance) necessarily *exists* with everything, it cannot, from this, be concluded that such a superimposed factor or appearance is not the naturelessness (that is, non-existent nature) of character explicitly indicated in the topic sentence.

A second point depends upon Tibetan syntax: If someone says, "It follows with respect to the subject, such a superimposed factor, that the nature of character of the brief indication does not exist because [that subject] is the naturelessness of character of the brief indication," the proper answer is, "There is no entailment." (*de chos can mdor bstan gyi mtshan nyid ngo bo nyid med par thal mdor bstan gyi mtshan nyid ngo bo nyid med pa yin pa'i phyir na ma khyab*). The play is around the fact that one might think that the challenge means: "It follows that the subject, such a superimposed factor, is the naturelessness of character of the brief indication because of being the naturelessness of character of the brief indication." Because of the construction *med par thal* in this instance, the subject does not function in the "thesis" of the consequence, the seeming predicate containing within it both subject and predicate.

> character as the referents of conceptual consciousnesses is not taught,[a] except in the sense of the meaning of the character-non-nature at this point **arriving at**, or getting down to, emptiness.

By indicating that imputational natures here are both the **nature** of character and the **character-non-nature**, Gung-tang and A-ku Lo-drö-gya-tso reveal that the reason why scholars usually hesitate to identify the **character-non-nature** as (1) the establishment of objects by way of their own character as the referents of conceptual consciousnesses and (2) the superimposed factor or appearance of such is just because it is the **nature** in terms of character that is being refuted. However, this very identification has to be made in their system; otherwise, the character-non-nature would end up as being emptiness and thus the ultimate-non-nature.

Indeed, the *Sūtra Unraveling the Thought*, as has been shown, does not intend to discourse on emptiness when it speaks of the character-non-nature since it (1) identifies imputational natures (and not thoroughly established natures) as character-non-natures, (2) says that imputational natures are "posited by names and terminology and do not subsist by way of their own character" (whereas thoroughly established natures are the opposite) and (3) compares character-non-natures with a flower in the sky, which is only imputed by conceptuality, whereas thoroughly established natures are established by way of their own character. Therefore, when Buddha declares that imputational natures "are said to be 'character-non-natures,'" he is saying that imputational natures are **those which** are character-non-natures. "Non-nature" is significantly read as meaning "that which lacks nature." Buddha is not teaching emptiness at this point; rather, he is identifying that of which other-powered natures are empty.

The critical acumen that drew us into a web of problems rescues us back out of them with the result that, if one can still think on the topic, our original intuitive reading of the sūtra re-emerges. In accordance with A-ku Lo-drö-gya-tso's cogent reading, the question should be rendered for the sake of clarity as,

---

[a] A-ku Lo-drö-gya-tso (80.6) also says that **establishment** of objects by way of their own character as the referents of conceptual consciousnesses is not taught. This is an odd observation since it would seem that only a fool could think that such establishment is **taught**, that is, advocated, here. However, this is the point of a short debate in Gung-tang's *Difficult Points* which serves as the basis for A-ku Lo-drö-gya-tso's remark. Gung-tang (106.13) says that establishment of objects by way of their own character as the referents of conceptual consciousnesses cannot be considered to be taught in the topic sentence just because it is the nature of character at that point. He says that in fact the opposite is true: since it is the nature of character at this point, it is necessarily not taught at this point. Otherwise, it would absurdly follow that the parallel could be drawn that external objects are asserted in the Mind-Only School's own system just because externality is the object of refutation in their own system. His meaning is that just because a sūtra mentions something, this does not mean that it **teaches** it. A-ku Lo-drö-gya-tso is mirroring this point.

"What is the non-existent nature in terms of character?" or, put another way, "What is the nature in terms of character that is non-existent?" or "What are those that are natureless in terms of character?" Seen this way, the extensive indication becomes:

> Paramārthasamudgata, concerning that, what are the non-existent natures of phenomena in terms of character? Those which are imputational characters. Why? It is thus: Those [imputational characters] are characters posited by names and terminology and do not subsist by way of their own character. Therefore, they are said to be the "non-existent natures in terms of character."

To avoid the pitfalls of the question seeming to be about emptiness as is the case with the translation as "What is the naturelessness of phenomena in terms of character?" I have used "What are character-non-natures of phenomena?"

Issue #101: Are the three natures and the three non-natures equivalent?

Through making a host of distinctions Gung-tang and A-ku Lo-drö-gya-tso have answered Gön-chok-jik-may-wang-bo's qualm about the Go-mang textbook which seems to be saying that the character-non-nature is the subtle selflessness of phenomena and hence the teaching of the ultimate-non-nature is redundant. It seems to me that Gung-ru Chö-jung and Jam-yang-shay-ba did not appreciate that the term "character-non-nature" actually means the "non-existent nature in terms of character" and thus were led into holding that the character-non-nature is the subtle selflessness of phenomena. Specifically, in a passage in which Jam-yang-shay-ba dispels objections to his own position,[304] he openly says that the character-non-nature explicitly indicated on this occasion in the *Sūtra Unraveling the Thought* is the thoroughly established nature. Also, in the process of doing this, he presents the counter-intuitive view that the three non-natures and the three natures are not equivalent. He gives no reasoning for this position except to cite the passage on the three natures in Chapter Six of the *Sūtra Unraveling the Thought* and the passages on the three non-natures in Chapter Seven, as if any and all competent readers could catch his point! About the three natures he cites the "Questions of Guṇākara Chapter":

> Guṇākara, there are three characters of phenomena. What are these three? They are the imputational character, the other-powered character, and the thoroughly established character. Guṇākara, what is the imputational character of phenomena? It is that which is posited by nominal terminology as the entities and attributes of phenomena due to imputing whatsoever conventions.
>
> Guṇākara, what is the other-powered character of phenomena? It

is just the dependent arising of phenomena. It is thus: Because this exists, that arises; because this is produced, that is produced. It is thus: This ranges from: "Due to the condition of ignorance, compositional factors [are produced]..." up to "In this way, just the great aggregates of suffering arise."

Guṇākara, what is the thoroughly established character of phenomena? It is that which is the suchness of phenomena, that which Bodhisattvas realize through the cause of effort and through the cause of proper mental application.

He then refers to the presentation of the three non-natures in the "Questions of Paramārthasamudgata Chapter" which I will cite in full:

"Paramārthasamudgata, thinking of three non-natures of phenomena—character-non-nature, production-non-nature, and ultimate-non-nature—I taught [in the middle wheel of the teaching], 'All phenomena are natureless.'

"Paramārthasamudgata, concerning that, what are character-non-natures of phenomena? Those which are imputational characters.

"Why? It is thus: Those [imputational characters] are characters posited by names and terminology[a] and do not subsist by way of their own character. Therefore, they are said to be 'character-non-natures.'

"What are production-non-natures of phenomena?[b] Those which are the other-powered characters of phenomena.

"Why? It is thus: Those [other-powered characters] arise through the force of other conditions and not by themselves.[c] Therefore, they are said to be 'production-non-natures.'

"What are ultimate-non-natures? Those dependently arisen phenomena—which are natureless due to being natureless in terms of production—are also natureless due to being natureless in terms of the ultimate.

"Why? Paramārthasamudgata, that which is an object of observation of purification in phenomena I teach to be the ultimate, and other-powered characters are not the object of observation of purification. Therefore, they are said to be 'ultimate-non-natures.'

"Moreover, that which is the thoroughly established character of phenomena is also called 'the ultimate-non-nature.' Why? Paramārthasamudgata, that which in phenomena is the selflessness of phenomena is called their 'non-nature.' It is the ultimate, and the ultimate is

---

[a] See issue #104.

[b] Roughly, this means, "What phenomena are without the nature of self-production?" See issues #76, 77. About "phenomena," see #71.

[c] See issue #67.

> distinguished by just the naturelessness of all phenomena; therefore, it is called the 'ultimate-non-nature.'

Jam-ȳang-shay-b̄a mysteriously adds that Asaṅga also treats the three non-natures and the three natures separately in his *Actuality of the Grounds,* also known as the *Grounds of Yogic Practice,* but to my astonishment he says no more. Somehow it is supposed to be obvious from these passages in the sixth and seventh chapters of the *Sūtra Unraveling the Thought* that the three non-natures and the three natures are not equivalent!

It is interesting to note that Jam-ȳang-shay-b̄a did not crib this point of the non-equivalence of the three natures and the three non-natures from his predecessor Gung-ru Chö-jung and that neither Gung-tang nor A-ku L̄o-drö-gya-tso ever mentions Jam-ȳang-shay-b̄a's point. Perhaps this is because it differs so radically from the attempt to rewrite the other statements from Gung-ru Chö-jung and Jam-ȳang-shay-b̄a, treated above, so that they would seem **not** to indicate that the character-non-nature is to be posited as the thoroughly established nature. My own opinion is that the three non-natures and the three natures are respectively equivalent—whatever is an imputational nature is a character-non-nature, and whatever is a character-non-nature is an imputational nature, and so on.

It is important to keep in mind that Gung-ru Chö-jung and Jam-ȳang-shay-b̄a are trying to right inadequacies in D̄zong-ka-b̄a's explanation:

- D̄zong-ka-b̄a's treating imputational natures here as "being the referent of conceptual consciousnesses" not only incurs the problem of a lower school's realizing that this is not established by way of its own character but also the problem of treating only existent imputational natures, whereas D̄zong-ka-b̄a himself says that imputational natures here are of two varieties, existent and non-existent.
- His treating the nature of character that is non-existent in imputational natures as just establishment by way of its own character does not allow the "own-character" of Paramārthasamudgata's question to be the same as the "character" in the character-non-nature of Buddha's answer, as D̄zong-ka-b̄a himself suggests it should be.

Their attempts to correct these problems, however, embroil them in the almost unimaginable complexities we have seen.

Issue #102: Does the extensive explanation of imputational natures' character-non-nature delineate the thoroughly established nature?

Jik-may-dam-chö-gya-tso[305] reports that the Mongolian scholar and follower of Jay-d̄zün Chö-ḡyi-gyel-tsen, Tsay-d̄en-hla-ram-b̄a, holds that the extensive explanation of imputational natures' character-non-nature does indeed delineate the thoroughly established nature. This means that the passage:

> Concerning that, what are character-non-natures of phenomena? Those which are imputational characters.
>
> Why? It is thus: Those [imputational characters] are characters posited by names and terminology and do not subsist by way of their own character. Therefore, they are said to be "character-non-natures."

delineates that the imputational nature's establishment by way of its own character—the object of negation—is non-existent in its basis of negation, an other-powered nature. Tsay-d̄en-hla-ram-b̄a, well aware of Ḡön-chok-jik-may-w̄ang-b̄o's and Gung-tang's criticism that then there would be no need for Buddha to speak of the ultimate-non-nature, says that the sūtra goes on to show that the thoroughly established nature is the ultimate-non-nature in order to make known that the thoroughly established nature is posited as a **mere negative** of its object of negation, the self of phenomena. He admits that the section on the thoroughly established nature as the ultimate-non-nature does not newly delineate the thoroughly established nature but holds that it is not purposeless, for it emphasizes that the thoroughly established nature is the mere elimination of its object of negation.

My feeling is that Tsay-d̄en-hla-ram-b̄a's opinion incurs the fault that when, in the process of meditating on selflessness, one ascertains the object of negation, one also would absurdly be delineating selflessness. Indeed, in order to realize **with valid cognition** that the establishment of objects by way of their own character as the referents of conceptual consciousnesses is the object of negation, one must realize emptiness, but, prior to that, this can be realized with a correctly assuming consciousness.

Issue #103: Could the character-non-nature explicitly taught in the brief indication be emptiness but the character-non-nature explicitly taught in the extensive explanation be an imputational nature?

Jik-may-dam-chö-gya-tso[306] reports that another scholar holds that:

- the character-non-nature taught on the occasion of the brief indication is indeed emptiness,
- but the character-non-nature explicitly taught on the occasion of the extensive explanation is an imputational nature.

No reason is given for this seemingly odd assertion, but it seems to me that a likely reason is that:

1. In the brief indication the character-non-nature, which looks like a mere absence of establishment by way of its own character, is only implicitly understood to be taken in terms of the imputational nature, and thus the reference is to the non-establishment of the imputational nature by way of its own character, which is emptiness.
2. However, the extensive explanation **explicitly** mentions the imputational nature, putting the focus not on its mere absence but on itself, that is to say, the imputational nature that is without nature in terms of character.

In answer to this position, Jik-may-dam-chö-gya-tso makes the cogent objection that except for the fact that the brief indication does not associate the character-non-nature with illustrations (that is, imputational natures), it teaches in a brief way what is delineated in the extensive explanation and thus what they both teach has to be similar.[a] He adds that since the sūtra indicates that the character-non-nature is just posited by terms and conceptuality and is not something established from its own side without depending on imputation by terms and conceptuality (as emptiness is), it is best to take the character-non-nature of both the brief and extensive explanations in the sūtra as being an imputational nature and thus not an emptiness.

Ser-shül Lo-sang-pün-tsok[307] similarly says that even the first non-nature in the extensive explanation—which in Tibetan is *kun btags mtshan nyid ngo bo nyid med pa* and could be understood as:

- imputational natures' character-non-nature
- or character-non-nature in imputational natures
- or imputational natures that are character-non-natures—

is predominantly understood (in the third way) to refer to the imputational nature itself. However, he adds that when debating, if the context is set as factors imputed in the manner of entity and attributes, then it might have to be said (in accordance with either of the first two ways) that it is the ultimate truth, emptiness. For otherwise even the non-establishment—of factors imputed in the manner of entity and attribute—by way of their own character[b] would absurdly not be the ultimate.

I take his point to be that since the latter phrase (translated as "the non-establishment—of factors imputed in the manner of entity and attribute—by way of their own character) is standardly taken in the first or second way and not as "factors imputed in the manner of entity and attribute which are not established by way of their own character," then the first non-nature in the

[a] Paṇ-chen Sö-nam-drak-ba (*Garland of Blue Lotuses*, 13b.2-13b.5) makes the similar point that the brief indication *implicitly* indicates the reasons for the three non-natures simply because the extensive explanation extensively explains just what the brief indication implicitly indicates.

[b] *ngo bo dang khyad par la kun brtags pa'i kun brtags de rang gi mtshan nyid kyis [ma] grub pa.*

extensive explanation[a] might have to be taken this way. S̄er-s̄hül adds that nevertheless his readers should examine what Jam-ȳang-shay-b̄a and his followers have said on the issue; the implication is that he has not come to a conclusion.

Nonetheless, it seems to me that, as Jik-may-dam-chö-gya-tso points out, since the *Sūtra Unraveling the Thought* itself says that the character-non-nature is just posited by terms and conceptuality and is not established by way of its own character, there is no way that the character-non-nature can be emptiness. For Ge-luk-b̄a scholars uniformly hold that since other-powered natures are established by way of their own character and are not just posited by terms and conceptuality, then the thoroughly established nature, emptiness, must also be established by way of its own character and not just posited by terms and conceptuality.

Looking Back

The Gung-ru Chö-jung, Jam-ȳang-shay-b̄a, Gung-tang, and A-ku L̄o-drö-gya-tso tradition of the Go-mang College of Dre-b̄ung Monastic University in Hla-s̄a and D̄ra-s̄hi-kyil Monastic University in northeastern Tibet as well as their affiliate monasteries attempts to forge, with considerable creativity, a magnificent consistency with regard to the mention of "own-character" in Paramārthasamudgata's question and with regard to the mention of "nature of character" in Buddha's subsequent answer as well as D̄zong-ka-b̄a's remarks about those terms. In other readings "nature of character" is only establishment by way of its own character, and imputational natures are factors imputed in the manner of entities and attributes.[b] Thus, in these other systems, it makes excellent sense, without any entangled and convoluted explanations, for Buddha to say that the imputational nature is called a "character-non-nature" (that which is not established by way of its own character) because of only being imputed by conceptuality and not being established by way of its own character. However, they undergo great difficulties in trying to explain how, according to their reading of Paramārthasamudgata's question, in the first wheel of doctrine Buddha taught that the aggregates and so forth are established by way of their own character (for even they admit that indeed the aggregates **are** established by way of their own character).

Since no one seems to have the perfectly fitting solution, the various renditions and comparison of them serve to draw a practitioner into the topic, provided that the issue does not become so complex that the mind is fractured into unusable bits of information and dis-information and also provided that the issue does not come to be seen as so hopelessly complex that the matter is left entirely in favor of blind faith, assuming that Buddha and D̄zong-ka-b̄a must

---

[a] *kun btags mtshan nyid ngo bo nyid med pa.*

[b] I prefer keeping D̄zong-ka-b̄a's often repeated "being the referent of a conceptual consciousness."

have had something consistent in mind which, nevertheless, is inaccessible to us. Indeed, frustration with such a plethora of distinctions, next to impossible to remember, appears to be a cause leading to simple-minded devotion to mundane deities that is observed in Tibetan monastic communities.

To provide a handle on the topic, the next chapter offers a quick review of the riddle from the perspective of Go-mang scholars.

14. Review: Two Riddles

Ḡzong-ka-ḡa was a genius at creating consistency in systems of thought, but sometimes he provided only brief expositions of some topics and at other times only suggested his views. Ge-luk-ḡa scholars—like others following a founder's words—have been drawn into the complex problems of extending his thought into those areas that he did not clearly explicate or of re-thinking what was clear but did not manifest the presumed consistency. The working premise is that Ḡzong-ka-ḡa's work is sensible and carefully crafted but is subject to the highly creative strategy of "positing his thought" as long as consonance with the corpus of his work is maintained.

The attempt at resolving apparent contradictions itself fuels increasing interest in the topics, this being a central reason why the Ge-luk-ḡa system of education, centered around scholastic debate, has been so influential throughout much of Inner Asia. I too have been drawn into the considerable ambiguity surrounding his usage of "own-character" and "imputational nature"—the process beginning like being teased by a riddle, then probing a mystery, then finding oneself in a maze, and finally the walls of the maze occasionally becoming transparent when the scope of the problem comes into view.

As has been shown in copious detail, the Go-mang tradition offers intriguing and highly convoluted explanations of these terms, and therefore in this chapter let us review its readings of (1) seven passages in which "own-character" or its variants appear and (2) ten passages where the term "imputational nature" or its variants appear.

The First Riddle

What is the consistent reading of "own-character" (and its possible variants in this context, "nature of character," "inherent existence," "establishment by way of its own character," and so forth) that could satisfy all the following references? This turns into the mystery, "Is there such a consistent reading?" and, when the multiple meanings needed are located, turns into a maze of possibilities.

1. Paramārthasamudgata's statement in the *Sūtra Unraveling the Thought* (*Emptiness in Mind-Only,* 75) that in the first wheel Buddha taught that the aggregates have their own character:[a]

   The Supramundane Victor spoke, in many ways, of the **own-character** of the aggregates. He also spoke of [their] character

[a] In this chapter I will mostly use Tibetan script in the notes.
བཅོམ་ལྡན་འདས་ཀྱིས་རྣམ་གྲངས་དུ་མར་ཕུང་པོ་རྣམས་ཀྱི་རང་གི་མཚན་ཉིད་ཀྱང་བཀའ་སྩལ། སྐྱེ་བའི་མཚན་ཉིད་དང་། འཇིག་པའི་མཚན་ཉིད་དང་། སྤང་བ་དང་ཡོངས་སུ་ཤེས་པ་ཡང་བཀའ་སྩལ།

of production, character of disintegration, abandonment, and thorough knowledge.

2. Ḏzong-ka-ḇa's statements (*Emptiness in Mind-Only,* 78) about what is taught in the three wheels of doctrine:[a]

 If the statements in some sūtras [that is, in the middle wheel of the teaching] that all phenomena are **nature**less, and so forth, and the statements in some sūtras [in the first wheel of the teaching] that the aggregates and so forth have an **own-character**, and so forth, were left as they are verbally, they would be contradictory.

 And (*Emptiness in Mind-Only,* 127):[b]

 The bases being posited as interpretable or definitive are the three—the statements [in the first wheel] that phenomena equally[c] have **nature in the sense of being established by way of their own character**, the statements [in the middle wheel] that phenomena equally do not have **such**, and the good differentiation [in the final wheel] of those [phenomena] that have [**such establishment**] and those that do not.[d]

 According to Jam-ȳang-shay-ḇa, that should read:

 The bases being posited as interpretable or definitive are the three—the statements equally [present throughout the sūtras of the first wheel] that phenomena have **nature in the sense of being established by way of their own character**, the statements equally [present throughout the sūtras of the middle wheel] that phenomena do not have **such**, and the good differentiation [in the final wheel] of those [phenomena] that have [**such establishment**] and those that do not.

3. Ke-drup's statement in his *Opening the Eyes of the Fortunate* about what is taught in the three wheels of doctrine:[e]

 Furthermore, in the first wheel the aggregates and so forth are said to be equally **existent by way of their own character**,

---

[a] མདོ་སྡེ་ཁ་ཅིག་ཏུ་ཆོས་ཐམས་ཅད་ངོ་བོ་ཉིད་མེད་པ་སོགས་སུ་གསུངས་པ་དང་། ཁ་ཅིག་ཏུ་ཕུང་པོ་ལ་སོགས་པའི་རང་གི་མཚན་ཉིད་ལ་སོགས་པ་ཡོད་པར་གསུངས་པ་གཉིས་སྒྲ་སོར་བཞག་ན་འགལ་ནའང་འགལ་བ་མེད་དགོས་པ།

[b] དྲང་ངེས་སུ་འཇོག་པའི་གཞི་ནི་ཆོས་རྣམས་ལ་རང་གི་མཚན་ཉིད་ཀྱིས་གྲུབ་པའི་ངོ་བོ་ཉིད་ཡོད་མཉམ་དུ་གསུངས་པ་དང་མེད་མཉམ་དུ་གསུངས་པ་དང་ཡོད་མེད་ལེགས་པར་ཕྱེ་བ་གསུམ་ཡིན་པ།

[c] See issues #44, 55.

[d] See issue #108.

[e] དེ་ཡང་འཁོར་ལོ་དང་པོར་ཕུང་སོགས་རང་གི་མཚན་ཉིད་ཀྱིས་ཡོད་མཉམ་དང་། བར་པ་ལས་ཐམས་ཅད་རང་བཞིན་མེད་མཉམ་དུ་གསུངས་ཀྱི། རང་བཞིན་ཡོད་མེད་དངོས་སུ་ཕྱེ་ནས་མ་གསུངས་པས་དྲང་དོན།: 200.4.

and in the middle wheel all are said to be equally **without inherent existence**. [In both cases Buddha] did not speak within explicitly differentiating whether [the aggregates and so forth] **inherently exist or not**; hence, [the first two wheels of doctrine] require interpretation.

4. Ḏzong-ka-ḇa's refutation (*Emptiness in Mind-Only,* 78-79) of Wonch'uk's explanation in which Ḏzong-ka-ḇa says that "own-character" could not possibly refer to the unique character of phenomena:[a]

> In the Chinese *Great Commentary*[b] [on the *Sūtra Unraveling the Thought* by the Korean scholar Wonch'uk], and so forth, "**own-character**"[c] here [in this passage in the *Sūtra Unraveling the Thought*] is explained as the unique character [of the aggregates and so forth], but this is not right.[d] For the sūtra itself at the point of [speaking about] imputational factors[e] clearly speaks of **establishment by way of [the object's] own character** [and does not speak of the unique character], and since even imputational factors have a unique characterization, there would be the fallacy that the character-non-nature could not be explained with respect to imputational factors.[f]

5. The passage in the *Sūtra Unraveling the Thought* to which Ḏzong-ka-ḇa (*Emptiness in Mind-Only,* 86) must be referring in the statement just cited:[g]

> It is thus: Those [imputational characters] are characters posited by names and terminology[h] and **do not subsist by way of their own character**. Therefore, they are said to be "character-non-natures."

6. Ḏzong-ka-ḇa's spelling out (*Emptiness in Mind-Only,* 86) the type of nature that imputational natures do not have:[i]

---

a རྒྱ་ནག་གི་འགྲེལ་ཆེན་སོགས་ལས་ཐུན་མོང་མ་ཡིན་པའི་མཚན་ཉིད་ལ་བཤད་པ་ནི་རིགས་པ་མ་ཡིན་ཏེ། མདོ་ཉིད་ལས་ཀུན་བཏགས་ཀྱི་སྐབས་སུ་རང་གི་མཚན་ཉིད་ཀྱིས་གྲུབ་པ་ལ་གསལ་བར་གསུངས་པའི་ཕྱིར་དང་། ཀུན་བཏགས་ལའང་ཐུན་མོང་མ་ཡིན་པའི་མཚན་བྱེད་ཡོད་པས་མཚན་ཉིད་ངོ་བོ་ཉིད་མེད་པ་ཀུན་བཏགས་ལ་བཤད་དུ་མི་རུང་བའི་སྐྱོན་དུ་འགྱུར་བའི་ཕྱིར་རོ།།

b See issue #8.

c See issues #27-55, 94.

d See issues #48, 39.

e See issue #50.

f See issue #48.

g འདི་ལྟར་དེ་ནི་མིང་དང་བརྡས་རྣམ་པར་བཞག་པའི་མཚན་ཉིད་ཡིན་གྱི་རང་གི་མཚན་ཉིད་ཀྱིས་རྣམ་པར་གནས་པ་ནི་མ་ཡིན་པས་དེའི་ཕྱིར་དེ་ནི་མཚན་ཉིད་ངོ་བོ་ཉིད་མེད་པ་ཉིད་ཅེས་བྱའོ།

h See issue #104.

i ཀུན་བཏགས་ལ་མེད་རྒྱུའི་མཚན་ཉིད་ཀྱི་ངོ་བོ་ཉིད་ནི་རང་གི་མཚན་ཉིད་ཀྱིས་གྲུབ་པའམ་གནས་པ་ལ་བྱའོ།། འདིར་རང་གི་མཚན་ཉིད་ཀྱིས་ཡོད་མེད་བསྟན་ཚོད་ནི་མིང་དང་བརྡ་ལ་ལྟོས་ནས་བཞག་མ་བཞག་ཡིན་ལ།

> The nature of **character** that imputational factors[a] do not have is to be taken as **establishment, or subsisting, by way of their own character**.[b] Here, the measure indicated[c] with respect to existing or not **existing by way of [an object's] own character** is: not to be posited or to be posited in dependence upon names and terminology.[d]

7. The character-non-nature explicitly mentioned at the point of the topic sentence in this section of the *Sūtra Unraveling the Thought:*[e]

> Paramārthasamudgata, thinking of three non-natures of phenomena—character-non-nature, production-non-nature, and ultimate-non-nature—I taught [in the middle wheel of the teaching], "All phenomena are natureless."

"Answer" of the Go-mang Tradition

Six meanings for "own-character" and so forth need be considered:

a. the unique character (of an object)[f]
b. establishment by way of its own character[g]
c. established by way of its own character as the referent of a conceptual consciousness[h]
d. true establishment[i]
e. establishment from its own side[j]
f. the superimposed factor (or appearance) of an object as established by way of its own character as the referent of a conceptual consciousness.[k]

According to the tradition of Gung-ru Chö-jung and Jam-ȳang-shay-b̄a and their followers, Gung-tang and A-ku L̄o-drö-gya-tso, there is no one answer. Rather, a variety of identifications is required. As I (with trepidation) read their

---

[a] See issue #83.

[b] See issues #29, 94.

[c] *bstan tshod;* see issue #96.

[d] See issues #105-109.

[e] དོན་དམ་ཡང་དག་འཕགས། ངས་ཆོས་རྣམས་ཀྱི་ངོ་བོ་ཉིད་མེད་པ་ཉིད་རྣམ་པ་གསུམ་པོ་འདི་ལྟ་སྟེ། མཚན་ཉིད་ངོ་བོ་ཉིད་མེད་པ་ཉིད་དང་སྐྱེ་བ་ངོ་བོ་ཉིད་མེད་པ་ཉིད་དང་དོན་དམ་པ་ངོ་བོ་ཉིད་མེད་པ་ཉིད་ལ་དགོངས་ནས་ཆོས་ཐམས་ཅད་ངོ་བོ་ཉིད་མེད་པའོ།། ཞེས་བསྟན་ཏོ།

[f] ཐུན་མོང་མ་ཡིན་པའི་མཚན་ཉིད།

[g] རང་གི་མཚན་ཉིད་ཀྱིས་གྲུབ་པ།

[h] རང་འཛིན་རྟོག་པའི་ཞེན་གཞིར་རང་གི་མཚན་ཉིད་ཀྱིས་གྲུབ་པ།

[i] བདེན་པར་གྲུབ་པ།

[j] རང་ངོས་ནས་གྲུབ་པ།

[k] རང་འཛིན་རྟོག་པའི་ཞེན་གཞིར་རང་གི་མཚན་ཀྱིས་གྲུབ་པར་སྒྲོ་བཏགས་པ།

explanations, the references to "own-character" in those seven passages are to be taken this way:

1. Paramārthasamudgata's statement in the *Sūtra Unraveling the Thought* that in the first wheel Buddha taught that the aggregates have their own character:

   > The Supramundane Victor spoke, in many ways, of the own-character of the aggregates [***c:* establishment by way of their own character as the referents of conceptual consciousnesses**]. He also spoke of [their] character of production, character of disintegration, abandonment, and thorough knowledge.

2. D̄zong-ka-b̄a's statements about what is taught in the three wheels of doctrine:

   > If the statements in some sūtras [that is, in the middle wheel of the teaching] that all phenomena are natureless [***b:* without establishment by way of their own character** and ***e:* without establishment from their own side**], and so forth, and the statements in some sūtras [in the first wheel of the teaching] that the aggregates and so forth have an own-character [***c:* establishment by way of their own character as the referents of conceptual consciousnesses**], and so forth, were left as they are verbally, they would be contradictory.

   And:

   > The bases being posited as interpretable or definitive are the three—the statements [in the first wheel] that phenomena equally have nature in the sense of being established by way of their own character [***c:* establishment by way of their own character as the referents of conceptual consciousnesses**], the statements [in the middle wheel] that phenomena equally do not have such [***b:* establishment by way of their own character** and ***e:* establishment from their own side**], and the good differentiation [in the final wheel] of those [phenomena] that have [such establishment] [***b:* establishment by way of their own character**] and those that do not.

3. Ke-drup's statement in his *Opening the Eyes of the Fortunate* about what is taught in the three wheels of doctrine:

   > Furthermore, in the first wheel the aggregates and so forth are said to be equally existent by way of their own character [***c:***

are established by way of their own character as the referents of conceptual consciousnesses], and in the middle wheel all are said to be equally without inherent existence [***b:*** **are not established by way of their own character** and ***e:*** **do not exist from their own side**]. [In both cases Buddha] did not speak within explicitly differentiating whether [the aggregates and so forth] inherently exist or not [***b:*** **exist by way of their own character or not**]; hence, [the first two wheels of doctrine] require interpretation.

4. Ḏzong-ka-ḇa's refutation of Wonch'uk's explanation in which Ḏzong-ka-ḇa says that "own-character" could not possibly refer to the unique character of phenomena:

> In the Chinese *Great Commentary* [on the *Sūtra Unraveling the Thought* by the Korean scholar Wonch'uk], and so forth, "own-character" [***c:*** **establishment of objects by way of their own character as the referents of conceptual consciousnesses**] here [in this passage in the *Sūtra Unraveling the Thought*] is explained as the unique character [of the aggregates and so forth], but this is not right. For, the sūtra itself at the point of [speaking about] imputational factors clearly speaks of establishment by way of [the object's] own character [***c:*** **establishment of objects by way of their own character as the referents of conceptual consciousnesses**] [and does not speak of the unique character], and since even imputational factors have a unique characterization, there would be the fallacy that the character-non-nature could not be explained with respect to imputational factors.

5. The passage in the *Sūtra Unraveling the Thought* to which Ḏzong-ka-ḇa must be referring in the statement just cited:

> It is thus: Those [imputational characters] are characters posited by names and terminology and do not subsist by way of their own character [***b:*** **do not exist by way of their own character**]. Therefore, they are said to be "character-non-natures" [***b:*** **establishment by way of their own character**].

The distinction must be made that "character-nature," or "nature of character," itself means ***b:*** **establishment by way of its own character and not being posited by name and term**, but that which is the nature of character is primarily ***f:*** **the superimposed factor or appearance of objects as established by way of their own character as the referents of conceptual consciousnesses** and secondarily ***c:*** **the establishment of objects by way of their own character as the**

referents of conceptual consciousnesses. (Those two are also non-natures of character, that is to say, the natures of character that are not established by way of their own character.) The distinction is between the *meaning* of "nature of character" and the *illustrations* of "nature of character."

6. Ḏzong-ka-ḇa's spelling out the type of nature that imputational natures do not have:

   > The nature in terms of character [*b:* **establishment by way of their own character**] that imputational factors do not have is to be taken as establishment, or subsisting, by way of their own character [*b:* **establishment by way of their own character**]. Here, the measure indicated with respect to existing or not existing by way of [the object's] own character [*b:* **establishment or not by way of its own character**] is: not to be posited or to be posited in dependence upon names and terminology.

7. The character-non-nature explicitly mentioned at the point of the topic sentence in this section of the *Sūtra Unraveling the Thought*:

   > Paramārthasamudgata, thinking of three non-natures of phenomena—character-non-nature [*b:* **establishment of objects by way of their own character**], production-non-nature, and ultimate-non-nature—I taught [in the middle wheel of the teaching], "All phenomena are natureless."

Again, it is important to make the distinction that "character-nature," or "nature of character," itself means *b:* **objects' establishment by way of their own character and not being posited by names and terminology,** but that which is the nature of character is primarily *f:* **the superimposed factor or appearance of objects as established by way of their own character as the referents of conceptual consciousnesses** and secondarily *c:* **the establishment of objects by way of their own character as the referents of conceptual consciousnesses.**

A Few Comments

The way the second quote in number two is taken is very unusual, three different referents being required:

> The bases being posited as interpretable or definitive are the three—the statements [in the first wheel] that phenomena equally have nature in the sense of being established by way of their own character [*c:* **establishment by way of their own character as the referents of conceptual consciousnesses**], the statements [in the middle wheel] that

> phenomena equally do not have such [*b:* **establishment by way of their own character** and *e:* **establishment from their own side**], and the good differentiation [in the final wheel] of those [phenomena] that have [such establishment] [*b:* **establishment by way of their own character**] and those that do not.

The first quote in number two is similar but deals with only the first two wheels of doctrine:

> If the statements in some sūtras [that is, in the middle wheel of the teaching] that all phenomena are natureless [*b:* **without establishment by way of their own character** and *e:* **without establishment from their own side**], and so forth, and the statements in some sūtras [in the first wheel of the teaching] that the aggregates and so forth have an own-character [*c:* **establishment by way of their own character as the referents of conceptual consciousnesses**], and so forth, were left as they are, they would be contradictory.

When the necessary switches in reference are seen, Jam-ȳang-shay-b̄a's rendition of Paramārthasamudgata's question is seen in all its subtlety:

> Supramundane Victor, in the first wheel of the teaching, as specified here in my question, you pronounced many times the words of sūtra, "The entities of phenomena[a] ranging from forms through the thirty-seven harmonies with enlightenment as well as [their attributes of] production, cessation, and so forth that are established by way of their own character exist, exist." In the middle wheel of the teaching, as specified here in my question, you pronounced many times the words of sūtra, "Production, cessation, and so forth that are established by way of their own character do not exist, do not exist, in phenomena ranging from forms through omniscient consciousnesses." If those two were left literally as they are, they would be contradictory, but since the Teacher does not have contradiction, of what were you thinking when you said such in the middle wheel?

Jam-ȳang-shay-b̄a speaks of "the first wheel of the teaching, **as specified here in my question**" because there are presentations of the three wheels of doctrine other than that found in the *Sūtra Unraveling the Thought.* Also, he specifies the different lists of phenomena about which Buddha was speaking in the first and second wheels of doctrine within stressing the aspects of entity and attributes—"the **entities** of phenomena ranging from forms through the thirty-seven harmonies with enlightenment as well as [their **attributes** of] production,

[a] Jam-ȳang-shay-b̄a makes what seems to be an unnecessary specification of "compounded phenomena" which A-ku L̄o-drö-gya-tso's *Precious Lamp* (59.6) changes to "phenomena"; I have rendered it in accordance with the latter.

cessation, and so forth" and "phenomena ranging from forms through omniscient consciousnesses."

He uses the phrase "pronounced the words of sūtra" of establishment and non-establishment of objects by way of their own character. This is because the seeming contradiction rests, not in a teaching in the first wheel that phenomena are established by way of their own character and in a teaching in the middle wheel that phenomena are not so established, but in the face value of the words themselves as well as in the different meanings that those words have in their respective contexts.

Another "Answer"

At a point when I found all of these wandering meanings to be quite befuddling, I suddenly remembered that a traditional way to answer conundrums is to ask the author even if that person had long since passed away. So, I closed my eyes and asked Ḏzong-ka-ḇa. The answer came quickly, "There is no need to be so rigid." In other words, plug in whichever one will make sense in that particular sentence without worrying about over-all consistency in the rigid sense of having only a single identification, since the meaning, for the most part, is obvious. There is no need for me to say that I am not making any claims for actually having contacted the author, but this advice, surfacing from within my subconscious, became a clue that a few years later led to the simple discovery that:

- Ḏzong-ka-ḇa took the meaning of "character" in Buddha's answer, "Those [imputational characters] are character-non-natures," (where it obviously means "establishment by way of its own character" because Buddha goes on to says that imputational natures "do not subsist by way of their own character") and **loosely** applied it back to the mention of "own-character" in Paramārthasamudgata's question
- But Gung-ru Chö-jung and Jam-ȳang-shay-ḇa (as well as their followers Gung-tang and A-ku Ḻo-drö-gya-tso), taking Ḏzong-ka-ḇa's identification rigidly, searched for a more appropriate meaning of "own-character" in Paramārthasamudgata's question and cogently chose "established by way of its own character as the referent of a conceptual consciousness" and **rigidly** applied it forward to the meaning of "character" in Buddha's answer—"Those [imputational characters] are character-non-natures."

Indeed, in his criticism of Wonch'uk Ḏzong-ka-ḇa himself implies that the "own-character" of the question and the "character" of the answer should be equated, but, as we have seen, if either of these readings are taken rigidly, they run into insurmountable problems. Seeing this, I have been led into making my own identifications, employing a more flexible approach:

1. Paramārthasamudgata's statement in the *Sūtra Unraveling the Thought* that in the first wheel Buddha taught that the aggregates have their own character:

> The Supramundane Victor spoke, in many ways, of the own-character of the aggregates [***a:*** **unique character** within the context of ***c:*** **being established by way of its own character as the referent of a conceptual consciousness**]. He also spoke of [their] character of production, character of disintegration, abandonment, and thorough knowledge.

2. Dzong-ka-ba's statements about what is taught in the three wheels of doctrine:

> If the statements in some sūtras [in the middle wheel of the teaching] that all phenomena are natureless [***b:*** **without establishment by way of their own character** and ***e:*** **without establishment from their own side**], and so forth, and the statements in some sūtras [in the first wheel of the teaching] that the aggregates and so forth have an own-character [***a:*** **unique character** within the context of ***c:*** **being established by way of its own character as the referent of a conceptual consciousness**], and so forth, were left as they are, they would be contradictory.

And:

> The bases being posited as interpretable or definitive are the three—the statements [in the first wheel] that phenomena equally have nature in the sense of being established by way of their own character [**their being or appearing as the referents of terms and conceptual consciousnesses is *b:* established by way of its own character**], the statements [in the middle wheel] that phenomena equally do not have such [***b:*** **establishment by way of their own character** and ***e:*** **establishment from their own side**], and the good differentiation [in the final wheel] of those [phenomena] that have [such establishment] [***b:*** **establishment by way of their own character**] and those that do not.

3. Ke-drup's statement in his *Opening the Eyes of the Fortunate* about what is taught in the three wheels of doctrine:

> Furthermore, in the first wheel the aggregates and so forth are said to be equally existent by way of their own character [**their being or appearing as the referents of terms and**

conceptual consciousnesses is *b:* established by way of its own character], and in the middle wheel all are said to be equally without inherent existence [***b:* are not established by way of their own character** and ***e:* do not exist from their own side**]. [In both cases Buddha] did not speak within explicitly differentiating whether [the aggregates and so forth] inherently exist or not [***b:* exist by way of their own character or not**]; hence, [the first two wheels of the teaching] require interpretation.

4. Dzong-ka-ba's refutation of Wonch'uk's explanation in which Dzong-ka-ba says that "own-character" could not possibly refer to the unique character of phenomena:

 In the Chinese *Great Commentary* [on the *Sūtra Unraveling the Thought* by the Korean scholar Wonch'uk], and so forth, "own-character" [***a:* unique character** within the context of ***c:* being established by way of its own character as the referent of a conceptual consciousness**] here [in this passage in the *Sūtra Unraveling the Thought*] is explained as [**merely**] the unique character [of the aggregates and so forth], but this is not right. For, the sūtra itself at the point of [speaking about] imputational factors clearly speaks of establishment by way of [the object's] own character [that is to say, **that objects' being or appearing as the referents of terms and conceptual consciousnesses is *b:* established by way of its own character**] [and does not speak of the unique character], and since even imputational factors have a unique characterization, there would be the fallacy that the character-non-nature could not be explained with respect to imputational factors.

5. The passage in the *Sūtra Unraveling the Thought* to which Dzong-ka-ba must be referring in the statement just cited:

 It is thus: Those [imputational characters] are characters posited by names and terminology and do not subsist by way of their own character [***b:* do not exist by way of their own character**]. Therefore, they are said to be "character-non-natures" [***b:* establishment by way of their own character**].

6. Dzong-ka-ba's spelling out the type of nature that imputational natures do not have:

 The nature of character [***b:* establishment by way of their own character**] that imputational natures do not have is to be taken as establishment, or subsisting, by way of their own

> character [*b:* **establishment by way of their own character**]. Here, the measure indicated with respect to <u>existing or not existing by way of [the object's] own character</u> [*b:* **establishment or not by way of its own character**] is: not to be posited or to be posited in dependence upon names and terminology.

7. The character-non-nature explicitly mentioned at the point of the topic sentence in this section of the *Sūtra Unraveling the Thought*:

> Paramārthasamudgata, thinking of three non-natures of phenomena—character-non-nature [*b:* **establishment of objects by way of their own character**], production-non-nature, and ultimate-non-nature—I taught, "All phenomena are natureless."

The Second Riddle

The second riddle is even more complicated to unravel. It is: What is the consistent reading of "imputational natures" (or its variants) that could satisfy all the following references? As before, this turns into the mystery, "Is there such a consistent reading?" and, when the multiple meanings needed are being located, turns into a maze of those multiple meanings.

1. The imputational natures that the *Sūtra Unraveling the Thought* says (*Emptiness in Mind-Only,* 86) are character-non-natures:[a]

> **Those** [**imputational characters**] are characters posited by names and terminology and do not subsist by way of their own character. Therefore, **they** are said to be "character-non-natures."

2. The sixth chapter of the *Sūtra Unraveling the Thought*, the "Questions of Guṇākara," where it says that imputational natures are to be identified in terms of a factor of appearance wrongly superimposed by a mistaken awareness:[b]

> The **imputational character** is to be viewed as like the flaws of dark spots that form in the eye[-sight] of one with the disease of dim-sightedness.

And:[c]

---

a དེ་ནི་མིང་དང་བརྡས་རྣམ་པར་བཞག་པའི་མཚན་ཉིད་ཡིན་གྱི་རང་གི་མཚན་ཉིད་ཀྱིས་རྣམ་པར་གནས་པ་ནི་མ་ཡིན་པས་དེའི་ཕྱིར་དེ་ནི་མཚན་ཉིད་ངོ་བོ་ཉིད་མེད་པ་ཉིད་ཅེས་བྱའོ།

b རབ་རིབ་ཅན་གྱི་མིག་ལ་རབ་རིབ་ཀྱི་སྐྱོན་ཆགས་པ་དེ་ལྟ་བུར་ནི་ཀུན་བརྟགས་པའི་མཚན་ཉིད་བལྟ་བར་བྱའོ།།: as cited in Gung-tang's *Difficult Points,* 109.16.

c ཤེལ་ཤིན་ཏུ་གསལ་བ་ལ་ནོར་བུ་རིན་པོ་ཆེ་ཨིནྡྲ་ནི་ལ་དང་། མཐོན་ཀ་ཆེན་པོ་དང་། པད་མ་རཱ་ག་ དང་།

> Apprehending the **imputational character** in other-powered characters should be viewed as like wrongly apprehending a very clear crystal as precious jewels—sapphire, the blue gem, ruby, emerald, or gold.

3. Ḏzong-ka-ḇa's remarks (*Emptiness in Mind-Only,* 110) restricting the scope of imputational natures here:[a]

> With respect to the **imputational factor** of which [other-powered natures] are empty, on both occasions of identifying the **imputational factor** in the sūtra it does not speak of any other imputational factor than just **factors imputed in the manner of entities and attributes**. I will explain the reason for this later.

His later explanation (*Emptiness in Mind-Only,* 217) of the reason:[b]

> Although among **imputational factors** in general there are many, such as all generally characterized phenomena, space, and so forth, the reason why these are not [explicitly] mentioned in the *Sūtra Unraveling the Thought* is that they are not relevant on the occasion of the **imputational factor** the emptiness of **which** is posited as the thoroughly established nature. Although many of those are existents that cannot be posited by names and terminology, they are not established by way of their own character because of being only imputed by conceptuality.

4. The imputational natures that Ḏzong-ka-ḇa has in mind when he (*Emptiness in Mind-Only,* 195) says that they must be identified in order to know the selflessness of phenomena well:[c]

> Therefore, if you do not know what this **imputational factor** that is a superimposed factor of a self of phenomena on other-powered natures is, you will not know in a decisive way the

---

མ་ནད་དང་། གསེར་དུ་ལོག་པར་འཛིན་པ་དེ་ལྟ་བུར་ནི་གཞན་གྱི་དབང་གི་མཚན་ཉིད་ལ་ཀུན་བརྟགས་པའི་མཚན་ཉིད་དུ་འཛིན་པར་བལྟ་བར་བྱའོ།།: as cited in Gung-tang's *Difficult Points,* 109.17.

a གང་གིས་སྟོང་པའི་ཀུན་བརྟགས་ནི་མདོ་འདིའི་ཀུན་བརྟགས་ངོས་བཟུང་བའི་སྐབས་གཉིས་ཀར་ངོ་བོ་དང་ཁྱད་པར་དུ་བཏགས་པ་ཙམ་མིན་པའི་ཀུན་བརྟགས་གཞན་མ་གསུངས་པའི་རྒྱུ་མཚན་ནི་འཆད་པར་འགྱུར་རོ།།

b སྤྱིར་ཀུན་བརྟགས་ལ་སྤྱི་མཚན་ཐམས་ཅད་དང་ནམ་མཁའ་ལ་སོགས་པ་དུ་མ་ཞིག་ཡོད་ཀྱང་དགོངས་འགྲེལ་ལས་མ་གསུངས་པ་ནི། ཀུན་བརྟགས་གང་གིས་སྟོང་པ་ཡོངས་གྲུབ་ཏུ་འཇོག་པའི་སྐབས་སུ་དེ་དག་མི་མཁོ་བས་སོ།། དེ་དག་གི་མང་པོ་ཞིག་མིང་དང་བརྡས་འཇོག་མི་ནུས་པའི་ཡོད་པ་ཡིན་ཡང་རང་གི་མཚན་ཉིད་ཀྱིས་གྲུབ་པ་མིན་ཏེ་རྟོག་པས་བཏགས་པ་ཙམ་ཡིན་པའི་ཕྱིར།

c གཞན་དབང་ལ་ཆོས་བདག་སྒྲོ་བཏགས་པའི་ཀུན་བརྟགས་འདི་ཇི་ལྟར་ཡིན་མི་ཤེས་ན་ལུགས་འདིའི་ཆོས་ཀྱི་བདག་འཛིན་དང་ཆོས་ཀྱི་བདག་མེད་མཐའ་ཆོད་པར་མི་ཤེས་སོ།།

conception of a self of phenomena and the selflessness of phenomena in this [Mind-Only] system.

5. Dzong-ka-ba's identification (*Emptiness in Mind-Only,* 195) of the imputational nature that, when conceived to be established by way of its own character, is the self of phenomena, saying it is not just imputational natures in general but a specific one:[a]

> Those **imputational factors**—which are such that a consciousness conceiving **imputational factors** to be established by way of their own character is asserted to be a consciousness conceiving a self of phenomena—are the nominally and terminologically imputed factors [in the imputation of] the aggregates and so forth as entities, "This is form," and as attributes, "This is the production of form," and so forth.

6. Dzong-ka-ba's distinction (*Emptiness in Mind-Only,* 210) that there are two types of imputational natures, those established and those not established by valid cognition:[b]

> Thus, form and so forth being the referents of conceptual consciousnesses is an **imputational factor** posited by name and terminology, but, since it is established by valid cognition, it cannot be refuted. However, that it is established by way of the thing's own character is an **imputational factor** posited only nominally that does not occur among objects of knowledge [that is, does not exist]. Hence, among **what are posited by names and terminology** there are two [types], those established by valid cognition and those not established by valid cognition. Still, this system asserts that once something is only posited by names and terminology, cause and effect are not suitable to occur in it.

7. The *Sūtra Unraveling the Thought*'s usage (*Emptiness in Mind-Only,* 93) of a flower in the sky as an example for imputational natures:[c]

> It is thus: for example, **character-non-natures [that is, imputational natures]** are to be viewed as like a flower in the sky.

---

a ཀུན་བཏགས་རང་གི་མཚན་ཉིད་ཀྱིས་གྲུབ་པར་འཛིན་པ་ཆོས་ཀྱི་བདག་འཛིན་དུ་འདོད་པའི་ཀུན་བཏགས་ནི་ཕུང་པོ་ལ་སོགས་པ་ལ་འདི་གཟུགས་སོ་ཞེས་ངོ་བོ་དང་འདི་གཟུགས་ཀྱི་སྐྱེ་བའོ་ཞེས་སོགས་ཁྱད་པར་དུ་མིང་དང་བརྡར་བཏགས་པའི་ངོ་བོའོ།།

b དེ་ལྟར་ན་གཟུགས་སོགས་རྟོག་པའི་ཞེན་གཞི་ཡིན་པ་དེ་མིང་དང་བརྡས་བཞག་པའི་ཀུན་བཏགས་ཡིན་མོད་ཀྱང་ཚད་མས་གྲུབ་པས་དགག་མི་ནུས་ལ། དེ་ཉིད་དངོས་པོ་དེ་དག་གི་རང་གི་མཚན་ཉིད་ཀྱིས་གྲུབ་པ་ནི་མིང་ཙམ་གྱིས་བཞག་པའི་ཀུན་བཏགས་ཤེས་བྱ་ལ་མི་སྲིད་པ་ཡིན་པས་མིང་དང་བརྡས་བཞག་པ་ལ་ཚད་མས་གྲུབ་མ་གྲུབ་གཉིས་ཡོད་དོ།། འོན་ཀྱང་མིང་དང་བརྡས་བཞག་པ་ཙམ་ཡིན་ཕྱིན་ཆད་དེ་ལ་རྒྱུ་འབྲས་མི་རུང་བར་འདི་པ་འདོད་དོ།།

c དེ་ལ་འདི་ལྟ་སྟེ་དཔེར་ན་ནམ་མཁའི་མེ་ཏོག་ཇི་ལྟ་བ་དེ་ལྟ་བུར་ནི་མཚན་ཉིད་ངོ་བོ་ཉིད་མེད་པ་ཉིད་བལྟ་བར་བྱའོ།།

8. Dzong-ka-ba's commentary (*Emptiness in Mind-Only,* 94) on that:[a]

> The similarity of **imputational factors** with a flower in the sky[b] is an example of their merely being imputed by conceptuality and is not an example of their not occurring among objects of knowledge [that is, existents].

9. Dzong-ka-ba's and Ke-drup's statements that Proponents of Sūtra cannot realize that such imputational natures are not established by way of their own character. Dzong-ka-ba (*Emptiness in Mind-Only,* 198) says:[c]

> Also, even if it were being refuted that the **self-isolate of the conceived object [of a conceptual consciousness]** is established by way of its own character, since it is confirmed even for Proponents of Sūtra that the objects of comprehension of an inferential valid cognition are generally characterized phenomena [and] do not exist as [functioning] things, this is not feasible.

Ke-drup's *Opening the Eyes of the Fortunate* says:[d]

> Concerning this, even Proponents of Sūtra have established that the **mere appearance that is the appearance to a conceptual consciousness that form and so forth are established by way of their own character as referents of the conventions of entity and attribute** is a **superimposed factor** that is not established by way of its own character. Furthermore, they have already established that such a conceptual consciousness is a consciousness mistaken with respect to that appearance.[e] Hence, there is no way that realization that this

---

a ཀུན་བཏགས་ནམ་མཁའི་མེ་ཏོག་དང་འདྲ་བ་ནི་རྟོག་པས་བཏགས་པ་ཙམ་གྱི་དཔེ་ཡིན་གྱི་ཤེས་བྱ་ལ་མི་སྲིད་པའི་དཔེ་མིན་ནོ།།

b As Jik-may-dam-chö-gya-tso (*Port of Entry,* 198.4) says, due to an eye disease (*rab rib*) the figure of a flower appears in the sky in the perspective of such a perception, but in fact there is no flower in the sky; just so, imputational natures are established as merely imputed by conceptuality. He identifies this explanation as from Wonch'uk's commentary (Golden Reprint, vol. 128, 820.1).

c ཞེན་ཡུལ་གྱི་རང་ལྡོག་རང་མཚན་གྱིས་གྲུབ་པ་འགོག་ན་འང་རྗེས་དཔག་ཚད་མའི་གཞལ་བྱ་སྤྱི་མཚན་དངོས་པོར་མེད་པར་མདོ་སྡེ་པས་ཀྱང་གྲུབ་པས་མི་འཐད་དོ།།

d དེ་ལ་གཟུགས་སོགས་ངོ་བོ་དང་ཁྱད་པར་གྱི་ཐ་སྙད་ཀྱི་གཞིར་རང་གི་མཚན་ཉིད་ཀྱིས་གྲུབ་པར་རྟོག་པ་ལ་སྣང་བའི་སྣང་བ་ཙམ་ནི་རང་གི་མཚན་ཉིད་ཀྱིས་མ་གྲུབ་པའི་སྒྲོ་བཏགས་སུ་མདོ་སྡེ་པས་ཀྱང་གྲུབ་ཟིན་ཅིང་། རྟོག་པ་དེ་སྣང་བ་དེ་ལ་འཁྲུལ་ཤེས་སུ་འང་དེས་གྲུབ་ཟིན་པས། རྟོག་པའི་སྣང་བ་དེ་རྟོག་པ་ལ་སྣང་བ་ལྟར་རང་གི་མཚན་ཉིད་ཀྱིས་གྲུབ་པས་སྟོང་པར་རྟོགས་པ་ཆོས་ཀྱི་བདག་མེད་རྟོགས་པར་འོང་དོན་མེད་དོ།

e It is mistaken in the sense that the appearing object (*snang yul*) of any conceptual consciousness, such as the image of a house that appears to a conceptual consciousness thinking of a house, appears to be a house, much as the image of a face in a mirror *appears* to be a face

> conceptual appearance is empty of being established by way of its own character in accordance with how it appears to a conceptual consciousness could constitute realization of the selflessness of phenomena [in the Mind-Only School].[308]

10. Dzong-ka-ba's reference (*Emptiness in Mind-Only,* 239) to imputational phenomena as if these are the imputational natures being considered:[a]

> Since **imputational phenomena** are not established by way of their own character, they are non-natures ultimately [that is, are without the nature of existing ultimately or by way of their own character].[b]

The "Answer" of the Go-mang Tradition

As possibilities, we need to consider the following thirteen meanings:

a. being the referent of a conceptual consciousness[c]
b. establishment by way of its own character as the referent of a conceptual consciousness[d]
c. the superimposed factor or appearance as established by way of its own character as the referent of a conceptual consciousness[e]
d. the superimposed factor or appearance of objects even to sense consciousnesses as established by way of their own character as the referent of a conceptual consciousness[f]
e. the appearance of objects even to sense consciousnesses as being the referents of conceptual consciousnesses[g]
f. imputational natures (in general, including uncompounded space and so forth as well as non-existent imputational natures such as the horns of a

---

even if one does not assent to that appearance.

[a] ཀུན་བརྟགས་ཀྱི་ཆོས་རྣམས་རང་གི་མཚན་ཉིད་ཀྱིས་མ་གྲུབ་པས་དོན་དམ་པར་ངོ་བོ་མེད་པ།

[b] The Tibetan (*Emptiness in Mind-Only,* 447) is: *kun btags kyi chos rnams rang gi mtshan nyid kyis ma grub pas don dam par ngo bo med pa dang.* Both Gung-ru Chö-jung (20b.5) and Jam-ȳang-shay-b̄a (52.5) misquote the passage as *kun btags kyi chos rnams rang gi mtshan nyid kyis ma grub pas* ***mtshan nyid*** *ngo bo med pa dang,* taking it to mean:

> Since the phenomena that are the bases of imputing the imputational nature are not established by way of their own character as the referents of conceptual consciousnesses, they are non-natures ultimately [that is, are without the nature of existing ultimately or by way of their own character].

[c] རྟོག་པའི་ཞེན་གཞིར་ཡིན་པ། or རང་འཛིན་རྟོག་པའི་ཞེན་གཞིར་ཡིན་པ།

[d] རང་འཛིན་རྟོག་པའི་ཞེན་གཞིར་རང་གི་མཚན་ཉིད་ཀྱིས་གྲུབ་པ།

[e] རང་འཛིན་རྟོག་པའི་ཞེན་གཞིར་རང་གི་མཚན་གྱིས་གྲུབ་པར་སྒྲོ་བཏགས་པའམ་སྣང་བ།

[f] དབང་ཤེས་ལ་ཡང་རང་འཛིན་རྟོག་པའི་ཞེན་གཞིར་རང་གི་མཚན་ཉིད་ཀྱིས་གྲུབ་པར་སྒྲོ་བཏགས་པའམ་སྣང་བ།

[g] དབང་ཤེས་ལ་ཡང་རྟོག་པའི་ཞེན་གཞིར་ཡིན་པར་སྣང་བ། also དབང་ཤེས་ལ་ཡང་རང་འཛིན་རྟོག་པའི་ཞེན་གཞིར་ཡིན་པར་སྣང་བ།

rabbit or establishment of objects by way of their own character as the referents of conceptual consciousnesses)[a]

g. imputational nature (just the general category, not its specific instances, technically called the generality-isolate or, more evocatively, the conceptually isolated generality)[b]
h. establishment (of something) by way of its own character[c]
i. establishment (of something) in accordance with the superimposed factor (or appearance) of being established by way of its own character as the referent of a conceptual consciousness[d]
j. all existent imputational natures[e] (including uncompounded space and so forth)
k. something only posited by conceptuality and not established by way of its own character[f]
l. the superimposed factor or appearance to a conceptual consciousness as established by way of its own character as the referent of a conceptual consciousness[g]
m. the appearing objects of inferential cognition.[h]

As before, according to the tradition of Gung-ru Chö-jung, Jam-ȳang-shay-b̄a, Gung-tang, and A-ku L̄o-drö-gya-tso, there is no one answer, flexibility being required. As I (with more trepidation than with the first puzzle) read their explanation, the references to "imputational natures," or the like, in those ten passages are:

1. The imputational natures that the *Sūtra Unraveling the Thought* says are character-non-natures:

> Those [imputational characters] [***b:*** **establishment by way of its own character as the referent of a conceptual consciousness** and ***c:*** **the superimposed factor or appearance as established by way of its own character as the referent of a conceptual consciousness**] are characters posited by names and terminology and do not subsist by way of their own character. Therefore, they [same ***b*** and ***c***] are said to be "character-non-natures."

2. The sixth chapter of the *Sūtra Unraveling the Thought*, the "Questions of

a ཀུན་བཏགས་ཐམས་ཅད།
b ཀུན་བཏགས།
c རང་གི་མཚན་ཉིད་ཀྱིས་གྲུབ་པ།
d རང་འཛིན་རྟོག་པའི་ཞེན་གཞིར་རང་གི་མཚན་ཉིད་ཀྱིས་གྲུབ་པར་སྒྲོ་བཏགས་པ་ལྟར་དུ་གྲུབ་པ།
e ཡོད་རྒྱུའི་ཀུན་བཏགས།
f རྟོག་པས་བཏགས་པ་ཙམ་ཡིན་གྱི་རང་གི་མཚན་ཉིད་ཀྱིས་མ་གྲུབ་པ།
g རྟོག་པ་ལ་རང་འཛིན་རྟོག་པའི་ཞེན་གཞིར་རང་གི་མཚན་ཉིད་ཀྱིས་གྲུབ་པར་སྒྲོ་བཏགས་པའམ་སྣང་བ།
h རྗེས་དཔག་གི་སྣང་ཡུལ།

Gunākara," where it says that imputational natures are to be identified in terms of a factor of appearance wrongly superimposed by a mistaken awareness:

> The imputational character [***i:*** **establishment in accordance with the superimposed factor or appearance of being established by way of its own character as the referent of a conceptual consciousness** and ***c:*** **the superimposed factor or appearance as established by way of its own character as the referent of a conceptual consciousness**] is to be viewed as like the flaws of dark spots that form in the eye[-sight] of one with the disease of dim-sightedness.

And:

> Apprehending the imputational character [***i:*** **establishment in accordance with the superimposed factor or appearance of being established by way of its own character as the referent of a conceptual consciousness** and ***c:*** **the superimposed factor or appearance as established by way of its own character as the referent of a conceptual consciousness**] in other-powered characters should be viewed as like wrongly apprehending a very clear crystal as precious jewels—sapphire, the blue gem, ruby, emerald, or gold.

3. D̄zong-ka-b̄a's remarks restricting the scope of imputational natures here:

> With respect to that imputational factor [***b:*** **establishment by way of its own character as the referent of a conceptual consciousness**] of which [other-powered natures] are empty, on both occasions of identifying the imputational factor [***b:*** **establishment by way of its own character as the referent of a conceptual consciousness** and ***c:*** **the superimposed factor or appearance as established by way of its own character as the referent of a conceptual consciousness**] in the sūtra it does not speak of any other imputational factor than just factors imputed in the manner of entities and attributes [***b:*** **establishment by way of its own character as the referent of a conceptual consciousness** and ***c:*** **the superimposed factor or appearance as established by way of its own character as the referent of a conceptual consciousness**]. I will explain the reason for this later.

His later explanation of the reason:

> Although among imputational factors in general [*f:* **imputational natures (in general, including uncompounded space and so forth as well as non-existent imputational natures such as the horns of a rabbit or establishment of objects by way of their own character as the referents of conceptual consciousnesses)**] there are many, such as all generally characterized phenomena, space, and so forth, the reason why these are not [explicitly] mentioned in the *Sūtra Unraveling the Thought* is that they are not relevant on the occasion of the imputational factor [*b:* **establishment by way of its own character as the referent of a conceptual consciousness** and *c:* **the superimposed factor or appearance as established by way of its own character as the referent of a conceptual consciousness**] the emptiness of which [*b:* **establishment by way of its own character as the referent of a conceptual consciousness**] is posited as the thoroughly established nature. Although many of those are existents that cannot be posited by names and terminology, they are not established by way of their own character because of being only imputed by conceptuality.

4. The imputational natures that Dzong-ka-ba has in mind when he says that they must be identified in order to know the selflessness of phenomena well:

> If you do not know what this imputational factor [*c:* **the superimposed factor or appearance as established by way of its own character as the referent of a conceptual consciousness**] that is a superimposed factor of a self of phenomena on other-powered natures is, you will not know in a decisive way the conception of a self of phenomena and the selflessness of phenomena of this [Mind-Only] system.

5. Dzong-ka-ba's identification of the imputational nature that, when conceived to be established by way of its own character, is the self of phenomena, saying it is not just the imputational nature in general but a specific one:

> Those imputational factors—which are such that a consciousness conceiving imputational factors [*b:* **establishment by way of its own character as the referent of a conceptual consciousness**] to be established by way of their own character is asserted to be a consciousness conceiving a self of phenomena—are the nominally and terminologically imputed entities [in the imputation of] the aggregates and so forth as

entities, "This is form," and as attributes, "This is the production of form," and so forth.

6. Ḏzong-ka-ḇa's distinction that there are two types of imputational natures, those established and those not established by valid cognition:

 Thus, form and so forth being the referents of conceptual consciousnesses is an imputational factor [*a:* **an object's being the referent of a conceptual consciousness**] posited through name and terminology, but, since it is established by valid cognition, it cannot be refuted. However, that it is established by way of the thing's own character is an imputational factor [*k:* **something only posited by conceptuality and not established by way of its own character**] posited only nominally that does not occur among objects of knowledge [that is, does not exist]. Hence, among what are posited by names and terminology [*f:* **imputational natures (in general, including uncompounded space and so forth as well as non-existent imputational natures such as the horns of a rabbit or establishment of objects by way of their own character as the referents of conceptual consciousnesses)**] there are two [types], those established by valid cognition and those not established by valid cognition. Still, this system asserts that once something is only posited by names and terminology, cause and effect are not suitable to occur in it.

7. The *Sūtra Unraveling the Thought*'s usage of a flower in the sky as an example for imputational natures:

 It is thus: for example, character-non-natures [that is, imputational natures] [*b:* **establishment by way of its own character as the referent of a conceptual consciousness** and *c:* **the superimposed factor or appearance as established by way of its own character as the referent of a conceptual consciousness**] are to be viewed as like a flower in the sky, for example.

8. Ḏzong-ka-ḇa's commentary on that:

 The similarity of imputational factors [*b:* **establishment by way of its own character as the referent of a conceptual consciousness** and *c:* **the superimposed factor or appearance as established by way of its own character as the referent of a conceptual consciousness**] with a flower in the sky is an example of their merely being imputed by conceptuality and is not an example of their not occurring among objects of knowledge [that is, existents]. (***b*** does not exist, but ***c*** does.)

9. Ḏzong-ka-ḇa's and Ke-drup's statements that Proponents of Sūtra cannot realize that such imputational natures are not established by way of their own character. Ḏzong-ka-ḇa says:

    Also, even if it were being refuted that the self-isolate of the conceived object [of a conceptual consciousness] [***m:*** **the appearing objects of inferential cognition (these being sound-generalities and meaning-generalities)**[a] or ***a:*** **being the referent of a conceptual consciousness**[b]] is established by way of its own character, since it is established even for the Sūtra School that the objects of comprehension of an inferential valid cognition are generally characterized phenomena [and] do not exist as [functioning] things, this is not feasible.

    Ke-drup's *Opening the Eyes of the Fortunate* says:

    Concerning this, even Proponents of Sūtra have established that the mere appearance that is the appearance to a conceptual consciousness that form and so forth are established by way of their own character as referents of the conventions of entity and attribute [***l:*** **the superimposed factor or appearance to a conceptual consciousness as established by way of its own character as the referent of a conceptual consciousness**] is a superimposed factor [***k:*** **something only posited by conceptuality and not established by way of its own character**] that is not established by way of its own character. Furthermore, they have already established that such a conceptual consciousness is a consciousness mistaken with respect to that appearance. Hence, there is no way that realization that this conceptual appearance is empty of being established by way of its own character in accordance with how it appears to a conceptual consciousness could constitute realization of the selflessness of phenomena [in the Mind-Only School].

10. Ḏzong-ka-ḇa's reference to imputational phenomena as if these are the imputational natures being considered:

    Since imputational phenomena are not established by way of their own character, they are non-natures ultimately [that is,

---

[a] Gung-ru Chö-jung's *Garland of White Lotuses,* 19b.3.

[b] A-ku Lo-drö-gya-tso's *Precious Lamp,* 238.4: *gzugs sogs ming brda'i yul yin pa'i cha lta bu.* He draws this from Gung-tang (*Difficult Points,* 120.20).

> are without the nature of existing ultimately or by way of their own character].

Usually, "imputational phenomena" would be identified as ***j:* all existent imputational natures, including uncompounded space and so forth**, but Gung-ru Chö-jung and Jam-ȳang-shay-b̄a misquote the passage such that it reads:

> Since the phenomena that are the bases of imputing the imputational nature [***b:* establishment by way of its own character as the referent of a conceptual consciousness**] are not established by way of their own character as the referents of conceptual consciousnesses, they are non-natures ultimately [that is, are without the nature of existing ultimately or by way of their own character].

That is how I read the explication by the Go-mang tradition.

Another "Answer"

My own identifications of "imputational nature" and so forth in these passages, offered with a mask of bravado, are:

1. The imputational natures that the *Sūtra Unraveling the Thought* says are character-non-natures:

   > Those [imputational characters] [***a:* being, or appearing as, the referent of a conceptual consciousness**] are characters posited by names and terminology and do not subsist by way of their own character. Therefore, they [same ***a***] are said to be "character-non-natures."

   (In the list of thirteen possibilities, I have, in effect, combined ***a*** and ***c***.)

2. The sixth chapter of the *Sūtra Unraveling the Thought*, the "Questions of Guṇākara," where it says that imputational natures are to be identified in terms of a factor of appearance wrongly superimposed by a mistaken awareness:

   > The imputational character [***c:* the superimposed factor or appearance as established by way of its own character as the referent of a conceptual consciousness**] is to be viewed as like the flaws of dark spots that form in the eye[-sight] of one with the disease of dim-sightedness.

   And:

   > Apprehending the imputational character [***b:* establishment**

by way of its own character as the referent of a conceptual consciousness] in other-powered characters should be viewed as like wrongly apprehending a very clear crystal as precious jewels—sapphire, the blue gem, ruby, emerald, or gold.

3. Ḏzong-ka-ḇa's remarks restricting the scope of imputational natures here:

> With respect to that imputational factor [*b:* **establishment by way of its own character as the referent of a conceptual consciousness**] of which [other-powered natures] are empty, on both occasions of identifying the imputational factor [*a:* **being, or appearing as, the referent of a conceptual consciousness**] in the sūtra it does not speak of any other imputational factor than just factors imputed in the manner of entities and attributes [*a:* **being, or appearing as, the referent of a conceptual consciousness** and *b:* **establishment by way of its own character as the referent of a conceptual consciousness**]. I will explain the reason for this later.

His later explanation of the reason:

> Although among imputational factors in general [*f:* **imputational natures (in general, including uncompounded space and so forth as well as non-existent imputational natures such as the horns of a rabbit or establishment of objects by way of their own character as the referents of conceptual consciousnesses)**] there are many, such as all generally characterized phenomena, space, and so forth, the reason why these are not [explicitly] mentioned in the *Sūtra Unraveling the Thought* is that they are not relevant on the occasion of the imputational factor [*b:* **establishment by way of its own character as the referent of a conceptual consciousness**] the emptiness of which [*b:* **establishment by way of its own character as the referent of a conceptual consciousness**] is posited as the thoroughly established nature. Although many of those are existents that cannot be posited by names and terminology, they are not established by way of their own character because of being only imputed by conceptuality.

4. The imputational natures that Ḏzong-ka-ḇa has in mind when he says that they must be identified in order to know the selflessness of phenomena well:

> If you do not know what this imputational factor [*c:* **the superimposed factor or appearance as established by way of its own character as the referent of a conceptual**

consciousness] that is a superimposed factor of a self of phenomena on other-powered phenomena is, you will not know in a decisive way the conception of a self of phenomena and the selflessness of phenomena of this [Mind-Only] system.

5. Dzong-ka-ba's identification of the imputational nature that, when conceived to be established by way of its own character, is the self of phenomena, saying it is not just the imputational nature in general but a specific one:

> Those imputational factors—which are such that a consciousness conceiving imputational factors [***a:*** **being, or appearing as, the referent of a conceptual consciousness**] to be established by way of their own character is asserted to be a consciousness conceiving a self of phenomena—are the nominally and terminologically imputed entities [in the imputation of] the aggregates and so forth as entities, "This is form," and as attributes, "This is the production of form," and so forth.

6. Dzong-ka-ba's distinction that there are two types of imputational natures, those established and those not established by valid cognition:

> Thus, form and so forth being the referents of conceptual consciousnesses is an imputational factor [***a:*** **being, or appearing as, the referent of a conceptual consciousness**] posited through name and terminology, but, since it is established by valid cognition, it cannot be refuted. However, that it is established by way of the thing's own character is an imputational factor [***k:*** **something only posited by conceptuality and not established by way of its own character**] posited only nominally that does not occur among objects of knowledge [that is, does not exist]. Hence, among what are posited by names and terminology [***f:*** **imputational natures (in general, including uncompounded space and so forth as well as non-existent imputational natures such as the horns of a rabbit or establishment of objects by way of their own character as the referents of conceptual consciousnesses)**] there are two [types], those established by valid cognition and those not established by valid cognition. Still, this system asserts that once something is only posited by names and terminology, cause and effect are not suitable to occur in it.

7. The *Sūtra Unraveling the Thought's* usage of a flower in the sky as an example for imputational natures:

   It is thus: for example, character-non-natures [that is, imputational natures] [*a:* **being, or appearing as, the referent of a conceptual consciousness** and *b:* **establishment by way of its own character as the referent of a conceptual consciousness**] are to be viewed as like a flower in the sky, for example.

8. D̄zong-ka-b̄a's commentary on that:

   The similarity of imputational factors [*a:* **being, or appearing as, the referent of a conceptual consciousness** and *b:* **establishment by way of its own character as the referent of a conceptual consciousness**] with a flower in the sky is an example of their merely being imputed by conceptuality and is not an example of their not occurring among objects of knowledge [that is, existents]. (***a*** exists, but ***b*** does not exist.)

9. D̄zong-ka-b̄a's and Ke-drup's statements that Proponents of Sūtra cannot realize that such imputational natures are not established by way of their own character. D̄zong-ka-b̄a says:

   Also, even if it were being refuted that the self-isolate of the conceived object [of a conceptual consciousness] [*m:* **the appearing objects of inferential cognition (these being sound-generalities and meaning-generalities)**] is established by way of its own character, since it is established even for the Sūtra School that the objects of comprehension of an inferential valid cognition are generally characterized phenomena [and] do not exist as [functioning] things, this is not feasible.

   Ke-drup's *Opening the Eyes of the Fortunate* says:

   The mere appearance that is the appearance to a conceptual consciousness of forms and so forth as established by way of their own character as bases of the conventions of entity and attribute [*l:* **the superimposed factor or appearance to a conceptual consciousness as established by way of its own character as the referent of a conceptual consciousness**] has already been established even by Proponents of Sūtra as a superimposed factor [*k:* **something only posited by conceptuality and not established by way of its own character**] which is not established by way of its own character, and this conceptual consciousness has already been established by them as a consciousness mistaken with respect to that appearance. Hence, there is no way for realization that this conceptual appearance is empty of being established by way of its own character to be a realization of the selflessness of phenomena.

10. Ḏzong-ka-ḇa's reference to imputational phenomena as if these are the imputational natures being considered:

    Since imputational phenomena [*j:* **all existent imputational natures, including uncompounded space and so forth**] are not established by way of their own character, they are non-natures ultimately [that is, are without the nature of existing ultimately or by way of their own character].

    Here Ḏzong-ka-ḇa speaks about imputational phenomena in general in the context of taking the three natures as a rubric categorizing all phenomena and of applying the statements in the Perfection of Wisdom Sūtras that all phenomena do not ultimately exist to these three categories.

The Import

Even though the technique of examining Ḏzong-ka-ḇa's usage of terminology yields considerable doubt about the identification of terms in particular contexts, such qualms arise only by juxtaposing those particular usages to the principles of his system. The exercise of such juxtaposition is fundamental to scholastic debate in the monastic colleges, causing scholars to use the basic principles of Ḏzong-ka-ḇa's perspective in an active, creative way. They thereby make the founder's mode of thought their own in a way that far surpasses mere repetition.

Thus, despite the difficulties involved in trying even to determine what such complex traditions of exegesis take to be the referents of these terms, basic and undisputed principles of Ḏzong-ka-ḇa's presentation of the topic emerge with considerable clarity. It is possible to miss the woods for the trees, but when one steps back and surveys the wider scene, it is clear that:

1. Phenomena are referents of conceptual consciousnesses and of terms.
2. However, they falsely appear to both sense consciousnesses and conceptual consciousnesses to be established by way of their own character as the referents of conceptual consciousnesses and of terms.
3. Assent to this false appearance constitutes the obstructions of omniscience and underlies all afflictive emotions.
4. Objects' emptiness of being established by way of their own character as

the referents of conceptual consciousnesses and of terms is a subtle selflessness of phenomena.

5. Realization of this emptiness and prolonged meditation on it in the manner of direct perception remove both the afflictive obstructions and the obstructions to omniscience.

15. Posited by Names and Terminology

Issue #104: In "posited by names and terminology" is "terminology" not redundant?

In the main translation of the *Sūtra Unraveling the Thought,* found in the Peking edition and so forth, the Sanskrit compound *nāmasaṃketa*[309] is treated as a conjunctive compound and thus is translated into Tibetan as *ming **dang** brda'* ("name **and** terminology").[a] Jam-ȳang-shay-b̄a[310] holds that "name"[b] in this context means a term expressing an object,[c] and although "terminology"[d] usually has the same meaning as "name," in order to avoid redundancy he takes it to mean a conceptual consciousness apprehending an object.[e] Tsay-d̄en-hla-ram-b̄a[311] takes "terminology" more narrowly as a conceptual consciousness mindful of associating name and object,[f] and another scholar[312] similarly takes it as a conceptual consciousness understanding a verbal convention at the time of using verbal conventions.[g] These explanations of "terminology" are well-founded in the tradition, since a common dictum is that names and conceptual consciousnesses engage their objects in a similar, eliminative manner, unable to engage their objects holistically as direction perception does.

Issue #105: What does D̄zong-ka-b̄a mean when he says that some imputational natures are only imputed by conceptuality but are not posited by names and terminology?

As is discussed in detail in Chapter 13 of *Reflections on Reality,* D̄zong-ka-b̄a appears to contradict himself:

1. He (*Emptiness in Mind-Only,* 86) indicates that even non-existents, never

---

[a] The *stog* palace translation of the *Sūtra Unraveling the Thought* treats the compound as a genitive *tatpuruṣa,* and thus the term is translated as *ming **gi** brda'* ("terminology **of** name" or "nominal terminology").

[b] *ming.*

[c] *rang zhes rjod pa'i sgra.*

[d] *brda'.*

[e] *rang 'dzin rtog pa.*

[f] *ming don 'brel bar dran pa'i rtog pa.* A-ku L̄o-drö-gya-tso (*Precious Lamp,* 15a.3) finds support for this position in Sthiramati's commentary on Maitreya's *Differentiation of the Middle and the Extremes* and reports that Tsay-d̄en-hla-ram-b̄a cites Gen-dün-drup's *Great Treatise on Valid Cognition: Adornment of Reasoning.*

[g] *tha snyad dus su tha snyad go ba'i tha snyad:* literally, "the convention that is the understanding of a convention at the time of a convention."

mind all existent imputational natures, are among what are "posited in dependence upon names and terminology":

> The nature of character that imputational factors[a] do not have is to be taken as establishment, or subsisting, by way of their own character.[b] Here, the measure indicated[c] with respect to existing or not existing by way of [an object's] own character is: not to be posited or to be posited in dependence upon names and terminology.[d]
>
> Furthermore, that which is posited [in dependence upon names and terminology] is not necessarily existent [since, for instance, the horns of a rabbit or a difference of entity between subject and object are posited in dependence upon names and terminology but do not exist].

In confirmation of this, in the section on the Consequence School much later in *The Essence of Eloquence* he says:

> [Yogic Practitioners] propound that, since [imputational natures] can be posited by names and terminology, [imputational natures] are not established by way of their own character.

Ḏzong-ka-ḇa says that the reason why the Proponents of Mind-Only propound that imputational natures are not established by way of their own character is that they can be posited by names and terminology; he does not say that some imputational natures can and some cannot.

2. However, late in the section on the Mind-Only School Ḏzong-ka-ḇa (*Emptiness in Mind-Only,* 217-218) posits three classes of objects when, as has been cited here numerous times above, he says:

> Although among imputational factors in general there are many, such as all generally characterized phenomena and space, and so forth, the reason why these are not [explicitly] mentioned in the *Sūtra Unraveling the Thought*[e] is that they are not relevant on the occasion of the imputational factor, the emptiness of which is posited as the thoroughly

[a] See issue #83.

[b] See issues #29, 94.

[c] *bstan tshod;* see issue #96.

[d] See issues #105-109.

[e] See issue #139, for six mentions of space in the *Sūtra Unraveling the Thought* as an example for the thoroughly established nature. The point here is that space is not relevant on the occasion of identifying the thoroughly established nature.

> established nature.[a] Although many of those are existents that cannot be posited by names and terminology, they are not established by way of their own character because of being only imputed by conceptuality.

In order to unravel their founder's meaning, Gung-ru Chö-jung and Jam-ȳang-shay-b̄a make a difference between "only posited by names and terminology"[b] and "posited by only names and terminology."[c] They explain that in the latter passage he is referring to "posited by only names and terminology":

> Although among imputational factors in general there are many, such as all generally characterized phenomena and space, and so forth, the reason why these are not [explicitly] mentioned in the *Sūtra Unraveling the Thought* is that they are not relevant on the occasion of the imputational factor, the emptiness of which is posited as the thoroughly established nature. Although many of those are existents that cannot be posited by names and terminology **[that is, are not posited by only names and terminology]**, they are not established by way of their own character because of being only imputed by conceptuality.

However, they hold that in the following passages he (*Emptiness in Mind-Only*, 86) means "only posited by names and terminology":

> The nature of character that imputational factors do not have is to be taken as establishment, or subsisting, by way of their own character. Here, the measure indicated with respect to existing or not existing by way of [an object's] own character is: not to be posited or to be posited in dependence upon names and terminology **[that is, only posited by names and terminology]**.
>
> Furthermore, that which is posited [in dependence upon names and terminology] is not necessarily existent [since, for instance, the horns of a rabbit or a difference of entity between subject and object are posited in dependence upon names and terminology but do not exist].

and:

> [Yogic Practitioners] propound that, since [imputational natures] can be posited by names and terminology **[that is, are only posited by names and terminology]**, [imputational natures] are not established by way of their own character.

This is how they cogently resolve Ḏzong-ka-b̄a's seemingly contradictory

---

[a] See issues #85, 89-92.

[b] *ming brdas bzhag tsam.*

[c] *ming brda tsam gyis bzhag pa.*

statements on the meaning of being posited by names and terminology.

Another explanation. Paṇ-chen S̄ö-nam-drak-b̄a[313] avers that the context itself of D̄zong-ka-b̄a's remarks needs to be considered. He holds that when D̄zong-ka-b̄a (*Emptiness in Mind-Only,* 86) says:

> Here, the measure indicated with respect to existing or not existing by way of [an object's] own character is: not to be posited or to be posited in dependence upon names and terminology.

his frame of reference is **just** those imputational natures explicitly indicated in the *Sūtra Unraveling the Thought*—imputational factors in the imputation of entity and attribute—and not imputational natures in general, including uncompounded space, and so forth. Thus, there is no contradiction with the first citation above, which indicates that some imputational natures are not posited in dependence upon names and terminology.

Therefore, for Paṇ-chen S̄ö-nam-drak-b̄a, D̄zong-ka-b̄a is saying:

- **in terms of phenomena such as forms**, that which is established by way of its own character and a phenomenon that is not posited by names and terminology are equivalent
- **in terms of imputational factors in the imputation of entity and attribute**, a phenomenon that is not established by way of its own character and a phenomenon that is posited by names and terminology are equivalent.

When taken this way, the second position does not conflict with D̄zong-ka-b̄a's also holding that other imputational natures such as uncompounded space:

- are not established by way of their own character
- are not posited by names and terminology
- but are only imputed by conceptuality.

I find Paṇ-chen S̄ö-nam-drak-b̄a's explanation also to be plausible, even though it is not entirely satisfactory as we shall now see.

Gung-tang's Refutation of Others' Explanations

The topic of what it means for something to be posited by names and terminology is complicated by several factors that become clear upon considering Gung-tang's interesting but frustrating refutation of others' attempts to delineate its meaning.[314] I say frustrating because his excursion does not tell us much in a positive sense about what this slippery term means. He makes a mess of others' assertions by challenging how they might account for the fact that uncompounded space and so forth are, in the Go-mang tradition's terms, only posited by names and terminology, but unfortunately his own explanation of this point is founded in the circularity that being only posited by names and terminology merely means not established by way of its own character. Still, his diversion highlights many issues.

Issue #106: Are non-existent imputational natures only imputed by conceptuality?

Gung-tang begins with a discussion of being only imputed by conceptuality. He notes that in some Ge-luk-b̄a monastic textbooks[a] an erroneous distinction is made such that:

1. existent imputational natures[b] (such as uncompounded space or an object's being the referent of a conceptual consciousness) are only imputed by conceptuality, but
2. non-existent imputational natures[c] (such as the horns of a rabbit or the establishment of an object by way of its own character as the referent of a conceptual consciousness) are not only imputed by conceptuality.

Gung-tang reports that according to these scholars non-existent imputational natures are not posited by conceptuality[d] since, according to them, they are not posited by an awareness[e] (and conceptual consciousnesses are instances of awareness). This, in turn, is due to the commonly accepted notion that non-existent imputational natures are not objects of knowledge[f] and hence not suitable to be taken as an object of an awareness.[g]

Their reasoning is based on the commonly accepted fact that since object of knowledge and existent are equivalent, non-existent imputational natures cannot be objects of knowledge; the horns of a rabbit, for instance, are non-existent and thus not objects of knowledge. Also, since the commonly accepted definition (or defining nature) of an object of knowledge is "that which is suitable to be taken as an object of an awareness," the horns of a rabbit cannot be suitable to be taken as an object of an awareness. With these points Gung-tang agrees, but these scholars draw what is for him the unwarranted conclusion that

---

a Jik-may-dam-chö-gya-tso (*Port of Entry,* 174.3) identifies these as the textbooks of the L̄o-s̄el-l̄ing College and the Jang-d̄zay College; he reports that they hold that a non-existent imputational nature is not posited by a conceptual consciousness (*rtogs pas ma bzhag pa*) but is posited by a conceptual consciousness apprehending it (***rang 'dzin** rtog pas bzhag pa*)—a have-your-cake-and-eat-it-too distinction.

b *yod rgyu'i kun btags.* These are also called "enumerated imputational natures" (*rnam grangs pa'i kun btags*); Gung-tang's *Difficult Points,* 111.1.

c *med rgyu'i kun btags.* These are also called "imputational natures whose character is nihil" (*mtshan nyid yongs su chad pa'i kun btags*).

d *rtog pas ma bzhag pa,* 111.3.

e *blos ma bzhag pa,* 111.4.

f *shes bya, jñeya.*

g *blo'i yul du bya rung ba.*

once something is not suitable to be taken as an object of an awareness, it could not be **posited** by an awareness and hence not **posited** by conceptuality (that is, a conceptual awareness), and thus could not be only imputed by conceptuality.

Gung-tang[315] answers by referring to the important principle in Ḏzong-ka-ḇa's system that in the Mind-Only School and the Middle Way School it is not suitable to consider that everything that is only imputed by conceptuality necessarily exists. From this statement it can be seen that, for Ḏzong-ka-ḇa, non-existents (such as the horns of a rabbit and the establishment of an object by way of its own character as the referent of a conceptual consciousness) also are only imputed by conceptuality. As cited earlier, Ḏzong-ka-ḇa (*Emptiness in Mind-Only,* 86) says:

> The nature of character that imputational factors do not have is to be taken as establishment, or subsisting, by way of their own character. Here, the measure indicated with respect to existing or not existing by way of [an object's] own character is: not to be posited or to be posited in dependence upon names and terminology.
>
> **Furthermore, that which is posited [in dependence upon names and terminology] is not necessarily existent.**

Ḏzong-ka-ḇa clearly says that what is posited by names and terminology does not necessarily exist, and thus there must be non-existents that are posited by names and terminology.

He (*Emptiness in Mind-Only,* 210) makes the same point in a passage which, though not cited by Gung-tang, is relevant:

> Thus, form and so forth being the referents of conceptual consciousnesses[a] is an imputational factor posited by name and terminology, but, since it is established by valid cognition, it cannot be refuted. However, that it is established **by way of the thing's own character** is an imputational factor posited only nominally that does not occur among objects of knowledge [that is, does not exist]. **Hence, among what are posited by names and terminology there are two [types], those established by valid cognition and those not established by valid cognition.**[b]

Ḏzong-ka-ḇa clearly speaks of two classes of what are posited by names and terminology—those that exist and those that do not.

Employing the distinction made by Gung-ru Chö-jung and Jam-ȳang-shay-ḇa above, we could say that non-existent imputational natures, though not objects of knowledge, are both only posited by names and terminology and posited by only names and terminology and, similarly, are both only imputed by conceptuality and imputed by only conceptuality. The point is that "only

a See issues #78-82.

b See issue #88.

posited by names and terminology" and "only imputed by conceptuality" are applicable not just to a certain class of existents but also to non-existents.

Gung-tang's discussion inches us closer to considering what these terms mean.

Issue #107: Does something's being posited by names and terminology entail that its appearance to the mind depends upon language? Or, does a bullock see space?

Gung-tang next considers other Ge-luk-b̄as' attempts to understand what D̄zong-ka-b̄a intends when he says that there are many existent imputational natures that are only imputed by conceptuality but cannot be posited by names and terminology. The reference is to D̄zong-ka-b̄a's (*Emptiness in Mind-Only,* 217-218) statement:

> Although among imputational factors in general there are many, such as all generally characterized phenomena and space, and so forth, the reason why these are not [explicitly] mentioned in the *Sūtra Unraveling the Thought*[a] is that they are not relevant on the occasion of the imputational factor, the emptiness of which is posited as the thoroughly established nature.[b] Although many of those are existents that **cannot** be posited by names and terminology, they are not established by way of their own character because of being only imputed by conceptuality.

Given what D̄zong-ka-b̄a says, it is understandable that scholars such as Paṇ-chen S̄ö-nam-drak-b̄a[316] hold that uncompounded space, sound's emptiness of permanence, and so forth are not posited by names and terminology. Remember that Jam-ȳang-shay-b̄a, whom Gung-tang is following, tries to get around the problems posed by D̄zong-ka-b̄a's statement by making a distinction between being "only posited by names and terminology" and "posited by only names and terminology." Jam-ȳang-shay-b̄a's position, as delineated by the Khalkha Mongolian Nga-w̄ang-b̄el-den, is that existent imputational natures are only posited by names and terminology but not posited by only names and

[a] D̄zong-ka-b̄a says that space is "not mentioned in the *Sūtra Unraveling the Thought,*" but Jik-may-dam-chö-gya-tso (*Port of Entry,* 620.6, 625.4-625.6) points out that space is indeed mentioned in the *Sūtra Unraveling the Thought* (see issue #139, for six occurrences in the sūtra) as an example for the thoroughly established nature. Thus he cogently interprets D̄zong-ka-b̄a as meaning that the sūtra at the point of the extensive indication identifying imputational natures does not explicitly say that space, and so forth, are imputational natures since, except for imputational natures in the manner of entity and attribute, space and so forth are not relevant on the occasion of identifying the thoroughly established nature.

[b] See issues #85, 89-92.

terminology,[a] and hence when Ḍzong-ka-ḅa says that "many of those are existents that **cannot** be posited by names and terminology," he means that they cannot be posited by only names and terminology, even though they are only posited by names and terminology. Paṇ-chen S̄ö-nam-drak-ḅa, however, does not make any such distinction and, instead of this, holds that uncompounded space and sound's emptiness of permanence are not posited by names and terminology.

Gung-tang explains that the reason why scholars such as Paṇ-chen S̄ö-nam-drak-ḅa say that uncompounded space is not posited by names and terminology is that it does not **need** to be posited by such. For instance, when a bullock, who (need it be mentioned?) does not know the terminology "space," comes to the edge of a high cliff, a generic image of a vacuity that is a negation of obstructive contact (that is, an image of uncompounded space) appears to the bullock's mind, whereupon he becomes frightened, and the dawning of such an aspect to the bullock's mind does not depend on name and terminology. These scholars hold that Ḍzong-ka-ḅa was thinking of such existent imputational natures when he said that there are many existent imputational natures that are only imputed by conceptuality but cannot (that is, do not have to) be posited by names and terminology.

Based on two fundamental points, Gung-tang concludes that these scholars are mistaken—his response saying a good deal about what "to be posited by names and terminology" does not entail. According to Gung-tang, contrary to Paṇ-chen S̄ö-nam-drak-ḅa's opinion, something's being posited by names and terminology does not entail that its appearance to the mind depends upon language. The progression of his argument is this:

1. The *Sūtra Unraveling the Thought* gives, as an illustration of imputational natures in this context, the establishment of objects by way of their own character as the referents of conceptual consciousnesses and goes on to give as the reason why such imputational natures are without a nature of character that "Those are characters posited by names and terminology."
2. An image of such establishment appears even to persons who do not know language, because the arising of the appearance of objects in this false aspect does not depend on language.
3. Therefore, the mere fact that something is posited by names and terminology does not entail that its appearance to the mind depends upon language.

[a] My opinion is that *such* existent imputational natures, that is, those not relevant on this occasion—these being uncompounded space and so forth but *not* an object's being the referent of terms and so forth—are only posited by names and terminology but not posited by only names and terminology. I take Gung-ru Chö-jung and Jam-ȳang-shay-ḅa's meaning to be that an object's being the referent of terms and so forth means both only posited by names and terminology and also posited by only names and terminology.

By grounding his point in the *Sūtra Unraveling the Thought* and in the basic Ge-luk-b̄a position that the false appearance of objects as if established by way of their own character as the referents of conceptual consciousnesses occurs even to babies and so forth who do not know language, Gung-tang makes his point—that something's being posited by names and terminology does not require that its appearance to the mind depend upon language—unassailable.

He concludes from this that it is not contradictory for sound's emptiness of permanence to be only posited by names and terminology and yet not be posited by only names and terminology. For the term "only" in "only posited by names and terminology" eliminates that sound's emptiness of permanence is established by way of its own character, and indeed it must be asserted that sound's emptiness of permanence is not established by way of its own character, since it is a mere negation of permanence. However, the term "only" in "posited by only names and terminology" would indicate that sound's emptiness of permanence could be posited by the mere phrase, "Sound is empty of permanence," and could be posited merely through the arbitrary force of conceiving it to be empty of permanence rather than being posited by way of reasoning through the forceful power of facts.[a] Indeed, it is unsuitable to assert that sound's emptiness of permanence is posited merely arbitrarily since, unlike arbitrarily calling the round orb in the sky with a rabbit in it "moon" (Indians saw a rabbit, not a man), sound's emptiness of permanence must be established by reasoning through the force of facts,[b] specifically, for instance, through the fact of its being a product. Sound's emptiness of permanence, therefore, is put as an object of inference through the force of facts,[317] whereas the suitability of calling the orb in the sky with a rabbit in it "moon" is put as an object of inference through renown, since its being called "moon" is established merely through wish.

Gung-tang[318] adds also that it is contradictory for these scholars to assert that sound's emptiness of permanence is not posited by names and terminology but is only posited by conceptuality, since "terminology" in "posited by names and terminology" is conceptuality (a conceptual consciousness) and thus there is no reason why the two—"only posited by names and terminology" and "only posited by conceptuality"—cannot be co-extensive. Also, Gung-tang avers that those scholars should make a difference between "only posited by conceptuality" and "posited by only conceptuality"; otherwise, they would have to say that sound's emptiness of permanence is posited by only conceptuality since even they say that it is only posited by conceptuality. In that case, they absurdly

---

a *dngos po'i stobs shugs kyi rigs pa*, 112.14. Nga-w̄ang-b̄el-den (*Stating the Mode of Explanation in the Textbooks on the Middle Way and the Perfection of Wisdom in the L̄o-s̄el-ling and Go-mang Colleges* (453.7) reports, in explaining the view of Paṇ-chen S̄ö-nam-drak-b̄a, that Ja-drel-ge-s̄hay Tsül-trim-ñam-gyel (*bya bral dge bshes tshul khrims rnam rgyal*) has a similar view.

b *dngos stobs kyi rigs pa*, 112.17.

would have to give up holding that sound's emptiness of permanence has to be proven by reasoning through the power of facts. However, as mentioned above, this is inadmissible, since everyone agrees that sound must be proven to be empty of permanence by a correct reason of the power of facts, such as that it is a product.

From this discussion, we glean that something's being only posited by names and terminology does not entail that it is arbitrarily established by language or conceptual thought. This point is made even more clearly by A-ku Lo-drö-gya-tso[319] who reports that Jay-d̄zün Chö-ḡyi-gyel-tsen and Paṇ-chen Sö-nam-drak-b̄a do not differentiate between being "posited by only names and terminology" and being "only posited by names and terminology" and hold that something's being posited by names and terminology means that its appearing as an object of awareness depends on names and terminology appearing as an object of awareness. He shows that Jay-d̄zün-b̄a holds this from a debate in his *General Meaning of (D̄zong-ka-b̄a's) "Differentiating the Interpretable and the Definitive"* in which he says:[320]

> It [absurdly] follows that the subject, uncompounded space, is posited by names and terminology because of being an imputational nature. If that is accepted, it [absurdly] follows with respect to the subject, uncompounded space, that its appearing as an object of awareness depends on names and terminology appearing as an object of awareness. This cannot be accepted because there are cases of space's appearing as an object of awareness even though the names and terminology for space have not appeared as an object of awareness.

Jay-d̄zün-b̄a, trying to make sense out of D̄zong-ka-b̄a's statement that there are many existent imputational natures that are only imputed by conceptuality but cannot be posited by names and terminology, is willing to accept that uncompounded space is only imputed by conceptuality but not willing to accept that it is posited by names and terminology because it does not have to appear to the mind through saying or thinking, "Uncompounded space." His eighteenth-century follower, D̄ra-d̄i Ge-s̄hay Rin-chen-dön-drup,[a] adds that through the mere verbalization of the name "uncompounded space" one **cannot** understand uncompounded space. Thus, for them, whatever is merely imputed by conceptuality is not necessarily only posited by names and terminology. Somehow, "imputed by conceptuality" is wider than "posited by names and terminology."[321]

---

[a] *Ornament for the Thought,* 22.14: *de'i ming brjod pa tsam gyis de go mi nus.*

Issue #108: Is any existent posited by (only) names and terminology?

We are led into wondering whether, in Jay-d̄zün Chö-ḡyi-gyel-tsen's reading, any existent is posited by names and terminology. We see one answer[322] when he points to the fact that D̄zong-ka-b̄a himself indicates that in the *Sūtra Unraveling the Thought* the exemplification of imputational natures by a flower in the sky demonstrates not that imputational natures do not exist but are only imputed by conceptuality:

> The similarity of imputational factors with a flower in the sky is an example of their merely being imputed by conceptuality and is not an example of their not occurring among objects of knowledge [that is, existents.]

D̄zong-ka-b̄a thereby indicates that there are imputational natures that do exist. Furthermore, he specifies that a form's being the referent of the term "form" is an imputational nature posited by names and terminology when he (*Emptiness in Mind-Only,* 210) says:

> Thus, form and so forth being the referents of conceptual consciousnesses is an imputational factor posited by name and terminology, but, since it is established by valid cognition, it cannot be refuted.

D̄ra-d̄i Ge-s̄hay, makes the point more clearly:[a]

> Since form and so forth as referents of names and conventions must be understood in dependence upon names and terminology appearing as objects of awareness, [forms and so forth] are only posited as such by names and terminology.[b]

and:[323]

> The factor of space's having become the referent of the term "space" is an imputational nature that can be posited by names and terminology.

He adds that this is true not just for space but for anything that exists.

This explanation that some existent imputational natures—namely, forms and so forth as referents of names and conventions—are posited by names and

[a] *Ornament for the Thought,* 21.14: *ming dang tha snyad kyi gzhir gzugs sogs 'di dag ming brda blo yul du shar ba la ltos nas go dgos.* Notice that he cleverly avoids using "being" (*yin pa*). His position is reported by A-ku L̄o-drö-gya-tso (*Precious Lamp,* 81.4).

[b] Correspondingly, D̄ra-d̄i Ge-s̄hay (*Ornament for the Thought,* 18) asserts that the meaning of being established by way of its own character is that the object is established from its own inherent nature as what it is without relying on being posited by names and terminology as such: *der ming brdas bzhag pa la mi ltos pas gzhi der rang gi ngo bo'i rang bzhin nas grub pa.*

terminology in addition to being only imputed by conceptuality makes good sense out of Ḏzong-ka-ḇa's (*Emptiness in Mind-Only,* 217-218) statement:

> Although among imputational factors in general there are many, such as all generally characterized phenomena and space, and so forth, the reason why these are not [explicitly] mentioned in the *Sūtra Unraveling the Thought* is that they are not relevant on the occasion of the imputational factor, the emptiness of which is posited as the thoroughly established nature. Although many of those are existents that **cannot** be posited by names and terminology, they are not established by way of their own character because of being only imputed by conceptuality.

Ḏzong-ka-ḇa's saying that **many** imputational natures cannot be posited by names and terminology but are only imputed by conceptuality suggests that there are **some** imputational natures that are both. Also, since the imputational natures listed in this citation are just existent imputational natures, it would seem that Ḏzong-ka-ḇa means that there are some **existent** imputational natures that are both posited by names and terminology and only imputed by conceptuality. Jay-ḏzün Chö-ḡyi-gyel-tsen and Ḏra-ḏi Ge-s̄hay provide us with at least one, forms and so forth as referents of names and conventions—one that is especially relevant to the discussion in the *Sūtra Unraveling the Thought.*

As long as we take "names and terminology appearing as objects of awareness" as including past conceptualization and verbalization, I agree with them. Otherwise, how could we posit that objects appear—even to those who do not know language—to be established by way of their own character as the referents of their respective names and conceptual consciousnesses?

I find Jay-ḏzün Chö-ḡyi-gyel-tsen's and Ḏra-ḏi Ge-s̄hay's explanations to be helpful because Ḏzong-ka-ḇa is not saying that only non-existents are posited by names and terminology or, in Jam-ȳang-shay-ḇa's vocabulary, posited by only names and terminology. Indeed, being the referent of terms and thoughts is established through the usage of language but misappears as if subsisting in objects themselves; thus, it is posited by only names and terminology. This is why I find Nga-w̄ang-ḇel-den's explanation that it is Jam-ȳang-shay-ḇa's position that no existent imputational natures are posited by only names and terminology to be off the mark.

Why does Nga-w̄ang-ḇel-den hold such a strange position? According to him, this is the reason why Ḏzong-ka-ḇa refers to "existents"—not because **some** existent imputational natures are posited by only names and terminology but because **all** existent imputational natures are necessarily not posited by only names and terminology. Thus, it is just non-existent imputational natures that are both only imputed by conceptuality and posited by only names and terminology.

Nga-w̄ang-ḇel-den's explanation of Jam-ȳang-shay-ḇa's reading of Ḏzong-ka-ḇa's statement is inventive, and it is likely that he makes this distinction because he views dependence on names and terminology appearing as objects of awareness to be restricted to **current** conceptualization and verbalization—not including influences carried over from past lives. His explanation thereby accounts for how the appearance of objects as established by way of their own character as the referents of terms and conceptual consciousnesses could occur to babies and animals, since, according to his restrictive reading, even though such an appearance is only posited by names and terminology it is not posited by only names and terminology, since the latter requires dependence on names and terminology appearing as objects of awareness and that, according to him, is restricted to **current** conceptualization and verbalization. Most likely, Nga-w̄ang-b̄el-den felt that this allowed him to retain the Ge-luk-b̄a foundational point that the existent imputational nature that is an image of establishment of objects by way of their own character as the referents of conceptual consciousnesses appears even to persons who do not know language.

Indeed, such must appear even to them because the conception of a self of phenomena exists innately in **all** sentient beings—animals, babies, and so forth included—since it is the final root of cyclic existence. It is through assenting to this false appearance of phenomena that beings are drawn into misconceptions of the substantial existence of persons, which, in turn, draw them into cyclic existence. However, it would have been more cogent for Nga-w̄ang-b̄el-den to hold that the mere fact that something is posited by names and terminology means that its appearance to the mind depends upon **current *or* past** usage of language. I think that Nga-w̄ang-b̄el-den has added an unnecessary facet to Jam-ȳang-shay-b̄a's explanation, whose followers should reject the opinion that only non-existents are posited by only names and terminology.[a]

Issue #109: Is what is posited by only names and terminology an object of comprehension of an inference of renown?

As explained just above, D̄ra-d̄i Ge-s̄hay Rin-chen-dön-drup's opinion is that:

- forms and so forth being referents of names and conventions is posited by names and terminology
- forms and so forth being posited by names and terminology means that being referents of names and conventions must be understood through names and terminology appearing as objects of awareness.

A-ku L̄o-drö-gya-tso[b] avers that this stance seems to lead D̄ra-d̄i Ge-s̄hay to hold that such an imputational nature is an "object of comprehension of an

[a] My position is buttressed by a clear statement by Ke-drup on the topic; see *Reflections on Reality,* 217-219.

[b] A-ku L̄o-drö-gya-tso (*Precious Lamp,* 81.5) says that whether such is the case needs to be investigated relative to what D̄ra-d̄i Ge-s̄hay offers as the syllogistic rendering of the extensive explanation.

inference of renown." To unpack his meaning, let us consider a similar stance by Paṇ-chen S̄ö-nam-drak-b̄a.[324] He holds that forms and so forth being the referents of a conceptual consciousness is posited by names and terminology, and from his declaring[325] that this "names and terminology" is synonymous with the "names and terminology" of the statement, "The one with the rabbit in it is posited by **names and terminology** as suitable to be expressed with the term 'moon,'" it can be concluded that, for Paṇ-chen S̄ö-nam-drak-b̄a, forms and so forth being the referents of a conceptual consciousness is, in Gung-ru Chö-jung and Jam-ȳang-shay-b̄a's vocabulary, posited by only names and terminology. Paṇ-chen S̄ö-nam-drak-b̄a[326] humbly says that the intelligent should analyze in detail whether whatever is posited by names and terminology is necessarily a case of something that is linguistically established,[a] that is, a linguistic artifact, but, in seeming self-contradiction, he[327] says that a form's being the referent of a conceptual consciousness apprehending form is not linguistically established.

Paṇ-chen S̄ö-nam-drak-b̄a appears to be in a quandary, but I think that with his first statement he has hit on an important key, even though in the second statement he backs off of it. Namely, just as the suitability to call any object by any name is a linguistic artifact but sometimes appears to be fixed in the order of things, so an object's being the referent of a word or of a conceptual consciousness is a linguistic artifact that appears to subsist in the object by way of its own character but does not. The problem in trying to extend this formula to **all** existent imputational natures such as uncompounded space can be cleared up by making Jam-ȳang-shay-b̄a's distinction between what is posited by only names and terminology and what is only posited by names and terminology. The former are linguistic artifacts, whereas the latter are not.

Since I find Jam-ȳang-shay-b̄a's distinction helpful, I agree with A-ku L̄o-drö-gya-tso's notion that the dilemma in which scholars such as Paṇ-chen S̄ö-nam-drak-b̄a find themselves is due to their not appreciating the difference between being posited by only names and terminology and being only posited by names and terminology. In his explanation of Jam-ȳang-shay-b̄a's position, A-ku L̄o-drö-gya-tso explains that the term "only" in

> "The suitability to express the thing with a rabbit in it by the term 'moon' is posited by only names and terminology"

eliminates that what posits such is anything other than names and terminology, such as reasoning through the force of facts, whereas the term "only" in

> "Imputational natures are only posited by names and terminology"

eliminates that they are established by way of their own character. The two have different modes of elimination.

When A-ku L̄o-drö-gya-tso indicates that terminological suitability—

[a] *sgra byung grags pa.*

which is an existent imputational nature—is posited by only names and terminology, he differs from Nga-w̄ang-b̄el-den, who reads Jam-ȳang-shay-b̄a as saying that no existents are posited by only names and terminology. One would think that A-ku L̄o-drö-gya-tso would proceed to crown his point by explicitly and emphatically declaring that the imputational natures relevant on this occasion, such as an object's appearance as established by way of its own character as the referent of a conceptual consciousness, also are posited by only names and terminology, but we frustratingly are left with his dropping the topic despite having brought us this far.

Instead of ascending to such a meaningful crescendo by revealing the meaning of the sūtra to be that the imputational natures relevant here are posited by only names and terminology (and hence linguistic artifacts), A-ku L̄o-drö-gya-tso takes the negative route of continuing his criticism of Jay-d̄zün Chö-ḡyi-gyel-tsen and Paṇ-chen S̄ö-nam-drak-b̄a. Indeed, he cogently points out that if, for something to be posited by only names and terminology, its appearance as an object of awareness required that names and terminology appear as objects of awareness, then for something to be only imputed by conceptuality its appearance as an object of awareness would absurdly require that conceptuality appear as an object of awareness, and no one wants to say such. As was mentioned earlier, even Jay-d̄zün Chö-ḡyi-gyel-tsen and Paṇ-chen S̄ö-nam-drak-b̄a assert that uncompounded space is not established by way of its own character and is only imputed by conceptuality, even though the appearance of uncompounded space to the mind of a bullock, for instance, does not depend upon terminology and conceptuality. A-ku L̄o-drö-gya-tso's implicit point is that if they can accept that something's being only imputed by conceptuality does not require conceptuality to appear as an object of awareness, they should also accept that something's being only posited by names and terminology does not require that names and terminology appear as an object of awareness.

Again, A-ku L̄o-drö-gya-tso does not go on to discuss whether something being posited by only names and terminology means that its appearance to the mind depends upon names and terminology appearing as an object of awareness, although we can speculate that he would not favor this, since he would follow Gung-tang in restricting the meaning of this only to **current** conceptualization and verbalization. My own opinion is that something being posited by only names and terminology means that its appearance to the mind depends upon names and terminology appearing as an object of awareness, but I extend the meaning of "names and terminology appearing as an object of awareness" to include both past and current conceptualization and verbalization. The association of names and objects over the course of past lives influences how objects appear even during unlanguaged lives or parts of a life.

Because of A-ku L̄o-drö-gya-tso's failure to discuss just what being posited by only names and terminology means, his own well-taken recommendation—that Paṇ-chen S̄ö-nam-drak-b̄a's and Jay-d̄zün Chö-ḡyi-gyel-tsen's followers accept Jam-ȳang-shay-b̄a's distinction (between what is posited by only names and terminology and what is only posited by names and terminology) in order to understand D̄zong-ka-b̄a's point that there are existent imputational natures that cannot be posited by names and terminology but are only imputed by conceptuality—is not fully developed.[a] I agree that Jam-ȳang-shay-b̄a's distinction is well taken, but it needs to be fleshed out so that the topic that is relevant here in the *Sūtra Unraveling the Thought* can come to life. The diversion into considering what "only imputed by conceptuality" and "only posited by names and terminology" mean comes to life only when the force of analysis of these terms is brought back to bear on the meaning of the sūtra's mention that imputational natures are "posited by names and terminology" (that is, in Jam-ȳang-shay-b̄a's terminology "posited by only names and terminology"). However, Gung-ru Chö-jung, Jam-ȳang-shay-b̄a, Gung-tang, and A-ku L̄o-drö-gya-tso shy away from this. One expects them to launch into a discussion of linguistically molded phenomena—such as being the referent of words and conceptual consciousnesses and the appearance of objects as established by way of their own character as the referents of their respective conceptual consciousnesses—and I find it disappointing that they do not. Instead of that, they continue their unrelenting probing of what the *Sūtra Unraveling the Thought* does not concern itself with—being only posited by names and terminology.

Still, we have learned much. The Go-mang tradition cogently concludes that we cannot say that the meaning of something's being only posited by names and terminology or being posited in dependence upon a conceptual consciousness is that its appearing to the mind depends upon language, or the like, appearing to the mind. For them, the meaning of something's being only posited by names and terminology (or being posited in dependence upon a conceptual consciousness) is merely that it is not established by way of its own character. Therefore, to understand what the *Sūtra Unraveling the Thought* means when it says that imputational natures are "posited by names and terminology," it is imperative to determine what "establishment by way of its own character" means in the Mind-Only School. This is the slippery topic of the next chapter.

---

[a] A-ku L̄o-drö-gya-tso (83.3) is willing to explain away the Second Dalai Lama's statement that whatever is an imputational nature is not necessarily positable by names and terminology as meaning that there are some imputational natures, such as sound's emptiness of permanence, that are not posited by only names and terminology, since the Second Dalai Lama later says, in explaining this point, that sound's emptiness of permanence and the aggregates' selflessness cannot be posited by the mere phrases, "Sound is empty of permanence," and "The aggregates are selfless."

16. Probing Establishment by Way of Its Own Character

One Mode of Conception Containing but Not Being Another

Dzong-ka-ba (*Emptiness in Mind-Only,* 86-87) first indicates that the meanings of "established by way of its own character" in the Mind-Only School and the Consequence School differ:

> Moreover, the mode of positing [something in dependence upon names and terminology in this Mind-Only system] is very different from the Consequence School's positing existents through the force of nominal conventions [even if the terminology is similar]. Therefore, the meaning of existing and not existing by way of [the object's] own character[a] [here in the Mind-Only School] also does not agree [with the interpretation of the Consequence School].

Immediately thereafter, he indicates that the two types of conception are somehow related:

> However, if one has the conception of [an object as] existing by way of its own character [as described] in this Mind-Only system, one also has the conception of its being established by way of its own character [as described] in the Consequence School. Nevertheless, there are cases in which, though [Proponents of Mind-Only] did not conceive certain bases [that is, imputational natures] in accordance with the former [description], they would be conceiving such in accordance with the latter [description by the Consequence School, since the Mind-Only School, for instance, holds that anything existent is findable when the object imputed is sought and this is the meaning of "establishment of an object by way of its own character" for the Consequence School].

His point must be that the grosser (Mind-Only School) version of the conception somehow has within it the subtler (Consequence School) version, but the subtler does not have within it the grosser one.

Issue #110: Can a wrong consciousness also be right?

Dzong-ka-ba **seems** to be saying that a consciousness conceiving that an object is established by way of its own character in accordance with the description in

[a] See issues #113-116.

the Mind-Only School also conceives that the object is established by way of its own character in accordance with the description in the Consequence School. However, Jay-d̄zün Chö-ḡyi-gyel-tsen,[328] Gung-ru Chö-jung,[329] and Jam-ȳang-shay-b̄a[330] suggest that D̄zong-ka-b̄a could (or should) not have intended this. They hold that his statement does not mean (even if it seems so) that whatever is a consciousness conceiving something to be established by way of its own character in accordance with the description by the Mind-Only School **also is** a consciousness conceiving such in accordance with the description by the Consequence School. For from the viewpoint of the Mind-Only School:

- a consciousness that conceives imputational natures to be established by way of their own character (in accordance with its description in their own system) is a **wrong consciousness**,[a] since, indeed, imputational natures are not established by way of their own character
- but a consciousness that conceives imputational natures to be established by way of their own character (in accordance with the description in the Consequence School) is a **factually concordant consciousness**[b] in that it is merely conceiving imputational natures to be established from their own side.

As Gung-tang[331] adds, there is no way that one consciousness could be both a wrong consciousness and a factually concordant consciousness, and thus D̄zong-ka-b̄a's meaning could not possibly be that a consciousness conceiving something to be established by way of its own character in accordance with the description by the Mind-Only School **also is** a consciousness conceiving such in accordance with the description by the Consequence School.

Rather, Gung-ru Chö-jung—with Jam-ȳang-shay-b̄a and Gung-tang following him—makes a difficult-to-comprehend distinction:

- What D̄zong-ka-b̄a means is that the mode of conception of any consciousness that conceives something to be established by way of its own character in accordance with the description by the Mind-Only School also **contains within it such a mode of conception**[c] in accordance with the description by the Consequence School—it does not actually conceive the latter.

Though D̄zong-ka-b̄a's passage might seem to suggest that one consciousness is both, his thought must be posited. According to their re-writing, he is saying:

---

[a] *log shes.*

[b] *blo don mthun.*

[c] *'dzin tshul tshang ba.* This distinction is found also in W̄el-mang Ḡön-chok-gyel-tsen's *Notes on (Ḡön-chok-jik-may-w̄ang-b̄o's) Lectures,* 401.2. S̄er-s̄hül (*Notes,* 18b.1-18b.5) cites a passage from Ke-drup's *Opening the Eyes of the Fortunate* that supports the Go-mang position.

> The mode of conception of a consciousness conceiving something to be established by way of its own character in accordance with the description in the Mind-Only School **also contains within it** the mode of conception of such as described by the Consequence School. However, the mode of conception of a consciousness conceiving something to be established by way of its own character in accordance with the description in the Consequence School does not necessarily **contain within it** that described by the Mind-Only School, as is the case with the Mind-Only School's assertion that it is correct to conceive imputational natures to be established from their own side but mistaken to view them as being established by way of their own character.

Gung-tang[332] proceeds to bring into considerable relief the implications of the distinction that a consciousness could contain within it the mode of apprehension of another consciousness and yet not be an instance of that consciousness. He does this by considering the issue of a consciousness that seems, on the surface, to be half right and half wrong—one that conceives imputational natures to be established from their own side (which is true) and not to be posited by names and terminology (which is untrue). In the Mind-Only School, imputational natures are both established from their own side and only posited by names and terminology; hence, a mind that conceives imputational natures to be established from their own side **without** depending upon being posited by names and terminology is a wrong consciousness. Still, it contains within it the mode of conceiving imputational natures to be established from their own side, and since imputational natures are indeed established from their own side, this **mode of conception** is factually concordant. Despite this, in order to avoid having to hold that this consciousness is right (or both right and wrong), Gung-tang refuses to say that it conceives imputational natures to be established from their own side, because the object of the mode of apprehension of this consciousness—this being imputational natures that are established from their own side without depending upon being posited by names and terminology—does not exist. The object of the mode of apprehension of a wrong consciousness simply does not exist, and thus this consciousness, despite **containing within it** the mode of apprehension of imputational natures as established from their own side (which indeed is true), does not conceive such. This is how he tries to have his cake and eat it too. As Gung-ru Chö-jung[333] and Jam-ȳang-shay-b̄a[334] say, a mind that conceives imputational natures to be established from their own side without depending upon being posited by names and terminology is not a mind that conceives imputational natures to be established from their own side.

Gung-ru Chö-jung and Jam-ȳang-shay-b̄a (unconvincingly) illustrate how a consciousness can contain within it a mode of apprehension without apprehending such by pointing to a classificatory problem if one accepted the opposite opinion. A consciousness conceiving the person to be permanent, unitary, and under its own power contains within its mode of apprehension the conception of the person as (1) permanent, (2) unitary in the sense of being partless, and (3) being under its own power in the sense of being independent, and thus its conceived object is called a "triply qualified self." Nevertheless, it is not, for instance, a consciousness conceiving the person to be permanent, for it is not a "view holding to an extreme" but a coarse[335] conception of a self of persons and thus a false view of the transitory collection. Among the five types of afflicted views, a view holding to an extreme and a false view of the transitory collection are mutually exclusive—whatever is the one is not the other. Hence, a consciousness conceiving the person to be permanent, unitary, and under its own power **contains within its mode of apprehension** the conception of the person as permanent, the conception of the person as unitary, and the conception of the person as being under its own power but it does not conceive these three (individually). They use this illustration to show how to split a hair so as to maintain that a consciousness could contain a mode of apprehension without apprehending such, thereby avoiding the problem of having to hold that one consciousness is both a wrong consciousness and a factually concordant consciousness. However, this illustration strikes me as weak because it seems merely to revolve around trying to maintain a classificatory scheme—the mutual exclusivity of a view holding to an extreme and a false view of the transitory collection—and one may wonder whether that scheme is inadequate in the first place.

Gung-tang[336] offers a better illustration that focuses on the basic problem. He says that a (wrong) conceptual consciousness that conceives form and a valid cognition apprehending form to exist as other substantial entities **contains within it** a (right) mode of apprehension conceiving that form exists, but it does not **conceive** that form exists. Rather, it conceives of subject and object within superimposing a difference of substantial entity beyond and on top of the mode of apprehension of existence; hence, it is called a view of an extreme of existence and is said to have fallen to an extreme of existence. However, the existence of form is not any type of object of that consciousness. Thus, even though a consciousness that conceives a form and a valid cognition apprehending a form to **exist** as other substantial entities contains within it a mode of apprehension of a consciousness that is factually concordant (that is, contains within it the mode of conception that form exists), it itself is a factually discordant, wrong consciousness. Gung-tang cogently says that within its mode of apprehension there is not the slightest factually concordant factor that is not polluted with wrongness.

He identifies this stance—of its being impossible for a wrong consciousness to have within it the slightest factually concordant factor that is not polluted with wrongness—as having an Indian source in a controversy between Devendrabuddhi and Dharmottara. Whereas Devendrabuddhi holds that a wrong consciousness could have a factor that is factually concordant, Dharmottara (here the favored party) holds the opposite. About a situation in which a person sees a white conch as yellow but with that perception is able to get at the object (such as picking it up), Devendrabuddhi holds that despite its being a wrong consciousness, there is a factually concordant factor within its mode of apprehension. He says:[337]

> Since the sought object is attained through [a consciousness] that is mistaken with respect to yellowness but not mistaken with respect to shape, [this factor] is posited as just a direct perception[a] [and hence is unmistaken].

Dharmottara, on the other hand, holds that within the mode of apprehension of a wrong consciousness there is not the slightest factor that gets at its object or is factually concordant. Speaking about a tree, misperceived as moving as when riding on a boat, he says:[338]

> *Question:* If it is a wrong consciousness, how does it get at the tree?
>
> *Answer:* It does not in the least get at [its object].

and:

> Through that which is a wrong consciousness, an aim is not accomplished.

Gung-tang shows that Dharmottara's opinion is accepted by D̄zong-ka-b̄a and his spiritual sons by citing Gyel-tsap's *Commentary on (Dignāga's) "Compilation of Prime Cognition"* in which he says:

> Though it is indeed difficult to know the thought of the great beings, the excellent leaders assert that the latter is correct; therefore, [the topic] should be asserted in accordance with the latter.[b]

Gung-tang concludes his quite cogent argument with these citations of sources.

Still, the position—that a wrong consciousness cannot have a factually concordant factor even if that wrong consciousness contains within it a factually concordant mode of apprehension—appears to be double-talk. Gung-tang's commentator, A-ku L̄o-drö-gya-tso, recognizing the difficulties with such a

---

[a] *mngon sum, pratyakṣa.*

[b] Gung-tang points out that Gyel-tsap's statement is from the viewpoint of the Sūtra School and adds that it can be known from Jam-ȳang-shay-b̄a's commentary on the second chapter of Dharmakīrti's *Commentary on (Dignāga's) "Compilation of Prime Cognition"* that even Devendrabuddhi's assertion is not very unsuitable in the Mind-Only School. Gung-tang's saying "not *very* unsuitable" may be his way of suggesting that Jam-ȳang-shay-b̄a missed the point.

position, makes a further hair-splitting distinction that brings more precision to the point:[a]

> There is no wrong consciousness that contains within it the mode of apprehension of a factually concordant consciousness, but with respect to whatever is a factually concordant consciousness, it is not necessarily the case that there is no wrong consciousness that contains within it its mode of apprehension [that is, that contains within it the mode of apprehension of something that is a factually concordant consciousness].

His device is to switch from "factually concordant consciousness" to "**something that is** a factually concordant consciousness." Thus, although there is no wrong consciousness that contains within it the mode of apprehension of a factually concordant consciousness, there are wrong consciousnesses that contain within them the mode of apprehension of **something (else) that is** a factually concordant consciousness. If we put this together with Gung-tang's example, the distinction becomes clear:

1. A consciousness conceiving a form and a valid cognition apprehending that form to exist is a factually concordant consciousness.
2. A consciousness that conceives a form and a valid cognition apprehending that form to **exist** as other substantial entities is a wrong consciousness, but it **contains within it** the mode of apprehension conceiving that the form and the consciousness exist.
3. Thus, it contains within it the mode of apprehension of **something (else) that is** a factually concordant consciousness, but it does not contain within it the mode of apprehension of a factually concordant consciousness and does not **conceive** that form exists.

It might seem better to hold that a wrong consciousness could have within it a factor of correctness, but then it would be necessary to give up the powerful point that it has no part that is not infected with wrongness. The distinction is aimed at preserving this cogent point of great impact. A fitting "conclusion" to a sticky problem!

Summation

Let us cite again Ḏzong-ka-b̄a's rendition (*Emptiness in Mind-Only,* 86-87) of the issue:

> Moreover, the mode of positing [something in dependence upon names and terminology in this Mind-Only system] is very different from the Consequence School's positing existents through the force of

[a] *Precious Lamp,* 85.5-85.6: *blo don mthun gyi 'dzin tshul tshang ba'i log shes med kyang/ blo don mthun yin na/ khyod kyi 'dzin tshul tshang ba'i log shes med pas ma khab zer dgos so//.*

> nominal conventions [even if the terminology is similar]. Therefore, the meaning of existing and not existing by way of [the object's] own character [here in the Mind-Only School] also does not agree [with the interpretation of the Consequence School]. However, if one has the conception of [an object as] existing by way of its own character [as described] in this Mind-Only system, one also has the conception of its being established by way of its own character [as described] in the Consequence School. Nevertheless, there are cases in which, though [Proponents of Mind-Only] did not conceive certain bases [that is, imputational natures] in accordance with the former [description], they would be conceiving such in accordance with the latter [description by the Consequence School, since the Mind-Only School, for instance, holds that anything existent is findable when the object imputed is sought and this is the meaning of "establishment of an object by way of its own character" for the Consequence School].

As Gung-tang says,[339] though both Proponents of Mind-Only and Consequentialists say that imputational phenomena are only imputed by conceptuality and are not established by way of their own character, what the term "only" eliminates and what it means to be established by way of their own character differ greatly in their respective systems. Both the Consequentialists and the Proponents of Mind-Only assert that imputational phenomena are not established by way of their own character in accordance with what that means in their own system; however, they assert that imputational phenomena are established by way of their own character in accordance with the meaning described in the Consequence School, that is, that when the object designated is sought, it is found.

Also, when Dzong-ka-ba says that "if one has the conception of [an object as] existing by way of its own character [as described] in this Mind-Only system, one also has the conception of its being established by way of its own character [as described] in the Consequence School," this means that a consciousness conceiving the former necessarily **contains** the mode of apprehension of the latter. For the reasons detailed above, it does not mean that whatever is a consciousness conceiving the former is a consciousness conceiving the latter.

As Gung-ru Chö-jung[340] and Jam-yang-shay-ba[341] sum up the issue, Proponents of Mind-Only do not conceive imputational phenomena to be established by way of their own character in accordance with their own assertion of such, but they do conceive this in accordance with the assertion of the Consequence School. For although they do not assert that imputational natures are established from their own side without being only imputed by conceptuality, they assert that existent imputational natures are indeed established from their own side simply because they hold that these exist.

Issue #111: Could Dzong-ka-ba's statement be taken another way?

Bel-jor-hlün-drup[a] of Še-ra Jay College and Paṇ-chen Šö-nam-drak-ba of Lo-sel-ling College, rather than holding that the mode of conception of one consciousness is contained in another, repeat Dzong-ka-ba's own framing of the issue, which is that if **one has** a consciousness conceiving that something is established by way of its own character in accordance with how that is asserted by Proponents of Mind-Only, **one has** a consciousness conceiving that something is established by way of its own character in accordance with how that is asserted by Consequentialists. Bel-jor-hlün-drup's successor, Jay-dzün Chö-ḡyi-gyel-tsen[b] refines this position slightly such that if a person **possesses in his/her continuum** a consciousness conceiving that something is established by way of its own character in accordance with how that is asserted by Proponents of Mind-Only, that person also **possesses in her/his continuum** a consciousness conceiving that something is established by way of its own character in accordance with how that is asserted by Consequentialists; for the Consequentialists this means to conceive that when the object imputed in the imputation of a convention is sought, something is found. This assertion, at least at first glance, does not require the entanglements of the Go-mang position.[c]

---

[a]   Bel-jor-hlün-drup's *Lamp for the Teaching* (15.1) says:

Therefore, the two, Consequentialists and Proponents of Cognition, also do not agree on the meaning of [something's] existing or not existing by way of its own character. This is because the Consequentialists assert that if there existed [something found] when the imputed object in the imputation of conventions was sought, then it would exist by way of its own character, [whereby] the Proponents of Cognition assert that that which exists by way of its own entity without being posited by the force of conventions exists by way of its own character.

However, if one has the conception of something as existing by way of its own character in accordance with the system of the Proponents of Cognition, one must have the conception of [that thing] as established by way of its own character in accordance with the Consequentialist system. This is because, if a phenomenon is conceived to exist from its own side without being posited through the force of conventions, then that phenomenon must be conceived to exist [that is, to be found] when the imputed object in the imputation of conventions is sought.

[b]   Jay-dzün Chö-ḡyi-gyel-tsen's *General-Meaning Commentary*, 12b.7-13a.2; his position is cited by Jik-may-dam-chö-gya-tso (*Port of Entry*, 177.6). Jay-dzün Chö-ḡyi-gyel-tsen's follower, Dra-di Ge-shay Rin-chen-dön-drup (*Ornament for the Thought*, 24.3) presents the same opinion and then goes on to explain that whoever is a person who conceives establishment by way of its own character necessarily is a person who conceives establishment from its own side.

[c]   For this reason it is easy to appreciate that Sha-mar Ge-dün-den-dzin-gya-tso, the author of *Clearing Away Mental Darkness* (as reported in Jik-may-dam-chö-gya-tso's *Port of Entry*, 177.6) finds this presentation more commodious than that of the Go-mang tradition.

Issue #112: When *does a person have both of these conceptions?*

Still, Gung-ru Chö-jung[a] asks a penetrating question of this explanation: **When** does one have both of these conceptions? He avers that their position requires that the person possess these **simultaneously in manifest form**[342] in his/her continuum, in which case a person absurdly would simultaneously have a manifest consciousness conceiving a self of phenomena (that is, that imputational natures in the imputation of entity and attribute are established by way of their own character) and a factually concordant consciousness (that is, that imputational natures in the imputation of entity and attribute are established from their own side). This is absurd because of the general dictum that only one mental consciousness can operate manifestly at exactly the same time.

Gung-ru Chö-jung's criticism points up the fact that none of these scholars have explicated **how** persons could possess these two consciousnesses in their continuum—simultaneously or not, and under what conditions. They do not even give an illustration of it. Their explanation seems to be no more than an uninflated trial balloon with the result that the lack of explanation highlights the bravery of the Go-mang position, despite its complications.

Established by Way of Its Own Character

Issue #113: According to the Sūtra School are all phenomena established by way of their own character?

B̄el-jor-hlün-drup and Jay-d̄zün Chö-ḡyi-gyel-tsen (former and later textbook authors of the Jay College of S̄e-ra Monastic University) have a basic disagreement as to whether Proponents of Sūtra assert that all phenomena (including imputational natures such as uncompounded space) are established by way of their own character. It will be remembered that Jay-d̄zün Chö-ḡyi-gyel-tsen holds that in both the Sūtra School and the Autonomy School all phenomena are established by way of their own character, but his predecessor B̄el-jor-hlün-drup clearly holds that in the Sūtra School imputational natures are **not** established by way of their own character. B̄el-jor-hlün-drup, like the scholars of the Go-mang tradition, agrees that Autonomists assert that all phenomena are established by way of their own character but holds that Proponents of Sūtra do not:[343]

Even though Proponents of Cognition do not conceive some bases

---

[a] Gung-ru Chö-jung's *Garland of White Lotuses,* 28b.3-29a.2. Why Jam-ȳang-shay-b̄a drops this from his cribbing of Gung-ru Chö-jung is a mystery. Does the reasoning somehow double back on another of his positions?

> [such as uncompounded space] to exist by way of their own character in accordance with how they assert [the meaning of such], they still have a conception of those as established by way of their own character in accordance with the assertions of the Consequentialists. For even though the **Proponents of Sūtra** and of Mind-Only do not assert that imputational natures exist by way of their own character, they do assert that [with respect to all existing phenomena] there is something found when the imputed object in the imputation of conventions is sought. This is so because [all non-Consequentialists], from the schools of others [that is, non-Buddhists] up to and including the Autonomy School, assert that if something exists, it is necessarily [found] to exist when the imputed object in the imputation of conventions is sought.

Jay-d̄zün Chö-ḡyi-gyel-tsen,[344] on the other hand, holds that:

- both the Sūtra School and the Autonomy School hold that all phenomena are established by way of their own character,
- but these schools do not hold that imputational natures are established by way of their own character **in accordance with how this is presented in the Mind-Only School**, for the latter holds that this means that an object is **only** imputed by conceptuality and is established from its own side, and the word "only" eliminates that it is established by way of its own character.[a]

Issue #114: What does "established by way of its own character" mean in the Mind-Only School?

Despite having considered interesting peripheral problems, we still have not arrived at what "established by way of its own character" means. As A-ku L̄o-drö-gya-tso summarizes the issue,[b] in the Autonomy and Consequence Schools, the meaning of something's being established by way of its own character is that it is findable when the object designated is sought—the Consequence School refuting this in each and every phenomenon and the Autonomy School (as well as all other schools) affirming such a status of all phenomena. He says

[a] Paṇ-chen S̄ö-nam-drak-b̄a (*Garland of Blue Lotuses,* 32b.6-33a.1) briefly indicates that it is by way of not having the artificial apprehension of self—in the sense of conceiving, in reliance on mistaken scriptures and/or reasonings, that imputational natures are established by way of their own character—that Proponents of Mind-Only could conceive something to be established by way of its own character in accordance with the description by the Consequence School though not in accordance with the description in their own school.

[b] *Precious Lamp,* 83.5. His presentation is based on a less detailed presentation in Gung-ru Chö-jung's *Garland of White Lotuses* (28a.1-28a.5); Jam-ȳang-shay-b̄a, for no apparent reason, eliminated this part when he revised Gung-ru Chö-jung's textbook.

that in the Mind-Only School, "established by way of its own character" means that the object is established without being only posited by names and terminology. He adds that in the two Hearer Schools—the Great Exposition and Sūtra schools—"established by way of its own character" means that the object is established by way of its own character as the referent of a conceptual consciousness. (The latter is in reference to those schools' implied assertion that **all** phenomena are "established by way of their own character," not to their more particular assertion that impermanent phenomena are established by way of their own character but permanent phenomena are not established by way of their own character.)

Notice that with respect to the Autonomy and Consequence Schools A-ku Lo-drö-gya-tso gives a positive description of what it means for something to be established by way of its own character—it is findable when the object designated is sought. He does not just say that it means the opposite of a lighter status of objects. However, for the Mind-Only School, he merely says that the meaning of something's being established by way of its own character is that it is established without being only posited by names and terminology—that is to say, it exists but is not just posited by names and terminology. Indeed, these scholars do not dare say anything else. They are left with only eliminating possibilities; let us consider how Jam-ȳang-shay-b̄a knocks down a likely candidate.

Issue #115: Could "established by way of its own character" mean established through the force of its own measure of subsistence?

Earlier (128), it was pointed out that even though the Great Exposition School and the Sūtra School do not assert that permanent phenomena are established by way of their own character, they assert that permanent phenomena are established **through the force of their own measure of subsistence.**[a] Thus, when it is said that these two Lesser Vehicle schools assert that even permanent phenomena are **established by way of their own character** as the referents of conceptual consciousnesses, this means that they assert that permanent phenomena are established this way **through the force of their own measure of subsistence**. Thus, it is inviting to identify "establishment by way of its own character" as meaning "establishment through the force of its own measure of subsistence."

Jam-ȳang-shay-b̄a[345] indicates that such is not suitable. He does not give his reasons, but presumably "establishment through the force of its own measure of subsistence" cannot be the meaning of "establishment by way of its own character" in the Sūtra School simply because the Sūtra School is capable of refuting that permanent phenomena are established by way of their own character. The

---

a *rang gi gnas tshod kyi dbang gis grub pa.*

problem is that if establishment of an object by way of its own character referred to its being established through the force of its own measure of subsistence, then when the Sūtra School refutes that permanent phenomena are the former, they would also be refuting the latter, due to which it could not be said that they assert that all phenomena, including existent imputational natures, are established through the force of their own measure of subsistence or established from their own side. That this is unacceptable is due to the basic assertion by all of the non-Consequence Schools that all existents inherently exist, in the sense that when they are sought among their bases of designation, they are found. Otherwise, why would they debate against the Consequentialists' point that everything exists conventionally but not ultimately? They would not.

Issue #116: Could any meaning of "established by way of its own character" meet the criteria it must satisfy?

The lack of an evocative description of what it means for something to be established by way of its own character leaves the issue in an unsatisfying state of circularity. The last chapter ended with the statement that the meaning of something's being only posited by names and terminology is merely that it is not established by way of its own character and that, therefore, it was imperative to determine what "establishment by way of its own character" means in the Mind-Only School. However, now that the most likely candidate—that when the object designated is sought analytically, it can be found—has been eliminated, we have seen that Gung-ru Chö-jung, Jam-ȳang-shay-b̄a, Gung-tang, and A-ku L̄o-drö-gya-tso are left with propounding that the meaning of something's being "established by way of its own character" is merely that it is established without being only posited by names and terminology. The circularity of the explanation is discouraging, even though the process of arriving at the point of appreciating why nothing else would work is informative.

The problem is the complex criteria that any meaning of "established by way of its own character" must meet:

1. It must be something that the Mind-Only School asserts that imputational natures, both existent and non-existent, do not have.
2. It must be something that the Mind-Only School asserts of both other-powered natures and thoroughly established natures.
3. It must be something that the Consequence School refutes with respect to all phenomena.
4. It must be something such that when Proponents of Mind-Only realize its absence with respect to the imputational natures, they do not realize emptiness as it is described in the Consequence School.
5. It must be something the absence of which the Sūtra School cannot realize with respect to imputational natures, or at least with respect to objects'

establishment as the referents of names and conceptual consciousnesses.

A-ku L̄o-drö-gya-tso's ingenious (if not evocative) choice that "established by way of its own character" means "established without being only posited by names and terminology" can be viewed as having a two-pronged meaning. Anything that is established by way of its own character is both A (established) and B (not only posited by names and terminology). This description of "established by way of its own character" meets the first three criteria easily:

1. The Mind-Only School clearly asserts that imputational natures are not **both** A and B, for they assert that existent imputational natures are A but not B—that is to say, they do not assert that existent imputational natures are both established and not only posited by names and terminology (since, even though existent imputational natures are established, they **are** only posited by names and terminology—and they assert that non-existent imputational natures are not A and are not B—they are not established and are only posited by names and terminology.
2. The Mind-Only School clearly asserts that other-powered natures are both A and B. For, the *Sūtra Unraveling the Thought* implies that other-powered natures are not only posited by names and terminology but are established by way of their own character when it **singles out** imputational natures as posited by names and terminology and not subsisting by way of their own character. Ge-luk-b̄a scholars see the Mind-Only School as extending this status to thoroughly established natures on the assumption that if impermanent phenomena are so established, then their final nature must be too.
3. The Consequence School clearly refutes that any phenomenon is both A and B—that is to say, established and not only posited by names and terminology—since it asserts that each and every phenomenon is A but not B. In the Consequence School, all phenomena are both established and only posited by names and terminology.

Seeming problems appear with respect to the fourth and fifth criteria:

4. When Proponents of Mind-Only realize that an imputational nature, such as an object's establishment as the referent of names and conceptual consciousnesses, is not "established without being only posited by names and terminology," they do this based on the fact that this is established and is also only posited by names and terminology. Since this is how the Consequentialists assert that all phenomena exist, would the Proponents of Mind-Only not be realizing a status of phenomena that could only be realized with valid cognition upon realizing emptiness as it is described by the Consequentialists? It seems to me that the only way around this problem is to make the distinction that for the Proponents of Mind-Only "established" means "established from its own side,"[346] and thus they are asserting that existent imputational natures are both established from their own side

and only posited by names and terminology—the first part of this being a position that is diametrically opposed to the Consequentialists' assertion that nothing is established from its own side.[a]

5. The Sūtra School Following Reasoning seems to be a big problem. For even if they assert that all phenomena are established by way of their own character as the referents of their respective conceptual consciousnesses, they assert that imputational natures, such as uncompounded space or an object's establishment as the referent of words and conceptual consciousnesses, are **not** established by way of their own character, whereas other-powered natures are established by way of their own character. Thus, it seems that they hold that existent imputational natures are not "established without being only posited by names and terminology"—A-ku Lo-drö-gya-tso's proposed meaning for "established by way of its own character"—since existent imputational natures, though established, are not not only posited by names and terminology, that is, they **are** only posited by names and terminology. Hence, it would absurdly seem that Proponents of Sūtra would realize emptiness as it is described in the Mind-Only School, in which case it would absurdly not be suitable to posit the Sūtra School as having a lower view, whereby the presentation of four schools of tenets would absurdly fall apart.

This is the type of issue that is put to considerable analysis in the debating courtyards of the monastic colleges. My own defense of A-ku Lo-drö-gya-tso's position would be to call on Ye-shay-tup-den's point[b] that Proponents of Sūtra cannot make a distinction between (1) an object and (2) an object as a referent of words and conceptual consciousnesses, and thus they do not consider the latter to be an imputational nature. Hence, when they realize that imputational natures are not established by way of their own character, they do not realize that this most important imputational nature in the Mind-Only School—an object as a referent of words and conceptual consciousnesses—is not established by way of its own character, that is, is not established without being only posited by names and terminology. They cannot separate an object from its serving as the referent of words and conceptual consciousnesses, and thus even if they realize that existent imputational natures are not established by way of their

[a] If by "established" A-ku Lo-drö-gya-tso means "established from its own side," we would have to make a few revisions in the first three statements, but none of them are devastating to his explication.

Paṇ-chen Sö-nam-drak-ba (*Garland of Blue Lotuses*, 32b.1-32b.5) raises the interesting objection that being established from the side of its own mode of subsistence without being merely posited through the force of conceptuality cannot be the distinctive meaning of "established by way of its own character" in the Mind-Only School because the Consequentialists also assert this. Unfortunately, he is vague on just what the Proponents of Mind-Only assert.

[b] See *Reflections on Reality*, 430.

own character, they cannot realize that serving as the referent of words and conceptual consciousnesses is not established by way of its own character since they do not recognize this as an imputational nature. That is how I would handle a challenge to A-ku Lo-drö-gya-tso's position.

Even though in doing this I am making use of a distinction put forward by Ken-sur Ye-shay-tup-den, he himself offered another solution—a double meaning. He suggested that the meaning of other-powered natures' being established by way of their own character might be that they are produced from causes and conditions and that the meaning of thoroughly established natures' being established by way of their own character might be that they are the final mode of subsistence of phenomena. At the time, unaware of the difficulty of the issue, I was stunned by the weakness of his positing the meaning of establishment of the object by way of its own character in such a two-pronged manner. It seemed simplistic, since he was merely taking what other-powered natures are (that is, things produced from causes and conditions) and what thoroughly established natures are (the emptinesses that are the final mode of subsistence of things) and claiming these as the meaning of their respective establishment by way of their own character. After all, it is **obvious** that "establishment of an object by way of its own character" must refer to a more substantial mode of existence than something's being established within being only posited by names and terminology. In time, however, I have come to appreciate that the prime modes of explanation are (1) the circularity of the above explanation by Jam-yang-shay-ba, Gung-tang, A-ku Lo-drö-gya-tso, and so forth, or (2) Ken-sur Ye-shay-tup-den's ingenious (albeit weak) solution.[a]

Above, I indicated how I would try to defend A-ku Lo-drö-gya-tso's stance; however, my own candidate is that since in the Mind-Only School both other-powered and thoroughly established natures are appearing objects[b] of directly perceiving consciousnesses, the meaning of their being established by way of their own character is that they are established from their own side and have a sufficiently substantial level of existence that they can serve as the appearing objects of directly perceiving consciousnesses. (The tenet that thoroughly established natures are susceptible to direct perception is not held by the Sūtra School, which holds that only the impermanent can be directly perceived, but this tenet is held by the Mind-Only School.) As counter-evidence to my proposition that in the Mind-Only School the meaning of something's being established by way of its own character is that, within being established from its own

---

[a] Both prongs of his "solution" require the qualification of "established from their own side," since otherwise the Consequentialists would absurdly hold (1) that other-powered natures are established by way of their own character, since they assert that other-powered natures are produced from causes and conditions, and (2) that thoroughly established natures, that is, emptinesses, are established by way of their own character, since they assert that emptiness is the final nature of phenomena.

[b] *snang yul.*

side, it can serve as an appearing object of a directly perceiving consciousness, one could cite that even imputational phenomena such as uncompounded space are appearing objects of a Buddha's omniscient consciousness; however, I can answer that many explanations are confined to the realm of non-Buddhas and do not have to include a Buddha's extraordinary mode of perception.

At first blush more damaging, one could cite that an object's being the referent of a conceptual consciousness appears even to directly perceiving sense consciousnesses and hence is the appearing object of direct perception but is not established by way of its own character. However, there is a common distinction between something merely appearing to a consciousness and its being the "appearing object" of that consciousness. For instance, Ge-luk-b̄a scholars assert that a pot appears to a conceptual consciousness apprehending a pot even though the appearing object of such a conceptual consciousness is merely the generic image (or meaning-generality)[a] of the pot. (They make the amazing assertion that a pot actually appears to such a conceptual consciousness; they do this so that inferential consciousnesses, which are necessarily conceptual, can be cases of explicit realization[b] and not implicit realization.)[c] Also, although the impermanence of a pot appears to an eye consciousness that directly perceives a pot, it is not the appearing object of that consciousness.[d] This is because, although it appears to such an eye consciousness, it is not ascertained, not noticed. Still, I would have to admit that the fact—that a pot is the referent of a conceptual consciousness apprehending a pot—appears to an eye consciousness and is ascertained, or noticed, since it is in dependence upon such an appearance that a subsequent mental consciousness conceives a pot to be established by way of its own character as the referent of a conceptual consciousness, in the sense that it assents to the appearance of pot's being the referent of a conceptual consciousness as if such subsisted right in the nature of the pot. To get around this, I might try to hold that since the appearance—to an eye consciousness—of pot as the referent of a conceptual consciousness is not the **main** object of

---

a *don spyi, arthasāmānya.*

b *dngos rtogs.*

c *shugs rtogs.*

d A-ku L̄o-drö-gya-tso (*Precious Lamp,* 95.2-95.4) similarly makes a distinction between an "object that appears" (*snang ba'i yul*) and an "appearing object" (*snang yul*):

> Since sound's impermanence is one substantial entity with sound in terms of their having undifferentiable establishment and abiding, sound's impermanence is an **object that appears** to a direct perception apprehending sound, but it is not its **appearing object** because it is not sound. [Whatever is not sound] is necessarily not [the appearing object of a direct perception apprehending sound] because whatever is an appearing object of an ear consciousness apprehending sound is necessarily sound. This is because Dharmakīrti's *Commentary on (Dignāga's) "Compilation of Prime Cognition"* says, "Because the minds of the sense powers are definite and...."

that consciousness, it is not its appearing object. Also, even though Proponents of Sūtra assert that imputational natures such as uncompounded space do not have a sufficiently substantial level of existence that they can serve as the appearing objects of directly perceiving consciousnesses, they simply cannot distinguish between an object and its establishment as a referent of words and conceptual consciousnesses, and thus they do not even hold the latter to be an imputational nature.

Still, my attempt smells of merely trying to find something significant that the two types of phenomena that are established by way of their own character—other-powered and thoroughly established natures—have in common according to the Mind-Only School, and this has to be refined in so many ways that it loses meaning. The basic problem is that even though it is obvious that establishment by way of an object's own character is a more substantial level of existence than being established within the context of being only posited by names and terminology, this more substantial level of existence is difficult to define. The reason for this is that a broad range of phenomena is included within what is only posited by names and terminology—uncompounded space, being the referent of words and conceptual consciousnesses, and so forth—and it is clear that some of these are not linguistically dependent. Thus, one is hard put to come up with something that "being only posited by names and terminology" means, except that the object is not established by way of its own character. This is probably why Jam-ȳang-shay-b̄a, Gung-tang, and A-ku L̄o-drö-gya-tso have remained with the circular explanation.

Their dilemma arises from straying from the immediate topic of the *Sūtra Unraveling the Thought* which is concerned with the status, not of uncompounded space and so forth, but of the linguistically dependent phenomenon of being the referent of terms and conceptual consciousnesses and the linguistically dependent pseudo-phenomenon of being established by way of its own character as the referent of terms and conceptual consciousnesses. It is admirable that these scholars have not shrunk from taking the theory of three natures, which are supposed to contain all phenomena, and the notion of two levels of existence—established by way of its own character and posited by names and terminology—and have tried to determine how certain problematic phenomena exist. Still, it is important to note how far they are from the *Sūtra Unraveling the Thought* even though the issue and the mode of approach are derived from Indian Buddhism as is evidenced by Hsüan-tsang's emphasis on just this type of problem after his return from India in 645.[a]

Tibetan scholars, even more so, do not treat the issue merely by citing Indian treatises; rather, the dynamics of the architecture of a system suggested by Indian texts have taken over. The system is a living phenomenon that is only **suggested** by Indian texts—merely its rough features being constructed through consulting them. Speculation—carrying out the implications of a

[a] See *Reflections on Reality*, 45.

system—is the order of the day. To avoid speculating on such issues merely because more clarification is not available in Indian texts would be to miss the primary intention of these collegiate traditions—to stimulate the metaphysical imagination.

I am deeply impressed with their inventiveness, perseverance, and willingness to face complexity, but one would expect them to return from this peripheral diversion to the basic issue, to bring the background gained from the diversion to bear on the central issue—factors imputed in the manner of entity and attribute—by way of discussing how the usage of language over beginningless lives "creates" the fact that phenomena are objects of terms and thoughts and "creates" the illusion that this fact is established in objects by way of their own character. However, they do not return to the central issue; the perplexing peripheral issue is where the matter is left.

17. Enforcing Consistency

In this final chapter on imputational natures, we will consider several peripheral points that Gung-tang[347] raises with respect to identifying the status that imputational natures lack. These distinctions, considered implicit in the *Sūtra Unraveling the Thought*, are introduced in an effort to preserve the difference between schools of tenets. Much attention is given to distinguishing the Mind-Only School, which Asaṅga founded based on the *Sūtra Unraveling the Thought*, from the Middle Way School against which he debated in many of his works, though it is said that his commentary on Maitreya's *Sublime Continuum of the Great Vehicle* evinces the viewpoint of the Consequence School. Also, much attention is devoted to distinguishing Asaṅga's philosophy from the views of the Sūtra School. The Sūtra School, in standard Ge-luk-b̄a presentations, has two subdivisions mainly comprised of followers of Vasubandhu and followers of Dharmakīrti. Since Vasubandhu was Asaṅga's younger half-brother, and Dharmakīrti was an indirect student of Dignāga, who was Vasubandhu's student, the concern with Asaṅga's views in relation to these sub-schools is a case of determining a relationship with what were—at Asaṅga's time—future developments.

The subdivision of the Sūtra School that is of particular concern to Ge-luk-b̄a scholars in this context is the one called the Sūtra School Following Reasoning, which presents a view of truly established external objects yet within following certain parts of Dignāga's and Dharmakīrti's teachings. The vocabulary in which many of these distinctions are drawn is, to a great extent, a Tibetan development of the Dignāga-Dharmakīrti school of logic and epistemology. Later terminology from India and Tibet is used as a device to convey subtleties considered to be embedded in the *Sūtra Unraveling the Thought* and in Asaṅga's works. The thoroughness with which Tibetan scholars pursue this task is a testament to their ingenuity.

Issue #117: Does D̄zong-ka-b̄a slip up when he identifies the "nature of character" as inherent existence?

In the last chapter it was made clear that in standard Ge-luk-b̄a presentations of the Mind-Only School, inherent existence is definitely not equivalent with established by way of its own character. However, D̄zong-ka-b̄a himself, the founder of the Ge-luk-b̄a order, seems to slip up when, in the Great Exposition of Special Insight[a] section of his *Great Exposition of the Stages of the Path*,[b] he puts forth the opinion that the nature of character that the *Sūtra Unraveling the*

a *lhag mthong chen mo.*

b *lam rim chen mo.*

Thought says imputational natures lack is inherent existence. He says:[348]

> Concerning that, the character that is non-existent is own-character or **inherent existence**. Although the Proponents of Mind-Only assert a non-existence of such with respect to imputational natures, [they hold that] other-powered natures have that character and hence have **inherent existence**.

By saying "own-character or inherent existence," Dzong-ka-ba indeed seems to equate establishment by way of an object's own character and inherent existence. However, Gung-tang points out that although Dzong-ka-ba is describing an assertion of the Mind-Only School, he is speaking from the viewpoint of the Consequence School, which does not differentiate between the two.

Jik-may-dam-chö-gya-tso[349] disagrees with Gung-tang's explanation. First, he points out that Gung-tang in effect is saying that Dzong-ka-ba let the viewpoint of the Consequence School slip into—that is to say, corrupt—his explanation of the Mind-Only School, and thus if this somehow is suitable, one would have to hold the absurd position that such would be appropriate whenever the Consequentialists state the views of another system. This is why Jik-may-dam-chö-gya-tso chooses to take Dzong-ka-ba at face value here. To do this, he holds the radically different position that the Mind-Only School indeed holds that imputational natures are not inherently existent,[a] although they do hold that imputational natures are objectively established.[b] He cogently points to a statement by Sthiramati in his *Explanation of (Vasubandhu's) "Commentary on (Maitreya's) 'Differentiation of the Middle and the Extremes'"* that implies that imputational natures do not inherently exist. Sthiramati says:[350]

> In order to refute the deprecation of everything by those who think that all phenomena are utterly, utterly without an inherent nature[c] like the horns of a rabbit, [the text] says, "Unreal comprehensive conceptuality exists." "Inherently"[d] is an extra word [to be added to "exists"].

Jik-may-dam-chö-gya-tso's point is that since Sthiramati is indicating that **other-powered natures** such as "unreal comprehensive conceptuality" are inherently established, the implication is that imputational natures are not inherently established.

Jik-may-dam-chö-gya-tso's opinion is at variance with the widely accepted

---

[a] *rang bzhin gyis grub pa;* Jik-may-dam-chö-gya-tso also holds that imputational natures are not even established from their own side (*rang ngos nas grub pa*), as will be explained below.

[b] *yul steng nas grub pa.*

[c] *rang bzhin ye med, sarvathā niḥsvabhāvāḥ.* This qualification of "exists" is a prime source for determining that in the Mind-Only system other-powered natures are established by way of their own character.

[d] *rang bzhin gyis, svabhāvatas.*

assertion among Ge-luk-b̄a scholars that in the Mind-Only School **all** phenomena, including existent imputational natures, are inherently established. Jik-may-dam-chö-gya-tso's suggestion is inventively provocative especially since he contradicts D̄zong-ka-b̄a's own explanation of this quotation when, in commentary just following the citation, he glosses "inherently existent" with "established by way of its own character":

> The phrase "ideation exists" is not complete just by itself; therefore, a remainder must be added, and it is this: "inherently." Thus, ideation is not just existent but is **inherently** existent or existent in the sense of being **established by way of its own character**.

Still, Jik-may-dam-chö-gya-tso's point is well taken, for indeed the only source indicating that Proponents of Mind-Only assert that imputational natures are inherently existent is the Consequentialist Chandrakīrti's claim that all other schools assert that all phenomena are inherently existent; in the literature of the Mind-Only School in India such an open statement simply cannot be found. The same also is true, of course, for Jik-may-dam-chö-gya-tso's own claim that the Proponents of Mind-Only assert that imputational natures are objectively established. We see at work in both explanations an agenda brought over from the Consequence School that may obscure rather than reveal the internal directionality of the tenets of the Mind-Only School, which is to undercut the status of imputational natures.

Jik-may-dam-chö-gya-tso finds one piece of evidence in D̄zong-ka-b̄a's writings that in the Mind-Only School existent imputational natures probably are also not established from their own side,[a] a startling claim in the face of the chorus of Ge-luk-b̄a scholars who with one voice hold the opposite. He points to D̄zong-ka-b̄a's statement in his Great Exposition of Special Insight:

> That they assert that those two [other-powered natures and thoroughly established natures] have a character or inherent nature in the sense of being **established by way of their own nature**[b] appears mainly to depend on the *Sūtra Unraveling the Thought.*

D̄zong-ka-b̄a **singles out** other-powered natures and thoroughly established natures as "established by way of their own nature," a term equivalent to "established from its own side,"[c] thereby suggesting that, in his exposition of the Mind-Only School, existent imputational natures do not have such a "character or inherent nature."

As delightfully provocative as Jik-may-dam-chö-gya-tso's comment is, it contravenes D̄zong-ka-b̄a's oft-repeated statements that (1) except in the Consequence School no school can posit the existence of a phenomenon unless it is

---

a *rang ngos nas ma grub pa.*

b *rang gi ngo bos grub pa'i mtshan nyid dam rang bzhin.*

c The term *rang ngos nas grub pa* is taken to be a contraction of *rang gi ngo bos grub pa.*

established from its own side, in the sense that something from among its bases of imputation must be posited as it and (2) just this is inherent existence. Also, since Ḏzong-ka-ḇa repeatedly says that in the Consequence School what is being negated in the doctrine of emptiness is inherent existence, then according to Jik-may-dam-chö-gya-tso's notion, the Proponents of Mind-Only would realize emptiness (as it is described in the Consequence School) with respect to imputational natures. Āryadeva's *Four Hundred* says:[351]

> That which is the viewer of one thing
> Is explained to be the viewer of all.
> That which is the emptiness of one
> Is the emptiness of all.

and Ge-luk-ḇa scholars standardly take this stanza as establishing the dictum that upon inferentially realizing the emptiness of one thing, one can—through the functioning of that reasoning—realize the emptiness of any other object just by turning one's mind to it, without using any further reasoning. For this reason, there is no way that a Proponent of Mind-Only could realize emptiness, as it is presented in the Consequence School, with respect to one phenomenon and not realize it with respect to other phenomena. These points are so indisputable that I take Jik-may-dam-chö-gya-tso to be teasing other scholars about what had become a too established, frozen perspective within Ge-luk-ḇa scholarship in which it is often taken for granted that, *of course,* the Mind-Only School asserts that imputational natures are inherently established. Also, he may be challenging Ge-luk-ḇa exegetes to find a source in the Mind-Only section of Ḏzong-ka-ḇa's *The Essence of Eloquence* that imputational natures inherently exist. (I take Ḏzong-ka-ḇa's restraint as evincing respect for the directionality of the system—the undercutting of imputational natures—despite how Consequentialists such as Chandrakīrti reacted to the system.)

Issue #118: Does Jam-ȳang-shay-ḇa slip up when he identifies the "nature of character" as inherent existence?

Jam-ȳang-shay-ḇa, in describing the Consequence School's identification of which from among the three wheels of doctrine require interpretation, makes the same seeming faux pas in his *Great Exposition of Tenets* when, in describing the position of the Consequence School on a statement in the *Sūtra Unraveling the Thought,* he says:[352]

> Of the three wheels [identified] in the *Sūtra Unraveling the Thought:*
>
> 1. The first wheel explains that the four truths and so forth exist by way of their own character
> 2. The last wheel explains that imputational natures do not exist

> inherently[a] and that other-powered phenomena and thoroughly established phenomena exist ultimately and inherently.
>
> [According to the Consequence School] these two types of sūtras require interpretation.

In the second item, instead of speaking about establishment by way of an object's own character, Jam-ȳang-shay-b̄a speaks of inherent existence, but again, Gung-tang says, this is from the perspective of the Consequence School, which does not differentiate between establishment by way of an object's own character and inherent existence. Gung-tang[353] points out that both D̄zong-ka-b̄a and Jam-ȳang-shay-b̄a must have meant such because otherwise their exposition would incur the faults of two absurd consequences.

- If the *Sūtra Unraveling the Thought* taught that imputational natures are without inherent existence, then, according to the Consequence School, the *Sūtra Unraveling the Thought* would have taught emptiness as it is described in the Consequence School.
- If the *Sūtra Unraveling the Thought* taught that imputational natures are without inherent existence, then, according to the Mind-Only School, the sūtra would have taught that imputational natures do not exist at all, since, in the system of the Mind-Only School, everything that exists at least inherently exists.

Issue #119: What does D̄zong-ka-b̄a mean when he says that according to the Mind-Only School all phenomena are established by way of their own character?

Gung-tang holds that the same perspective—that is, that the author is speaking from within the context of the Consequence School—is to be applied to D̄zong-ka-b̄a's statement in *The Essence of Eloquence* in the section on the Consequence School that the lower schools, including Mind-Only, all assert that whatever exists—including existent imputational natures—necessarily exists by way of its own character:[354]

> When, not being satisfied with just the imputation of the [verbal] convention "person," [the person] is posited upon analyzing and examining the status of the basis of imputation to which that [verbal] convention is imputed, it is being posited that the person is established by way of its own character. All of our own schools from the Great Exposition School through the Middle Way Autonomy School similarly assert such.

---

[a] *rang bzhin med pa, svabhāva-asat.*

According to Gung-tang, Ḏzong-ka-ḇa is indicating that, in all of the non-Consequentialist schools, any phenomenon must be found upon examining the imputed object and that, in the Consequence School, such a status is called "establishment by way of an object's own character." He is not saying that this is what establishment by way of an object's own character means in the Mind-Only School; rather, this is what it means in the Consequence School, and from its viewpoint all the other schools come to assert that all phenomena are established this way.[355]

The Proponents of Mind-Only assert that imputational natures are not established by way of their own character by reason of the fact that they are only posited by names and terminology, but they nevertheless assert that when those phenomena are sought from the side of their respective bases of imputation, they are found. Thus, from the Consequentialists' own viewpoint, the Proponents of Mind-Only are still within the boundaries of asserting that imputational natures are established by way of their own character. That this is Ḏzong-ka-ḇa's opinion is clear from a hypothetical objection and response in the section on the Consequence School in *The Essence of Eloquence:*[356]

> *Objection:* If, within the import of their asserting establishment by valid cognition, [we are, according to your explanation, to understand that] our own schools from the Proponents of the Great Exposition through to the Middle Way Autonomy School assert such establishment by way of the object's own character, then this contradicts [your own] earlier explanation that the Yogic Practitioners, while asserting the existence of imputational natures in the imputation of forms and so forth as entities and attributes, refute that [imputational natures] are established by way of their own character but [hold that imputational natures] are posited by names and terminology.
>
> *Answer:* There is no fault. [Yogic Practitioners] propound that, since [imputational natures] can be posited by names and terminology, [imputational natures] are not established by way of their own character [and thus this is what the Yogic Practitioners mean by imputational natures' not being established by way of their own character]. However, since they do not assert that [an imputational nature] is not found when the basis of imputation in imputing its name is sought, they have the conception that [imputational natures] are established by way of their own character as described by this [Consequentialist system, even though not as it is described in their own system].

Ḏzong-ka-ḇa clearly says that although Proponents of Mind-Only do not conceive imputational natures to be established by way of their own character as this is described in their own system, they do have such as it is described in the Consequence School. Therefore, when his statements are put together, there is no way to say, as might seem from the first quote, that it is his opinion that in the Mind-Only School establishment by way of an object's own character is the same as inherent existence.

Also, since D̄zong-ka-b̄a clearly says that in the Mind-Only School imputational natures are not established by way of their own character, it is impossible to hold that, according to him, this school propounds that all phenomena are established by way of their own character but that other-powered and thoroughly established natures are truly established and imputational natures are not. Rather, true establishment and establishment by way of an object's own character are equivalent. Gung-tang's argument is most cogent.

Issue #120: What does Dharmakīrti mean when he says that all objects are specifically characterized phenomena?

Gung-tang[357] points out that some scholars[a] mistakenly hold that all objects of comprehension (all existents) are specifically characterized phenomena (or established by way of their own character), basing this opinion on Dharmakīrti's statement in his *Commentary on (Dignāga's) "Compilation of Prime Cognition"* that[b] "The specifically characterized are the sole objects of comprehension." He says that if this line is taken their way, it would contradict Dharmakīrti's own dictum,[358] "Because there are two [types of] objects of comprehension, there are two [types of] valid cognitions."

The two types of objects of comprehension are specifically characterized phenomena (which have uncommon characteristics that can serve as appearing objects of directly perceiving consciousnesses) and generally characterized phenomena (which do not have uncommon characteristics that can serve as appearing objects of directly perceiving consciousnesses). The two types of valid cognition are direct perception and inference, which take, respectively, the two objects of comprehension as their appearing objects. If Dharmakīrti's passage were taken as these other scholars do, then generally characterized phenomena such as uncompounded space would not exist, a consequence of which would be that there would not be two types of valid cognition; namely, there would be no inference. Since this is clearly unacceptable in Dharmakīrti's system, we must read the first citation in the larger context of his system, and thus Kedrup[359] explains Dharmakīrti's meaning is that objects of comprehension that are not mentally imputed are solely the specifically characterized, the particular context being that only the specifically characterized have the capacity to bring about sought-after aims. Hence, even in the branch of the Mind-Only School

---

a These are most likely non-Ge-luk-b̄a scholars.

b *rang gi mtshan nyid gcig bzhal bya.* Stanza III.53d (Miyasaka's II.53d, pp. 48-49): *meyaṃ tv ekaṃ svalakṣaṇaṃ //.* The stanza reads: *gal te dngos chos nyid nyams na / dngos por 'dzin pa sngon 'gro can / de shes yin phyir nyes 'di med / rang gi mtshan nyid gcig gzhal bya /, bhāvadharmatvahāniś ced bhāvagrahaṇapūrvakaṃ / tajjñānam ity adoṣo 'yaṃ meyaṃ tv ekaṃ svalakṣaṇaṃ //.*

that follows Dignāga and Dharmakīrti, it cannot be said that all objects of comprehension (all phenomena) are established by way of their own character.

Issue #121: When Dzong-ka-ba suggests that in the Sūtra School existent imputational natures are established by way of their own character as the referents of their respective conceptual consciousnesses, what does "established by way of their own character" mean?

Still another of Dzong-ka-ba's statements leads some scholars to assume that he maintains that in the Sūtra School Following Reasoning all phenomena are established by way of their own character. However, Gung-tang[360] makes a cogent case that actually this particular statement clearly does not say such. In speaking about how the lower schools posit objects, Dzong-ka-ba (*Emptiness in Mind-Only,* 210) says:

> The two Proponents of [Truly Existent External] Objects [that is, the Great Exposition and the Sūtra schools] do not know how to posit forms and so forth as existing if their being established by way of their own character as the referents of conceptual consciousnesses and as the foundations of imputing terminology is negated. This is not the own-character that is renowned to the Epistemologists.[a]

In the system of the Epistemologists (which here means the Proponents of Sūtra Following Reasoning), objects of comprehension are of two types, specifically characterized phenomena and generally characterized phenomena, which are mutually exclusive contradictories—it being impossible for one to be the other. The general source for this tenet is the statement by Dharmakīrti just cited, "Because there are two [types of] objects of comprehension, there are two [types of] valid cognitions." Dzong-ka-ba is saying that the status of establishment by way of an object's own character as the referent of a conceptual consciousness is not limited to specifically characterized phenomena, which in the Sūtra School are only impermanent phenomena.

In other words, in their system even though some phenomena—specifically, generally characterized phenomena such as uncompounded space—are not established by way of their own character, in the estimation of the Proponents of Mind-Only, they **come to assert** (but do not **explicitly** assert) that all phenomena, both generally and specifically characterized phenomena, are established by way of their own character as the referents of conceptual consciousnesses and as foundations of the imputation of terminology. Here in the final sentence of the quote, "established by way of their own character" refers

[a] *tshad ma pa, prāmāṇika.* See also issue #40.

not to specifically characterized or impermanent phenomena but to establishment through the force of objects' own status.

Ḏzong-ka-ḇa is saying that in the Great Exposition and the Sūtra schools, for something to be posited as existing, it must be established through the force of its own status, or measure of subsistence, as a referent of names and terminology. Thus, even if these schools refute that generally characterized phenomena are established by way of their own character as such is described in their own systems, these schools can still posit those objects as existing, as long as these objects are established by way of their own character as the referents of conceptual consciousnesses. Hence, even though it is true that the Great Exposition School and the Sūtra School cannot posit something as existing if it is not established by way of its own character as the referent of a conceptual consciousness, this does not entail that, for them, whatever exists is necessarily established by way of its own character. That this is Ḏzong-ka-ḇa's opinion is clearly stated in Ke-drup's *Opening the Eyes of the Fortunate*:[361]

> The statement here that Proponents of Sūtra and so forth do not know how to posit something as existing if it is negated that it is established by way of its own character as a foundation of the imputation of terminology is not in reference to the "establishment by way of an object's own character" [or specifically characterized phenomenon][a] that is renowned to the Proponents of Sūtra on the occasion of [Dharmakīrti's] statement, "Because there are two [types of] objects of comprehension, there are two [types of] valid cognitions." The Proponents of Sūtra do not assert that space's being the referent of a name for space is a functioning [impermanent] thing; hence it is not something established by way of its own character [or a specifically characterized phenomenon] as on the occasion of [Dharmakīrti's] statement, "Because there are two [types of] object of comprehension, there are two [types of] valid cognitions." Nevertheless, they posit it as existing. Still, they assert that space is established through the force of its own measure of subsistence as the referent of a name for space. If it were not established as such, they would not know how to posit space as existing.

Although the Proponents of Sūtra do not **explicitly** assert that imputational phenomena are "established **by way of their own character** as the referents of conceptual consciousnesses," by pressure of the logic of the Mind-Only School they come to have asserted such in terms of meaning. Still, what a school explicitly asserts and what it comes to have asserted by logical pressure are not to be confused. As Ke-drup's *Opening the Eyes of the Fortunate* says:[362]

---

a *rang mtshan, svalakṣaṇa.*

> The Proponents of Sūtra assert that space, nirvana, and so forth are established through their own measure of subsistence as the bases to which the names for space, the extinguishment of contaminations, and so forth refer. Though the Proponents of Sūtra themselves do not designate the name "established by way of its own character" [or "specifically characterized phenomenon"] to those [phenomena], the Proponents of Sūtra have come to assert the meaning of being "established by way of its own character" according to the Proponents of Mind-Only. [This is what D̄zong-ka-b̄a] means. Realization of this [point] is very important.

With such commentary, D̄zong-ka-b̄a's statements make good sense.

Issue #122: In the Mind-Only School are imputational natures established from their own side as the referents of conceptual consciousnesses? Tell me it isn't true!

Still, many of these points themselves lead to a difficult issue. It has been said that in the non-Consequentialist schools whatever exists is (1) established from its own side, (2) inherently exists, and (3) is established through its own measure of subsistence. It has also been said that imputational natures, such as an object's being the referent of a conceptual consciousness and the referent of the term expressing it, exist. Thus, once "existence" means establishment of an object from its own side, it would seem that in the Mind-Only School even imputational natures would be established from their own side as the referents of conceptual consciousnesses and as the referents of terms and thus would also be inherently established as such and established through their own measure of subsistence as such.

This, indeed, is the opinion of Paṇ-chen S̄ö-nam-drak-b̄a. When I first heard from the Ken-sur Ye-s̄hay-tup-d̄en that this is Paṇ-chen S̄ö-nam-drak-b̄a's position, I was amazed at and pitied the self-made trap that Paṇ-chen S̄ö-nam-drak-b̄a had set for himself. It is a cardinal point of the Mind-Only School that objects are not established **by way of their own character** as the referents of conceptual consciousnesses, and to turn around and propound that objects, nevertheless, are established **from their own side** as the referents of conceptual consciousnesses is to split a hair and thereby make yourself bald!

I wanted to find a viable way to posit Paṇ-chen S̄ö-nam-drak-b̄a's thought, but I could not figure out any way to get him out of this mess. Once it is allowed that existence, in the Mind-Only School, means existence from the object's own side and once it is allowed that a phenomenon's being the referent of a conceptual consciousness exists, it seemingly must be said that a phenomenon is established from its own side as the referent of a conceptual consciousness. How awful for the Mind-Only School to be put in the position of holding this just so that it can be different from the Consequence School!

Relief came when I found that Gung-tang[363] does not accept that this is the position of the Mind-Only School. He admits that it is indeed the case that, in general, in the Mind-Only School, "establishment from the object's own side" and "existence" are equivalent and that such are not equivalent with "establishment by way of its own character." However, he says that "establishment from its own side as (that is, **in**)[a] the referent of a conceptual consciousness" and "establishment by way of its own character as (that is, **in**) the referent of a conceptual consciousness" are equivalent. Hence, even though forms and so forth are referents of conceptual consciousnesses, they are not established from their own side as (that is, **in**) the referents of conceptual consciousnesses. Gung-tang does this through a brilliant if slippery grammatical analysis of the phrase *ming brda 'jug pa'i gnas su grub pa,* which is usually taken to mean "established **as** the referent of names and terminology."[364] He identifies the particle *su* not as an adverbial accusative but as a locative, whereby the phrase comes to mean "established **in** the referent of names and terminology." He says that here the force of the locative case is such that if forms and so forth are established from their own side **in** the referents of conceptual consciousnesses, their being the referents of conceptual consciousnesses could not be dependent upon being imputed there by names and terminology. In a brilliant defensive move, he says that this is why Ke-drup, in the citation just above, specifies the Proponents of Sūtra when he says:

> The Proponents of Sūtra assert that space, nirvana, and so forth are established through their own measure of subsistence as [that is, **in**] the bases to which the names for space, the extinguishment of contaminations, and so forth refer.

Ke-drup specifies just the Sūtra School, not both the Sūtra and the Mind-Only schools, thereby indicating that he does not hold that in the Mind-Only School space, nirvana, and so forth are established through their own measure of subsistence as (that is, **in**) the referents of the names for space, the extinguishment of contaminations, and so forth. By stretching grammar, Gung-tang has rescued good sense in the face of a perplexing quandary.

Issue #123: Do Proponents of Sūtra realize that imputational natures are not established by way of their own character?

Gung-tang[365] raises a related difficult point: Once, from the viewpoint of the Mind-Only School, it is said that the Sūtra School asserts that phenomena, even existent imputational natures, are **established by way of their own**

---

[a] As will be shortly explained, Gung-tang reads the phrase in this second way; according to him, it means "establishment from its own side ***in*** the referent of a conceptual consciousness."

character as the referents of conceptual consciousnesses, can it be said that, from the viewpoint of the Mind-Only School, Proponents of Sūtra even realize that existent imputational natures such as uncompounded space are not established by way of their own character? If they realized that space and so forth are not established by way of their own character, the problem is that they should have realized that space and so forth are not established by way of their own character as the referents of conceptual consciousnesses—a realization that is supposed to be beyond their own system.

It is for this very reason that the Second Dalai Lama[366] and Paṇ-chen Sö-nam-drak-ba̅ hold that Proponents of Sūtra do not realize that imputational natures are not established by way of their own character. Their position stems from a general operative principle that if someone ascertains something as empty of a generality (such as sound), that person ascertains that it is empty of being an instance of that generality (such as the sound of a conch). Gung-tang accepts the principle but maintains that these scholars misapply it in this context to mean that if someone ascertains something as empty of a generality (that is, establishment by way of an object's own character), then that person ascertains that it is empty of an instance of that generality (that is, establishment by way of an object's own character as the referent of a conceptual consciousness).

The principle, worded in a loose way, is enunciated in the *Illumination of the Path of Liberation* by Gyel-tsap, one of D̄zong-ka-ba̅'s two main disciples, in his commentary on Dharmakīrti's *Commentary on (Dignāga's) "Compilation of Prime Cognition"*:

> It is established that if something is ascertained as empty of a generality, it necessarily is ascertained as empty of [any] instance [of that generality].

Based on this principle, the Second Dalai Lama and Paṇ-chen Sö-nam-drak-ba̅ hold that if Proponents of Sūtra really did ascertain that space and so forth are not established by way of their own character, they should not even have doubt that space and so forth are not established by way of their own character as the referents of conceptual consciousnesses.

Gung-tang does not mention these scholars by name and, instead of that, has a hypothetical objector put forth the position that, from the viewpoint of the Mind-Only School, even if Proponents of Sūtra **assert** that space and so forth are not established by way of their own character, they have not actually realized such. Gung-tang's answer[367] is that the objector has not understood the principle, which actually refers only to things that do not differ with respect to the mode of emptiness of the respective entity. For instance, if a person ascertains something to be empty of sound, that person has established that it is necessarily empty of the sound of a conch, and if someone realizes that a place is without fire, that person must have ascertained that it is without sandalwood fire. However, in the case of establishment by way of an object's own character and establishment by way of an object's own character as the referent of a conceptual consciousness, although the terms are similar merely in that they involve the words "establishment by way of an object's own character," the way that their respective meanings appear to the mind is very different.

Gung-tang[a] points out that a person who has realized that a pot is impermanent could not possibly have doubts surmising that maybe the pot is permanent—that is, that it does not disintegrate—but has not necessarily realized that the pot is empty of being permanent, unitary, and self-powered. Similarly, a person who has realized that a pot has parts would not have doubt wondering whether or not a pot is unitary, that is, does not have parts, but has not necessarily realized that the pot is empty of being permanent, unitary, and self-powered. However, according to the objector's explanation, this person would have to have realized such, since, according to the objector, once someone realized the generality, that is, that it is empty of permanence or empty of not having parts, that person would have to have realized also that it is empty of an instance of those, namely, such a triply qualified nature. Gung-tang then cites the absurdities that whoever realized that a pot has a mouth, a base, and so forth would have realized that it is empty of being permanent, unitary, and self-powered and that, therefore, all sentient beings would have realized the emptiness of permanence, unity, and self-poweredness.

In a positive vein, Gung-tang[368] points out that Proponents of Sūtra have realized that imputational natures are existent but non-effective things, in which case they have realized that imputational natures are generally characterized phenomena, and to realize that something is a generally characterized phenomenon, one must realize that it is not established by way of its own character. Hence, Proponents of Sūtra have indeed realized that imputational natures are not established by way of their own character; still, this does not entail that they have realized that imputational natures are not established by way of their own character as the referents of conceptual consciousnesses.

Issue #124: Don't Proponents of Sūtra realize that imputational natures are imputational natures?

Furthermore, as Gung-tang says,[369] despite the fact that Proponents of Sūtra do not realize that imputational natures are not established by way of their own character as the referents of conceptual consciousnesses, they realize that imputational natures are not established by way of their own character because they realize imputational natures to be imputational natures. For to do so, they must

---

[a] Gung-tang's *Difficult Points,* 119.10. On 119.9, read *dang* ***rang*** *'dzin* for *dang 'dzin* in accordance with the Ngawang Gelek edition, 530.2. On the next line, read ***'dra'ang*** *don gyi spyi blo ngor* for ***'dra'*** *don gyi spyi blo dor,* in accordance with the Ngawang Gelek edition, 530.2. On 119.11, read *rtag gcig* for *rtag* ***pa*** *gcig* in accordance with the Ngawang Gelek edition, 530.3.

realize that imputational natures are only imputed by conceptuality, since the definition of an imputational nature is something only imputed by conceptuality, and they cannot realize that an imputational nature is something only imputed by conceptuality in any way except by understanding what is eliminated by the word "only"—namely, that it is established by way of its own character.[a]

Issue #125: What is "the self-isolate of the conceived object of a conceptual consciousness"? How to handle a cryptic passage?

That Dzong-ka-ba holds that Proponents of Sūtra have realized that imputational natures are not established by way of their own character is evident in a cryptic passage (*Emptiness in Mind-Only,* 198):

> Also, even if it were being refuted that the self-isolate of the conceived object [of a conceptual consciousness] is established by way of its own character, since it is confirmed even for Proponents of Sūtra that the objects of comprehension of an inferential valid cognition are generally characterized phenomena [and] do not exist as [functioning] things, this is not feasible. (*zhen yul gyi rang ldog rang mtshan gyis grub pa 'gog na'ang rjes dpag tshad ma'i gzhal bya spyi mtshan dngos por med par mdo sde pas kyang grub pas mi 'thad do*)

Let us first discuss the terms used in this citation. The "conceived object of a conceptual consciousness"[b] is the object that the conceptual consciousness is getting at; for instance, a conceptual consciousness apprehending a pot through the medium of an image (or, more technically, "meaning-generality")[c] of a pot is conceiving of a pot, not an image of a pot, and thus the pot itself is the conceived object of that consciousness. The image of the pot (or meaning-generality of the pot) is the appearing object[d] of that consciousness but not its conceived object.

With respect to "the self-isolate of the conceived object of a conceptual

---

[a] Gung-tang (121.10) goes on to raise the extremely difficult point of whether the Autonomists realize that imputational natures are not established by way of their own character in the Mind-Only School's sense of that term. As he says, Autonomists hold that imputational natures are established by way of their own character in the Consequentialists' sense of that term, that is, that imputational natures can be found when sought among their bases of designation, but do they realize that imputational natures are not established by way of their own character in the Mind-Only School's sense of that term? He says that he will analyze the issue in the section on the Autonomy School, but he stopped his composition before finishing the section on the Mind-Only School.

[b] [*rtog pa'i*] *zhen yul.*

[c] *don spyi, arthasāmānya.*

[d] *snang yul.*

consciousness," let us first consider the "self-isolate of pot,"[a] "meaning-isolate of pot,"[b] and "illustration-isolate of pot"[c] in the way that these terms are used in elementary logic and epistemology texts called "Collected Topics of Prime Cognition."[d] In that systemization, the "self-isolate of pot" is merely pot itself, not instances of pot, such as a copper pot, or the definition (that is, basic meaning) of pot—that which has a bulbous belly, is flat bottomed, and able to hold fluid. Similarly, the "meaning-isolate of pot" is just the basic meaning of pot—that which has a bulbous belly, is flat bottomed, and able to hold fluid—not pot itself and not instances or illustrations, such as a copper pot. Also, an "illustration-isolate of pot" is just something that illustrates or characterizes what a pot is through possessing its full meaning—a copper pot, a gold pot, a bronze pot, and so forth—not pot itself or its meaning.

"Isolates" are ways of conceptually zeroing in on a particular aspect of an object to the exclusion of other aspects. They are abstractions and thus are considered to be existent imputational natures and hence permanent, not in the sense of existing forever but in the sense of not being produced by causes and conditions and not disintegrating moment by moment. Hence, the "self-isolate of pot" (or the self-isolate of anything) is an abstraction and not established by way of its own character even if that which is posited as being the self-isolate of pot is just pot, which is not an abstraction and is established by way of its own character. Similarly, the "illustration-isolate of pot" is an abstraction and not established by way of its own character, but things, such as copper and gold pots, that are posited as illustration-isolates of pot are definitely impermanent and established by way of their own character.

In the citation that we are considering, D̄zong-ka-b̄a uses the term "self-isolate" in a looser manner. For just prior to this passage, when he speaks of the illustration-isolate of a conceived object, he seemingly equates such with other-powered natures. In the stricter usage of the term, the illustration-isolate of anything is an abstraction and thus an existent imputational nature, but D̄zong-ka-b̄a uses the term to refer to those things that **are** the illustration-isolates—those things that **are** illustrations—of conceived objects. Since anything, either permanent or impermanent, can be a conceived object of a conceptual consciousness, other-powered natures are among the conceived objects of conceptual consciousnesses and thus are illustration-isolates of conceived objects. Since other-powered natures are not generally characterized phenomena, they could not be the referent of D̄zong-ka-b̄a's reference to "the self-isolate of the conceived object [of a conceptual consciousness]."

Therefore, in my estimation, here the "self-isolate of the conceived object

---

a *bum pa'i rang ldog.*

b *bum pa'i don ldog.*

c *bum pa'i gzhi ldog.*

d *bsdus grwa.* See Daniel E. Perdue, *Debate in Tibetan Buddhism* (Ithaca, N.Y.: Snow Lion, 1992), 411-479.

[of a conceptual consciousness]" is the appearing object of a conceptual consciousness—a meaning-generality or sound-generality,[a] that is, a conceptual image through the route of which a conceptual consciousness understands its object. My reading is buttressed by Gung-ru Chö-jung's[370] cogent identification of the "objects of comprehension of an inferential valid cognition" as the appearing objects of inferential cognition, these being sound-generalities and meaning-generalities,[b] which are the appearing objects of conceptual consciousnesses.

A-ku Lo-drö-gya-tso,[c] however, says that when Dzong-ka-ba speaks of "the self-isolate of a conceived object [of a conceptual consciousness]," he does not just mean the self-isolate but "the factor, for instance, of forms and so forth **being** objects of names and terminology." Contrary to the copious evidence suggesting that Dzong-ka-ba holds that Proponents of Sūtra do not realize that being the referent of a conceptual consciousness is not established by way of its own character,[d] A-ku Lo-drö-gya-tso claims that the Proponents of Sūtra are capable of realizing that the factor, for instance, of forms and so forth **being** objects of names and terminology is an imputation and is not established by way of its own character. Indeed, Ke-drup makes a related point in the passage cited above from his *Opening the Eyes of the Fortunate* that gives credence to A-ku Lo-drö-gya-tso's opinion:

> The Proponents of Sūtra do not assert that space's **being** the referent of a name for space is a functioning [impermanent] thing; hence it is not something established by way of its own character.

Again: As reasons why Proponents of Sūtra have realized that the self-isolate of a conceived object of a conceptual consciousness is not established by way of its own character, Dzong-ka-ba cites that they have realized such to be a generally characterized phenomenon and not to exist as a functioning, impermanent thing. A-ku Lo-drö-gya-tso understandably (but, according to me, wrongly) identifies Dzong-ka-ba's mention of "the self-isolate of a conceived object of a conceptual consciousness" as referring to "the factor, for instance, of forms and so forth **being** objects of names and terminology" because it is a standard tenet of Ge-luk-ba textbooks on elementary logic and epistemology that although a pot is impermanent, its **being** impermanent is an abstraction and thus an existent imputational nature and, hence, "permanent." Similarly, a pot is a pot, but a pot's **being** a pot is an abstraction, an existent imputational nature, and "permanent," that is, a non-disintegrating phenomenon. Thus, from the viewpoint of Ge-luk-ba texts on elementary logic and epistemology there is no

---

[a] *sgra spyi, śabdasāmānya.*

[b] *don spyi, arthasāmānya.*

[c] A-ku Lo-drö-gya-tso's *Precious Lamp,* 238.4: *gzugs sogs ming brda'i yul yin pa'i cha lta bu.* He draws this from Gung-tang (*Difficult Points,* 120.20).

[d] See *Reflections on Reality,* 199.

question that even Proponents of Sūtra have realized that a pot's **being** an object of names and terminology is an abstraction and an existent imputational nature. However, they have not realized that a pot is not established by way of its own character as an object of names and terminology. This latter realization is a principal advance made in the tenets of the Mind-Only School, and according to A-ku Lo-drö-gya-tso, it must be worded this way and not as the realization that being the referent of a conceptual consciousness is not established by way of its own character, for even Proponents of Sūtra realize this.

However, unlike A-ku Lo-drö-gya-tso, I do not want to ignore the copious evidence that, according to Dzong-ka-ba, the Proponents of Sūtra do not realize that objects are established by way of their own character as the referents of their respective conceptual consciousnesses and do not realize that being the referent of a conceptual consciousness is not established by way of its own character. Therefore, I have to find a way to explain away the discrepancy with the texts on elementary logic and epistemology. Such a maneuver was suggested in the late 1970's by La-di Rin-bo-chay; he averred that a distinction needs to be made between the system of the Collected Topics on elementary logic and epistemology and the system of the Interpretable and the Definitive. In other words, in the former system being the referent of a conceptual consciousness is recognized as an abstraction in the system of the Sūtra School Following Reasoning but in the latter system is not recognized as such. At the time I thought the maneuver to be a desperate whimper, but I have come to appreciate the complexities behind the weak move. Indeed the device abrogates the dictum that a seamless whole must be found; at minimum, it introduces a basic cleavage into the seamless whole. In one way, it strikes me as paltry to allow the assertion that Proponents of Sūtra realize that a form's being a form is an abstraction to interfere with these basic points, and in another way I am deeply impressed by these scholars' willingness to pursue consistency at any cost. My own opinion is, as stated earlier (218), that:

1. Although the Proponents of Sūtra realize that **being** a form, for instance, is not established by way of its own character, they are unable to distinguish between the appearance of a form and the appearance (even in direct perception) of a form's being the referent of terms and thoughts.
2. Hence, since they hold that forms are established by way of their own character, they come to hold that forms' being the referents of terms and thoughts is established by way of its own character.

In any case, it is clear that Proponents of Sūtra do indeed realize that imputational natures (such as uncompounded space) are not established by way of their own character. Basically, realization that something does not exist by way of its own character could not entail realization that it is not established by way of its own character as the referent of a conceptual consciousness; this is simply because the latter is the subtle selflessness of phenomena in the Mind-Only

School, and there must be a progression from the Sūtra School to the Mind-Only School. Otherwise, if realization of the one entailed realization of the other, it would have to be said that Proponents of Sūtra do not even realize that the self-isolate of a conceived object of a conceptual consciousness is not established by way of its own character. If they had not realized this, Ḏzong-ka-ḇa would not say that proving such to them would be a case of proving to them what is already established for them. Thus, his opinion is clear on this point.

Issue #126: How to keep Ḏzong-ka-ḇa from contradicting one's own exposition of his system?

Gung-tang and A-ku Ḻo-drö-gya-tso refuse to allow that Ḏzong-ka-ḇa, despite copious evidence to the contrary, holds that in the Mind-Only School the distinctive realization that constitutes realization of emptiness is that objects' **being** the referent of thoughts and terms is not established by way of its own character. For they hold that Proponents of Sūtra realize this. Thus, they are faced with having to twist their founder's words into saying what they seem not to say. For instance,[371] in presenting a possible defense that the Sūtra School might make to the Mind-Only School's refutation, Ḏzong-ka-ḇa (*Emptiness in Mind-Only,* 209-210) says:

> The Hearer schools [that is, the Great Exposition and Sūtra schools] say [in reply]:
>
>> If the explicit object of the imputation of terminology [that is, a term-generality or meaning-generality] were established by way of its own character in the entity of that object, then there would be faults such as that without depending upon making the association of the terminology [with the object through being taught the name of the object], an awareness of the name would be generated, and so forth. However, such fallacies do not accrue to the establishment, by way of its own character, of form and so forth being the foundations of the imputation of terminology and the referents of conceptual consciousnesses.
>
> Though they say this, it is similar.

In the last sentence of the Sūtra School's hypothetical defense of their own position, Ḏzong-ka-ḇa has them saying that form and so forth **being** the foundations of the imputation of terminology and the referents of conceptual consciousnesses is established by way of its own character. From this, it would be seemingly proper to draw the conclusion that in the Sūtra School the self-isolate of the conceived object of a conceptual consciousness—which A-ku Ḻo-drö-gya-tso creatively explains is the factor of forms and so forth **being** objects of names and terminology—is also established by way of its own character, but this, of course, contradicts what they claim Dzong-ka-ba says a few pages earlier.

Gung-tang,[372] trying to forge consistency within his own explanation, suggests that Dzong-ka-ba's statement is imprecise. Dzong-ka-ba's meaning, he says, is that:

> If the explicit object of a conceptual consciousness, the appearance of a term-generality or a meaning-generality, were established by way of its own character in the entity of that [object], then there would be the faults that without depending upon making the connection of the terminology [to the object through being taught the name of the object, it would absurdly follow that an awareness of the name would be generated, and so forth]. However, such fallacies do not accrue to form's establishment by way of its own character as being the referent of a conceptual consciousness apprehending form.

In the final sentence Gung-tang switches the grammar so that "establishment by way of its own character" goes, not with "being" as in Dzong-ka-ba's phraseology, but with "form." Through the rerendering of Dzong-ka-ba's sentence, he artfully tries to maintain the position that Dzong-ka-ba does indeed hold that, in the Sūtra School, form's **being** a foundation of names and terminology is asserted not to be established by way of its own character. My own opinion is that it would be better to find a way to show that Proponents of Sūtra do indeed assert that form's **being** a foundation of names and terminology is asserted to be established by way of its own character.

Concluding Remark

It seems to me that Gung-tang is cogent when he explains that in the controversial passage cited at the beginning of this chapter (308) Dzong-ka-ba is merely speaking within the context of the assertions of the Consequence School and, due to this, conflates vocabulary that he usually distinguishes. Still, Jik-may-dam-chö-gya-tso's objection to this reading (308) points to a more fundamental problem in relating Dzong-ka-ba's thought to its Indian precursors.

With these sometimes crucial and sometimes peripheral distinctions, we have come to the end of these scholars' presentations of the character-non-nature—that is, that imputational natures are without a nature of character. We have seen a thorough-going concern with making sense, consistent with developments in Indian Buddhism, of the statement in this section of the *Sūtra Unraveling the Thought* about imputational natures:

> Paramārthasamudgata, thinking of three non-natures of phenomena—character-non-nature, production-non-nature, and ultimate-non-nature—I taught [in the middle wheel of the teaching], "All phenomena are natureless."
>
> Paramārthasamudgata, concerning that, what are character-non-natures of phenomena? Those which are imputational characters.
>
> Why? It is thus: Those [imputational characters] are characters posited by names and terminology and do not subsist by way of their own character. Therefore, they are said to be "character-non-natures."

With these refinements about other-powered natures and imputational natures as background, we now turn to ultimate-non-natures.

18. The First Ultimate-Non-Nature

The *Sūtra Unraveling the Thought* treats the third non-nature in two ways, one with respect to other-powered natures and another with respect to thoroughly established natures. Other-powered natures are ultimate-non-natures in that they are **not** the ultimate, whereas thoroughly established natures are ultimate-non-natures in that they **are** both the ultimate and the very absence, or non-existence, of the object of negation in selflessness.

Other-Powered Natures as Ultimate-Non-Natures

The *Sūtra Unraveling the Thought* (*Emptiness in Mind-Only,* 88) initially discusses the ultimate-non-nature with respect to other-powered natures, also called "other-powered characters":[a]

> What are ultimate-non-natures? Those dependently arisen phenomena—which are natureless due to being natureless in terms of production—are also natureless due to being natureless in terms of the ultimate.

---

[a] The discussion of the first mode of positing the ultimate-non-nature in this and the next chapter is drawn from:

Second Dalai Lama's *Lamp Illuminating the Meaning,* 19.1-20.3.

Go-mang and Ḏra-s̄hi-kyil

Gung-ru Chö-jung's *Garland of White Lotuses,* 31a.2-35a.2.
Jam-ȳang-shay-ḇa's *Great Exposition of the Interpretable and the Definitive,* 71.4-81.5.
Jam-ȳang-shay-ḇa's *Brief Decisive Analysis,* 505.4-508.4.
Jam-ȳang-shay-ḇa's *Notes,* 313.3-318.5.
W̄el-mang Ḡön-chok-gyel-tsen's *Notes on (Ḡön-chok-jik-may-w̄ang-ḇo's) Lectures,* 401.5-401.6.
Gung-tang's *Annotations,* 25.3-28.5 (*za*).
Gung-tang's *Difficult Points,* 129.18-143.12.
Dön-drup-gyel-tsen's *Four Intertwined Commentaries,* 54.1-58.6.
A-ku L̄o-drö-gya-tso's *Precious Lamp,* 94.2-105.6.
Jik-may-dam-chö-gya-tso's *Port of Entry,* 182.4-191.2.
Pa-bong-ka-ḇa's *Brief Notes on Jo-ni Paṇḍita's Lectures,* 412.2-412.5.

L̄o-s̄el-l̄ing and S̄har-ḏzay

Paṇ-chen S̄ö-nam-drak-ḇa's *Garland of Blue Lotuses,* 33b.4-34a.4.

S̄e-ra Jay

B̄el-jor-hlün-drup's *Lamp for the Teaching,* 17.2-18.7.
Jay-ḏzün Chö-ḡyi-gyel-tsen's *General-Meaning Commentary,* 14b.6-16a.4.
S̄er-s̄hül's *Notes,* 19a.1-19b.1.
Ḏa-drin-rap-ḏen's *Annotations,* 17.4-21.3.

S̄e-ra M̄ay

L̄o-sang-trin-lay-ye-s̄hay's *Summarized Meaning,* 156.15-156.16.

> Why? Paramārthasamudgata, that which is an object of observation of purification in phenomena I teach to be the ultimate, and other-powered characters are not the object of observation of purification. Therefore, they are said to be "ultimate-non-natures."

Since other-powered natures are not what is observed and realized in order to become purified of the obstructions to enlightenment, they are not the ultimate; only the thoroughly established nature—emptiness—is the ultimate. Therefore, other-powered natures are said to be without the nature of the ultimate; they are ultimate-non-natures. In this vein, Ḏzong-ka-ḇa (*Emptiness in Mind-Only,* 88-89) says:

> Because other-powered natures do not exist as the ultimate nature, they are said to be "ultimate-non-natures." For the ultimate is that through observation of which and familiarization with which obstructions[a] are removed, but obstructions cannot be removed through observing and familiarizing with other-powered natures.

Jam-ȳang-shay-ḇa[373] frames the point syllogistically:

> With respect to the subjects, other-powered natures, there is a reason for calling them ultimate-non-natures because they are described this way due to the fact that the main object of observation [of a path] of purification—which is such that meditation on it by a Superior's exalted wisdom of meditative equipoise directly realizing the selflessness of phenomena purifies the obstructions to omniscience—is the ultimate and other-powered natures are not established as such.

Ḏzong-ka-ḇa's and Jam-ȳang-shay-ḇa's exposition is taken directly from the *Sūtra Unraveling the Thought* where, as cited just above, Buddha says:

> Paramārthasamudgata, that which is an object of observation of purification in phenomena I teach to be the ultimate, and other-powered characters are not the object of observation of purification. Therefore, they are said to be "ultimate-non-natures."

This clear statement that other-powered natures are not objects of observation of a path of purification and hence not the ultimate militates against the notion, found in much scholarship outside the Tibetan sphere, that a purified version of other-powered natures is the thoroughly established nature. For instance, A. K. Chatterjee[374] says, "The *paratantra,* when it is disinfected of the *parikalpita,* becomes the *pariniṣpánna.*" Alan Sponberg explains K'uei-chi's view similarly:[375]

> A key element in K'uei-chi's model, one derived directly from the *Mahāyānasaṃgraha* (MS: II: 29), is the notion of the Dependent having

[a] See issues #153-167.

> two parts or aspects, one defiled and one pure, the first corresponding to the Imaginary and the second corresponding to the Consummate.

Gadjin Nagao explains the same source:[376]

> In the "lump of clay containing gold" simile (*kañcanagarbhā mṛttikā*), the "clay is an embryo of gold".... The gold-bearing ore appears simply as clay, for no gold is visible. When the clay is burned, it disappears and gold becomes manifest.

Asaṅga's *Summary of the Great Vehicle* itself lends support to their reading:[377]

> In consideration of what did the Supramundane Victor say in the *Sūtra of Manifest Knowledge,* "There are three phenomena—those included in thoroughly afflicted factors, those included in purified factors, and those included in factors of both of those"? He said this in consideration that:
>
> - Imputational natures existing in other-powered natures are included in thoroughly afflicted factors.
> - Thoroughly established natures existing [in other-powered natures] are included in purified factors.
> - Other-powered natures themselves are included in factors of both of those.
>
> What example is there for this meaning? An example is gold existing in a lump of earth. For example, in gold existing in a lump of earth three [factors] are observed—earth-constituent, earth, and gold. With respect to this, non-existent earth is observed in the earth-constituent,[a] but the existent gold is not observed. It is as follows: When burned by fire, earth does not appear, but gold appears. When the earth-constituent appears as earth, it appears wrongly; when it appears as gold, it appears exactly as it is. Hence, the earth-constituent is included in factors of both.
>
> Likewise, when cognition[b] is not burned by the fire of non-conceptual exalted wisdom, it appears as the unreal imputational nature,[c] but does not appear as the real thoroughly established nature. However, when cognition is burned by the fire of non-conceptual exalted wisdom, that cognition appears as the real thoroughly established nature, but does not appear as the unreal imputational nature. Hence, those other-powered natures—cognitions of unreal ideation[d]—are

[a] The earth-constituent is the general category of all hard things; thus, it includes both gold and earth, or soil.

[b] *rnam par rig pa, vijñapti.*

[c] *yang dag pa ma yin pa kun brtags pa'i ngo bo nyid, abhūtaparikalpitasvabhāva.*

[d] *yang dag ma yin kun tu rtog pa'i rnam par rig pa, abhūtaparikalpavijñapti.*

> included in factors of both, like the earth-constituent when gold exists in a lump of earth.

The earth-constituent that appears to be just earth (soil) but is actually gold is the other-powered nature. Its seeming to be merely soil is a deceptive appearance (the superimposed imputational nature), whereas its being gold, which appears when subjected to fire, is its true reality (the thoroughly established nature).

Extrapolating from this example and Asaṅga's explanation of its import, the above-mentioned scholars view the other-powered nature as pivotal in that it itself is perceived in two ways—in false and true aspects—and thus actually is the thoroughly established nature. However, Ḏzong-ka-ḇa and his followers, drawing from the passage from the *Sūtra Unraveling the Thought* cited above, hold that an other-powered nature is merely the **basis** of the misimagined imputational nature and the **basis** of the thoroughly established nature; it itself is neither of these.

Issue #127: Is an other-powered nature's ultimate-non-nature an actual *ultimate-non-nature?*

That other-powered natures are not the ultimate is driven home by Gung-tang's[378] point that the only **actual** ultimate-non-nature is thoroughly established natures' ultimate-non-nature, for thoroughly established natures are both the ultimate and the non-existence of the nature of what is negated in selflessness. Due to this, an other-powered nature's ultimate-non-nature is not an **actual** ultimate-non-nature.

Gung-tang is refining Jam-ȳang-shay-ḇa's[379] dual opinion that:

- Because other-powered natures are not both ultimates and non-existences of the entity of a self of phenomena, **in general** other-powered natures are not ultimate-non-natures, despite being called so in the *Sūtra Unraveling the Thought.*
- Other-powered natures are ultimate-non-natures **as explicitly indicated in the brief indication** in the *Sūtra Unraveling the Thought* simply because there is a way of positing other-powered natures as ultimate-non-natures.

Whereas Jam-ȳang-shay-ḇa draws a distinction between what is so in general and what is indicated in the *Sūtra Unraveling the Thought,* Gung-tang feels no need to make this distinction, for even in the sūtra itself other-powered natures are said to be ultimate-non-natures only in order to clear away the qualm that they might be the ultimate. The actual ultimate-non-nature is just emptiness, the thoroughly established nature.

Issue #128: If there are two modes of positing the ultimate-non-nature, are there two modes of ultimate-non-nature?

In a debate on my final day at Tibet's Dre-b̄ung Monastic University in November, 1988, I took the position that although there are two **modes of positing** the ultimate-non-nature,[a] the ultimate-non-nature as posited in the first mode is not an **actual** ultimate-non-nature and hence not an ultimate-non-nature—the latter clearly being Gung-tang's position. My opponent then presented me with the stimulating quibble of having to decide whether, since there are two **modes of positing** the ultimate-non-nature, there are two **modes** of ultimate-non-nature.[b] Sitting on the small rocks of the debating courtyard of the L̄o-s̄el-l̄ing College[c] (the rocks are said to have magically appeared there) on a bright, hot day in the midst of thin shade and conscious of the expanse of Hla-s̄a Valley and of the many theatres of debate taking place in the courtyard that day, I found the ingenuity of the challenge to be an esthetic epiphany, unbearably cute. I paused in a reverie of delight, pleasantly searching my mind for an answer worthy of the resourcefulness of the challenge but could only respond dryly that there are not two **modes** of ultimate-non-nature. (If there were, I would have had to admit that the first one is an **actual** ultimate-non-nature.) Sufficient as the answer was, the moment passed, but its flavor has remained. This was no spiritual insight, just delight in his ingenuity.

The Qualm

Issue #129: Since existent imputational natures, such as uncompounded space, are also not final objects of observation of a path of purification, why are they too not called ultimate-non-natures? Why does Buddha single out other-powered natures?

The reason for saying that other-powered natures are also "ultimate-non-natures" is to clear away the qualm that they might be the ultimate. But, why single out other-powered natures? Why not mention that imputational natures also are not the ultimate and thus ultimate-non-natures? About this, D̄zong-ka-b̄a (*Emptiness in Mind-Only,* 89-90) says:

> *Question:* Why are imputational factors not also posited [at this point in the *Sūtra Unraveling the Thought*] as ultimate-non-natures?

[a] *don dam pa ngo bo nyid med pa 'jog tshul gnyis.*

[b] *don dam pa ngo bo nyid med tshul gnyis.*

[c] At that time the debating courtyard was shared with the Go-mang College since its was in shambles.

Answer: If [something] were posited as [an ultimate-non-nature] merely through not being an object of observation of purification, that would be true [that is, imputational natures also would have to be posited as ultimate-non-natures]. However, in the context of refuting a misconception, other-powered natures are posited as ultimate-non-natures due to not being objects of observation of purification, whereas imputational factors are not posited [as ultimate-non-natures].

Question: How is that?

Answer: When one understands that obstructions are purified through meditation observing other-powered natures' emptiness of the imputational factor [—for example, through meditating on other-powered natures' emptiness of being established by way of their own character as the referents of words and of conceptual consciousnesses—], there arises the qualm that since, in that case, [the pure exalted wisdom] must also observe the other-powered natures that are the substrata [of the quality of emptiness, those other-powered natures] also would be objects of observation of purification, due to which they would be ultimates. [Thus, such a qualm needs to be alleviated with respect to other-powered natures.] However, such a qualm does not occur with respect to imputational factors.

The fault of that qualm does not exist. It is like the fact that just as although the conception that sound is permanent is overcome by ascertaining sound as impermanent, it is not contradictory that the conception of permanence is not overcome through [merely] observing sound.

But just what is the misconception being countered? The long history of scholarship on D̄zong-ka-b̄a's text has yielded seven readings of the issue:

1. **Jam-yang-shay-b̄a:** Since other-powered natures are observed in the process of realizing their emptiness, the qualm could arise that other-powered natures would have to be final objects of observation of a path of purification.
2. **Gung-ru Chö-jung, Gung-tang, and A-ku L̄o-drö-gya-tso:** Autonomists and Consequentialists would have the qualm that, since in the Mind-Only School other-powered natures are truly established, their mode of being established as objects of observation of a path of purification would have to be their final mode of subsistence, in which case other-powered natures could not be anything other than final objects of observation by a path of purification.
3. **Ḡön-chok-jik-may-w̄ang-b̄o:** The qualm arises with respect to other-powered natures because they are established by way of their own character, whereas it does not arise with respect to imputational natures since they are not established by way of their own character.

4. **Jik-may-dam-chö-gya-tso:** In dependence upon the sūtra's mode of teaching that other-powered natures are bases of emptiness it is more difficult to generate the qualm that imputational natures might be final objects of observation of a path of purification.
5. **Ge-u-tsang:** Those who are practicing the mind-only view might have the qualm that mind-only is a final object of observation by a path of purification.
6. **Unnamed:** There would be no qualm that the *non-existent* imputational nature that is the object negated in selflessness might be the final object of observation by a path of purification; thus, such a qualm arises only with respect to other-powered natures.
7. **Unnamed:** Other-powered natures are posited as ultimate-non-natures but imputational natures are not because other-powered natures are the *main* basis of the debate about true existence between the Proponents of Mind-Only and the Proponents of the Middle.

Let us consider these, one by one.

Issue #130: Does the qualm stem from the fact that other-powered natures are observed in the process of realizing their emptiness and thus might seem to be final objects of observation of a path of purification?

According to Jam-ȳang-shay-b̄a:[380] The *Sūtra Unraveling the Thought* has taught that other-powered natures' emptiness of being established in accordance with factors imputed in the manner of entity and attribute is the final object of observation by a path of purification, in which case the qualm arises that since other-powered natures must be observed (as the bases of such an emptiness), those other-powered natures would also be final objects of observation of a path of purification, that is, that which removes obstructions. Let us reframe Jam-ȳang-shay-b̄a's point in the light of the opinion of one of his followers, Jik-may-dam-chö-gya-tso, to be discussed in detail below (338, #133):

> The *Sūtra Unraveling the Thought* does not speak of realizing that **imputational** natures are empty of the imputational nature; rather, it speaks of realizing that **other-powered** natures are empty of the imputational nature.

For instance, the *Sūtra Unraveling the Thought* says:[381]

> Guṇākara, it is like this: For example, other-powered characters should be viewed as being [under the influence of] the predispositions for conventions that are the imputational nature, like a very clear crystal that is in contact with a color. It is like this: For example,

> other-powered characters that are apprehended as the imputational character should be viewed as being like the mistaken apprehension of the very clear crystal as a sapphire, a great sapphire, a ruby, an emerald, or gold. Guṇākara, it is like this: For example, the very clear crystal should be viewed as an other-powered character. Guṇākara, it is like this: For example, just as the very clear crystal is not thoroughly established as having the character of a sapphire, a *mahānīla,* a ruby, an emerald, or gold, and is without those natures in permanent, permanent time and in everlasting, everlasting time, so other-powered characters are not thoroughly established in permanent, permanent time and in everlasting, everlasting time as having the imputational character, and are without that nature; just that non-establishment or naturelessness is to be viewed as the thoroughly established character.... In dependence upon the non-existence of the manifest conception of that other-powered character as being the imputational character, the thoroughly established character is known.

Jam-ȳang-shay-b̄a's point is that since the basis of a thoroughly established nature is an other-powered nature, there is a greater likelihood that persons would have qualms that other-powered natures would be final objects of observation of a path of purification than they would with respect to imputational natures, and, therefore, the qualm has to be eliminated with respect to other-powered natures, there not being any such great qualm concerning imputational natures.[a]

A source of the difficulty in explaining D̄zong-ka-b̄a's meaning is that **all** phenomena, including both existent imputational natures (such as uncompounded space) and thoroughly established natures, are empty of being established by way of their own character as the referents of conceptual consciousnesses, but the *Sūtra Unraveling the Thought* in this kind of passage speaks only of realizing that other-powered natures are empty. The format that the sūtra employs for describing the process of realizing emptiness—a division of phenomena into the three natures and the positing of emptiness with respect to other-powered natures—has ramifications that run counter to the basic doctrine that a practitioner must realize the emptiness of **all** phenomena, which the sūtra itself clearly indicates when it describes the eighteen emptinesses in its eighth chapter.[382]

Jam-ȳang-shay-b̄a's line of explanation does indeed seem to reflect what

[a] D̄a-drin-rap-d̄en (*Annotations,* 19.2) similarly speaks of "stronger" (*shugs che*) qualms with respect to other-powered natures, but he describes the qualm itself in accordance with Ge-u-tsang's explanation (with amplification), presented below (339, issue #134). In his *Brief Decisive Analysis* (507.6) Jam-ȳang-shay-b̄a says that such a qualm would **not** be generated in the discriminating (*rtog ldan la skye ba med*) concerning imputational natures, but here in his *Great Exposition of the Interpretable and the Definitive* he suggests that there is **less** qualm concerning imputational natures.

Ḏzong-ka-b̄a is saying. For the context is the sūtra's teaching that thoroughly established natures are other-powered natures' emptinesses of the imputational nature, and, therefore, since other-powered natures must serve as objects of observation—bases with respect to which the thoroughly established nature is realized—it might seem that other-powered natures are final objects of observation of such a path of purification.

Issue #131: Or, is this a qualm that Autonomists and Consequentialists would have?

Would anyone versed in technical terminology have such a qualm as Jam-ȳang-shay-b̄a describes it? Anyone who knew that merely to be the object of observation by a path of purification does not entail being a **final** object of observation by a path of purification would not think that other-powered natures, just because they are the former, would have to be the latter. Thus, to provide a more plausible context for the qualm, Gung-tang[383] and A-ku Lo-drö-gya-tso[384] lay out its background in a different way despite being followers of Jam-ȳang-shay-b̄a; they base their explanation on one by Jam-ȳang-shay-b̄a's predecessor Gung-ru Chö-jung.[385] According to these scholars, Autonomists and Consequentialists would have the qualm that:

- Since in the Mind-Only School other-powered natures are **truly established**, their mode of being established as objects of observation of a path of purification would have to be their **final mode of subsistence**.
- In that case, other-powered natures could not be anything other than **final objects of observation** (that is, that which is comprehended) by a path of purification.
- Imputational natures, on the other hand, are **not truly established** according to the Mind-Only School but are said to be falsely established.
- Thus even though imputational natures such as uncompounded space are indeed **objects of observation of a path of purification** (that is, they are bases with respect to which emptiness is realized), they are **not** *truly established* as objects of observation of a path of purification.
- Hence Autonomists and Consequentialists do not have the qualm that in the Mind-Only School imputational natures would absurdly be **final objects of a path of purification**.

When Autonomists and Consequentialists fling at the Proponents of Mind-Only the absurd consequence that since, according to the Mind-Only system, other-powered natures are truly established, they would have to be final objects of observation of a path of purification, the Proponents of Mind-Only answer that, even though other-powered natures and thoroughly established natures are similarly truly established as objects of observation of a path of purification, they differ with respect to whether a consciousness meditating on them does or does not have the capacity to eradicate misconceptions of the status of persons and phenomena through having a mode of apprehension that is contradictory to such misconceptions. For example, both sound and sound's impermanence are similar in appearing to a direct perception apprehending sound and both are similar in being truly established, but through observing and thereupon meditating on sound the conception of its permanence cannot be overcome, whereas through observing and thereupon meditating on the impermanence of sound the conception of its permanence can be overcome.[a] In the same way, observation and meditation on other-powered natures cannot overcome the misconceptions of a self of phenomena or of a self of persons, and, therefore, other-powered natures are not final objects of observation of a path of purification. It is because this qualm needs to be settled that the *Sūtra Unraveling the Thought* explains that other-powered natures are ultimate-non-natures—that is to say, are not the ultimate—and does not say such about imputational natures, even though the latter are equally not the ultimate. That is Gung-tang's and A-ku Lo-drö-gya-tso's presentation of why the *Sūtra Unraveling the Thought* singles out other-powered natures to indicate that they are non-natures in terms of the ultimate, that is, that they are not the ultimate.

This presentation of the qualm and how it is resolved is attractive in that it resonates with positions known (as least in Ge-luk-b̄a texts) to be held by the Mind-Only and Middle Way schools; however, I do not think that it is

[a] Gung-tang (*Annotations*, 26.7, and *Difficult Points*, 134.2), following Gung-ru Chö-jung's *Garland of White Lotuses* (34b.4) says, "Although sound and sound's impermanence are similar in being appearing objects of a direct perception apprehending sound..." (*sgra dang sgra mi rtag pa sgra 'dzin mngon sum gyi snang yul du mtshungs kyang*). Then in the next sentence he says, "Distinctions are needed with respect to appearing objects" (*snang yul la zhib cha dgos*); however, he does not go into what those distinctions might be. A-ku Lo-drö-gya-tso (*Precious Lamp*, 95.2-95.4) clarifies the matter by making a distinction between an "object that appears" (*snang ba'i yul*) and an "appearing object" (*snang yul*):

> Since sound's impermanence is one substantial entity with sound in terms of their having undifferentiable establishment and abiding, [sound's impermanence] is an object that appears to a direct perception apprehending sound, but it is not its appearing object because it is not sound. [Whatever is not sound is necessarily not the appearing object of a direct perception apprehending sound] because whatever is an appearing object of an ear consciousness apprehending sound is necessarily sound. This is because Dharmakīrti's *Commentary on (Dignāga's) "Compilation of Prime Cognition"* says, "Because the minds of the sense powers are definite and...."

As may be remembered, I attempted to make this same distinction earlier (304) when explaining that although a form's being the referent of a conceptual consciousness appears to an eye consciousness, it is not an appearing object of that consciousness. This was in an attempt to assert that establishment from its own side as an appearing object of a directly perceiving consciousness (*mngon sum gyi snang yul du rang ngos nas grub pa*) might be the meaning of an object's being established by way of its own character.

air-tight. For, as Gung-tang clearly points out, the principle that whatever is truly established as an object of observation by a path of purification must be truly established as a **final** object of observation (that is, what is comprehended) by a path of purification is enunciated in the Middle Way School and not in the Mind-Only School, and if, in explaining this qualm, it is permissible to use another school's perspective, then why not also recognize that although the Proponents of Mind-Only do not explicitly assert that imputational natures are truly established, from the perspective of the Middle Way School the Proponents of Mind-Only do indeed come to assert such. For Ge-luk-b̄a scholars hold that the measure of true establishment in the Autonomy School is the establishment of objects by way of their own unique mode of subsistence without being posited through the force of appearing to a flawless awareness, and they univocally explain that Autonomists hold that Proponents of Mind-Only come to assert that all phenomena are established this way.

Also, in the Consequence School the measure of true establishment is inherent existence, and, according to the Consequentialists, the other schools assert that all phenomena are inherently existent. Thus, from the perspective of both branches of the Middle Way School, Proponents of Mind-Only are seen as being forced to accept that even imputational natures are truly established, and since existent imputational natures are objects of observation of a path of purification (in that they also are bases of emptiness), they must be truly established as such and thus would have to be **final** objects of observation of a path of purification.

The very reasoning that Gung-ru Chö-jung, Gung-tang, and A-ku L̄o-drö-gya-tso use in describing the qualm as occurring to Autonomists and Consequentialists doubles back on them, making it impossible for them to explain why Buddha called only other-powered natures and not imputational natures ultimate-non-natures. I do not see how these scholars can avoid this problem.[a]

Issue #132: Does the qualm stem from the fact that other-powered natures are established by way of their own character?

Gung-tang's resurrection of Gung-ru Chö-jung's explanation is an implicit criticism of Jam-ȳang-shay-b̄a's exposition, and most likely in relation to this, Gung-tang's fellow student, W̄el-mang Ḡön-chok-gyel-tsen[386] (in notes taken from lectures on D̄zong-ka-b̄a's text by Ḡön-chok-jik-may-w̄ang-b̄o, who was

[a] It might seem out of place to view Buddha as responding to a position of schools of thought that took shape long after his own death, but in these traditions it is held that Buddha taught the basic doctrines of all four schools, and, indeed, the *Sūtra Unraveling the Thought*, as we have seen, is critical of positions held by the Middle Way School. Of course, another attractive scenario is that the *Sūtra Unraveling the Thought* was written after the emergence of the Middle Way School and here is indeed responding to a qualm that Proponents of the Middle would have.

recognized as Jam-ȳang-shay-b̄a's reincarnation) makes the distinction that the qualm, as explained by Jam-ȳang-shay-b̄a, arises with respect to other-powered natures because they are established by way of their own character, whereas it would not arise with respect to imputational natures since they are not established by way of their own character.[a] Though, like Gung-tang, W̄el-mang Ḡön-chok-gyel-tsen stresses the true establishment of other-powered natures, he says nothing about the qualm's being generated in Proponents of the Middle. Also, unlike Jam-ȳang-shay-b̄a, who says that it is **more difficult** for such a qualm to arise with respect to imputational natures, W̄el-mang Ḡön-chok-gyel-tsen holds that there is **no sensible way** for such a qualm to occur with respect to imputational natures since they are not truly established.[b] His reasoning must be that if even other-powered natures are established by way of their own character, there is no way that the ultimate could not be so established, thus effectively eliminating existent imputational natures from being suspected as being ultimates even if they are indeed bases of emptiness.

Issue #133: Does the qualm stem from the fact that the Sūtra *teaches that other-powered natures are bases of emptiness?*

W̄el-mang Ḡön-chok-gyel-tsen's presentation is teasingly brief, and fortunately another of Jam-ȳang-shay-b̄a's followers, Jik-may-dam-chö-gya-tso,[387] rallies to Jam-ȳang-shay-b̄a's defense with a more carefully worded re-framing of his presentation. He stresses the focal point that the qualm arises around **how** the *Sūtra Unraveling the Thought* explains the process of meditating on emptiness. The sūtra repeatedly explains that one must take other-powered natures as bases of emptiness and must realize that they are empty of being established in accordance with exaggerated factors imputed in the manner of entity and attribute. Because, in the process of meditating, one must take cognizance of other-powered natures as objects of observation with respect to which emptiness is realized, the qualm arises that since these are objects of observation of an exalted wisdom, they might be ultimates.

Since the sūtra explains the process of meditating on emptiness in terms of realizing that other-powered natures are empty of the imputational nature and never speaks of realizing that imputational natures are empty of the imputational nature, it is more difficult **in dependence upon the sūtra's mode of teaching** to generate such a qualm with respect to imputational natures.[c]

[a] Jik-may-dam-chö-gya-tso (*Port of Entry,* 188.3) reports that this is also the thought of a commentary called *zur rgyan.* He reports another view that combines this emphasis on true establishment with the fact that other-powered natures are the **chief** bases of thoroughly established natures, this being in D̄ra-d̄i Ge-s̄hay Rin-chen-dön-drup's *Ornament for the Thought* (*dgongs rgyan*).

[b] *kun btags bden med yin pas de 'dra'i dogs pa skye don med.*

[c] Jik-may-dam-chö-gya-tso's *Port of Entry,* 184.6: *mdo des bstan tshul la brten nas kun*

Jik-may-dam-chö-gya-tso adds that when positing the **actual** ultimate-non-nature (in the sense of a phenomenon's not being the ultimate), it must be done in accordance with its main reference, and thus other-powered natures and ultimate-non-natures are co-extensive. This means that although imputational natures are without the nature of being the ultimate, they are not **actual** ultimate-non-natures on this occasion of the *Sūtra Unraveling the Thought.*

I find this explanation to ring true to the sūtra, for through emphasizing the sūtra's style of teaching Jik-may-dam-chö-gya-tso has found a way to bridge the gap between the explicit doctrines of the sūtra and implications that the sūtra does not address. That his highly nuanced explanation is so imbedded in the context of the *Sūtra Unraveling the Thought* is indeed impressive.

Issue #134: Does the qualm arise in practitioners of the Mind-Only view?

Gung-tang[388] and A-ku Ḻo-drö-gya-tso[389] reject another explanation found in a commentary on Ḏzong-ka-ḇa's text by G̱e-u-tsang,[390] who, while being a follower of Jay-ḏzün Chö-g̱yi-gyel-tsen of the Jay College of S̱e-ra Monastic University, presents this issue innovatively, independently of Jay-ḏzün Chö-g̱yi-gyel-tsen. The controversy says a great deal about presentations of the Mind-Only School at their time as well as in scholarship on Mind-Only especially in Europe, the United States, and Japan.

G̱e-u-tsang[391] attributes the qualm—that other-powered natures might be a final object of observation by a path of purification—not to Proponents of the Middle (as Gung-ru Chö-jung, Gung-tang, and A-ku Ḻo-drö-gya-tso do) but to those who are practicing the Mind-Only view. He says that just as when light reflected in water suddenly appears on a wall, one has the sense that it is shining forth from the wall but in fact is just the luster of the water itself, so when a practitioner ascertains the ultimate according to the Mind-Only School, there is a time when all coarse appearances of external objects vanish (since one has understood that all objects are not different entities from the mind). Because there is nothing other to be seen separate from the mind, there is a strong possibility that one would have the qualm that the mind is a final object found by a consciousness analyzing the ultimate, that is, a final object of observation by a path of purification.

His reason for saying this is that the qualm that the *Sūtra Unraveling the Thought* is countering (when it identifies that other-powered natures are not the ultimate) is concerned with other-powered natures, the chief of which is the **mind**. In many texts of the Mind-Only School, the identification of other-powered natures is done mainly in terms of the mind, such as when Maitreya's

btags la de 'dra'i dogs pa skyed dka' ba.

Differentiation of the Middle and the Extremes says,[a] "Unreal comprehensive conceptuality exists," in which "conceptuality" (here meaning any dualistic consciousness) is intended to stand for other-powered natures in general. Also, when one understands that a difference of entity between subject and object does not exist, one sees the appearance of objects as the self-effulgence of the mind, and hence one might think that the mind is a final object of observation by a path of purification. Thus, because the mind is the principal other-powered nature, when the *Sūtra Unraveling the Thought* explains that other-powered natures are without the nature of the ultimate, it is clearing up a qualm that arises from having practiced the Mind-Only view, namely that the mind might be the ultimate. Ge-u-tsang's explanation, based on practical application of doctrine in meditation, makes a great deal of sense.

A-ku Lo-drö-gya-tso,[392] in responding to Ge-u-tsang, admits that it is true that such a qualm can arise, but he disputes that this is the qualm being dispelled **here in the sūtra**. He maintains that the qualm being countered in the sūtra is based on the tenets of the Mind-Only School itself, which does not assert in any way that the mind is the ultimate, whereas the qualm, as Ge-u-tsang has described it, would mostly not arise with respect to the Mind-Only School's own assertions, since, A-ku Lo-drö-gya-tso claims, the school **clearly** does not assert that the mind is the ultimate and also does not even assert that the mind is an object of observation by a path of purification. Gung-tang,[393] whom A-ku Lo-drö-gya-tso is following, complains that many Tibetans at his time as well as earlier have held that seeing the entity of the mind—its mere luminous and knowing nature—upon the ceasing of other appearances is what it means to find the view of Mind-Only and that, furthermore, many have even identified this as the final view of the Middle Way School as well as the view of even the Great Seal[b] of clear light.

Since according to all major Ge-luk-ba scholars, seeing the luminous and knowing nature of the mind is not the final view of either the Mind-Only School, the Middle Way School, or the Great Seal of clear light, it seems to me that one reason, if not the main reason, why A-ku Lo-drö-gya-tso objects to Ge-u-tsang's explanation of the qualm is that he wants to stress the unfoundedness of this identification of the view of the Mind-Only School that he sees in other orders of Tibetan Buddhism. (Whether other orders actually hold this position or whether this is a reductionist rendition of their view needs to be examined carefully.)

A-ku Lo-drö-gya-tso, by holding that such a qualm would not be from one familiar with Mind-Only tenets, puts down what he perceives to be a popular presentation of Mind-Only in no uncertain fashion; he uses his commentary on the sūtra as a dramatic opportunity to discredit this view as based on not even knowing a basic tenet of the Mind-Only School. I suggest that he over-states

a I.2a. For discussion of this, see *Emptiness in Mind-Only*, 182ff.

b *phyag rgya chen po, mahāmudrā*.

his point for the sake of impact. The background of his point—that is, that the *Sūtra Unraveling the Thought* speaks of the ultimate only in negative ways—is well taken, but I doubt that this is sufficient reason to hold that the *Sūtra Unraveling the Thought* could not be addressing such a qualm.

Issue #135: Is there no qualm that the non-existent imputational nature negated in selflessness might be the final object of observation by a path of purification?

To re-state the problem: In the *Sūtra Unraveling the Thought* other-powered natures are posited as ultimate-non-natures due to not being established as final objects of observation of a path of purification, and thus why are imputational natures not also posited as ultimate-non-natures since they also are not established as final objects of observation of a path of purification?

Gung-ru Chö-jung[394] presents and then rejects another explanation of the reason behind this. According to this faulty explanation, when Ḏzong-ka-ḇa says, "Such a qualm does not occur with respect to imputational factors," the term "imputational factors" refers only to the object of negation, that is, the establishment of objects by way of their own character as the referents of conceptual consciousnesses, which is a non-existent imputational nature. Gung-ru Chö-jung cogently objects that since a path of purification realizes the **absence** of such an imputational factor, no one would have the qualm that such establishment is what is being **comprehended** by a path of purification. According to Gung-ru Chö-jung, this explanation itself suggests that indeed (existent) imputational natures **are** to be posited as ultimate-non-natures because it does not lay out any special reason or purpose why (existent) imputational natures are not posited as ultimate-non-natures.

That is the gist of Gung-ru Chö-jung's well-founded objection to this reading. Indeed, once the basic meditative structure of the sūtra is to advocate realization of other-powered natures as empty of a (non-existent) imputational nature, it is obvious that no one would have the qualm that such imputational natures are objects of observation of a path of purification and hence ultimates. Still, Indian, Chinese, and Tibetan scholars' emphasis on **existent** imputational natures is a focus added to the *Sūtra Unraveling the Thought* and is not integral to the sūtra itself, which often appears to be speaking only about non-existent imputational natures and, specifically, those non-existent imputational natures that are negated in the doctrine of selflessness. Tibetan scholars like Gung-ru Chö-jung, out of a concern for a thorough-going seamless system, concentrate on permanent phenomena—such as uncompounded space—and thus have invented the category of existent imputational natures.

I propose another, but not entirely satisfactory, "solution": let us consider uncompounded space and so forth to be other-powered natures that do not fulfill the etymology of "other-powered" (since they are not under the influence of other causes and conditions in the sense of being produced from them) but are put in this class precisely because they are bases of the thoroughly established nature. In support of my position, I could use the by now familiar gambit that even though not all other-powered natures are dependent-arisings (despite the fact that the *Sūtra Unraveling the Thought* gives this as part of the reason why they are called production-non-natures), the **main** other-powered natures are. A good deal of the nearly obsessive entanglements that these scholars create about "existent imputational natures" could thereby be avoided.

In terms of Ge-luk-b̄a scholarship, the suggestion that I offer is radical, since I could not possibly pretend to be positing D̄zong-ka-b̄a's thought because he clearly holds that uncompounded space and so forth are not other-powered natures and are existent imputational natures. Still, according to Jam-ȳang-shay-b̄a and so forth, D̄zong-ka-b̄a holds that any phenomenon is **its own** other-powered nature, even if that phenomenon itself is an existent imputational nature and thus is not an actual other-powered nature.

Issue #136: Is it that other-powered natures are the main *basis of the debate about true existence between the Proponents of Mind-Only and the Proponents of the Middle?*

As Gung-ru Chö-jung explains,[395] another reading of the reason why other-powered natures are posited as ultimate-non-natures but imputational natures are not is that other-powered natures are "the **main** basis of the debate about true existence between the Proponents of Mind-Only and the Proponents of the Middle." Gung-ru Chö-jung criticizes the verbal framing of this explanation by making the cogent point that according to the Mind-Only School, the Autonomists and Consequentialists are **not** Proponents of the Middle.[a] This is because, from the perspective of the Mind-Only School, the Autonomists and the Consequentialists have fallen to an extreme by maintaining that other-powered natures are not truly established (whereas they actually are), and thus their view cannot be a view of the middle. From their perspective, only the Proponents of Mind-Only are the Proponents of the Middle; Autonomists and Consequentialists should be called Proponents of Non-Nature.

Aside from this verbal fault, Gung-ru Chö-jung does not offer other criticisms of this explanation, but Jay-d̄zün Chö-ḡyi-gyel-tsen does. He draws the unwanted consequence that whatever is a basis of an emptiness that serves as an object of observation of an uninterrupted path purifying the obstructions to omniscience would absurdly have to be one of the **main** bases of debate between the upper and lower Buddhist systems of tenets about whether they are truly established or not. He does not explicitly give the further reason, merely

[a] *dbu ma pa, mādhyamika.*

saying that the rebuttal is easy to understand—his point surely being that then such paths absurdly would not realize the emptiness of the uncompounded.

It seems to me that Jay-d̄zün Chö-ḡyi-gyel-tsen's criticism stems from the fact that the two sections in the *Sūtra Unraveling the Thought* on the ultimate-non-nature are concerned with distinguishing what is not and what is the ultimate nature of phenomena, this being for the sake of identifying the final object of meditation for purifying the obstructions to omniscience. From the unchallengeable fact that when other-powered natures are negatively identified as without the nature of the ultimate, they are also positively indicated as being bases of emptinesses, he draws the somewhat shaky conclusion that the bases of emptinesses are restricted to being just other-powered natures. It seems to me that all that is being claimed is that the **main** bases of emptiness are other-powered natures—these being the impermanent phenomena with respect to which ordinary beings generate mistaken notions thereby drawing themselves into a diseased state of existence.

Issue #137: Is there less qualm or no qualm that imputational natures are ultimate-non-natures?

Gung-tang[396] criticizes a position that A-ku L̄o-drö-gya-tso[397] attributes to the Second Dalai Lama, Gen-dün-gya-tso, but also is represented to some extent in the presentations of B̄el-jor-hlün-drup,[398] Paṇ-chen S̄ö-nam-drak-b̄a,[399] and even Gung-tang's prime source, Jam-ȳang-shay-b̄a. Gung-tang agrees with the Second Dalai Lama's presentation that each and every phenomenon is posited as its own other-powered nature (whether it is impermanent or permanent, or whether it is an other-powered nature, an imputational nature, or a thoroughly established nature), since it is the basis of its own emptiness. However, Gung-tang does not agree with the Second Dalai Lama's description of the qualm that Buddha is countering when he singles out other-powered natures as natureless in terms of the ultimate. The Second Dalai Lama's formulation is not, from Gung-tang's point of view, well framed. The Second Dalai Lama is taken as describing the situation this way:

> When delineating the mode of subsistence of each and every phenomenon in terms of having posited them as their own other-powered nature, there is a greater chance of developing the qualm that the basis of emptiness itself might be the final object of observation by a path of purification with respect to other-powered natures, whereas there is less chance of developing such a qualm with respect to imputational natures.

The Second Dalai Lama himself says:[400]

> The bases of emptiness—other-powered natures—are empty of that

> factor imputed in the manner of imputation as entity and attribute. When this emptiness is taught to be the main object of observation by a path of purification, there [might] be the qualm that since, in that case, one must observe the other-powered natures that are the substrata—the bases—of emptiness, those other-powered natures also would be objects of observation of purification. Since this qualm is to be eliminated, other-powered natures are described this way [as ultimate-non-natures], but such does not need to be analyzed with respect to imputational natures.

The Second Dalai Lama does indeed seem to have correctly reframed Ḏzong-ka-ḇa's statement (*Emptiness in Mind-Only,* 89), which I will cite again in order to highlight Gung-tang's objection:

> When one understands that obstructions are purified through meditation observing other-powered natures' emptiness of the imputational factor [—for example, through meditating on other-powered natures' emptiness of being established by way of their own character as the referents of words and of conceptual consciousnesses—], there arises the qualm that since, in that case, [the pure exalted wisdom] must also observe the other-powered natures that are the substrata [of the quality of emptiness, those other-powered natures] also would be objects of observation of purification, due to which they would be ultimates. [Thus, such a qualm needs to be alleviated with respect to other-powered natures.] However, such a qualm does not occur with respect to imputational factors.

Gung-tang's problem centers around the Second Dalai Lama's statement that there is no qualm with respect to imputational natures that are factors imputed in the manner of entity and attribute (as established by way of their own character),[a] which is a far cry from saying that there is no qualm with respect to imputational natures **in general** (which are indeed bases of emptiness). Gung-tang allows that the Second Dalai Lama's explanation is passable (for indeed no one in their right mind would wonder whether the object negated in selflessness is the ultimate), but he nevertheless suggests that it does not represent Ḏzong-ka-ḇa's actual thought. For "**final** object of observation" refers to the object of

[a] Gung-tang does not add this qualification, but A-ku Ḻo-drö-gya-tso (100.1-100.6) emphasizes that since factors imputed in the manner of entity and attribute do exist, they cannot be the object of negation of emptiness. He admits, therefore, that it is possible to have the qualm that factors imputed in the manner of entity and attribute might be a final object of observation by a path of purification but goes on to say that Gung-tang means that an "intelligent person" would not have such a qualm. A-ku Ḻo-drö-gya-tso does not explain what Gung-tang could have meant by saying that factors imputed in the manner of entity and attribute is the main object of negation by reasoning. I have added this parenthetical expression in an effort to indicate what he might have meant.

the mode of apprehension of a path of purification—emptiness—and not merely to the objects of observation, which do indeed include all phenomena; and since the meaning of "final object of observation" is so limited, there is not much chance of a (well-educated) qualm that whatever is merely an object of observation by a path of purification would have to be the object of its mode of apprehension.

Gung-tang also complains that since factors imputed in the manner of entity and attribute (as established by way of their own character) are the main object of negation by reasoning, an intelligent person would not have **even the slightest** qualm, never mind **less** qualm, that it would be the final object of observation by a path of purification, that is to say, the final fact that is being established by reasoning. This part of his objection must be directed not at the Second Dalai Lama, who says that "such does not need to be analyzed with respect to imputational natures," but at Jam-ȳang-shay-b̄a who says:[401]

> There is a **greater** likelihood of qualms that other-powered natures would be final objects of observation of a path of purification extinguishing obstructions [than that imputational natures would be], and, therefore, the qualm has to be eliminated with respect to other-powered natures, there not being **any such great** qualm concerning imputational natures that needs to be eliminated.

The Second Dalai Lama, B̄el-jor-hlün-drup, and Paṇ-chen S̄ö-nam-drak-b̄a all explain that there is **no** such qualm about imputational natures; it is Jay-d̄zün Chö-ḡyi-gye̱l-tsen's innovation to speak of there being a **possibility**, and Jam-ȳang-shay-b̄a's innovation to speak of there being **less** qualm with respect to imputational natures.[a]

In drawing out the meaning of Gung-tang's position, A-ku L̄o-drö-gya-tso[402] argues that there could not be **any** qualm that imputational natures might be the final object of observation by a path of purification, because D̄zong-ka-b̄a (*Emptiness in Mind-Only,* 89) clearly says that imputational natures cannot be such:

> However, in the context of refuting a misconception, other-powered natures are posited as ultimate-non-natures due to not being objects of observation of purification, whereas imputational factors are not posited [as ultimate-non-natures].

---

[a] Jik-may-dam-chö-gya-tso (*Port of Entry,* 189.6) reports that Tsül-kang Lek-b̄a-dön-drup speaks of levels of difficulty in generating such a qualm but does not explain what makes the one easier to generate and the other more difficult. Pa-bong-ka-b̄a's *Brief Notes on Jo-ni Paṇḍita's Lectures* (412.3) says that there are greater qualms about other-powered natures because they are truly established and are objects of observation of a path of purification; he thereby suggests that there would be lesser qualms about imputational natures, but he does not explain how such would occur.

and (*Emptiness in Mind-Only,* 89):

> When one understands that obstructions are purified through meditation observing other-powered natures' emptiness of the imputational factor [—for example, through meditating on other-powered natures' emptiness of being established by way of their own character as the referents of words and of conceptual consciousnesses—], there arises the qualm that since, in that case, [the pure exalted wisdom] must also observe the other-powered natures that are the substrata [of the quality of emptiness, those other-powered natures] also would be objects of observation of purification, due to which they would be ultimates. [Thus, such a qualm needs to be alleviated with respect to other-powered natures.] However, such a qualm **does not occur** with respect to imputational factors.

Dzong-ka-ba clearly says that there is **no** such qualm about imputational natures.[a] Using this reasoning, one of Jay-dzün Chö-gyi-gyel-tsen's followers, Day-lek-nyi-ma,[403] maintains that because a path consciousness directly realizing the thoroughly established nature that is other-powered natures' emptiness of the imputational nature does not observe the imputational nature **that is the object of negation**, the discriminative would not have the qualm that such an imputational nature would be an object of observation by a path of purification, but it is not that the discriminative would not have qualms that imputational natures **in general** would be objects of observation of a path of purification. For as Jay-dzün Chö-gyi-gyel-tsen explains,[b] there are paths of purification that observe imputational natures (such as uncompounded space) in the process of realizing that imputational natures are empty of a self of phenomena.

Gung-tang's analysis, with A-ku Lo-drö-gya-tso's clarifications, seems to be devastating, but it must be recognized that the Second Dalai Lama et al. are seeking to explain Dzong-ka-ba's thought, and it seems to me that Gung-tang's criticism applies equally to what Dzong-ka-ba says. Gung-tang and A-ku Lo-drö-gya-tso (despite being followers of Jam-yang-shay-ba who frames the qualm as the Second Dalai Lama does[c]) find more clarity in the opinion of

[a] Jik-may-dam-chö-gya-tso (*Port of Entry,* 190.4) points out that in the textbook literature of the Jang-dzay College of Gan-den Monastic University, it is said that imputational natures are ultimate-non-natures and that in Jam-yang-shay-ba's *Notes* (315.3) both modes of ultimate-non-natures are posited with respect to each and every phenomenon. Indirectly indicating his disapproval of these positions, Jik-may-dam-chö-gya-tso politely calls for analysis of them in the light of Dzong-ka-ba's statement here that imputational natures are not posited as ultimate-non-natures.

[b] He says, "An exalted wisdom—purifying the obstructions to omniscience—that realizes that imputational natures are not established by way of their own character as the referents of conceptual consciousnesses observes imputational natures." For the reference and more context, see p. 355.

[c] A-ku Lo-drö-gya-tso (99.5) says that Jam-yang-shay-ba does not draw out the point in

Jam-ȳang-shay-b̄a's predecessor, Gung-ru Chö-jung, whose opinion is that the qualm would come from Proponents of the Middle viewing the tenet of the Mind-Only School that other-powered natures are truly established as objects of observation of a path of purification and hence, from the viewpoint of the Middle Way School, would have to be final objects of observation of a path of purification. It is clear that Gung-tang's and A-ku L̄o-drö-gya-tso's scholastic loyalty to Jam-ȳang-shay-b̄a did not prevent creative and decisive criticism.

Issue #138: Is a qualm a doubt?

As was detailed earlier (335, #131), Gung-tang, though primarily following Jam-ȳang-shay-b̄a's textbook literature, revives Gung-ru Chö-jung's explanation that the qualm that the *Sūtra Unraveling the Thought* is countering when it says that other-powered natures are ultimate-non-natures is generated in Autonomists and Consequentialists. Tsay-d̄en-hla-ram-b̄a,[a] a Mongolian scholar following the textbooks of Jay-d̄zün Chö-ḡyi-gyel-tsen of the Jay College of S̄e-ra and critic of Gung-tang, objects to Gung-ru Chö-jung's and Gung-tang's opinion.

Tsay-d̄en-hla-ram-b̄a takes a "qualm"[b] to be a "doubt"[c] and rightly says that Autonomists and Consequentialists have decided[404]—and thus have no doubts—that for the Mind-Only School truly established other-powered natures are objects of observation of a path of purification and that a truly established thoroughly established nature is the object of the mode of apprehension of a path of purification. Also, he rightly says that the Autonomists and the Consequentialists one-pointedly hold that once truly established other-powered natures are objects of observation of a path of purification, they could not be anything but final objects of observation of a path of purification and be able to bear reasoned analysis. Tsay-d̄en-hla-ram-b̄a concludes that, therefore, it would seem that Autonomists and Consequentialists could not have any "qualms," that is, doubts, that for the Proponents of Mind-Only other-powered natures

all its clarity, as does Gung-ru Chö-jung. On this issue, Gung-tang's *Difficult Points,* even though cryptic, is much more refined that his *Annotations;* A-ku L̄o-drö-gya-tso's lucid exposition (98.3-99.3) of Gung-tang's meaning is very helpful.

[a] As reported and refuted in A-ku L̄o-drö-gya-tso's *Precious Lamp,* 101.5-102.5. Jik-may-dam-chö-gya-tso (*Port of Entry,* 190.6-191.1) reports that Tsay-d̄en-hla-ram-b̄a gives "quite a number of reasons" (*rgyu mtshan mang tsam*) why the qualm would not arise in Autonomists and Consequentialists, but he does not list them, and I have not been able to locate Tsay-d̄en-hla-ram-b̄a's text. Jik-may-dam-chö-gya-tso reports that in the *Clearing Away Mental Darkness* Sha-m̄ar Ge-dün-d̄en-dzin-gya-tso says that Tsay-d̄en-hla-ram-b̄a's reasons are not much to the point; he also refers his readers to A-ku L̄o-drö-gya-tso's *Precious Lamp* for a defense of the position that the qualm would arise in Autonomists and Consequentialists; the latter is utilized in this discussion.

[b] *dogs pa.*

[c] *the tshom.*

would have to be final objects of observation of a path of purification. This is how he criticizes Gung-tang and hence Gung-tang's source, Gung-ru Chö-jung.

A-ku Lo-drö-gya-tso[405] decisively responds that Tsay-den-hla-ram-ba has confused qualms and doubts. The qualm that the Autonomists and Consequentialists have on this occasion is a **uni-directional conception** that such indeed would be the case for the Proponents of Mind-Only, and the sūtra is dispelling the Autonomists' and Consequentialists' thought that the Proponents of Mind-Only have such a fault. Doubt, on the other hand, requires a **two**-pointedness of mind, wondering whether a topic is this way or that way. Dzong-ka-ba himself (*Emptiness in Mind-Only,* 89) says that the qualm here is a misconception;[a] he does not say that it is a doubt:

> If [something] were posited as [an ultimate-non-nature] merely through not being an object of observation of purification, that would be true [that is, imputational natures also would have to be posited as ultimate-non-natures]. However, in the context of refuting a misconception, other-powered natures are posited as ultimate-non-natures due to not being objects of observation of purification, whereas imputational factors are not posited [as ultimate-non-natures].

Since Tsay-den-hla-ram-ba is attempting to explain Dzong-ka-ba's position, the citation is devastating.

Tsay-den-hla-ram-ba's purpose in refuting Gung-ru Chö-jung and Gung-tang is to support Ge-u-tsang's explanation of the qualm. Though Tsay-den-hla-ram-ba's attack is seriously flawed, it strikes me that, despite the esthetic elegance of Gung-ru Chö-jung's, Gung-tang's, and A-ku Lo-drö-gya-tso's position, their reading need not be the only position, for they have not shown any reasons why the holder of the qualm being answered here **must** be so well educated about the fact that in the *Sūtra Unraveling the Thought* the thoroughly established nature is a mere absence, a mere elimination of an object of negation. Though their explanation fits in well with Dzong-ka-ba's highly developed emphasis on the Mind-Only School's assertion of other-powered natures as being established by way of their own character, this does not appear to be a topic emphasized in the sūtra at this particular point. It seems to me that this sūtra passage that posits other-powered natures, and not imputational natures, as ultimate-non-natures can be seen as emphasizing the frequently reiterated point that other-powered natures are not the ultimate—they are not their own final mode of subsistence. Also, since beings usually conceive not just the mind but any other-powered nature to be its own real nature, it is relevant to emphasize, at least for beginners, that each and every other-powered nature is not its own ultimate.

Indeed, Gung-tang, in a surprising about-face, makes this very point when

[a] *log rtog.*

he explains the reason behind Buddha's positing other-powered natures as ultimate-non-natures. After having striven so hard to establish that the qualm that is being alleviated is a highly educated philosophical response to Mind-Only tenets, he reverses himself and indicates a far more basic meaning behind Buddha's identification.[406] He explains that Buddha's teaching the first mode of positing the ultimate-non-nature—that is, that other-powered natures are without the nature of being the ultimate—is for the sake of trainees' understanding the fact that they must delineate the second mode of positing the ultimate-non-nature, specifically the thoroughly established nature that is the ultimate-non-nature. For it is necessary to desist from adhering to the present mode of appearance as if it were the mode of subsistence of things and necessary to examine the meaning of emptiness, the actual mode of being of things. Gung-tang describes the plight of cyclic existence as being based on untrained assent to the false mode of appearance of phenomena and offers a straightforwardly simple and penetratingly profound exposition that Buddha taught the first mode of positing the ultimate-non-nature so that his listeners would realize that other-powered natures do not constitute the ultimate and thereby would be stimulated to seek the actual ultimate which Buddha is about to describe in the second mode of positing the ultimate-non-nature.

Gung-tang's moving description, infused with spiritual import, indicates that the qualm giving rise to the teaching of the first mode of positing the ultimate-non-nature does not have to be from persons who are familiar with the tenets of the sūtra (despite his own earlier indication to the contrary). Moreover, from contemporary non-Tibetan presentations of the thoroughly established nature that identify the ultimate as a purified version of the other-powered nature,[a] we can see that the sūtra's clear statements that the thoroughly established nature is a mere selflessness are still being ignored; thus, the qualm that other-powered natures are ultimates needs, also today, to be addressed by underlining the import of Buddha's presentation of the first mode of positing the ultimate-non-nature—other-powered natures are not final objects of observation of a path of purification and hence are not ultimates.

[a] This is why they translate *parinispanna* (*yongs grub*) not as "thoroughly established" but as "consummated."

19. Ramifications

Three pivotal points have surfaced in the discussion of why Buddha singled out other-powered natures as ultimate-non-natures. We have seen that:

1. Other-powered natures such as pots, bodies, and minds are not the ultimate.
2. The ultimate, or thoroughly established nature, is a mere absence of the imputational nature in other-powered natures.
3. Existent imputational natures such as uncompounded space are also not the ultimate, but there is less qualm that they might be the ultimate and thus were not singled out to be described as "ultimate-non-natures."

Existent Imputational Natures as Bases of Emptiness

Issue #139: If the three natures include all phenomena, what is uncompounded space?

The problem is:

- The *Sūtra Unraveling the Thought* speaks of other-powered natures as being dependent-arisings—impermanent phenomena arisen from causes and conditions—and as being the bases of the emptiness that is the thoroughly established nature.
- However, all phenomena—both the impermanent and the permanent—are empty of being established by way of their own character as the referents of conceptual consciousnesses and thus are bases of emptiness, and since permanent phenomena, such as uncompounded space, are not impermanent dependent-arisings, they cannot be other-powered natures even though they are bases of emptiness.
- Even though space—a mere absence of obstructive contact—is uncompounded and is used as an example, or analog, for understanding that the thoroughly established nature is a mere elimination of an object of negation, it itself is not a thoroughly established nature.
- The only category left in the all-inclusive division of phenomena into the three natures is that of imputational natures. Therefore, imputational natures are divided into the existent—including such permanent phenomena as uncompounded space and non-analytical cessations—and the non-existent.
- However, the *Sūtra Unraveling the Thought* does not make such a division explicitly, and thus it needs to be examined whether the *Sūtra* is even concerned with permanent phenomena such as uncompounded space. Is the

concern (fixation) with how to categorize such a phenomenon solely the creation of later scholars who are attempting to discover the seamlessly logical system of the sūtra?

There is no question that the **emphasis** on how to categorize phenomena such as uncompounded space that manifests in Indian, Chinese, and Tibetan treatises is not present in the *Sūtra Unraveling the Thought.* However, the sūtra itself mentions space at least six times,[407] and thus one would expect that it also would be taken into account in the doctrine of the three natures.

The sūtra first mentions space at the end of chapter four, the "Questions of Subhūti," as an example of the all-pervasiveness and non-difference of the ultimate:[408]

> Therefore, Subhūti, you should know by this form of explanation also that that which has a character that is everywhere of one taste is the ultimate. Subhūti, it is like this: For example, space is signless, non-conceptual, and non-increasing with respect to the manifold various aspects of instances of forms; it has the character of being of one taste everywhere. Similarly, with respect to the phenomena that have different characters, the ultimate is to be viewed as having a nature that is everywhere of one taste.

The same theme is repeated in chapter seven, the "Questions of Paramārthasamudgata":

> Just as, for example, space is distinguished by merely the naturelessness of form [that is, as being a mere absence of forms] and pervades everywhere, so the ultimate-non-nature is to be viewed as distinguished by the selflessness of phenomena and as pervading everything.

Near the end of the same chapter, the all-pervasiveness of space is used to exemplify the presence of Buddha's teaching on the ultimate that occurs even in all of his non-literal teachings requiring interpretation that do not, on the surface, appear to be directed toward the ultimate:[409]

> For example, space is everywhere of one taste and also does not obstruct activities. Similarly, this definitive teaching by the One-Gone-Thus, stemming from the naturelessness of phenomena through to phenomena being naturally passed beyond sorrow, is of one taste in all sūtras of interpretable meaning. It also does not obstruct any effort with regard to the Hearer Vehicle, the Solitary Realizer Vehicle, or the Great Vehicle.

That space is used as an example not just for the rarefied topic of the ultimate but also for how the **teaching** of the ultimate pervades all of Buddha's other teachings suggests that it is a well-known example.

In the eighth chapter,[410] the "Questions of Maitreya," space is mentioned twice in the context of the first of the four formless absorptions, the sphere of limitless space, a topic well-known in Buddhist meditative lore. In the ninth chapter, the "Questions of Avalokiteshvara," the example of space is turned around and used, not to exemplify something that pervades but something that is pervaded; here, it is an example for assumptions of bad states that are pervaded by a cloud-like Truth Body:[411]

> Because the great cloud-like Truth Body pervades and covers the collection of assumptions of bad states that are like space, the tenth ground is called the "Cloud of Doctrine."

These six mentions of space indicate that it is used fairly frequently as an example, but it is nowhere mentioned in a list of phenomena, nor is it explicitly ever said to be uncompounded. Still, that it is used this many times as an example indicates that it is a well-known phenomenon and should be taken into account in the division of all phenomena into the three natures. Also, the fact that it is described in the seventh chapter as a mere absence of forms strongly suggests that it is uncompounded.

We could speculate that the reason why space is never considered as a base of emptiness (which would raise the obvious point that it is not an other-powered nature and the resultant quandary of where it should be included among the three natures) is that the *Sūtra Unraveling the Thought* is primarily concerned with a practical doctrine of meditation on emptiness and thus concentrates, even exclusively, on other-powered natures as the bases with respect to which the emptiness of the non-existent imputational nature is to be realized. I do not offer this explanation as an excuse for philosophical sloppiness in the sūtra; rather, it provides a context for me to suggest, contrary to Ge-luk-b̄a scholars, that uncompounded space and other such permanent phenomena could be considered a sub-category of other-powered natures without inventing a category of existent imputational natures. The problem with doing this is that I must admit that uncompounded space, despite being **categorized** as an other-powered nature, neither is a dependent-arising nor is established by way of its own character—salient features of other-powered natures. However, it **is** a basis of emptiness, this being another primary feature of other-powered natures, and thus I might claim that space is not just categorized as an other-powered nature while actually being something else; rather, it **is** an actual other-powered nature. In this way, because of being bases of emptiness, space and so forth could be other-powered natures without having to be dependent-arisings or established by way of their own character.

In my scenario, imputational natures would be only non-existent factors such as an object's being established by way of its own character as the referent of a conceptual consciousness and thus are not objects of knowledge and hence not existents—they are only factors of exaggerated adherence. Indeed, this reflects an important usage of the term "imputational nature" in the *Sūtra Unraveling the Thought.* Still, I would have to admit that then the three natures would not be a division of objects of knowledge, that is, existents, since imputational natures would not include any existents. Also, I would find it difficult to explain the sūtra's own reference to deprecating imputational natures, since if they do not exist, how could they be deprecated? The *Sūtra Unraveling the Thought* (*Emptiness in Mind-Only,* 95) says:[412]

> Even though they have interest in that doctrine [of the profound thoroughly established nature], they do not understand, just as it is, the profound reality that I have set forth with a thought behind it. With respect to the meaning of these doctrines, they adhere to the terms as only literal: "All these phenomena are only natureless. All these phenomena are only unproduced, only unceasing, only quiescent from the start, only naturally thoroughly passed beyond sorrow." Due to that, they acquire the view that all phenomena do not exist and the view that [establishment of objects by way of their own][413] character does not exist. Moreover, having acquired the view of nihilism and the view of the non-existence of [establishment of objects by way of their own] character, they deprecate all phenomena in terms of all of the characters—deprecating the imputational character of phenomena and also deprecating the other-powered character and thoroughly established character of phenomena.

Perhaps I could suggest that the sūtra means that imagination of the non-existent could not occur without an existent base that is being imagined to have a false status.

Another problem with my notion that uncompounded space and so forth are actual other-powered natures, in the sense that they are bases of emptiness, is that thoroughly established natures—since they themselves are also empty of being established by way of their own character as the referents of conceptual consciousnesses—are bases of emptinesses and hence would have to be actual other-powered natures, thereby raising the question of why there are three natures and not just one. Perhaps, however, I could consider "other-powered nature" here as referring to an object's own other-powered nature, which—as we will see below in the case of existent imputational natures and thoroughly established natures—does not have to be an **actual** other-powered nature. But this has problems too, since thoroughly established natures would be ultimate-non-natures, in the sense of not being the ultimate, and hence would absurdly not be ultimate-non-natures, in the sense of being the ultimate.

By seeing the difficulties of my innovative scenario we can appreciate why Ḏzong-ka-ḇa and his followers have opted for creatively finding a category called existent imputational natures as if it already exists in the *Sūtra Unraveling the Thought.* Their gambit, like mine, far from eliminating all problems, opens up others. Let us consider the problems stemming from their solution.

Issue #140: Is there an actual *other-powered nature of uncompounded space?*

Since the three natures are both (1) a rubric for classifying phenomena—each phenomenon being only one from among the three—and (2) a rubric for understanding the multiple natures of individual phenomena, there must be a way to posit the other-powered nature even of uncompounded space. In Gung-tang's consideration of this problem,[414] he first scrutinizes D̄ra-d̄i Ge-s̄hay Rin-chen-dön-drup's reformulation of the basic point of this section. D̄ra-d̄i Ge-s̄hay frames it this way:

> With respect to the subjects [of this syllogism], the other-powered natures of all phenomena, there is a reason why they are called ultimate-non-natures, because they are called such due to the fact that the final object of observation that extinguishes obstructions and is with [each and every] phenomenon is the ultimate and they [that is, other-powered natures] are not established as such a [final] object of observation.

Though in an earlier work, his *Annotations*,[415] Gung-tang points out that D̄ra-d̄i Ge-s̄hay's framing of the basic point does not differ from Jam-ȳang-shay-b̄a's, in his *Difficult Points* he questions in what sense Rin-chen-dön-drup is speaking of the "other-powered natures of **all** phenomena."[a] Gung-tang reports that many earlier scholars posit an **actual** other-powered nature with respect to all phenomena, compounded and uncompounded, by considering a valid consciousness cognizing uncompounded space, for instance, to be the other-powered nature of uncompounded space. Since a valid consciousness cognizing uncompounded space is an impermanent phenomenon produced from causes and conditions, these scholars are able to posit an **actual** other-powered nature even with respect to permanent phenomena such as uncompounded space, which itself is a mere absence of obstructive contact and thus not produced from causes and conditions. Gung-tang considers this position to be invalid because, as will be explained later in this chapter, the phenomenon itself must be posited as its own other-powered nature even if it is not an **actual** other-powered nature.

Gung-tang[416] suspects that D̄ra-d̄i Ge-s̄hay holds that a valid consciousness apprehending any permanent phenomenon (except emptiness) is the other-powered nature of that phenomenon because D̄ra-d̄i Ge-s̄hay is a follower of

---

[a] Gung-tang himself posits only impermanent phenomena produced from causes and conditions as *actual* other-powered natures. For A-ku L̄o-drö-gya-tso's brilliant expansion of the etymology of "other-powered" even to uncompounded, permanent phenomena, see *Reflections on Reality*, 180-183.

Jay-d̄zün Chö-ḡyi-gyel-tsen, the textbook author of the Jay College of S̄e-ra Monastic University, who holds such a position. For instance, Jay-d̄zün Chö-ḡyi-gyel-tsen says:[a]

> In the explicit teaching of the *Sūtra Unraveling the Thought*, when the thoroughly established nature of compounded and uncompounded phenomena is delineated, **only the other-powered natures** of those [phenomena] are taken as bases of emptiness, whereupon the thoroughly established nature that is the selflessness of phenomena is delineated. Hence, since an exalted wisdom of purification must observe other-powered natures, which are bases of emptiness, other-powered natures become objects of observation [of a path] of purification, due to which there is the greater qualm that other-powered natures are ultimates. However, it is not that in general such a qualm is never generated with respect to imputational natures because an exalted wisdom—purifying the obstructions to omniscience—that realizes that imputational natures are not established by way of their own character as the referents of conceptual consciousnesses observes imputational natures.... The *Sūtra Unraveling the Thought* does not explicitly take those [imputational natures] as bases of emptiness; ...[rather] **the other-powered natures of those** [imputational natures] are taken as bases of emptiness, whereupon their emptinesses are explicitly delineated.[b]

---

[a] Jay-d̄zün Chö-ḡyi-gyel-tsen's *General-Meaning Commentary*, 15b.6-16b.3; cited in A-ku L̄o-drö-gya-tso's *Precious Lamp*, 99.2. Jay-d̄zün Chö-ḡyi-gyel-tsen (14b.6) titles this general section *gzhan dbang don dam* ***par*** *ngo bo nyid med pa bshad pa*, whereas he himself later uses the more common expression *gzhan dbang don dam* ***pa*** *ngo bo nyid med pa bshad pa*. D̄zong-ka-b̄a uses the former term (minus *bshad pa*) once when he (*Emptiness in Mind-Only*, 239) says:

> Since imputational phenomena are not established by way of their own character, they are non-natures ultimately [that is, are without the nature of existing ultimately or by way of their own character]. **Since other-powered phenomena are not established as the ultimate which is the object of purification, they are non-natures ultimately [that is, are without the nature of being the ultimate].** Also, since thoroughly established phenomena are the ultimate [which is the object observed by a path of purification] and also are the non-existence of phenomena as entities of self, they are non-natures ultimately [that is, are without the nature of that ultimacy which is the self of phenomena].

[b] Literally, the text reads:

> *Objection:* It [absurdly] follows that the *Sūtra Unraveling the Thought* does not explicitly delineate the emptiness of uncompounded phenomena such as imputational natures because it does not explicitly delineate the emptiness of those within explicitly taking them as bases of emptiness. You have asserted the reason.
>
> *Response:* [That the *Sūtra Unraveling the Thought* does not explicitly delineate the emptiness of uncompounded phenomena such as imputational natures within

By taking this tack, Jay-d̄zün Chö-ḡyi-gyel-tsen is able to hold that although the *Sūtra Unraveling the Thought* does not explicitly take imputational natures as bases of emptiness, it nevertheless explicitly delineates the emptiness of imputational natures, since it explicitly takes their other-powered natures as bases of emptiness. For him, there is an **actual** other-powered nature of uncompounded space, this being a valid cognition apprehending uncompounded space.

Despite Jay-d̄zün Chö-ḡyi-gyel-tsen's seemingly clear statement that the *Sūtra Unraveling the Thought* does not explicitly take imputational natures as bases of emptiness, one of his followers, S̄er-s̄hül L̄o-sang-pün-tsok,[417] maintains that Jay-d̄zün Chö-ḡyi-gyel-tsen did not mean to say this at all. He points to the fact that in D̄zong-ka-b̄a's writings it is said again and again that in both the Mind-Only and the Middle Way schools, when the selflessness of phenomena is delineated, it must be demonstrated with respect to those bases about which sentient beings adhere to self—"self" in this case meaning establishment by way of the object's own character as the referent of terms and conceptual consciousnesses—and sentient beings do indeed adhere to uncompounded phenomena as being established this way. Therefore, S̄er-s̄hül claims that when Jay-d̄zün Chö-ḡyi-gyel-tsen says that "**only** the other-powered natures of those [phenomena] are taken as bases of emptiness," the word "only" merely eliminates that other-powered natures are **not** taken as bases of emptinesses and that it does not eliminate that uncompounded phenomena are taken as their own bases of emptinesses.[418] Even if we were to accept this rewriting of that part of Jay-d̄zün Chö-ḡyi-gyel-tsen's explanation, we would have to point out that S̄er-s̄hül L̄o-sang-pün-tsok does not address Jay-d̄zün Chö-ḡyi-gyel-tsen's even clearer statement that "The *Sūtra Unraveling the Thought* does not explicitly take those [imputational natures] as bases of emptiness." S̄er-s̄hül's creative rewriting of Jay-d̄zün Chö-ḡyi-gyel-tsen's statement indicates how seriously he takes Gung-tang's criticisms of this exposition of the thoroughly established nature of uncompounded phenomena.

Tsay-d̄en-hla-ram-b̄a,[419] another follower of Jay-d̄zün Chö-ḡyi-gyel-tsen, offers the nuanced exposition that when one delineates the final reality—that is, the emptiness or thoroughly established nature—of uncompounded space, space itself and not some other phenomenon is the **actual** basis of that emptiness.[a] However, he posits that uncompounded space must have an actual other-powered nature as its **root** basis of emptiness.[b] This is because every uncompounded phenomenon has an other-powered nature that is its basis of

explicitly taking them as bases of emptiness] does not entail [that the *Sūtra Unraveling the Thought* does not explicitly delineate the emptiness of those] because on [this] occasion in the *Sūtra Unraveling the Thought* their emptiness is explicitly delineated within their other-powered natures being taken as bases of emptiness.

a *dngos kyi stong gzhi.*

b *rtsa ba'i stong gzhi.*

imputation, and for uncompounded space this is an appearance of betweenness,[a] without which uncompounded space and hence its emptiness could not be apprehended. He proffers the distinctions that:

- Although a compounded other-powered nature's emptiness of the imputational nature is posited as the thoroughly established nature of that compounded phenomenon, an uncompounded phenomenon's other-powered nature's emptiness of the imputational nature is not to be posited as the thoroughly established nature of that uncompounded phenomenon.
- Rather, an uncompounded phenomenon's **root** other-powered nature's emptiness of the imputational nature is posited as the thoroughly established nature of that uncompounded phenomenon.
- Although the real nature of uncompounded space is the real nature that is **with its** other-powered nature, it is not the real nature **of** the other-powered nature of uncompounded space.[b]

In order to make these distinctions and yet defend Jay-d̄zün Chö-ḡyi-gyel-tsen, he has to claim that the opposite statement in Jay-d̄zün Chö-ḡyi-gyel-tsen's *General-Meaning Commentary*—that the real nature of uncompounded space is the real nature **of** the other-powered nature of uncompounded space—is merely a misprint.

Gung-tang[420] frames his criticism as a response to a sixteenth-century follower of Jay-d̄zün Chö-ḡyi-gyel-tsen, Gom-day-nam-ka-gyel-tsen,[c] as well as others. According to Gom-day-nam-ka-gyel-tsen, the reason why there is less chance of having the qualm that imputational natures might be final objects of observation of a path of purification is that the *Sūtra Unraveling the Thought* **explicitly**[421] takes only other-powered natures as bases of emptiness and does not take uncompounded phenomena such as imputational natures as bases of emptiness. His opinion reflects a literal reading of Jay-d̄zün Chö-ḡyi-gyel-tsen's opinion cited just above, unlike Tsay-d̄en-hla-ram-b̄a's and S̄er-s̄hül L̄o-sang-pün-tsok's creative re-writings.

Gung-tang strongly objects to Gom-day-nam-ka-gyel-tsen's reading as being a case of having lost the point of this section of the *Sūtra Unraveling the Thought*, for uncompounded phenomena other than emptinesses are included in the eighteen constituents, and the sūtra applies the threefold explanation of an imputational nature, an other-powered nature, and a thoroughly established nature to the eighteen constituents. The sūtra, after explaining this threefold division and the corresponding three non-natures with respect to the mental and physical aggregates, says, "Such is also likewise the case with respect to each of the eighteen constituents." Thus, from among the eighteen constituents, the

---

[a] *bar snang.*

[b] *nam mkha'i chos nyid de'i gzhan dbang gi steng gi chos nyid yin yang nam mkha'i gzhan dbang gi chos nyid min.*

[c] *sgom sde nam mkha' rgyal mtshan,* 1532-1592.

phenomena-constituent—which includes all permanent phenomena—is to be taken as a basis of emptiness, and the emptiness that is the negation of the imputational nature (which is the phenomena-constituent's establishment by way of its own character as the referent of a conceptual consciousness) is its thoroughly established nature. Since this is the way that a phenomenon is treated as a basis of emptiness, the *Sūtra Unraveling the Thought* does indeed explicitly treat uncompounded phenomena as bases of emptiness. Gung-tang's point is well taken.

According to him, the phenomenon itself is a basis of emptiness, and in this sense the phenomenon itself is called an "other-powered nature" even if it is not an **actual** other-powered nature produced from causes and conditions. If, as Gom-day-nam-ka-gyel-tsen wants, the sūtra is taken as meaning that **actual** other-powered natures related with uncompounded phenomena—that is, the valid consciousnesses apprehending them—are to be taken as bases of emptiness, then the same absurdly would have to be applied to all the remaining eighteen constituents, in which case it would have to be said that the sūtra takes none of them themselves as bases of emptiness. For the other-powered nature of even compounded phenomena such as pots and so forth absurdly would have to be the valid consciousnesses apprehending them. This is how, according to Gung-tang, Gom-day-nam-ka-gyel-tsen and so forth have lost the meaning of this section of the sūtra.

I find Gung-tang's refutation profoundly contextual and to the point; the seventh chapter of the *Sūtra Unraveling the Thought* is clear about how to treat each and every phenomenon in terms of the three natures. The phenomenon itself is to be considered its other-powered nature even though, indeed, this presents difficulties with respect to permanent phenomena, which are not produced from causes and conditions and thus do not fulfill the actual meaning of an "other-powered nature" as being dependently arisen from causes and conditions. However, rather than undermining this central presentation of the three natures of each phenomenon by positing some other, impermanent phenomenon as the other-powered nature of a permanent phenomenon—that is, the valid consciousness apprehending it—it is better to retain the more fundamental point that even uncompounded phenomena are their own other-powered natures by holding that they are not **actual** other-powered natures, which, by the sūtra's own definition, are necessarily produced from causes and conditions. For even uncompounded phenomena fulfill a good deal of the etymology of "other-powered nature" as found in Asaṅga's *Summary of the Great Vehicle:*[422]

> Why are they called "other-powered natures"? Since they are produced from their respective seeds that are predisposing latencies, they are under the other-influence of conditions.[423] Having been produced, their entities cannot remain more than an instant. Hence, they are called "other-powered."

Asaṅga indicates that other-powered natures are not self-powered or autonomous for two reasons:

1. because they are produced under the influence of causes and conditions—specifically the seeds of perception that give rise to them—these being other than themselves
2. because they do not have the power to remain even for a second instant.

A-ku L̄o-drö-gya-tso[424] adapts these two points to permanent phenomena by drawing a parallel between impermanent and permanent phenomena:

1. Even though uncompounded phenomena are not **produced** from causes, they are factors of appearance that **dawn** to the mind through the force of the maturation of internal, predisposing latencies.
2. Even though uncompounded phenomena do not **depend** on conditions that produce them, they must **abide in dependence** upon their respective final reality[a] just as clouds depend upon the sky. The thoroughly established nature of uncompounded phenomena is their final reality that immutably serves as their basis, and they themselves are posited as their own other-powered natures.

In a sense, therefore, uncompounded space is the "other-powered nature" of uncompounded space, for as Gung-tang[425] notes, the other-powered nature of sound has to be just sound—that is, sound alone is the other-powered nature of sound—even if the impermanence of sound does not have to be just sound. In the same way the other-powered nature of an uncompounded phenomenon can be said to be that very uncompounded phenomenon itself.

Issue #141: Is the real nature of an imputational nature not an emptiness?

As just explained, contrary to Jay-d̄zün Chö-ḡyi-gyel-tsen, Gung-tang concludes that since uncompounded phenomena are included in the eighteen constituents, which explicitly are among the bases with respect to which the thoroughly established nature is taught, the *Sūtra Unraveling the Thought* explicitly teaches the emptiness of both compounded and uncompounded phenomena. This fact also invalidates the opinion of an unnamed scholar (whom Gung-ru Chö-jung and Jam-ȳang-shay-b̄a[426] cite and refute) that the reason why an ultimate-non-nature is set forth with respect to other-powered natures and not with respect to imputational natures is that the real nature of other-powered natures is an emptiness whereas the real nature of imputational natures is not. For, once the *Sūtra Unraveling the Thought* posits a thoroughly established nature with respect to the eighteen constituents, among which is a category called

---

[a] *chos nyid, dharmatā.*

"phenomena" that includes all permanent phenomena such as uncompounded space, the real nature of such existent imputational natures must be a fully qualified emptiness. Jam-ȳang-shay-b̄a makes reference to the fact that Vasubandhu, in his commentary on Maitreya's *Differentiation of the Middle and the Extremes* speaks of the sixteen emptinesses, among which are the emptiness of non-effective (that is, permanent) things and the emptiness of the nature of non-effective things. Also, among the twenty emptinesses is an emptiness of the uncompounded. Therefore, the non-establishment of uncompounded phenomena by way of their own character as the referents of conceptual consciousnesses is a fully qualified emptiness, and thus the reason why the *Sūtra Unraveling the Thought* speaks of other-powered natures, and not imputational natures, as being ultimate-non-natures cannot be that the real nature of other-powered natures is emptiness whereas the real nature of imputational phenomena, that is, permanent phenomena, is not. As Jay-d̄zün Chö-ḡyi-gyel-tsen[427] concisely puts it, if something exists, its emptiness necessarily exists, and hence its real nature necessarily exists.

Issue #142: Does the real nature of uncompounded space fulfill the meaning of a real nature?

Jay-d̄zün Chö-ḡyi-gyel-tsen reports a more refined (but incorrect) notion that although a real nature of uncompounded phenomena exists, it does not fulfill the meaning of a real nature, in which case it has to be said that the real nature of imputational natures is not a real nature. In rejecting this attempt to get around the issue, Jay-d̄zün Chö-ḡyi-gyel-tsen draws the same absurd consequence that, if this were the case, then the eighteen and twenty emptinesses, which are determined by way of the phenomena that are empty—these including the uncompounded—would not be feasible.[428]

Issue #143: Since uncompounded space is not truly established but its emptiness is, why does D̄zong-ka-b̄a say that if the real nature of an object is truly established, the object also must be truly established?

The position that the real nature of an imputational nature is indeed an emptiness presents an interesting problem:

> Because an emptiness is truly established, an imputational nature such as uncompounded space, since it is the basis of an emptiness, also would (absurdly) have to be truly established.

Indeed, this is just what D̄zong-ka-b̄a seems to be saying in his *Explanation of (Nāgārjuna's) "Treatise on the Middle": Ocean of Reasoning,* when he says:[429]

> Both Proponents of Mind-Only and Proponents of the Middle agree with respect to this fact that when a real nature is truly established, the qualificand that is the substratum of it must be something that is truly established. This is because it is contradictory for a falsity to act as the basis of the truly established.

Ḏzong-ka-ḇa indicates that, in the Mind-Only and Middle Way systems, there must be an equivalency in terms of the presence of true existence or the absence of true existence between a phenomenon and its emptiness.

However, if this is to be taken at face value, then since in the Mind-Only School an emptiness is truly established, its basis—which, if we consider uncompounded space, is an imputational nature—would also have to be truly established. This has to be a reason why Paṇ-chen Sö-nam-drak-ḇa concludes that because we know that in the Mind-Only School an imputational nature does not truly exist (since the *Sūtra Unraveling the Thought* itself says, "Those [imputational characters] are characters posited by names and terminology and do not subsist by way of their own character,") an imputational nature cannot be the basis of its own emptiness, and, instead, a valid cognition apprehending it is the basis of the emptiness of an imputational nature.

Gung-ru Chö-jung,[430] however, creatively gets around Ḏzong-ka-ḇa's statement by maintaining that Ḏzong-ka-ḇa here uses the term "true establishment" to refer not to actual true establishment but to what is refuted in the respective systems of the Mind-Only and Middle Way schools. In this forced reading, Ḏzong-ka-ḇa "actually" is saying:

> According to the Mind-Only School, if an emptiness were established by way of its own character as the referent of a conceptual consciousness, then its basis would also have to be established by way of its own character as the referent of a conceptual consciousness.

This stinks of rank apologetic, since elsewhere in the same text Ḏzong-ka-ḇa says:

> The scholars of the Yogic Practice School also saw that for a truly existent thoroughly established nature the other-powered nature that is its basis must be truly existent.

Gung-tang[431] takes a different tack that smells but not so bad. He maintains that Ḏzong-ka-ḇa's reference is indeed to actual true establishment but is limited to the sphere of compounded phenomena, since it is admittedly the case that in the Mind-Only and Middle Way systems there is an equivalency in terms of the true existence or the absence of true existence between a compounded phenomenon and its emptiness, the former holding that both are truly established and the latter that they are not.

Taken either way, Ḏzong-ka-ḇa, at minimum, is not clear. Still, it strikes me as far better to attempt to explain away (or correct) Dzong-ka-ba's remark as either Gung-ru Chö-jung or Gung-tang do than to resort to asserting that permanent phenomena such as uncompounded space are not bases of their own emptiness.[432]

Jam-yang-shay-ba's Refutation of Gung-ru Chö-jung

Issue #144: Do Solitary Realizers comprehend that objects are not established by way of their own character as the referents of their respective conceptual consciousnesses?

Jam-yang-shay-ba's *Great Exposition of the Interpretable and the Definitive* owes much to Gung-ru Chö-jung's *Garland of White Lotuses* and can, in many respects, be considered an edited (and corrected) version of that text. For instance, although Jam-yang-shay-ba[433] agrees with Gung-ru Chö-jung (his predecessor as author of the textbook literature of the Go-mang College of Drebung) that the position that the real nature of imputational phenomena is not an emptiness is to be refuted, he criticizes points within Gung-ru Chö-jung's refutation. Jam-yang-shay-ba does not mention Gung-ru Chö-jung by name, probably to indicate respect for his scholarship, which A-ku Lo-drö-gya-tso[434] says was so good that Jam-yang-shay-ba used his commentary on Dzong-ka-ba's text as the basis for most of his own *Great Exposition of the Interpretable and the Definitive.* The delicacy of Jam-yang-shay-ba's situation can be seen in his saying:

> [These positions] will be analyzed by a lackadaisical one [that is, Jam-yang-shay-ba himself] through the kindness of the subtle paths of reasoning in the scriptures of the father, the foremost venerable Dzong-ka-ba, and his spiritual sons as well as the paths of reasoning in the scriptures of the great chariots of this [Mind-Only] system of the country of Superiors [India]. May those who possess analysis and investigation put aside partisanship and perceive this with fine intelligence.

Calling himself lazy, Jam-yang-shay-ba assumes a humble attitude and asks his readers—the scholars of Go-mang College—for an unbiased attitude open to criticism of their textbook literature.

Jam-yang-shay-ba's appeal is to calm reasoning, but the story of how his textbooks came to supplant those of Gung-ru Chö-jung shows it was done under pressure. The Mongol "King of Tibet," Hla-sang[a] Khan, who was a patron

[a] *hla bzang.*

of Jam-ȳang-shay-b̄a, murdered the regent and president Day-s̄i-s̄ang-gyay-gya-tso,[a] in 1706 just outside of Dre-b̄ung. It is reported[435] that he did so hurriedly because his lama, Jam-ȳang-shay-b̄a, was on his way to see him and he knew that the lama would not approve. Jam-yang-shay-ba, who had gone to Central Tibet at age twenty-one, became abbot of the Go-mang College of Dre-b̄ung Monastic University at age fifty-three. Six years later in 1707, just the next year after his patron, Hla-sang Khan, murdered the Regent, he returned to Am-do, where in 1710 he founded a new monastic university to the southeast of Ḡum-bum[b] Monastic University, which was built in 1588 at the site of D̄zong-ka-b̄a's birthplace. Jam-ȳang-shay-b̄a's new center of learning was called Dra-s̄hi-kyil. Not long after Jam-ȳang-shay-b̄a's return to Am-do, his textbook literature was adopted by Go-mang College due to pressure from Hla-sang Khan, thereby supplanting that of Gung-ru Chö-jung. It is reported[436] that his return to Am-do was to escape a hot situation at Go-mang due to the fact that he was trying to get his textbooks adopted.

Indeed, the subsequent adoption of his works by Go-mang was the result of pressure from the government headed by his patron, whose assassination of the Regent must have given Gung-ru Chö-jung's followers second thoughts, at minimum.[c] Jam-ȳang-shay-b̄a's situation, therefore, was both delicate and explosive. One would expect that the intense political and social allegiances associated with a scholar such as Jam-ȳang-shay-b̄a would have an effect on his assertions on particular topics. However, aside from the important fact that such activity promotes new and differing opinions, I cannot trace particular influences on specific points. One of the reasons why Jam-ȳang-shay-b̄a came to have great influence was undoubtedly his wide scholarship; indeed, it would be next to impossible for someone who decided mainly for political reasons to write such works as these to maintain sufficient interest to keep up the pretense.

To the point at hand: Gung-ru Chö-jung[d] frames his response to the position that the real nature of imputational phenomena is not an emptiness around a discussion of the path of seeing. The meditative equipoise of a path of

[a] *sde srid sangs rgyas rgya mtsho.*

[b] *sku 'bum.*

[c] It is widely known that the Fifth Dalai Lama tried to get his works adopted as the textbook literature of L̄o-s̄el-l̄ing College at Dre-b̄ung and that Paṇ-chen S̄ö-nam-drak-b̄a's textbooks were burned just outside one of the debating courtyards of Go-mang College. Two contemporary scholars have reported that monks of the L̄o-s̄el-l̄ing College even avoid walking near that spot. L̄o-s̄el-l̄ing nevertheless was able to keep from adopting the Fifth Dalai Lama's textbooks, which were ultimately adopted by the relatively insignificant Day-yang College of Dre-b̄ung.

[d] Gung-ru Chö-jung's *Garland of White Lotuses,* 31b.5-32a.3. Jam-ȳang-shay-b̄a (72.5-73.5) cites this passage accurately but helpfully emends ***gnyis*** *pa ma grub na* (*Garland of White Lotuses,* 32a.2) to ***gsum*** *pa ma grub na.* In the course of the citation Jam-ȳang-shay-b̄a makes three side comments that render the passage difficult to follow unless one has Gung-ru Chö-jung's text.

seeing is divided into three parts, an "uninterrupted path" that abandons acquired obstructions, a "path of release" that is the state of having abandoned those acquired obstructions, and a meditative equipoise of a path of seeing that is neither an uninterrupted path nor a path of release, such as meditative equipoise on emptiness again after an exalted wisdom subsequent to meditative equipoise. An uninterrupted path is so named because without interruption or interval a yogi immediately passes on to a path of release that is a condition of having been released from those obstructions.

The uninterrupted path of a path of seeing corresponds to phases called the eight forbearances, and the path of release corresponds to phases called the eight knowledges.

Chart 2: Sixteen Moments of Forbearance and Knowledge
(read from bottom to top)

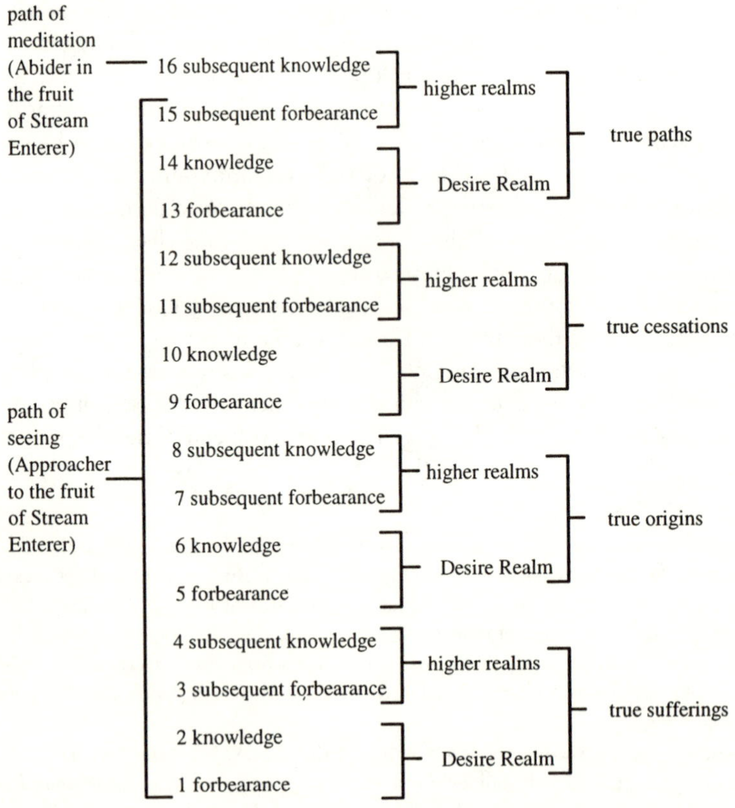

During the eight forbearances, the realization of emptiness is applied to objects and subjects—specifically to the four noble truths and the subjects that realize emptiness with respect to them. Through direct realization of the emptinesses that qualify these objects, acquired misconceptions with respect to the four noble truths are simultaneously abandoned. The initial direct realization of emptiness causes the acquired (not the innate) conception of self to be abandoned simultaneously with respect to true sufferings (such as an afflicted being wandering in cyclic existence), true origins (such as a consciousness conceiving self), true cessations (such as the absence of an affliction brought about by cultivation of its antidote), and true paths (such as a consciousness realizing emptiness). The emptiness of the wisdom consciousness cognizing these is also realized at the same time; this realization is nevertheless called "subsequent" because in the lower systems of tenets there is a step-by-step procedure, even though in the Mind-Only School an actual temporal sequence does not occur.

The eight knowledges, the knowledge that those acquired conceptions of self have been abandoned, are the path of release. The presentation of eight parts to the uninterrupted path and eight parts to the path of release details phenomena, qualified by emptiness, that a yogi realizes to be empty. Therefore, Gung-ru Chö-jung, in response to the position that the real nature of imputational phenomena is not an emptiness, introduces the topic of what sort of emptiness a Solitary Realizer would realize on the uninterrupted path of a path of seeing in that part called doctrinal forbearance with respect to true cessations.[a] He chooses true cessations as the reference because they are imputational phenomena,[b] and he says that, if the real nature of imputational phenomena is not an emptiness, then this phase of a Solitary Realizer's path of seeing would not have any emptiness to realize.[c] He gives three reasons, all of which Jam-ȳang-shay-b̄a finds objectionable. The first is:

> If the real nature of imputational phenomena is not an emptiness, then true cessations' emptiness of being established by way of their own

[a] *'gog pa chos bzod.*

[b] That this is the reason is confirmed by Jay-d̄zün Chö-ḡyi-gyel-tsen's *General-Meaning Commentary* (15a.6), "It [absurdly] follows that the emptiness of a true cessation is not an emptiness because the emptiness of an imputational nature is not an emptiness." Nevertheless, I am puzzled by the fact that, as will be seen in the next chapter (422), both Jay-d̄zün Chö-ḡyi-gyel-tsen and Jam-ȳang-shay-b̄a hold that in the Mind-Only School true cessations are thusnesses and hence emptinesses; it would seem, therefore, that true cessations are thoroughly established natures and not imputational natures. For a clear statement by Jay-d̄zün Chö-ḡyi-gyel-tsen to this effect, see his *General-Meaning Commentary,* 17b.1).

[c] Jay-d̄zün Chö-ḡyi-gyel-tsen's *General-Meaning Commentary* (15a.6-15a.7) presents this same reasoning but applies it not to Solitary Realizers but to Great Vehicle practitioners. This may suggest that Gung-ru Chö-jung's commentary pre-dates Jay-d̄zün Chö-ḡyi-gyel-tsen's.

> character as the referents of conceptual consciousnesses would absurdly not be what is realized by Solitary Realizers at this point.

Gung-ru Chö-jung thereby indicates that Solitary Realizers do indeed realize that objects are not established by way of their own character as the referents of conceptual consciousnesses. Jam-ȳang-shay-b̄a cogently objects that since such non-establishment is a selflessness of phenomena, Solitary Realizers would, if Gung-ru Chö-jung were right, be mainly abandoning the subtle conception of a self of phenomena. In that case, when Solitary Realizers reached the path of no more learning, they absurdly would have abandoned the subtle conception of a self of phenomena, in which case they would be Buddha Superiors. However, this is impossible since they are of the Lesser Vehicle; Solitary Realizers who are definite in their lineage do not realize the subtle selflessness of phenomena, as is attested in numerous sources.

According to Jam-ȳang-shay-b̄a, in the Mind-Only School both Hearers and Solitary Realizers simply realize at this point that true cessations are empty of being substantially existent in the sense of being self-sufficiently existent. This is because they are in one-pointed meditative equipoise on the selflessness of persons with respect to all phenomena. Jam-ȳang-shay-b̄a adds that the assertions that Hearers and Solitary Realizers on the uninterrupted path of a path of seeing do not differ in terms of the obstructions that are their objects of abandonment and in terms of the selflessness that is being realized is made not only in the Mind-Only School but also by the Kashmiri Proponents of the Great Exposition, the Sūtra School, and the Sūtra Autonomy School.[a] Thereby, he establishes that, contrary to Gung-ru Chö-jung's opinion, Solitary Realizers do not realize the subtle selflessness of phenomena.

Jam-ȳang-shay-b̄a politely communicates the point that Gung-ru Chö-jung has made the egregious error of treating the path-structure in the Mind-Only School in the format of the Yogic Autonomy Middle Way School, in which:

- Hearers mainly meditate on the selflessness of persons.
- Solitary Realizers mainly meditate on a coarse selflessness of phenomena (the absence of a difference of entity of subject and object and a phenomenon's not being established by way of its own character as the referent of a conceptual consciousness).
- Bodhisattvas mainly mediate on the subtle selflessness of phenomena, which is their emptiness of true existence.[b]

---

[a] To establish these points, Jam-ȳang-shay-b̄a (76.1-76.6) decisively cites passages from the *Presentation of Tenets* by the Second Dalai Lama Gen-dün-gya-tso and from D̄zong-ka-b̄a's *Great Exposition of Secret Mantra.* For the latter, see Tsong-ka-pa, *Tantra in Tibet,* (London: George Allen and Unwin, 1977), 93, last paragraph.

[b] For Ḡön-chok-jik-may-w̄ang-b̄o's presentation of these points, see Geshe Lhundup Sopa and Jeffrey Hopkins, *Cutting Through Appearances: The Practice and Theory of Tibetan Buddhism* (second edition, Ithaca, N.Y.: Snow Lion, 1989), 289-296.

All major Ge-luk-b̄a textbooks agree on this presentation of the path-structure for the Mind-Only School. Gung-ru Chö-jung simply goofed. His faux pas most likely results from the perspective of Yogic Autonomy system unconsciously slipping into his discussion of the Mind-Only School.

Issue #145: Do beings innately misconceive true cessations to be external objects?

The next issue between Jam-ȳang-shay-b̄a and Gung-ru Chö-jung is a topic of considerable controversy among Ge-luk-b̄a scholars. To restate:

> Gung-ru Chö-jung is refuting the view that the real nature of imputational natures such as uncompounded space, is not an emptiness; in his first reasoning he shows that, if that were the case, then Solitary Realizers would have no emptiness to realize during that phase of the uninterrupted path of a path of seeing called "doctrinal forbearance with respect to true cessations." Jam-ȳang-shay-b̄a agrees with him that the real nature of imputational natures is indeed an emptiness, but he does not agree with his reasoning, as was discussed above.

Having disposed of Gung-ru Chö-jung's first reason, Jam-ȳang-shay-b̄a now attacks the second—that Solitary Realizers could not be realizing true cessations' emptiness of being external objects because there are no **innate** consciousnesses that apprehend true cessations to be external objects.

Again, Jam-ȳang-shay-b̄a agrees that Solitary Realizers do not mainly meditate on the emptiness of external objects, but he gives a different two-part reason:

1. according to the Mind-Only School, Solitary Realizers do not realize the selflessness of phenomena, and
2. the emptiness of external objects is a subtle selflessness of phenomena.

In addition, Jam-ȳang-shay-b̄a[437] objects to Gung-ru Chö-jung's opinion that there are no innate consciousnesses that apprehend true cessations to be external objects. Gung-ru Chö-jung bases his opinion on a reading of Ke-drup's *Opening the Eyes of the Fortunate,* which Jam-ȳang-shay-b̄a takes apart through citing parallels to Ke-drup's statement. Jam-ȳang-shay-b̄a's argument initially seems strained, then somewhat convincing though hard to follow, and finally unconvincing when placed in the context of Ke-drup's remarks.

First: Gung-ru Chö-jung misquotes Ke-drup as saying,[a] "There are no innate consciousnesses that conceive uncompounded space to be an external object." Ke-drup seems to be saying that, although it would be possible to be led

---

[a] Gung-ru Chö-jung's *Garland of White Lotuses,* 32a.1: *nam mkha' phyir rol don du 'dzin pa'i blo lhan skyes mi srid do.*

by false reasoning or mistaken scriptures to misconceive uncompounded space to be an object that is a different entity from the consciousness apprehending it, this is never done innately, without such a background. However, as Jam-ȳang-shay-b̄a[438] points out, Ke-drup's *Opening the Eyes of the Fortunate* actually says,[a] "There are no innate consciousnesses that conceive uncompounded space to be an external, **material** object." Jam-ȳang-shay-b̄a agrees with Ke-drup that there are no innate consciousnesses that conceive uncompounded space to be an external, **material** object, but he insists that Ke-drup does not say anything to contradict that there are innate misapprehensions of uncompounded space as established in accordance with an appearance as an external object that is merely a different entity from the awareness to which it appears—without the qualification of "material."

Jam-ȳang-shay-b̄a maintains that for Ke-drup such misapprehension does indeed occur among common beings who have not entered into a system of tenets. Hence, such misapprehension is included among objects to be abandoned by the path of meditation of the Great Vehicle, and uncompounded space's emptiness of being established as an external object is a subtle selflessness of phenomena, only realized by practitioners of the Great Vehicle.

Jam-ȳang-shay-b̄a makes the cogent case that the emptiness of uncompounded space does not refer to its emptiness of being established as an external, **material** object because, otherwise, those who have realized that uncompounded space is empty of being established as an external, **material** object (for example, Proponents of Sūtra) absurdly would have realized that space is empty of being established as an external object. Since Proponents of Sūtra certainly have realized that uncompounded space is devoid of compounded phenomena in general, there is no question that they have realized that it is devoid of material phenomena. However, they could not have realized the selflessness of phenomena as it is presented in the Mind-Only School; otherwise, the presentation of four schools of tenets for Indian Buddhism, graduated by way of their view of selflessness, would fall to the ground.

Still, Ke-drup, in speaking about Yogic Autonomists in his *General Presentation of the Tantra Sets*,[b] does seem to indicate that "external object" and "material phenomenon" are not to be differentiated when he says:

> Forms, sounds, and so forth are not factualities other than the mind; they assert that external objects, or material phenomena, are not established bases [that is, do not exist].[c]

[a] Jam-ȳang-shay-b̄a's *Great Exposition of the Interpretable and the Definitive*, 78.2: *nam mkha' phyir rol gyi bem por 'dzin pa'i blo lhan skyes mi srid do.* See also the translation in Cabezón, *A Dose of Emptiness*, 67.

[b] See Ferdinand D. Lessing and Alex Wayman, *Mkhas Grub Rje's Fundamentals of the Buddhist Tantras* (The Hague: Mouton, 1968; reprint, Delhi: Motilal Banarsidass, 1978), 93.

[c] *gzugs sgra sogs sems las don gzhan ma yin te/ phyi don nam/ bem po gzhi ma grub par 'dod*

Nevertheless, Jam-ȳang-shay-b̄a argues that Ke-drup means that Shāntarakṣhita and Kamalashīla do not assert that forms and sounds, as well as odors, tastes, and tangible objects, are factualities other than the mind since these are not asserted as **either** external objects that are factualities other than the mind **or** as material phenomena that are factualities other than the mind. In what to me seems to be a diversion from the issue, Jam-ȳang-shay-b̄a insists that Ke-drup's "and so forth" does not include permanent phenomena; indeed, if it did, Ke-drup would be saying that Shāntarakṣhita and Kamalashīla do not assert that permanent phenomena such as uncompounded space are either external objects that are factualities other than the mind or are material phenomena that are factualities other than the mind. It appears that Jam-ȳang-shay-b̄a's meaning is that since no intelligent person would have qualms that uncompounded space is a material phenomenon, Ke-drup would be eliminating something that is not even speculatively a choice. However, it seems to be that Gung-ru Chö-jung would not read Ke-drup's "and so forth" as including permanent phenomena or even mental phenomena.

In order to dispel the notion that he is merely creatively explaining away Ke-drup's thought by claiming that Ke-drup does not intend to include all phenomena, including uncompounded objects, in the term "and so forth" and, instead, is referring only to physical phenomena, Jam-ȳang-shay-b̄a attempts to clinch the issue by drawing the absurd consequence that it would have to be said that, from Ke-drup's point of view, Bhāvaviveka asserts that all phenomena or all compounded phenomena, including mental phenomena, are material. For Ke-drup, just prior to the above citation, says:

> The masters Bhāvaviveka, Jñānagarbha, and so forth assert that forms, sounds, and so forth are external, material objects that are factualities other than the mind.[a]

Jam-ȳang-shay-b̄a's point is that it is obvious that although Bhāvaviveka asserts that physical phenomena are external, material objects, he does not assert that permanent phenomena such as uncompounded space or even compounded phenomena such as consciousnesses are material phenomena. Hence, it is clear that here the term "and so forth" in such contexts does not include permanent phenomena and thus the same can be adduced for Ke-drup's usage of "and so forth" in the subsequent statement about Yogic Autonomists. All of this somehow goes to back up Jam-ȳang-shay-b̄a's notion that Ke-drup does not equate external object with material external object in his *Opening the Eyes of the Fortunate* and leaves room for an innate misapprehension of uncompounded space

do//: Jam-ȳang-shay-b̄a's *Great Exposition of the Interpretable and the Definitive*, 78.3.

[a] *slob dpon legs ldan 'byed dang ye shes snying po sogs ni gzugs sgra sogs sems las don gzhan pa'i phyi rol gyi don bem por bzhed la:* Jam-ȳang-shay-b̄a's *Great Exposition of the Interpretable and the Definitive*, 79.1.

as an external object (that is to say, merely a different entity from the consciousness apprehending it) in the Mind-Only School.

Jam-ȳang-shay-b̄a's point that any object, permanent or impermanent, can be innately misconceived to be a separate entity from the consciousness apprehending it is well taken, but it seems to me that his attempt to re-explain Ke-drup falls flat. Specifically, Ke-drup is explaining D̄zong-ka-b̄a's statement (*Emptiness in Mind-Only,* 218-219):

> When one does not know—with respect to the statements in Asaṅga's *Summary of the Great Vehicle* that all declarations in the Mother Sūtras of "does not exist" refute the imputational factor—this mode of refuting the imputation [that objects are established by way of their own character as the referents of conceptual consciousnesses and as the referents of terms] in the *Sūtra Unraveling the Thought,* one [wrongly] explains [all the statements of "does not exist" in the Mother Sūtras] as only [refuting] the imputation of other substantial entities of apprehended-object and apprehending-subject. Thereby, many great unsuitabilities also have to be propounded with respect to the system of the Yogic Practitioners....

Ke-drup gives an example of just the type of absurdity that would be entailed:

> If one does not know such a mode of refuting the extreme of superimposition, it comes that one must propound many very absurd consequences even with respect to the Cognition Proponents' own system concerning the meaning of the statements in Asaṅga's *Summary of the Great Vehicle,*[a] and so forth, that the statements in the Mother Sūtras that [all phenomena] "do not exist" are in consideration of imputational natures. This is because it comes that one would have to make explanations relating [such statements] to only refuting wrong conceptions that would never arise for an intelligent person; **one would be explaining that, for instance, "Even the statements [in the Perfection of Wisdom Sūtras] that space does not exist would be in consideration that space does not exist as an external object."** [However] if one understands this [mode of refuting the extreme of superimposition], one becomes skilled in a mode of exegesis that "In consideration that space is not established by way of its own character as a foundation of the name 'space,' it is said [in the Perfection of Wisdom Sūtras] that space is not perceived, and also the name of space is not perceived, and so forth." The conception that space exists through the

[a] Jik-may-dam-chö-gya-tso (*Port of Entry,* 666.6) identifies the passage as:

> How is one to understand the imputational nature in the teaching of the Very Extensive Great Vehicle [Sūtras] taught by the Buddha? It is to be understood through the teachings in the framework (*rnam grangs*) of non-existence.

> force of space's own mode of subsistence as a foundation of such a convention exists innately even among common beings. Also, this is a conception of a self of phenomena in the system of these [Proponents of Mind-Only], whereas there are no innate awarenesses conceiving space to be an external, material object.
>
> Similarly, if one understands this [mode of refuting the extreme of superimposition], one becomes skilled in the mode of explanations in this fashion—in Asaṅga's *Summary of the Great Vehicle* and Dignāga's *Condensation of the Meaning of the "Eight Thousand Stanza Perfection of Wisdom Sūtra"*—of the meaning of the sūtra passages in the Mother Sūtras that "A Bodhisattva is not seen in reality; a name of a Bodhisattva is also not seen in reality." Otherwise [that is, if one does not understand this way of refuting the extreme of superimposition], one has not seen even a portion of the mode of explaining the meaning of the sutras of the [leading figures of the Great Vehicle, called] great chariots.

Ke-drup clearly explains that D̄zong-ka-b̄a's point is that emptiness of phenomena such as uncompounded space does not refer to their not being external objects but refers to their not being established by way of their own character as foundations of names. Since Ke-drup manifestly identifies how the emptiness of space is to be considered, it is hard to accept Jam-ȳang-shay-b̄a's claim that Ke-drup does not consider that external objects involve materiality.

In this vein, Jik-may-dam-chö-gya-tso,[439] a follower of Jam-ȳang-shay-b̄a who diverges from him on this point, suggests that the emptiness of externality refers to the emptiness of apprehended-object and apprehending-subject with the latter being an effect of the forms and so forth that are apprehended-objects. In other words, externality—as framed by Ke-drup's remarks—refers to material objects, forms and so forth, that generate consciousnesses of them.

I agree with Jik-may-dam-chö-gya-tso about how to take Ke-drup's text but am stimulated by Jam-ȳang-shay-b̄a's more general point that any phenomenon, whether permanent or impermanent, can be innately misapprehended to be a separate entity from the consciousness apprehending it. Indeed, it seems to me that Jam-ȳang-shay-b̄a is, in a convoluted way, criticizing D̄zong-ka-b̄a for suggesting (and Ke-drup for openly declaring) that an emptiness of externality could not be posited with respect to permanent phenomena such as uncompounded space.

The third point of difference between Gung-ru Chö-jung and Jam-ȳang-shay-b̄a—the former's holding that the emptiness realized by Hearers and that realized by Solitary Realizers must be different—has already been considered (365ff.). Jam-ȳang-shay-b̄a cogently holds that in the Mind-Only School they are the same. One of the reasons why Jam-ȳang-shay-b̄a wrote the textbooks that came to be adopted at the Go-mang College must be that he wanted to present careful analysis of issues on which Gung-ru Chö-jung's works were susceptible to criticism. It is reported[440] that Jam-ȳang-shay-b̄a's extreme devotion to citation of sources indeed stems from seeking to supplant Gung-ru Chö-jung as textbook author. The change from one set of textbooks to another must have been momentous, given the allegiance cultivated for the textbook author, who is elevated to a level near divinity. That Jam-ȳang-shay-b̄a cribbed many points from his predecessor must have provided a sense of continuity within reformation.

Issue #146: Do Proponents of Sūtra assert that external objects are truly established?

A-ku L̄o-drö-gya-tso[441] makes the interesting observation that in the Sūtra School since external objects include uncompounded phenomena, which are necessarily not truly established, it cannot be said that the Sūtra School holds that external objects, in general, are truly established. This is based on the rule that if a category includes both permanent and impermanent phenomena, permanence predominates, and it is widely accepted among Ge-luk-b̄a scholars that in the Sūtra School permanent phenomena are **not** truly established. From this point of view, he shows that Gung-ru Chö-jung's definition of a Proponent of Sūtra as being a person propounding Buddhist tenets who asserts that both external objects and self-knowing consciousnesses are truly established is wrong because external objects, in general, are not truly established. He indicates that Gung-ru Chö-jung's error stems from his mistaken association of external objects with material things, as discussed just above (for indeed if external objects were merely material phenomena, all external objects would be impermanent and hence truly established). A-ku L̄o-drö-gya-tso notes that when Jam-ȳang-shay-b̄a's reincarnation, Ḡön-chok-jik-may-w̄ang-b̄o, gives a similarly inappropriate definition of a Proponent of Sūtra he is merely repeating Gung-ru Chö-jung's error. In Ḡön-chok-jik-may-w̄ang-b̄o's *Precious Garland of Tenets* the definition of a Proponent of Sūtra is incorrectly given as:[442]

> a person propounding Lesser Vehicle tenets who asserts the true existence of both external objects and self-cognizing consciousness.

A-ku L̄o-drö-gya-tso adds that since not all Proponents of Sūtra—specifically those following scripture—assert self-cognizing consciousness, the second part of the definition is also inappropriate.

Meditating on the Emptiness of Emptiness

Issue #147: Are thoroughly established natures empty of the imputational nature that is the self of phenomena? If so, is the thoroughly established nature the mode of being of the thoroughly established nature? Is emptiness the mode of being of emptiness?

To restate earlier points: The qualm that other-powered natures are their own final object of observation by a path of purification needs to be cleared away, and thus Buddha taught that other-powered natures are ultimate-non-natures, that is, non-natures in terms of the ultimate. It would, therefore, seem that such a qualm would have to be cleared away with respect to conventional phenomena but not with respect to the real nature of things, emptiness, the thoroughly established nature, since emptiness **is** the final object of observation by a path of purification and hence **is** the ultimate. Thus, it seems that there would be no reason at all to teach that thoroughly established natures are natureless in terms of the ultimate.

Indeed, when one is investigating the mode of subsistence of a pot, a pot's emptiness is the final object of observation by a path of purification in relation to it, but when one is investigating the mode of subsistence of the emptiness of a pot—when one is meditating on the fact that the emptiness of a pot is not a different entity from the consciousness apprehending it or that it is not established by way of its own character as the referent of a conceptual consciousness—the emptiness of a pot is not the final object of observation by a path of purification; rather, it is a basis of its own emptiness, and the emptiness of the emptiness[a] of a pot is the final object of the path of purification. In this sense,

[a] The *Sūtra Unraveling the Thought* mentions the emptiness of emptiness in chapter 8:

"Supramundane Victor, how many kinds of signs — which Bodhisattvas who thoroughly realize doctrines and meanings in that way are engaged in removing — do you speak of? By what are they eliminated?"

"Maitreya, there are ten [kinds]; they are eliminated by emptiness. What are the ten? They are: (1) when one thoroughly knows the meanings of doctrines, then the various signs of verbal expressions are eliminated by the emptiness of all phenomena; (2) when one thoroughly knows the meaning of the suchness of abiding, then the signs that are a continuation of production, cessation, abiding, and transformation are eliminated by the emptiness of character and the emptiness of what is beginningless and endless; (3) when one thoroughly knows objects that are apprehenders, then the signs of the view of the transitory collection and the signs of 'I' are eliminated by the emptiness of the internal and the emptiness of the unapprehendable; (4) when one thoroughly knows objects that are apprehended, then the signs of viewing enjoyment are eliminated by the emptiness of the external; (5)

even thoroughly established natures are without the nature of being **their own** ultimate. (More on this in issue #127.)

Issue #148: Is emptiness the object found by a wisdom consciousness realizing the emptiness of emptiness?

Gung-tang[443] goes on to make the subtle distinction that even if a wisdom consciousness realizing the emptiness of emptiness is a wisdom consciousness realizing emptiness, emptiness is not the object found by a wisdom consciousness realizing the emptiness of emptiness. This is because emptiness is not the ultimate in relation to emptiness, nor is emptiness the thoroughly established nature in relation to emptiness. Instead, emptiness is its own other-powered nature, not in the actual sense of being produced from causes and conditions but in the sense of being the basis of its own emptiness, its own thoroughly established nature.[444] Still, Gung-tang maintains that a wisdom consciousness realizing the emptiness of emptiness is a wisdom consciousness realizing emptiness even if emptiness is not the object found by a wisdom consciousness realizing the emptiness of emptiness.

Ask yourself, "Does a wisdom consciousness realizing the emptiness of emptiness realize emptiness?" Yes, for it certainly does not realize some conventional phenomenon; after all, the emptiness of emptiness is an emptiness! Also, "Does a wisdom consciousness realizing the emptiness of emptiness find emptiness?" Again, yes; "to realize" means "to find," although it does not mean to find the object being sought by ultimate analysis. Still, in order to stress the important doctrine that emptiness is also empty, Gung-tang holds that

---

when one thoroughly knows objects that are resources—possessing the services of women and men and of possessions as objects of enjoyment—then the signs of internal happiness and the signs of external apprehended-objects are eliminated by the emptiness of the external and internal and by the emptiness of nature; (6) when one thoroughly knows the objects that are abodes, then the signs of the immeasurable are eliminated by the emptiness of the great; (7) in dependence upon [thoroughly knowing] formlessness, the internal signs of blissful liberation are eliminated by the emptiness of compounded phenomena; (8) when one thoroughly knows the objects of the suchness of character, then the signs of selflessness of persons, the signs of selflessness of phenomena, the signs of cognition-only, and the signs of the ultimate are eliminated by the emptiness of what has passed beyond the extremes, by the emptiness of non-things, by the emptiness of inherent existence of non-things, and by the emptiness of the ultimate; (9) when one thoroughly knows the objects of pure suchness, then the signs of the uncompounded and the signs of the indestructible are eliminated by the emptiness of uncompounded phenomena and the emptiness of the indestructible; and (10) when one takes to mind the suchness that is an antidote to these signs, then the signs of emptiness are eliminated by the **emptiness of emptiness.**"

See Powers, *Wisdom of Buddha,* 187-191.

emptiness is not its "object found."[a] The distinction preserves a basic point.

Issue #149: What is the object found by a totally non-dualistic consciousness directly realizing the emptiness of emptiness?

Ge-luk-b̄a scholars often take particular delight in putting one of their own basic tenets in jeopardy. Analysis is stretched to the point where a fundamental posture distinguishing the view of their sect from that of another comes into question. To accomplish such a self-devastating move, A-ku L̄o-drö-gya-tso[445] looks into the ramifications of this distinction that:

- a wisdom consciousness realizing the emptiness of emptiness is a wisdom consciousness realizing emptiness
- but emptiness is not the object found by a wisdom consciousness realizing the emptiness of emptiness (since the emptiness of emptiness is).

He considers what this means for a consciousness of meditative equipoise of a path of seeing. The fundamental positions that he turns against themselves are:

1. Even though the emptiness of one phenomenon is similar in type to another emptiness in just being the absence of the same object of negation, the emptiness of one phenomenon is not the emptiness of another phenomenon much as the impermanence of a table is not the impermanence of a chair; thus the emptiness of one phenomenon is different from the emptiness of another phenomenon. Consequently, the final object of observation by a path of purification purifying the misconception of a self of form is just the emptiness of form and not the emptiness of some other object.
2. A wisdom consciousness directly realizing emptiness necessarily realizes the emptinesses of **all** phenomena in direct perception with subject (the wisdom consciousness realizing emptiness) and object (emptiness) so fused that they are like water in water. Thus, to a consciousness of meditative equipoise realizing all these different emptinesses, their difference does not appear. All emptinesses are realized without any sense of difference.
3. The state of non-dualistic meditative equipoise of a path of seeing is divided into two parts—an uninterrupted path that overcomes a level of obstructions and a path of release that is a state of having overcome those obstructions—and both of these realize the emptinesses of all existents, and thus both must realize the emptiness of emptiness too.

It might seem better to leave such an exalted, non-dualistic state to the realm of analogy and mystery, but it is a hallmark of a system of education centered around debate to extend conceptual probing as far as possible, and this is just

[a] Gung-tang's *Difficult Points,* 134.1: *rnyed don.*

what A-ku Lo-drö-gya-tso does: With the above point as his basis, he examines the object found by an uninterrupted path of a path of seeing that realizes the emptiness of emptiness.

Since any consciousness of non-dualistic meditative equipoise realizes the emptinesses of **all** phenomena, it would seem that to focus critical attention on a consciousness of non-dualistic meditative equipoise that realizes the emptiness of a **specific** phenomenon such as the emptiness of emptiness would be unwarranted and even dangerously narrow since such a separation clearly is a creation for the sake of discussion. However, an uninterrupted path of a path of seeing does indeed realize the emptinesses of all phenomena, and, therefore, it must realize the emptiness of emptiness as well as the emptiness of the emptiness of emptiness, ad infinitum (there being no problem with an infinite regress since all these are realized simultaneously). Hence, A-ku Lo-drö-gya-tso has some justification for speaking of an uninterrupted path of a path of seeing that realizes the emptiness of emptiness, even if he is teetering on the edge of the cliff of ridiculousness by focusing on only one of the infinite objects that such a consciousness directly perceives (without any sense of difference!)

What is the object found by an uninterrupted path of a path of seeing realizing the emptiness of emptiness? Following Gung-tang's point that emptiness is not the object found by a wisdom consciousness realizing the emptiness of emptiness, A-ku Lo-drö-gya-tso says that it would have to be that the object found by an uninterrupted path of a path of seeing realizing the emptiness of emptiness must be the emptiness of emptiness and not the emptinesses of all phenomena. Otherwise, the emptinesses of all phenomena would have to be objects found by, for instance, an exalted wisdom realizing the emptiness of form, in which case the emptinesses of all phenomena would be final objects of observation of a path of purification concerning form. This would contradict the above dictum that the final object of observation by a path of purification purifying the misconception of a self of form is just the emptiness of form and not the emptiness of some other object.

It is a fundamental Ge-luk-ba tenet that although realization of the emptiness of one phenomenon opens the way for realization of the emptinesses of all phenomena, the emptiness of one thing is not the emptiness of another thing, and thus the final object of a path of purification with respect to one thing is not the final object of observation of purification with respect to another thing. By considering what is found by a path of seeing realizing the emptiness of emptiness, A-ku Lo-drö-gya-tso demonstrates how easily one could be put in the position of asserting just the opposite of this fundamental tenet—the opposite position being that the emptiness of **any** phenomenon is the final object of a path of purification with respect to any other object. He thereby creates an appreciation of the tenuousness of even this fundamental tenet and an appreciation of the logic of the diametrically opposite position—namely, it might be that the emptiness of one thing is indeed the emptiness of any other thing.

It seems to me that since even conceptual realization of the emptiness of one thing allows for realization of the emptiness of any other thing through the functioning of that same reasoning and without relying on any further reasoning, **from an important point of view** the object of observation by a path of purification with respect to one thing is, loosely speaking, the object of observation by a path of purification with respect to another thing. Moreover, in direct cognition of ultimate truth, the emptinesses of all things are realized simultaneously without any sense of their difference. That Ge-luk-b̄as emphasize that the thoroughly established nature (emptiness or ultimate truth) of one thing is **not** the emptiness of another thing reflects their emphasis on philosophically or ontologically oriented styles of description founded in the perceptions of an ordinary, unrealized being over psychologically based styles of description that evoke a sense of the experience of realization. This preference accords with the Ge-luk-b̄a emphasis on giving a level of valid status to ordinary appearance to the point where it determines much of the general philosophical orientation although, of course, it does not militate against describing a yogi's perceptions as exceptions to the general state. As Jam-ȳang-shay-b̄a says:[446]

> [A Buddha can] transform a moment into an eon and an eon into a moment. And, even though [a Buddha can] set all world systems into a single minute particle or a single hair-pore, their respective sizes are not changed, and, like space, they are not crowded.

Issue #150: Is emptiness ever a conventional truth?

A-ku L̄o-drö-gya-tso[447] takes the discussion one step further, saying that, because of this difficulty, the distinction has to be made that although emptiness is an existent in relation to emptiness, it is not either of the two truths—conventional or ultimate—in relation to emptiness.[a] His reasoning has to be that even though an emptiness is an ultimate truth, it is not the ultimate truth of emptiness (since the emptiness of emptiness is the ultimate truth of emptiness), and it obviously is not the conventional truth of emptiness. Again, A-ku L̄o-drö-gya-tso has juxtaposed doctrines such that his analysis is on the edge of wreaking havoc with a basic principle—that whatever exists is necessarily one of the two truths—for, if this dictum is so, one would expect that any existent in relation to an object would be one of the two truths in relation to that object.

The difficulties ensuing on any position with respect to this issue make clear the background of a carefully worded statement by the present Dalai Lama in his *Key to the Middle Way:*[448]

> Therefore, when a tree, for instance, is analyzed, the tree is not found, but its mode of being, or emptiness, is found. Then, when that emptiness is analyzed, that emptiness also is not found, but the emptiness of

---

a *stong nyid stong nyid kyi steng gi yod pa yin yang de'i steng gi bden gnyis gang rung min.*

> that emptiness is found. This is called an emptiness of an emptiness. Thus, a tree is a conventional truth, and its mode of being is an ultimate truth. Further, when that ultimate truth becomes the basis of analysis and when its mode of being is posited, then that ultimate truth becomes the basis of qualification in relation to the quality that is its mode of being. Thus, there is even an explanation that in these circumstances an emptiness can be viewed as a conventional truth.

From the perspective of A-ku L̄o-drö-gya-tso's exposition, we can appreciate why the Dalai Lama merely reports that "there is even an explanation" that in such a situation an emptiness is a conventional truth.

In the vocabulary of the three natures, when one meditates on the thoroughly established nature of the thoroughly established nature, the thoroughly established nature can be viewed to be the other-powered nature of the thoroughly established nature, since it is the basis of its own emptiness. Does this make the thoroughly established nature an other-powered nature?

A-ku L̄o-drö-gya-tso concludes this delightful diversion not with a decisive resolution but by saying that there are many such distinctions and points to be examined. Indeed, upon allowing consideration of such abstruse ramifications, the embroilments would seem endless. At first, such diversions seem to have lost the profound tone of meaningful exploration, but there is esthetic pleasure in taking principles of inquiry beyond their usual sphere to the point where they crash, such that one is unable to posit a sensible way out. Some Ge-luk-b̄a scholars describe this as an experiencing of the non-finding of objects as put forth in the Consequence School (although it is difficult to say that merely probing a topic in such a way that it gets one into trouble constitutes ultimate analysis). Others, at the point of entanglement, despair of rescuing anything practical for individual meditation and turn to cultic involvement with mundane "deities" for relief from the impending collapse of a worldview and for an opportunity to project their psychological problems onto psycho-religious dramas of competing protector deities. The turn to cultic practices strikes me as stemming from an unrealistic expectation of verbalization—either expecting too much from the words of a specific writer or expecting too much from one's own conceptualization. It also constitutes a revolt against the psychological dryness of too much verbalization such that one is no longer able to apply the philosophy to one's own experience. It is like turning on a soap opera after reading abstract philosophy.

A telling point about Ge-luk-b̄a scholarship is that although its stated aim is meditative realization, its basic paradigm of exposition is not bounded by gaining sufficient understanding so that one can meditate. Although meditation is supposed to be the purpose of inquiry, the format of the texts does not allow for concluding a topic by appealing to a need for practical application. This, indeed, would open the door to shoddy thought. That there is no such boundary put on the workings of the intellect has meant that Tibetan culture could spawn great works of philosophical literature and great oral philosophical cultures. The extremism of the region is just what has saved it from mediocrity, even if the conceptual entanglement that it has released can indeed become a formidable obstacle to meditation. Here, in A-ku Lo-drö-gya-tso's far-flung inquiry the exploration also opens up appreciation of others' systems, relieving the pressure of the untutored assumption that there are water-tight answers for all problems.

Issue #151: If a thoroughly established nature is not its own ultimate, should a thoroughly established nature be posited as an ultimate-non-nature?

Because a thoroughly established nature is not its own ultimate, should we posit a thoroughly established nature as an ultimate-non-nature? Such a move certainly would stand the *Sūtra Unraveling the Thought* on its head, since it is mainly making the point that **other-powered natures** are ultimate-non-natures because they are not the ultimate, whereas thoroughly established natures are ultimate-non-natures because they **are** the ultimate. Juxtaposing this central point with the important fact that a thoroughly established nature is not its own thoroughly established nature is, to say the least, disruptive, but such a consideration is not entirely foreign to the thought of the *Sūtra Unraveling the Thought,* since the emptiness of emptiness is frequently mentioned in the Perfection of Wisdom Sūtras and the *Sūtra Unraveling the Thought* was taught in the context of those sūtras, and, as mentioned above (see 368, footnote a), itself speaks of the emptiness of emptiness.

In his *Notes,*[449] Jam-ȳang-shay-b̄a attempts to get around these difficulties by positing two presentations of the three non-natures, one being what is explicitly expressed in the *Sūtra Unraveling the Thought* and the other being a more general one. Through this technique, he attempts to preserve the integrity of the *Sūtra Unraveling the Thought* by not forcing it to say what it clearly does not. Specifically, in the ultimate-non-nature as it is explicitly presented in the *Sūtra Unraveling the Thought,* "ultimate" and "nature" both refer to the ultimate,[450] which is the final object of observation by a path of purification and the mode of subsistence.[a] In addition, stemming from an assessment of the implications mentioned above, Jam-ȳang-shay-b̄a[451] presents an alternative assertion that he admits is not what is explicitly indicated in the sūtra; he changes the terminology of "mode of subsistence" slightly and alters the explanation dramatically. In this reading, "nature" refers to (objects') **establishment as their own** mode of abiding.[b] It indeed is the case that other-powered natures are not

[a] *gnas lugs* or *sdod lugs.*

[b] *rang rang gi sdod lugs su grub pa.*

established as their own mode of abiding, but also imputational natures and thoroughly established natures are not established as their own mode of abiding. Just as a table is not its own mode of abiding, but the emptiness of a table is the mode of abiding of a table, so uncompounded space or a thoroughly established nature is not its own mode of abiding, but the emptiness of uncompounded space or the emptiness of a thoroughly established nature is. Using this reading of "ultimate-non-nature," it indeed could be applied to all phenomena and not just to other-powered natures. Still, Jam-ȳang-shay-b̄a admits that this exposition flies in the face of the *Sūtra Unraveling the Thought* (*Emptiness in Mind-Only,* 88), which says:[452]

> Paramārthasamudgata, that which is an object of observation of purification in phenomena I teach to be the ultimate, and other-powered characters are not the object of observation of purification. Therefore, they are said to be "ultimate-non-natures."

The sūtra clearly glosses the term "ultimate" with "the object of observation of purification," which, far from being the establishment of objects as their own mode of abiding, is the **non**-establishment of objects as their own mode of abiding. Thus, this way of depicting the ultimate-non-nature is clearly not what is explicitly set forth in the *Sūtra Unraveling the Thought.* Hence, Jam-ȳang-shay-b̄a posits it as the meaning of a more general presentation of the ultimate-non-nature.

Although I can see why Jam-ȳang-shay-b̄a has been led to positing a second set of three non-natures beyond what is explicitly taught in the *Sūtra Unraveling the Thought,* I question its practicality. For, the impetus for positing the three natures and three non-natures is to structure meditation. The very purpose of the first mode of positing the ultimate-non-nature, that is, that other-powered natures are without the nature of the ultimate, is to lead to the second mode of positing the ultimate-non-nature in which it is pointed out that thoroughly established natures are the ultimate. However, when in the first mode "ultimate" and "nature" are taken as **establishment as their own mode of abiding**, even this first ultimate-non-nature is emptiness, as Jam-ȳang-shay-b̄a himself says. In that case, the second mode of positing the ultimate-non-nature becomes redundant. Since the doctrine of three natures and three non-natures arises out of the practical, religious context detailed above, to posit another form of these outside of such a context seems purposeless. Indeed, it is significant that (1) Jam-ȳang-shay-b̄a makes this presentation only in his *Notes* and not in his *Great Exposition of the Interpretable and the Definitive,* and (2) none of the scholars following him picks up on this dual presentation. One of his followers, Jik-may-dam-chö-gya-tso,[453] indirectly indicates his displeasure with this assertion by calling for analysis of it, and I heartily agree.

Issue #152: Oddity of oddities, could an other-powered nature's ultimate-non-nature be an emptiness?

Gung-tang[454] raises the at first surprising and then intriguing question of whether an other-powered nature's ultimate-non-nature—an other-powered nature's **non**-establishment as an object of observation by a path of purification—could be an emptiness (and thus, absurdly, a thoroughly established nature).[a] On more than just the surface, it seems odd that, once other-powered natures are singled out as **not** being the ultimate, it would even be considered whether their non-establishment as the ultimate would be the ultimate! However, other-powered natures do not even appear to a wisdom consciousness directly perceiving emptiness, and thus, as Gung-tang himself says, the non-establishment of other-powered natures in the face of an uninterrupted path of the path of seeing (for instance) is an emptiness. The issue is a flabbergasting, delightful example of juxtaposing doctrinal points from different perspectives in order to stimulate thought.

Gung-tang admits that:

- an other-powered nature's **non**-establishment as a final object of observation by a path of purification is indeed the meaning of an other-powered nature's ultimate-non-nature
- and an other-powered nature's non-establishment in the face of perception by a path of purification, such as an uninterrupted path of a path of seeing, is indeed an emptiness.

However, he does not want to be drawn into the seemingly avoidable conclusion that an other-powered nature's ultimate-non-nature is an emptiness (and the unmentioned consequence that an other-powered nature's ultimate-non-nature would be a thoroughly established nature). For that would conflate the two types of ultimate-non-nature. To maneuver out of this predicament he claims that even though the above two facts might seem to entail that an other-powered nature's ultimate-non-nature is an emptiness, they do not. The claim is forced, but the reasons he cites for this seeming inconsistency are solid—namely:

---

[a] Most likely Gung-tang was stimulated to consider this point by a statement in Jam-ȳang-shay-b̄a's *Notes* (316.1) that "The two ultimate-non-natures formulated in terms of both modes of positing it are similar in being posited as the mode of subsistence" (*'jog tshul gnyis ka'i dbang du byas pa'i don dam pa ngo bo nyid med pa gnyis gnas lugs su 'jog*). Gung-tang has ferreted out Jam-ȳang-shay-b̄a's meaning, but he makes a qualification that allows him not to hold this distinctly uncomfortable position.

Jik-may-dam-chö-gya-tso (*Port of Entry,* 186.1) notes the discrepancy between Jam-ȳang-shay-b̄a's and Gung-tang's positions and suggests that it is better to assert the point according to Gung-tang. Still, he does not discuss the issue in any detail.

1. There is no consciousness conceiving "self" that conceives an other-powered nature to be an emptiness.
2. To understand that other-powered natures are not emptinesses, it is not necessary to realize emptiness.
3. Correspondingly, to realize other-powered natures' emptiness of being external objects, it is necessary to realize emptiness.
4. Even Proponents of Sūtra assert that other-powered natures are able to bear analysis as to whether they are established or not as external objects (they assert that other-powered natures are able to bear such analysis).

From these, he draws the conclusion that an other-powered nature's non-establishment in the face of a path of purification, such as an uninterrupted path of a path of seeing, and an other-powered nature's non-establishment as a final object of observation by a path of purification are by no means parallel. The first is an emptiness, whereas the second is not.

Undoubtedly, Gung-tang makes this distinction in order to avoid having to hold that when Buddha taught the first mode of ultimate-non-nature, he taught emptiness, for indeed the teaching that other-powered natures are **not** the ultimate is a prelude to teaching the actual ultimate. By juxtaposing an assertion from another context—namely, that an other-powered nature's non-establishment in the face of a path of purification, such as an uninterrupted path of a path of seeing, is an emptiness—he shows that relevant issues can complicate what otherwise looks straightforward. The distinction[a] that he uses to short-circuit the problem puts all the more emphasis on the basic point that other-powered natures are not ultimates, since this is the point that is being preserved.

[a] The distinction is that an other-powered nature's non-establishment in the face of a path of purification, such as an uninterrupted path of a path of seeing, and an other-powered nature's non-establishment as a final object of observation by a path of purification are by no means parallel.

20. Two Ultimate-Non-Natures

Overview of Thoroughly Established Natures

Definition of a thoroughly established nature:[455] a thusness that is an emptiness of establishment in accordance with superimposition by either of the two apprehensions of self.[a] Or: a thusness that is a final object of observation of a path of purification.[b]

Equivalents: thoroughly established nature, emptiness, thusness, limit of reality, signlessness, ultimate truth, element of attributes.

Divisions by way of entity: thoroughly established natures in terms of selflessness of persons and of selflessness of phenomena.[c]

Terminological divisions comprising the basis, path, and fruit: object, practice, and attainment thoroughly established natures[d]—which are equivalent with object ultimate (emptiness that is the object of meditation), practice ultimate (the path that is the means of meditating on emptiness), and attainment ultimate (the nirvāṇa that is the fruit of having meditated). These are called a terminological division because practice thoroughly established natures are not actual thoroughly established natures, since they are consciousnesses.

Divisions by way of associating object and subject: non-erroneous thoroughly established natures (such as a Superior's exalted wisdom of non-conceptual meditative equipoise) and immutable thoroughly established natures (such as the noumenon).[e] Non-erroneous thoroughly established natures are not actual thoroughly established natures because they are consciousnesses; rather, they are called "thoroughly established natures" by way of their object, emptiness.

Etymologies: It is called thoroughly established because of not changing into another aspect, being a final object of observation of a path of purification, and being the supreme of all virtuous phenomena.[f] It is called thusness (*de bzhin nyid, tathatā*) because of always abiding without changing into anything other than being established as the final mode of subsistence. It is called limit of

[a] Jik-may-dam-chö-gya-tso's *Port of Entry*, 238.2: *bdag 'dzin gnyis gang rung gis sgro btags pa ltar grub pas stong pa'i de bzhin nyid.*

[b] Ibid., 238.3: *rnam dag lam gyi dmigs pa mthar thug tu gyur pa'i de bzhin nyid.*

[c] Ibid., 238.5: *gang zag gi bdag med dang chos kyi bdag med kyi dbang du byas pa'i yongs grub.*

[d] Ibid., 239.1: *don dang sgrub pa dang thob pa yongs grub.*

[e] Ibid., 239.2: *phyin ci ma log pa'i yongs grub dang 'gyur med yongs grub.*

[f] Ibid., 239.3: *rnam pa gzhan du mi 'gyur ba dang rnam dag lam gyi dmigs pa mthar thug dang dge ba'i chos thams cad kyi mchog yin pas na yongs grub ces bya.*

reality (*yang dag mtha', bhūtakoṭi*) because of really abiding as the final non-perverse mode of subsistence. It is called signlessness (*mtshan ma med pa, animitta*) because of being the final mode of subsistence in which the signs of the proliferations that are the object of negation are ceased. It is called ultimate (*don dam, paramārtha*) because of being the final object of activity of a Superior's exalted wisdom of meditative equipoise. It is called element of attributes (*chos dbyings, dharmadhātu*) because of serving as the element—that is, the cause—of a Superior's attributes when, upon being observed, it is meditated upon.

The Selflessness of Persons

Issue #153: Is the selflessness of persons an actual ultimate-non-nature?

An issue of controversy about the ultimate-non-nature is whether it comprises only the selflessness of phenomena or whether it also includes the selflessness of persons.[456] As presented by Ge-luk-ba scholars, in the Mind-Only system, the selflessness of phenomena itself is twofold—the emptiness of a difference of entity between subject and object and the emptiness of objects' being established by way of their own character as the referents of conceptual consciousnesses—but this is not the point being questioned; rather, the issue is whether the ultimate-non-nature, or thoroughly established nature, includes not just these two versions of the selflessness of phenomena but also the selflessness of persons.

In approaching this question it is important to realize that it is agreed that:

- The selflessness of phenomena applies to **both** persons and other phenomena, since these two types of the selflessness of phenomena apply equally to persons and other phenomena such as mind, body, house, and so forth.
- Still, a person's selflessness of phenomena is not a selflessness of persons despite the fact that it is a selflessness and is of a person; rather, it is a selflessness of phenomena qualifying a person. (Since persons are indeed phenomena,[a] this usage of terminology is reasonable, though counter-intuitive when first encountered.)

The term "selflessness of persons" is reserved for a coarser level of emptiness that, according to most but not all Ge-luk-ba scholars,[b] applies only to persons—specifically, a person's not being established as a substantial or self-sufficient entity. Therefore, the controversy is over whether the selflessness of persons—a person's not being established as a substantial or self-sufficient

[a] *chos, dharma.*

[b] Jam-ȳang-shay-b̄a and his followers are the exceptions.

entity—is a thoroughly established nature and an ultimate-non-nature.

Here is the brunt of the issue:

- Ge-luk-b̄a scholars uniformly hold that the three natures are to be treated in two ways, one in terms of the selflessness of phenomena (which is the main object of meditation by practitioners of the Great Vehicle) and another in terms of the selflessness of persons (which is the main object of meditation by practitioners of the Lesser Vehicle, that is, Hearers and Solitary Realizers). Thus, everyone agrees that there is an ultimate-non-nature **in terms of** the selflessness of phenomena and ultimate-non-nature **in terms of** the selflessness of persons.[a]
- Ge-luk-b̄a scholars differ, however, on whether the thoroughly established nature in terms of the selflessness of persons is an **actual** thoroughly established nature or not. The Jay College of S̄e-ra Monastic University and the Jang-d̄zay College of Ganden Monastic University, who follow Jay-d̄zün Chö-ḡyi-gyel-tsen, and the Go-mang College of Dre-b̄ung Monastic University and D̄ra-s̄hi-kyil Monastic University, who follow Gung-ru Chö-jung, Jam-ȳang-shay-b̄a, Gung-tang, and so forth, hold that the thoroughly established nature in terms of the selflessness of persons is an **actual** thoroughly established nature, but the Second Dalai Lama as well as the L̄o-s̄el-l̄ing College of Dre-b̄ung and the S̄har-d̄zay[b] College of Gan-den, following Paṇ-chen S̄ö-nam-drak-b̄a, hold that it is not.

Go-mang and L̄o-s̄el-l̄ing, both on the eastern side of the Great Assembly Hall at Dre-b̄ung and only forty paces from each other, debate the issue with fervor, both sides finding evidence for their opinion. The issue is almost entirely terminological, but in treating it several fundamental issues come to be highlighted.

Let us list the evidence—both scriptural sources and reasonings—cited by those who hold that the selflessness of persons is not an actual thoroughly established nature. Paṇ-chen S̄ö-nam-drak-b̄a and his followers, for instance, point to the *Sūtra Unraveling the Thought* itself (*Emptiness in Mind-Only,* 90) as indicating that the actual thoroughly established nature consists of only the selflessness of phenomena:[457]

> Moreover, that which is the thoroughly established character of phenomena is also called "the ultimate-non-nature." Why? Paramārthasamudgata, that which in phenomena is the **selflessness of phenomena** is called their "non-nature." It is the ultimate, and the ultimate is distinguished by just the naturelessness of all phenomena; therefore, it is called the "ultimate-non-nature."

---

[a] *chos kyi bdag med kyi **dbang du byas pa'i** don dam pa ngo bo nyid med pa dang gang zag gi bdag med kyi **dbang du byas pa'i** don dam pa ngo bo nyid med pa.*

[b] *shar rtse* (East Point).

Paṇ-chen Sö-nam-drak-b̄a takes this passage as indicating that a thoroughly established nature is **necessarily** a thusness that is a negation of a self of phenomena.[a]

Also, although Paṇ-chen Sö-nam-drak-b̄a does not cite it here, the *Sūtra Unraveling the Thought* (*Emptiness in Mind-Only,* 94) similarly says:

> Just as, for example, space is distinguished by the mere naturelessness of form [that is, as a mere absence of forms] and pervades everywhere, so from between those [two][458] ultimate-non-natures, one [that is, the thoroughly established nature] is to be viewed as distinguished by the **selflessness of phenomena** and as pervading everything.

and (*Emptiness in Mind-Only,* 107):

> That which is:
>
> - the thorough non-establishment—of just those [other-powered natures which are] the objects of activity of conceptuality, the foundations of imputational characters, and those which have the signs of compositional phenomena—as that imputational character,
> - just the naturelessness of only that [imputational] nature,
> - **the absence of self in phenomena,**
> - thusness, and
> - the object of observation of purification
>
> is the thoroughly established character.

In addition, Maitreya's *Differentiation of the Middle and the Extremes* (*Emptiness in Mind-Only,* 162-163) says:[b]

> The objects of activity [of the path][459] of purification are twofold;
> It [that is, the thoroughly established nature] is expressed as solely one
> [of those, that is, the selflessness of phenomena].

Furthermore, there are statements by Dzong-ka-b̄a (*Emptiness in Mind-Only,* 90-91) that suggest the same:

> Since the thoroughly established nature of phenomena—the **selflessness of phenomena**—is the object of observation of purification, it is

---

[a] Paṇ-chen Sö-nam-drak-b̄a's *Garland of Blue Lotuses,* 34b.2: *yongs grub yin na chos bdag bkag pa'i de bzhin nyid yin pas khyab par bstan pa'i phyir.*

[b] Translated here in accordance with Paṇ-chen Sö-nam-drak-b̄a's reading of it. III.12cd; Peking 5522, vol. 108, 20.3.7. The Sanskrit from Nagao (*Madhyāntavibhāga,* 42) is:

> *viśuddhi-gocaraṃ dvedhā ekasmād eva kīrttitaṃ* [Pandeya: *kīrtitaṃ*]/

See also Pandeya, *Madhyānta-vibhāga,* 99. For a translation see Stefan Anacker, *Seven Works of Vasubandhu,* 238.

> the ultimate. Also, since it is distinguished by, that is to say, is posited by way of the mere **naturelessness of a self in phenomena**, it is also called "the non-nature of phenomena," whereby it is called "the ultimate-non-nature."

And (*Emptiness in Mind-Only,* 91-92):

> Also, when giving examples [of the three non-natures, the *Sūtra Unraveling the Thought*] says that just as space is posited as the **mere** absence of form [that is, a mere absence of obstructive contact], so [the thoroughly established nature] is posited as selflessness. Therefore, it is very clear that the thoroughly established nature, which is the **selflessness of phenomena**, is posited as the non-affirming negation of [dualistic] proliferations that is a mere elimination of a self of phenomena, with compounded phenomena[a] as that which possesses the quality [of emptiness].

And (*Emptiness in Mind-Only,* 108):

> "[The absence of self] in phenomena..." identifies as the thoroughly established nature just that **selflessness of phenomena** called "thusness" through observation of and meditation on which obstructions are purified. What is the selflessness of phenomena? It is "just the naturelessness [of the imputational nature that is the object of negation in the view of selflessness]."

Since the three citations from D̄zong-ka-b̄a's *The Essence of Eloquence* speak of the thoroughly established nature as specifically referring to the selflessness of phenomena, it might seem to be D̄zong-ka-b̄a's opinion that the thoroughly established nature is limited to the selflessness of phenomena.

In addition, D̄zong-ka-b̄a's two main disciples, Ke-drup and Gyel-tsap, seem to say the same. Ke-drup's *Opening the Eyes of the Fortunate* says:[460]

> The Proponents of Mind-Only and the Middle Way Autonomists do not assert that a selflessness of persons is an ultimate truth, and also

---

[a] With respect to D̄zong-ka-b̄a's specifying "compounded phenomena" as the basis of negation despite the fact that all phenomena, including the uncompounded, are without a self of phenomena, Jik-may-dam-chö-gya-tso (*Port of Entry,* 270.2) points out that:

- Gung-ru Chö-jung explains that this is due to the fact that compounded phenomena are the **main** ones,
- whereas Jam-ȳang-shay-b̄a and Gung-tang explain that D̄zong-ka-b̄a is deliberately reversing the Jo-nang-b̄a positing of compounded phenomena as the **object** of negation (with the thoroughly established nature as the basis of negation) and indicating that compounded phenomena must be taken as the **bases** of negation and an imputational nature must be posited as the object of negation.

Jik-may-dam-chö-gya-tso takes both explanations to be suitable.

> they assert that the reasonings refuting a self of persons are reasonings analyzing a conventionality.

And Gyel-tsap's *Explanation of (Dharmakīrti's) Commentary on (Dignāga's) "Compilation of Prime Cognition": Unerring Illumination of the Path to Liberation* says:[461]

> The immutable thoroughly established nature is the final object of observation which is such that, when observed and thereupon meditated, all obstructions to omniscience are extinguished.

In this way, the *Sūtra Unraveling the Thought,* Dzong-ka-ba, and his two chief disciples provide seemingly excellent scriptural sources for the opinion that the selflessness of persons is not an actual thoroughly established nature.

Jik-may-dam-chö-gya-tso details their three reasonings:[462]

1. It [absurdly] follows that a subtle selflessness of persons is a middle because of being an emptiness. If you accept that a subtle selflessness of persons is a middle, then it [absurdly] follows that a Proponent of Sūtra has found the view of the middle because [according to you] a subtle selflessness of persons is a middle and [according to you] a Proponent of Sūtra is a person who has found the view of the middle. If you accept that a Proponent of Sūtra has found the view of the middle, then it [absurdly] follows that a Proponent of Sūtra is a Proponent of the Middle (*dbu ma pa, mādhyamika*)[a] because you have asserted that a Proponent of Sūtra has found the view of the middle. You cannot accept that a Proponent of Sūtra has found the view of the middle because a Proponent of Sūtra is not a Proponent of Mind-Only.

2. Also, it [absurdly] follows with respect to a subtle selflessness of persons that it is an emptiness of persons because [according to you] its way of being an emptiness is logical. If you accept that a subtle selflessness of persons is an emptiness of persons, then it [absurdly] follows that a subtle selflessness of persons is a mode of subsistence of persons because you have asserted that a subtle selflessness of persons is an emptiness of persons. If you accept that a subtle selflessness of persons is a mode of subsistence of persons, then it [absurdly] follows with respect to a Proponent of Sūtra that he/she realizes a mode of subsistence of persons because you have asserted that a subtle selflessness of persons is a mode of subsistence of persons. You cannot accept that a Proponent of Sūtra

[a] According to Proponents of Mind-Only, all Proponents of the Middle are Proponents of Mind-Only because only the Mind-Only School presents the true middle between the extremes of superimposition and deprecation.

realizes a mode of subsistence of persons because he/she is a person who makes erroneous superimpositions about the mode of subsistence of persons, since he/she is a person who conceives that persons are established by way of their own character as the referents of conceptual consciousnesses apprehending them, and non-establishment as such is the subtle mode of subsistence.

3. Also, it [absurdly] follows that a subtle selflessness of persons is an element of attributes because of being an emptiness. If you accept that a subtle selflessness of persons is an element of attributes, then it [absurdly] follows that the element of attributes has divisions that are different entities and types because you have asserted that a subtle selflessness of persons is an element of attributes. You cannot accept that the element of attributes has divisions that are different entities and types because [Maitreya's *Ornament for Clear Realization*] says, "The element of attributes has no divisions."

Now let us consider the responses to these impressive scriptures and reasonings by those such as Jay-d̄zün Chö-ḡyi-gyel-tsen, Gung-ru Chö-jung, Jam-ȳang-shay-b̄a, Gung-tang, and so forth who hold that the selflessness of persons is an actual thoroughly established nature.

The quote that Paṇ-chen S̄ö-nam-drak-b̄a cites from the *Sūtra Unraveling the Thought* unambiguously limits the thoroughly established nature to the selflessness of phenomena,[463] but Gung-tang,[464] who holds that the thoroughly established nature consists of **both** the selflessness of persons and the selflessness of phenomena, gets around the sūtra's restrictive qualification by saying that the ultimate-non-nature that is **explicitly** indicated in the *Sūtra Unraveling the Thought* at this point is necessarily the subtle selflessness of phenomena,[465] but the ultimate-non-nature that is a subtle selflessness of persons is indicated **implicitly**. Gung-tang's reason is that, as explained earlier, when Buddha explicitly explains the basis in his thought behind his earlier teaching of the middle wheel of doctrine, his description also implicitly explains the basis in his thought behind his teaching the first wheel of doctrine, this being the ultimate-non-nature in terms of the selflessness of persons. In this vein, D̄zong-ka-b̄a says about Paramārthasamudgata's question:

> Through that, [Paramārthasamudgata] implicitly[a] asks of what [Buddha] was thinking when [in the first wheel of the teaching] he spoke of the existence of own-character and so forth.[b]

Also, when Buddha answers Paramārthasamudgata's explicit question about the middle wheel, explaining that the basis in his thought—when he taught the middle wheel—was the ultimate-non-nature in terms of the selflessness of

a See issue #56.

b See issues #21-24.

phenomena, he **implicitly** indicates that the basis in his thought when he set forth the first wheel of doctrine was the ultimate-non-nature in terms of the selflessness of persons. Once this is the case, there has to be an ultimate-non-nature in terms of the selflessness of persons.

Indeed, Ge-luk-b̄a scholars are in agreement that there has to be an ultimate-non-nature in terms of the selflessness of persons, but Paṇ-chen S̄ö-nam-drak-b̄a proceeds to hold that the ultimate-non-nature in terms of the selflessness of persons is not an **actual**[a] ultimate-non-nature, whereas Jay-d̄zün Chö-ḡyi-gyel-tsen, Gung-ru Chö-jung, Jam-ȳang-shay-b̄a, Gung-tang, and A-ku L̄o-drö-gya-tso maintain that it is. Their point that actual ultimate-non-natures cannot be confined to the selflessness of phenomena is based on the importance of the sūtra's explanation of what Buddha had in the back of his mind, so to speak, not just when he taught the middle wheel of doctrine but also when he taught the first wheel of doctrine. Thus, when Buddha explains his thought behind the middle wheel of doctrine through appealing to the doctrine of three natures and three non-natures in terms of the selflessness of phenomena, he implicitly makes a similar explanation of his thought behind the first wheel of doctrine in terms of the selflessness of persons. Also, Paramārthasamudgata's question is concerned with **both** the first and second wheels of doctrines—as we know from his describing both sets of teachings and from the fact that when he later recounts Buddha's meaning, he explains initially that the first wheel requires interpretation and then that the second wheel requires interpretation. Once this issue is so important to the sūtra, it is likely that the ultimate-non-nature in terms of the selflessness of persons should be considered an **actual** ultimate-non-nature and not just an extension of the usage of the term "ultimate-non-nature" beyond its proper bounds.

From this perspective, Jay-d̄zün Chö-ḡyi-gyel-tsen[466] also explains away the passage cited above from the *Sūtra Unraveling the Thought* that seems to confine the thoroughly established nature to the selflessness of phenomena by holding that it indicates only that the thoroughly established nature **explicitly indicated** in the *Sūtra Unraveling the Thought* must be a selflessness of phenomena. In other words, the sūtra also implicitly indicates that a subtle selflessness of persons is a thoroughly established nature. As Jik-may-dam-chö-gya-tso puts it,[467] the *Sūtra Unraveling the Thought,* aside from saying that a subtle selflessness of phenomena is a thoroughly established nature, does not say that a selflessness of persons is not a thoroughly established nature, and he[468] uses the same defense with respect to the passages from D̄zong-ka-b̄a given above (386) by indicating that, except for saying that the selflessness of phenomena is a thoroughly established nature, they are not clear on the issue.

Using another passage in the seventh chapter of the *Sūtra Unraveling the Thought,* Jam-ȳang-shay-ba[469] similarly builds a case that both the (subtle) selflessness of persons and the selflessness of phenomena are thoroughly established

a *dngos.*

natures. There, Buddha speaks of the general mode of procedure of the path of realization as being the understanding that other-powered natures are natureless in terms of character and natureless in terms of the ultimate, after which the thoroughly established nature is realized, and then Buddha applies this procedure of the path to **all three** vehicles, not just to the Great Vehicle. By indicating that the principal object of meditation of Hearers and Solitary Realizers also falls within the rubric of meditating on this general pattern of path-cultivation, the sūtra itself indicates that their object of meditation is also a thoroughly established nature. That is Jam-ȳang-shay-b̄a's argument, and his point is well taken, but, as is clear from the sūtra passage cited below, it does not identify that Hearers and Solitary Realizers meditate on the selflessness of persons. The *Sūtra Unraveling the Thought* never specifies that Bodhisattvas meditate on one thoroughly established nature and that Hearers and Solitary Realizers meditate on another; however, it does clearly say that some Hearers do not attain the enlightenment of a Buddha, and Asaṅga's *Summary of Manifest Knowledge* identifies Hearers' and Solitary Realizers' object of meditation as being the selflessness of persons.

First, about persons with the lineage—that is, inclinations—of Hearers and Solitary Realizers, the sūtra says:[470]

> Because, hearing these doctrines, they do not conceive other-powered natures in the manner of the imputational character, they believe, thoroughly differentiate, and realize properly that [other-powered natures] are natureless in terms of production, natureless in terms of character,[a] and natureless in terms of the ultimate.... Moreover, on this basis, they thoroughly develop aversion toward all compositional phenomena, become completely free from desire, become completely released, and become thoroughly released from the afflictions that are the afflictive emotions, the afflictions that are actions, and the afflictions that are births.
>
> With respect to that, Paramārthasamudgata, through just this path and through just this procedure, even sentient beings who have the lineage of the Hearer Vehicle attain the unsurpassed accomplishment and blissful nirvana. Through just this path and through just this procedure, sentient beings who have the lineage of the Solitary Realizer Vehicle and those who have the lineage of the Vehicle of a One-Gone-Thus attain the unsurpassed accomplishment and blissful nirvana. The path of thorough purification of Hearers, Solitary Realizers, and

[a] It seems that this phrase has to be explained as meaning that they realize that other-powered natures are not established by way of their own character as the imputational nature. Otherwise, it would be indicating that other-powered natures themselves are not established by way of their own character, a position which would contradict the sūtra itself (see also issues #27, 155).

> Bodhisattvas is only this one, and their purification is also one—there is no second. In consideration of this, I explain that there is only one vehicle, but it is not that, in the realms of sentient beings, there do not exist various types of sentient beings who naturally have dull faculties, middling faculties, and sharp faculties.
>
> Paramārthasamudgata, even though all the Buddhas exert themselves, a person who has the lineage of a Hearer who proceeds solely to peacefulness is unable to attain the unsurpassed, perfect enlightenment upon being set in the supreme of enlightenments. Why is this? It is thus: Due to very limited compassion and great fear of suffering, such beings are naturally of inferior lineage. Just as their compassion is very limited, so they have turned away from others' welfare. Just as they are very afraid of suffering, so they have turned away from the thorough compoundedness of all compositional phenomena. I do not describe those who have turned away from others' welfare and have turned away from the thorough compoundedness of compositional phenomena as unsurpassably, perfectly enlightened. Therefore, they are called "those who seek peace for themselves alone."

Though the passage makes it seem that Hearers, Solitary Realizers, and Bodhisattvas meditate on the same ultimate-non-nature or thoroughly established nature, Asaṅga indicates in his *Summary of Manifest Knowledge* that the former two meditate on the selflessness of persons and the latter meditate on the selflessness of phenomena. With this qualification, it can be seen that a focal point of the *Sūtra Unraveling the Thought* is that practitioners of all three vehicles meditate on **some sort** of thoroughly established nature through contemplating other-powered natures' emptiness of **some sort** of imputational nature.

In this light, it can be seen that the position that a selflessness of persons is an actual ultimate-non-nature arises from consideration of the context of the *Sūtra Unraveling the Thought,* though, as we have seen, the sūtra also appears to put forward the opposite position. Thus, although the terminology of the three natures and the three non-natures is not highlighted in the literature of Lesser Vehicle schools of tenets, it is reasonable that according to the Mind-Only School the vocabulary of three natures and three non-natures is appropriately applied to Buddha's teachings about the Lesser Vehicle practitioners.

Issue #154: Is the selflessness of persons an emptiness?

Paṇ-chen S̄ö-nam-drak-b̄a,[471] in addition to holding that a selflessness of persons is not an **actual** ultimate-non-nature and is merely an ultimate-non-nature **in terms of** the selflessness of persons, also holds that although a selflessness of persons is an emptiness **in terms of** a selflessness of persons, it is not an emptiness. He thereby reserves even the vocabulary of "emptiness" for the Great

Vehicle schools. Specifically, he maintains that although the two selflessnesses—that is, of persons and of phenomena—are objects of the mode of apprehension of the exalted wisdom of meditative equipoise of Lesser and Great Vehicle Superiors respectively,[472] the thoroughly established nature is solely the selflessness of phenomena. He bases his opinion on a passage from Maitreya's *Differentiation of the Middle and the Extremes* (*Emptiness in Mind-Only,* 162-163), which I shall cite in accordance with his reading of it:[a]

> The objects of activity [of the path][473] of purification are twofold;
> It [that is, the thoroughly established nature] is expressed as solely one [of those, that is, the selflessness of phenomena].

For Paṇ-chen Sö-nam-drak-b̄a, the fact that the basis in Buddha's thought when he set forth the first wheel of doctrine was the ultimate-non-nature in terms of the selflessness of persons only goes to prove that there is an ultimate-non-nature, or thoroughly established nature, **in terms of** the selflessness of persons; it does not establish that such is an **actual** thoroughly established nature. For, according to him, this passage shows that the thoroughly established nature is composed solely of the selflessness of phenomena.

Gung-tang,[474] most likely utilizing Jay-d̄zün Chö-ḡyi-gyel-tsen's[475] refutation of this exposition (Jay-d̄zün Chö-ḡyi-gyel-tsen does not mention Paṇ-chen S̄ö-nam-drak-b̄a by name), answers that the latter has severely misread the passage, since it actually says:[b]

> The objects of activity [of the path][476] of purification are twofold.
> [Both][477] are said to be only the **single** [thoroughly established nature].[478]

According to this reading, the passage indicates that although the objects of activity of a path of purification are twofold, namely, the two subtle[c] selflessnesses with different objects of negation, both of them must be posited as solely the thoroughly established nature from among the three natures. Vasubandhu's commentary (*Emptiness in Mind-Only,* 163) supports this reading:[d]

[a] III.12cd; Peking 5522, vol. 108, 20.3.7. The Sanskrit from Nagao (*Madhyāntavibhāga,* 42) is:

viśuddhi-gocaraṃ dvedhā ekasmād eva kīrttitaṃ [Pandeya: *kīrtitaṃ*]/

See also Pandeya, *Madhyānta-vibhāga,* 99.

[b] The Sanskrit uses the general singular and thus does not clear up the matter. A literal translation of the Sanskrit, *viśuddhi-gocaraṃ dvedhā ekasmād eva kīrttitaṃ* (Nagao, 42), is:

> The object of activity of purification is twofold.
> It is said to be only the one [thoroughly established nature].

[c] The word "subtle" is from Jam-ȳang-shay-b̄a's *Brief Decisive Analysis,* 510.4.

[d] Peking 5528, vol. 108, 126.3.4. The Sanskrit from Nagao (*Madhyāntavibhāga,* 42) is:

*pariniṣpannād eva svabhāvān [*Pandeya*: svabhāvāt/] na hy anyasvabhāvo viśuddhi-jñāna-dvaya-gocaro bhavati/*

> The suchness that is the object of activity of purification is of two types...[they are] said to be the thoroughly established nature. The other natures [that is, imputational and other-powered natures][479] are not objects of the **two** types of exalted wisdom purifying [obstructions].

Vasubandhu clearly identifies "The objects of activity [of the path] of purification" as being the "objects of the **two** types of exalted wisdom purifying [obstructions]," about which D̄zong-ka-b̄a (*Emptiness in Mind-Only,* 163) says:

> The two exalted wisdoms are the exalted wisdoms purifying the two obstructions [to liberation and to omniscience].

Since Ge-luk-b̄a scholars unanimously hold that in the Mind-Only School the exalted wisdom purifying the obstructions to liberation realizes the selflessness of persons, Paṇ-chen S̄ö-nam-drak-b̄a's reading appears to be at odds with D̄zong-ka-b̄a's, though perhaps not intentionally so.[a]

Simply put, according to Jay-d̄zün Chö-ḡyi-gyel-tsen and Gung-tang, Paṇ-chen S̄ö-nam-drak-b̄a misread the line, as is even more obvious from Gung-tang's[480] decisive citation of Sthiramati's *Explanation of (Vasubandhu's) Commentary on (Maitreya's) "Differentiation of the Middle and the Extremes,"* "These **twofold** objects of activity of purification are expressed by the sole thoroughly established nature." Sthiramati clearly glosses the line as indicating that **both** selflessnesses are thoroughly established natures.[b] The evidence seems to be overwhelming, but Paṇ-chen S̄ö-nam-drak-b̄a's followers persist to this day in citing Maitreya's text in support of their textbook's position.

Gung-tang[481] cites further evidence internal to Maitreya's text indicating that both selflessnesses are similarly posited as thoroughly established natures, as elements of (a Superior's) attributes,[c] emptinesses, and so forth. The *Differentiation of the Middle and the Extremes* says:[d]

See also Pandeya, *Madhyānta-vibhāga,* 99. For a translation see Stefan Anacker, *Seven Works of Vasubandhu,* 238. Cited in Jik-may-dam-chö-gya-tso's *Port of Entry,* 269.5.

[a] There is nothing in Paṇ-chen S̄ö-nam-drak-b̄a's writing to indicate that he wants to interpret the lines in a way different from Vasubandhu and Sthiramati.

[b] Gung-tang's *Difficult Points* (144.11) mentions another misreading of Maitreya's lines in which "objects of activity" (*spyod yul, gocaraṃ*) is taken as referring to objects of observation (*dmigs yul, ālambana*). The meaning is then taken to be that although the objects of observation of paths of purification are twofold—other-powered natures and imputational natures—the object of their mode of apprehension (*'dzin stangs kyi yul*) is only the thoroughly established nature. As Gung-tang says, that this is not the meaning of Maitreya's lines can be known from the explanation already given. The misreading arises from making a distinction that is foreign to the text, though not to Ge-luk-b̄a exegesis.

[c] *chos dbyings, dharmadhātu.*

[d] I.20ab; Peking 5522, vol. 108, 20.1.2. The Sanskrit from Nagao (*Madhyāntavibhāga,* 26) is:

> Here the non-actuality of persons
> And of phenomena is emptiness.

Also, Sthiramati's *Explanation of (Vasubandhu's) Commentary on (Maitreya's) "Differentiation of the Middle and the Extremes"* says:[482]

> Since the objects of the **two** types of exalted wisdom are real natures,[a] the suchness that is the object of activity [of the path] of purification is posited by just the thoroughly established nature.

Issue #155: If the selflessness of persons is not an actual thoroughly established nature, is it an imputational nature?

Paṇ-chen S̄ö-nam-drak-b̄a's position, though perhaps not supported by his citation of Maitreya's text, has the attractive feature of limiting the designation of the **actual** thoroughly established nature and the **actual** ultimate-non-nature to the Great Vehicle assertion of a selflessness of phenomena. However, Gung-tang pursues consequences of Paṇ-chen S̄ö-nam-drak-b̄a's position that may be even more unattractive than disagreeing with Vasubandhu and Sthiramati.

In effect, Gung-tang[483] asks Paṇ-chen S̄ö-nam-drak-b̄a: "Since in the Mind-Only School all phenomena are included in the three natures, what from among the three natures is the selflessness of persons?" Paṇ-chen S̄ö-nam-drak-b̄a has already declared that a selflessness of persons is not an actual thoroughly established nature; the only other possibilities, therefore, are that it is either an other-powered nature or an imputational nature. Since a selflessness of persons is not an impermanent phenomenon produced upon the aggregation of causes and conditions, it cannot be an other-powered nature, and since all permanent phenomena except thoroughly established natures are included among existent imputational natures, a selflessness of persons must be an imputational nature. Thus, Paṇ-chen S̄ö-nam-drak-b̄a has to maintain the distinctly uncomfortable position that Hearers and Solitary Realizers meditate on an **imputational** nature in order to overcome the obstructions to liberation from cyclic existence! The final object of observation of their path purifying the afflictive obstructions is an imputational nature! And, indeed, this is just what Paṇ-chen S̄ö-nam-drak-b̄a's followers hold.

Gung-tang continues: In addition, if the selflessness of persons is an imputational nature, then it must not be truly existent, since the *Sūtra Unraveling the*

> *pudgalasyātha* [Pandeya: *pudgalasyā'tha*] *dharmmāṇām* [Pandeya: *dharmāṇām*] *abhāvaḥ śūnyatā 'tra hi/*

See also Pandeya, *Madhyānta-vibhāga,* 45. For a translation see Stefan Anacker, *Seven Works of Vasubandhu,* 220. Jay-d̄zün Chö-ḡyi-gyel-tsen (*General-Meaning Commentary,* 18a.4) also cites this passage.

[a] *chos nyid, dharmatā.*

Thought itself says that imputational natures are "characters posited by names and terminology and do not subsist by way of their own character."[484] Moreover, if the selflessness of persons—the main object of meditation of Hearers and Solitary Realizers—is not truly existent, then since the nirvana that they attain is the true cessation that is the extinguishment of the obstructions to liberation from cyclic existence into the entity of the selflessness of persons, there is no way that their nirvana can be truly existent: a highly uncomfortable position in the Mind-Only School where even other-powered natures, such as tables, are truly existent. Furthermore, once a nirvana is not truly existent, cyclic existence also cannot be truly existent, and once cyclic existence does not truly exist, then other-powered natures also would not truly exist. However, the *Sūtra Unraveling the Thought* itself (*Emptiness in Mind-Only,* 97) makes it abundantly clear that whatever is produced from causes and conditions is established by way of its own character, when it says that imputational natures are not established by way of their own character because they are not produced from causes and conditions:[485]

> Concerning that, thinking of just character-non-natures [that is, thinking of just imputational factors which are not established by way of their own character], I taught that all phenomena are unproduced, unceasing, quiescent from the start, naturally thoroughly passed beyond sorrow.
>
> Why? Paramārthasamudgata, it is thus: That which does not exist by way of its own character is not produced.

Since the reason why imputational natures are not established by way of their own character is that they are not produced, it is clear in the sūtra itself that whatever is produced must be established by way of its own character.

By showing these most uncomfortable consequences, Gung-tang ravages Paṇ-chen S̄ö-nam-drak-b̄a's position that a selflessness of persons is not an actual thoroughly established nature. He points out that this reasoning is at the root of the assertion that other-powered natures and thoroughly established natures are **equally** truly existent. Along these lines, Gung-tang[486] caps this part of his argument with a quote from D̄zong-ka-b̄a's *Ocean of Reasoning, Explanation of (Nāgārjuna's) "Treatise on the Middle":*

> Even the Proponents of [Truly Existent] Things from among our own schools in the Country of Superiors [that is, India] do not make a difference between cyclic existence and nirvana as to whether they truly exist or not.

Still, when Jay-d̄zün Chö-ḡyi-gyel-tsen[487] cites this same passage to show that true cessations are truly established, he adds that when D̄zong-ka-b̄a speaks of "Proponents of [Truly Existent] Things," he cannot (or should not) be referring to Proponents of Sūtra (Following Reasoning), since they indeed assert that cyclic existence is truly established because of being specifically characterized (*rang mtshan, svalakṣaṇa*), but nirvana is not truly established because of being generally characterized (*spyi mtshan, sāmānyalakṣaṇa*).

Issue #156: How to deal with Ke-drup's statement that the selflessness of persons is not an ultimate truth?

Thus, for Jam-ȳang-shay-b̄a, Gung-tang, and A-ku L̄o-drö-gya-tso, in the Mind-Only School a subtle selflessness of persons is an emptiness, a suchness, a thusness,[a] an ultimate truth, and a thoroughly established nature. As has been seen, they cite both scripture and reasoning; moreover, lacking a crystal-clear statement from D̄zong-ka-b̄a on the issue, they have culled D̄zong-ka-b̄a's writings for hints at his position. The evidence leads them to a conclusion that is diametrically opposed to Paṇ-chen S̄ö-nam-drak-b̄a's position. However, a statement by Ke-drup, one of D̄zong-ka-b̄a's two most influential students, indicates that the selflessness of persons is not an ultimate truth. As cited above (387), in his *Opening the Eyes of the Fortunate* Ke-drup says:[488]

> The Proponents of Mind-Only and the Middle Way Autonomists do not assert that a selflessness of persons is an ultimate truth, and also they assert that the reasonings refuting a self of persons are reasonings analyzing a conventionality.

Ke-drup in no uncertain terms says that a selflessness of persons is a conventional truth, not an ultimate truth, and thus that the reasonings proving it are reasonings analyzing a conventionality, not an ultimate. Moreover, he goes out of his way to accept openly the consequence that the reasonings proving a selflessness of persons are not concerned with analyzing an ultimate, as one might expect. Jay-d̄zün Chö-ḡyi-gyel-tsen[489] asserts that, indeed, the thought of Ke-drup's *Opening the Eyes of the Fortunate* is that the selflessness of persons is a thoroughly established nature but not an emptiness, but he openly disagrees with Ke-drup and holds that the selflessness of persons is an emptiness.

Following Jam-ȳang-shay-b̄a, Gung-tang,[490] instead of disagreeing with Ke-drup, goes to considerable lengths to explain that Ke-drup's position is being misunderstood. Despite the seeming clarity of Ke-drup's stance, Gung-tang attempts to explain it away by taking Ke-drup's reference as being to the **coarse** selflessness of persons that is the third of the four views that testify to a doctrine's being Buddhist:

---

[a] Jay-d̄zün Chö-ḡyi-gyel-tsen (*General-Meaning Commentary*, 17b.6) cites a passage from Asaṅga's *Summary of Manifest Knowledge* that says that Hearers attain cessation upon observing thusness, this indicating that Asaṅga considers that a selflessness of persons is a thusness and hence an emptiness. In the same text (18a.2) he also cites another passage from Asaṅga's *Summary of Manifest Knowledge* to the effect that the two selflessnesses are thusnesses. See these and other sources at the end of issue #166.

1. All compounded phenomena are impermanent.
2. All contaminated things are miserable.
3. All phenomena are selfless.
4. Nirvāṇa is peace.

Since these four views are said to be held in common by all Buddhist schools including even the sub-schools of the Great Exposition School that assert an inexpressible person, selflessness here refers to the absence of a permanent, unitary, independent self, this being the coarse and not the subtle selflessness of persons in the Mind-Only School. As Jam-ȳang-shay-b̄a[491] points out, Ke-drup's remark is indeed within the context of speaking about such a permanent, unitary, independent self, for Ke-drup goes on to say:[492]

> The Proponents of True Existence assert that the negation of a permanent, unitary, independent person is the meaning of a mere selflessness of persons and hence they must assert and do indeed assert that, through familiarizing with realization of just this, an innate conception of a self of persons is entirely abandoned. Therefore, Chandrakīrti's *Supplement to (Nāgārjuna's) "Treatise on the Middle"* says:[493]
>
> > [You propound] that when selflessness is realized
> > One abandons [only] the permanent self,[a] [but] it is not asserted
> > As the base of the conception of self. Hence, it is fantastic to propound
> > That through knowing [such a] selflessness the view of self is eradicated.
> >
> > That while seeing a snake living in a hole in a wall of your house,
> > Your fears can be removed and the fright of a snake abandoned
> > By [someone's saying] "There is no elephant here,"
> > Is, alas, laughable to others!
>
> Certain of our own schools assert that the conception of a permanent, unitary, independent person is an innate view of a self of persons, and some assert that although that is an acquired [conception of self], realization that [the person] does not exist as apprehended by that [misconception] abandons even the innate view of a self of persons.

Jam-ȳang-shay-b̄a's point is that Ke-drup is speaking about unacceptable assertions by certain Buddhist schools that realization of such a coarse selflessness of persons is sufficient and that hence when Ke-drup says that a selflessness of persons is a conventional truth and thus that the reasonings proving it are

[a] In his *Great Exposition of Tenets* Jam-ȳang-shay-b̄a indicates that this is an outflow of asserting the emptiness of a substantially existent person that has a character different from the character of the aggregates; see Hopkins, *Maps of the Profound*, 646-647.

reasonings analyzing a conventionality, he is referring only to such a **coarse** selflessness of persons and the reasonings proving it, and not to the subtle selflessness of persons and its reasonings. Thus, according to Jam-ȳang-shay-b̄a and Gung-tang, although from Ke-drup's remark it rightly can be concluded that a coarse selflessness of persons is not a thoroughly established nature, to extend this to a subtle selflessness of persons is unwarranted.

Issue #157: Does any Buddhist school assert that the conception of a permanent, unitary, independent person is innate?

Jam-ȳang-shay-b̄a's and Gung-tang's case is powerfully presented, but it needs to be asked which Buddhist schools assert that (as Ke-drup says) "the conception of a permanent, unitary, independent person is an **innate** view of a self of persons"? Is this not only an **acquired** misconception?

Gung-tang[494] cogently answers that the five Saṃmitīya sub-schools of the Great Exposition School that assert an inexpressible person propound that the conception of a permanent, unitary, independent person is an **innate** view of a self of persons. Although these five schools do not assert that a person is empty of being substantially existent in the sense of being self-sufficient, they also do not assert that a person substantially exists in the sense of being self-sufficient. As Jam-ȳang-shay-b̄a says in his *Great Exposition of Tenets*,[495] these five schools see that if the person is asserted to be a different entity from the mental and physical aggregates, it would incur the faults of the non-Buddhist assertion of a self, but they also see that if the person were one with the mental and physical aggregates, it would be plural since the aggregates are plural, and hence they assert that a person is inexpressible.

Gung-tang's point is that even these sub-schools maintain that only an **innate** misconception of the nature of the person draws one into cyclic existence, and thus, for these schools, the conception that a person is permanent, unitary, and independent has an innate form.[a] Thus, for them, the non-existence of such a self is the selflessness of persons, and since they assert this level of selflessness, they are Buddhist even from the viewpoint of philosophical assertion.[b]

---

[a] Jam-ȳang-shay-b̄a, in his *Great Exposition of the Middle*, states that **all** Buddhist schools assert that such a conception is only acquired, but Gung-tang (*Difficult Points*, 149.11-149.15) explains this away by interpreting it as referring to **most** Buddhist schools.

[b] In his *Great Exposition of Tenets* (Hopkins, *Maps of the Profound*, 219ff.; *kha*, 8b.8-10b.1) Jam-ȳang-shay-b̄a explains that the Vātsīputrīyas do not assert a self-sufficient, substantially existent person because they, like the other Proponents of a Person (*gang zag smra ba, pudgalavādin*), hold that the person is inexpressible as either substantially existent or imputedly existent, or as the same as or different from the aggregates, whereas a self-sufficient, substantially existent person is necessarily able to stand by itself separate from the aggregates. Ḡön-chok-jik-may-ŵang-b̄o, who is identified as Jam-ȳang-shay-b̄a's reincarnation, agrees

Issue #158: What is the "generality-isolate of the selflessness of persons"?

Jam-ȳang-shay-b̄a[496] literally says that Ke-drup's statement is "evidently in reference to the generality-isolate of the selflessness of persons or, in another way, to the non-existence of a permanent, unitary, and independent self."[a] What does he mean by "generality-isolate"? Usually, "generality-isolate"[b] is said to have the same connotation as "self-isolate,"[c] a technical term referring to an object itself without any reference to its instances or its defining nature. The terminology provides a way for conceptually zeroing in on facets of an object, excluding all others. Thus, only pot—and not copper pot, and so forth, or that which is flat bottomed, bulbous, and capable of holding fluid—is the self-isolate of pot.

Taken this way, Jam-ȳang-shay-b̄a seems to be saying that the coarse selflessness of persons is the general selflessness of persons. However, Gung-tang[497] cogently explains that here Jam-ȳang-shay-b̄a's usage of the term "generality-isolate" does not mean "self-isolate" but instead refers to the mere selflessness that is among the four seals testifying to a doctrine's being Buddhist and is asserted **in general**[d] by all four schools of tenets.

Gung-tang explains that since selflessness is the ultimate, selflessness itself[e] must be the ultimate, and A-ku L̄o-drö-gya-tso[f] adds that the self-isolated[g]

with his predecessor that the selflessness mentioned in the four seals refers to "the absence of a permanent, unitary, self-powered self," but he does not agree with Jam-ȳang-shay-b̄a's position that the Vātsīputrīyas do not assert a substantially existent person. In holding that the Vātsīputrīyas assert a substantially existent person, Ḡön-chok-jik-may-w̄ang-b̄o is probably following his teacher, J̄ang-ḡya Röl-b̄ay-dor-jay, who, in his *Presentation of Tenets* (77.5-84.12) gives a long refutation of Jam-ȳang-shay-b̄a on this topic. Nevertheless, Ḡön-chok-jik-may-w̄ang-b̄o does not accept J̄ang-ḡya's conclusion (84.4.) that the Vātsīputrīyas, though Buddhist, are not actual proponents of Buddhist tenets. Ḡön-chok-jik-may-w̄ang-b̄o maintains that they are actual proponents of Buddhist tenets by holding—as does Jam-ȳang-shay-b̄a—that the selflessness indicated in the four seals refers to the absence of a permanent, unitary, self-powered self. See Sopa and Hopkins, *Cutting Through Appearances* (Ithaca, N.Y.: Snow Lion, 1989), 176-178.

[a] *gang zag gi bdag med spyi ldog la dgongs pa'am/ yang na/ rtag gcig rang dbang can kyi bdag med la dgongs par mngon.*

[b] *spyi ldog.*

[c] *rang ldog.*

[d] The word "general" is taken from A-ku L̄o-drö-gya-tso's *Precious Lamp*, 110.2: *rang sde grub mtha' spyi 'dod pa'i bdag med.*

[e] *bdag med rang nyid.*

[f] A-ku L̄o-drö-gya-tso's *Precious Lamp*, 110.5: *rang ldog stong nyid yin pa'i phyir dang/ de'i gang zag gi bdag 'dzin rang ldog bdag 'dzin phra mo yin pa'i phyir.*

[g] I am presuming that A-ku L̄o-drö-gya-tso is making a difference between "the self-isolate **of** a selflessness of the person" (*gang zag bdag med* ***gi*** *rang ldog*) and "the self-isolated selflessness of the person" (*gang zag bdag med rang ldog*), since it is widely accepted that the

selflessness of the person is an emptiness and that the self-isolated conception of a self of persons is a **subtle** conception of a self of persons. Their point is that Ke-drup's reference is to the non-existence of a permanent, unitary, and independent self, which is a **coarse** selflessness, and, hence, if this were also the self-isolated selflessness of persons, the non-existence of a permanent, unitary, and independent self would absurdly have to be an ultimate truth and an emptiness, since the self-isolated selflessness of persons is an emptiness; however, that it is not so is just the point that Ke-drup is making, for he says:

> The Proponents of Mind-Only and the Middle Way Autonomists do not assert that a selflessness of persons is an ultimate truth, and also they assert that the reasonings refuting a self of persons are reasonings analyzing a conventionality.

Through this route, Gung-tang and A-ku Lo-drö-gya-tso give a plausible explanation of Jam-ȳang-shay-b̄a's meaning when he speaks of the "generality-isolate of the selflessness of persons," but why does Jam-ȳang-shay-b̄a say that Ke-drup's statement is "evidently in reference to the generality-isolate of the selflessness of persons **or, in another way,** to the non-existence of a permanent, unitary, and independent self"? Jam-ȳang-shay-b̄a's choice of words suggests that he is giving two possible explanations, not one. Gung-tang and A-ku Lo-drö-gya-tso, on the other hand, have reduced the first to the second, but if we challenged them, perhaps they would answer that "or, in another way" does not indicate a second possibility but a re-phrasing of the first. At the least, this is what Jam-ȳang-shay-b̄a **should** have meant by "or, in another way."

Issue #159: Has someone who has realized the coarse selflessness of persons realized the selflessness of persons?

In a terminological aside, Jam-ȳang-shay-b̄a[a] goes on to explain that one who has realized that a person is empty of being permanent, unitary, and independent has realized a fully qualified **mere** selflessness of persons, and hence, even though one has realized a fully qualified **mere** selflessness of persons, one has not necessarily realized the non-existence of a self-sufficient, substantially existent self—which is the **subtle** selflessness of persons. Since he holds that someone who has realized the **coarse** selflessness of persons has realized selflessness of persons (in literal translation without an article), a coarse conception of a self of persons must be asserted to be (in literal translation without an article) conception of a self of persons.[b]

---

self-isolate of pot (*bum pa'i rang ldog*) is not pot.

[a]   Jam-ȳang-shay-b̄a's *Great Exposition of the Interpretable and the Definitive*, 110.2: *gang zag gi bdag med tsam mtshan nyid tshang ba rtogs kyang rang rkya thub pa'i rdzas yod kyi bdag med rtogs mi dgos.*

[b]   110.4: *gang zag gi bdag med rags pa rtogs pas kyang gang zag gi bdag med rtogs 'dug pa.*

In English, which makes extensive use of qualifying articles, it seems easy to say that someone who has realized the **coarse** selflessness of persons has realized **a** selflessness of persons; however, the terminological problem does not entirely disappear, for we can ask, "Has someone who has realized the **coarse** selflessness of persons realized **the** selflessness of persons?" The answer is certainly that context dictates the meaning of "the," but in the debating courtyards of Tibetan monastic universities, a yes or no answer has to be given. At least for the Tibetan version of the question, Jam-ȳang-shay-b̄a answers yes. Still, we can extrapolate from the explanations given by Gung-tang and A-ku L̄o-drö-gya-tso in the previous paragraph that someone who has realized the **coarse** selflessness of persons has not realized the self-isolated selflessness of persons, since the latter is an emptiness, an ultimate truth, and a thoroughly established nature.

Issue #160: Why do Chandrakīrti, Ke-drup, and D̄zong-ka-b̄a speak of other Buddhist schools as asserting what is only a coarse *selflessness of persons?*

The above explanation has drawn from a series of five axiomatic notions that are fundamental to Ge-luk-b̄a presentations of the process of removing ignorance by cultivating a correct view. However, they are put in question by statements by the founder of their sect, D̄zong-ka-b̄a, and one of his two chief students, Ke-drup, as well as by their chief Indian source, Chandrakīrti. The five axiomatic notions are:

1. Persons are drawn into cyclic existence through **innate** misconceptions of the nature of persons and phenomena, not merely through **acquired** misconceptions gained from wrong scriptures and reasonings. Otherwise, bugs and babies would be liberated.
2. The conception of the person as being permanent, unitary, and independent is solely an acquired misconception.
3. A correct view sufficiently powerful to overcome the process of cyclic existence must counteract **innate** ignorance.
4. It is not sufficient, therefore, merely to refute what is misconceived merely by an acquired level of ignorant misapprehension.
5. In other words, a subtler level of misconception cannot be refuted by refuting a coarser one.

However, when Chandrakīrti, D̄zong-ka-b̄a, and Ke-drup speak of other Buddhist schools' own assertions on the selflessness of persons, they describe what has come in Ge-luk-b̄a scholastic literature to be considered only a **coarse** selflessness even in those systems.

In the stanzas cited above (398), Chandrakīrti leaves no room for anything but an emptiness of a **permanent** self when he describes the selflessness of persons in the lower Buddhist schools; he does not mention that they assert an emptiness of a substantially existent person in the sense of being self-sufficient. In a similar vein, Ke-drup, as cited above (398), takes pains to detail that these schools hold that the conception of a permanent, unitary, independent person is an **innate** view of a self of persons, or that even if they hold that it is only a conception acquired from study of false scripture and reasoning, realization of its emptiness nevertheless can overcome the **innate** view of a self of persons that even babies and animals have.

Dzong-ka-ba is even more explicit in limiting the non-Consequentialist schools to asserting a selflessness that is merely the emptiness of a permanent, unitary, independent person. In the introductory chapter to his *Great Exposition of Secret Mantra,* he says (with his seeming blunder highlighted in boldface):[498]

> The Proponents of Sūtra, Kashmiri Proponents of the Great Exposition, Proponents of Mind-Only, and Middle Way [Autonomists] hold that Hearers and Solitary Realizers do not realize that a person, even though empty of inherent existence in the sense of lacking existence by way of its own character, appears like a magician's illusion to exist inherently. They say that a cognition of a selflessness of persons involves realization that persons do not have a substantially existent entity **such as is imputed by non-Buddhists**.

Dzong-ka-ba's statement is problematic since, according to the traditions of scholarship following him, those Buddhist systems do not accept that in order to achieve liberation from cyclic existence it is sufficient to realize and become accustomed to the non-existence of self **as such is imputed by non-Buddhists**. Rather, a subtler conception of substantial existence that exists **innately** in beings must be overcome. In his introduction to Dzong-ka-ba's exposition, the Fourteenth Dalai Lama speaks to this deficiency in Dzong-ka-ba's explanation:[499]

> When he describes the type of selflessness that they realize, he says that they do not realize that the person is empty of existence by way of its own character but realize that the person is empty of a substantial existence **as is imputed by the non-Buddhists**. He seems to be saying that according to the Great Exposition and Sūtra systems of tenets themselves, one need only realize that a person is empty of being a permanent, unitary, independent entity. However, we have to say that the Autonomists, Proponents of Mind-Only, Proponents of Sūtra, and Proponents of the Great Exposition do not assert that cognition of a person's emptiness of being permanent, unitary, and independent opposes the **innate** misconception of self. In their own systems the conception of the person as permanent, unitary, and independent is only

> artificial, intellectually acquired, not innate.... Ḏzong-ka-ḇa here and in other places seems to say that in the lower systems themselves the subtle selflessness of the person is described as a person's not being permanent, unitary, and independent.

After this analysis of how Ḏzong-ka-ḇa's statement does not fit together with other indisputable assertions of those schools, the Dalai Lama explains how some Tibetan scholars explain away the apparent inconsistency:[500]

> Many scholars say that Ḏzong-ka-ḇa's reference is to the implications of the lower systems as seen from the viewpoint of the Consequence School. This means that when Consequentialists consider the reasons proving selflessness that are set forth in the lower systems, they find that the person's inherent existence or existence by way of its own character is taken for granted and that their reasoning for refuting self has the capacity only to refute the existence of a person that has a character different from the character of mind and body.

The Dalai Lama reports that many Tibetan scholars explain away the problem by asserting that Ḏzong-ka-ḇa is speaking not about the actual explicit assertions of those schools but about the implications of their assertions **as viewed by the Consequence School**.

Since according to basic, highly cogent perspectives of Ge-luk-ḇa presentations of liberation, no school of tenets can violate the above principles, it is easy to understand why some Tibetan scholars prefer to pass off Chandrakīrti's, Ḏzong-ka-ḇa's, and Ke-drup's seeming blunders by holding that they were speaking from the perspective of the Consequence School. For when the Consequence School considers what the other Buddhist schools describe as the **subtle innate** misconception of a self of persons, it only appears to be a **coarse acquired** misconception.

The reason why the Dalai Lama merely reports how other scholars attempt to explain away the problem by claiming that Ḏzong-ka-ḇa was speaking from the perspective of the Consequence School and why he does not give it explicit approval can be seen through Jam-ȳang-shay-ḇa's treatment of the topic.[501] He is reluctant to explain away these descriptions of the lower schools' assertion that the selflessness of persons is an emptiness of a permanent, unitary, and independent person not only because Chandrakīrti and Ḏzong-ka-ḇa describe it this way but also because Ke-drup, as cited above (398), takes pains to detail the meaning of this assertion in terms that do not leave room for such an exposition. Specifically, Ke-drup says:[502]

> Certain of our own schools assert that the conception of a permanent, unitary, independent person is an innate view of a self of persons, and some assert that although that is an acquired [conception of self], realization that [the person] does not exist as apprehended by that

[misconception] abandons even the innate view of a self of persons.

Since Ke-drup clearly is explaining these schools' own assertions and is not speaking merely from the perspective of the Consequence School, Jam-ȳang-shay-b̄a heroically (if desperately) tries to explain what this could possibly mean. He says:[503]

> Proponents of Mind-Only and so forth assert that, even through having meditated on the selflessness of persons imputed by [non-Buddhist] Forders,[a] the innate conception of a self of persons can be abandoned. That this is so follows because they assert that among the selflessnesses that occur initially on the path of seeing directly realizing the selflessness of persons, there is the non-existence of a permanent, unitary, and independent self.[b]

Jam-ȳang-shay-b̄a does not explain how a path of seeing realizing directly the selflessness of persons has a coarse level of selflessness as its object at the beginning and a subtler level afterwards, or how, according to the other alternative explanation, realization of the coarser level could abandon the **innate** conception of a self of persons. He proceeds to cite the first of the two stanzas from Chandrakīrti's *Supplement to (Nāgārjuna's) "Treatise on the Middle"* given above (398) and to mention D̄zong-ka-b̄a's frequent descriptions of the selflessness of persons in the Mind-Only School and so forth as being the emptiness of a permanent, unitary, and independent self, after which he concludes this part of his tantalizing commentary with a disclaimer, saying, "This is what I think."[c]

To recapitulate: Despite the superficial neatness of explaining away Chandrakīrti's, D̄zong-ka-b̄a's, and Ke-drup's seeming deviation from a well-structured system by claiming that they are speaking from the perspective of the Consequence School, such a maneuver ignores the fact that they do not at all seem to be adopting the perspective of another school but show clear signs of attempting to explain non-Consequentialist schools on their own grounds.[d] The strength of Jam-ȳang-shay-b̄a's explanation is that he tries to accommodate this fact; the weakness is that he only hints at an avenue of explanation without detailing it. That, after giving a hint, he withdraws from further discussion is an esthetically pleasing admission of the difficulties involved—a bit like a fan dancer showing a little more than previous dancers and then disappearing behind a curtain with a wink.

However, Jam-ȳang-shay-b̄a returns to this issue in a later work, his *Great*

---

a *mu stegs pa, tīrthika.*

b *der thal/ gang zag gi bdag med mngon sum du rtogs pa'i mthong lam du thog mar 'byung ba'i bdag med la rtag gcig rang dbang can gyi bdag med cig 'dod pa'i phyir.*

c Jam-ȳang-shay-b̄a's *Great Exposition of the Interpretable and the Definitive*, 109.2: *snyam.*

d I assume that this is why the Dalai Lama merely reports these scholars' apologetic and does not endorse it.

Exposition of Tenets, completed in 1699 fourteen years after publication of his *Great Exposition of the Interpretable and the Definitive,* which has been our source here. Before giving his much more refined explanation, let us set the scene:

- It is clear from the two stanzas cited above in Chandrakīrti's *Supplement to (Nāgārjuna's) "Treatise on the Middle"* (398) that Chandrakīrti himself is concerned with the difference between acquired and innate levels of misconception, or at least with different levels of ignorance; hence, we cannot explain concern with such as being a later development, although the issue certainly received more explicit attention in Tibet. We are left with having to opine either that Chandrakīrti was attempting to belittle the other Buddhist systems by intentionally misrepresenting their positions or that those systems were not as highly developed in their Indian setting as they came to be in Tibetan commentaries, or both.
- There is no question that D̄zong-ka-b̄a is centrally concerned with identifying the difference between coarser and subtler as well as acquired and innate levels of misconception; thus, his statements that picture the non-Consequentialist systems as promoting nothing more than realization of the non-existence of an acquired level of self that leads to release from cyclic existence would have to be a gigantic blunder, impossible given the frequency with which he addresses this issue, as well as his over-all concern with consistency. It might seem that D̄zong-ka-b̄a is merely following the lead of Chandrakīrti's *Supplement,* and that Chandrakīrti, from the perspective of his more subtle estimation of what is refuted in the selflessness of persons, always speaks of the other systems from the viewpoint of his own system, but this reading does not take into account Ke-drup's offering the same as those systems' own position. There is no getting around the fact that Ke-drup is presenting those schools' own position by providing detail where Chandrakīrti and D̄zong-ka-b̄a did not. Also, it seems unlikely that he would not have understood that Chandrakīrti and D̄zong-ka-b̄a are speaking from the perspective of the Consequence School, if indeed that is the case. The quandary does not come just from trying to find a seamless structure of consistent meaning in the systems of writers sometimes separated by centuries; rather, the problem is that the inconsistency is too gross not to have been noticed.

In answer to this quandary Jaṃ-ȳang-shay-b̄a in his *Great Exposition of Tenets* differentiates four levels of misapprehension of persons:[504]

> Furthermore, with respect to selflessnesses of persons there are:
>
> 1. a very coarse selflessness of persons: the non-existence of a permanent, unitary, and self-powered self in accordance with the description in Chandrakīrti's *Supplement:*[505]

> The [Sāṃkhya] Forders impute a self that is the experiencer [of pleasure, pain, and so forth], a permanent thing,
> Non-creator [of transformations], without [the three] qualities [of the nature—mental potency, motion, and darkness—], inactive.

As explained earlier, this selflessness is asserted even by the Vatsīputrīyas [who assert an inexpressible self].

2. a selflessness of persons a little subtler than that: the non-existence of a substantially existent person having a character discordant with the aggregates such that the two—the aggregates and the self—are apprehended as servants and master, or the controlled and the controller, like cattle and a herdsman. Autonomists and below assert that this type of self is the conceived object of innate consciousnesses conceiving a self [of persons].
3. a selflessness of persons a little subtler than that: a person's emptiness of apprehension in which even though the aggregates and the self have a concordant character, they are apprehended as being like servants and master.[a] This [type of self] is what is explicitly indicated in the statement in Chandrakīrti's *Supplement* [when speaking about the coarse level of misconception of self that is extinguished on the fourth Bodhisattva ground],[506] "What is related with the view of a self is thoroughly extinguished."[b]

Coarse and subtle versions are to be distinguished with respect to [the conception of the person as being substantially existent in the sense of being self-sufficient, described in items 2 and 3, in which the aggregates and the self are conceived as being like servants and master]. Regarding the former [that is, the coarser version described in item 2], once [the self] has a character discordant with the character of the aggregates, it is asserted to be permanent even if this is not [said so] in words, because [such systems] are speaking of a person that does not have the characteristics of compounded phenomena. This is why [when] Chandrakīrti [speaks about the innate misapprehension of self as it is presented by non-Consequentialist schools, he] says:[507]

---

[a] Jam-ȳang-shay-b̄a's *Great Exposition of the Middle* (179b.5ff.) describes this level with the more apt metaphor of salespersons and head salesperson, since a head salesperson has the character of a salesperson and is also the other salespersons' boss.

[b] With bracketed commentary from D̄zong-ka-b̄a's *Illumination of the Thought* this line reads:

> [The coarse level of consciousnesses conceiving that persons are substantially existent in the sense of being self-sufficient and of the "mine" as being objects of use of such a person, this being] what is related with [or preceded by] the [subtle] view of self [as inherently existent] is thoroughly extinguished.

> [You propound] that when selflessness is realized,
> One abandons the *permanent* self.[a]

4. a very subtle selflessness of persons: the absence of inherent existence of persons.

Jam-ȳang-shay-b̄a's new distinction is that when the self and the mental and physical aggregates are misapprehended as having a discordant character (as in the second item), the self cannot be impermanent and hence must be permanent. He offers this as the reason why Chandrakīrti and D̄zong-ka-b̄a speak of the lower schools as only speaking of the non-existence of a permanent self.

Issue #161: Is the basis of a division into a coarse and subtle selflessness of persons a selflessness of persons undifferentiated into coarse and subtle?

As may not be remembered after so much entanglement, this discussion began with:

1. Ke-drup's statement:

   > The Proponents of Mind-Only and the Middle Way Autonomists do not assert that a selflessness of persons is an ultimate truth, and also they assert that the reasonings refuting a self of persons are reasonings analyzing a conventionality.

2. Jam-ȳang-shay-b̄a's exposition that Ke-drup speaks "evidently in reference to the generality-isolate of the selflessness of persons or, in another way, to the non-existence of a permanent, unitary, and independent self."
3. Gung-tang's explanation that in Jam-ȳang-shay-b̄a's statement the term "generality-isolate" does not mean "self-isolate" but merely refers to a selflessness of persons accepted **in general** by all Buddhist schools of tenets, that is to say, the emptiness of a permanent, unitary, independent person.

Gung-tang[508] also disposes of certain other unnamed scholars' explanations that Jam-ȳang-shay-b̄a's reference is to a selflessness of persons undifferentiated into coarse and subtle. Let us turn to this.

In one way, it might seem as if the basis of a division (that is, what is divided) into a coarse and subtle selflessness of persons is a selflessness of persons undifferentiated into coarse and subtle; however, as A-ku L̄o-drö-gya-tso[509] points out, in that case a subtle selflessness of persons would have to be a selflessness of persons undifferentiated into coarse and subtle, but, of course, it is

[a] For the Fourteenth Dalai Lama's clear contextualization of this, see Hopkins, *Maps of the Profound,* 728, fnt. a.

not.[a] For example, if tables undifferentiated into wooden and metal were what is divided into wooden and metal tables, then a wooden table absurdly would have to a table undifferentiated into wooden and metal. As Gung-tang[510] says, when self that is undifferentiated into coarse and subtle is refuted, self is refuted.[b] His point is that if a selflessness of persons undifferentiated into coarse and subtle were the basis of division into the coarse and subtle selflessnesses of persons, then when the coarse self was refuted, the subtle self absurdly would be refuted.

Issue #162: Is a selflessness of persons a thoroughly established nature but not an ultimate truth?

These points have been peripheral to Gung-tang's showing that even in Ke-drup's exposition, despite seeming indications otherwise, both the selflessness of persons and the selflessness of phenomena are thoroughly established natures and ultimate truths. A prominent scholar from the Jay College of S̄e-ra Monastic University, Gom-day-nam-ka-gyel-tsen, concurs in part with this explanation, but he takes Ke-drup differently.[511] He agrees that it is the thought of Ke-drup's *Opening the Eyes of the Fortunate* that the selflessness of persons is an **actual** thoroughly established nature because Ke-drup says:[c]

> A thoroughly established nature is a thusness[d] that is an emptiness of establishment in accordance with what is superimposed by the **two** types of consciousnesses conceiving self [that is, those conceiving a self of persons and a self of phenomena] in other-powered natures.

However, based on the passage from Ke-drup's same work cited above,

> The Proponents of Mind-Only and the Middle Way Autonomists do

---

[a] A-ku L̄o-drö-gya-tso (110.6-111.2) mentions that this is the very reasoning that Jam-ȳang-shay-b̄a uses to refute the great S̄a-ḡya scholar D̄ak-tsang S̄hay-rap-rin-chen's assertion that in the Middle Way School uninvestigated and unanalyzed objects of knowledge are the bases of division into the two truths; see Hopkins, *Maps of the Profound,* 608. D̄ak-tsang S̄hay-rap-rin-chen's point is that objects of knowledge are not found under ultimate investigation and analysis and thus even ultimate truths in the Middle Way School are uninvestigated and unanalyzed objects of knowledge, but Jam-ȳang-shay-b̄a retorts that ultimate truths are found under investigation and analysis and thus are not uninvestigated and unanalyzed objects of knowledge. In that context, it seems to me that D̄ak-tsang and Jam-ȳang-shay-b̄a are using the term "uninvestigated and unanalyzed objects of knowledge" differently.

[b] A-ku L̄o-drö-gya-tso (*Precious Lamp,* 110.6) intriguingly draws the parallel between the fact that true sufferings undifferentiated into coarse and subtle are true sufferings and a selflessness of persons undifferentiated into coarse and subtle is a **subtle** selflessness of persons. Unfortunately, he says no more on the topic.

[c] See also the translation in Cabezón, *A Dose of Emptiness,* 68.

[d] *de bzhin nyid, tathatā.*

> not assert that a selflessness of persons is an ultimate truth, and also they assert that the reasonings refuting a self of persons are reasonings analyzing a conventionality.

he holds that, for Ke-drup, a selflessness of persons is not an ultimate truth.[a] He obviously does not opt for the explanation that Ke-drup's reference is merely to a coarse level of the selflessness of persons, as Jam-ȳang-shay-b̄a does. (Gom-day-nam-ka-gyel-tsen's position is indeed reasonable, given that although Ke-drup is speaking about the non-existence of a permanent, unitary, independent self, there is, as has been shown, a long history of the language of the coarse and subtle selflessnesses being mixed.) Thus, even though in the first quote Ke-drup seems clearly to speak of both selflessnesses as being thusnesses, Gom-day-nam-ka-gyel-tsen concludes that since Ke-drup says that a selflessness of persons is not an ultimate truth, it also cannot be an **actual** thusness and hence is only a thusness **in terms of a selflessness of persons**.

In response, Gung-tang[512] enunciates the principle that in the Mind-Only School whatever is uncompounded and truly established is necessarily an emptiness, and hence has to be an ultimate. He backs this up with a statement from Maitreya's *Differentiation of the Middle and the Extremes* (*Emptiness in Mind-Only,* 182) that limits the truly established to other-powered natures (which are indicated by the chief of them, conceptuality) and to emptiness:[513]

> Unreal ideation [—ideation being the main other-powered nature—] exists [by way of its own character in that it is produced from causes and conditions].
> Duality [of subject and object in accordance with their appearance as if distant and cut off] does not exist in that [ideation].
> [The thoroughly established nature which is the] emptiness [of being distant and cut off] exists [by way of its own character as the mode of subsistence] in this [ideation].

---

[a] Gom-day-nam-ka-gyel-tsen's position accords with that of Jay-d̄zün Chö-ḡyi-gyel-tsen's *General-Meaning Commentary* (17a.5) which explains that, according to the system of exegesis in Ke-drup's *Opening the Eyes of the Fortunate,* a thusness that is the emptiness of a self of persons (that is, a person's emptiness of being substantially existent in the sense of being self-sufficient) is not a thusness. The reason why Jay-d̄zün Chö-ḡyi-gyel-tsen explains Ke-drup's system this way is that Maitreya's *Differentiation of the Middle and the Extremes* describes an emptiness as being a thusness, limit of reality, signlessness, ultimate, and element of attributes, and thus since Jay-d̄zün Chö-ḡyi-gyel-tsen reads Ke-drup as saying that the selflessness of persons is not an emptiness, it cannot be any of these either. From this, one can see why Jam-ȳang-shay-b̄a and Gung-tang are intent on creatively reading Ke-drup so that he does not say that the selflessness of persons is not an emptiness. Jay-d̄zün Chö-ḡyi-gyel-tsen (*General-Meaning Commentary,* 18a.2), on the other hand, merely disagrees with Ke-drup's presentation in this text, pointing to the fact that Asaṅga, for instance, in his *Summary of Manifest Knowledge* says, "What is the thusness of virtuous practices? The two types of selflessness and...."

Maitreya, in speaking about what exists—which is taken here to mean what truly exists or exists by way of its own character—mentions only other-powered natures and emptinesses. Gung-tang, based on the principle that a selflessness must be truly established, concludes that a selflessness of persons must be an emptiness.

In response to those who accept that a selflessness of persons is an emptiness but who hold that it is not an ultimate, he cites the statement in Maitreya's *Differentiation of the Middle and the Extremes* that indicates that emptiness, ultimate, and so forth are equivalent and synonymous:[a]

> In brief, emptiness, thusness,
> Limit of reality, signlessness,
> Ultimate, and element of [a Superior's]
> Qualities are synonymous.

Also, Gung-tang[514] cites the principle enunciated in the *Sūtra Unraveling the Thought* that a final object of observation by a path of purification is a thoroughly established nature,[515] "That which is an object of observation of purification[b] in phenomena I teach to be the ultimate." Since Hearers and Solitary Realizers mainly take the selflessness of persons as their object of meditation to purify the obstructions to liberation from cyclic existence, it is a final object of observation of a path of purification and, consequently, an **object** (*don, artha*) of a **highest** (*dam pa, parama*), non-conceptual, exalted wisdom of meditative equipoise. Hence, the selflessness of persons is an ultimate, which in Sanskrit is *paramārtha* (*dam pa'i don, paramasya artha*), that is, an object of the highest (consciousness).

Gung-tang[516] concludes his case with a citation of Asaṅga's *Summary of Manifest Knowledge* that, through giving a definition of a thusness, indicates implicitly that a selflessness of persons is a thusness:

> A thusness into which contaminated phenomena are ceased through observation of it has a character of cessation.

Since the selflessness of persons is a final object of observation through meditation on which a true cessation that is an extinguishment of the obstructions to liberation from cyclic existence is attained, it must be a thusness.

Issue #163: Why does Ke-drup say that a selflessness of persons is an other-powered nature?

Gung-tang's reasoning seems impeccable, but the issue is much more complex, as can be seen through the next step in his argument, this being an attempt to

---

a *don gcig ming gi rnam grangs.*

b *rnam par dag pa'i dmigs pa, viśuddhālambana* (Lamotte, *Saṃdhinirmocana*, 69 [6], n. 1).

handle a strange explanation by Ke-drup. In the section on the Middle Way School in his *Opening the Eyes of the Fortunate,* Ke-drup speaks of a great self-contradiction within the tenets of the Mind-Only School, but, in doing so, he seems to misrepresent severely a central tenet of the Mind-Only School. Specifically, he says that a selflessness of persons is an other-powered nature; yet, we know that in the Mind-Only School other-powered natures are necessarily impermanent phenomena produced from causes and conditions, whereas a (subtle) selflessness of persons is a mere absence of self-sufficient, substantial existence in a person and thus is permanent and not produced from causes and conditions. Ke-drup says:[517]

> Having asserted (1) that whatever is an other-powered nature and a conventional truth necessarily is an object of observation that increases the thorough afflictions and (2) that an object of observation through observation of which obstructions are removed is only a thoroughly established nature, the Proponents of Mind-Only expound that any object of observation of a Hearer's or Solitary Realizer's exalted wisdom abandoning the afflictive emotions without residue is necessarily an other-powered nature and that observation of the thoroughly established nature [by Hearers and Solitary Realizers] does not occur. This is a great internal contradiction in their tenets.

Hearers and Solitary Realizers mainly meditate on the selflessness of persons in order to abandon the obstructions to liberation from cyclic existence, and Ke-drup says that the Mind-Only School holds that a selflessness of persons is an other-powered nature and not a thoroughly established nature. Indeed, this position fits together with the seeming meaning of Ke-drup's statement cited above:

> The Proponents of Mind-Only and the Middle Way Autonomists do not assert that a selflessness of persons is an ultimate truth, and also they assert that the reasonings refuting a self of persons are reasonings analyzing a conventionality.

In this passage, Ke-drup openly says that a selflessness of persons is not an ultimate truth, due to which it, of course, could not be a thoroughly established nature; however, as we have seen, Gung-tang and so forth explain away this passage by showing that it refers to a coarse level of the selflessness of persons. Indeed, Ke-drup himself says that a (subtle) selflessness of persons is a thusness:

> A thoroughly established nature is a thusness that is an emptiness of establishment in accordance with what is superimposed by the **two** types of consciousnesses conceiving self [that is, those conceiving a self of persons and a self of phenomena] in other-powered natures.

Once a selflessness of persons is a thusness, it should be an ultimate truth and a thoroughly established nature. Ke-drup appears to be inconsistent.

Even if we conceded for the moment that, according to Ke-drup's presentation of the Mind-Only system, a subtle selflessness of persons is not a thoroughly established nature, why does he not say that it is an imputational nature? Indeed, Paṇ-chen S̄ö-nam-drak-b̄a does just this; as will be remembered (see issues #153-155), he holds that:

1. A (subtle) selflessness of persons is a thoroughly established nature **in terms of the selflessness of persons** but is not a thoroughly established nature and, instead, is an imputational nature.
2. A selflessness of persons is not a dependent-arising produced from causes and conditions and hence cannot be an other-powered nature; also, all permanent phenomena, except thoroughly established natures, are existent imputational natures.
3. Thus, the obvious choice—once it is maintained that the selflessness of persons is not a thoroughly established nature—is that it is an imputational nature.

Ke-drup's failure to use the same reasoning is mind-boggling.

Gung-tang attempts to explain away this seeming blunder by claiming that Ke-drup is speaking from the perspective of the Middle Way School. Gung-tang says:[518]

> Since [this explanation of the Mind-Only position] occurs during the exposition of the system of the Middle Way School, Ke-drup is indicating an internal contradiction forced on them through a reasoning **from the viewpoint of the Middle Way School**. Namely:
>
> - Although even Proponents of [Truly Existent External] Objects **realize** merely such a selflessness of persons, even the Proponents of Mind-Only have no other choice than to assert it as a thoroughly established nature that is the **final mode of subsistence of phenomena**.
> - However, they also have no other choice than [to assert] that whatever is not fit to be [both] a thoroughly established nature and truly established must be an other-powered nature.
>
> However, since in the system of the Proponents of Mind-Only themselves they must not have internal contradictions, they assert that a selflessness of persons is both an object of observation of a path of purification and a thoroughly established nature. If that were not the case, it would [absurdly] follow that there would be no object of observation through observation of which Hearers and Solitary Realizers could purify obstructions because (1) such [an object of observation] has to be a thoroughly established nature, (2) a selflessness of persons

would not be a thoroughly established nature, and (3) there is not something other than the selflessness of persons that could be posited as the final object of observation for them.

The internal contradiction comes because, according to the Middle Way School, whatever is an object of observation for removing obstructions must be a thoroughly established nature that is a **final mode of subsistence** of the phenomenon in question and yet the Proponents of Mind-Only hold that because the selflessness of persons is the main object of meditation by Hearers and Solitary Realizers, it is a thoroughly established nature despite its not being the **final mode of subsistence** of persons, this being the selflessness of phenomena in their system. In the Mind-Only School, a person's emptiness of being substantially existent in the sense of being self-sufficient is not the final mode of subsistence of persons (which has to be a selflessness of phenomena) and thus, from the perspective of the Middle Way School, is not fit to be a thoroughly established nature, and, furthermore, since a selflessness of persons must be truly established, it cannot be an imputational nature and thus, in the Mind-Only system, would have to be an other-powered nature.

A-ku Lo-drö-gya-tso calls Gung-tang's explanation a "great good explanation,"[a] and indeed it forges sense where sense seems to be lacking. Nevertheless, it is troubling that Ke-drup clearly is setting forth an assertion by the Proponents of Mind-Only themselves, not one forced on them from another system's perspective. Wondering what Ke-drup could have had in mind, I have come up with an involved but perhaps more attractive explanation arrived at through considering the assertions on the selflessness of persons in the system of the Sūtra School Following Reasoning, that is, following Dignāga and Dharmakīrti.

Like the Proponents of Mind-Only, the Proponents of Sūtra Following Reasoning hold that the object explicitly comprehended by an uninterrupted path belonging to a path of seeing or a path of meditation must be perceived directly, but, unlike the Proponents of Mind-Only, they maintain that whatever is perceived directly must be an impermanent, specifically characterized phenomenon, and since such are always compounded phenomena, they must be other-powered natures. Because a selflessness or emptiness is an uncompounded phenomenon, it is not a specifically characterized phenomenon and thus cannot be realized directly. Consequently, the Proponents of Sūtra assert that a yogic direct perception does not **explicitly** realize selflessness; rather, it realizes the mind and body as no longer qualified with such a self. Thus, compounded phenomena—the mental and physical aggregates—are directly realized by a yogic direct perception, whereby the emptiness of a self of persons is **implicitly** realized. This fact greatly distinguishes the Proponents of Sūtra from the Great Vehicle schools, which assert direct cognition of emptiness itself. As

---

[a] *Precious Lamp*, 109.6: *legs bshad chen mo*.

Ḡön-chok-jik-may-w̄ang-b̄o says in his *Precious Garland of Tenets:*[519]

> Because the appearing object of direct perception must be a specifically characterized object, the Proponents of Sūtra do not assert that the subtle selflessness of persons is the object of the mode of apprehension by an uninterrupted path of a Hearer's [or anyone's] path of seeing. This is because they assert that the subtle selflessness of persons is realized **implicitly** by Hearers [and so forth] through **explicit** comprehension of compositional phenomena [namely, the mental and physical aggregates] that are devoid of a self of persons.

Although Ke-drup clearly presents the Proponents of Mind-Only as holding that the selflessness of **phenomena** is explicitly realized in meditative equipoise, I would suggest that perhaps he maintains that their assertion on the realization of the selflessness of **persons** is like that of the Proponents of Sūtra Following Reasoning. In that case, the explicit object of comprehension of a Hearer's path of purification is aggregates that are devoid of a self of persons and thus, being impermanent and compounded, are other-powered natures. The self-contradiction in the tenets of the Mind-Only School, therefore, is that they hold that a final object of observation of purification—that is, the object explicitly realized by a path of purification—is a thoroughly established nature and yet at the same time hold that what a Hearer's uninterrupted path explicitly realizes is not the selflessness of persons but aggregates devoid of a self of persons, the selflessness of persons being realized only implicitly. Thus, although the selflessness of persons is not an other-powered nature, the final object of observation of a Hearer's path of purification is an other-powered nature. This is how I posit Ke-drup's thought when he says that in the Mind-Only system the selflessness of persons is an other-powered nature. However, I might have to admit that this is merely a case of the perspective of the Sūtra School Following Reasoning slipping into his discussion of the Mind-Only School, if I want to maintain that the subtle selflessness of persons is a thoroughly established nature, that is, a final object of observation of a path of purification of the afflictive obstructions.

Issue #164: Is a reasoning consciousness realizing the selflessness of persons a reasoning consciousness that has found the ultimate*?*

Gung-tang has defended Jam-ȳang-shay-b̄a's position that a selflessness of persons is a thoroughly established nature and an ultimate-non-nature, but then in a brilliant and straightforward analysis, he exposes the weakness of his own position, the blame for which he lays at a self-contradiction in Mind-Only tenets.[520] Here Gung-tang responds to the first reasoning mentioned above (388) in support of the position, which backs up the position held by Paṇ-chen S̄ö-nam-drak-b̄a and so forth, that a selflessness of persons is not an actual thoroughly established nature. That reasoning, in Jik-may-dam-chö-gya-tso's rendering, is:

> It [absurdly] follows that a subtle selflessness of persons is a middle because of being an emptiness. If you accept that a subtle selflessness of persons is a middle, then it [absurdly] follows that a Proponent of Sūtra has found the view of the middle because [according to you] a subtle selflessness of persons is a middle and [according to you] a Proponent of Sūtra is a person who has found the view of the middle. If you accept that a Proponent of Sūtra has found the view of the middle, then it [absurdly] follows that a Proponent of Sūtra is a Proponent of the Middle (*dbu ma pa, mādhyamika*)[a] because you have asserted that a Proponent of Sūtra has found the view of the middle. You cannot accept that a Proponent of Sūtra has found the view of the middle because a Proponent of Sūtra is not a Proponent of Mind-Only.

Gung-tang's response revolves around usage of vocabulary standard in this highly developed scholastic tradition and can be rendered only in its formal language, which for those accustomed to it is distinctly evocative but for others is stilted:

1. Gung-tang maintains that a selflessness of persons is an object **found** by a reasoning consciousness analyzing the ultimate[b] and hence that a reasoning consciousness realizing a selflessness of persons is a reasoning consciousness **analyzing** an ultimate.[c]
2. Therefore, he is willing to admit that the object—with respect to which a reasoning consciousness realizing the selflessness of persons in the continuum of a Hearer sectarian (that is, a Proponent of the Great Exposition or a Proponent of Sūtra) has become a reasoning consciousness—is found by that consciousness and that this object is an ultimate.[d]
3. But he is not willing to allow that a reasoning consciousness realizing the selflessness of persons in the continuum of a Hearer sectarian is a reasoning consciousness that has **found the ultimate upon analysis.**[e]

He says that the reason why Hearer sectarians have not found the ultimate is that they have not found the view of the middle, and the basic reason for this,

---

a According to Proponents of Mind-Only, all Proponents of the Middle are Proponents of Mind-Only because only the Mind-Only School presents the true middle between the extremes of superimposition and deprecation.

b *don dam dpyod pa'i rigs shes kyis rnyed don.*

c *don dam dpyod pa'i rigs shes.*

d *khyod gang la rigs shes su song ba'i yul de khyod kyis rnyed pa gang zhig/ yul de don dam yin pa.*

e *don dam dpyad nas rnyed pa'i rigs shes.*

in turn, is that they are proponents of tenets that have fallen to extremes of permanence and/or annihilation. Gung-tang does not spell out the latter point, but his meaning has to be that since Proponents of the Great Exposition and Proponents of Sūtra hold that objects are established by way of their own character as the referents of conceptual consciousnesses and that subject and object are different entities, they have fallen to an extreme of over-reification, called an extreme of permanence, and hence do not have a view of the middle. How could one say that a Hearer sectarian with an extreme view has found the ultimate even if that Hearer has realized (and thus found) the selflessness of persons!

The problem is that the Jam-ȳang-shay-b̄a tradition holds a view realizing the selflessness of persons to be a view realizing a thoroughly established nature, an ultimate truth, and an ultimate, but this same view of a selflessness of persons is propounded by lower schools of tenets that hold the opposite to the Mind-Only view of the selflessness of phenomena. This is why Jam-ȳang-shay-b̄a and his followers find it impossible to hold that these lower systems propound a view of the middle or that their followers find, or realize, the ultimate. The line has to be drawn somewhere, and Gung-tang refuses to admit that a reasoning consciousness realizing the selflessness of persons in the continuum of a Proponent of the Great Exposition or a Proponent of Sūtra is a reasoning consciousness that has **found the ultimate**, even though it has found the selflessness of persons which is an ultimate. As A-ku L̄o-drö-gya-tso adds,[a] one therefore has to say that an uninterrupted path of the Lesser Vehicle (this being a path consciousness realizing the selflessness of persons), upon having analyzed the ultimate, does not find it.

Gung-tang admits that "these are not comfortable in the mind, but they are internal contradictions in the tenets [of the Mind-Only School]."[b] He cites a passage in Ke-drup's *Opening the Eyes of the Fortunate* that presents a similar picture of self-contradiction in Mind-Only tenets. In that passage Ke-drup explains that there is no disagreement among scholars of the Mind-Only and Middle Way schools that whatever is a true cessation is necessarily a thusness, but the Proponents of Mind-Only have a "very heavy, great burden of self-contradiction"[521] in that:

- They explicitly assert that Hearer Superiors directly realize true cessation.
- They explicitly assert that Hearer Superiors do not directly realize the real nature.[c]

---

[a] A-ku L̄o-drö-gya-tso's *Precious Lamp,* 112.2: *theg dman gyi bar chad med lam gyis don dam dpyad nas ma rnyed.*

[b] Gung-tang's *Difficult Points,* 150.17: *'di dag blor bde ba mi 'dug kyang grub mtha'i nang 'gal yin.* See also Gung-tang's *Annotations,* 31.5.

[c] *chos nyid, dharmatā.* I also translate this as "noumenon."

- However, they implicitly have to assert that whoever directly realizes a true cessation necessarily directly realizes the real nature.

Gung-tang, by exposing the difficulties in Jam-ȳang-shay-b̄a's and his own position that a selflessness of persons is a thoroughly established nature and an ultimate, reveals possible reasons behind Paṇ-chen S̄ö-nam-drak-b̄a's assertion right from the start that a selflessness of persons is a thoroughly established nature **in terms of a selflessness of persons** but is not a thoroughly established nature or an ultimate. By this simple device, Paṇ-chen S̄ö-nam-drak-b̄a avoids all of these problems, but in the process he has to maintain the at least equally uncomfortable positions that a selflessness of persons is an imputational nature, that the object of observation by a path of purification of obstructions for Hearers and Solitary Realizers is an imputational nature, and that a selflessness of persons does not truly exist and is not established by way of its own character.

Issue #165: Is the selflessness of persons the mode of subsistence of persons?

Jay-d̄zün Chö-ḡyi-gyel-tsen[522] takes a position between these two. He does this in response to the second reasoning, cited above (388), which backs up the position held by Paṇ-chen S̄ö-nam-drak-b̄a and others, that a selflessness of persons is not an actual thoroughly established nature:

> Also, it [absurdly] follows with respect to a subtle selflessness of persons that it is an emptiness of persons because [according to you] its way of being an emptiness is logical. If you accept that a subtle selflessness of persons is an emptiness of persons, then it [absurdly] follows that a subtle selflessness of persons is a mode of subsistence of persons because you have asserted that a subtle selflessness of persons is an emptiness of persons. If you accept that a subtle selflessness of persons is a mode of subsistence of persons, then it [absurdly] follows with respect to a Proponent of Sūtra that he/she realizes a mode of subsistence of persons because you have asserted that a subtle selflessness of persons is a mode of subsistence of persons. You cannot accept that a Proponent of Sūtra realizes a mode of subsistence of persons because he/she is a person who makes erroneous superimpositions about the mode of subsistence of persons, since he/she is a person who conceives that persons are established by way of their own character as the referents of conceptual consciousnesses apprehending them, and non-establishment as such is the subtle mode of subsistence.

Like Jam-ȳang-shay-b̄a but unlike Paṇ-chen S̄ö-nam-drak-b̄a, Jay-d̄zün Chö-ḡyi-gyel-tsen holds that a selflessness of persons is an **actual** thoroughly established nature and an ultimate truth. Still, Jay-d̄zün Chö-ḡyi-gyel-tsen[523] (unlike

Jam-ȳang-shay-b̄a and his commentator Gung-tang) is willing to take the further step that the selflessness of persons is a mode of subsistence of persons and thus that Proponents of Sūtra realize a mode of subsistence of persons, even though not the **subtle** mode of subsistence. Jay-d̄zün Chö-ḡyi-gyel-tsen's maneuver is intended for the sake of maintaining that although Proponents of Sūtra make false superimpositions with respect to persons' selflessness of phenomena, they do not make false superimpositions with respect to the mode of subsistence of persons, that is, the selflessness of persons (even though he implicitly concedes that they make false superimpositions with respect to the **subtle** mode of subsistence of persons and other phenomena). Since this is where he chooses to draw the line, his response to the above reasoning is that the final reason does not entail the consequence—namely, the facts (1) that a Proponent of Sūtra is a person who conceives that persons are established by way of their own character as the referents of conceptual consciousnesses apprehending them and (2) that non-establishment as such is the subtle mode of subsistence do not entail that a Proponent of Sūtra is a person who makes erroneous superimpositions about the mode of subsistence of persons.

In a similar fashion,[524] Jay-d̄zün Chö-ḡyi-gyel-tsen maintains that a view realizing the selflessness of persons is a view of the middle, but he is not willing to concede that a **person** dwelling in a view realizing the selflessness of persons is a **person** dwelling in the view of the middle, since the latter is constituted only by Proponents of Mind-Only.

It seems to me that the basic tension stems from an ambiguity in the *Sūtra Unraveling the Thought* itself, for it has tendencies in both directions. On the one hand, the sūtra emphasizes that Hearers and Solitary Realizers utilize just this path of meditation on the three natures and three non-natures, and thus one would think, as Jay-d̄zün Chö-ḡyi-gyel-tsen does, that if the selflessness of persons is a thoroughly established nature of persons and an ultimate truth of persons, it would also be the mode of subsistence of persons. Yet, on the other hand, the *Sūtra Unraveling the Thought* (as in the first four chapters) repeatedly indicates that Hearers and Solitary Realizers do not get at the final nature of things, and thus it is not comfortable to hold that according to the Mind-Only School the proponents of lower schools of tenets realize a thoroughly established nature, an ultimate truth, or a mode of subsistence of persons. Tibetan scholars have faced this problem only to find no comfortable solution.

In this case, juxtaposition of tenets causes the system to crash on itself with considerable clatter. Nevertheless, the viewing of the rubble is accomplished through applying the principles of the doctrine of three natures and three non-natures in the Greater and Lesser Vehicles, thereby serving to increase familiarity with basic postures of the Mind-Only School. When one turns the focus back on the structural principles used to expose the tangle, it is revealed that one's understanding has advanced.

Issue #166: Is the selflessness of persons an element of attributes?

Now let us turn to the third reasoning, cited above (388), that backs up the position held by Paṇ-chen Sö-nam-drak-b̄a and so forth, that a selflessness of persons is not an actual thoroughly established nature:

> Also, it [absurdly] follows that a subtle selflessness of persons is an element of attributes because of being an emptiness. If you accept that a subtle selflessness of persons is an element of attributes, then it [absurdly] follows that the element of attributes has divisions that are different entities and types because you have asserted that a subtle selflessness of persons is an element of attributes. You cannot accept that the element of attributes has divisions that are different entities and types because [Maitreya's *Ornament for Clear Realization*] says:[a]
>
> The element of attributes[b] has no divisions.
> Therefore the lineages cannot be different.
> Divisions of lineage are thoroughly imputed
> Through differences in the dependent phenomena.

I would add that the *Sūtra Unraveling the Thought* in a similar vein speaks sixteen times about suchness being of **one** taste, thereby seeming to rule out that there would be two types of selflessness within that one taste. For instance, at the end of the fourth chapter it says:

> Subhūti, you should know by this form of explanation also that that which has a character everywhere of one taste is the ultimate. Subhūti, it is like this: For example, space is signless, non-conceptual, and non-increasing with respect to the manifold various aspects of instances of forms; it has the character of being of one taste everywhere. Similarly, with respect to the phenomena that have different characters, the ultimate is to be viewed as having a nature that is everywhere of one taste.

We can surmise—from Jik-may-dam-chö-gya-tso's rendering of the third reasoning behind Paṇ-chen Sö-nam-drak-b̄a's view—that the latter found it more attractive to hold that the selflessness of persons is not an **actual** element of attributes even though it is an element of attributes **in terms of the selflessness of persons**.

To refute this position, Jik-may-dam-chö-gya-tso[525] quotes statements by Maitreya, Asaṅga, Vasubandhu, Sthiramati, D̄zong-ka-b̄a, Gyel-tsap, and

[a] Ge-luk-b̄a scholars generally take this text to be of the Yogic Autonomy Middle Way School with occasional passages that reflect views of the Consequence School; hence, its relevance at this point would have to be in terms of general perspective in the Great Vehicle schools.

[b] *chos dbyings, dharmadhātu.*

Ke-drup that espouse the contrary "with one voice." As cited above (393), Maitreya's *Differentiation of the Middle and the Extremes* (*Emptiness in Mind-Only*, 162-163) says:

> The objects of activity [of the path] of purification are twofold.
> [Both] are said to be only the **single** [thoroughly established nature].

and Vasubandhu's commentary (*Emptiness in Mind-Only*, 163) explains:

> The suchness that is the object of activity of purification is of two types...[they are] said to be the thoroughly established nature. The other natures [that is, imputational and other-powered natures][526] are not objects of the **two** types of exalted wisdom purifying [obstructions].

and Sthiramati's sub-commentary rephrases:

> These **twofold** objects of activity of purification are expressed by the sole thoroughly established nature.

Asaṅga's *Summary of Manifest Knowledge* similarly says:

> What is the thusness of virtuous phenomena? The **two** types of selflessness, emptiness, signlessness, limit of reality, the ultimate; the element of attributes also is it.

and his *Grounds of Bodhisattvas:*

> Selflessness in persons and phenomena, the ultimate, thusness of phenomena, profound.

and his *Compendium of Ascertainments:*

> All selflessnesses—whatsoever selflessnesses of persons and whatsoever selflessnesses of phenomena—are, in general, called "emptiness."

Dzong-ka-ba's *The Essence of Eloquence* (*Emptiness in Mind-Only*, 224) says:

> The emptiness of the imputational factor—a self of persons—in other-powered natures—the aggregates—is posited as the thoroughly established nature that is the selflessness of persons.

Ke-drup's *Opening the Eyes of the Fortunate* says:

> A thoroughly established nature is a thusness that is an emptiness of establishment in accordance with what is superimposed by the **two** types of consciousnesses conceiving self in other-powered natures. The definition [of a thoroughly established nature] is also just that.

Gyel-tsap's *Explanation of (Dharmakīrti's) Commentary on (Dignāga's) "Compilation of Prime Cognition": Unerring Illumination of the Path to Liberation* says:

> Emptiness that is a selflessness in persons and phenomena is known directly by Superiors' individual meditative equipoise.

Jik-may-dam-chö-gya-tso concludes with an observation that, except for minor differences, Jay-d̄zün Chö-ḡyi-gyel-tsen and Jam-ȳang-shay-b̄a agree in how they present the opinion that the selflessness of persons is indeed an actual element of attributes.

Issue #167: How to deal with Ke-drup's contradictions?

As detailed above (issue #156), when Ke-drup seemingly blunders by indicating that:

> The Proponents of Mind-Only and the Middle Way Autonomists do not assert that a selflessness of persons is an ultimate truth, and also they assert that the reasonings refuting a self of persons are reasonings analyzing a conventionality.

Jam-ȳang-shay-b̄a explains this away by showing (or manufacturing) that Ke-drup is actually referring to the coarse selflessness of persons. Jay-d̄zün Chö-ḡyi-gyel-tsen,[527] however, takes Ke-drup's *Opening the Eyes of the Fortunate* at face value as teaching that the selflessness of persons is indeed **not** an actual thoroughly established nature but that Ke-drup is wrong about this. Jay-d̄zün Chö-ḡyi-gyel-tsen indirectly admits that this involves Ke-drup in a manifest self-contradiction, for Ke-drup also holds that:[528]

> No scholar of the Mind-Only School or Middle Way School disagrees with the assertion that whatever is a true cessation is a thusness.

If any true cessation is a thusness (and hence an emptiness and so forth), then a true cessation achieved by a Hearer or Solitary Realizer is also a thusness. Moreover, if any true cessation is a thusness, then, even more so, any selflessness would have to be a thusness, but, as we have seen, Ke-drup says that a selflessness of persons is not an ultimate (and hence not an emptiness, thusness, and so forth). Jay-d̄zün Chö-ḡyi-gyel-tsen, by taking Ke-drup's original statement (that the selflessness of persons is not an ultimate) at face value has to accept that Ke-drup incurs self-contradiction, whereas, two centuries later, Jam-ȳang-shay-b̄a avoids this problem by explaining away Ke-drup's original statement.

Jay-d̄zün Chö-ḡyi-gyel-tsen proceeds to point out that Ke-drup himself, in his commentary on Maitreya's *Ornament for Clear Realization,* indicates that according to the Autonomy School true cessations are not asserted to be emptinesses, thus contradicting the above-quoted statement to the opposite effect. Jay-d̄zün Chö-ḡyi-gyel-tsen clearly does not fear admitting that Ke-drup had not worked out the implications of his exposition, but it needs to be noticed that Jam-ȳang-shay-b̄a often employs merely a facade of pretending to construct a seamless harmony in the views of D̄zong-ka-b̄a and his student Ke-drup in the process of making an esthetically delightful display of his own ingenuity. In this case, however, I do not have a confident sense that this is all that Jam-ȳang-shay-b̄a is doing, despite its being likely that if Ke-drup was referring only to the coarse selflessness of persons, he would, at some point, have made clear his opinion on the subtle selflessness of persons. For me, the issues still dangle with no satisfactory conclusion despite Jam-ȳang-shay-b̄a's skillful attempts to forge consistency—impressive in the breadth of material juxtaposed in the process.

21. Comparing Schools on the Three Non-Natures

Issue #168: How do the Mind-Only, Autonomy, and Consequence schools take the three non-natures?

Following Gung-tang,[529] A-ku Lo-drö-gya-tso[530] lists the differing presentations of the three non-natures by the Mind-Only, Autonomy, and Consequence schools:

Character-non-natures

For the Proponents of Mind-Only, imputational natures, aside from only being posited by names and terminology, are natureless in the sense of not being established by way of their own character.

For the Autonomists, imputational natures, aside from being only factors wrongly imputed to be truly established, are natureless in the sense of not ultimately being established by way of their own character.

For the Consequentialists, imputational natures, aside from merely being factors imputed by nominal conventions, are natureless in the sense of not being established from their own side.

Other-powered natures

For the Proponents of Mind-Only, other-powered natures are natureless in terms of production because they are not produced causelessly.[a]

For the Autonomists, other-powered natures are natureless in terms of production because they do not have production that is established by way of its own character ultimately.

For the Consequentialists, other-powered natures are natureless in terms of production because they do not have production that is established from its own side.

Thoroughly established natures

For the Proponents of Mind-Only, when a thoroughly established nature is posited as ultimate-non-nature, the basis of the quality of emptiness is an other-powered nature such as a pot, which is other than its own thoroughly established nature (though not a different entity from it). Since the thoroughly established nature of a table is the ultimate[b] and is the mere

[a] Jik-may-dam-chö-gya-tso (*Port of Entry,* 197.5) points out that in his *Annotations* (34.1) Gung-tang explains this as referring to production from self but corrects this in his *Difficult Points* (135.10) to causeless production.

[b] Jik-may-dam-chö-gya-tso (*Port of Entry,* 197.6) points out that in his *Annotations* (34.3) Gung-tang (mistakenly) explains that "ultimate" here refers to the object of negation but in his *Difficult Points* (135.12) (correctly) explains that "ultimate" here refers to the actual

negation of the table's establishment as "self" (which, in terms of the self of phenomena, is its establishment by way of its own character as the referent of a conceptual consciousness or its establishment as a different entity from the consciousness apprehending it), it is called an "ultimate-non-nature."

For the Autonomists, the object of negation is not inherent existence but true existence. Gung-tang[531] emphasizes that the explanation of the term "ultimate" in "ultimate-non-nature" as referring to the object of negation and not to the fact that the thoroughly established nature is the ultimate is mainly from the viewpoint of the Consequence School. For the Autonomist Kamalashīla in his *Illumination of the Middle* posits the thoroughly established nature as the "ultimate-non-nature" in accordance with the *Sūtra Unraveling the Thought,* saying that it is the ultimate in the sense that it is the final object of observation by a path of purification and is a naturelessness in the sense that it is the mere negation of true establishment with respect to its bases of emptiness. In Kamalashīla's rendition, the term "ultimate" in "ultimate-non-nature" refers to the fact that the thoroughly established nature is the ultimate.[a]

---

ultimate—that is to say, it indicates that the thoroughly established nature is the actual ultimate. In other words, does the fact that thoroughly established natures are ultimate-non-natures mean that thoroughly established natures are not established **as** the entity of the object of negation—that is, are not established by way of their own character as the referents of conceptual consciousnesses—or does it mean that thoroughly established natures are themselves the very non-establishment of objects by way of their own character as the referents of conceptual consciousnesses. I agree with Gung-tang's later explanation that it is the latter, for the *Sūtra Unraveling the Thought* clearly speaks of the thoroughly established nature as being the selflessness of phenomena and as being posited by way of such non-establishment:

> Moreover, that which is the thoroughly established character of phenomena is also called "the ultimate-non-nature." Why? Paramārthasamudgata, that which in phenomena is the selflessness of phenomena is called their "naturelessness." It is the ultimate, and the ultimate is distinguished by the mere naturelessness of all phenomena; therefore, it is called the "ultimate-non-nature."

[a] This seemingly contradicts Jam-ÿang-shay-b̄a's statement (84.3) that the Autonomists and Consequentialists assert that the term "ultimate" in "ultimate-non-nature" refers to the object of negation:

> Though the two—the Autonomists and the Consequentialists—explain it that way, on this occasion [the context] is the system of the Proponents of Mind-Only....

Gung-tang tries to explain away Jam-ÿang-shay-b̄a's *faux pas* by saying that Jam-ÿang-shay-b̄a's reference is **mainly** to the Consequentialists, but Gung-tang does not clarify the resultant suggestion that in a minor way this reading is used in the Autonomy School. We have, however, seen that Gung-tang does not hesitate to re-explain Jam-ÿang-shay-b̄a's positions; thus, I doubt that he uses the term "mainly" merely in order not to refute Jam-ÿang-shay-b̄a directly and thus leave some common ground with his position, but I have not been able to figure out his point, if it is not just weak apologetic.

For the Consequentialists, the term "ultimate" in "ultimate-non-nature" is taken as referring to inherent existence, the object of negation; thus, the term "ultimate" defines the type of nature of which the thoroughly established nature is the negation. Therefore, in the Consequence School, even though the thoroughly established nature is indeed the ultimate, the term "ultimate" in "ultimate-non-nature" is taken as referring not to this fact but to the ultimate establishment or the inherent existence that is the object of negation. Thus, according to the Consequence School, it would be preferable to translate the term as "naturelessness of the ultimate" (although, admittedly, the mere shift in translation does not remove all ambiguity). That the thoroughly established nature is a naturelessness of the ultimate means that it itself is without inherent existence, and thus the object of negation, inherent existence, is posited with respect to the thoroughly established nature and not some other phenomenon. The thoroughly established nature itself is the basis of negation.

It seems to me that even in the Mind-Only School since the thoroughly established nature itself is not established as a self of phenomena (that is, is not established by way of its own character as the referent of a conceptual consciousness), it also can be said that in the Mind-Only School the thoroughly established nature is without the nature of the object of negation even if the Proponents of Mind-Only do not explicitly take the usage of the term "ultimate-non-nature" in the *Sūtra Unraveling the Thought* this way. Also, in the Consequence School, the thoroughly established nature of a phenomenon is constituted by the absence of inherent existence of that phenomenon and hence is the naturelessness of that phenomenon's inherent existence—the basis of emptiness here being the phenomenon and not the thoroughly established nature itself. Therefore, A-ku L̄o-drö-gya-tso's depiction of their respective treatments of the "ultimate-non-natures" as being radically different from the viewpoint of whether the thoroughly established nature can be taken as the basis that is without the respective nature is exaggerated.

Nevertheless, the Mind-Only School does not take true existence or inherent existence to be the object of negation. This is D̄zong-ka-b̄a's point when he says (*Emptiness in Mind-Only,* 93):

> Since this thoroughly established nature is the mere elimination of the nature of self in phenomena,[a] it is called "the ultimate-non-nature of phenomena." However, this is a system that does not assert that the

[a] *chos rnams kyi bdag gi ngo bo.* Notice that here D̄zong-ka-b̄a does not confine the thoroughly established nature to the absence of a self of *phenomena* (which would be *chos bdag gi ngo bo* or *chos kyi bdag gi ngo bo* and not *chos* ***rnams*** *kyi bdag gi ngo bo*) but speaks of it as an absence of self in /of phenomena, and hence it is open to the reading that for him not just the absence of a self of phenomena but also an absence of a self of persons could be the thoroughly established nature. See issues #153-167.

> thoroughly established nature is natureless due to the entity of the negation itself not being established by way of its own character[a] [for in the Mind-Only School emptiness, the thoroughly established nature, **is** ultimately established by way of its own character].

In the Mind-Only School, emptiness, the thoroughly established nature, is established by way of its own character. Dzong-ka-ba is contrasting this assertion with that of the Consequence School, which rejects that the thoroughly established nature is established by way of its own character.

As A-ku Lo-drö-gya-tso[532] points out, the reason why Dzong-ka-ba, in presenting the assertions of the Mind-Only School, interjects the assertions of the Middle Way School (and particularly the Consequence School) is that, for Dzong-ka-ba, the Consequence School represents the final thought of the Perfection of Wisdom Sūtras.

Issue #169: What do "ultimate" and "nature" mean in the two ultimate-non-natures?

According to the Mind-Only School, in the first mode of positing the ultimate-non-nature, other-powered natures are said to be ultimate-non-natures because the ultimate consists of final objects of observation of paths of purification and other-powered natures are not such. Therefore, the nature that other-powered natures here lack is the ultimate, since they are not ultimates. As Jam-yang-shay-ba[533] says, Buddha taught that other-powered natures are ultimate-non-natures in order to promote realization that other-powered natures, although appearing to common beings to be their own final mode of subsistence, are not their own final mode of subsistence.

In the second mode of positing the ultimate-non-nature, thoroughly established natures are said to be ultimate-non-natures because they are the ultimate and are the very lack of a self of phenomena, that is, the absence of objects' being established by way of their own character as the referents of conceptual consciousnesses. Here, "nature" is the self of phenomena that is the object negated, whereas in the first mode of positing the ultimate-non-nature "nature" is the ultimate. Thus, as Jam-yang-shay-ba[534] says, the "nature" of the first mode and the "nature" of the second mode are contradictory.

In the first mode (this being the positing of other-powered natures as ultimate-non-natures), "ultimate" and "nature" both refer to the ultimate,[535] which is the final object of observation by a path of purification and the mode of subsistence.[b] In the second mode of positing the ultimate-non-nature (this being

---

[a] See issue #168.

[b] *gnas lugs* or *sdod lugs*. Jam-yang-shay-ba (*Notes*, 315.4-315.6) also presents an alternative assertion that changes the terminology of "mode of subsistence" slightly and alters the reading dramatically (and unjustifiably). According to this reading, in the first mode of positing

the positing of thoroughly established natures as ultimate-non-natures), "ultimate" and "nature" do not have the same meaning, for "ultimate" means "final object of observation by a path of purification" and "nature" means "the object of negation." Therefore, in the two modes of positing the ultimate-non-nature, "ultimate" in both cases refers to the final object of observation by a path of purification,[a] and "nature" in the first mode also refers to the ultimate but in

---

the ultimate-non-nature, "nature" refers to objects' **establishment as their own** mode of subsistence (*rang rang gi sdod lugs su grub pa*). I find this explanation to be unacceptable, since although it is the case that other-powered natures are not established as their own mode of subsistence, imputational natures and thoroughly established natures also are not established as their own mode of subsistence. For just as a table is not its own mode of subsistence, but the emptiness of a table is a table's mode of subsistence, so uncompounded space is not its own mode of subsistence, but the emptiness of uncompounded space is uncompounded space's mode of subsistence, and similarly a thoroughly established nature is not its own mode of subsistence, but the emptiness of a thoroughly established nature is a thoroughly established nature's mode of subsistence. If Jam-ȳang-shay-b̄a's alternative reading were a proper explanation of the first mode of positing the ultimate-non-nature, it indeed could be applied to all phenomena and not just to other-powered natures, but this reading flies in the face of the *Sūtra Unraveling the Thought,* which says (Lamotte, *Saṃdhinirmocana,* 68 [6], and 194; Dön-drup-gyel-tsen's *Four Intertwined Commentaries,* 7.3-7.5; and Powers, *Wisdom of Buddha,* 101):

> Paramārthasamudgata, that which is the object of observation of purification in phenomena I teach to be the ultimate, and other-powered characters are not the object of observation of purification. Therefore, they are said to be "without the nature of the ultimate."

The sūtra clearly glosses the term "ultimate" with "the object of observation of purification," which, far from being the establishment of objects as their own mode of subsistence, is the **non**-establishment of objects as their own mode of subsistence. Thus, this way of depicting the first mode of positing the ultimate-non-nature is clearly not what is explicitly set forth in the *Sūtra Unraveling the Thought.*

In his *Notes* (313.3-315.2) Jam-ȳang-shay-b̄a makes a distinction between modes of positing the ultimate-non-nature by using the phrase "as explicitly expressed in the *Sūtra Unraveling the Thought*" to refer to one of them, presumably to distinguish it from this more general exposition of the three natures (this being the radically different one that I have just indicated is not what the *Sūtra Unraveling the Thought* explicitly teaches). None of his followers, however, takes up this distinction. Indeed, Jam-ȳang-shay-b̄a himself objects to this system of presentation if one holds that it reflects what the *Sūtra Unraveling the Thought* explicitly indicates about these two modes. I see no point in making a double exposition of the three natures—that is, one that is explicitly presented in the *Sūtra Unraveling the Thought* and a more general one.

[a] W̄el-mang Ḡön-chok-gyel-tsen (*Notes on Ḡön-chok-jik-may-w̄ang-b̄o's Lectures,* 401.5) presents the (unfounded) opinion that in the second mode "ultimate" refers to the self of phenomena. Indeed, if the "nature" of the second mode of positing the ultimate-non-nature were establishment **as** the entity of the object of negation, then such a mode of ultimate-non-nature would have to be applied to **all** phenomena, not just thoroughly established natures, but this is clearly not what the *Sūtra Unraveling the Thought* is explicitly indicating.

the second mode refers to the object of negation.

Issue #170: Since external objects are thoroughly negated, how do Buddhas—who have removed all predispositions giving rise to appearances—perceive their own extraordinary bodies and perceive suffering sentient beings?

As Jik-may-dam-chö-gya-tso[536] says, the **production** of the signs and beauties of a Buddha's body and so forth occurs through the force of uncontaminated predispositions, and Buddhas' cognition of all phenomena comes through the force of having completed the two collections of merit and wisdom.[537] Thus, their cognition of their own and other Buddhas' qualities as well as their intimate knowledge of sentient beings occurs neither from predispositions for these appearances nor from external objects impinging on consciousness but as a result of having cultivated merit and wisdom. These salutary practices allow internally possessed uncontaminated forces to blossom, providing a means to know all that can be known.

From this description, the conclusion can be drawn that the externality being refuted refers to the falsely imagined process of, for instance, a patch of blue producing an eye consciousness apprehending blue with the resultant appearance that apprehended-object and apprehending-subject seem to be distant and cut off. It is not being negated that there are other sentient beings, for they can be known—not by a web of shared predispositions—but by having brought health to the mind by practice of merit and wisdom.[a]

Rather, the *Sūtra Unraveling the Thought* speaks within the context of dividing all phenomena into the three classes of the three natures and applying three types of naturelessness individually to them.

[a] From this viewpoint, Yoshifumi Ueda concludes that the Yogic Practice School of Asaṅga and Vasubandhu does not refute external objects, and instead restricts the meaning of "consciousness-only" to the relation between subject and object **in the case of an unenlightened being**. See *Emptiness in Mind-Only*, Appendix 2, 520ff.

PART FOUR: *DIFFERENTIATING SCRIPTURES*

22. Strategies for Interpretation

Although examinations into whether scriptures are definitive or require interpretation are well known in the Mind-Only School and Middle Way School, it is not that such distinctions are absent in the Great Exposition School and Sūtra School. As Jam-ȳang-shay-ba̅ says, there are a variety of positions on this question among the Lesser Vehicle schools:[538]

- Some subdivisions of the Great Exposition assert, in accordance with the description in Bhāvaviveka's *Blaze of Reasoning*, that all of [Buddha's] word is just definitive meaning,[a] that is, to be taken literally.
- Other subdivisions of the Great Exposition assert that there are both definitive meanings and meanings requiring interpretation.
- All later Proponents of the Great Exposition, including even the Vatsīputrīyas, assert that even Perfection of Wisdom Sūtras require interpretation.

The latter take statements in the Perfection of Wisdom Sūtras about the absence of true existence, no production, naturelessness, no attainment, no abandonment, and the non-existence of things as referring to how truth, production, and so forth are asserted by non-Buddhist schools, such as the Sāṃkhyas. He gives examples:[539]

> Even most Proponents of Sūtra Following Scripture and Proponents of Sūtra Following Reasoning assert that the Great Vehicle scriptural collections are the Word [of Buddha] requiring interpretation.... According to some Proponents of Sūtra such as Saṅghagupta there is a thought behind the words of the Perfection of Wisdom Sūtras and so forth saying "All phenomena do not exist, do not exist," because it would be unsuitable for the meaning of the statement that "Phenomena do not exist" to be that phenomena utterly do not exist, and, therefore, scripture and reasoning establish that the meaning is to be taken as referring to the lowliness and smallness of [impermanent] objects.... With respect to the statements in the Perfection of Wisdom Sūtras [that all phenomena] are nothings[b] and so forth, since effective things are momentary, they are said to be nothings and so forth, these being terms of lowliness.... Also, since non-effective things are plentiful and effective things are fewer, [all phenomena] are called "non-things." And they are called natureless, unproduced, unceased, and so forth because of not being produced beforehand and passing away

a *nges don, nītārtha.*

b *dngos med.*

> afterwards, as, for example, when someone with little wealth is said to have no wealth.

Jam-ȳang-shay-b̄a pokes fun at Tibetans who claim that no such distinctions are made in the Lesser Vehicle schools:[540]

> Tibetans who have said with the cry of a bewildered ox that the Hearer schools assert that the Great Vehicle is the Word [of Buddha] but that there are no [sūtras] requiring interpretation should hear this fearless lion's roar[a] and take heed!

Interpretation in the Great Vehicle Schools

Jam-ȳang-shay-b̄a[541] details five strategies used in the Mind-Only and Middle Way schools as analytical procedures to differentiate what requires interpretation and what is definitive,[b] these being the four reliances, four reasonings, four thoughts, four indirect intentions, and a general fourfold format. He says that **both** words and meanings are differentiated by the four reliances and the four reasonings, and thus it is not just scriptures that are taken to require interpretation and to be definitive but also meanings, or phenomena, themselves. Phenomena themselves are to be tested to determine whether they are definitive or require interpretation with regard to their final mode of being, even though in the Mind-Only School the main mode of interpretation, as will be seen below, is concerned with means of expression (scriptures).

---

[a] The title of Jam-ȳang-shay-b̄a's root text is *Presentation of Tenets: Lion's Roar Eradicating Error, Precious Lamp Illuminating the Genuine Path to Omniscience.*

[b] Gung-tang makes a critical difference between *gsung rab* ***kyi*** *drang nges 'byed pa* and *gsung rab* ***la*** *drang nges 'byed pa*; I translate the former as "differentiating the interpretable and definitive **within** the scriptures" and the latter as "differentiating the interpretable and definitive **with respect to** the scriptures"; admittedly, the English is no clearer than the Tibetan. According to him (*Difficult Points,* 38.4), the former, "differentiating the interpretable and definitive **within** the scriptures," means to identify what are interpretable and what are definitive scriptures from among the scriptures (*gsung rab kyi nang nas 'drang don gyi gsung rab dang nges don gyi gsung rab gang yin so sor ngos bzung ba la byed*) whereas the latter, "differentiating the interpretable and the definitive **with respect to** the scriptures," means to differentiate the interpretable and the definitive with respect to the **meaning** of the scriptures, this requiring extensive delineation of the presentation of the two truths, which itself requires realization of emptiness. Therefore, the latter cannot be required for realization of emptiness, whereas the former can. The latter is called (37.7) "differentiating the interpretable and the definitive on the level of the meaning that is expressed within the scriptures" (*brjod bya don gyi drang nges 'byed pa*), whereas the former is called (38.5) "differentiating the interpretable and the definitive on the level of the words that are the means of expression" (*rjod byed tshig gi drang nges 'byed pa*). See *Reflections on Reality,* 99.

Four Reliances

The first of the five strategies are the four reliances, which are expressed in sūtra:

> Rely on doctrine, but do not rely on persons.
> Rely on meaning, but do not rely on words.
> Rely on definitive meaning, but do not rely on interpretable meaning.
> Rely on exalted wisdom, but do not rely on consciousness.

The movement is toward non-conceptual realization of the ultimate, approached through analysis.

Four Reasonings

The four reasonings are general Buddhist approaches to knowledge through investigating causation, function, affirmation or contradiction by valid cognition, and the nature of objects.[542]

1. The reasoning of dependence[a] is from the viewpoint that the arising of effects depends on causes and conditions.
2. The reasoning of performance of function[b] is from the viewpoint that phenomena perform their respective functions, such as fire performing the function of burning.
3. The reasoning of tenable proof[c] is to prove a meaning without contradicting valid cognition—direct, inferential, or believable scripture.
4. The reasoning of nature[d] is to examine from the viewpoint of (1) natures renowned in the world, such as heat being the nature of fire and moisture being the nature of water,[e] (2) inconceivable natures such as placing a world-system in a single hair-pore, and so forth.

Four Thoughts

Scriptures are differentiated into the interpretable and the definitive by the four thoughts and the four indirect intentions. The four thoughts[f] are the actual

---

a *ltos pa'i rigs pa, apekṣāyukti.*

b *bya ba byed pa'i rigs pa, kāryakāraṇayukti.*

c *'thad pas sgrub pa'i rigs pa, upapattisādhanayukti.*

d *chos nyid kyi rigs pa, dharmatāyukti.*

e This suggests that Buddhists are content with the fact that moisture is the nature of water and do not look to a creator deity who makes water wet.

f *dgongs pa bzhi, catvāro 'bhiprāyā.* For the four thoughts and four indirect intentions, see Étienne Lamotte, *La Somme du grand véhicule d'Asaṅga,* reprint, 2 vols., Publications de l'Institute Orientaliste de Louvain 8 (Louvain: Université de Louvain, 1973), vol. 1, 129-132 (II.31), and vol. 2, 41-42; and John P. Keenan, *The Summary of the Great Vehicle by*

facts in consideration of which Buddha made statements that are not literally acceptable. They involve determining what Buddha's own thought on the topic is. Jam-ȳang-shay-ba̅ gives examples for each:[543]

1. Thinking of sameness:[a] For instance, when Shākyamuni Buddha said, "At that time, I was the Buddha Vipashyi," the meaning he had in mind is not that the person qualified by being Shākyamuni Buddha was the person qualified by being the Buddha Vipashyi; rather, he made that statement in consideration of the sameness in truth body.
2. Thinking of another meaning:[b] For instance, Buddha's statement "All phenomena are natureless" is not literally acceptable according to the Mind-Only School; rather, what he had in mind was the three natures and their respective non-natures.
3. Thinking of another time:[c] For instance, Buddha's statement "Through merely planting wish-prayers you will be born in the Blissful Pure Land" is not literally acceptable since it was made in consideration that one would be born there at another time upon the accumulation of numerous causes and conditions beyond the making of wish-prayers.
4. Thinking of a person's attitude:[d] For instance, Buddha praised a particular root of virtue such as charity for one person, but derided satisfaction with that for another.

These four are concerned with the truth behind non-literal statements, but are not concerned with the purpose, or intention, for Buddha's teaching this way, which are the focus of the next set of four.

Four Indirect Intentions

A sūtra having a thought behind it is also a sūtra having an indirect intention,[e] and vice versa, and thus the two sets of four are to be understood as being from different viewpoints. According to Jam-ȳang-shay-ba̅,[544] sūtras whose thought must be explained as other than the literal reading, as in "This was said in consideration of such and such," are those having a thought (that is, something else in Buddha's own thought), whereas non-literal sūtras such that they call for explanation in the manner of "This does not teach straight out, but the thought indicated with indirect speech is such and such," are those having indirect

Bodhisattva Asaṅga: Translated from the Chinese of Paramārtha (Berkeley, Calif.: Numata Center for Buddhist Translation and Research, 1992), 55-56.

a *mnyam pa nyid la dgongs pa, samatābhiprāya.*

b *don gzhan la dgongs pa, arthāntarābhiprāya.*

c *dus gzhan la dgongs pa, kālāntarābhiprāya.*

d *gang zag gi bsam pa la dgongs pa, pudgalāntarābhiprāya.*

e *ldem dgongs, abhisaṃdhaya.*

intention. Jam-ȳang-shay-b̄a cites Asvabhāva's[a] *Connected Explanation of (Asaṅga's) "Summary of the Great Vehicle"*:

> Thought is only what is set in [Buddha's] mind; it is not asserted relative to another. Indirect intention is relative to another's apprehension.

Nga-w̄ang-b̄el-den[545] explains:

> "Thought" (*dgongs pa, abhiprāya*) is posited from the viewpoint of indicating the basis in [Buddha's] thought, "Thinking of this, [such and such] was said," and "indirect intention" (*ldem dgongs, abhisaṃdhaya*) is posited from the viewpoint of indicating purpose, "[Such and such] was said for this purpose." Since thought and indirect intention are assigned by way of different modes of positing **with respect to the same non-literal sūtra**, [a sūtra having an] indirect intention and [a sūtra having an] indirect thought must be asserted as mutually inclusive.[b] The basis in [Buddha's] thought is just what the Teacher [that is, Buddha] has set in [his own] mind and is not relative to another—the trainee—whereas purpose definitely must rely on another, the trainee, since it is for the sake of nurturing another.... Whatever is a non-literal sūtra [passage] is necessarily both [a passage] indirectly intending transformation and [a passage having] a thought of another meaning.

In this way, the four indirect intentions provide models of interpretation centered around what Buddha intends for his listeners:

1. Indirectly intending entry:[c] For instance, when Buddha teaches that "Forms and so forth exist" to communicate that forms and so forth are established by way of their own character as the referents of their respective terms and conceptual consciousnesses, this non-factual teaching is given so that Hearers could overcome fear of a too flimsy status of phenomena if they were taught the truth, the aim being their entry into the teaching and, thereby, the practice of virtue.
2. Indirectly intending the characters:[d] For instance, when Buddha teaches that all phenomena are natureless, this non-literal teaching is in consideration of the three individual types of naturelessness of the three characters—namely, that imputational natures are character-non-natures, other-powered natures are production-non-natures and ultimate-non-natures, and that thoroughly established natures are ultimate-non-natures.

---

a *ngo bo nyid med pa.*

b *don gcig.*

c *gzhug pa la ldem por dgongs pa, avatāranābhisaṃdhi.*

d *mtshan nyid la ldem por dgongs pa, lakṣaṇābhisaṃdhi.*

3. Indirectly intending an antidote:[a] For instance, Buddha gives teachings in order to overcome eight faults:[546]
   - As an antidote to scorning the Buddha, Shākyamuni Buddha said, for instance, "At that time, I was the Buddha Vipashyi."
   - As an antidote to scorning scriptural doctrines, Buddha gave the non-literal teaching, for instance, "If you worship and serve Buddhas equal in number to the grains of sand of the Ganges, from that point realization of the Great Vehicle will be generated."[b]
   - As an antidote to the defilement of laziness, Buddha—using a thought of another time—said, "Through merely planting wish-prayers you will be born in the Blissful Pure Land." This is not literally acceptable, since the statement was made in consideration that one would be born there at another time upon the accumulation of numerous causes and conditions beyond the mere making of wish-prayers. Similarly, Buddha made the non-literal statement, "By merely uttering the name of the One-Gone-Thus Chandraprabhāvimāla[c] you will be definite with respect to unsurpassed enlightenment," whereas such is not sufficient to make one definite with respect to unsurpassed enlightenment. For the time being, however, such statements encourage effort at these (actually inadequate) practices.
   - As an antidote to being satisfied with only a little, for instance, Buddha derided giving and so forth for some, but praised them for others.
   - As an antidote to desirous behavior, for instance, Buddha praised the wealth of Buddha Lands.
   - As an antidote to prideful behavior, for instance, Buddha praised the wonders of certain Buddhas.
   - As an antidote to regret, for instance, Buddha said that "Those who harm Buddhas and Bodhisattvas will be reborn in high status."
   - As an antidote to defilements of indefiniteness and reversibility, for instance, Buddha prophesied that Hearers would attain the highest enlightenment and spoke of one final vehicle, whereas according to the Mind-Only School Following Scripture not all Hearers eventually switch to the Great Vehicle, a situation requiring that there are three final vehicles.

---

[a] *gnyen po la ldem por dgongs pa, pratipakṣābhisaṃdhi*.

[b] The point here is likely that Buddha inflated the value of practice in order to counter a deflation of its value.

[c] *zla 'od dri med;* the Sanskrit is a guess.

4. Indirectly intending transformation:[a] In this case, renowned bad literature is to be transformed, or translated, into means of teaching profound meaning; for instance:

 Know essencelessness as the essence,
 Abide nicely in the obverse,
 Be intensely afflicted with afflictions,
 And holy enlightenment will be attained.

 These four lines are to be transformed as follows:[547]

 - "Know essencelessness as the essence" is to be taken as realization thinking, "Undistracted[b] one-pointed stability of mind is supreme, excellent, and chief." This indicates the four levels of the Great Vehicle path of preparation—heat, peak, forbearance, and supreme mundane qualities.
 - "Abide nicely in the obverse" is to be taken as not falling from direct realization of impurity, misery, impermanence, and selflessness—which are the obverse of apprehension of purity, bliss, permanence, and self; this indicates the Great Vehicle path of seeing.
 - "Be intensely afflicted with afflictions" is to be taken as making oneself physically tired through much asceticism for the sake of abandoning what is to be abandoned by the path of meditation; this indicates the path of meditation from the second ground through the tenth.
 - "Holy enlightenment will be attained" is to be taken as meaning that if one does as described above, holy enlightenment will be attained.

Principal Fourfold Mode of Interpretation in *The Essence of Eloquence*

The full title of D̄zong-ka-b̄a's text, *Treatise Differentiating Interpretable and Definitive Meanings: The Essence of Eloquence,* indicates that through delineating emptiness—the essence of Buddha's eloquent teachings—in the Mind-Only, Autonomy, and Consequence schools one will understand what those schools posit as definitive and as requiring interpretation. With respect to the Mind-Only School Following Scripture, D̄zong-ka-b̄a accomplishes this:

- through citing scriptures teaching that imputational natures are not established by way of their own character and teaching that apprehended-object

---

[a] *sbyor ba la ldem por dgongs pa/ bsgyur ba la ldem por dgongs pa, pariṇāmābhisaṃdhi.*

[b] "Essencelessness" is taken to mean "undistractedness."

and apprehending-subject are not established as separate substantial entities,[a]

- and through detailing reasoning employed by Mind-Only masters proving that imputational natures are not established by way of their own character and proving that external objects do not exist.[b]

According to Ḏzong-ka-ḇa, interpretation of scripture in that school is based on the literality and non-literality of passages, the basis of which is a determination of what actually exists. As the doctrine of the three natures is central to this school's presentation of what do and do not exist as well as the status of what exists, the determination of emptiness—the thoroughly established character—is of special importance. Emptiness is the final object of observation of a path of purification, and, therefore, its delineation forces the requirement that scriptures speaking of contradictory modes of being, such as those that teach of a difference of entity between object and subject, must be interpreted. That Asaṅga, the founder of the Yogic Practice School, holds a non-difference of entity between subject and object to be the final mode of subsistence of phenomena is, for this reason, of pivotal importance not only in his presentation of liberation from obstructions but also in his interpretation of scripture, his hermeneutic.

According to Ge-luk-ḇa scholars, the ontological position of no external objects (idealism) and its correlate of an emptiness of a difference of entity between subject and object forces interpretation of Buddha's teachings. In the first wheel of doctrine as described in the *Sūtra Unraveling the Thought* Buddha taught external objects and taught that objects are established by way of their own character as the referents of their respective conceptual consciousnesses. However, since it is shown by reasoning that objects are empty of externality and empty of being established by way of their own character as the referents of their respective conceptual consciousnesses, these first-wheel teachings are not definitive—that is, cannot be taken literally—and must be interpreted otherwise. Also, in the middle wheel of doctrine Buddha taught on the literal level that nothing is established by way of its own character; however, since it is established by reasoning that other-powered natures and emptinesses are established by way of their own character, this teaching also is not definitive, cannot be taken literally, and must be interpreted otherwise.

The reasoned and scripturally established position of no external objects forces the requirement that these superficially contradictory teachings be considered non-literal and thus requiring interpretation. Buddha's intention in teaching these non-ontologically founded doctrines is shown to be in response to specific trainees' temporary inability to realize the deepest doctrine and their

---

a See *Emptiness in Mind-Only,* 115-131, and *Reflections on Reality,* 103ff.

b See *Emptiness in Mind-Only,* 206-219 and 324-332; *Reflections on Reality,* 465-487; and *Maps of the Profound,* 405-414.

need for another, provisional, doctrine in order to advance.

This mode of interpretation is standardized in Ge-luk-b̄a expositions as a process of making four distinctions:

1. determining **the basis in Buddha's thought**[a] when Buddha taught a literally unacceptable doctrine. In the case of teaching external objects this is the fact that objects appear due to the maturation of internal seeds of perception.
2. determining **the purpose**[b] in Buddha's teaching such. In the case of teaching external objects, it is in order that these trainees, although temporarily incapable of realizing the most profound reality, might realize that there is no seer and so forth except for a consciousness seeing forms and so forth.
3. determining **the scripture and reasoning that refute the literal reading of the text.**[c] In the case of teaching external objects, scriptures that refute this teaching are, for instance, the *Sūtra on the Ten Grounds* and the *Sūtra Unraveling the Thought,* and the reasoning is, for instance, the threefold reasoning about names and objects.
4. determining **the thought**[d] of the text itself. In the case of teaching external objects, the thought of the text is that external objects exist.

Let us consider these with regard to the first two wheels of doctrine in more detail.

The Basis in Buddha's Thought in the First Wheel of Doctrine

The "basis of thought" (*dgongs gzhi*), which I usually translate as "the basis in Buddha's thought," refers to what Buddha has set in mind when he speaks a teaching that is not literally acceptable. "Thought," however, does not refer to conceptual thinking since a Buddha has no conceptuality; rather, it means a non-conceptual factor of realization.

In this way, the basis in Buddha's thought does not refer to something that Buddha is indirectly or implicitly teaching but is the basis in fact from which Buddha is speaking. When Buddha says something non-factual such as that a patch of blue and the eye consciousness apprehending it are different entities, he is speaking from something which, though factual, is not expressed—even indirectly or implicitly—by his words teaching that these two are different entities.

In the case of this first-wheel teaching that subject and object are different entities, the basis in Buddha's thought is the fact that objects appear due to the maturation of internal seeds of perception. Buddha knows that internal seeds or

[a] *dgongs gzhi.*

[b] *dgos pa.*

[c] *dngos la gnod byed.*

[d] *dgongs pa.*

predispositions cause the appearance of objects, but, since certain trainees are unfit for this teaching, he presently does not teach this to them either directly, indirectly, or implicitly but instead teaches them external causation. Indeed, in time, when those trainees have matured, he will teach them that objects appear due to the maturation of internal seeds of perception, but this fact does not make this first category—the basis in Buddha's thought—into what Buddha has in mind, or intends, to teach these trainees later.[a]

That Ge-luk-b̄a scholars speak of something being in Buddha's thought when he speaks a non-literal doctrine indicates that for them a Buddha is not in a contentless state of mind but in a state of realization of what is. Also, that is not just emptiness but also all other existent phenomena, such as minds, bodies, persons, and so forth. What a Buddha has in mind is not damaged by reasoning but is indeed supported by reasoning; this reasoned validation shows that what exists is not merely a matter of wish but rather that there are criteria for determining what exists. Also, since the basis in Buddha's thought is something that he will eventually teach, it is clear that not all doctrines are equal in terms of validation by correct cognition even if, at certain times under certain circumstances, many different doctrines can be useful in leading trainees. There are non-final and final teachings. (No one, of course, claims that the words expressing a doctrine such as emptiness are emptiness itself; still, emptiness is the referent of the word "emptiness," even though it is not established by way of its own character as a referent of the term "emptiness" or established as the referent of a conceptual consciousness apprehending it as "emptiness.")

It is unsuitable to translate *dgongs gzhi* as "intention" or as "indirect intention," for intention, whether direct or indirect, is included in the third category, purpose, and the non-intentionality of this first category has already been

---

[a] This point is surprising and bothered me for a number of years, but Ge-luk-b̄a scholars whom I have consulted have consistently spoken of this category as merely what Buddha has set in mind (*thugs la bzhag pa*). The only possible evidence to the contrary that I have encountered is one statement by Gung-tang (*Difficult Points*, 85.16) that the basis in Buddha's thought—when he taught that objects are established by way of their own character as referents of conceptual consciousnesses and terms—is the selflessness of persons, since soon after giving the former non-factually based teaching, he intends to teach the selflessness of persons. "The selflessness of persons is posited as the basis in [Buddha's] thought when he said in the first wheel that [phenomena] are established by way of their own character as the referents of their respective conceptual consciousnesses."

Still, even though this is the only instance (that I have found) of explicitly connecting this first category of the basis in Buddha's thought with an intention to teach this doctrine later, it is certainly to be admitted that whatever is construed as a basis in Buddha's thought is indeed something to be taught to trainees eventually in the future. The question is whether in the fourfold format this category is primarily used in an intentional sense, that is, as referring to a doctrine that Buddha plans to teach at a later time. It is clear to me that Ge-luk-b̄a scholars almost never use the category this way. Consider, for instance, Nga-w̄ang-b̄el-den's distinction between the four thoughts and the four indirect intentions given above (437).

shown.[a] This is supported by the fact that the purpose is always identified by terms such as "so that trainees might realize," whereas the basis in Buddha's thought is always identified by a mere fact such as that objects appear due to the maturation of internal seeds of perception.

In sum, as Jam-ȳang-shay-b̄a puts it, in the first wheel of doctrine Buddha[548] spoke of apprehended-object and apprehending-subject as separate substantial entities in consideration of (1) predispositions that ripen as consciousnesses and the objects they apprehend and (2) appearances of forms and so forth. In other words, Buddha's own thought is that consciousnesses having the appearance of external objects arise in dependence upon predispositions making the appearance of external objects. As Vasubandhu's *The Twenty* says:[b]

> The Subduer spoke about these—
> The seeds from which cognitions respectively arise
> And the appearances [of forms]—
> In a dualistic way as [internal and external] sense-spheres[c] of those [cognitions].

Nga-w̄ang-b̄el-den explains that in consideration[549] of the existence of (1) seeds making the appearance of forms and (2) appearances as forms, Buddha gave the non-factual teaching that an eye consciousness and the visible form it perceives are external objects. Specifically, Buddha spoke of a visible form and an eye consciousness apprehending it as cause and effect, and because fully qualified cause and effect are necessarily different substantial entities, this amounts to saying that apprehended-object and apprehending-subject are different substantial entities. Hence, the thought of the speaker[d] and the thought of what he

---

a The same holds for "having a thought [behind it]" (*dgongs pa can*).

b Stanza 9; the Sanskrit in Lévi (*Vijñaptimātratāsiddhi,* 5.25) is:

yataḥ svabījādvijñaptiryadābhāsā pravartate/
dvividhāyatanatvena te tasyā munirabravīt//

See also Chatterjee, *Vijñapti-Mātratā-Siddhi,* 9.1. See Hopkins, *Emptiness in Mind-Only,* 234. Vasubandhu's own commentary on this stanza is:

> Regarding (1) the seeds—the respective seeds that have undergone a type of transformation [that is, have thoroughly ripened]—from which the cognitions that perceive forms arise and (2) those appearances, the Supramundane Victor respectively spoke of an eye-sense-sphere and a form-sense-sphere of that cognition.

The bracketed material is from Vinītadeva's *Explanation of (Vasubandhu's) [Auto] Commentary on the "Twenty Stanza Treatise"* (*rab tu byed pa nyi shu pa'i 'grel bshad, prakaraṇaviṃśakāṭīkā*), P5566, vol. 113, 318.4.4; Vinītadeva glosses *pariṇāmaviśeṣaprāptād* with what in the extant Tibetan is *yongs su smin pa.* See also Stefan Anacker, *Seven Works of Vasubandhu* (Delhi: Motilal Banarsidass, 1984), 165; and Thomas A. Kochumuttom, *A Buddhist Doctrine of Experience* (Delhi: Motilal Banarsidass, 1982), 265.

c *skye mched, āyatana.*

d *gsung ba po'i dgongs pa.*

said[a] differ, since he was not, at that time, communicating his own deeper understanding. This is like, for example, the fact that when Buddha spoke of the mental and physical aggregates as a burden and the person as the carrier of the burden, this amounts to speaking of the aggregates and the person as different entities.

The Purpose of the First Wheel of Doctrine

The purpose is the intention behind Buddha's uttering words which, if taken literally, cannot bear examination. The purpose is always explained in terms of certain trainees' temporarily being unable to understand a certain truth and thus needing to be led toward that deeper truth by thinking something else. For instance, the purpose or intention behind Buddha's teaching a self-sufficient or substantially established self is said to be so that trainees who are temporarily unable to posit a continuum of moral cause and effect without such a substantial person could enter into the practice of adopting virtue and discarding non-virtue, these practices being basic to spiritual development.

With respect to the purpose of Buddha's teaching the blatantly non-factual doctrine of the existence of external objects in the first wheel of doctrine,[550] Vasubandhu's *The Twenty* says:[b]

> That form-sense-spheres and so forth exist [as external objects][551]
> Was said through the force of a thought behind it[c]
> With regard to beings tamed by that,
> Like [the teaching of] spontaneously arisen sentient beings [as substantially established or permanent].

Buddha[552] said that forms and so forth are established as external objects in order that Hearers who are temporarily unfit to be taught the selflessness of phenomena could abandon their fear of the truth so that they could enter the teaching. This is like Buddha's saying—in consideration of sentient beings of the intermediate state—that spontaneously produced sentient beings substantially exist, this being for the sake of teaching those having nihilistic views that there is a basis for the connection of actions and effects.

Nga-w̄ang-b̄el-den points out that the intention,[553] or purpose, behind Buddha's teaching that an eye consciousness seeing a visible form arises in dependence upon an eye sense power and a form is for the sake of entering into

---

a *gsung rab kyi dgongs pa.*

b Stanza 8. The Sanskrit in Lévi (*Vijñaptimātratāsiddhi,* 5.25) is:

rūpādyāyatanāstitvaṃ tadvineyajanaṃ prati/
abhiprāyavaśāduktamupapādukasatvavat//

See also Chatterjee, *Vijñapti-Mātratā-Siddhi,* 8.5. See also Anacker, *Seven Works of Vasubandhu,* 165; and Kochumuttom, *Buddhist Doctrine of Experience,* 264-265.

c *dgongs pa.*

realizing that a **person's** seeing a form is merely imputed to the **eye consciousness'** seeing a form and thus that a seeing person who exists apprehendable as a separate substantial entity from an eye consciousness does not exist. In this way it is for the sake of trainees who for the time being are unfit to be taught the selflessness of phenomena, so that they will enter into realization of the selflessness of persons.

Damage to the Explicit Teaching of the First Wheel of Doctrine

The third category involved in delineating that a scripture requires interpretation is the fact that there are refutations of the literal reading of the text. This is the pivot of the process of interpretation in that the literal reading of the scripture must be established as literally unacceptable by a means of valid knowledge before one is drawn into examining the basis in Buddha's thought and purpose of Buddha's saying such on the literal level. Through reasoning and citation of other scripture, it is determined that the thought of the text—the thought of the literal reading of the text—is not fit to be what Buddha has in his own mind. This leads to positing what Buddha had in mind and what his purpose was.

The conflict between what Buddha said and what he had in mind does not refer to his thinking one thing but mistakenly or inadequately expressing it, for a Buddha has no mistake in speech. Rather, the conflict is between something a Buddha said that is literally unacceptable and what a Buddha knows to be true. The conflict is resolved by considering the purpose for saying such. It is said that the fact that a Buddha operates with such purpose clearly in mind shows that a Buddha is omniscient.

The impetus for determining what a Buddha had in mind and for determining what the purpose was comes from the fact that there are other scriptures and reasonings that damage, that is to say, contradict, what is indicated on the literal level by the words of the teaching. Between scripture and reasoning, reasoning is more important since if a scripture were the main means of determining that another scripture requires interpretation, the process would lead to an infinite regress. Buddha himself in the *Sūtra Unraveling the Thought* says that the teaching that all phenomena are not established by way of their own character requires interpretation, whereas in the *Teachings of Akṣhayamati Sūtra* he says that this very teaching is definitive. Dzong-ka-ba therefore concludes that reasoning alone is the arbiter.[a] Although suchness—emptiness—is very profound, it is accessible to reasoning, and thus proper reasoning, difficult as it may be, can determine whether statements about reality are true or not. Hence, the reasoning that is the means of differentiating whether a doctrine is definitive or interpretable is primarily the reasoning about emptiness.

In the first wheel of doctrine the existence of sense-spheres that are external

[a] See *Emptiness in Mind-Only,* 70-71, and *Reflections on Reality,* 96-100.

objects is a topic expressed, and it indeed is the literal reading of the first wheel. However, this position is damaged by both scripture and reasoning. As Jam-ȳang-shay-b̄a says:[554]

> Scriptural damage to this is, for instance, contradiction by:
>
> - the statement in the *Sūtra on the Ten Grounds*,[555] "O Conqueror Children, it is thus: These three realms are mind-only."
> - sūtra passages[a] teaching that imputational natures are not established by way of their own character.
>
> With respect to [damage by] reasoning,[b] Vasubandhu's *The Twenty* says:[c]
>
> > Due to simultaneous conjunction with six [particles]
> > A particle has six parts.
> > Also, if the six were in the same place,
> > Even a mass would be of the size of a particle.
>
> and Dharmakīrti's *Ascertainment of Prime Cognition* says:[d]
>
> > Because of the certainty of simultaneous observation,
> > Blue and an awareness of it are not other.
>
> and so forth, and Dharmakīrti's *Commentary on (Dignāga's) "Compilation of Prime Cognition"* says:
>
> > When things are analyzed,
> > They do not exist as things in suchness
> > Because they do not have
> > A nature of one or many.
>
> and Asaṅga's *Summary of the Great Vehicle* says:[e]
>
> > Because an awareness does not exist prior to name,
> > Because manifold, and because unrestricted,
> > There are the contradictions of being in the essence of that, of many entities,
> > And of the mixture of entities. Therefore, it is proven.

---

[a] Such as the seventh chapter of the *Sūtra Unraveling the Thought* explained in detail in these three volumes.

[b] For a presentation of eleven reasonings, see *Reflections on Reality*, 465-487.

[c] Stanza 12. For this reasoning see *Reflections on Reality*, 476-478.

[d] For this reasoning see *Reflections on Reality*, 483-487.

[e] Chap. 2; P5549, vol. 112, 224.4.1; Lamotte, *La somme*, vol. 1, 36 (24); vol. 2, 118-119; and Keenan, *Summary*, 50-51. For this reasoning see *Reflections on Reality*, 400-403 and 466-469.

The Thought of the First Wheel of Doctrine

The "thought" is the thought of the text,[a] a category distinct from the basis in Buddha's thought or the "thought of the speaker."[b] When the literal reading is unacceptable, one has to make a distinction between Buddha's own thought and the thought of the literal reading of the text. That such a distinction is made stresses the point that despite the fact that the Great Vehicle is said to be baseless in the sense that no phenomenon justifiably serves as a basis of the conception that it is established by way of its own character as the referent of a conceptual consciousness or of a verbalizing term, some doctrines are founded in valid cognition and some are not, and an enlightened being has valid cognition of specific facts from which that being speaks.

The thought,[556] or the meaning, of the first wheel of doctrine is the existence of sense-spheres that are external objects, whereas the basis in Buddha's thought is the existence of a seed, or predisposition, from the ripening of which an eye consciousness and the appearance of a visible form arise. Thus, in the first wheel of doctrine the thought of the sūtras and the basis in Buddha's thought are contradictory. As Ḏzong-ka-ḇa's *The Essence of Eloquence* says:[c]

> The Sovereign of Subduers did not accept to teach the intended trainees of these [first-wheel] sūtras the basis in [his own] thought—which is that although external objects do not exist, the appearance of objects arises through the force of internal, ripened predispositions. Hence, this is not to be expressed to those trainees and is not the thought [of the first wheel of doctrine], and this is an occasion such that those of the Lesser Vehicle are not suitable as vessels to realize this.

In sum, Buddha spoke from a basis of specific understanding; his skill in means wrought changes in what he said according to his audience, but it is not that there was no basis in his own thought. Thus, his word needs to be explained in terms of both the needs of the listener and his own grounding in actual fact. When the existential need of the trainee required that the teaching be at odds with the ontological fact, his teaching is subject to refutation by other scripture and reasoning. Thus, the interpretation of scripture revolves around the basis in Buddha's thought (the ontological fact), the purpose (the existential need of the trainee), and damage to the explicit teaching (refutation by valid sources of knowledge).

---

[a] *gsung rab kyi dgongs pa.*

[b] *gsung ba po'i dgongs pa.*

[c] See Hopkins, *Emptiness in Mind-Only,* 254. The lack of equivalence between the basis in Buddha's thought with respect to the first wheel of doctrine and the thought of the first wheel of doctrine is emphasized because, as will be seen below, there is such an equivalence with regard to the middle wheel of doctrine.

Basis in Buddha's Thought in the Middle Wheel of Doctrine

About the second wheel of doctrine Jam-ÿang-shay-b̄a makes the point that, even for the Proponents of Mind-Only, the Perfection of Wisdom Sūtras and so forth are the supreme of sūtras but are non-literal:[557]

> The middle wheel of doctrine indicated here [in the *Sūtra Unraveling the Thought*] is the supreme of sūtra sets extensively teaching the Great Vehicle profound path through limitless forms, but it is of non-literal interpretable meaning because of the sūtra words in those sūtras [saying] that all phenomena ranging from forms through to exalted knowers-of-all-aspects are, without difference, natureless. They have a basis in [Buddha's] thought because they are in consideration of the [respective three] naturelessnesses of the [three] characters. The *Sūtra Unraveling the Thought* says:[558]
>
>> Paramārthasamudgata, thinking of three non-natures of phenomena—character-non-nature,[a] production-non-nature,[b] and ultimate-non-nature[c]—I taught [in the middle wheel of the teaching],[559] "All phenomena are natureless."[560]
>
> and Vasubandhu's *The Thirty*[d] also says:[561]
>
>> Thinking of three types of non-nature
>> Of the three types of natures [respectively],[562]
>> He taught [in the Perfection of Wisdom Sūtras][563]
>> That all phenomena are natureless.
>
> and Asaṅga's *Compendium of Ascertainments* also says:[564]
>
>> *Question:* Thinking of what did the Supramundane Victor say [in the middle wheel][565] that all phenomena are natureless?
>>
>> *Answer:* Here and there[e] he said such through the force of taming[f] [trainees],[566] thinking of three types of non-nature.

---

[a] *mtshan nyid ngo bo nyid med pa nyid, lakṣaṇaniḥsvabhāvatā* (Lamotte, *Samdhinirmocana,* 67 [3], n. 3).

[b] *skye ba ngo bo nyid med pa nyid, utpattiniḥsvabhāvatā* (ibid., 67 [3], n. 4).

[c] *don dam pa ngo bo nyid med pa nyid, paramārthaniḥsvabhāvatā* (ibid., 67 [3], n. 5).

[d] See issue #61.

[e] Jik-may-dam-chö-gya-tso (*Port of Entry,* 160.4) cogently suggests that "here and there" (*de dang der*) may mean either "in this and that sūtra" (*mdo de dang der*) or "to this and that trainee" (*gdul bya de dang der*).

[f] Jik-may-dam-chö-gya-tso (ibid., 164.2) reports that D̄ra-d̄i Ge-s̄hay Rin-chen-dön-drup (*pra sti dge bshes rin chen don grub, Ornament for the Thought,* 18.16) interprets "through the force of taming" (*'dul ba'i dbang gis*) as "through the force of taming trainees having the lineage of the Middle Way School by means of the literal reading" (*gdul bya dbu*

Nga-w̄ang-b̄el-den explains:[567]

> Imputational natures are described as character-non-natures because of not being established by way of their own character. Moreover, the meaning of not being established by way of their own character is to be taken as not being established without reliance on names and terminology;[a] it is not to be taken, as the [Consequentialist] Proponents of Non-Nature do, as not established from their own side.
>
> Other-powered natures are described as production-non-natures, that is, as not being produced under their own power. Moreover, the meaning of not being produced under their own power is to be taken as not being produced without depending on causes and conditions.
>
> Thoroughly established natures are described as ultimate-non-natures because of being the ultimate, and the ultimate is just distinguished by [that is to say, is posited[b] by way of] the non-existence of the nature of self that is the object of negation [in the selflessness of phenomena].

Jam-ȳang-shay-b̄a gives another set of thoughts behind Buddha's teaching that all phenomena are natureless:

> Moreover, [the teaching that all phenomena are natureless] is in consideration of [the naturelessness of] the three characteristics of compounded things [that is, that things are not produced under their own power, do not abide under their own power, and do not disintegrate under their own power],[568] and in consideration of the non-existence [of natures] as conceived by childish beings [who conceive forms and so forth to be pure, blissful, permanent, and self and to be separate entities from the consciousnesses apprehending them].[569] Maitreya's *Ornament for the Great Vehicle Sūtras* says:[570]
>
> > Because [things] are not [produced in the future from] themselves
> > And because [having ceased, past objects are] not [produced again] as having their own nature

ma pa'i rigs can sgras zin des 'dul ba'i dbang gis). However, Jik-may-dam-chö-gya-tso points out that D̄zong-ka-b̄a himself in the section on the Consequence School glosses "through the force of taming" (*'dul ba'i dbang gis*) with "through the force of trainees' thought" (*gdul bya'i bsam pa'i dbang gis;* Sarnath gtsang edition, 207). It seems to me that both expositions are suitable.

[a] *brda;* to avoid redundancy with "names" this is taken to mean conceptuality (*rtog pa*). See issue #104.

[b] D̄zong-ka-b̄a (Hopkins, *Emptiness in Mind-Only,* 91) glosses the frequently used technical term *rab tu phye ba* with *bzhag pa,* which merely has the sense of "posit"; his reading, therefore, runs contrary to Lamotte's translation (194.6) as "***est manifesté*** par l'irréalité de toutes les choses."

And because [present objects] do not abide [for a second moment] in their own entity
And because [the natures of objects] conceived [by childish beings] do not exist,
Naturelessness was asserted [in the Perfection of Wisdom Sūtras].

and Asaṅga's *Summary of Manifest Knowledge*[571] says:

What is the thought behind the statements in the Very Extensive [Perfection of Wisdom Sūtras] that all phenomena are natureless? [That is said] because:

- [things] do not arise [in the future] by themselves
- [past objects, having ceased,] are not [produced again] as having their own nature
- [present objects] do not abide [for a second moment] in their own entity, and
- [objects] do not have characters as they are apprehended by childish beings.

Dharmakīrti (*Emptiness in Mind-Only,* 190-193) takes a different tack, explaining that, in consideration of the non-existence of apprehended-object and apprehending-subject as other substantial entities the Perfection of Wisdom Sūtras speak of all phenomena as natureless. As Jam-ȳang-shay-b̄a says:[572]

The basis in [Buddha's] thought for the statements in the middle wheel of doctrine that all phenomena are natureless and are without the nature of production, cessation, and so forth is the non-existence of production and so forth in accordance with how apprehended-object and apprehending-subject appear dualistically to an awareness polluted by dualistic appearance differentiating the production and so forth of things.

Dharmakīrti also presents a way of explaining what in consideration of which the Perfection of Wisdom Sūtras speak of all phenomena as natureless, or without true existence, which is shared between the Mind-Only School and the Sūtra School. Here, the basis in Buddha's thought is the absence of true existence of the factors of agent and object in the context of taking a definition as an agent (in the sense of being the means of characterization) and the definiendum (that is, the object characterized) as the object. For if such factors of object and agent were truly established, definiendum and definition—such as a pot and that which is bulbous, flat-based, and able to hold water—would absurdly not be just one basis that is merely differentiated by way of conceptuality.

The Purpose of the Middle Wheel of Doctrine

Jik-may-dam-chö-gya-tso lists various opinions about those for whom the middle wheel of doctrine was taught:[573]

- According to both Paṇ-chen S̄ö-nam-drak-b̄a and Jay-d̄zün Chö-ḡyi-gyel-tsen, the middle wheel is for the sake of taking care of Proponents of Mind-Only who have sharp faculties, this being because they can understand the three natures and non-natures without further elaboration as is found in the third wheel of doctrine.
- According to Jam-ȳang-shay-b̄a's textbook,[a] the middle wheel is for the sake of leading Consequentialists and so forth, this being because they can posit the cause and effect of actions (and thus the value of virtuous practice) only within a denial of the inherent existence of phenomena.
- According to J̄ang-ḡya,[b] the middle wheel is for the sake of stopping the ten distracting conceptualizations. Nga-w̄ang-b̄el-den's *Annotations* lists the ten as:[574]

    Two Distracting Conceptualizations Depending on a Self of Persons

    1. Conceptualization of the non-existence of effective things—conceiving that the aggregates do not exist
    2. Conceptualization of effective things—conceiving that a permanent, unitary, self-powered self exists

    Eight Distracting Conceptualizations Depending on a Self of Phenomena

    3. Conceptualization of superimposition—conceiving that apprehended-object and apprehending-subject are different substantial entities
    4. Conceptualization of deprecation—conceiving that other-powered natures do not exist
    5. Conceptualization of oneness—conceiving that other-powered natures and their noumenon are one isolate
    6. Conceptualization of difference—conceiving that other-powered natures and their noumenon are different entities
    7. Conceptualization of entity—conceiving that the object verbalized by the name "form" is ultimately established as the entity of form
    8. Conceptualization of attribute—conceiving that the objects verbalized by the name "production," "cessation," and so forth are ultimately established as attributes of form

---

[a] The reference is likely to Jam-ȳang-shay-b̄a's *Great Exposition of the Interpretable and the Definitive.*

[b] Jam-ȳang-shay-b̄a also posits this; see Hopkins, *Maps of the Profound,* 342 and 344.

9. Conceptualization of an object as like the name—when hearing how the name "form" is imputed, conceiving that an awareness perceiving the object verbalized is non-mistaken
10. Conceptualization of a name as like the object—when observing an object such as a form and so forth, conceiving that an awareness perceiving its name is non-mistaken in how it is observed.

- According to unnamed "others" the middle wheel is for the sake of stopping the view of permanence in which the first wheel is held to be literal.[a]

A complication is that the **literal level** of the middle wheel says that objects are natureless in that they are not established by way of their own character or not established from their own side, and this literal-level teaching must be for someone's sake, but whose? It obviously is not for Proponents of Mind-Only, since they assert that other-powered natures and thoroughly established natures are established by way of their own character and assert that all phenomena **are** established from their own side. The literal level is said, therefore, to be especially intended for Consequentialists, who can posit the cause and effect of actions only within what—for the Proponents of Mind-Only—is a deprecation of the status of phenomena.[b]

Damage to the Literal Teaching of the Middle Wheel of Doctrine

As with the first wheel of doctrine, the damage to taking literally the middle wheel of doctrine is twofold, scripture and reasoning. As Jam-ȳang-shay-b̄a says:[575]

> Scriptural damage exists because [the statement that all phenomena are natureless] contradicts many sūtra passages [of the wheel of doctrine] of good differentiation; for instance, the *Sūtra Unraveling the Thought* (*Emptiness in Mind-Only,* 95) says:[576]
>
> > Even though they have interest in that doctrine [of the profound thoroughly established nature], they do not understand, just as it is, the profound reality that I have set forth with a thought behind it. With respect to the meaning of these doctrines, they adhere to the terms as only literal: "All these phenomena are only natureless. All these phenomena are only unproduced, only unceasing, only quiescent from the

[a] Jam-ȳang-shay-b̄a declares this explanation to be wrong; see Hopkins, *Maps of the Profound,* 342.

[b] For a detailed presentation of ramifications of this issue, see *Reflections on Reality,* 136-140.

> start, only naturally thoroughly passed beyond sorrow." Due to that, they acquire the view that all phenomena do not exist and the view that [establishment of objects by way of their own] character does not exist. Moreover, having acquired the view of nihilism and the view of the non-existence of [establishment of objects by way of their own] character, they deprecate all phenomena in terms of all of the characters—deprecating the imputational character of phenomena and also deprecating the other-powered character and thoroughly established character of phenomena.
>
> Why? Paramārthasamudgata, it is thus: If the other-powered character and the thoroughly established character exist [by way of their own character], the imputational character is known [that is, is possible]. However, those who perceive the other-powered character and the thoroughly established character as without character [that is to say, as not being established by way of their own character] also deprecate the imputational character. Therefore, those [persons] are said to deprecate even all three aspects of characters.

The damage by reasoning is the reasonings refuting the extreme of deprecation.... According to the literal reading, [this statement that all phenomena are natureless] deprecates all three characters [that is, imputational natures, other-powered natures, and thoroughly established natures]....[577] Asaṅga's *Grounds of Bodhisattvas* (*Emptiness in Mind-Only,* 146) says:[578]

> Therefore, some persons [that is, only Consequentialists], who have heard sūtras that are difficult to understand, profound, imbued with the Great Vehicle, endowed with the profound emptiness, and taught with a meaning in [Buddha's] thought [that is other than the literal reading] do not know, just as it is, the real meaning that is expounded. This being so, they make improper imputations and, with mere conceptions produced from illogicality upon improper analysis, view and propound, "Whoever view that all these [phenomena] are exhausted as mere imputations [by conceptuality] and that this is suchness are correctly viewing [the nature of phenomena]."
>
> Since, according to them, even the mere things that are the bases of imputation do not exist [by way of their own character], the imputing [persons, conceptual consciousnesses, and terms] themselves also come to be non-existent in all ways, in which case how could a suchness that is a mere imputation

> exist! Thereby, through this avenue, they deprecate both suchness and imputed [phenomena]. Since through that format they deprecate imputation and suchness, it is said that they are to be known as the chief of those having nihilistic views.

Nga-w̄ang-b̄el-den describes how Consequentialists take the Perfection of Wisdom Sūtras:[579]

> Having heard the words of Perfection of Wisdom Sūtras that are difficult to understand, they—not knowing that these have a basis in [Buddha's] thought—apprehend them as literal. Then, [Consequentialists] say:
>
> > Except for only being imputed by conceptuality, all phenomena do not inherently exist, and this absence of inherent existence is suchness. Therefore, the view of the absence of inherent existence is the correct view.
>
> If bases of imputation did not exist, imputing [that is, persons, conceptual consciousnesses, and terms that impute] also would not exist, whereby both taking all phenomena to be merely imputed and taking just that [absence of inherent existence] to be the meaning of suchness would be impossible. Hence, that is the chief view of annihilation.

Jam-ȳang-shay-b̄a[580] explains that, according to the Mind-Only, Sūtra, and Great Exposition schools, all effective things must truly exist,[a] and thus within the context of effective things whatever does not truly exist must not exist. This is why these schools debate against the assertion of the Consequence School that other-powered natures are only imputed by conceptuality, since, if that were the case, then other-powered natures could not be truly established. To their way of thinking, the bases of emptiness for the thoroughly established nature, the imputers of imputations, and the bondage and release of cyclic existence and nirvāṇa require the true existence of other-powered natures.

D̄zong-ka-b̄a (*Emptiness in Mind-Only,* 158-171, 294-301) explains at length divergent meanings of "conventionally existing" and "ultimately/truly existing," which Jam-ȳang-shay-b̄a summarizes:[581]

> Although there are many modes of explaining "conventionally existing" and "ultimately existing," the chief are two:
>
> 1. To be established as a phenomenon posited through the force of name and terminology is to be conventionally established [or to conventionally exist], and to be established but not as a phenomenon posited through the force of name and terminology is to be ultimately established [or to ultimately exist]. This mode of

---

[a] "Truly established" would be more appropriate for the Great Exposition School.

establishment is the one about which Proponents of Mind-Only and Proponents of the Middle debate when they analyze whether [an object] is conventionally or ultimately established. The Proponents of Mind-Only assert that imputational phenomena are conventionally established in the sense of being established as phenomena posited through the force of name and terminology, and they assert that other-powered natures and thoroughly established natures are ultimately established in the sense of being established but not as phenomena posited through the force of name and terminology. They assert that if other-powered natures and thoroughly established natures are not established that way, other-powered natures would not be fit to be causes and effects and able to perform functions, and thoroughly established natures would not be fit to be the mode of subsistence, as [indicated by] the many previously mentioned scriptural passages and reasonings.

2. To be established as a conventional basis suitable to give rise to thorough afflictions is said to exist conventionally and to exist as a conventional truth [and to be established as an object of observation of a path of purification is said to exist ultimately and to exist as an ultimate truth].

Thus, here in the discussion about other-powered natures their true existence refers to the first mode, not the second, for otherwise other-powered natures would be ultimate truths.[a]

The Thought of the Middle Wheel of Doctrine

The "thought" here is the thought of the literal reading of the text,[b] which is that all of these do not truly exist or are not established from their own side. As mentioned above, with regard to the middle wheel of doctrine the thought of the text—rather than the thought of the literal reading of the text—is exactly the same as the basis in Buddha's thought. Thus, whereas in the first wheel of doctrine the thought of the sūtras and the basis in Buddha's thought are contradictory, here in the middle wheel of doctrine the thought of the sūtras and the basis in Buddha's thought are equivalent. The problem is with the literal reading of the middle wheel.

---

[a] For discussion of the thoughts behind Buddha's statements that all phenomena are unproduced, unceasing, quiescent from the start, and naturally thoroughly passed beyond sorrow, see *Emptiness in Mind-Only*, 97-103, and *Maps of the Profound*, 334-337. For Buddha's statements about attaining forbearance with respect to the doctrine of non-production, see *Emptiness in Mind-Only*, 173-176, and *Maps of the Profound*, 337-342, the latter including discussion of other topics such as the thought behind the teaching of one final vehicle.

[b] *sgras zin kyi dgongs pa.*

How to Explain the Teaching of One Final Vehicle?

The style of interpretation allows for stimulating and esthetically delightful expositions of what is behind doctrines in the Perfection of Wisdom Sūtras that, on the literal level, are discordant with basic postures of the Mind-Only School. For instance, how can the teaching of one final vehicle—that all sentient beings eventually attain Buddhahood—be explained in the Mind-Only School Following Scripture, which asserts that there are three final vehicles. Among those with the capacity for liberation, some achieve only the path of no more learning of a Hearer or Solitary Realizer and do not attain Buddhahood; others proceed on to Buddhahood. Thus, there are three final vehicles and five lineages—those definite in each of the three vehicles, those indefinite (who switch from one vehicle to another), and those without a capacity for liberation.

What did Buddha have in his own mind as the factual basis for this non-factual teaching of only one final vehicle? India—with its penchant for elaboration in art, architecture, religion, and literature—provides not just one answer but a number of different facts that can be claimed to be what Buddha himself had in mind. As Nga-w̄ang-b̄el-den explains in his *Annotations for (Jam-ȳang-shay-b̄a's) "Great Exposition of Tenets,"*[582] according to Maitreya's *Ornament for the Great Vehicle Sūtras* there are seven bases in Buddha's thought behind his teaching of one final vehicle:

1. the fact that the element of attributes is the same for Hearers, Solitary Realizers, and Bodhisattvas
2. the fact that Hearers, Solitary Realizers, and Bodhisattvas are the same in being selfless
3. the fact that the release from cyclic existence that is a fruit of the Hearer, Solitary Realizer, and Bodhisattva vehicles is the same
4. the fact that even two separate lineages—that is, some of those having indefinite lineage and those definite in the Great Vehicle lineage—engage in one Great Vehicle path
5. the fact that two attitudes of similarity are attained:
   - a Buddha's attitude of sameness—gained from the first Bodhisattva ground—this being non-dualism with respect to one's own and sentient beings' [final] natures
   - the attitude gained for just a moment by some who are definite in the Hearer lineage who temporarily practice the Bodhisattva deeds but give them up, enter the Hearer Vehicle, and then when they have attained a Hearer nirvāṇa, through the Buddha's power think, "I will become fully purified through practicing the Bodhisattva deeds," in accordance with the Buddha's own previous thought, "I became buddhafied through practicing the Bodhisattva deeds."

6. the fact that many times emanations of the Buddha display the manner of attaining nirvāṇa by way of the Hearer Vehicle
7. the fact that there is no vehicle surpassing the Great Vehicle.

As Jam-ȳang-shay-b̄a points out,[583] the statement in Maitreya's *Ornament for the Great Vehicle Sūtras:*

> Because of the sameness of the [element of] attributes, selflessness,
> And release, because of different lineages,
> Because of attainment of two attitudes, because of emanations,
> Because of finality, just one vehicle.

accords with the *Sūtra Unraveling the Thought:*

> Mañjushrī, Ones-Gone-Thus, Hearers, and Solitary Realizers are similar and equal with respect to the body of release.

and the seventh chapter [of the *Sūtra Unraveling the Thought*]:[584]

> This is the sole path of purification of Hearers, Solitary Realizers, and Bodhisattvas, and the purification is also one; there is no second. In consideration of this, I teach one vehicle.

Then, what is the purpose of teaching one final vehicle when there are actually three? It is for the sake of leading Hearers having indefinite lineage into Great Vehicle practice and for the sake of nurturing Bodhisattvas having indefinite lineage such that they remain in the Great Vehicle.

Definitions of the Interpretable and the Definitive

In this way, according to the *Sūtra Unraveling the Thought,* the final wheel of doctrine of good differentiation is definitive in the sense of being literal, and the other two wheels of doctrine require interpretation in the sense that they are not literal. In the *Sūtra Unraveling the Thought* the Bodhisattva Paramārthasamudgata recounts to Buddha the import of his teaching:[585]

> Initially, in the area of Varaṇāsi in the Deer Park called "Sage's Propounding,"[a] the Supramundane Victor thoroughly turned a wheel of doctrine for those engaged in the Hearer Vehicle,[b] fantastic[a] and

[a] *drang song smra ba, ṛṣivadana* (Étienne Lamotte, *Saṃdhinirmocanasūtra: L'explication des mystères* [Louvain: Université de Louvain, 1935], 85 [30], n. 3). A-ku L̄o-drö-gya-tso (*Precious Lamp,* 141.5) cites an explanation in the *Great Exposition* (*bye brag bshad mdzod chen mo, mahāvibhāṣa*) that it is called Sage's Propounding because it is a place where Buddha, the supreme of sages, propounded doctrine.

[b] *nyan thos kyi theg pa la yang dag par zhugs pa, śrāvakayānasaṃprasthita* (Lamotte, *Saṃdhinirmocana,* 85 [30], n. 5). Jik-may-dam-chö-gya-tso (*Port of Entry,* 228.4) explains that "vehicle" here means the scriptural collections of the Hearers, these being the Hearer vehicle as verbalizing words (*rjod byed tshig gi theg pa*).

marvelous[b] which none—god or human—had previously turned in a similar fashion in the world, through teaching the aspects of the four noble truths. Furthermore, that wheel of doctrine thoroughly turned by the Supramundane Victor is surpassable,[c] affords an occasion [for refutation],[d] requires interpretation,[e] and serves as a basis for controversy.[f]

Based[g] on just the naturelessness of all phenomena and based on just the absence of production, the absence of cessation, quiescence from the start, and naturally passed beyond sorrow, the Supramundane Victor turned a second wheel of doctrine, for those engaged in the Great Vehicle,[h] very fantastic and marvelous, through the aspect of speaking on emptiness.[i] Furthermore, that wheel of doctrine turned by the Supramundane Victor is surpassable, affords an occasion [for refutation], requires interpretation, and serves as a basis for controversy.

However,[j] based on just the naturelessness of phenomena and based on just the absence of production, the absence of cessation, quiescence from the start, and naturally passed beyond sorrow, the Supramundane Victor turned a third wheel of doctrine for those engaged in all vehicles,[k] possessed of good differentiation,[l] fantastic and marvelous.[m] This wheel of doctrine turned by the Supramundane Victor is

---

a *ngo mtshar, āścarya* (Lamotte, *Saṃdhinirmocana,* 86 [30], n. 8).

b *rmad du byung ba, adbhūta* (ibid., 86 [30], n. 9).

c *bla na mchis pa, sa-uttara* (ibid., 86 [30], n. 14).

d *skabs mchis pa, sa-avakāśa* (ibid., 86 [30], n. 15).

e *drang ba'i don, neyārtha* (ibid., 86 [30], n. 16).

f *rtsod pa'i bzhi'i gnas, vivādādhikaraṇa* (ibid., 86 [30], n. 17).

g *brtsams, ārabhya* (ibid., 86 [30], n. 18). Gung-tang (*Difficult Points,* 236.10) explains that *brtsams* here means "taking such and such as substrata" (*khyad gzhir bzung ba*), although in other places it means that "the thought comes down to such and such" (*dgongs pa der 'bab pa tsam*). For the Go-mang tradition of Gung-ru Chö-jung, Jam-ȳang-shay-b̄a, Gung-tang, and A-ku L̄o-drö-gya-tso, the second wheel—taking these as its substrata—teaches on the literal level that all phenomena are not established from their own side.

h *theg pa chen po la yang dag par zhugs pa, mahāyānasaṃprasthita* (Lamotte, *Samdhinirmocana,* 86 [30], n. 19).

i *stong pa nyid smos pa'i rnam pas, śūnyatāvādākāreṇa* (ibid., 86 [30], n. 20).

j Jik-may-dam-chö-gya-tso (*Port of Entry,* 294.2) points out the disjunctive function of the Tibetan *lags kyi* that follows the description of the middle wheel but not the first, since both require interpretation; it serves to separate out the third wheel.

k *theg pa thams cad la yang dag par zhugs pa, sarvayānasaṃprasthita* (Lamotte, *Saṃdhinirmocana,* 86 [30], n. 21).

l *legs par rnam par phye ba dang ldan pa, suvibhakta* (ibid., 86 [30], n. 22).

m The *stog* Palace edition of the sūtra (70.4) reads "extremely fantastic and extremely marvelous" (***ha cang yang*** *ngo mtshar la/* ***ha cang yang*** *rmad du byung ba*). Gung-tang (*Difficult Points,* 247.1-247.5) rejects similar readings (***shin tu*** *ngo mtshar rmad du byung ba*) in:

unsurpassable, does not afford an occasion [for refutation], is of definitive meaning,[a] and does not serve as a basis for controversy.

For the sake of facility in scholastic debate the meaning of being definitive and of requiring interpretation is reduced to its nub. According to Ḡön-chok-jik-may-w̄ang-b̄o, in the Mind-Only School the definition of a sūtra of interpretable meaning is:[586]

They posit a sūtra whose explicit teaching is not suitable to be asserted

- the *rtag brtan* edition (this most likely being an early-seventeenth-century block-print edition prepared at *rtag brtan phun tshogs gling* Monastery built by the great Jo-nang-b̄a master Tāranātha, who was second only in importance to S̄hay-rap-gyel-tsen to the Jo-nang-b̄a School; the monastery was taken over by the Ge-luk-b̄a order in 1650); and
- in Wonch'uk's commentary. (Although Jik-may-dam-chö-gya-tso, 307.5, reports that Wonch'uk's text does not have this reading, the Peking edition [5517, vol. 106, chap. 5, 170.1.8] does.)

Gung-tang says that he rejects such readings because they contradict many other editions as well as the *Sūtra Unraveling the Thought* as it is cited in Asaṅga's *Compendium of Ascertainments.* I would add that calling the final wheel of doctrine "*extremely* fantastic and *extremely* marvelous" goes against the basic Ge-luk-b̄a position that even for the Proponents of Mind-Only the middle wheel is the supreme teaching for the Bodhisattvas who are sharper than those for whom the third wheel was specifically taught. This is because these sharp Bodhisattvas can understand the doctrine of the three natures and the three non-natures just from hearing the Perfection of Wisdom Sūtras, and so forth (see Gung-tang's *Difficult Points,* 245.10-247.1). For this reason, the version of sūtra accepted in Ge-luk-b̄a circles speaks **only** of the middle wheel as being "*very* fantastic and marvelous."

In the seventh chapter of the *Sūtra Unraveling the Thought,* Buddha speaks about the various types of sentient beings to whom he teaches doctrine, among whom the supreme are these sharp Bodhisattvas (Lamotte, *Saṃdhinirmocana,* 75 [17], and 199; and Powers, *Wisdom of Buddha,* 115):

> Paramārthasamudgata, with respect to this, thinking of just these three types of non-nature, the One-Gone-Thus, by way of the aspect of setting forth sūtras of interpretable meaning, taught the doctrine [of the middle wheel] in this way, "All phenomena are natureless; all phenomena are unproduced, unceasing, quiescent from the start, and naturally thoroughly passed beyond sorrow." Regarding that, [when] sentient beings who have generated roots of virtue, have purified the obstructions, have ripened their continuums, have great faith, and have accumulated great collections of merit and wisdom hear this doctrine, they understand—**just as it is**—this which I explained with a thought behind it, and they develop faith in that doctrine. They also realize, by means of their exalted wisdom, **the meaning just as it is**. Also, through cultivating their realization they very quickly attain the very final state.

It is said that these sharp Bodhisattvas can realize the meaning of the middle wheel of doctrine—that is, the three natures and three non-natures—without relying on an exposition such as that found in the *Sūtra Unraveling the Thought.*

[a] *nges pa'i don, nītārtha* (Lamotte, *Saṃdhinirmocana,* 86 [30], n. 23).

> literally as a sūtra requiring interpretation, and they posit a sūtra whose explicit teaching is suitable to be asserted literally as a definitive sūtra.

Whether the subject matter of the sūtra is explicitly concerned with emptiness or not makes no difference; rather, the determination of what requires interpretation and what is definitive is by way of whether the passage can be accepted literally or not. A sūtra that speaks of the five aggregates—forms, feelings, discriminations, compositional factors, and consciousnesses—is definitive, since it is literally acceptable.

The same dividing line of literal acceptability and unacceptability also applies to passages concerned with the ultimate—emptiness or selflessness. In this vein, D̄zong-ka-b̄a (*Emptiness in Mind-Only,* 241) says that differentiation of the interpretable and the definitive in the Mind-Only School is by way of whether there is damage to the literal reading:

> [In the Mind-Only School], the differentiation between interpretable and definitive scriptures that are set forth stemming from the ultimate derives from whether there is or is not damage by reasoning to the literal reading.

Thus, when the *Sūtra Unraveling the Thought* speaks of the interpretable and the definitive, its concern is **solely** with passages concerned with the ultimate—selflessness. As D̄zong-ka-b̄a says (*Emptiness in Mind-Only,* 242), the three wheels as set forth at this point in the *Sūtra Unraveling the Thought* are constituted only by passages setting forth selflessness:

> The three stages of wheels of doctrine mentioned in the *Sūtra Unraveling the Thought* are posited, not by way of the assemblies of [Buddha's] circle[a] or by way of periods in the Teacher's life[b] and so forth but by way of topics of expression. Furthermore, those are in terms of delineating the meaning of selflessness.

Thus, although in general literality is the means for determining what is interpretable and what is definitive, the application of this principle at this point of considering the *Sūtra Unraveling the Thought* is always in relation to the ultimate. Hence, even though the definitions of the interpretable and the definitive given above do not speak of a dual qualification—being explicitly concerned with the ultimate and being literally acceptable—this comes to be the case in so far as the *Sūtra Unraveling the Thought* is the focus, and it appears to be the almost exclusive focus of hermeneutics in the Mind Only School. An outflow of this is that according to the *Sūtra Unraveling the Thought* the three wheels of

---

[a] Jik-may-dam-chö-gya-tso (*Port of Entry,* 705.5) identifies the Jo-nang-b̄as as the proponents of this notion.

[b] Jik-may-dam-chö-gya-tso (ibid., 705.6) identifies Chim, the Translator Tro, and the Translator Chak (*mchims khro chag*) as the proponents of this notion.

doctrine do not contain all of Buddha's teaching, just all teachings concerned with the ultimate. Hence, the three wheels are not ways to parcel his life teachings into three classes.

From this perspective Jam-ȳang-shay-b̄a gives instances of the three wheels of doctrine along with sūtras that are concordant with them or included among them:[587]

- actual first wheel of doctrine: *Wheel of Doctrine of the Four Truths*
- sūtras partially concordant with the first wheel: the *Four Groups of Scriptures on Discipline,*[a] *Four Establishments through Mindfulness Sūtra,* the *brgya ba rtogs brjod brgya ba* in the *Extensive Sport Sūtra,* and so forth
- actual middle wheel of doctrine: those in the class of Perfection of Wisdom Sūtras
- sūtras partially concordant with the middle wheel: *Diamond Cutter Sūtra, King of Meditative Stabilizations Sūtra, Buddhāvataṃsaka Sūtra, Pile of Jewels Sūtra,* and so forth.
- actual final wheel of doctrine: *Sūtra Unraveling the Thought* and particularly its Chapter of Questions by Paramārthasamudgata
- sūtras included in the class of final wheel: *Sūtra on the Heavily Adorned* and so forth.

Jam-ȳang-shay-b̄a adds that even though the Middle Way School considers the *Descent into Laṅkā Sūtra,* the *Sūtra on the Ten Grounds,* the *Matrix-of-One-Gone-Thus Sūtra,* and so forth to be in the middle wheel of doctrine, for the Mind-Only School these are included in the final wheel of doctrine, since they cite these to prove that the class of the Perfection of Wisdom Sūtras requires interpretation.

In this way, the delineation of emptiness in the Mind-Only School determines which teachings require interpretation and which are definitive. That the differentiation of scriptures depends on the view of emptiness illustrates how D̄zong-ka-b̄a's title, *Treatise Differentiating the Interpretable and the Definitive: The Essence of Eloquence,* while seeming to place the distinguishing of scriptures as the central topic, actually indicates its principal focus, emptiness. The presentation of emptiness, in turn, is accomplished through extensive analysis, even though the principal sūtra, the *Sūtra Unraveling the Thought,* does not—in the actual run of words—itself contain any reasonings proving emptiness. Begun in commentarial traditions in Inḍia and extended into even more of an art form in Tibet and the Mongolias, the vividly distinct articulations of reasoning—around which social units formed—provide copious evidence that among scholars of even one sect there was no monolithic power exerting control from an all-powerful center. In a culture of often great provincialism, intellectual diversity and difference were deliberately encouraged.

[a] *lung sde bzhi.*

Appendix: Wonch'uk's Influence in Tibet

The Korean scholar Wonch'uk[a] was born in 612 or 613 in Hsin-lo and ordained as a novice at the age of three; at fifteen he traveled to Ch'ang-an,[b] China, capital of the T'ang dynasty (618-908), where he remained for the rest of his life, dying at Fo-shou-chi Monastery on August 25, 696. He wrote a ten-fascicle commentary on the *Sūtra Unraveling the Thought* that was eventually translated into Tibetan sometime between 815 and 824[c] and thus was available in Tibet when Ḏzong-ka-ḇa wrote *The Essence of Eloquence* at the turn of the fifteenth century (1407-1408).[d]

Ḏzong-ka-ḇa explicitly refers to Wonch'uk's text nine times—three by his name,[e] five by "Chinese *Great Commentary*,"[f] and once within "the commentaries."[g] There are also two times when, without attribution, he uses Wonch'uk's text as a source for outlines of passages from the *Sūtra Unraveling the Thought*.[h] The number of references and the fact that he does so by name or title of his text eight times are particularly significant, since Ḏzong-ka-ḇa only obliquely refers to one other text written in Chinese—a commentary on the sūtra by Paramārtha that, most likely, he knew only through Wonch'uk's commentary. Also, he does not even mention the name of any Tibetan scholar, including the one whom he is principally refuting, S̄hay-rap-gyel-tsen (1292-1361), whose opinions he frequently rebukes.[i] Ḏzong-ka-ḇa's open references to Wonch'uk

---

a For a more detailed presentation of Wonch'uk's biography, see *Emptiness in Mind-Only*, 39ff.

b Presently called Xian.

c For a discussion of how the text came to be translated by Fa-ch'eng, see *Emptiness in Mind-Only*, 44.

d It may be that Ḏzong-ka-ḇa was the first in Tibet to react in detail to Wonch'uk's commentary. I have made inquiries as to whether Wonch'uk is cited by scholars of other Tibetan schools and to date have learned of none.

e Twice as *wen tsheg* (*Emptiness in Mind-Only*, Translation, 119/ Text, 387; 125/389) and once as *sde snod gsum pa wen tsheg* (Tripiṭaka Wonch'uk, 123/388).

f It is apparent that Ḏzong-ka-ḇa was unaware that Wonch'uk was born in Korea; it is likely that by using the nomenclature of "the Chinese *Great Commentary*" (*rgya nag gi 'grel chen; Emptiness in Mind-Only*, 78/370, 98/381, 101/382, 123/388, 126/389), he intends to distinguish Wonch'uk's commentary from another long commentary extant in Tibetan (for discussion of its authorship see *Emptiness in Mind-Only*, Appendix 1, p. 453ff.). Ḏzong-ka-ḇa cites this commentary only once, in order to refute it (see *Emptiness in Mind-Only*, 156). Ḏzong-ka-ḇa does not cite Jñānagarbha's commentary (Peking 5535, vol. 109), which is only on the eighth chapter, nor does he mention a short one attributed to Asaṅga (Peking 5481, vol. 104). His attention is clearly on Wonch'uk's text.

g *'grel pa rnams; Emptiness in Mind-Only*, 80/370.

h *Emptiness in Mind-Only*, 86/373 and 118/387.

i See *Emptiness in Mind-Only*, 54-55, and *Reflections on Reality*, 271-391.

most likely derive from deference to his wide-ranging scholarship and from a wish to correct the opinions of the scholar who wrote the longest commentary on the *Sūtra Unraveling the Thought.* Among the eleven references, Ḏzong-ka-ḇa disagrees with Wonch'uk six times (items 1, 2, 8, 10, 11), refines his opinion four times (items 5, 6, 7, 9), and agrees with Wonch'uk two times (3, 4).

It is highly likely that through Wonch'uk's text Ḏzong-ka-ḇa became aware of the scholarship of Bodhiruci, Dharmapāla, Paramārtha, and Hsüan-tsang, all of whom the Tibetan scholar mentions in his separate presentation of the mind-basis-of-all and afflicted mentality,[a] written in his twenties.[588] Also, Ernst Steinkellner[589] cogently speculates that the Tibetan technique of employing elaborate sectioning and subsectioning of texts may stem from similarly elaborate sectioning in Wonch'uk's commentary. If this is so, Wonch'uk also gave rise to a predominant style of scholarly organization in Tibetan texts that was employed to greater and lesser degrees by scholars in all of the major sects.

Throughout the first four chapters of *The Essence of Eloquence*, Ḏzong-ka-ḇa, while relying on Wonch'uk's presentation, seeks to refine many points, and subsequently Tibetan and Mongolian commentators subject his critiques—as well as other points in limited parts of the *Sūtra Unraveling the Thought*—to extensive analysis. Through extended discussions they often draw attention to facets of the sūtra that otherwise could easily be missed, and at other times they endow the sūtra with retroactive meanings created by analyzing it in the light of subsequent scholastic developments.

In analyzing Ḏzong-ka-ḇa's critiques, some commentators return to Wonch'uk's text and, in the guise of "defending" Ḏzong-ka-ḇa's points, actually give highly critical analyses by pointing out potential flaws in his presentation. Even when they valiantly explain away difficulties, they sometimes do this to the point where they give credence to Wonch'uk's reading. Also, they identify the actual passages in Wonch'uk's text when Ḏzong-ka-ḇa uses it as a source, especially if the reference does not appear in the corresponding place in the chapter of the *Sūtra Unraveling the Thought* under consideration.

We will first consider all of Ḏzong-ka-ḇa's explicit and implicit references to Wonch'uk's commentary and then consider representative references by other Ge-luk-ḇa scholars.

---

[a] *Extensive Commentary on the Difficult Points of the Mind-Basis-of-All and Afflicted Mentality: Ocean of Eloquence* (*yid dang kun gzhi'i dka' ba'i gnas rgya cher 'grel pa legs par bshad pa'i rgya mtsho*). See the excellent translation by Gareth Sparham in collaboration with Shōtarō Iida, *Ocean of Eloquence: Tsong kha pa's Commentary on the Yogācāra Doctrine of Mind* (Albany, N.Y.: State University of New York Press, 1993). In that text, Ḏzong-ka-ḇa cites Wonch'uk with regard to the history of Great Vehicle masters (pp. 48-49) and the number of consciousnesses asserted by Mind-Only masters (pp. 153-156).

1. References to Wonch'uk in Ḏzong-ka-ḇa's *The Essence of Eloquence*

First Reference: "Chinese *Great Commentary.*"
Disagrees with Wonch'uk about the meaning of a term, but the commentators are left with a morass

Ḏzong-ka-ḇa (59-133) disagrees with Wonch'uk's definition of "own-character" (*rang mtshan, svalakṣaṇa*) that appears in Paramārthasamudgata's question:

> The Supramundane Victor [initially] spoke, in many ways, of the **own-character** of the aggregates [of forms, feelings, discriminations, compositional factors, and consciousnesses, these being that in which one travels in cyclic existence].[590]

Wonch'uk takes the term "own-character" in Paramārthasamudgata's description of the first wheel of doctrine as referring to the unique character or definition of a phenomenon as when Buddha speaks of a phenomenon and then of its unique character that distinguishes it from other phenomena. In the case of form, for instance, it is that which is obstructive. In the case of consciousness, it is that which knows.

Ḏzong-ka-ḇa criticizes Wonch'uk's reading, saying "own-character" means "establishment by way of its own character." His attempt at correction is based on Buddha's usage of a similar term in his answer:

> Those [imputational natures] are characters posited by names and terminology and **do not subsist by way of their own character**. Therefore, they are said to be "non-natures in terms of character."

Here in the answer "character" in "non-natures in terms of character" unquestionably refers to "establishment by way of [their] own character." Ḏzong-ka-ḇa identifies the "own-character" of Paramārthasamudgata's question as having the same meaning as the "character" in Buddha's answer, which he himself identifies as "establishment by way of [its] own character."

This identification leads his commentators into a morass of difficulties. The problem revolves around the fact that in the Mind-Only School the aggregates are indeed "established by way of their own character," and thus Buddha's teaching in the first wheel of doctrine would not require interpretation, whereas it is a fundamental point of the *Sūtra Unraveling the Thought* that the first and second wheels of doctrine require interpretation. What to do?

- Jay-ḏzün Chö-ḡyi-gyel-tsen (1469-1546) leaves as is Ḏzong-ka-ḇa's identification of "own-character" as "established by way of its own character."

He cryptically suggests that the first wheel **also** teaches that phenomena are established by way of their own character as the referents of their respective conceptual consciousnesses.

- Paṇ-chen S̄ö-nam-drak-b̄a[591] likewise leaves D̄zong-ka-b̄a's identification as is but adds that a difference of entity between subject and object is **also** taught. Some of his contemporary followers (e.g., Kensur Ye-s̄hay-tup-d̄en and Ge-s̄hay Ḡön-chok-tsay-ring) add that when Buddha teaches "establishment by way of its own character," the establishment of objects by way of their own character as the referents of words and conceptual consciousnesses is **also** communicated. Thus, it seems that in Jay-d̄zün Chö-ḡyi-gyel-tsen and Paṇ-chen S̄ö-nam-drak-b̄a's traditions any passage that teaches that forms, for instance, are established by way of their own character **also** teaches that forms are established by way of their own character as the referents of their respective words and conceptual consciousnesses or are external objects. Hence, even though such a passage is factually correct in teaching that forms are established by way of their own character, it does not follow that the passage is literally acceptable and thus of definitive meaning, since it **also** teaches a false status of objects.
- Gung-ru Chö-jung and Jam-ȳang-shay-b̄a, however, strictly limit the meaning of "own-character" in Paramārthasamudgata's question to the establishment of objects by way of their own character as the referents of conceptual consciousnesses and hold that this is what D̄zong-ka-b̄a meant by "established by way of its own character." Thus, they conclude that what D̄zong-ka-b̄a means is that first-wheel sūtras teach, relative to certain trainees, that each and every phenomenon, whether compounded or uncompounded, is established by way of its own character **as the referent of its respective conceptual consciousness.**

In Gung-tang's commentary, a hypothetical objection is made to Gung-ru Chö-jung and Jam-ȳang-shay-b̄a's identification of "own-character" as "established by way of its own character **as the referent of its respective conceptual consciousness**"; the objector wants to remain with D̄zong-ka-b̄a's identification as "established by way of its own character." The objector says that the context of the first wheel of doctrine is to indicate that whatever topic is under discussion is established by way of its own character as the referent of a conceptual consciousness, even though the words for this are not present. Thus, the term "own-character" does not have to indicate this; it can be left, as D̄zong-ka-b̄a says, as meaning the establishment of objects by way of their own character. Hence, when the *Sūtra Unraveling the Thought* speaks of the own-character of the aggregates, we should take not just aggregates but aggregates **established by way of their own character** as the topic under discussion which, due to the mode of pronouncement, come to be communicated as established by way of their own character as referents of conceptual consciousnesses. This is the case, for instance, with all of the attributes of the aggregates—production, disintegration, abandonment, and thorough knowledge—which are, in their literal reading, not to be taken as what is negated; rather, the terms for the attributes ("production" and so forth) are those phenomena in their actuality; nevertheless, the context of the teaching is that these are established by way of their own character as the referents of words and conceptual consciousnesses. Thus, just as production is taken to be actual production that, due to context, is pronounced as being established by way of its own character as the referent of a term or thought about it, so aggregates established by way of their own character are actual aggregates established by way of their own character that, due to context, are pronounced as being established by way of their own character as the referents of conceptual consciousnesses.

Gung-tang's answer. Gung-tang responds that the establishment of the aggregates by way of their own character is an **attribute** of the aggregates, not the **entity** of the aggregates, and thus the teaching that the establishment of the aggregates by way of their own character is itself established by way of its own character as the referent of a conceptual consciousness would not constitute a teaching about the **entity** of the aggregates but would be a teaching about an **attribute** of the aggregates.

Gung-tang's own "solution." He is left with having to posit Ď̄zong-ka-b̄a's "actual" meaning when he used those words. He[592] avers that when Ď̄zong-ka-b̄a, having criticized Wonch'uk for taking "own-character" as meaning the unique character of an object, says that, instead of this, the term refers to establishment by way of its own character, he is using a code word for establishment of objects by way of their own character as the referents of conceptual consciousnesses—not actual establishment of objects by way of their own character. As evidence for his opinion, Gung-tang says that if "own-character" meant merely establishment of objects by way of their own character, then since the mental and physical aggregates are indeed established by way of their own character, it would be inappropriate for Paramārthasamudgata to ask about the basis in Buddha's thought when he taught such.

Gung-tang is reduced to saying that Ď̄zong-ka-b̄a could not have made such an egregious mistake about the reason for Paramārthasamudgata's questioning the teaching in the first wheel of doctrine and hence he could not have meant what his mere words seem to say. It is likely that Gung-tang is indicating that this is what Ď̄zong-ka-b̄a **should** have meant.

Remark

The objector's opinion so strenuously refuted by Gung-tang shows how to revive Wonch'uk's exposition of "own-character" as the entity or unique defining nature of an object without contravening Ď̄zong-ka-b̄a's point that an imputational nature has a unique defining character. Gung-tang does not face the issue that if, like Wonch'uk, we consider "own-character" to be the entity or unique defining nature of an object, his objection—which revolves around the fault that "own-character" if it means "establishment by way of its own character" refers to an attribute and not to the entity—no longer holds. For, just like the objector, we can posit that everything taught in the first wheel of doctrine is within the context of its being established by way of its own character as the referent of terms and conceptual consciousnesses. Then, we can use Wonch'uk's definition of "own-character" as the entity or unique nature of an object, and not have to twist it into something else. As in Ḏzong-ka-ḇa's reading, this false status of objects constitutes what is negated in emptiness; however, unlike Ḏzong-ka-ḇa's explanation, it is not indicated by the term "own-character" in Paramārthasamudgata's question; rather, this false status of objects is the context in which everything in the first wheel is taught.

Indeed, this seems to be just what the *Sūtra Unraveling the Thought* is saying, for the failing of the first wheel is not that it teaches a plethora of phenomena but that it does not teach that all phenomena have the same taste in the ultimate—the thoroughly established nature that is the imputational nature's emptiness of being established by way of its own character. It does not teach that all phenomena are of one taste in the ultimate. The first wheel lacks this teaching of the ultimate as the general character of all phenomena.

I surmise that Gung-tang intends to suggest this revival of Wonch'uk's reading of "own-character" as the unique defining nature of an object within emphasizing that the teachings in the first wheel of doctrine are made within the context of communicating that these phenomena are established by way of their own character as the referents of their respective terms and thoughts about them.

So why did Ḏzong-ka-ḇa say what he did? It is likely that he was seeking to show that in the Mind Only School even though permanent phenomena such as uncompounded space are merely imputed by conceptuality, they do have their own defining natures, and thus their imputed existence is validated existence. In this, he is opposed by certain S̄a-ḡya scholars who say that imputed existence does not serve as validated existence. Ḏzong-ka-ḇa wants to show that the views of so-called "lower" schools function as stepping-stones to the so-called "highest" view, that of the Consequence School; this "final" view is that all phenomena exist imputedly, and such existence is validated existence. This is a cornerstone of his philosophical writing and is a source of more than considerable controversy between the Ge-luk-ḇa schools and other Tibetan schools.

Second Reference: Included in "the commentaries." Disagrees about the meaning of a set of terms, but the criticism is refined by commentators

With regard to Ḏzong-ka-ḇa's criticism of Wonch'uk's reading of "the various[a] and manifold[b] constituents" as **both** referring to the eighteen constituents (issue #16), Gung-tang points out that despite evidence in the seventh chapter of the *Sūtra Unraveling the Thought* supporting Ḏzong-ka-ḇa's reading as "the eighteen constituents and the six constituents," the order of that passage in the sūtra has to be reversed from "six and eighteen" to "eighteen and six." He also indicates that there are sources for Wonch'uk's reading in the Questions of Subhūti chapter of the *Sūtra Unraveling the Thought,* in "Asaṅga's *Compendium of Ascertainments*" (Wonch'uk refers to the *Grounds of Yogic Practice*), in the *Myrobalan Sūtra,* and in Maitreya's *Ornament for the Great Vehicle Sūtras.* Another commentator, A-ku Ḻo-drö-gya-tso[593] tries to save Ḏzong-ka-ḇa's point by making the distinction that although the usage of these two terms **at the point of Paramārthasamudgata's question** does not accord with Wonch'uk's explanation, it is also permissible to explain these terms as they are set forth in the *Sūtra Unraveling the Thought* (in general or in the Subhūti Chapter).[594] They thereby give credence to Wonch'uk's exegesis, even if they criticize it for being misplaced.

Third Reference: implicit. Uses as a source for an outline of a scriptural passage

Apparently following Wonch'uk's[595] structuring of Buddha's description of the character-non-nature in the *Sūtra Unraveling the Thought,* Ḏzong-ka-ḇa divides it into a (rhetorical) question, an answer, a (rhetorical) questioning of the reason, and an answer to that question. He then advises that this format should be used also with respect to the other two non-natures. (See *Emptiness in Mind-Only,* 85-86, 263, and *Reflections on Reality,* 154-156.)

Fourth Reference: "Chinese Great Commentary." Uses as a source for the meaning of a term

The *Sūtra Unraveling the Thought* states that the ultimate-non-nature is distinguished by the selflessness of phenomena and only subsists **in permanent, permanent time**[c] **and everlasting, everlasting time.**[d] Ḏzong-ka-ḇa approvingly cites Wonch'uk's explanation that these mean former time and later time. (See *Emptiness in Mind-Only,* 98.)

---

a *tha dad pa, nānātva.*

b *du ma, anekatva.*

c *rtag pa'i dus.*

d *ther zug gi dus.*

Jik-may-dam-chö-gya-tso identifies the gloss as being in Wonch'uk's commentary near the end of the Subhūti Chapter in the *Sūtra Unraveling the Thought*. Drawing from Wonch'uk, he points out that, according to context, "permanent time" and "everlasting time" have various meanings, and he lists them. (See *Emptiness in Mind-Only*, 98-99, fnt. e.)

Fifth Reference: "Chinese *Great Commentary.*"

Cites as the source for the resolution of an apparent conflict between the *Sūtra Unraveling the Thought* and Asaṅga's *Summary of Manifest Knowledge* and refines Wonch'uk's explanation. B̄el-jor-hlün-drup fleshes out the point, and Jik-may-dam-chö-gya-tso covers up an omission that serves as evidence counter to his own tradition's explanation of "production by itself."

The Perfection of Wisdom Sūtras say that all phenomena are unproduced, unceasing, quiescent from the start, and naturally thoroughly passed beyond sorrow. In identifying what was behind Buddha's teaching, the *Sūtra Unraveling the Thought* at this point speaks of only imputational natures and the thoroughly established nature. However, Asaṅga in his *Summary of Manifest Knowledge* says that Buddha taught such in consideration of **all three** natures. About this, Wonch'uk says:[596]

> The teaching, in dependence upon imputational natures, in treatises such as the *Very Extensive One Hundred Stanzas* and so forth[a] that all phenomena are natureless, unproduced, unceasing, and so forth indicates that dependently arisen objects are not non-existent. Therefore, these sūtras also, thinking of the three natures in general, teach that all phenomena are natureless and, thinking of the first and last natures, teach [that all phenomena] are unproduced, and so forth.

D̄zong-ka-b̄a (see *Emptiness in Mind-Only*, 100-103) reframes Wonch'uk's statement, in the course of which he implicitly criticizes Wonch'uk for referring to the mere existence of dependent-arisings and not their "existence by way of their own character." Still, the remainder of his explanation accords exactly with Wonch'uk's text.

In more detail:

- The *Sūtra Unraveling the Thought* is indicating that since other-powered natures have production and cessation that **exist by way of their own character**, the statements in the *Sūtra Unraveling the Thought* concerning no production and no cessation are not in consideration of other-powered natures. Also, since most other-powered natures are included within the

---

[a] *bstan bcos shin tu rgyas pa brgya pa la sogs pa.*

class of thoroughly afflicted phenomena, they are not treated as what was behind Buddha's teaching that phenomena are quiescent from the start and naturally thoroughly passed beyond sorrow.

- Asaṅga, on the other hand, seeks to demonstrate a correspondence between how each of the three natures is natureless and how they also are not produced, not ceasing, quiescent from the start, and primordially passed beyond sorrow.

Bel-jor-hlün-drup's *Lamp for the Teaching* fleshes out Asaṅga's presentation:

- Imputational natures are said to be "unproduced" because they are not produced by way of their own character. They are said to be "unceased" because they do not cease by way of their own character. They are said to be quiescent from the start and naturally passed beyond sorrow because they are not afflicted phenomena since they are uncompounded.
- Other-powered natures are said to be "unproduced, unceasing," because they are not produced by their own power without depending on conditions and do not cease by their own power. Other-powered natures are said to be "quiescent from the start and naturally passed beyond sorrow" because without depending on conditions they do not exist as thoroughly afflicted phenomena.
- Thoroughly established natures are said to be "not produced, not ceasing" because they are not produced and do not cease as the nature that is a self of phenomena, or because they are the suchness that is not produced and does not cease as either a self of persons or a self of phenomena. They are said to be "quiescent from the start" and "naturally passed beyond sorrow" because they are without afflictions that are the nature of a self of phenomena, that is, without afflictions that are established by way of their own character as referents of conceptual consciousnesses. On this occasion, "sorrow" is the afflictive emotions. Or, in another way, thoroughly established natures are said to be "quiescence from the start" and "naturally passed beyond sorrow" because of being naturally passed beyond the afflictions in the sense of not being either established as a substantially existent person or established by way of their own character as the referents of conceptual consciousnesses and words.

When Wonch'uk presents Asaṅga's exposition of the production that other-powered entities lack, he gives a double meaning to the type of production that is lacking:

> Because other-powered entities are produced in dependence upon others but do not have the meaning **(1) of being produced by themselves and (2) of being produced causelessly**, [Asaṅga's] treatise, the *Summary of Manifest Knowledge,* and so forth say that stemming from the three aspects of natures, [Buddha] taught that all phenomena are

> natureless, unproduced, unceasing, quiescent from the start, and naturally thoroughly passed beyond sorrow.

Gung-tang (see issue #68),[597] however, cogently holds that in the *Sūtra Unraveling the Thought* "production by itself"[a] means intrinsic production as in the Nihilist School, and it is intriguing that Dzong-ka-ba does not criticize Wonch'uk for describing Asaṅga's view of the production that other-powered entities lack as "being produced by themselves **and** being produced causelessly," since Wonch'uk indeed does not seem to be giving two ways of referring to causeless production but seems to offer two **different** explanations. The two versions could only be production from self and causeless production, since at least in the Tibetan translation he uses the term **by** (*kyis*) for the first type and connects the two with "and" (*dang*). Jik-may-dam-chö-gya-tso[598] recognizes the problem, and thus when he recapitulates Wonch'uk's meaning, he gets around the situation by switching "and" to "or" (*'am*), thereby making the second explanation into a gloss of the first and thus makes the reference into being just causeless production.

Sixth Reference: implicit. Adapts an outline of a sūtra passage

Unlike Dzong-ka-ba's sixfold division (*Emptiness in Mind-Only,* 118) of the sūtra passage about the first wheel of doctrine—place, trainees, entity, subjects of expression, praise, and its not being of definitive meaning—Wonch'uk divides a slightly longer passage (beginning with an initial statement, "Then, at that time, the Bodhisattva Paramārthasamudgata also offered this to the Supramundane Victor," and then continuing through what Dzong-ka-ba cited[b]) into two parts with several subdivisions. Wonch'uk's twofold arrangement[599] with these subdivisions and their corresponding passages in the *Sūtra Unraveling the Thought* is:

1. Indicating that the [first] wheel of doctrine itself is lofty[c]
   a. Indicating the petitioner and the respondent: "Then, at that time, the Bodhisattva Paramārthasamudgata also offered this to the Supramundane Victor"
   b. Indicating the time when it was spoken: "initially"
   c. Indicating the place where it was spoken: "in the area of Varaṇāsi in the Deer Park [called] 'Sage's Propounding'"
   d. Indicating those for whom it was spoken: "for those engaged in the Hearer vehicle"
   e. Indicating the wheel of doctrine: "thoroughly turned a wheel of

---

a *bdag nyid kyis skye ba.*

b *Emptiness in Mind-Only,* 115.

c *yang dag par.*

doctrine through teaching the aspects of the four noble truths"

2. Indicating that the [first] wheel of doctrine is inferior and not of definitive meaning: "fantastic and marvelous which none—god or human—had turned in a similar fashion in the world [but] that wheel of doctrine thoroughly turned by the Supramundane Victor is surpassable, provides an opportunity [for refutation], is of interpretable meaning, and serves as a basis for controversy"

Dzong-ka-ba not only does not use Wonch'uk's twofold division of the sūtra passage but also (1) eliminates the category of indicating the petitioner and respondent as well as that of time and (2) adds the category of praise. He also changes Wonch'uk's category of "indicating the wheel of doctrine" into two categories, entity and subjects of expression. Dzong-ka-ba does all this without mentioning Wonch'uk, but immediately after this (see the next reference) he cites Wonch'uk's explanation.

Seventh Reference: "Wonch'uk (wen tsheg)." Draws on and refines explanations of terms

Dzong-ka-ba (*Emptiness in Mind-Only,* 119, fnt. a) gives two versions of the four qualities mentioned in the *Sūtra Unraveling the Thought* to describe the first turning of the wheel of doctrine. In the first list, he paraphrases Wonch'uk's explanation;[600] in the second list, he gives his own rendition of the four. Wonch'uk himself says:

> Because this wheel of doctrine holds back [or hides] emptiness and teaches [everything] as just existent, it (1) is of interpretable meaning. Because it fully teaches the causes and effects of cyclic existence and nirvāṇa as well as the selflessness of persons and does not teach the reasoning of the emptiness of phenomena, this teaching of [the first wheel of doctrine] (2) is a teaching that has a special [doctrine] higher than it, (3) is a teaching in relation to which there is occasion for [realization of a doctrine][a] more special and is susceptible to destruction by others, and (4) is a source of controversy among the twenty sects [of Hearers].

Gung-tang explains the reason for Wonch'uk's change in order

Gung-tang shows his own prowess by elaborately defending Dzong-ka-ba but admits that he is unsuccessful, suggesting that Dzong-ka-ba does not fully represent Wonch'uk's intention or meaning. Wonch'uk puts first what is mentioned in the sūtra as the third quality of this wheel of doctrine—its being of interpretable meaning. As Gung-tang[601] says, this is because Wonch'uk sees the

[a] This addition is Gung-tang's exposition of Wonch'uk's meaning; see below.

sūtra's first, second, and fourth qualities as being consequences of the first wheel's being of interpretable meaning.

In the first list of four, D̄zong-ka-b̄a (*Emptiness in Mind-Only,* 121) essentially paraphrases Wonch'uk, except that he rearranges Wonch'uk's explanation in accordance with the order of the four points in the sūtra:

> With respect to those, Wonch'uk explains:
>
> 1. "Surpassable" means that there is a special doctrine higher than this
> 2. "Affords an occasion" means that there is an occasion of a doctrine more special than this[a]
> 3. Because it does not teach emptiness and teaches [that everything] exists, it requires interpretation
> 4. That it has controversy means that it is susceptible to destruction by others [through debate][602] and serves as a source of controversy among Hearer sectarians

Gung-tang explains in what sense Wonch'uk and D̄zong-ka-b̄a agree

Then, in his own listing of the four points, D̄zong-ka-b̄a objects only to Wonch'uk's rendering of the second; however, he rewords **all** four points. As Gung-tang[603] says, "Since [D̄zong-ka-b̄a] did not make a refutation of the other three, they accord in **meaning** with his own system." Most likely, Gung-tang is suggesting that even if three of D̄zong-ka-b̄a's list agree with Wonch'uk's in meaning, the phraseology is markedly different.

It seems to me that D̄zong-ka-b̄a also does not accept the meaning of Wonch'uk's rendition of the third quality, unless by "exists" Wonch'uk intends not mere existence but **existence by way of its own character**, since D̄zong-ka-b̄a repeatedly says that the issue is not with existence but with existence by way of its own character. Also, D̄zong-ka-b̄a cannot accept the first part of the fourth quality as Wonch'uk presents it, since D̄zong-ka-b̄a considers the first wheel's susceptibility to destruction by others through debate to be the meaning of the second quality. He would not, however, have any substantial quarrel with Wonch'uk's description of the first quality.

Gung-tang pretends to defend D̄zong-ka-b̄a's misplacement of a term when reporting Wonch'uk's presentation

In Gung-tang's *Difficult Points*[b] a hypothetical opponent points out that

---

[a] In order to avoid redundancy with the first quality, Gung-tang (*Difficult Points,* 240.6) explains Wonch'uk's presentation of this quality as meaning that there is an occasion **of realization** of a doctrine more special than this.

[b] Gung-tang's *Difficult Points,* 238.5-240.12.

Wonch'uk himself takes "destruction by others" as part of his explanation of the sūtra's second quality, that is, "affords an occasion." According to this hypothetical critic, D̄zong-ka-b̄a has misread "destruction by others" to be part of the sūtra's fourth quality due to the ambiguity of the Tibetan translation of Wonch'uk's rearrangement of these four into his own list. Speaking about the second and fourth qualities of the first wheel (which, in D̄zong-ka-b̄a's re-ordering of Wonch'uk's passage, are the third and fourth qualities), Wonch'uk[604] says:

> *skabs khyad par can yod pa'i bstan pa dang/* ***gzhan dag gis gzhig par bya ba dang/*** *sde pa nyis shu po rtsod par smra ba dag gi gnas su gyur pa yin no//*

The ambiguity revolves around whether the second phrase, "is susceptible to destruction by others" (*gzhan dag gis gzhig par bya ba*) goes with the material before it, "is a teaching in relation to which there is occasion for something more special" (*skabs khyad par can yod pa'i bstan pa*) or after it, "is a source of controversy among the twenty sects [of Hearers]" (*sde pa nyis shu po rtsod par smra ba dag gi gnas su gyur pa*). Putting it with the material preceding it, the passage reads:

> (3) is a teaching in relation to which there is occasion for something more special and is susceptible to destruction by others, and (4) is a source of controversy among the twenty sects [of Hearers].

Putting it with the material following it, D̄zong-ka-b̄a takes the passage as saying:

> (3) is a teaching in relation to which there is occasion for something more special, and (4) is susceptible to destruction by others and is a source of controversy among the twenty sects [of Hearers].

D̄zong-ka-b̄a puts the second phrase ("is susceptible to destruction by others") with the material following it, but the hypothetical critic objects that it should be put with the material preceding it, citing as evidence Wonch'uk's later explanation of "does not afford an occasion" with regard to the third wheel, where there is no grammatical ambiguity in the Tibetan. The critic's point is extremely well taken, for, about the third wheel, Wonch'uk[605] does indeed say:

> Because this is supremely fantastic and there is no other exceeding it, it is unsurpassable. **Because it does not afford an occasion for something more superior later and does not afford an occasion for [later] destruction, it does not afford an occasion.** Because it teaches existence and non-existence completely, it is of definitive meaning, and it is not a source of controversy. (*'di mchog tu rmad du byung zhing de las lhag pa gzhan med pas bla na ma mchis pa dang /* ***phyis mchog tu***

> ***'gyur ba'i skabs dang gzhig pa'i skabs med pas skabs ma mchis pa*** *dang / yod med rdzogs par bstan pas nges pa'i don dang / rtsod pa smra ba'i gzhi'i gnas min pa'o//*)

In the middle sentence, Wonch'uk clearly puts "occasion for something more superior later" (*phyis mchog tu 'gyur ba'i skabs*) and "occasion for [later] destruction" (*gzhig pa'i skabs*) together in one negative reason clause, from which it can be determined that this is how the earlier passage about the first wheel should be read (but, of course, without the negative).

Gung-tang gives an elaborate "defense" of Ḏzong-ka-ḇa's apparent slip with regard to the first wheel. In order to maintain the pretense that Ḏzong-ka-ḇa did not make an error (and in order to indicate his own powers of creative exposition), Gung-tang makes the claim that in Wonch'uk's text "is susceptible to destruction by others" (*gzhan dag gis gzhig par bya ba* or *gzhan gyis gzhig nus pa*) does indeed go with what follows it, "is a source of controversy among the twenty sects" (*sde pa nyis shu po rtsod...*) and not with the preceding, "is a teaching that has a special [doctrine] higher than it" (*skabs khyad par can yod pa'i bstan pa*), despite the fact that *phyis gzhig pa'i skabs med pa* goes with *skabs med pa*. He does this by analyzing Wonch'uk's meaning of "affording an occasion" as being that there is an occasion **of a higher realization** and thus having nothing to do with external debate. He also thereby has to claim that "does not afford an occasion for destruction" (*gzhig pa'i skabs med pa*), which is undeniably tied to "it does not afford an occasion" (*skabs med pa*), refers not to destruction in debate but to the third wheel's not being discarded upon realizing a higher meaning. However, as Gung-tang himself admits, this brings him into conflict with Ḏzong-ka-ḇa's statement that except for the **former** of the two reasons for "not affording an occasion" his own presentation agrees with Wonch'uk's, for Ḏzong-ka-ḇa explains the **latter** of the two reasons "does not afford an occasion for later destruction" (*gzhig pa'i skabs med pa*) as not affording an occasion for destruction in debate and not as "not being discarded upon realizing a higher meaning" as Gung-tang takes Wonch'uk's meaning. Gung-tang thereby admits the weakness of his otherwise ingenious defense of Ḏzong-ka-ḇa. The admission can be understood only through realizing that he is self-consciously and humorously operating under the dictum that Ḏzong-ka-ḇa somehow has to be made right even when he is not.

Eighth Reference: "Tripiṭaka Wonch'uk (*sde snod gsum pa wen tsheg*)."

Disagrees with Wonch'uk about the meaning of a set of terms

Ḏzong-ka-ḇa (*Emptiness in Mind-Only,* 123, 275) implicitly criticizes Wonch'uk for merely saying that the four qualities of the middle wheel of doctrine—being surpassable, affording an occasion, requiring interpretation, and serving as a basis for controversy—are so "in relation to the third wheel." Though this is indeed the case because the third wheel is not surpassable, does not afford an occasion, is definitive, and does not serve as a basis for controversy, Dzong-ka-ba considers Wonch'uk's commentary to be insufficient. He also passes off Paramārtha's explanation, cited by Wonch'uk, as not good and thus does not even cite it or explain his disdain. Dzong-ka-ba's opinion is that the four should be presented as was done for the first wheel:

- Surpassable means that there are other teachings of definitive meaning higher than this.
- Affording an occasion means that it affords an occasion for the assessment of fault by other disputants.
- Requiring interpretation means that its meaning must be interpreted otherwise.
- Serving as a basis for controversy means that, since Buddha did not clearly differentiate the status of what from among the three natures exists by way of its own character and what does not, there is controversy about the meaning.

Ninth Reference: "Chinese *Great Commentary.*" Praises the translation of a term but implicitly disagrees about its meaning

Dzong-ka-ba praises Wonch'uk's translation of a term regarding the middle wheel of doctrine in the *Sūtra Unraveling the Thought.* Dzong-ka-ba's own citation (*Emptiness in Mind-Only,* 116) of the sūtra (with the phrase under scrutiny highlighted) is:

> Based[a] on just the naturelessness of all phenomena and based on just the absence of production, the absence of cessation, quiescence from the start, and naturally passed beyond sorrow, the Supramundane Victor turned a second wheel of doctrine, for those engaged in the Great Vehicle,[b] very fantastic and marvelous, **through the aspect of speaking on emptiness.**[c] Furthermore, that wheel of doctrine turned by the

[a] *brtsams, ārabhya* (Lamotte, *Saṃdhinirmocana,* 86 [30], n. 18). Gung-tang (*Difficult Points,* 236.10) explains that *brtsams* here means "taking such and such as substrata" (*khyad gzhir bzung ba*), although in other places it means that "the thought comes down to such and such" (*dgongs pa der 'bab pa tsam*).

For the Go-mang tradition of Gung-ru Chö-jung, Jam-yang-shay-ba, Gung-tang, and A-ku Lo-drö-gya-tso, the second wheel—taking these as its substrata—teaches on the literal level that all phenomena are not established from their own side.

[b] *theg pa chen po la yang dag par zhugs pa, mahāyānasaṃprasthita* (Lamotte, *Saṃdhinirmocana,* 86 [30], n. 19).

[c] *stong pa nyid smos pa'i rnam pas, śūnyatāvādākāreṇa* (ibid., 86 [30], n. 20).

> Supramundane Victor is surpassable, affords an occasion [for refutation], requires interpretation, and serves as a basis for controversy.

Ḏzong-ka-ḇa (*Emptiness in Mind-Only,* 123) praises Wonch'uk's rendition:

> In the Chinese *Great Commentary* [by Wonch'uk], "**in a non-manifest manner**"[a] also appears [in his citation of the *Sūtra Unraveling the Thought* instead of "through the aspect of speaking on emptiness."[b] Wonch'uk] explains that it means holding back [or hiding][606] the existent.[c] That translation is good.

However, Ḏzong-ka-ḇa refines the significance:

> The meaning is that while the latter two wheels are similar in teaching "stemming from naturelessness" as the subject of expression, the difference in the mode of teaching is that the middle wheel does not differentiate [clearly][607] what has nature and what does not, as explained before, due to which the sūtra says, "in a non-manifest manner," whereas since the latter wheel differentiates these, the sūtra says, "possessed of good differentiation."

He is clearly building on and refining Wonch'uk's commentary.

Tenth Reference: "Wonch'uk (*wen tsheg*)." Disagrees with Wonch'uk about the meaning of a term

Ḏzong-ka-ḇa (*Emptiness in Mind-Only,* 125) quotes Wonch'uk with regard to the four qualities of the third wheel of doctrine and laconically faults the first part of his twofold rendition of the second quality. Ḏzong-ka-ḇa reports Wonch'uk's opinion and criticizes only this part of it:

> Wonch'uk explains:[608]

a Wonch'uk (Peking 5517, vol. 106, chap. 5, 169.2.3): *mi mngon pa'i rnam pas.* Gung-ru Chö-jung's *Garland of White Lotuses* (64b.4) and Jam-ȳang-shay-ḇa's *Great Exposition of the Interpretable and the Definitive* (133.6), when citing Wonch'uk, add *stong pa nyid,* making *stong pa nyid mi mngon pa'i rnam pas;* Wonch'uk's text itself reads: *rang bzhin gyis yongs su myang ngan las 'das pa nyid las brtsams nas 'di ltar mi mngon pa'i rnam pas yang dag pa'i chos kyi 'khor lo bskor ba.*

b *stong pa nyid smos pa'i rnam pas.* The *stog* Palace edition of the *Sūtra Unraveling the Thought* (70.1) has still another reading: "through the aspect of elaborations" (*spros pa'i rnam pas*). Jik-may-dam-chö-gya-tso (*Port of Entry,* 292.2) points out that the *ska cog* translation of the *Sūtra Unraveling the Thought* reads "having elaborations" (*spros pa dang bcas pa*).

c Wonch'uk (Peking 5517, vol. 106, chap. 5, 169.3.2) explains that the first wheel hides emptiness and teaches existence, whereas the second wheel hides existence and teaches emptiness. Ḏzong-ka-ḇa considers the rendering of "in a non-manifest manner" preferable to "through the aspect of speaking," but he does not accept the meaning that Wonch'uk assigns to the expression.

> Because this is supremely marvelous and there is no other exceeding it, it is unsurpassable. Because it does not afford an occasion for some more superior [realization][609] later and does not afford an occasion for [later][a] destruction, it does not afford an occasion. Because it teaches existence and non-existence completely, it is of definitive meaning, and it is not a source of controversy.

> Except for [Wonch'uk's unsuitable explanation of] the former [of the two meanings] of no occasion [that is, "it does not afford an occasion for some more superior (realization) later"], his explanations [of the other three qualities][610] appear to be similar in meaning with the opposite of my earlier explanation of the meaning of surpassable and so forth [with respect to the first wheel and thus are suitable].

Dzong-ka-ba's earlier version of the four (*Emptiness in Mind-Only,* 121) with regard to the first two wheels of doctrine is:

1. There are other [teachings] of definitive meaning higher than this.
2. It affords an occasion[b] for [the assessment of] fault by other disputants when its meaning is asserted in accordance with how it is taught. This is even translated as "susceptible to dispute" in [Paramārtha's] Chinese commentary;[c] hence, the meaning is such [and not as Wonch'uk explains it].[611]

---

[a] Wonch'uk (Peking 5517, vol. 106, chap. 5, 170.2.2) has a second "later" (*phyis*), as is confirmed by Gung-tang's *Difficult Points* (240.14), whereas Dzong-ka-ba omits the second, citing only *phyis mchog tu 'gyur ba'i skabs dang gzhig pa'i skabs med pas.*

[b] As Jik-may-dam-chö-gya-tso (*Port of Entry,* 290.2) explains, "affords an occasion" (*skabs mchis pa*) means "suitable for the assessment of censure" (*klan ka 'jug rung*) and thus allowing for fallacies through reasonings refuting the extreme of superimposition by opponents such as the Proponents of Mind-Only (*sems tsam sogs rgol bas sgro 'dogs kyi mtha' 'gog pa'i rigs pa dag gis rgol ba'i skyon kyi go skabs yod pa*).

[c] This is the text written by Paramārtha (*yang dag bden pa;* 499-569), called *Commentary on the "Sūtra Unraveling the Words"* (*tshig nges par 'grel ba'i mdo'i 'grel pa*); see Wonch'uk (Peking 5517, vol. 106, chap. 5, 170.2.7, and so forth) for citation of the title. The translation into Tibetan of Paramārtha's explanation, as cited by Wonch'uk (170.3.1 and 170.3.4; see also Jik-may-dam-chö-gya-tso's *Port of Entry,* 290.4), uses the term "susceptible to dispute" (*rgol ba dang bcas pa*) in place of "affords an opportunity" (*skabs mchis pa*). Dzong-ka-ba's own usage of "affords an opportunity" (*skabs mchis pa*) indicates his preference in terms of the **words**; he agrees, however, that Paramārtha's version communicates the **meaning**, and thus he says, "This is even translated as 'susceptible to dispute' in the Chinese commentary [by Paramārtha]; hence, the **meaning** is such [and not as Wonch'uk explains it]."

One might think that by "Chinese commentary" Dzong-ka-ba is referring to Wonch'uk's commentary, but in all five instances of referring to Wonch'uk's text without giving his name (there being three others when he refers to him by name and one when the text is included within "the commentaries") he refers to it as the "Chinese **Great** Commentary" (*rgya nag gi 'grel* ***chen***), and furthermore he has just finished listing Wonch'uk's

3. Its meaning must be interpreted otherwise.
4. Since the Teacher [Buddha] did not clearly differentiate the status [of what from among the three natures exists by way of its own character and what does not],[612] there is controversy about the meaning.

A-ku L̄o-drö-gya-tso's explanation[613] of these four in a way that is applicable to the first two wheels of doctrine is particularly clear since it focuses on the literal reading:[a]

1. Due to the mode of teaching the literal reading, there are other sūtras of definitive meaning above it.
2. When asserted in accordance with the literal reading, there are opportunities for the assessment of fault by other disputants.
3. Since the literal reading is not literal,[b] it requires interpretation.
4. Since whether the three natures are truly existent is not clarified, there are controversies about the literal reading among followers who assert the literal reading.

Thus, the third wheel is the opposite:

1. Due to the mode of teaching the literal reading, there are no other sūtras of definitive meaning above it.
2. When asserted in accordance with the literal reading, there is no opportunity for the assessment of fault by other disputants.
3. Since the literal reading is literal, it is definitive.
4. Since whether the three natures are truly existent is clarified, there are no

---

assertions on these four points; thus I have taken "Chinese commentary" as referring to Paramārtha's commentary. Indeed, D̄zong-ka-b̄a's reference is extremely cryptic, to be deciphered only by searching for "susceptible to dispute" (*rgol ba dang bcas pa*) in Wonch'uk's text and finding that it occurs only in Wonch'uk's citation of Paramārtha's text. (Wonch'uk repeatedly cites Paramārtha's text—sometimes agreeing with it, sometimes disagreeing, and sometimes not expressing an opinion.) In sum, D̄zong-ka-b̄a is saying that Wonch'uk should have followed Paramārtha on this point.

Paramārtha's commentary on the *Sūtra Unraveling the Thought* seems not to be extant in Chinese, and also a translation into Tibetan is not found in any Tibetan catalogues (thanks to Paul Hackett for the search). Wonch'uk (for example, Peking 5517, vol. 106, chap. 5, 169.4) also refers to a text called "the master Paramārtha's *Purification of Forgetfulness* (*slob dpon yang dag bden pa'i brjed byang*)—an essay written in order to refresh the memory; this latter text seems to me to be in addition to Paramārtha's commentary on the sūtra and not just another name for it, but I could not confirm my hunch, since it was not found either in Tibetan or in Chinese (thanks to Paul Groner for the latter search). Gung-tang (for example, 241.8) refers to Paramārtha's *Purification of Forgetfulness,* but it may be that his sole source for this is Wonch'uk's citations.

A-ku L̄o-drö-gya-tso (*Precious Lamp,* 172.5) refers to another text by Paramārtha called *Purification of Forgetfulness* which teaches the views of the different sects.

[a] *sgras zin.*

[b] *sgra ji bzhin pa.*

controversies about the literal reading among followers who assert the literal reading.

Gung-tang implicitly disagrees with how Dzong-ka-ba seems to take part of Wonch'uk's explanation

Dzong-ka-ba says that except for the first part of the second quality in Wonch'uk's explanation ("it does not afford an occasion for some more superior [realization] later"), his explanation agrees with Wonch'uk's. However, Gung-tang reads the meaning of the second part of the second quality in Wonch'uk's explanation "does not afford an occasion for [later][a] destruction" as that it "is not susceptible to developing higher realization that overwhelms one's earlier realization." Gung-tang cogently says that the type of destruction mentioned here does not refer to being overwhelmed in debate, because there would be no sense in Wonch'uk's using the temporal reference "later," since if the position were so susceptible, it would always be so; rather, destruction refers to developing higher realization that overwhelms one's earlier realization.

Gung-tang admits that his reading makes it not accord in meaning with Dzong-ka-ba's presentation, which is that "It affords an occasion for [the assessment of] fault by other disputants when its meaning is asserted in accordance with how it is taught." Thus, he wonders whether, when Dzong-ka-ba says that Wonch'uk and he are in agreement about these qualities (except for Wonch'uk's exposition of the first part of the second), he is referring merely to the fact that both Wonch'uk and he explain that the third wheel is not susceptible to destruction, even if they disagree on what this means. However, it seems to me that since Dzong-ka-ba clearly says, "his **explanations** [of the other three qualities] appear to be **similar in meaning**," it is likely that Gung-tang is politely saying that Dzong-ka-ba erred.

However, Jik-may-dam-chö-gya-tso posits Dzong-ka-ba's thought

Jik-may-dam-chö-gya-tso,[614] on the other hand, explains the unsuitability of Wonch'uk's explanation as being that if it means that the third wheel does not allow for there being something superior to it, then (1) it is redundant with the earlier mention that "there is no other exceeding it" and (2) the second wheel would also "not afford an occasion." This latter point is that sharp Bodhisattvas can, without further explanation, understand the second wheel as teaching the three natures and three non-natures, and thus the second wheel teaches the three natures and three non-natures even if not on the literal level, and hence

[a] Wonch'uk (Peking 5517, vol. 106, chap. 5, 170.2.2) has a second "later" (*phyis*), as is confirmed by Gung-tang's *Difficult Points* (240.14), whereas Dzong-ka-ba omits the second, citing only *phyis mchog tu 'gyur ba'i skabs dang gzhig pa'i skabs med pas.*

the second wheel also does not afford an occasion for there being something superior to it, in this sense.

Eleventh Reference: "Chinese *Great Commentary.*" Disagrees about the nomenclature for the third wheel of doctrine

Dzong-ka-ba (*Emptiness in Mind-Only,* 126, 278) agrees with Wonch'uk that the first wheel is to be called the wheel of doctrine of the four truths and that the second is to be called the wheel of doctrine of no character but he does not agree that the third is to be called the "wheel of the ultimate, the definitive"; rather, he prefers "the wheel of good differentiation" based on the description (*Emptiness in Mind-Only,* 116) in the *Sūtra Unraveling the Thought:*

> The Supramundane Victor turned a third wheel of doctrine for those engaged in all vehicles,[a] **possessed of good differentiation,**[b] fantastic and marvelous.

However, Gung-tang (*Difficult Points,* 226.6) points out that the *Sūtra Unraveling the Thought* itself is also the source for Wonch'uk's calling the third wheel "the wheel of the ultimate, the definitive." Near the end of chapter 7, Paramārthasamudgata questions Buddha about the name of the teaching that Buddha has been giving:[615]

> Bodhisattva Paramārthasamudgata said to the Supramundane Victor: "Supramundane Victor, what is the name of this teaching in this form of doctrine, which comments on the thought behind your teachings? In what way should we apprehend this?"
>
> The Supramundane Victor said: "Paramārthasamudgata, this is 'the teaching of the ultimate, the definitive meaning.' This is to be apprehended as 'the teaching of the ultimate, the definitive meaning.'"

Gung-tang speculates that, according to Dzong-ka-ba, Buddha here gives the particular name of **this chapter of the sūtra** and not the name of the third wheel of doctrine, which, as "the wheel of good differentiation," is more parallel to the names of the other two wheels. I would add that perhaps Dzong-ka-ba seeks to preserve the point that the middle wheel teaches the ultimate, even if not on the literal level.

---

a *theg pa thams cad la yang dag par zhugs pa, sarvayānasaṃprasthita* (Lamotte, *Saṃdhinirmocana,* 86 [30], n. 21).

b *legs par rnam par phye ba dang ldan pa, suvibhakta* (ibid., 86 [30], n. 22).

2. References to Wonch'uk by Ge-luk-b̄a Scholars Other Than D̄zong-ka-b̄a

Jik-may-dam-chö-gya-tso explains the difference in the number of chapters in versions of the *Sūtra Unraveling the Thought*

See issue #8, p. 27, and *Emptiness in Mind-Only,* Appendix 1 and 2.

Gung-tang tries to defend the Second Dalai Lama for not mentioning a chapter of the *Sūtra Unraveling the Thought* by referring to a statement by Wonch'uk

See issue #9, p. 27.

Gung-tang criticizes Wonch'uk's two explanations of abandonment and thorough knowledge, but A-ku L̄o-drö-gya-tso posits Wonch'uk's thought

See issue #13, p. 33.

Gung-tang disagrees about the meaning of the last two of the seven attributes of the thirty-seven harmonies with enlightenment

See issue #18, p. 45.

Jik-may-dam-chö-gya-tso and so forth cite Wonch'uk as an organizational source for dividing Buddha's reply into four parts

In the *Sūtra Unraveling the Thought* Buddha explains that from two perspectives—imputational natures and thoroughly established natures—he taught in the Perfection of Wisdom Sūtras that all phenomena are unproduced, unceasing, quiescent from the start, and naturally thoroughly passed beyond sorrow. Based on Wonch'uk's exposition,[616] scholars such as Jik-may-dam-chö-gya-tso divide these two expositions into a brief indication,[a] an extensive explanation,[b] a giving of examples, and a summary sentence. See *Reflections on Reality,* 150, 158.

---

[a] *mdor bstan.*

[b] *rgyas bshad.*

Jik-may-dam-chö-gya-tso structures the three wheels of doctrine around nine viewpoints based on Wonch'uk's description

See *Emptiness in Mind-Only,* 274-277.

Gung-tang rejects Wonch'uk's citation of the *Sūtra Unraveling the Thought* concerning the third wheel where it reads "**extremely** fantastic and **extremely** marvelous"

First let us cite Dzong-ka-ba's quotation (*Emptiness in Mind-Only,* 116-117) of the sūtra passage in question:

> However,[a] based on just the naturelessness of phenomena and based on just the absence of production, the absence of cessation, quiescence from the start, and naturally passed beyond sorrow, the Supramundane Victor turned a third wheel of doctrine for those engaged in all vehicles,[b] possessed of good differentiation,[c] **fantastic and marvelous.** This wheel of doctrine turned by the Supramundane Victor is unsurpassable, does not afford an occasion [for refutation], is of definitive meaning,[d] and does not serve as a basis for controversy.

The *stog* Palace edition of the sūtra (70.4) reads "**extremely** fantastic and **extremely** marvelous" (***ha cang yang*** *ngo mtshar la/* ***ha cang yang*** *rmad du byung ba*). Gung-tang[617] rejects similar readings (***shin tu*** *ngo mtshar rmad du byung ba*) in:

- the *rtag brtan* edition[e]
- and Wonch'uk's commentary.[f]

Gung-tang says that he rejects such readings because they contradict many other editions as well as the *Sūtra Unraveling the Thought* as it is cited in

---

[a] Jik-may-dam-chö-gya-tso (*Port of Entry,* 294.2) points out the disjunctive function of the Tibetan *lags kyi* that follows the description of the middle wheel but not the first, since both require interpretation; it serves to separate out the third wheel.

[b] *theg pa thams cad la yang dag par zhugs pa, sarvayānasaṃprasthita* (Lamotte, *Saṃdhinirmocana,* 86 [30], n. 21).

[c] *legs par rnam par phye ba dang ldan pa, suvibhakta* (ibid., 86 [30], n. 22).

[d] *nges pa'i don, nītārtha* (Lamotte, *Saṃdhinirmocana,* 86 [30], n. 23).

[e] This most likely is an early-seventeenth-century block-print edition prepared at *rtag brtan phun tshogs gling* Monastery built by the great Jo-nang-ba master Tāranātha, who was second only in importance to Shay-rap-gyel-tsen to the Jo-nang-ba School; the monastery was taken over by the Ge-luk-ba order in 1650.

[f] Although Jik-may-dam-chö-gya-tso (*Port of Entry,* 307.5) reports that Wonch'uk's text does not have this reading, the Peking edition (5517, vol. 106, chap. 5, 170.1.8) does. There is no evidence that Jik-may-dam-chö-gya-tso is referring to the Chinese edition.

Asaṅga's *Compendium of Ascertainments.* I would add that calling the final wheel of doctrine "extremely fantastic and extremely marvelous" goes against the basic Ge-luk-b̄a position that even according to Proponents of Mind-Only the middle wheel is the supreme teaching for Bodhisattvas who are sharper than those for whom the third wheel was specifically taught. This is because these sharp Bodhisattvas can understand the doctrine of the three natures and the three non-natures just from hearing the Perfection of Wisdom Sūtras and so forth.[618] For this reason, the version of sūtra accepted in Ge-luk-b̄a circles speaks only of the middle wheel as being "**very** fantastic and marvelous," not the third wheel.

In the seventh chapter of the *Sūtra Unraveling the Thought,* Buddha speaks about the various types of sentient beings to whom he teaches doctrine, among whom the supreme are these sharp Bodhisattvas:[619]

> Paramārthasamudgata with respect to this, thinking of just these three types of non-nature, the One-Gone-Thus, by way of the aspect of setting forth sūtras of interpretable meaning, taught the doctrine [of the middle wheel] in this way, "All phenomena are natureless; all phenomena are unproduced, unceasing, quiescent from the start, and naturally thoroughly passed beyond sorrow." Regarding that, [when] sentient beings who have generated roots of virtue, have purified the obstructions, have ripened their continuums, have great faith, and have accumulated great collections of merit and wisdom hear this doctrine, they understand—just as it is—this which I explained with a thought behind it, and they develop faith in that doctrine. They also realize, by means of their exalted wisdom, **the meaning just as it is**. Also, through cultivating their realization they very quickly attain the very final state.

It is said that these sharp Bodhisattvas can realize the meaning of the middle wheel of doctrine—that is, the three natures and three non-natures—without relying on an exposition such as that found in the *Sūtra Unraveling the Thought.* Thus, Gung-tang's criticism is both textual and contextual.

Jik-may-dam-chö-gya-tso adds Wonch'uk's explanation for why those who take literally the middle wheel of doctrine misread sūtra

Concerning how the middle wheel of doctrine is misread when Proponents of Non-Nature take it literally, the *Sūtra Unraveling the Thought,* as cited by D̄zong-ka-b̄a (*Emptiness in Mind-Only,* 95-96), says:[620]

> Even though they have interest in that doctrine [of the profound thoroughly established nature], they do not understand, just as it is, the

> profound reality that I have set forth with a thought behind it.[a] With respect to the meaning of these doctrines, they adhere to the terms as only literal: "All these phenomena are only natureless. All these phenomena are only unproduced, only unceasing, only quiescent from the start, only naturally thoroughly passed beyond sorrow." Due to that, they acquire the view that all phenomena do not exist and the view that [establishment of objects by way of their own][621] character does not exist. Moreover, having acquired the view of nihilism and the view of the non-existence of [establishment of objects by way of their own] character, they deprecate all phenomena in terms of all of the characters—deprecating the imputational character of phenomena and also deprecating the other-powered character and thoroughly established character of phenomena.

With respect to the first sentence Jik-may-dam-chö-gya-tso[622] points out that as the reason why they do not understand the profound doctrine, Wonch'uk says that "they do not have a nature of honesty and just dwell in their own view." Jik-may-dam-chö-gya-tso takes these to mean that they are not unbiased and are attached to their own view.

Jik-may-dam-chö-gya-tso draws on Wonch'uk to explain the example of a flower in the sky

In the *Sūtra Unraveling the Thought* non-natures in terms of character, i.e., imputational natures, are compared to a flower in the sky. About this, Dzong-ka-ba (*Emptiness in Mind-Only,* 94) says:

> The similarity of imputational factors with a flower in the sky is an example of their merely being imputed by conceptuality and is not an example of their not occurring among objects of knowledge [that is, existents; hence, the exemplification does not indicate that all imputational factors do not exist.][b]

[a] Jik-may-dam-chö-gya-tso (*Port of Entry,* 202.1) glosses "set forth with a thought behind it" (*dgongs te bshad pa*) with "set forth non-literally" (*sgra ji bzhin pa min par bshad pa*).

[b] For instance, uncompounded space is an existent imputational nature, as is an object's being the referent of a term and of a conceptual consciousness (with the qualification that it is not established so **by way of its own character**). As Jik-may-dam-chö-gya-tso (*Port of Entry,* 198.5) says, if there were no imputedly existent phenomena, then all objects of knowledge would absurdly have to be substantially existent. See issues #88, 108.

A-ku Lo-drö-gya-tso (*Precious Lamp,* 112.4) points out that in the Mind-Only School and Consequence School a flower in the sky is taken as an example of conceptual imputation but not as an example of imputational natures not occurring among objects of knowledge, that is, existents, whereas in the Autonomy School it is taken as an example of the fact that the object negated in selflessness does not occur among objects of knowledge.

Jik-may-dam-chö-gya-tso[623] draws on Wonch'uk's commentary[624] to explain that just as due to an eye disease[a] the figure of a flower appears in the sky in the perspective of such a person's perception, but in fact there is no flower in the sky, so imputational natures are established as merely imputed by conceptuality. See *Reflections on Reality,* 156-158.

Jik-may-dam-chö-gya-tso cites Wonch'uk's explanation of entity and attribute and elaborates

In the *Sūtra Unraveling the Thought* the Bodhisattva Paramārthasamudgata speaks about imputation in the manner of entity and attributes during his re-rendering of the meaning of Buddha's answer (*Emptiness in Mind-Only,* 104):[625]

> That which is posited by names and terminology[b]—with respect to [other-powered natures which are] (1) the objects of activity of conceptuality,[c] (2) the foundations of imputational characters,[d] and (3) those which have the signs of compositional phenomena[e]—in the character of entities[f] or particulars [such as, "This is][626] a form aggregate,"[g] and that which is posited by names and terminology in the character of entities or the character of particulars[h] [that is, attributes, such as] "the production of the form aggregate," "the cessation of the form aggregate," "the abandonment and thorough knowledge of the form aggregate" are imputational characters.[i]

Jik-may-dam-chö-gya-tso cites Wonch'uk's[627] explanation of the sūtra's (curiously) speaking of **both** entity and particular—that is, attribute—on the occasion of **both** entity and particular:

> That which is posited by names and terminology...**in the character of entities or particulars** [such as, "This is] a form aggregate" and that

---

[a] *rab rib.*

[b] Jik-may-dam-chö-gya-tso (*Port of Entry,* 228.4) identifies the meaning of "That which is posited by names and terminology" as:

> establishment by way of its own character as an entity for imputation by terms and conceptual consciousnesses (*sgra rtog gis btags pa'i ngo bor rang gi mtshan nyid kyis grub pa*).

[c] *rnam par rtog pa'i spyod yul, vikalpagocara* (Lamotte, *Saṃdhinirmocana,* 81 [25], n. 12).

[d] *kun brtags pa'i mtshan nyid kyi gnas, parikalpitalakṣaṇāśraya* (ibid., 81 [25], n. 13).

[e] *'du byed kyi mtshan ma, saṃskāranimitta* (ibid., 81 [25], n. 14).

[f] *ngo bo nyid kyi mtshan nyid, svabhāvalakṣaṇa* (ibid., 81 [25], n. 16).

[g] "This is a form aggregate" is an illustration of the mode of imputation of entities, whereas the rest are illustrations of the mode of imputation of attributes.

[h] *bye brag gi mtshan nyid, viśeṣalakṣaṇa* (ibid., 81 [25], n. 17).

[i] Ḍa-drin-rap-ḍen (*Annotations,* 34.5.) adds that although these are imputed as form and so forth, they are not actual form and so forth.

> which is posited by names and terminology **in the character of entities or the character of particulars** [that is, attributes, such as] "the production of the form aggregate," "the cessation of the form aggregate," and "the abandonment and thorough knowledge of the form aggregate" are imputational characters.

Following Wonch'uk, Jik-may-dam-chö-gya-tso[628] ingeniously posits two types of imputation each with respect to entity and attribute:

Imputation of just the entity that is an imputation of entity (*ngo bo la kun btags pa'i kun btags su gyur pa'i ngo bo nyid la kun btags pa*)	"This is a form" (*'di ni gzugs so*)
Imputation of a particular that is an imputation of entity (*ngo bo la kun btags pa'i kun btags su gyur pa'i bye brag la kun btags pa*)	"This is a contaminated form" (*'di ni zag bcas kyi gzugs so*)
Imputation of just the entity that is an imputation of attribute (*khyad bar la kun btags pa'i kun btags su gyur pa'i ngo bo nyid la kun btags pa*)	"Form is produced" (*gzugs skye'o*)
Imputation of a particular that is an imputation of attribute (*khyad bar la kun btags pa'i kun btags su gyur pa'i bye brag la kun btags pa*)	"Form is produced momentarily" (*gzugs skad cig la skye'o*)

Jik-may-dam-chö-gya-tso disagrees about the meaning of "objects of activity of conceptuality"

In the same section of the *Sūtra Unraveling the Thought* the Bodhisattva Paramārthasamudgata similarly speaks about other-powered natures (*Emptiness in Mind-Only,* 106): [629]

> Those which are the objects of activity of conceptuality, the foundations of imputational characters, and have the signs of compositional phenomena are other-powered characters.

Ḏzong-ka-ḇa explains the terminology:

> The first [that is, "those which are the objects of activity of conceptuality"] indicates of what [type of consciousness other-powered natures] are objects. The second [that is, "the foundations of imputational characters"] indicates that they are the bases of imputation of the imputational factor. The third [that is, "those that have the signs of a compositional phenomenon"] indicates their own entities.

As Jik-may-dam-chö-gya-tso[630] points out, Wonch'uk[631] says that conceptuality refers to both (conceptual) main minds and mental factors. Then he cites Wonch'uk's two explanations of how other-powered natures are the objects of activity of conceptual consciousnesses:

- the form aggregate and so forth are the objects of conceptual consciousnesses
- the form aggregate and so forth are observed-object-conditions[a] of conceptual consciousnesses.

Wonch'uk himself prefers the first explanation. Jik-may-dam-chö-gya-tso refers to the fact that Gung-tang, in his *Annotations,* indicates that forms and so forth could only be taken as observed-object-conditions in the sense of appearing to conceptual consciousnesses[b] or as **imputed** object-of-observation-conditions[c]—his meaning being that they could not be **actual** conditions generating consciousnesses, since they would then be external objects. Gung-tang himself, as Jik-may-dam-chö-gya-tso[632] points out, takes object of activity[d] not as observed-object-condition but as object of observation,[e] with the caveat that whatever is the object of observation of an awareness is not necessarily an object of activity of that awareness:

- since otherwise all conventional phenomena would have to be the objects of activity of an exalted wisdom of a Superior's meditative equipoise directly realizing emptiness (because it is held that the objects of observation of a consciousness directly realizing emptiness are all phenomena, since they are the bases of emptiness even though they are not perceived), and
- since otherwise an omniscient consciousness would have to be an object of activity (that is to say, in the sphere) of a common consciousness of an ordinary being (because an ordinary being can think about an omniscient consciousness).

Jik-may-dam-chö-gya-tso[633] also refers to the fact that Wonch'uk[634] prefers the second of two expositions of the phrase "(having) the signs of a compositional phenomenon":

- having the signs of an object of a consciousness observing a compositional phenomenon
- having the signs of the aspects of a compounded phenomenon.

Jik-may-dam-chö-gya-tso praises the fact that Gung-tang prefers the first in order to include all phenomena. This must be because the looser meaning of "compositional phenomenon" includes permanent phenomena, whereas "compounded phenomenon" does not. Still, the term "compositional phenomenon" also could be taken in its stricter sense as compounded phenomenon if we say that the sūtra is referring to the **main** bases of emptiness.[635]

---

a *dmigs rkyen.*

b *snang ba'i dmigs rkyen.*

c *dmigs rkyen btags pa ba.*

d *spyod yul.*

e *dmigs yul.*

Jik-may-dam-chö-gya-tso disagrees about the meaning of the third wheel of doctrine being for those engaged in all vehicles

In the *Sūtra Unraveling the Thought* (*Emptiness in Mind-Only,* 116) Paramārthasamudgata, in relating back to Buddha the meaning of what he has said about the third wheel of doctrine, explicitly indicates that the third wheel of doctrine is for those "engaged in all vehicles," that is, the Hearer, Solitary Realizer, and Great Vehicles:

> Based on just the naturelessness of phenomena and based on just the absence of production, the absence of cessation, quiescence from the start, and naturally passed beyond sorrow, the Supramundane Victor turned a third wheel of doctrine **for those engaged in all vehicles**, possessed of good differentiation, fantastic and marvelous. This wheel of doctrine turned by the Supramundane Victor is unsurpassable, does not afford an occasion [for refutation], is of definitive meaning, and does not serve as a basis for controversy.

About this, D̄zong-ka-b̄a (*Emptiness in Mind-Only,* 224) says:

> Through the force of this exposition, one can understand that the meaning of the Low Vehicle sūtras is just the presentation of the three natures in which the emptiness of the imputational factor—a self of persons—in other-powered natures—the aggregates—is posited as the thoroughly established nature that is the selflessness of persons. Therefore, it is implicit to the exposition in the *Sūtra Unraveling the Thought* that the trainees for whom the first wheel was spoken are suitable as vessels for realizing the character-non-nature in terms of the selflessness of persons and are not suitable as vessels for realizing the character-non-nature[a] in terms of the selflessness of phenomena. This is the meaning of the statement that the wheel of doctrine of good differentiation is for the sake of those engaged in all vehicles.

The first sentence strongly suggests that the selflessness of persons is a thoroughly established nature, but some hold that it means only that the selflessness of persons is a thoroughly established nature **in terms of the selflessness of persons** but is not an actual thoroughly established nature (see issues #153-157).

According to Jik-may-dam-chö-gya-tso:[636]

1. Wonch'uk takes this as meaning that there are cases of all three types of trainees (Hearer, Solitary Realizer, and Bodhisattva) attaining the respective fruits of their paths **in dependence upon** the *Sūtra Unraveling the Thought.*

[a] See issue #95.

2. Jay-d̄zün Chö-ḡyi-gyel-tsen similarly says that the *Sūtra Unraveling the Thought* has trainees of both the Great and Lesser Vehicles.
3. The Second Dalai Lama, Gung-ru Chö-jung, and Jam-ȳang-shay-b̄a as well as the followers of the latter two say that this refers to those (**followers of the Great Vehicle**) who are able to realize—in dependence upon the explanation of the thought of the first two vehicles by the third vehicle—that the thoughts behind the first two vehicles contain the two selflessnesses (that is, the selflessness of persons and the selflessness of phenomena respectively).
4. The *Illumination of the Difficult to Realize*[a] says that, although the intended trainees of the *Sūtra Unraveling the Thought* are those who have the Great Vehicle lineage, those of duller faculties among them are fit to be led into another (that is, Lesser) vehicle.

The first two solutions allow that all three types of trainees could be trainees of the *Sūtra Unraveling the Thought,* whereas the last two limit the trainees of the *Sūtra Unraveling the Thought* to those of the Great Vehicle. Jik-may-dam-chö-gya-tso favors the third opinion.

A Final Remark

Wonch'uk's commentary on the *Sūtra Unraveling the Thought* drove important aspects of scholarship from the fifteenth to twentieth centuries in the Ge-luk-b̄a school,[b] especially in the Am-do Province. Ge-luk-b̄a scholars certainly did not use Wonch'uk as a straw man, turning his exposition into a distorted caricature; their comments and criticisms are totally devoid of invective, in contrast to how S̄hay-rap-gyel-tsen and many others are treated. Rather, they probed passages—taking their lead from those cited by D̄zong-ka-b̄a but also others—to determine Wonch'uk's actual opinions and to use these to expand D̄zong-ka-b̄a's points, or to refine them to make them fit their founder's system, or, for the same reason, to reject some. In this way, part of Wonch'uk's text became a focus of active scholarship concerned with meaning.

---

[a] *rtogs dka'i snang ba.*

[b] I specify this school, since I have yet to find any Tibetan scholars outside of Ge-luk who cite Wonch'uk.

Backnotes

1 Berkeley: University of California Press, 1999.

2 Gung-tang's *Difficult Points,* 18.10ff. For a brief biography of Gung-tang, see E. Gene Smith, *Tibetan Catalogue* (Seattle, Washington: University of Washington, 1969), vol. 1, 81-82.

3 Gung-tang's *Difficult Points,* 18.10-22.9.

4 *sangs rgyas bcom ldan 'das la zab mo rten cing 'brel bar 'byung ba gsung ba'i sgo nas bstod pa legs par bshad pa'i snying po.* For English translations see: Geshe Wangyal, in *The Door of Liberation* (New York: Lotsawa, 1978), 117-25; and Robert Thurman, in *Life and Teachings of Tsong Khapa* (Dharmsala, India: Library of Tibetan Works and Archives, 1982), 99-107.

5 Peking 6016, vol. 153 37.3.4; for Geshe Wangyal's translation of this passage, see his *The Door of Liberation,* 177; for Robert Thurman's translation, see his *Life and Teachings of Tsong Khapa,* 100.

6 Pa-bong-ka-b̄a's *Brief Notes on J̄o-ni Paṇḍita's Lectures,* 403.3.

7 Ye shes thabs mkhas edition, 323.5.

8 Ibid., 323.1.

9 A-ku L̄o-drö-gya-tso's *Precious Lamp,* 3.3.

10 *drang nges chen mo.*

11 Jam-ȳang-shay-b̄a's *Great Exposition of the Interpretable and the Definitive,* 5.2.

12 Jay-d̄zün Chö-ḡyi-gyel-tsen's *General-Meaning Commentary,* 3b.7.

13 Jay-d̄zün Chö-ḡyi-gyel-tsen (ibid., 4a.3) makes a similar point.

14 Paraphrasing Gung-tang's *Difficult Points,* 17.7-17.16.

15 Ibid., 18.7.

16 Ibid., 18.11.

17 Ibid., 7.10.

18 III.9bc.

19 III.70cd.

20 Gung-tang's *Difficult Points,* 8.18-11.1.

21 For more detailed presentations of the levels of cyclic existence, see Lati Rinbochay's explanation in Lati Rinbochay, Denma Lochö Rinbochay, Leah Zahler, Jeffrey Hopkins, *Meditative States in Tibetan Buddhism* (London: Wisdom Publications, 1983), 29-47; and Herbert V. Guenther, *The Jewel Ornament of Liberation by sGam-po-pa* (London: Rider, 1963; rpt. Berkeley: Shambhala, 1971), 55-73.

22 Dön-drup-gyel-tsen's *Four Intertwined Commentaries,* 33.1-33.3.

23 *dgongs pa nges par 'grel pa'i mdo, Saṃdhinirmocanasūtra;* Peking 774, vol. 29; Toh 106; Dharma vol. 18. The Tibetan text has been edited and translated into French by Étienne Lamotte in *Saṃdhinirmocanasūtra: L'explication des mystères* (Louvain: Université de Louvain, 1935). For an English translation, see C. John Powers, *Wisdom of Buddha: Saṁdhinirmocana Sūtra* (Berkeley, Calif.: Dharma, 1995).

24 Jay-d̄zün Chö-ḡyi-gyel-tsen's *General-Meaning Commentary,* 6b.2.

25 Gung-tang's *Difficult Points,* 73.13-74.6. See also Jik-may-dam-chö-gya-tso's *Port of Entry,* 132.5

26 Second Dalai Lama's *Lamp Illuminating the Meaning of [D̄zong-ka-b̄a's] Thought,* 11.3-12.1.

27 Gung-tang's *Difficult Points,* 74.18 and 75.11-75.13.

28 Jik-may-dam-chö-gya-tso's *Port of Entry,* 136.1.

29 Gung-tang's *Difficult Points,* 74.6-75.13.

30 In his *Ornament for the Essence, Explanation [of (Maitreya's) "Ornament of Clear Realization" and (Haribhadra's) Commentary]* (*rnam bshad snying po rgyan*).

31 Jik-may-dam-chö-gya-tso's *Port of Entry,* 137.6-138.1.

32 Jay-d̄zün Chö-ḡyi-gyel-tsen's *General-Meaning Commentary,* 6a.7-6b.6.

33 *Summarized Meaning,* 154.14, 155.3.

34 Gung-tang's *Annotations,* 6.6-7.6.

35 This section identifying the first-wheel sūtras giving rise to Paramārthasamudgata's

question is taken from Gung-tang's *Difficult Points,* 75.15-77.18 and A-ku Lo-drö-gya-tso's *Precious Lamp,* 51.3-53.4.

[36] Cited in Gung-tang's *Difficult Points,* 75.17.

[37] Jik-may-dam-chö-gya-tso's *Port of Entry,* 154.5-155.2.

[38] For a similar qualm, see A-ku Lo-drö-gya-tso's *Precious Lamp,* 51.3-52.1.

[39] Jik-may-dam-chö-gya-tso's *Port of Entry,* 156.1.

[40] A-ku Lo-drö-gya-tso's *Precious Lamp,* 53.1-53.2.

[41] Cited in Gung-tang's *Difficult Points,* 76.3.

[42] A-ku Lo-drö-gya-tso's *Precious Lamp,* 52.4.

[43] Cited in Gung-tang's *Difficult Points,* 76.11.

[44] A-ku Lo-drö-gya-tso's *Precious Lamp,* 52.2. Šer-šhül (*Notes,* 13b.4) repeats Gung-tang's presentation of these two interpretations.

[45] Gung-tang's *Difficult Points,* 79.1.

[46] A-ku Lo-drö-gya-tso's *Precious Lamp,* 52.5.

[47] Ibid., 52.3.

[48] Šer-šhül Lo-sang-pün-tsok's *Notes,* 13b.5.

[49] 39.6; also given in Wel-mang Gön-chok-gyel-tsen's *Notes on (Gön-chok-jik-may-wang-bo's) Lectures,* 395.6.

[50] See Alex Wayman, *Analysis of the Śrāvakabhūmi Manuscript,* University of California Publications in Classical Philology, vol. 17 (Berkeley, Calif.: University of California Press, 1961), 136-139, where Gyel-tsap is cited.

[51] See Vasubandhu's *Treasury of Manifest Knowledge,* III.119-128; and the *Visuddhi-magga,* XI (thanks to C. John Powers for these two citations). Jik-may-dam-chö-gya-tso (*Port of Entry,* 141.1) gives the same explanation.

[52] Oral commentary.

[53] Geshe Gedün Lodrö, *Calm Abiding and Special Insight: Spiritual Transformation through Meditation,* translated and edited by Jeffrey Hopkins (Ithaca, New York: Snow Lion Publications, 1998), 70-71.

[54] Jik-may-dam-chö-gya-tso's *Port of Entry,* 156.3-156.6.

[55] The discussion of the two terms is drawn from Gung-tang's *Difficult Points,* 86.14-89.10.

[56] Chap. 7; Lamotte, *Saṃdhinirmocana,* 81 [25], and 204; Dön-drup-gyel-tsen's *Four Intertwined Commentaries,* 22.5; and Powers, *Wisdom of Buddha,* 131.

[57] Gung-tang's *Difficult Points,* 87.7-87.11/37b.3.

[58] Peking 5517, vol. 106, chap. 5, 129.3.2. Cited in Jik-may-dam-chö-gya-tso's *Port of Entry,* 141.4.

[59] Gung-tang's *Difficult Points,* 87.11.

[60] Gung-tang's *Annotations,* 15.7.

[61] A-ku Lo-drö-gya-tso's *Precious Lamp,* 54.5.

[62] Ibid., 53.4.

[63] Gung-tang's *Difficult Points,* 88.18-89.10.

[64] *rgyal po la gtam bya ba rin po che'i phreng ba, rājaparikathāratnāvalī;* stanzas 80-81; Jeffrey Hopkins, *Buddhist Advice for Living and Liberation: Nāgārjuna's Precious Garland* (Ithaca, N.Y.: Snow Lion, 1998), 57-58 and 104-105.

[65] For Dzong-ka-ba's mention of this in his *Illumination of the Thought of (Chandrakīrti's) Supplement to (Nāgārjuna's) "Treatise on the Middle,"* see Tsong-ka-pa, Kensur Lekden, and Jeffrey Hopkins, *Compassion in Tibetan Buddhism* (London: Rider, 1980; repr. Ithaca, N.Y.: Snow Lion, 1980), 226.

[66] A-ku Lo-drö-gya-tso's *Precious Lamp,* 55.2-55.3.

[67] Gung-tang's *Difficult Points,* 79.1-79.7.

[68] Šer-šhül (*Notes,* 14b.1) repeats this explanation of these two.

[69] A-ku Lo-drö-gya-tso's *Precious Lamp,* 55.5.

[70] Ibid., 50.4.

[71] Gung-tang's *Difficult Points,* 80.2-80.12.

[72] Ibid., 79.14-79.15.

[73] Ibid., 79.7-80.2.

[74] Jik-may-dam-chö-gya-tso's *Port of Entry,* 154.1.

[75] For the general sources from which the continuing discussion of Paramārthasamud-

gata's question is drawn, see the footnote in chapter eight.

76 *Lamp for the Teaching*, 12.1.

77 Gung-ru Chö-jung's *Garland of White Lotuses*, 4b.5-6a.2.

78 Jam-ȳang-shay-b̄a's *Great Exposition of the Interpretable and the Definitive*, 26.3-28.6; see also Jam-ȳang-shay-b̄a's *Brief Decisive Analysis* (488.1-488.4) for a less refined presentation of similar material. Jay-d̄zün Chö-ḡyi-gyel-tsen makes a similar but shorter objection in his *General-Meaning Commentary* (8a.4-9a.2).

79 Jam-ȳang-shay-b̄a's *Great Exposition of the Interpretable and the Definitive*, 27.3.

80 This sentence is drawn from Gung-tang's *Difficult Points*, 89.13.

81 Stanza 390; Hopkins, *Buddhist Advice*, 26-27, 31, 48, 89, 90, 146.

82 Stanza 393; Ibid., 27, 393.

83 Jam-ȳang-shay-b̄a's *Great Exposition of the Interpretable and the Definitive*, 28.3.

84 Jay-d̄zün Chö-ḡyi-gyel-tsen's *General-Meaning Commentary*, 8b.5.

85 Second Dalai Lama's *Lamp Illuminating the Meaning of (D̄zong-ka-b̄a's) Thought*, 15.2-15.4.

86 Jay-d̄zün Chö-ḡyi-gyel-tsen's *General-Meaning Commentary*, 8b.6-9a.2.

87 Gung-ru Chö-jung's *Garland of White Lotuses*, 5b.1-6a.2.

88 Jam-ȳang-shay-b̄a's *Great Exposition of the Interpretable and the Definitive*, 27.6-28.3.

89 I.3ab.

90 Jik-may-dam-chö-gya-tso's *Port of Entry*, 156.3-156.6.

91 A-ku L̄o-drö-gya-tso's *Precious Lamp*, 64.1.

92 Jay-d̄zün Chö-ḡyi-gyel-tsen's *General-Meaning Commentary*, 9a.3-9a.5.

93 The Second Dalai Lama (*Lamp Illuminating the Meaning*, 12.5), except for the difference mentioned above, frames the question similarly.

94 Gung-ru Chö-jung's *Garland of White Lotuses*, 6a.2ff.

95 Jam-ȳang-shay-b̄a's *Great Exposition of the Interpretable and the Definitive*, 28.6ff; see also his *Brief Decisive Analysis*, 489.2-490 and 492.2-492.4.

96 Chap. 7; Lamotte, *Saṃdhinirmocana*, 67-68 [4], and 194; Dön-drup-gyel-tsen's *Four Intertwined Commentaries*, 7.1-7.2.

97 Jam-ȳang-shay-b̄a (*Great Exposition of the Interpretable and the Definitive*, 30.1/12b.6) omits this step from his cribbing of Gung-ru Chö-jung (*Garland of White Lotuses*, 6b.2) probably for the sake of economy of expression.

98 Chapter 1, stanza 217 (Miyasaka's III.217, pp. 146-147): *heyopādeyatattvasya sopāyasya prasiddhitaḥ / pradhānārthāvisaṃvādād anumānaṃ paratra vā //*; the bracketed material in the last two lines is drawn from Ke-drup's commentary, 135b.6. The Dalai Lama cites the last two lines in his *The Buddhism of Tibet and The Key to the Middle Way* (London: George Allen and Unwin, 1975; reprint, Ithaca, N.Y.: Snow Lion, 1987), 83.

99 Jam-ȳang-shay-b̄a's *Great Exposition of the Interpretable and the Definitive*, 30.3.

100 *bstan bcos bzhi brgya pa zhes bya ba'i tshig le'ur byas pa, catuḥśatakaśāstrakārikā;* P5246, vol. 95; stanza 280 which occurs in Chapter 12; parenthetical additions are from Gyel-tsap's commentary, 90b.3-91a.2; see *Yogic Deeds of Bodhisattvas: Gyel-tsap on Āryadeva's Four Hundred*, commentary by Geshe Sonam Rinchen, translated and edited by Ruth Sonam (Ithaca, N.Y.: Snow Lion Publications, 1994), 241-242.

101 *The Buddhism of Tibet and The Key to the Middle Way*, 83.

102 Jam-ȳang-shay-b̄a's *Brief Decisive Analysis*, 491.2.

103 Gung-ru Chö-jung's *Garland of White Lotuses*, 7a.1-7a.4.

104 Jam-ȳang-shay-b̄a's *Great Exposition of the Interpretable and the Definitive*, 30.4-30.6.

105 Gung-ru Chö-jung's *Garland of White Lotuses*, 7a.1-7a.4.

106 Jay-d̄zün Chö-ḡyi-gyel-tsen's *General-Meaning Commentary*, 9b.5.

107 Gung-ru Chö-jung's *Garland of White Lotuses*, 7b.1-7b.6.

108 Jam-ȳang-shay-b̄a's *Great Exposition of the Interpretable and the Definitive*, 31.3-32.3.

109 Gung-ru Chö-jung's *Garland of White Lotuses*, 7b.6.

110 Jam-ȳang-shay-b̄a's *Great Exposition of the Interpretable and the Definitive,* 32.2.

111 Ibid., 62.5-63.3.

112 Gung-tang's *Difficult Points,* 93.2, 108.9.

113 Jam-ȳang-shay-b̄a's *Great Exposition of the Interpretable and the Definitive,* 36.2-36.6.

114 Gung-ru Chö-jung's *Garland of White Lotuses,* 7b.6-8a.3. Jam-ȳang-shay-b̄a (*Great Exposition of the Interpretable and the Definitive,* 33.2) does not copy this reasoning.

115 Jay-d̄zün Chö-ḡyi-gyel-tsen's *General-Meaning Commentary,* 7a.4-7b.6 and 9b.7-10a.2.

116 Ibid., 9a.3.

117 Ibid., 9a.6-9b.1.

118 Ibid., 9b.7-10a.2; cited in A-ku L̄o-drö-gya-tso's *Precious Lamp,* 65.4.

119 A-ku L̄o-drö-gya-tso's *Precious Lamp,* 65.3-65.6.

120 Jay-d̄zün Chö-ḡyi-gyel-tsen's *General-Meaning Commentary,* 10a.2-10a.3.

121 Jik-may-dam-chö-gya-tso's *Port of Entry,* 145.1-145.4 and 146.3-146.5.

122 Recorded oral teaching.

123 Jik-may-dam-chö-gya-tso's *Port of Entry,* 145.4.

124 Gung-ru Chö-jung's *Garland of White Lotuses,* 15b.2-16b.1.

125 Ibid., 15b.2.

126 Cited in Gung-ru Chö-jung's *Garland of White Lotuses,* 16a.5.

127 Jay-d̄zün Chö-ḡyi-gyel-tsen's *General-Meaning Commentary,* 7a.6-8a.4.

128 S̄er-s̄hül's *Notes,* 13a.1-13b.4.

129 Paṇ-chen S̄ö-nam-drak-b̄a's *Garland of Blue Lotuses,* 10a.6-11b.6.

130 Ibid., 12b.3-13a.3.

131 Ibid., 12b.6.

132 Jay-d̄zün Chö-ḡyi-gyel-tsen's *General-Meaning Commentary,* 7a.6-8a.4.

133 Paṇ-chen S̄ö-nam-drak-b̄a's *Garland of Blue Lotuses,* 13a.3.

134 Ibid.

135 Ibid., 4b.1-5b.3; Paṇ-chen S̄ö-nam-drak-b̄a's opinion is discussed in Jik-may-dam-chö-gya-tso's *Port of Entry,* 708.1.

136 Paṇ-chen S̄ö-nam-drak-b̄a's *Garland of Blue Lotuses,* 5a.3.

137 For more on this topic, see A-ku L̄o-drö-gya-tso's *Precious Lamp,* 295.2, and Jik-may-dam-chö-gya-tso's *Port of Entry,* 708.3.

138 Paṇ-chen S̄ö-nam-drak-b̄a's *Garland of Blue Lotuses,* 10b.4.

139 Ibid., 12a.4-12b.3.

140 Oral teaching in Hamburg, Germany, 1971.

141 Gung-tang's *Difficult Points,* 18.14.

142 Jik-may-dam-chö-gya-tso's *Port of Entry,* 145.5.

143 Peking 5517, vol. 106, chap. 5, 128.5.7.

144 Jam-ȳang-shay-b̄a's *Great Exposition of the Interpretable and the Definitive,* 36b.1.

145 Jik-may-dam-chö-gya-tso's *Port of Entry,* 145.5-146.4. See 145.6 for *kho na.*

146 Ibid., 149.5.

147 Ibid., 149.6-150.1.

148 Gung-ru Chö-jung's *Garland of White Lotuses,* 8a.3-8b.1.

149 Jam-ȳang-shay-b̄a's *Great Exposition of the Interpretable and the Definitive,* 33.2-33.6.

150 Ngawang Gelek edition, 200.4; cited in Gung-tang's *Difficult Points,* 90.5, and in Jik-may-dam-chö-gya-tso's *Port of Entry,* 144.5.

151 Gung-tang's *Difficult Points,* 90.8. Jik-may-dam-chö-gya-tso (*Port of Entry,* 145.1) repeats Gung-tang's point.

152 Gung-ru Chö-jung's *Garland of White Lotuses,* 15a.6-15b.2.

153 Jam-ȳang-shay-b̄a's *Great Exposition of the Interpretable and the Definitive,"* 40.3-41.1.

154 A-ku L̄o-drö-gya-tso's *Precious Lamp,* 61.1-63.4.

155 Jam-ȳang-shay-b̄a's *Great Exposition of the Interpretable and the Definitive,* 40.5.

156 A-ku L̄o-drö-gya-tso's *Precious Lamp,* 62.4-62.6. He appears to be following Jam-ȳang-shay-b̄a's *Brief Decisive Analysis,* 492.4-493.3.

157 Peking 5517, vol. 106, chap. 5, 128.5.7.

158 Commenting on stanza 24. For the Sanskrit, see *Vijñaptimātratāsiddhi/ Deux traités de Vasubandhu: Viṃśatikā (La Vigtaine) et Triṃśikā (La Trentaine),* edited by Sylvain Lévi, in Bibliotheque de l'École des Hautes Études, fascicule 245 (Paris: Libraire Ancienne

Honoré Champion, 1925), 41.14; for the Tibetan, see Peking 5565, vol. 113, 311.4.4; also, Enga Teramoto, *Sthiramati's Triṃśikābhāṣyaṃ (Sum-cu-paḥi ḥGrel-pa) A Tibetan Text* (Kyoto: Association for Linguistic Study of Sacred Scriptures, 1933), 80.11.

159 Gung-tang's *Difficult Points,* 90.10ff.

160 Paraphrasing ibid., 91.9.

161 Powers, *Wisdom of Buddha,* 41-42.

162 Gung-tang's *Difficult Points,* 92.6.

163 Ibid., 92.10.

164 Jam-ȳang-shay-b̄a's *Great Exposition of the Interpretable and the Definitive,* 36.1-36.6.

165 Gung-tang's *Difficult Points,* 92.13-93.12.

166 A-ku L̄o-drö-gya-tso's *Precious Lamp,* 58.1-58.3.

167 Gung-ru Chö-jung's *Garland of White Lotuses,* 13a.1-15a.6.

168 Jam-ȳang-shay-b̄a's *Great Exposition of the Interpretable and the Definitive,* 38.1-40.2. Jam-ȳang-shay-b̄a's presentation of the following points, while based on Gung-ru Chö-jung's, is for the most part clearer.

169 See also the translation in José Ignacio Cabezón, *A Dose of Emptiness* (Albany, N.Y.: State University of New York Press, 1992), 66.

170 Gung-ru Chö-jung's *Garland of White Lotuses,* 10b.6-11b.5, especially 11a.5-11b.5. See also Gung-tang's *Difficult Points,* 95.15-96.4, A-ku L̄o-drö-gya-tso's *Precious Lamp,* 67.6-69.3, and Dön-drup-gyel-tsen's *Four Intertwined Commentaries,* 595.3.

171 Gung-ru Chö-jung's *Garland of White Lotuses,* 9b.3-10b.5.

172 Jik-may-dam-chö-gya-tso (*Port of Entry,* 150.1) reports this position.

173 Between the question just asked and this stanza there is another sentence, not cited by D̄zong-ka-b̄a, that says the same in prose. The bracketed additions are drawn from Nga-w̄ang-b̄el-den's *Annotations, dngos* 186.6-187.4, and Jam-ȳang-shay-b̄a's *Great Exposition of Tenets/ Explanation of 'Tenets', Sun of the Land of Samantabhadra Brilliantly Illuminating All of Our Own and Others' Tenets and the Meaning of the Profound [Emptiness], Ocean of Scripture and Reasoning Fulfilling All Hopes of All Beings* (*grub mtha' chen mo/ grub mtha'i rnam bshad rang gzhan grub mtha' kun dang zab don mchog tu gsal ba kun bzang zhing gi nyi ma lung rigs rgya mtsho skye dgu'i re ba kun skong*), (Musoorie, India: Dalama, 1962), *nga* 44b.6-45a.3.

174 Jik-may-dam-chö-gya-tso's *Port of Entry,* 150.5.

175 Gung-tang's *Difficult Points,* 96.9.

176 Gung-ru Chö-jung's *Garland of White Lotuses,* 13a.1-13a.5.

177 Jam-ȳang-shay-b̄a's *Great Exposition of the Interpretable and the Definitive,* 37.2.

178 Gung-tang's *Difficult Points,* 95.8-95.15.

179 *Ornament for the Thought,* 16.3-16.7.

180 Gung-ru Chö-jung's *Garland of White Lotuses,* 16b.2-17b.1.

181 Jam-ȳang-shay-b̄a's *Great Exposition of the Interpretable and the Definitive,* 41.3-43.5.

182 Gung-ru Chö-jung's *Garland of White Lotuses,* 17b.1-18a.5. At 17b.2, read *'dis mtshan nyid ngo ba nyid med pa cig dngos su bstan/ kun btags mtshan nyid ngo bo nyid med pa cig dngos su* ***ma*** *bstan pa'i phyir* for *'dis mtshan nyid ngo ba nyid med pa cig dngos su* ***ma*** *bstan/ kun btags mtshan nyid ngo bo nyid med pa cig dngos su bstan pa'i phyir* in accordance with the two occurrences of similar reasoning on 18a.3-18a.5, and in accordance with Jam-ȳang-shay-b̄a's *Great Exposition of the Interpretable and the Definitive,* 43.5.

183 Jam-ȳang-shay-b̄a's *Great Exposition of the Interpretable and the Definitive,* 43.4-44.4; also *Brief Decisive Analysis,* 497.1-497.6.

184 A-ku L̄o-drö-gya-tso's *Precious Lamp,* 69.6.

185 Second Dalai Lama's *Lamp Illuminating the Meaning of [D̄zong-ka-b̄a's] Thought,* 15.1-15.6.

186 The headings in bold print are added to the sūtra. The first heading is taken from Wonch'uk's *Extensive Commentary,* Peking 5517, vol. 116, 130.2.4.

187 Gung-ru Chö-jung's *Garland of White Lotuses,* 16b.4-17b.1.

188 Jam-ȳang-shay-b̄a's *Great Exposition of the Interpretable and the Definitive,* 43.1-43.4.

189 Peking 5517, vol. 116, 130.5.4ff.

190 Dra-d̄i Ge-s̄hay Rin-chen-dön-drup (*Ornament for the Thought,* 20.17-21.4)

combines the first two.

191 Gung-ru Chö-jung's *Garland of White Lotuses,* 17b.3-18a.2.

192 Jam-ȳang-shay-b̄a's *Great Exposition of the Interpretable and the Definitive,* 44.4.

193 Gung-tang's *Difficult Points,* 98.2-99.2. His exposition appears to be based to a great extent on Gung-ru Chö-jung's *Garland of White Lotuses* (18b.1-19a.3) which, however, is not openly associated with explaining why D̄zong-ka-b̄a cites the two Indian texts in a seemingly inappropriate context.

194 B̄el-jor-hlün-drup's *Lamp for the Teaching,* 13.2-13.6.

195 All three passages are given in Jam-ȳang-shay-b̄a's *Great Exposition of the Interpretable and the Definitive,* 48.1-48.3, but not in Gung-ru Chö-jung's *Garland of White Lotuses.* The first is cited in A-ku L̄o-drö-gya-tso's *Precious Lamp,* 71.4. The second is cited with the preceding two lines in Jik-may-dam-chö-gya-tso's *Port of Entry,* 162.6, along with a stanza from Āryadeva's *Four Hundred.* The first stanza is *mūlamadhyamakakārikāḥ* VII.33cd (J.W. de Jong, ed. [Madras: The Adyar Library and Research Centre, 1977], 11): *saṃskṛtasyāprasiddhau ca kathaṃ setsyaty asaṃskṛtam //.* The second stanza is *mūlamadhyamakakārikāḥ* XIII.8cd (de Jong edition, p. 18): *yeṣāṃ tu śūnyatādṛṣṭis tān asādhyān babhāṣire //.*

196 *'jig rten las 'das par bstod pa, lokātītastava,* stanza 23; Sanskrit in Lindtner, *Master of Wisdom,* 161: *sarvasaṃkalpanāśāya śūnyatāmṛtadeśanā / yasya tasyām api grāhas tvayāsāv avasāditaḥ //* (Tibetan on p.8).

197 Gung-tang's *Difficult Points,* 99.8.

198 Ibid., 99.9.

199 Gung-ru Chö-jung's *Garland of White Lotuses,* 19a.3.

200 Paraphrasing A-ku L̄o-drö-gya-tso's *Precious Lamp,* 70.3-71.1.

201 Ibid., 72.2.

202 Gung-tang (*Difficult Points,* 139.1; *Annotations,* 32.5) cites Rin-chen-n̄am-gyel's (*rin chen rnam rgyal*) *Ornament Beautifying the Essence of a One Gone to Bliss* (*bde gshegs snying po'i mdzes rgyan*) as his source for this point.

203 Gung-tang's *Difficult Points,* 138.2; *Annotations,* 33.5.

204 Jik-may-dam-chö-gya-tso's *Port of Entry,* 196.6-197.5.

205 Jik-may-dam-chö-gya-tso bases this explanation on the *ṭīk bshad de nyid snang ba.*

206 S̄hay-rap-gyel-tsen's *Ocean of Definitive Meaning,* 77.1.

207 *rtsod pa bzlog pa'i tshig le'ur byas pa, vigrahavyāvartanīkārikā,* stanza 29; D3828, *dbu ma,* vol. *tsa,* 28a.1; Tibetan in Lindtner, *Master of Wisdom,* 222; translated in Jeffrey Hopkins, *Meditation on Emptiness* (London: Wisdom, 1983; rev. ed., Boston, Ma.: Wisdom, 1996), 471.

208 Stanza XVI.25; Tibetan in Karen Lang, *Āryadeva's Catuḥśataka: On the Bodhisattva's Cultivation of Merit and Knowledge* (Copenhagen: Akademisk Forlag, 1986), 150; translated in Hopkins, *Meditation on Emptiness,* 475.

209 S̄hay-rap-gyel-tsen's *Ocean of Definitive Meaning,* 41.2.

210 Ibid., 52.3.

211 The source for these three is Jik-may-dam-chö-gya-tso's *Port of Entry,* 237.3.

212 Chap. 7; Lamotte, *Saṃdhinirmocana,* 68 [5], and 194; Dön-drup-gyel-tsen's *Four Intertwined Commentaries,* 7.2-7.3.

213 Jam-ȳang-shay-b̄a's *Great Exposition of the Interpretable and the Definitive,* 70.1.

214 Gung-tang's *Difficult Points,* 124.17.

215 Ibid., 125.4.

216 Ibid., 125.6.

217 Also Gung-ru Chö-jung's *Garland of White Lotuses,* 29b.6-30b.2, and Jam-ȳang-shay-b̄a's *Brief Decisive Analysis,* 504.6-505.4.

218 Chap. 7; Lamotte, *Saṃdhinirmocana,* 71-72 [11], and 196-197; Dön-drup-gyel-tsen's *Four Intertwined Commentaries,* 11.1-11.5.

219 Second Dalai Lama's *Lamp Illuminating the Meaning of [D̄zong-ka-b̄a's] Thought,* 18.5-19.1.

220 This sentence is drawn from Gung-ru Chö-jung's *Garland of White Lotuses,* 30b.4-31a.2.

221 W̄el-mang Ḡön-chok-gyel-tsen's *Notes on Ḡön-chok-jik-may-w̄ang-b̄o's Lectures,* 401.3.

222 As reported in Jik-may-dam-chö-gya-tso's *Port of Entry,* 182.2. This is likely the commentary by Jin-b̄a-dar-gyay (*sbyin pa dar*

rgyas), Brief Illumination of the Difficult Points of (Dzong-ka-ba's) "Differentiating the Interpretable and the Definitive": Mirror Illuminating the Good Explanations (drang nges rnam 'byed kyi dka' gnad gsal bar byed pa bsdus don legs bshad gsal ba'i me long).

223 A-ku Lo-drö-gya-tso's *Precious Lamp,* 88.4.

224 Peking 5539, vol. 111, 71.3.2. Tokyo *sde dge, sems tsam,* vol. 9 (*zi*), 8.4.7.

225 A-ku Lo-drö-gya-tso's *Precious Lamp,* 89.5. He is following Gung-tang's *Annotations,* 16.3/743.3.

226 Cited in A-ku Lo-drö-gya-tso's *Precious Lamp,* 90.2.

227 Ibid., 90.3.

228 Jam-yang-shay-ba's *Great Exposition of the Interpretable and the Definitive,* 44.5.

229 A-ku Lo-drö-gya-tso's *Precious Lamp,* 92.1.

230 Wel-mang Gön-chok-gyel-tsen's *Notes on (Gön-chok-jik-may-wang-bo's) Lectures,* 401.4.

231 This discussion is from Gung-ru Chö-jung's *Garland of White Lotuses,* 30b.2-31a.2.

232 Gung-tang's *Difficult Points,* 126.13ff.

233 *dbu ma la 'jug pa, madhyamakāvatāra,* stanza VI.97; Peking 5262, vol. 98 103.3.4ff; La Vallée Poussin's translation is in *Muséon,* n.s. v.12, p. 253. Brackets are from *Commentary on the 'Supplement'* (Peking 5263, vol. 98 136.3.8ff, and Nga-wang-bel-den's *Annotations* (*dbu* 66b.4ff).

234 See Hopkins, *Meditation on Emptiness,* 619-620, and Jeffrey Hopkins, *Maps of the Profound: Jam-yang-shay-ba's Great Exposition of Buddhist and Non-Buddhist Views on the Nature of Reality* (Ithaca, N.Y.: Snow Lion Publications, 2003), 820-822.

235 P731, vol. 19, 189.2.1. This is quoted in Dzong-ka-ba's *Essence* (P6142, vol. 153, 203.5.8).

236 Peking 5263, vol. 98, 136.4.7ff, commenting on VI.97; La Vallée Poussin's translation is in *Muséon,* n.s. v.12, p. 255. This is quoted in Dzong-ka-ba's *Illumination* (Peking 6143, vol. 154, 76.3.6ff) and in the section on the Consequence School in *The Essence* (Peking 6142, vol. 153, 204.5.3ff). See Nga-wang-bel-den's *Annotations, dbu,* 66b.6ff, and Jam-yang-shay-ba's *Great Exposition of the Middle,* 464a.2ff. Brackets are from Dzong-ka-ba's *Illumination.*

237 *Treatise,* XV.2cd.

238 Gung-tang's *Difficult Points,* 128.1.

239 Translated in Jeffrey Hopkins, *Emptiness Yoga* (Ithaca, N.Y.: Snow Lion Publications, 1987), 304 and 409.

240 Cited in Gung-tang's *Difficult Points,* 128.2.

241 Cited in ibid., 128.4.

242 Ibid., 128.14.

243 Jam-yang-shay-ba's *Great Exposition of the Interpretable and the Definitive,* 70.3.

244 Gung-tang's *Difficult Points,* 128.16-129.18.

245 Ye shes thabs mkhas edition, 154.20.

246 Ibid., 171.14.

247 Gung-tang's *Difficult Points,* 129.10.

248 Ye shes thabs mkhas edition, 150.4.

249 Da-drin-rap-den, *Annotations,* 209.1.

250 Jam-yang-shay-ba's *Great Exposition of the Interpretable and the Definitive,* 71.3.

251 As reported in A-ku Lo-drö-gya-tso's *Precious Lamp,* 75.6-77.4.

252 Ibid., 76.4.

253 Jik-may-dam-chö-gya-tso's *Port of Entry,* 573.4.

254 A-ku Lo-drö-gya-tso's *Precious Lamp,* 77.1.

255 Gung-ru Chö-jung's *Garland of White Lotuses,* 26b.4.

256 Jam-yang-shay-ba's *Great Exposition of the Interpretable and the Definitive,* 61.6/ 23b.5.

257 499.1.

258 Gung-tang's *Difficult Points,* 104.13-106.13; he is taking his lead from Gung-ru Chö-jung's *Garland of White Lotuses,* 19b.5-20a.4, and Jam-yang-shay-ba's *Great Exposition of the Interpretable and the Definitive,* 49.6-51.4.

259 Jam-yang-shay-ba's *Great Exposition of the Interpretable and the Definitive,* 54.1-54.5; Gung-ru Chö-jung does not make this point.

260 Chap. 7; Lamotte, *Saṃdhinirmocana,* 70 [10], and 196.

261 Chap. 7; Lamotte, *Saṃdhinirmocana,* 72-73 [13], and 197-198.

262 Chap. 7; Lamotte, 73 [14]; 198; Dön-drup-gyel-tsen's *Four Intertwined Commentaries,* 13.2-13.5.

263 Gung-ru Chö-jung's *Garland of White Lotuses,* 20a.4-20b.1; Jam-ȳang-shay-b̄a's *Great Exposition of the Interpretable and the Definitive,* 51.4-52.1.

264 Gung-ru Chö-jung's *Garland of White Lotuses,* 20b.1-21a.2.

265 Jam-ȳang-shay-b̄a's *Great Exposition of the Interpretable and the Definitive,* 52.1-52.5.

266 Gung-ru Chö-jung's *Garland of White Lotuses,* 21a.1.

267 Jam-ȳang-shay-b̄a's *Great Exposition of the Interpretable and the Definitive,* 54.1-54.5.

268 Gung-ru Chö-jung's *Garland of White Lotuses,* 21b.1-22b.1.

269 Jam-ȳang-shay-b̄a's *Great Exposition of the Interpretable and the Definitive,* 54.5-56.3.

270 IX.140.

271 Gung-ru Chö-jung's *Garland of White Lotuses,* 24a.2-24a.5.

272 Jam-ȳang-shay-b̄a's *Great Exposition of the Interpretable and the Definitive,* 57.6-58.4; *Brief Decisive Analysis,* 500.3-501.2.

273 Gung-ru Chö-jung's *Garland of White Lotuses,* 23a.3-23b.1.

274 Jam-ȳang-shay-b̄a's *Great Exposition of the Interpretable and the Definitive,* 57.3.

275 Gung-ru Chö-jung's *Garland of White Lotuses,* 24a.5-25a.1.

276 Jam-ȳang-shay-b̄a's *Great Exposition of the Interpretable and the Definitive,* 58.4-59.3.

277 Gung-ru Chö-jung's *Garland of White Lotuses,* 23b.3-24a.2.

278 Gung-tang's *Difficult Points,* 108.1-110.12. See also Jik-may-dam-chö-gya-tso's *Port of Entry,* 174.2-174.3.

279 Gung-tang's *Difficult Points,* 102.7-103.13; and 104.12-111.1; *Annotations,* 16.4-18.2/743.4-745.5.

280 Gung-ru Chö-jung's *Garland of White Lotuses,* 27a.2.

281 Jam-ȳang-shay-b̄a's *Great Exposition of the Interpretable and the Definitive,* 62.2, and *Brief Decisive Analysis,* 499.6.

282 See also the translation in Cabezón, *A Dose of Emptiness,* 54.

283 A-ku L̄o-drö-gya-tso's *Precious Lamp,* 77.6.

284 Jik-may-dam-chö-gya-tso (*Port of Entry,* 559.3-560.1) presents a distillation of this issue.

285 Jam-ȳang-shay-b̄a's *Great Exposition of the Interpretable and the Definitive,* 61.6.

286 Gung-tang's *Difficult Points,* 109.1ff.

287 A-ku L̄o-drö-gya-tso's *Precious Lamp,* 74.2.

288 Gung-tang's *Difficult Points,* 109.13.

289 Ibid., 108.12.

290 Ibid., 110.8.

291 Ibid., 110.10-110.11: read *med dgos* for *med* ***med*** *dgos.*

292 Ibid., 110.10-110.11: read *chos bdag* for *chos* ***btags.***

293 Ibid., 104.12ff.

294 Ibid., 104.13.

295 Gung-ru Chö-jung's *Garland of White Lotuses,* 27a.2.

296 Jam-ȳang-shay-b̄a's *Great Exposition of the Interpretable and the Definitive,* 62.3.

297 Jam-ȳang-shay-b̄a's *Great Exposition of the Interpretable and the Definitive,* 62.4.

298 Gung-tang's *Difficult Points,* 105.4; *Annotations,* 17.7.

299 Gung-ru Chö-jung's *Garland of White Lotuses,* 271.3.

300 Gung-tang's *Difficult Points,* 105.1.

301 Ibid., 106.18-107.5.

302 A-ku L̄o-drö-gya-tso's *Precious Lamp,* 78.5. See also Jam-ȳang-shay-b̄a's *Great Exposition of the Interpretable and the Definitive,* 67.6-68.1.

303 A-ku L̄o-drö-gya-tso's *Precious Lamp,* 80.5.

304 Jam-ȳang-shay-b̄a's *Great Exposition of the Interpretable and the Definitive,* 67.5-68.6.

305 Jik-may-dam-chö-gya-tso's *Port of Entry,* 167.6-168.2.

306 Ibid., 168.2-168.3.

307 S̄er-s̄hül's *Notes,* 14b.1-14b.4.

308 See also the translation in Cabezón, *A Dose of Emptiness,* 55.

309 Lamotte, *Saṃdhinirmocana,* 68 [4].

310 Jam-ȳang-shay-b̄a's *Great Exposition of the*

Interpretable and the Definitive, 60.2.

311 As reported in S̄er-s̄hül's *Notes,* 15a.3.

312 Reported in S̄er-s̄hül's *Notes* (15a.6) as being from *rta nag rnam 'grel.*

313 Paṇ-chen S̄ö-nam-drak-b̄a's *Garland of Blue Lotuses,* 31ab.3-32a.1.

314 Gung-tang's *Difficult Points,* 111.1-113.14.

315 Jik-may-dam-chö-gya-tso (*Port of Entry,* 174.5) makes the same point.

316 Paṇ-chen S̄ö-nam-drak-b̄a's *Garland of Blue Lotuses,* 29a.4-29b.5.

317 Jay-d̄zün Chö-ḡyi-gyel-tsen (*General-Meaning Commentary,* 11b.5-11b.7) makes a similar point.

318 Gung-tang's *Difficult Points,* 113.7.

319 A-ku L̄o-drö-gya-tso's *Precious Lamp,* 80.6-83.5.

320 Jay-d̄zün Chö-ḡyi-gyel-tsen's *General-Meaning Commentary,* 11b.4.

321 Ibid., 12a.1.

322 Ibid., 12a.2-12a.4.

323 D̄ra-d̄i Ge-s̄hay's *Ornament for the Thought,* 22.18.

324 As reported in A-ku L̄o-drö-gya-tso's *Precious Lamp,* 81.5-82.1.

325 Paṇ-chen S̄ö-nam-drak-b̄a's *Garland of Blue Lotuses,* 30a.2 and 31a.5.

326 Ibid., 31a.4-31b.3.

327 Ibid., 29b.1.

328 Jay-d̄zün Chö-ḡyi-gyel-tsen's *General-Meaning Commentary,* 12b.3-13a.2.

329 Gung-ru Chö-jung's *Garland of White Lotuses,* 27b.3-29b.4; for this point see 28a.5ff.

330 Jam-ȳang-shay-b̄a's *Great Exposition of the Interpretable and the Definitive,* 63a.3-67a.5; for this point see 65.6ff.

331 Gung-tang's *Difficult Points,* 122.12-123.5.

332 Ibid., 123.5.

333 Gung-ru Chö-jung's *Garland of White Lotuses,* 29a.3.

334 Jam-ȳang-shay-b̄a's *Great Exposition of the Interpretable and the Definitive,* 66.6.

335 In Gung-ru Chö-jung's *Garland of White Lotuses* (29b.1) read *bdag 'dzin* ***rags*** *pa* for *bdag 'dzin* ***dgos*** *pa* in accordance with Jam-ȳang-shay-b̄a's *Great Exposition of the Interpretable and the Definitive* (67.3).

336 Gung-tang's *Difficult Points,* 123.11.

337 As cited in ibid., 124.3.

338 As cited in ibid., 124.5.

339 Ibid., 121.16-122.12.

340 Gung-ru Chö-jung's *Garland of White Lotuses,* 29b.2-29b.4.

341 Jam-ȳang-shay-b̄a's *Great Exposition of the Interpretable and the Definitive,* 67.3-67-5.

342 Gung-ru Chö-jung's *Garland of White Lotuses,* 29a.2: *mngon gyur pa cig car du.*

343 B̄el-jor-hlün-drup's *Lamp for the Teaching,* 15.

344 Jay-d̄zün Chö-ḡyi-gyel-tsen's *General-Meaning Commentary,* 13a.2-13a.5; his position is cited in Jik-may-dam-chö-gya-tso's *Port of Entry,* 178.2.

345 Jam-ȳang-shay-b̄a's *Great Exposition of the Interpretable and the Definitive,* 65.3. Jik-may-dam-chö-gya-tso (*Port of Entry,* 176.5) makes a similarly brief statement.

346 Indeed, this is just what Gung-ru Chö-jung (*Garland of White Lotuses,* 28a.4) and Dra-d̄i Ge-s̄hay Rin-chen-dön-drup (*Ornament for the Thought,* 23.17) say.

347 Gung-tang's *Difficult Points,* 113.14ff.; also his *Annotations,* 22.4-23.1 (*wa*).

348 Cited in Gung-tang's *Difficult Points,* 113.16.

349 Jik-may-dam-chö-gya-tso's *Port of Entry,* 174.6-176.3.

350 Peking 5334, vol. 109, 138.1.5. For translations into English, see David Lasar Friedmann, *Sthiramati, Madhyāntavibhāgaṭīkā: Analysis of the Middle Path and the Extremes,* 10.16; and F. Th. Stcherbatsky, *Madhyāntavibhāga, Discourse on Discrimination between Middle and Extremes ascribed to Bodhisattva Maitreya and Commented by Vasubandhu and Sthiramati,* 17.19.

351 VIII.16; D3846, *dbu ma,* vol. *tsha,* 9b.6; Karen Lang, *Āryadeva's Catuḥśataka: On the Bodhisattva's Cultivation of Merit and Knowledge,* Indiske Studier 7 (Copenhagen: Akademisk Forlag, 1986), 82: *bhāvasyaikasya yo draṣṭā draṣṭā sarvasya sa smṛtaḥ / ekasya śūnyatā yaiva saiva sarvasya śūnyatā //.* See *Yogic Deeds of Bodhisattvas: Gyel-tsap on*

Āryadeva's Four Hundred, commentary by Geshe Sonam Rinchen, translated and edited by Ruth Sonam (Ithaca: Snow Lion Publications, 1994), 194.

352 See Hopkins, *Meditation on Emptiness,* 601, and *Maps of the Profound,* 812-813. Cited in Gung-tang's *Difficult Points,* 114.3.

353 Ibid., 114.6.

354 Ye shes thabs mkhas edition, 196.9. Cited in ibid., 114.13.

355 The last clause is drawn from Jik-may-dam-chö-gya-tso's *Port of Entry,* 177.3.

356 Cited in Gung-tang's *Difficult Points,* 115.6.

357 Ibid., 115.14.

358 *gzhal bya gnyis phyir tshad ma gnyis:* III.1a; Miyasaka's II.1a, pp. 42-43: *mānaṃ dvividhaṃ meyadvaividhyāt;* P5709, vol. 130, 88.3.4.

359 Ke-drup in his commentary on Dharmakīrti's *Commentary on (Dignāga's) "Compilation of Prime Cognition,"* cited in Jik-may-dam-chö-gya-tso's *Port of Entry,* 254.5.

360 Gung-tang's *Difficult Points,* 116.2-117.11.

361 As cited in Gung-tang's *Difficult Points,* 116.13.

362 As cited in ibid., 117.7.

363 Ibid., 118.1-118.15; also Jik-may-dam-chö-gya-tso's *Port of Entry,* 607.1.

364 Ibid., 118.12. I have added *grub pa* in order to supply more context.

365 Ibid., 118.15-120.16; also Jik-may-dam-chö-gya-tso's *Port of Entry,* 607.3.

366 Second Dalai Lama's *Lamp Illuminating the Meaning of [D̄zong-ka-b̄a's] Thought,* 18.1-18.2.

367 Gung-tang's *Difficult Points,* 119.4.

368 Ibid., 120.1.

369 Ibid., 121.7-121.10.

370 Gung-ru Chö-jung's *Garland of White Lotuses,* 19b.3.

371 For this discussion, see Gung-tang's *Difficult Points,* 120.16.

372 Ibid., 120.17-121.10.

373 Jam-ȳang-shay-b̄a's *Brief Decisive Analysis,* 506.4.

374 A. K. Chatterjee, *Readings in Yogācāra Buddhism* (Banaras Hindu University: Center of Advanced Study in Philosophy, 1971), 31.

375 "The Trisvabhāva Doctrine in India and China: A Study of Three Exegetical Models," *Bukkyō Bunka Kenkyū-jo Kiyō* 21 (1982): 104.

376 "The Buddhist Worldview as Elucidated in the Three-Nature Theory and Its Similes," *The Eastern Buddhist* 16 (1983): 9-10; the same analysis appears in Gadjin Nagao, "The Logic of Convertibility," in *Mādhyamika and Yogācāra* (Albany, N.Y.: State University of New York Press, 1991), 123-153.

377 Étienne Lamotte, *La Somme du grand véhicule d'Asaṅga,* reprint, 2 vols., Publications de l'Institute Orientaliste de Louvain 8 (Louvain: Université de Louvain, 1973), vol. 1, 39-40 (II.29), and vol. 2, 125-126. See also the translation by John P. Keenan, *The Summary of the Great Vehicle by Bodhisattva Asaṅga: Translated from the Chinese of Paramārtha* (Berkeley, Calif.: Numata Center for Buddhist Translation and Research, 1992), 53-54.

378 Gung-tang's *Difficult Points,* 129.18; Gung-tang's *Annotations,* 16.6.

379 Jam-ȳang-shay-b̄a's *Brief Decisive Analysis,* 505.4-506.4.

380 Jam-ȳang-shay-b̄a's *Great Exposition of the Interpretable and the Definitive,* 80.5.

381 See also Powers, *Wisdom of Buddha,* 85-86.

382 Ibid., *Wisdom of Buddha,* 189-191.

383 Gung-tang's *Annotations,* 26.5-26.1 and *Difficult Points,* 130.11- 131.7.

384 A-ku L̄o-drö-gya-tso's *Precious Lamp,* 94.3-95.4.

385 Gung-ru Chö-jung's *Garland of White Lotuses,* 33b.5-35a.2. His position is summarized in Jik-may-dam-chö-gya-tso's *Port of Entry,* 189.1-189.6.

386 W̄el-mang Ḡön-chok-gyel-tsen's *Notes on (Ḡön-chok-jik-may-w̄ang-b̄o's) Lectures,* 401.6.

387 Jik-may-dam-chö-gya-tso's *Port of Entry,* 184.1-185.2.

388 Gung-tang's *Annotations* (25.3-26.5) and *Difficult Points* (131.7-132.13). Jik-may-dam-chö-gya-tso includes this in a list of positions on the reason for the qualm (*Port of Entry,* 188.5).

389 A-ku L̄o-drö-gya-tso's *Precious Lamp,* 95.4-98.1.

390 *ske tshang/ske'u tshang.* A-ku Lo-drö-gya-tso's *Precious Lamp* (95.4) names him explicitly, whereas Gung-tang's *Annotations* (25.3) and *Difficult Points* (131.7) do not.

391 These two paragraphs are repeated from *Reflections on Reality,* 237-238, as background for the following discussion.

392 A-ku Lo-drö-gya-tso's *Precious Lamp,* 96.1.

393 Gung-tang's *Difficult Points,* 131.16.

394 Gung-ru Chö-jung's *Garland of White Lotuses,* 32a.6-33a.1.

395 Ibid., 33a.1-33a.3; Jik-may-dam-chö-gya-tso (*Port of Entry,* 186.2), most likely following Jay-dzün Chö-gyi-gyel-tsen's *General-Meaning Commentary* (15a.7-15b.2), reports a similar position.

396 Gung-tang's *Difficult Points,* 133.2-133.11; see also Jik-may-dam-chö-gya-tso (*Port of Entry,* 186.3-187.1) for a description of this position. See also Jay-dzün Chö-gyi-gyel-tsen's *General-Meaning Commentary,* 15b.2-15b.6.

397 A-ku Lo-drö-gya-tso's *Precious Lamp,* 99.3-100.3.

398 *Lamp for the Teaching,* 18.1-18.4.

399 Paṇ-chen Sö-nam-drak-ba's *Garland of Blue Lotuses,* 34a.1-34a.3.

400 Second Dalai Lama's *Lamp Illuminating the Meaning of [Dzong-ka-ba's] Thought,* 19.6; also cited in A-ku Lo-drö-gya-tso's *Precious Lamp,* 99.3.

401 Jam-yang-shay-ba's *Great Exposition of the Interpretable and the Definitive,* 80.5.

402 A-ku Lo-drö-gya-tso's *Precious Lamp* (100.1-100.3), in drawing out the implications of Gung-tang's *Annotations* (28.1).

403 *bde legs nyi ma.* Cited in Jik-may-dam-chö-gya-tso's *Port of Entry,* 187.4.

404 In A-ku Lo-drö-gya-tso's *Precious Lamp* (102.1), read *thag bcad **yin*** for *thag bcad **min**.*

405 Ibid., 102.3.

406 Gung-tang's *Difficult Points,* 151.6-152.13.

407 Thanks to C. John Powers for locating these references.

408 Powers, *Wisdom of Buddha,* 63-65.

409 Ibid., 137.

410 Ibid., 159 and 207.

411 Ibid., 229.

412 Chap. 7; Lamotte, *Saṃdhinirmocana,* 77 [20], and 200-201; Dön-drup-gyel-tsen's *Four Intertwined Commentaries,* 17.1-17.6; and Powers, *Wisdom of Buddha,* 119. See *Emptiness in "Mind-Only" Buddhism,* 95ff.

413 Da-drin-rap-den's *Annotations,* 27.3.

414 Gung-tang's *Difficult Points,* 132.14-133.2; see also Gung-tang's *Annotations,* 27.5-28.1.

415 27.6. Jik-may-dam-chö-gya-tso (*Port of Entry,* 190.4) mentions this discrepancy.

416 A-ku Lo-drö-gya-tso's *Precious Lamp,* 99.1.

417 Ser-shül's *Notes,* 19a.1-19b.1.

418 Ser-shül (ibid., 19a.6) refers his readers to Tsay-den-hla-ram-ba for more detail.

419 As reported in Jik-may-dam-chö-gya-tso's *Port of Entry,* 247.1.

420 Gung-tang's *Difficult Points,* 134.4-134.12; see also A-ku Lo-drö-gya-tso's *Precious Lamp,* 98.1-98.3, and Jik-may-dam-chö-gya-tso's *Port of Entry,* 188.1.

421 For "explicitly" (*dngos su*), see A-ku Lo-drö-gya-tso's *Precious Lamp,* 98.2.

422 See Étienne Lamotte, *La Somme du grand véhicule d'Asaṅga,* reprint, 2 vols., Publications de l'Institute Orientaliste de Louvain 8 (Louvain: Université de Louvain, 1973), vol. 1, 31 (II.15), and vol. 2, 107; and John P. Keenan, *The Summary of the Great Vehicle by Bodhisattva Asaṅga: Translated from the Chinese of Paramārtha* (Berkeley, Calif.: Numata Center for Buddhist Translation and Research, 1992), 46.

423 In A-ku Lo-drö-gya-tso's *Precious Lamp* (92.3) read *rkyen **kyi*** for *rkyen **kyis*** in accordance with Gung-tang's *Annotations* (752.6).

424 A-ku Lo-drö-gya-tso's *Precious Lamp,* 92.2-93.3. His explanation is almost entirely drawn from Gung-tang's *Annotations,* 23.7-24.5 (Ngawang Gelek edition: 752.5-753.4).

425 Gung-tang's *Annotations,* 92.6.

426 Jam-yang-shay-ba's *Great Exposition of the Interpretable and the Definitive,* 71.6-72.5. Jam-yang-shay-ba has reframed Gung-ru Chö-jung's explanation of the same (*Garland of White Lotuses,* 31b.1-31b.5). For the mere

mention of this position, see Jik-may-dam-chö-gya-tso's *Port of Entry,* 189.6.

[427] Jay-d̄zün Chö-ḡyi-gyel-tsen's *General-Meaning Commentary,* 15a.3.

[428] Jik-may-dam-chö-gya-tso (*Port of Entry,* 190.2) briefly mentions these two positions.

[429] Cited in Gung-ru Chö-jung's *Garland of White Lotuses,* 32a.4.

[430] Ibid., 32a.5.

[431] See A-ku L̄o-drö-gya-tso's *Precious Lamp,* 135.4.

[432] For a particularly lengthy treatment of this topic see Jik-may-dam-chö-gya-tso's *Port of Entry,* 251.5-257.6

[433] Jam-ȳang-shay-b̄a's *Great Exposition of the Interpretable and the Definitive,* 72.5-79.4.

[434] A-ku L̄o-drö-gya-tso's *Precious Lamp,* 102.5.

[435] By late Go-mang scholar Thupten Gyatso at the Tibetan Buddhist Learning Center in New Jersey.

[436] By the contemporary Inner Mongolian scholar, Gen D̄en-dzin, at Go-mang, Hla-s̄a, in the fall of 1988.

[437] Jam-ȳang-shay-b̄a's *Great Exposition of the Interpretable and the Definitive,* 76.6. See Jik-may-dam-chö-gya-tso's *Port of Entry,* 668.5.

[438] Ibid., 73.3.

[439] Jik-may-dam-chö-gya-tso's *Port of Entry,* 669.5.

[440] By the late Go-mang scholar Thupten Gyatso at the Tibetan Buddhist Learning Center in New Jersey.

[441] A-ku L̄o-drö-gya-tso's *Precious Lamp,* 104.1-105.6.

[442] Geshe Lhundup Sopa and Jeffrey Hopkins, *Cutting Through Appearances: The Practice and Theory of Tibetan Buddhism,* 221 (second edition).

[443] Gung-tang's *Difficult Points,* 133.18; see also Gung-tang's *Annotations,* 28.1-28.5.

[444] A-ku L̄o-drö-gya-tso's *Precious Lamp,* 101.1.

[445] Ibid., 100.6-101.5.

[446] Hopkins, *Maps of the Profound,* 1003.

[447] A-ku L̄o-drö-gya-tso's *Precious Lamp,* 101.5.

[448] In Tenzin Gyatso, *The Buddhism of Tibet* (London: George Allen and Unwin, 1983), 76.

[449] Jam-ȳang-shay-b̄a's *Notes,* 315.4-315.6.

[450] Jik-may-dam-chö-gya-tso's *Port of Entry,* 183.3-183.5.

[451] Jam-ȳang-shay-b̄a's *Notes,* 315.4-315.6.

[452] Chap. 7; Lamotte, *Saṃdhinirmocana,* 68 [6], and 194; Dön-drup-gyel-tsen's *Four Intertwined Commentaries,* 7.3-7.5.

[453] Jik-may-dam-chö-gya-tso's *Port of Entry,* 190.5.

[454] Gung-tang's *Difficult Points,* 130.2.

[455] The source for these three is Jik-may-dam-chö-gya-tso's *Port of Entry,* 237.3.

[456] For Jik-may-dam-chö-gya-tso's treatment of this topic ranging from Issue #153-167, see ibid., 266.6-274.5.

[457] Paṇ-chen S̄ö-nam-drak-b̄a's *Garland of Blue Lotuses,* 34a.4-34b.3. See also A-ku L̄o-drö-gya-tso's *Precious Lamp,* 108.1. Paṇ-chen S̄ö-nam-drak-b̄a himself cites only the first passage.

[458] Ibid., 199.6.

[459] D̄a-drin-rap-d̄en's *Annotations,* 82.5.

[460] Gung-tang's *Difficult Points,* 18.4; Jik-may-dam-chö-gya-tso's *Port of Entry,* 268.1.

[461] Jik-may-dam-chö-gya-tso's *Port of Entry,* 268.2.

[462] Ibid., 268.3-269.3. Paṇ-chen S̄ö-nam-drak-b̄a's text is particularly sparse on this topic, and thus Jik-may-dam-chö-gya-tso is likely drawing from oral tradition.

[463] S̄er-s̄hül's *Notes,* 19b.1.

[464] Gung-tang's *Difficult Points,* 143.14; see also Gung-tang's *Annotations,* 28.5 (note *'a*).

[465] The same position is presented in Jay-d̄zün Chö-ḡyi-gyel-tsen's *General-Meaning Commentary,* 16b.4.

[466] Ibid., 16b.4.

[467] Jik-may-dam-chö-gya-tso's *Port of Entry,* 269.4.

[468] Ibid., 270.2.

[469] Jam-ȳang-shay-b̄a's *Notes,* 319.5-320.3.

[470] Chap. 7; Lamotte, *Saṃdhinirmocana,* 72-73 [13-14], and 197-198.

[471] Paṇ-chen S̄ö-nam-drak-b̄a's *Garland of Blue Lotuses,* 34b.2. See also A-ku L̄o-drö-gya-tso's *Precious Lamp,* 108.1.

[472] Gung-tang's *Difficult Points,* 144.2.

[473] D̄a-drin-rap-d̄en's *Annotations,* 82.5.

[474] Gung-tang's *Difficult Points,* 144.6. See also Gung-tang's *Annotations,* 28.6-29.3 (note *'a*), and Jik-may-dam-chö-gya-tso's *Port of Entry,* 269.4.

[475] Jay-d̄zün Chö-ḡyi-gyel-tsen's *General-Meaning Commentary,* 19a.5-20b.1.

[476] Ibid., 82.5.

[477] Ibid., 82.5.

[478] Ibid., 82.5.

[479] D̄a-drin-rap-d̄en's *Annotations,* 82.6.

[480] Gung-tang's *Difficult Points,* 144.9.

[481] Ibid., 144.15.

[482] Cited as it appears in Jik-may-dam-chö-gya-tso's *Port of Entry,* 269.6.

[483] Gung-tang's *Difficult Points,* 144.18.

[484] Chap. 7; Lamotte, *Saṃdhinirmocana,* 67-68 [4], and 194; Dön-drup-gyel-tsen's *Four Intertwined Commentaries,* 7.1-7.2.

[485] Chap. 7; Lamotte, *Saṃdhinirmocana,* 69-70[8], and 195; Dön-drup-gyel-tsen's *Four Intertwined Commentaries,* 8.4-9.1.

[486] Gung-tang's *Difficult Points,* 145.11.

[487] Jay-d̄zün Chö-ḡyi-gyel-tsen's *General-Meaning Commentary,* 17b.3.

[488] Gung-tang's *Difficult Points,* 18.4. See also the translation in Cabezón, *A Dose of Emptiness,* 198.

[489] Jay-d̄zün Chö-ḡyi-gyel-tsen's *General-Meaning Commentary,* 16b.7-17a.3.

[490] Gung-tang's *Difficult Points,* 146.3-148.3, taking his lead from Jam-ȳang-shay-b̄a's *Great Exposition of the Interpretable and the Definitive,* 108.2-113.6.

[491] Jam-ȳang-shay-b̄a's *Great Exposition of the Interpretable and the Definitive,* 109.3.

[492] See also the translation in Cabezón, *A Dose of Emptiness,* 130.

[493] VI. 140-141,

[494] Gung-tang's *Difficult Points,* 149.4-150.1.

[495] See Hopkins, *Maps of the Profound,* 220.

[496] Jam-ȳang-shay-b̄a's *Great Exposition of the Interpretable and the Definitive,* 108.5; see also 110.1. Also, Jik-may-dam-chö-gya-tso's *Port of Entry,* 270.4.

[497] Gung-tang's *Difficult Points,* 146.10; see also Gung-tang's *Annotations,* 29.7.

[498] Adapted from D̄zong-ka-b̄a's exposition in H.H. the Dalai Lama, Tsong-ka-pa, and Jeffrey Hopkins, *Tantra in Tibet* (London: George Allen and Unwin, 1977; reprint, Ithaca, N.Y.: Snow Lion, 1987), 93.

[499] Adapted from *Tantra in Tibet,* 40-41.

[500] Ibid., 41.

[501] Jam-ȳang-shay-b̄a's *Great Exposition of the Interpretable and the Definitive,* 108.4-109.6.

[502] Ibid., 109.5.

[503] Ibid., 108.5.

[504] See Hopkins, *Maps of the Profound,* 650-652.

[505] VI.121. The bracketed material is drawn from Nga-w̄ang-b̄el-den's *Annotations, dbu ma pa, ya,* 29.3.

[506] IV.2d. The brackets are from D̄zong-ka-b̄a's *Illumination of the Thought.*

[507] Chandrakīrti's *Supplement,* VI.140a.

[508] Gung-tang's *Difficult Points,* 146.12.

[509] A-ku L̄o-drö-gya-tso's *Precious Lamp,* 110.5-111.2.

[510] Gung-tang's *Difficult Points,* 146.14.

[511] As presented in ibid., 146.15-147.3; see also his *Annotations,* 29.5. Gom-day-nam-ka-gyel-tsen is following Jay-d̄zün Chö-ḡyi-gyel-tsen's *General-Meaning Commentary,* 16b.7-17a.3.

[512] Gung-tang's *Difficult Points,* 147.3-148.3.

[513] I.1a-1c; Peking 5522, vol. 108, 19.4.5.

[514] Gung-tang's *Difficult Points,* 147.12.

[515] Chap. 7; Lamotte, *Saṃdhinirmocana,* 68 [6], and 194; Dön-drup-gyel-tsen's *Four Intertwined Commentaries,* 7.3-7.5.

[516] Gung-tang's *Difficult Points,* 147.17.

[517] Ibid., 148.5.

[518] Ibid., 148.11-149.4.

[519] Adapted from Sopa and Hopkins, *Cutting Through Appearances,* 238-239.

[520] Gung-tang's *Difficult Points,* 150.9-151.6.

[521] As cited in ibid., 151.5.

[522] Jay-d̄zün Chö-ḡyi-gyel-tsen's *General-Meaning Commentary,* 18a.5.

[523] Ibid., 18b.1.

[524] Ibid., 16b.5.

[525] Jik-may-dam-chö-gya-tso's *Port of Entry,* 273.2.

[526] D̄a-drin-rap-d̄en's *Annotations,* 82.6.

[527] Jay-d̄zün Chö-ḡyi-gyel-tsen's *General-Meaning Commentary,* 18b.4-18b.7.

[528] As cited in ibid., 18b.5.

[529] Gung-tang's *Difficult Points,* 135.7-136.9, and *Annotations,* 33.7-35.1.

[530] A-ku L̄o-drö-gya-tso's *Precious Lamp,* 106.6ff.

[531] Gung-tang's *Difficult Points,* 136.2

[532] A-ku L̄o-drö-gya-tso's *Precious Lamp,* 107.6.

[533] Jam-ȳang-shay-b̄a's *Notes,* 318.3.

[534] Ibid., 315.6-316.1.

[535] Jik-may-dam-chö-gya-tso's *Port of Entry,* 183.3-183.5.

[536] Ibid., 553.1.

[537] Ibid., 665.3 and 666.3.

[538] Hopkins, *Maps of the Profound,* 235; Taipei, 188.1.

[539] Ibid., 268-269; paraphrasing Taipei, 209.10.

[540] Ibid., 269; Taipei, 210.19.

[541] These are presented in detail in Jam-ȳang-shay-b̄a's *Great Exposition of Tenets;* see Hopkins, *Maps of the Profound,* 312-347, which in the Taipei edition is 241.16ff.

[542] For these, see Tsong-kha-pa, *The Great Treatise on the Stages of the Path to Enlightenment,* vol. 3, trans. and ed. Joshua W. C. Cutler and Guy Newland (Ithaca, N.Y.: Snow Lion, 2003), 329. D̄zong-ka-b̄a's explanation is cited in Nga-w̄ang-b̄el-den's *Annotations, dngos, nga,* 132.4.

[543] Jam-ȳang-shay-b̄a's *Great Exposition of Tenets,* Taipei, 245.19.

[544] Ibid., Taipei, 246.21.

[545] Nga-w̄ang-b̄el-den's *Annotations, dngos, ja,* 133.7 and 134.1.

[546] The exposition of the eight is from ibid., *dngos, ca,* 132.7, who quotes D̄zong-ka-b̄a's *Golden Rosary.*

[547] Ibid., *dngos, cha,* 133.4.

[548] Jam-ȳang-shay-b̄a's *Great Exposition of Tenets,* Taipei, 247.19. See Hopkins, *Maps of the Profound,* 324ff.

[549] This explanation is drawn from Nga-w̄ang-b̄el-den's *Annotations, dngos, ta,* 134.5.

[550] Jam-ȳang-shay-b̄a's *Great Exposition of Tenets,* Taipei, 248.1.

[551] S̄er-s̄hül's *Notes,* 54a.6.

[552] Nga-w̄ang-b̄el-den's *Annotations, dngos, ta,* 134.7.

[553] In this case, Nga-w̄ang-b̄el-den's *dgongs* clearly means "intended," since it refers to the purpose.

[554] Hopkins, *Maps of the Profound,* 326.

[555] *sa bcu pa, daśabhūmika;* chap. 6. P574, vol. 25, 263.3.8.

[556] Jam-ȳang-shay-b̄a's *Great Exposition of Tenets,* Taipei, 248.21.

[557] Ibid., Taipei, 249.9; see Hopkins, *Maps of the Profound,* 329ff.

[558] Lamotte, *Saṃdhinirmocanasūtra,* 67 [2], and 193; Dön-drup-gyel-tsen's *Four Intertwined Commentaries,* 6.2-6.5; and Powers, *Wisdom of Buddha,* 97. See Hopkins, *Emptiness in Mind-Only,* 82ff.

[559] D̄a-drin-rap-d̄en's *Annotations,* 11.6.

[560] Chap. 7; Lamotte, *Saṃdhinirmocanasūtra,* 67 [3], and 193; Dön-drup-gyel-tsen's *Four Intertwined Commentaries,* 6.6-7.1.

[561] Stanza 23; this is cited also by Wonch'uk (P5517, vol. 106, chap. 5, 130.4.8). For the Sanskrit, see Hopkins, *Emptiness in Mind-Only,* 371, footnote b. For other translations, see Stefan Anacker, *Seven Works of Vasubandhu* (Delhi: Motilal Banarsidass, 1984), 188; and Thomas A. Kochumuttom, *A Buddhist Doctrine of Experience* (Delhi: Motilal Banarsidass, 1982), 258.

[562] S̄er-s̄hül's *Notes,* 14b.5; and D̄a-drin-rap-d̄en's *Annotations,* 12.4.

[563] Jam-ȳang-shay-b̄a's *Great Exposition of the Interpretable and the Definitive,* 45.4; and S̄er-s̄hül's *Notes,* 14b.5.

[564] *rnam par gtan la dbab pa bsdu ba, viniścayasaṃgrahaṇī;* P5539, vol. 111, 71.2.8; Tokyo *sde dge, sems tsam,* vol. 9 (*zi*), 8.4.5.

[565] D̄a-drin-rap-d̄en's *Annotations,* 12.4.

[566] Ibid., 12.3.

[567] Nga-w̄ang-b̄el-den's *Annotations, dngos, na,* 135.4.

568 Ibid., 93.1.

569 A-ku Lo-drö-gya-tso's *Precious Lamp,* 220.3.

570 XI.50; P5521, vol. 108, 9.1.3; for the Sanskrit, see Hopkins, *Emptiness in Mind-Only,* 416, footnote a. The bracketed material is from A-ku Lo-drö-gya-tso's *Precious Lamp,* 220.2. See Sylvain Lévi, *Mahāyānasūtrālaṃkāra, exposé de la doctrine du grand véhicule selon le système Yogācāra* (Paris: Bibliothèque de l'École des Hautes Études, 1907), vol. 1, 67.16; vol. 2, 121. See Hopkins, *Emptiness in Mind-Only,* 172 and 302.

571 P5550, vol. 112, 266.1.2-266.1.4, in the first section, titled *lakṣaṇasamuccaya;* and Walpola Rahula, *Le Compendium de la super-doctrine (philosophie) (Abhidharmasamuccaya) d'Asaṅga* (Paris: École française d'Extrême-Orient, 1980), 141-142.

572 *Maps of the Profound,* 343-344; Taipei, 253.11.

573 Jik-may-dam-chö-gya-tso's *Port of Entry,* 706.2. The reasons given for the first two are my elaboration.

574 *dngos, sha,* 187.4. Drawing from Gyel-tsap's *Commentary on (Asaṅga's) Summary of Manifest Knowledge.* Quoted from Hopkins, *Maps of the Profound,* 394.

575 Jam-ȳang-shay-b̄a's *Great Exposition of Tenets,* Taipei, 250.3; see Hopkins, *Maps of the Profound,* 332-333.

576 Chap. 7; Lamotte, *Saṃdhinirmocana,* 77 [20], and 200-201; Dön-drup-gyel-tsen's *Four Intertwined Commentaries,* 17.1-17.6; and Powers, *Wisdom of Buddha,* 119.

577 The remainder of this section is drawn from *Maps of the Profound,* 362-374; Jam-ȳang-shay-b̄a's *Great Exposition of Tenets,* Taipei, 268.19.

578 P5538, vol. 110, 144.4.1-144.5.5; see also the translation in Willis, *On Knowing Reality,* 161; for the Sanskrit, see Hopkins, *Emptiness in Mind-Only,* 398, footnote a.

579 Nga-w̄ang-b̄el-den's *Annotations, dngos, tsa,* 147.8.

580 Hopkins, *Maps of the Profound,* 405; Taipei, 269.8.

581 Ibid., 370; this is part of a longer discussion in *Maps of the Profound,* 363-374.

582 *dngos, tsha,* 138.2; *Maps of the Profound,* 339-340.

583 Ibid., 339-340.

584 Chap. 7; Lamotte, 73 [14]; 198; Dön-drup-gyel-tsen's *Four Intertwined Commentaries,* 13.2-13.5.

585 Chap. 7; Étienne Lamotte, *Saṃdhinirmocanasūtra: L'explication des mystères* (Louvain: Université de Louvain, 1935), 85 [30], and 206; Dön-drup-gyel-tsen's *Four Intertwined Commentaries,* 27.1-28.2; see also the translation by Powers, *Wisdom of Buddha,* 139-141.

586 See Geshe Lhundup Sopa and Jeffrey Hopkins, *Cutting Through Appearances: The Practice and Theory of Tibetan Buddhism* (Ithaca, N.Y.: Snow Lion Publications, 1989), 277.

587 Hopkins, *Maps of the Profound,* 314-315; Taipei, 241.5.

588 For the date, see Gareth Sparham in collaboration with Shōtarō Iida, *Ocean of Eloquence: Tsong kha pa's Commentary on the Yogācāra Doctrine of Mind* (Albany, N.Y.: State University of New York Press, 1993), 17-18.

589 Ernst Steinkellner, "Who Is Byaṅ chub rdzu 'phrul? Tibetan and Non-Tibetan Commentaries on the *Saṃdhinomocanasūtra*—A Survey of the Literature," *Berliner Indologische Studien* 4, no. 5 (1989): 235.

590 D̄a-drin-rap-·en's *Annotations,* 8.5: *'khor ba 'khor sa.*

591 Paṇ-chen S̄ö-nam-drak-b̄a's *Garland of Blue Lotuses,* 10a.6-11b.6.

592 Gung-tang's *Difficult Points,* 92.6.

593 A-ku Lo-drö-gya-tso's *Precious Lamp,* 54.5.

594 For identification of the passage, see Jik-may-dam-chö-gya-tso's *Port of Entry,* 157.3. He disputes that the Questions of Subhūti Chapter actually treats the constituents this way and says that the fact that it does not is clear in Wonch'uk's commentary (see *Port of Entry,* 157.6).

595 Peking 5517, vol. 116, 130.5.4ff.

596 Peking 5517, vol. 106, chap. 5, 133.3.6; and Golden Reprint, vol. 128, 832.6.

597 Gung-tang's *Difficult Points,* 125.4.

598 Jik-may-dam-chö-gya-tso's *Port of Entry,* 212.40.

599 Wonch'uk's *Great Commentary,* Peking 5517, vol. 106, chap. 5, 164.1.5-169.2.2.

600 Peking 5517, vol. 106, chap. 5, 169.1.6-169.1.8.

601 Gung-tang's *Difficult Points,* 228.13.

602 Ibid., 42.5.

603 Ibid., 228.18.

604 Cited in ibid., 238.9.

605 Peking 5517, vol. 106, chap. 5, 170.2.2; cited by Ḏzong-ka-ḇa, *Emptiness in Mind-Only,* 125.

606 Jik-may-dam-chö-gya-tso's *Port of Entry,* 292.3; and Ḏa-drin-rap-ḏen's *Annotations,* 43.4.

607 Ḏa-drin-rap-ḏen's *Annotations,* 43.5.

608 Peking 5517, vol. 106, chap. 5, 170.2.2.

609 Gung-tang's *Difficult Points,* 240.11.

610 Ibid., 228.4.

611 S̄er-s̄hül's *Notes,* 21b.4.

612 Jik-may-dam-chö-gya-tso's *Port of Entry,* 291.1.

613 Ibid., 153.5.

614 Ibid., 296.4.

615 See also Powers, *Wisdom of Buddha,* 145.

616 Peking 5517, vol. 106, 130.5.4ff. Jik-may-dam-chö-gya-tso (*Port of Entry,* 159.1-160.2) uses Wonch'uk's detailed breakdown of this section.

617 Gung-tang's *Difficult Points,* 247.1-247.5.

618 See ibid., 245.10-247.1.

619 Lamotte, *Saṃdhinirmocana,* 75 [17], and 199; and Powers, *Wisdom of Buddha,* 115.

620 Chap. 7; Lamotte, *Saṃdhinirmocana,* 77 [20], and 200-201; Dön-drup-gyel-tsen's *Four Intertwined Commentaries,* 17.1-17.6; and Powers, *Wisdom of Buddha,* 119.

621 Ḏa-drin-rap-ḏen's *Annotations,* 27.3.

622 Jik-may-dam-chö-gya-tso's *Port of Entry,* 202.2.

623 Ibid., 198.4.

624 Golden Reprint, vol. 128, 820.1.

625 Chap. 7; Lamotte, *Saṃdhinirmocanasūtra,* 81 [25], and 203; Dön-drup-gyel-tsen's *Four Intertwined Commentaries,* 21.3-21.21.5; and Powers, *Wisdom of Buddha,* 131.

626 Ḏa-drin-rap-ḏen's *Annotations,* 34.2.

627 Golden Reprint, vol. 129, 141.5ff.

628 Jik-may-dam-chö-gya-tso's *Port of Entry,* 227.6, 236.2.

629 Chap. 7; Lamotte, *Saṃdhinirmocana,* 81 [25], and 203-204; Dön-drup-gyel-tsen's *Four Intertwined Commentaries,* 21.6; and Powers, *Wisdom of Buddha,* 131.

630 Jik-may-dam-chö-gya-tso's *Port of Entry,* 225.6.

631 Golden Reprint, vol. 129, 140.6.

632 Jik-may-dam-chö-gya-tso's *Port of Entry,* 265.2.

633 Ibid., 226.5.

634 Golden Reprint, vol. 129, 141.3.

635 See S̄er-s̄hül's *Notes,* 20a.2.

636 Jik-may-dam-chö-gya-tso's *Port of Entry,* 298.2.

Glossary

English	*Tibetan*	*Sanskrit*
A		
abandoner	spong byed	
absence of inherent existence	rang bzhin med pa	svabhāva-asat
action	las	karma
actual basis of emptiness	dngos kyi stong gzhi	
actually/directly/explicitly	dngos su	
affirming negative	ma yin dgag	paryudāsapratiṣe-dha
affixed through the force of the object itself	dngos dbang gis 'jug pa	
afflicted mentality/afflicted mentality	nyon mongs can gyi yid	kliṣṭamanas
afflictive emotion	nyon mongs	kleśa
afflictive obstruction	nyon sgrib	kleśāvaraṇa
affords an occasion [for refuta-tion]/affords an opportunity	skabs mchis pa	sa-avakāśa
Am-do	a mdo	
appear/manifest/dawn	shar ba	
appearance	snang ba	
appearance that a form is established by way of its own character as the referent of a conceptual consciousness apprehending a form	gzugs gzugs 'dzin rtog pa'i zhen gzhir rang gi mtshan nyid kyis grub par snang ba	
appearing object	snang yul	*pratibhāsaviṣaya
appearing object of inferential cogni-tion	rjes dpag gi snang yul	
appearing object-of-observation-condition	snang ba'i dmigs rkyen	
appearing to be distant and cut off	rgyang chad du snang ba	
apprehend/conceive	'dzin pa	
apprehended-object	gzung don	
apprehended-object and apprehend-ing-subject	gzung 'dzin	grāhya-grāhaka
arbitrary production/capricious pro-duction	'dod rgyal du skye ba	
argumentation/logic	rtog ge	tarka
arise through the power of other causes and conditions	rgyu rkyen gzhan gyi dbang gis byung ba	
arrogance	dregs pa	
artificial	kun btags	parikalpita

English	*Tibetan*	*Sanskrit*
as the ultimate	dam pa'i don du	
aspect	rnam pa	
aspiring faith	'thob 'dod kyi dad pa	
atom/dust/particle	rdul	aṇu
attention/intention	sems pa	cetanā
attribute/quality	chos	dharma
author of the *Ornament* / Prajñākara-gupta	rgyan mkhan po	
authoritative being	tshad ma'i skyes bu	pramāṇabhuta
autonomous production	rang dbang gis skye ba	
autonomously inherently produced	rang dbang du rang bzhin gyis skye	
autonomously produced	rang dbang gis skye	
Autonomy School	rang rgyud pa	svātantrika
B		
barbarian	kla klo	mlecca
base/foundation	gzhi	
based	brtsams	ārabhya
bases of composition	brtsams gzhi	
basic constituent/constituent	khams	dhātu
basic disposition of things	dngos po'i gshis	
basis in [Buddha's] thought	dgongs gzhi	
basis-of-all	kun gzhi	ālaya
being the referent of a conceptual consciousness	rtog pa'i zhen gzhi yin pa	
being the referent of a conceptual consciousness apprehending it	rang 'dzin rtog pa'i zhen gzhi yin pa	
betweenness/intermediate appearance	bar snang	
beyond consciousness	rnam shes las 'das pa	
Bliss-Arising (Maheśvara/Śiva)	bde 'byung	śambhu
Blissful [Pure Land]	bde ba can	sukhāvatī
blue that is the referent of the convention "blue"	sngon po'i tha snyad kyi gzhir gyur pa'i sngon po	
Bodiless Lord	lus med bdag po	anaṅgapati
body of attributes/Truth Body	chos sku	dharmakāya
brief indication	mdor bstan	
Buddha element or elemental Buddha	sangs rgyas kyi dbyings sam dbyings kyis sangs rgyas	
Buddha lineage	sangs rgyas kyi rigs	buddhagotra
Buddha Superior	sangs rgyas 'phags pa	
by way of its own character	rang gi mtshan nyid gyis	

English	*Tibetan*	*Sanskrit*
C		
called thoroughly established because of not changing into another aspect, being a final object of observation of a path of purification, and being the supreme of all virtuous phenomena	rnam pa gzhan du mi 'gyur ba dang rnam dag lam gyi dmigs pa mthar thug dang dge ba'i chos thams cad kyi mchog yin pas na yongs grub ces bya	
calm abiding	zhi gnas	śamatha
capacity to perform a function	don byed nus pa	
causeless production	rgyu med las skye ba	
character of a particular	bye brag gi mtshan nyid	viśeṣalakṣaṇa
character of entity	ngo bo nyid kyi mtshan nyid	svabhāvalakṣaṇa
character of objects of knowledge	shes bya'i mtshan nyid	jñeyalakṣaṇa
character or inherent nature in the sense of being established by way of their own nature	rang gi ngo bos grub pa'i mtshan nyid dam rang bzhin	
character-non-nature/natureless in terms of character	mtshan nyid ngo bo nyid med pa nyid	lakṣaṇaniḥsvabhā-vatā
child set on mother's lap	ma pang bu 'jug	
Chö-ding	chos sdings	
clear realization/clear realizer	mngon rtogs/mngon par rtogs pa	abhisamaya
clearer away	sel byed	
Cloud Mount	sprin la zhon	meghavāhana/ indra/śakra
cognition	rnam par rig pa/rnam rig	vijñapti
cognition of unreal ideation	yang dag ma yin kun tu rtog pa'i rnam par rig pa	abhūtaparikalpa-vijñapti
Collected Topics of Prime Cognition	bsdus grwa	
common locus of a phenomenon and non-momentary	chos dang skad cig ma ma yin pa'i gzhi mthun pa	
complete training in all the aspects/ complete realization of all the aspects	rnam rdzogs sbyor ba/rnam kun mngon par rdzogs par rtogs pa	sarvākārābhisaṃbo-dha
completely correct means of expres-sion	rjod byed rnam dag	
compositional thing	'du byed	saṃskāra
compounded thing	'dus byas	saṃskṛta
concealer/conventionality/fraudulence	kun rdzob	saṃvṛti
conceive/apprehend	'dzin pa	
conceived object	zhen yul	
conception/consciousness conceiving	'dzin pa	

English	*Tibetan*	*Sanskrit*
conception of a difference of substantial entity between apprehended-object and apprehending-subject	gzung 'dzin rdzas tha dad du 'dzin pa	*grāhyagrāhaka-dravyabhedagrāha
conception of a self of phenomena	chos kyi bdag tu 'dzin pa	dharmātmagraha
conceptual consciousness	rnam rtog/rtog pa	
conceptual consciousness apprehending it	rang 'dzin rtog pa	
conceptual consciousness associating name and meaning	ming don 'brel ba'i rtog pa	
conceptual consciousness having dualistic appearance	rtog pa la gnyis snang yod pa	
conceptual consciousness mindful of associating name and object	ming don 'brel bar dran pa'i rtog pa	
conceptual consciousness understanding a verbal convention at the time of using verbal conventions	tha snyad dus su tha snyad go ba'i tha snyad	
concordant with the fact	don dang mthun pa	
concrete	ling po	
Congregating [Solitary Realizers]	tshogs spyod pa	
consciousness	rnam shes/shes pa	vijñāna
consciousness conceiving/conception	'dzin pa	
consciousness food	rnam shes kyi zas	vijñāna-āhāra
Consequence School	thal 'gyur pa	prāsaṅgika
Consequence School perspective slipped in	thal 'gyur ba'i grub mtha' shor ba	
constituent/basic constituent	khams	dhātu
contact	reg pa	sparśa
contact food	reg pa'i zas	sparśa-āhāra
contains such a mode of conception	'dzin tshul tshang ba	
convention	kun rdzob/tha snyad	saṃvṛti/vyavahāra
conventional truth/obscurational truth	kun rdzob bden pa	saṃvṛtisatya
conventionality/concealer/fraudulence	kun rdzob	saṃvṛti
correctly assuming consciousness	yid dpyod	*manaḥparīkṣā
cyclic existence	'khor ba	saṃsāra
D		
damage/harm	gnod pa	bādhā
dawn/appear/manifest	shar ba	
deceptive phenomenon	bslu ba'i chos	
deceptive with respect to the meaning that it teaches	rang gi bstan don la slu ba	
decisive analysis commentary	mtha' dpyod	
definiendum	mtshon bya	lakṣya

English	*Tibetan*	*Sanskrit*
definite goodness	nges par legs pa	naiüśreyasa
definition	mtshan nyid	lakṣaṇa
definitive meaning	nges don/nges pa'i don	nītārtha
delineating the selflessness of phenomena by hearing and thinking in the basal state	gzhi chos kyi bdag med thos bsam gyis gtan la 'bebs pa	
dependent-arising	rten 'byung	pratītyasamutpāda
designation	gdags pa	
destroy into total disorder	rmeg med du bcom	
developmental lineage	rgyas 'gyur gyi rigs	
devoted	mos pa	
difference between the existence [that is, presence] of such and such and being such and such	yod pa dang yin pa'i khyad par	
different entity	ngo bo tha dad	
different factualities	don tha dad pa	
different substantial entity	rdzas tha dad	
differentiated by way of conceptually isolatable factors	ldog chas phye ba	
differentiating the interpretable and definitive with respect to the scriptures	gsung rab la drang nges 'byed pa	
differentiating the interpretable and definitive within the scriptures	gsung rab kyi drang nges 'byed pa	
differentiating the interpretable and the definitive on the level of the meaning that is expressed within the scriptures	brjod bya don gyi drang nges 'byed pa	
differentiating the interpretable and the definitive on the level of the words that are the means of expression	rjod byed tshig gi drang nges 'byed pa	
difficult points commentary	dka' 'grel	
dim-sightedness/eye disease	rab rib	
direct perception	mngon sum	pratyakṣa
directly/explicitly/actually	dngos su	
Discipline	'dul ba	vinaya
discordant mode of appearance and mode of abiding	snang tshul gnas tshul mi mthun pa	
discrimination	'du shes	saṃjñā
distant and cut off	rgyang chad	
distinctions are needed with respect to appearing objects	snang yul la zhib cha dgos	
distinguished	rab tu phye ba	

English	*Tibetan*	*Sanskrit*
do not subsist by way of their own character	rang gi mtshan nyid kyis rnam par gnas pa ni ma yin pa	svalakṣaṇena avyavasthitaṃ
doctrinal forbearance with respect to true cessation	'gog pa chos bzod	
doctrinal language	chos skad	
doubt	the tshom	
doubt not tending toward the fact	don mi gyur gyi the tshom	
doubt tending toward the fact	don gyur gyi the tshom	
Dre-b̄ung	'bras spungs	
dust/particle/atom	rdul	aṇu
E		
earlier Tibetans and other quarters	bod snga ma dang gzhan phyogs	
earth/ground	sa	bhūmi
effective thing/thing/functioning thing	dngos po	
effects of separation	bral ba'i 'bras bu	
effects that are produced	bskyed pa'i 'bras bu	
efficacious means/method	thabs	upāya
efficacious means of abandoning	spong ba'i thabs	
efficacious means of attaining a Nature Truth Body	ngo bo nyid sku thob pa'i thabs	
eighteen constituents	khams bco brgyad	
element of [a Superior's] attributes/ element of attributes	chos kyi dbyings	dharmadhātu
elimination-isolate	bcad ldog	
eliminator	gcod byed	
eloquence/well explained/good explanation	legs bshad	subhāṣita
emptiness	stong pa nyid	śūnyatā
emptiness of apprehended-objects and apprehending-subjects existing as different substantial entities	bzung 'dzin rdzas tha dad kyis stong pa	*grāhyagrāhaka-dravyabhedaśūnya
emptiness of external objects	phyi rol don gyis stong pa	bāhyārthaśūnya
emptiness of factors imputed in the manner of entity and attribute	ngo bo dang khyad bar du kun btags pas stong pa'i stong pa nyid	
emptiness of inherent existence	rang bzhin stong pa nyid / rang bzhin gyis grub pas stong pa'i stong pa nyid	
emptiness of nature/natural emptiness	ngo bo nyid kyis stong pa nyid	

English	*Tibetan*	*Sanskrit*
emptiness of non-entities	dngos po med pa stong pa nyid	
emptiness of the one-being-empty-of-the-other	gcig gis gcig stong pa'i stong nyid	
emptiness of the other—permanent, stable, eternal, everlasting	gzhan stong rtag brtan g.yung drung ther zug	
emptiness that is the [ultimate] nature of non-entities	dngos po med pa'i ngo bo nyid stong pa nyid	
emptiness that is the object observed by the path	lam gyi dmigs pa'i stong pa nyid	
emptiness that is the ultimate nature which is the opposite of conventionalities	kun rdzob las bzlog pa don dam pa'i ngo bo nyid	
Epistemologists	tshad ma pa	prāmāṇika
epistemology and logic	tshad ma	pramāṇa
equal doubt	cha mnyam pa'i the tshom	
equivalent/mutually inclusive	don gcig	
equivalent and synonymous	don gcig ming gi rnam grangs	
established by the force of its own measure of subsistence	rang gi gnas tshod kyi dbang gis grub pa	
established by way of its own character	rang gi mtshan nyid kyis grub pa	svalakṣaṇasiddha
established by way of its own measure of subsistence as the referent of a conceptual consciousness	rtog pa'i zhen gzhir rang gi gnas tshod kyi dbang gis grub pa	
established by way of its own nature	rang gi ngo bo nyid kyis grub pa	
established from their own side	rang ngos nas grub pa	*svarūpasiddha
establishment as its own mode of abiding	rang rang gi sdod lugs su grub pa	
establishment by way of its own character	rang gi mtshan nyid kyis grub pa	svalakṣaṇasiddhi
establishment by way of its own character as an entity for imputation by terms and conceptual consciousnesses	sgra rtog gis btags pa'i ngo bor rang gi mtshan nyid kyis grub pa	
establishment by way of its own character as the referent of a conceptual consciousness apprehending it	rang 'dzin rtog pa'i zhen gzhir rang gi mtshan nyid kyis grub pa	
establishment from its own side as an appearing object of a direct perception	*mngon sum gyi snang yul du rang ngos nas grub pa	

English	*Tibetan*	*Sanskrit*
establishment in accordance with the superimposed factor of being established by way of its own character as the referent of a conceptual consciousness	rang 'dzin rtog pa'i zhen gzhir rang gi mtshan nyid kyis grub par sgro btags pa ltar du grub pa	
establishment of form by way of its own character as the referent of a term expressing "form"	gzugs gzugs zhes rjod pa'i sgra 'jug pa'i 'jug gzhir rang gi mtshan nyid kyis grub pa	
establishment through the force of the object's measure of subsistence/ establishment through the force of the object's own status	rang gi gnas tshod kyi dbang gis grub pa	
establishment through the force of the object's own status/establishment through the force of the object's measure of subsistence	rang gi gnas tshod kyi dbang gis grub pa	
establishment without depending on imputation by terms and conceptual consciousnesses	sgra rtog gis btags pa la ma ltos par grub pa	
eternal	g.yung drung	
everlasting	ther zug	dhruvaṃ
everlasting everlasting time	ther zug ther zug gi dus	dhruvaṃ dhruvakālaṃ
exalted knower/exalted knowledge	mkhyen pa	
exalted wisdom/wisdom/pristine wisdom	ye shes	jñāna
exalted wisdom of individual self-knowledge	so sor rang rig pa'i ye shes	
exist	yod	vidyate
exist as [its own] reality/really exist	yang dag par yod pa	
existence [that is, presence] of such and such does not establish being such and such	yod pas yin par mi 'grub	
existent	yod pa	
existent imputational nature	yod rgyu'i kun btags	
existing as an object found by the reasoning consciousness distinguishing a conventionality	tha snyad dpyod pa'i rigs shes kyi rnyed don du yod pa	
explanation	rnam par bshad pa	
explicit realization	dngos rtogs	
explicit teaching	dngos bstan	
explicitly/actually/directly	dngos su	
explicitly arose	dngos su byung	

English	*Tibetan*	*Sanskrit*
explicitly ask a question	dngos su zhus	
explicitly taught	dngos su bstan	
extensive explanation	rgyas bshad	
external material objects that are factualities other than the mind	sems las don gzhan pa'i phyi rol gyi don bem po	
eye disease/dim-sightedness	rab rib	
eye sense power	mig gi dbang po	cakṣurindriya
F		
factor	cha shas	
factor for instance of forms and so forth being objects of names and terminology	gzugs sogs ming brda'i yul yin pa'i cha lta bu	
factually concordant consciousness	blo don mthun	
faith of clear delight	dang ba'i dad pa	
faith of conviction	yid ches kyi dad pa	
falsity	brdzun pa	mṛṣā
fantastic	ngo mtshar	āścarya
faulty mode of structuring the statement	sbyor lugs skyon can	
feeling	tshor ba	vedanā
final mind-only	mthar thug gi sems tsam	
final mode of subsistence	gnas lugs mthar thug	
final nature/real nature/noumenon	chos nyid	dharmatā
final object of observation by a path of purification	rnam dag lam gyi dmigs pa mthar thug	
final summary	mjug bsdu ba	
Foe Destroyer/Worthy One	dgra bcom pa	arhant
Following Reasoning	rigs pa'i rjes 'brangs	*nyāyānusārin
Following Scripture	lung gi rjes 'brangs	*āgamānusārin
forbearance	bzod pa	kṣānti
Forder	mu stegs can/mu stegs pa	tīrthika
form and so forth being a conceived object of a conceptual consciousness	gzugs sogs rtog pa'i zhen yul yin pa	
form and so forth being a referent of a conceptual consciousness	gzugs sogs rtog pa'i zhen gzhi yin pa	
Form Body	gzugs sku	rūpakāya
form's being the referent of a conceptual consciousness apprehending a form	gzugs gzugs 'dzin rtog pa'i zhen gzhi yin pa	

English	*Tibetan*	*Sanskrit*
form's establishment by way of its own character as the referent of a conceptual consciousness apprehending a form	gzugs gzugs 'dzin rtog pa'i zhen gzhir rang gi mtshan nyid kyis grub pa	
format/framework/synonym	rnam grangs	
forms and so forth in accordance with how they appear to ordinary consciousnesses of confined beings are imputational	tshur mthong gi shes pa rang dga' ba la snang tshod ltar gyi gzugs sogs kun btags yin	
foundation/base	gzhi	
foundations of imputational characters	kun brtags pa'i mtshan nyid kyi gnas	parikalpita-lakṣaṇāśraya
four great royal lineages	rgyal chen rigs bzhi	cāturmahārājakā-yika
four indirect intentions	ldem dgongs bzhi	catvāro 'bhisaṃ-dhaya
four thoughts	dgongs pa bzhi	catvāro 'bhiprāyā
framework/synonym/format	rnam grangs	
fraudulence/concealer/conventionality	kun rdzob	saṃvṛti
from the point of view of general characteristics and thorough investigation	spyi'i mtshan nyid dang yongs su brtags pa'i sgo nas	
from the point of view of thoroughly analyzing their own signs	rang gi mtshan ma yongs su brtags pa'i sgo nas	
from the side of the mode of subsistence of its own factuality	rang gi dngos po'i gnas tshul gyi ngos nas	
fruition	rnam smin	vipāka
fruitional consciousness	rnam smin rnam shes	vipakavijñāna
functioning thing/effective thing/thing	dngos po	
fundamental innate mind of clear light	gnyug ma lhan cig skyes pa'i 'od gsal gyi sems	
G		
Gan-den	dga' ldan	
Garlanded Belly	tha gu'i lto	dāmodara/viṣṇu
Ge-luk-b̄a	dge lugs pa	
general meaning commentary	spyi don	
generality-isolate of the selflessness of persons	gang zag gi bdag med spyi ldog	
generally characterized phenomenon	spyi mtshan	sāmānyalakṣaṇa
generated in the discriminating	rtog ldan la skye ba	
Glorious Stūpa of the Constellations	dpal ldan rgyu skar gyi mchod rten	

English	*Tibetan*	*Sanskrit*
go as efficacious means/serve as effica-cious means	thabs su 'gro ba	
God of Desire	'dod lha	kāmadeva
Golden Womb	gser gyi mngal	hiraṇyagarbha/ brahmā
good explanation/eloquence/well explained	legs bshad	subhāṣita
Grāmaghātaka	grong 'joms	grāmaghātaka
Great Exposition	bye brag bshad mdzod chen mo	mahāvibhāṣa
Great Exposition School	bye brag smra ba	vaibhāṣika
Great Fruit	'bras bu che ba	vṛhatphala
Great Middle Way	dbu ma chen po	
great seal	phyag rgya chen po	mahāmudrā
Great Vehicle	theg chen/theg pa chen po	mahāyāna
ground/earth	sa	bhūmi
grounds and paths	sa lam	
H		
harm/damage	gnod pa	bādhā
having another thought [behind it]	dgongs pa can	
heard	śruta	
Hearer	nyan thos	śrāvaka
heaven of thirty-three	sum cu rtsa gsum	trayastriṃśa
held within the words	tshig gis zin pa	
high status	mngon mtho	abhyudaya
high-and-mighty	'gying	
highest object	don dam pa	parama-artha
Hla-ṡa	lha sa	
hypothetical dispute	rgol ba khong nas bsus pa	
hypothetical qualm	dogs pa khong bslang/dogs pa khong slong	
I		
I	nga	ahaṃ
ideation/comprehensive imagination/ comprehensive construction	kun rtog/kun tu rtog pa	
ignorance	ma rig pa	avidyā
illustration	mtshan gzhi	
illustration-isolate/illustration simplic-iter	gzhi ldog	
immediately preceding condition	de ma thag rkyen	samanantara-pratyaya
implicit realization	shugs rtogs	

English	*Tibetan*	*Sanskrit*
implicitly ask a question	don gyis zhus	
imputational character	kun btags kyi mtshan nyid	parikalpitalakṣaṇa
imputational conventionality	btags pa'i kun rdzob	
imputational factor	kun btags	
imputational factors imputed in the manner of entity and attribute	ngo bo dang khyad par la kun btags pa'i kun btags	
imputational nature	kun btags kyi rang bzhin/kun btags kyi ngo bo nyid	parikalpitasvabhāva
imputational natures whose character is thoroughly nihil	mtshan nyid yongs su chad pa'i kun btags	
imputational words	'dogs pa'i tshig	prajñaptivāda
imputed object-of-observation-condition	dmigs rkyen btags pa pa	
imputed	btags pa/rnam brtags	prajñaptir
imputing	'dogs pa	prajñapti
indirect intention	ldem dgongs	abhisaṃdhaya
indirect intention of causing entry	gzhug pa ldem dgongs	
indirectly intending an antidote	gnyen po la ldem por dgongs pa	pratipakṣābhi-saṃdhi
indirectly intending entry	gzhug pa la ldem por dgongs pa	avatāranābhisaṃ-dhi
indirectly intending the characters	mtshan nyid la ldem por dgongs pa	lakṣaṇābhisaṃdhi
indirectly intending translation	sbyor ba la ldem por dgongs pa/bsgyur ba la ldem por dgongs pa	pariṇāmābhisaṃ-dhi
Indra	dbang po	
induced by valid cognition	tshad mas drang pa	
inexpressible things	brjod du med pa'i dngos po	
inference	rjes dpag	anumāna
inference by the power of the fact	dngos stobs rjes dpag	
inherent existence/inherent na-ture/nature	rang bzhin	svabhāva
inherent production	rang bzhin gyis skye ba	
inherently	rang bzhin gyis	svabhāvatas
inherently established	rang bzhin gyis grub pa	svabhāvasiddha
innate	lhan skyes	sahaja
inquiry	brtag pa	
integrally/on their own part	rang chas su	
intending an antidote	gnyen po la ldem por dgongs pa	pratipakṣābhisaṃ-dhi

English	*Tibetan*	*Sanskrit*
intending entry	gzhug pa la ldem por dgongs pa	avatāraṇābhisaṃdhi
intending the characters	mtshan nyid la ldem por dgongs pa	lakṣaṇābhisaṃdhi
intending translation	sbyor ba la ldem por dgongs pa/bsgyur ba la ldem por dgongs pa	pariṇāmābhisaṃdhi
intention/attention	sems pa	cetanā
intention food	sems pa'i zas	manaḥsaṃcetanāhāra
intentionality/will	sems pa	cetanā
intermediate appearance/betweenness	bar snang	
interpretable meaning/requires interpretation	drang ba'i don	neyārtha
intrinsic production	ngo bo nyid kyis skye ba	
isolate/conceptually isolatable phenomenon	ldog pa	
its own-character [that is, unique character] does not exist	rang gi mtshan nyid yod pa ma yin	
J		
Jaina	rgyal ba pa	jaina
Jambudvīpa	'dzam gling	jambudvīpa
Jo-nang-b̄a	jo nang pa	
Joyous Land	dga' ldan	tuṣita
just imputed by conceptuality/only imputed by conceptuality	rtog pas btags tsam	
just the mere absence of self and just the mere absence of inherent nature of compounded phenomena	'du byed rnams kyi bdag med pa tsam dang rang bzhin med pa tsam nyid	
K		
Kam	khams	
knower of all aspects	rnam mkhyen	sarvākārajñāna
knowing itself by itself	rang gis rang rig pa	
knowledge of all aspects	rnam pa thams cad mkhyen pa nyid	sarvākārajñatā
knowledge of bases	gzhi shes	vastujñāna
knowledge of paths	lam shes nyid	mārgajñatā
L		
land without combat	'thab bral	yāma
languaged person	brda la byang ba'i skyes bu	
Lesser Vehicle	theg dman	hīnayāna
limit of correctness/limit of reality	yang dag mtha'	bhūtakoṭi

English	*Tibetan*	*Sanskrit*
limitless consciousness	nam mkha' mtha' yas	ākāśānantya
limitless space	rnam shes mtha' yas	vijñānānantya
lineage	rigs	gotra
linguistic referentiality	brda byas pa	
linguistically established	sgra byung grags pa	
literal level/literal reading/literality	sgras zin	
Little Light	'od chung ba	parīttābhā
logic/argumentation	rtog ge	tarka
logic-epistemology	tshad ma	pramāṇa
logician	rtog ge pa	
Lokāyata/Hedonist	rgyang 'phan pa	lokāyata
Lord of Love	dga' rab dbang phyug	
Lord of Subduers	thub dbang	munīndra
M		
main meaning taught	bstan don gtso bo	
main object found by conventional valid cognitions	tha snyad pa'i tshad ma'i rnyed don gtso bo	
main object of observation of purification	rnam dag gi dmigs pa'i gtso bo/rnam dag dmigs pa'i gtso bo	
Majority School	phal chen sde pa	mahāsaṃghika
manifest/dawn/appear	shar ba	
Manifest Knowledge	chos mngon pa	abhidharma
manifestation	rnam 'gyur	
manifesting the manner/putting on a show	tshul mdzad pa	
manifold	du ma	anekatva
many forms/many synonyms	rnam grangs du ma	
marvelous	rmad du byung ba	adbhūta
matrix-of-one-gone-thus	de bzhin gshegs pa'i snying po	tathāgatagarbha
meaning	don	artha
meaning arrives at, or involves, emptiness	don stong nyid du 'gro ba	
meaning established through the pressure of reasoning	rigs pas 'phul gyis sgrub pa'i don	
meaning expressed/meaning communicated	brjod don	
meaning-generality	don spyi	arthasāmānya
meaning-isolate	don ldog	

English	*Tibetan*	*Sanskrit*
meaning of the character-non-nature explicitly indicated on this occasion	skabs 'dir dngos su bstan pa'i mtshan nyid ngo bo nyid med pa'i don	
means of abandoning	spong ba'i thabs	
means of questioning	dri ba zhu byed	
measure indicated	bstan tshod	
measure [that is, level] indicated by the words	tshig gis bstan tshod	
measure [that is, level] of meaning gotten at	don gyi thob tshod	
meditative equipoise with appearance	mnyam bzhag snang bcas	
meditative equipoise without appearance	mnyam bzhag snang med	
meditative stabilization	ting nge 'dzin	samādhi
mental consciousness	yid kyi shes pa	
mental continuum weighty with the good qualities of scripture and realization	rgyud lung rtogs kyi yon tan gyis lci ba	
mental conventionalities	shes pa'i kun rdzob	
mental dormancy	yid la nyal	
mental engagement/taking to mind	yid la byed pa	manaskāra
mental nourishment	yid kyi zas	
mere cognition	rnam rig tsam	vijñaptimātra
messenger of an evil devil	ngan bdud kyi pho nya	
method	thabs	upāya
Middle Way Autonomy School	dbu ma rang rgyud pa	svātantrika-mādhyamika
Middle Way Consequence School	dbu ma thal 'gyur pa	prāsaṅgika-mādhyamika
Middle Way School	dbu ma pa	mādhyamika
Mīmāṃsa/Analyzers/Ritualists	dpyod pa ba	mīmāṃsa
mind	sems	citta
mind-basis-of-all	kun gzhi rnam par shes pa/kun gzhi rnam shes	ālayavijñāna
mindful establishment	dran pa nyer bzhag	smṛtyupasthāna
Mind-Only School	sems tsam pa	cittamātra
misconception/wrong conception	log rtog	
mode of superimposition of the self of phenomena on other-powered natures	gzhan dbang la chos bdag sgro btags pa'i sgro 'dogs tshul	
momentary training	skad cig ma'i sbyor ba	kṣaṇikaprayoga

English	*Tibetan*	*Sanskrit*
more difficult in dependence upon the sūtra's mode of teaching to generate such a qualm with respect to imputational natures	mdo des bstan tshul la brten nas kun btags la de 'dra'i dogs pa skyed dka' ba	
morsels of food/morsel food	kham gyi zas	kavaḍaṃkāra-āhāra
mother	yum	mātṛ
Mṛgāramata	ri dags 'dzin gyi ma	mṛgāramata
mutually inclusive/equivalent	don gcig	
N		
Naiyāyika/Logicians	rig pa can pa	naiyāyika
name	ming	nāma
natural emptiness	rang bzhin gyis stong pa nyid	
natural lineage	rang bzhin gnas rigs	
nature/inherent existence/inherent nature	rang bzhin/ngo bo nyid	svabhāva
nature of self in phenomena	chos rnams kyi bdag gi ngo bo	
Nature Truth Body	ngo bo nyid sku	svabhāvikakāya
natureless/naturelessness/non-nature	ngo bo nyid med pa	niḥsvabhāvatā
natureless in terms of character/character-non-nature	mtshan nyid ngo bo nyid med pa	
negation/negative	dgag pa	pratiṣedha
Nirgrantha/Unclothed	gcer bu pa	nirgrantha
no sensible way for such a qualm to occur with respect to imputational natures since they are not truly established	kun btags bden med yin pas de 'dra'i dogs pa skye don med	
non-abiding nirvāṇa	mi gnas pa'i myang 'das	apratiṣṭhitanirvāṇa
non-affirming negation/non-affirming negative	med dgag	prasajyapratiṣedha
non-associated compositional factors	ldan min 'du byed	viprayuktasaṃskāra
non-erroneous thoroughly established natures and immutable thoroughly established natures	phyin ci ma log pa'i yongs grub dang 'gyur med yongs grub	
non-establishment by the force of its own measure of subsistence	rang gi gnas tshod kyi dbang gis ma grub pa	
non-establishment by way of its own character as a referent of a conceptual consciousness apprehending it	rang 'dzin rtog pa'i zhen gzhir rang gi mtshan nyid kyis ma grub pa	

English	*Tibetan*	*Sanskrit*
non-establishment by way of its own character as a referent of a term expressing it	rang zhes rjod pa'i sgra jug pa'i jug gzhir rang gi mtshan nyid kyis ma grub pa	
non-establishment—of factors imputed in the manner of entity and attribute—by way of their own character	ngo bo dang khyad par la kun brtags pa'i kun brtags de rang gi mtshan nyid kyis ma grub pa	
non-existence of a permanent, unitary, and independent self	rtag gcig rang dbang can kyi bdag med	
non-existence of pot	bum pa med pa	
non-existent imputational nature	med rgyu'i kun btags	
non-forgetfulness	mi brjed pa	
non-loss	mi bskyud pa	asaṃpramoṣatā
non-nature/naturelessness	ngo bo nyid med pa	niḥsvabhāva
non-nature ultimately/ultimately natureless	don dam par ngo bo nyid med pa	
non-non-pot	bum pa ma yin pa ma yin pa	
non-pot	bum pa ma yin pa	
non-religious	chos min	
not by themselves	bdag nyid kyis ma yin pa	na svatas
not established as the entity of mind	sems kyi bdag nyid du ma grub pa	
not exist in conventional terms	tha snyad du med pa	
not subsist by way of its own character	rang gi mtshan nyid kyis rnam par gnas pa ni ma yin pa	svalakṣaṇena avyavasthitaṃ
not subsisting by way of their own character	rang gi mtshan nyid gyis gnas pa ma yin	
not taught on the literal level	sgras zin la ma bstan	
nothingness	ci yang med	ākiṃcaya
noumenon/real nature/final nature	chos nyid	dharmatā
nourishment of consciousness	rnam shes kyi zas	vijñānāhāra
nourishment of intention	sems pa'i zas	manaḥsaṃcetanā-hāra
number of chapters	le'u gzhung tshad	
O		
object found by a reasoning consciousness analyzing the ultimate	don dam dpyod pa'i rigs shes kyis rnyed don	
object of activity	spyod yul	gocaraṃ
object of comprehension	gzhal bya	prameya
object of engagement	'jug yul	pravṛttiviṣaya

English	*Tibetan*	*Sanskrit*
object of expression/subject matter/topic expressed	brjod bya	
object of knowledge	shes bya	jñeya
object of observation	dmigs pa	ālambana
object of observation by a path of purification	rnam dag lam gyi dmigs pa/rnam dag lam gyi dmigs yul	
object of observation of purification	rnam par dag pa'i dmigs pa	viśuddhālambana
object of the highest [wisdom]	dam pa'i don	paramasya artha
object of the mode of apprehension	'dzin stangs kyi yul	
object of the ultimate	dam pa'i don	paramasyārtha
object, practice, and attainment thoroughly established natures	don dang sgrub pa dang thob pa yongs grub	
object that appears	snang ba'i yul	
object that is the conceived object of a conceptual consciousness	rtog pa'i zhen yul yin pa'i don	
object that is the referent of a conceptual consciousness	rtog pa'i zhen gzhi yin pa'i don	
object appearing in the aspect of dualistic appearance	yul de gnyis snang gi rnam par 'char ba	
objective establishment	yul steng nas grub pa	
objects of activity of conceptuality	rnam par rtog pa'i spyod yul	vikalpagocara
obscurational truth/conventional truth	kun rdzob bden pa	saṃvṛtisatya
observation of the disintegration of the aggregates	phung po'i 'jig pa dmigs pa	skandha-vināśopalambha
observation of the production of the aggregates	phung po'i skye ba dmigs pa	skandhotpādopalambha
observation of the signs of the aggregates	phung po'i mtshan ma dmigs pa	skandhanimittopalambha
observed-object condition	dmigs rkyen	ālaṃbanapratyaya
obstructions to omniscience	shes sgrib	jñeyāvaraṇa
obstructive	sra	
occasion of identifying the imputational eye	kun brtags kyi mig ngos 'dzin skabs	
olive	skyu ru ra	āmalakī
omniscient	kun mkhyen	
on their own part/integrally	rang chas su	
One Convention School	tha snyad gcig pa	ekavyavahārika
One Gone to Bliss	bde gshegs/bde bar gshegs pa	sugata
one who possesses the six goodnesses	legs pa drug dang ldan pa	bhagavan
only	tsam	mātra

English	*Tibetan*	*Sanskrit*
only imputed by conceptuality	rtog pas btags tsam	
only posited by conceptuality and not established by way of its own character	rtog pas btags pa tsam yin kyi rang gi mtshan nyid kyis ma grub pa	
only posited by names and terminology	ming brdas bzhag tsam	
opening exclamation for debate	thal skad	
opposite from non-pot	bum pa my yin pa las log pa	
ordinary mind	tha mal pa'i sems	
other-powered character	gzhan dbang gi mtshan nyid	paratantralakṣaṇa
other-powered nature	gzhan dbang gi ngo bo nyid/ gzhan dbang gi rang bzhin	paratantrasvabhāva
own-character	rang gi mtshan nyid	svalakṣaṇa
P		
particle/atom/dust	rdul	aṇu
path of accumulation	tshogs lam	saṃbhāramārga
path of liberation	thar lam	
path of meditation	sgom lam	bhāvanāmārga
path of no more learning	mi slob lam	aśaikṣamārga
path of preparation	sbyor lam	prayogamārga
path of seeing	mthong lam	darśanamārga
peak of cyclic existence	srid rtse	bhavāgra
peak training	rtse sbyor	mūrdhaprayoga
permanent permanent time	rtag pa rtag pa'i dus	nityaṃ nitya-kālaṃ
permanent, stable, everlasting	rtag pa brtan pa ther zug	
person	gang zag	pudgala
phenomena of forms and so forth appear to conceptual consciousnesses apprehending forms and so forth to be the referents of the conventions of entity and attribute from the side of the mode of subsistence of the intrinsic factuality of those forms and so forth	gzugs sogs kyi chos rnams gzugs sogs 'dzin pa'i rtog pa la ngo bo dang khyad par gyi tha snyad kyi gzhir gzugs sogs rang gi dngos po'i gnas tshul gyi ngos nas snang ba	
phenomenology	chos mngon pa	abhidharma
phenomenon/religion/practice/way	chos	dharma
phenomenon-constituent	chos kyi khams	dharmadhātu
phenomenon-sense-sphere	chos kyi skye mched	dharmāyatana
physical life support	lus rten	
physical manifestation	lus kyi rnam 'gyur	
play/sport	rol pa	līla

English	*Tibetan*	*Sanskrit*
pollutant	bslod byed	
posit/posited	rab tu phye ba/rab tu bzhag pa	
posited by a conceptual consciousness apprehending it	rang 'dzin rtog pas bzhag pa	
posited by a conceptual consciousness	rtog pas bzhag pa	
posited by an awareness	blos bzhag pa	
posited by only names and terminology	ming brda tsam gyis bzhag pa	
positive/positive phenomenon	sgrub pa	vidhi
possessed of good differentiation	legs par rnam par phye ba dang ldan pa	suvibhakta
practice/way/phenomenon/religion	chos	dharma
predisposing latency/predisposition	bag chags	vāsanā
predispositions of [perceptions of] similar type	rigs mthun gyi bag chags	
predispositions of maturation	rnam smin gyi bag chags	
predispositions of the branches of cyclic existence	srid pa'i yan lag gi bag chags	bhavāṅgavāsanā
predispositions of the view of self	bdag lta'i bag chags	ātmadṛṣṭivāsanā
predispositions of the view of the transitory collection	'jig tshogs la lta ba'i bag chags	
predispositions of verbalization	mngon brjod kyi bag chags	abhilāpavāsanā
predispositions of verbal repetition	zlos pa'i bag chags	
presumptions	rlom pa	
pristine wisdom/exalted wisdom/wisdom	ye shes	jñāna
produced by way of [its own] nature	ngo bo nyid kyis skyes pa	
produced from their own essence	rang gi bdag nyid las skye ba	
produced from their own natures	rang gi ngo bo nyid las skye ba	
produced from their own side	rang ngos nas skye ba	
produced through their own power	rang dbang gis skye ba	
production by itself	bdag nyid kyis skye ba	
production by way of its own entity	ngo bo nyid kyis skye ba	
production from itself	rang las skye ba	
production from themselves	bdag nyid las skye ba	
production-non-nature	skye ba ngo bo nyid med pa nyid	utpattiniḥsvabhāvatā
production through their own power	rang dbang gis skye ba	
Proponent of a Person	gang zag smra ba	pudgalavādin

English	*Tibetan*	*Sanskrit*
Proponent of Cognition	rnam rig pa	vijñaptika/ vijñapti-vādin
Proponent of Mind-Only	sems tsam pa	cittamātrin
Proponent of Non-Nature	ngo bo nyid med par smra ba	niḥsvabhāvavādin
Proponents of the Middle	dbu ma pa	mādhyamika
purpose	dgos pa	
putting on a show/manifesting the manner	tshul mdzad pa	
Q		
quality/attribute	chos	dharma
qualm	dogs pa	
quite a number of reasons	rgyu mtshan mang tsam	
R		
Ra-ka Precipice	rva kha brag	
rash	bab col	
real nature/noumenon/final nature	chos nyid	dharmatā
real nature of other-powered nature	gzhan dbang gi chos nyid	
real nature that is with its other-powered nature	gzhan dbang gi steng gi chos nyid	
reality	yang dag	samyak
really exist/exist as [its own] reality	yang dag par yod pa	
reasoning consciousness/rational consciousness	rigs shes	
reasoning consciousness analyzing an ultimate	don dam dpyod pa'i rigs shes	
reasoning consciousness that has found the ultimate upon analysis	don dam dpyad nas rnyed pa'i rigs shes	
reasoning of dependence	ltos pa'i rigs pa	apekṣāyukti
reasoning of nature	chos nyid kyi rigs pa	dharmatāyukti
reasoning of performance of function	bya ba byed pa'i rigs pa	kāryakāraṇayukti
reasoning of tenable proof	'thad pas sgrub pa'i rigs pa	upapattisādhana-yukti
reasoning through the forceful power of facts	dngos po'i stobs shugs kyi rigs pa	
reasons	rgyu mtshan	
refutation of the explicit teaching	dngos la gnod byed	
religion/practice/way/phenomenon	chos	dharma
requires interpretation/interpretable meaning	drang ba'i don	neyārtha
respectively/tentatively	re zhig	
Rhinoceros-like	bse ru lta bu	

English	*Tibetan*	*Sanskrit*
roar	nga ro	
root basis of emptiness	rtsa ba'i stong gzhi	
S		
Sage's Propounding	drang song smra ba	ṛṣivadana
Sa-gya	sa skya	
Sāṃkhya/Enumerators	grangs can pa	sāṃkhya
scriptural collection	sde snod	piṭaka
scriptures/high sayings	gsung rab	pravacana
secondary meaning taught	bstan don phal pa	
self	bdag	ātman
self-isolate	rang ldog	
self-isolate of a selflessness of persons	gang zag bdag med gi rang ldog	
self-isolate of pot	bum pa'i rang ldog	
self-isolated selflessness of the person	gang zag bdag med rang ldog	
self-powered production	bdag nyid kyi dbang gis skye ba	
self-production	rang skye ba	
sense-sphere	skye mched	āyatana
sense-sphere of form	gzugs kyi skye mched	rūpāyatana
separate annotations	zur mchan	
serial training	mthar gyis sbyor ba	anupūrvaprayoga
serve as efficacious means/go as efficacious means	thabs su 'gro ba	
serve as efficacious means of clearing away	sel ba'i thabs su 'gro ba	
serves as a basis for controversy	rtsod pa'i bzhi'i gnas	vivādādhikaraṇa
set forth non-literally	sgra ji bzhin pa min par bshad pa	
set forth with a thought behind it	dgongs te bshad pa	
set in mind	thugs la bzhag pa	
seven actualities	dngos po rnam pa bdun	
seven pronouncements	bka' stsal bdun	
Shakra	brgya byin	
Sha-lu	zha lu	
Shar-dzay	shar rtse	
signlessness	mtshan ma med pa	animitta
signs of compositional phenomena	'du byed kyi mtshan ma	saṃskāranimitta
simultaneous certification/simultaneous observation	lhan cig dmigs nges	
six constituents	khams drug	

English	*Tibetan*	*Sanskrit*
skill in means/skillful means	thabs mkhas/thabs la mkhas pa	upāyakauśalya
solid	mkhregs	
Solitary Realizer	rang rgyal	pratyekabuddha
sorrow	mya ngan	
Sūtra School	mdo sde pa	sautrāntika
sound/term	sgra	śabda
sound and sound's impermanence are similar in being appearing objects of a direct perception apprehending sound	sgra dang sgra mi rtag pa sgra 'dzin mngon sum gyi snang yul du mtshungs	
sound-generality	sgra spyi	śabdasāmānya
sounds of speech	ngag gi sgra	
source of attributes/source of phenomena	chos 'byung	
source of controversy among the twenty sects [of Hearers]	sde pa nyis shu po rtsod par smra ba dag gi gnas su gyur pa	
source of phenomena/source of attributes	chos 'byung	
spatial over-self	nam mkha'i bdag po	
special insight	lhag mthong	vipaśyanā
specific character	bye brag gi mtshan nyid	
specifically characterized phenomenon	rang mtshan	svalakṣaṇa
spoke the words of sūtra "..."	ces pa'i mdo tshig bka' stsal pa	
spoken for the sake of leading	drang ba'i phyir du gsungs pa	
sport/play	rol pa	līla
stable	brtan pa	
stable predispositions	bag chags brtan byung	
steel bow and steel arrow	lcags mda' lcags gzhu	
stronger	shugs che	
subject matter/object of expression/topic expressed	brjod bya	
substantially established	rdzas su ma grub pa	
suchness	de nyid/de kho na nyid	tattva
suffering of pervasive conditioning	khyab pa 'du byed kyi sdug bsngal	
suitable for the assessment of censure	klan ka 'jug rung	
suitable to be taken as an object of an awareness	blo'i yul du bya rung ba	

English	*Tibetan*	*Sanskrit*
superimposed factor of forms and so forth as established by way of their own character as the referents of conceptual consciousnesses	gzugs sogs rtog pa'i zhen gzhir rang mtshan gyis grub par sgro btags pa	
superimposed factor or appearance of an object as established by way of its own character as the referent of a conceptual consciousness	rang 'dzin rtog pa'i zhen gzhir rang gi mtshan nyid kyis grub pa sgro btags pa'am snang ba	
superimposed factor that a form is established by way of its own character as the referent of a conceptual consciousness apprehending a form	gzugs gzugs 'dzin rtog pa'i zhen gzhir rang gi mtshan nyid kyis grub par sgro btags pa'i cha	
Superior	'phags pa	ārya
Supramundane Mind-Only	'jig rten las 'das pa'i sems tsam	
Supramundane Victor	bcom ldan 'das	bhagavan
supreme actuality	dngos po mchog	
supreme of all sūtras	mdo sde kun gyi mchog	
surpassable	bla na mchis pa	sa-uttara
susceptible to destruction by others	gzhan dag gis gzhig par bya ba/gzhan gyis gzhig nus pa	
susceptible to dispute	rgol ba dang bcas pa	
synonym	ming gi rnam grangs	
synonym/framework/format	rnam grangs	
T		
taking [such and such] as substrata	khyad gzhir bzung ba	
taking to mind/mental engagement	yid la byed pa	manaskāra
teaching in relation to which there is occasion for something more special	skabs khyad par can yod pa'i bstan pa	
techniques of altruism	gzhan phan gyi thabs	
temporary clearer away	gnas skabs kyi sel byed	
tentatively/respectively	re zhig	
tentatively exist	re zhig yod pa	
term/sound	sgra	śabda
term expressing that object	rang zhes rjod pa'i sgra	
terminology/communication	brda'	
textbook literature	yig cha	
that which holds its own entity	rang gi ngo bo 'dzin pa	
that which is observed by valid cognition	tshad mas dmigs pa	
that which is only imputed by conceptuality	rtog pas btags tsam	
that which is suitable as form	gzugs su rung ba	

English	*Tibetan*	*Sanskrit*
thing/functioning thing/effective thing	dngos po	
thinking of another meaning/in consideration of another meaning	don gzhan la dgongs pa	arthāntarābhiprāya
thinking of another time/in consideration of another time	dus gzhan la dgongs pa	kālāntarābhiprāya
thinking of a person's attitude/in consideration of a person's thought	gang zag gi bsam pa la dgongs pa	pudgalāntarābhiprāya
thinking of sameness/in consideration of sameness	mnyam pa nyid la dgongs pa	samatābhiprāya
thorough examination	yongs su tshol ba	paryeṣanā
thorough knowledge	yongs su shes pa	parijñāna
thoroughly established character	yongs grub kyi mtshan nyid	pariniṣpannalakṣaṇa
thoroughly established nature	yongs su grub pa'i ngo bo nyid/yongs su grub pa'i rang bzhin	pariniṣpannasvabhāva
thoroughly established natures in terms of selflessness of persons and of selflessness of phenomena	gang zag gi bdag med dang chos kyi bdag med kyi dbang du byas pa'i yongs grub	
those engaged in all vehicles	theg pa thams cad la yang dag par zhugs pa	sarvayānasaṃprasthita
those engaged in the Great Vehicle	theg pa chen po la yang dag par zhugs pa	mahāyānasaṃprasthita
those engaged in the Hearer Vehicle	nyan thos kyi theg pa la yang dag par zhugs pa	śrāvakayānasaṃprasthita
Those Who Enjoy Emanation	'phrul dga'	nirmāṇarati
Those Who Make Use of Others' Emanations	gzhan 'phrul dbang byed	paranirmitavaśavartin
thought/thought behind it	dgongs pa	abhiprāya
thought comes down to that	dgongs pa der 'bab pa	
thought of the literal reading	sgras zin kyi dgongs pa	
thought of the scripture	gsung rab kyi dgongs pa	
thought of the speaker	gsung ba po'i dgongs pa	
three characters	mtshan nyid gsum	trilakṣaṇa
three natures	ngo bo nyid gsum	trisvabhāva
three non-natures	ngo bo nyid med pa gsum	
through the aspect of speaking on emptiness	stong pa nyid smos pa'i rnam pas	śūnyatāvādākāreṇa
thusness	de bzhin nyid	tathatā

English	*Tibetan*	*Sanskrit*
thusness that is a final object of observation of a path of purification	rnam dag lam gyi dmigs pa mthar thug tu gyur pa'i de bzhin nyid	
thusness that is a negation of a self of phenomena	chos bdag bkag pa'i de bzhin nyid	
thusness that is an emptiness of establishment in accordance with superimposition by either of the two apprehensions of self	bdag 'dzin gnyis gang rung gis sgro btags pa ltar grub pas stong pa'i de bzhin nyid	
topic expressed/subject matter/object of expression	brjod bya	
tracks	shul	
trainee	gdul bya	
Translation of the Treatises	bstan 'gyur	
true establishment	bden grub	
truly exist	bden par yod pa	
truth	bden pa	satya
Truth Body/Body of Attributes	chos sku	dharmakāya
truth of the highest object/ultimate truth	don dam pa'i bden pa	parama-arthasya satya
two modes of positing the ultimate-non-nature	don dam pa ngo bo nyid med pa 'jog tshul gnyis	
two modes of ultimate-non-nature	don dam pa ngo bo nyid med tshul gnyis	
U		
ultimate	dam pa	parama
ultimate	don dam pa	paramārtha
Ultimate Manifest Knowledge	don dam pa'i chos mngon pa	paramārthābhidharma
Ultimate Mind-Only	don dam pa'i sems tsam	
ultimate noumenon beyond dependent-arising	don dam rten 'brel las 'das pa'i chos nyid	
ultimate object	don dam pa	paramārtha
ultimate truth	don dam bden pa	paramārthasatya
ultimately able to perform a function	don dam par don byed nus pa	
ultimately exist	don dam par yod pa	
ultimate-naturelessness	don dam pa ngo bo nyid med pa	
ultimate-non-nature	don dam pa ngo bo nyid med pa nyid	paramārthaniḥsvabhāvatā

English	*Tibetan*	*Sanskrit*
ultimate-non-nature in terms of the selflessness of persons	gang zag gi bdag med kyi dbang du byas pa'i don dam pa ngo bo nyid med pa	
ultimate-non-nature in terms of the selflessness of phenomena	chos kyi bdag med kyi dbang du byas pa'i don dam pa ngo bo nyid med pa	
ultimately natureless/non-natures ultimately	don dam par ngo bo nyid med pa	
uncommon character/unique character/unique defining character	thun mong ma yin pa'i mtshan nyid	
uncommon proprietary condition	thun mong ma yin pa'i bdag rkyen	asādhāraṇādhipatipratyaya
unique character/unique defining character/uncommon character	thun mong ma yin pa'i mtshan nyid	
unmatched proponent	smra ba zla med	
unreal ideation	yang dag pa ma yin pa'i kun rtog / yang dag pa ma yin pa'i kun tu rtog pa /yang dag min kun rtog	abhūtaparikalpa
unreal imputational nature	yang dag pa ma yin pa kun brtags pa'i ngo bo nyid	abhūtaparikalpitasvabhāva
unsurpassed proponent	smra ba bla na med pa	
Upagupta	nyer sbas	upagupta
utterly without an inherent nature	rang bzhin ye med	sarvathā niḥsvabhāvās
V		
Vaisheṣhika/Particularists	bye brag pa	vaiśeṣika
valid cognition	tshad ma	pramāṇa
various	tha dad pa	nānātva
vehicle	theg pa	yāna
verbal conventionalities	brjod pa'i kun rdzob	
verbalization	brjod pa	
Very Extensive [Sūtras]	shin tu rgyas pa	vaipulya
very obscure objects of comprehension	shin tu lkog gyur gyi gzhal bya/gzhal bya shin tu lkog gyur	
view in the face of knowledge	rig ngo lta ba	
view of the basal state	gzhi'i lta ba	
view of the transitory	'jig lta	satkāyadṛṣṭi
W		
way/phenomenon/religion/practice	chos	dharma
well explained/good explanation/eloquence	legs bshad	subhāṣita

English	*Tibetan*	*Sanskrit*
wet and moistening	rlan zhing gsher ba	
wheel ascertaining the ultimate/wheel of the ultimate, the definitive	don dam rnam par nges pa'i 'khor lo	
will/intentionality	sems pa	cetanā
wind	rlung	prāṇa
wisdom/pristine wisdom/exalted wisdom	ye shes	jñāna
wish to know and wish to communicate	shes 'dod dang ston 'dod	
without a nature in terms of production	skye ba ngo bo nyid med pa	
without a nature of production	skye ba'i ngo bo nyid med pa	
without inherent nature	rang bzhin med pa	
without thingness	dngos po med pa	
wonderful features of high states	mtho ris kyi phun tshogs	
word/phrase	tshig	
word commentary	tshig 'grel	
worldly conventions	'jig rten gyi tha snyad	
worthy of worship	mchod 'od	arhat
Worthy One/Foe Destroyer	dgra bcom pa	arhant
wrong conception/misconception	log rtog	
wrong consciousness	log shes	viparyayajña
Y		
Yogic Practitioner	rnal 'byor spyod pa pa	yogācāra

List of Abbreviations

"Dharma" refers to the *sde dge* edition of the Tibetan canon published by Dharma Press: the *Nying-ma Edition of the sDe-dge bKa'-'gyur and bsTan-'gyur* (Oakland, Calif.: Dharma, 1980).

"Golden Reprint" refers to the *gser bris bstan 'gyur* (Sichuan, China: krung go'i mtho rim nang bstan slob gling gi bod brgyud nang bstan zhib 'jug khang, 1989).

"Karmapa *sde dge*" refers to the *sde dge mtshal par bka' 'gyur: A Facsimile Edition of the 18th Century Redaction of Si tu chos kyi 'byung gnas Prepared under the Direction of H.H. the 16th rgyal dbang karma pa* (Delhi: Delhi Karmapae Chodhey Gyalwae Sungrab Partun Khang, 1977).

"P," standing for "Peking edition," refers to the *Tibetan Tripiṭaka* (Tokyo-Kyoto: Tibetan Tripiṭaka Research Foundation, 1955-1962).

"*stog* Palace" refers to the *Tog Palace Manuscript of the Tibetan Kanjur* (Leh, Ladakh: Smanrtsis Shesrig Dpemdzod, 1979).

"Toh" refers to the *Complete Catalogue of the Tibetan Buddhist Canons,* edited by Hukuji Ui (Sendai, Japan: Tohoku University, 1934), and *A Catalogue of the Tohuku University Collection of Tibetan Works on Buddhism,* edited by Yensho Kanakura (Sendai, Japan: Tohoku University, 1953).

"Tokyo *sde dge*" refers to the *sDe dge Tibetan Tripiṭaka—bsTan ḥgyur preserved at the Faculty of Letters, University of Tokyo,* edited by Z. Yamaguchi, et al. (Tokyo: Tokyo University Press, 1977-1984).

Bibliography

Sūtras and tantras are listed alphabetically by English title in the first section of the bibliography. Indian and Tibetan treatises are listed alphabetically by author in the second section; other works are listed alphabetically by author in the third section. Works mentioned in the first or second sections are not repeated in the third section.

For an excellent bibliography of Yogācāra texts, see C. John Powers, *The Yogācāra School of Buddhism: A Bibliography,* American Theological Library Association Bibliography Series 27 (Metuchen, N.J., and London: American Theological Library Association and Scarecrow Press, 1991).

1. Sūtras and Tantras

Descent into Laṅkā Sūtra

laṅkāvatārasūtra

lang kar gshegs pa'i mdo

P775, vol. 29

Sanskrit: Bunyiu Nanjio. *Bibl. Otaniensis,* vol. 1. Kyoto: Otani University Press, 1923. Also: P. L. Vaidya. *Saddharmalaṅkāvatārasūtram.* Buddhist Sanskrit Texts 3. Darbhanga, India: Mithila Institute, 1963.

English translation: D. T. Suzuki. *The Lankavatara Sutra.* London: Routledge and Kegan Paul, 1932.

Eight Thousand Stanza Perfection of Wisdom Sūtra

aṣṭasāhasrikāprajñāpāramitā

shes rab kyi pha rol tu phyin pa brgyad stong pa

P734, vol. 21

Sanskrit: P. L. Vaidya. *Aṣṭasāhasrika Prajñāpāramitā, with Haribhadra's Commentary called Ālokā.* Buddhist Sanskrit Texts 4. Darbhanga, India: Mithila Institute, 1960.

English translation: E. Conze. *The Perfection of Wisdom in Eight Thousand Lines & Its Verse Summary.* Bolinas, Calif.: Four Seasons Foundation, 1973.

Great Drum Sūtra

mahābherīhārakaparivartasūtra

rnga bo che chen po'i le'u'i mdo

P888, vol. 35

Lion's Roar of Shrīmālādevī Sūtra

'phags pa lha mo dpal phreng gi seng ge'i sgra zhes bya ba theg pa chen po'i mdo

āryaśrīmālādevīsiṃhanādanāmamahāyanasūtra

P760.48, vol. 24

English translation: A. Wayman and H. Wayman. *The Lion's Roar of Queen Śrīmālā.* New York: Columbia University Press, 1974.

Mahāparinirvāṇa Sūtra

'phags pa yongs su mya ngan las 'das pa chen po'i mdo

P787, vols. 30-31; translated by wang phab shun, dge ba'i blo gros, rgya mtsho'i sde

P788, vol. 31; translated by Jinamitra, Jñānagarbha, lha'i zla ba

English translation from the Chinese: Kosho Yamamoto. *The Mahayana Mahāparinirvāṇa-sutra.* Ube, Japan: Karinbunko, 1973.

Matrix-of-One-Gone-Thus Sūtra

āryatathāgatagarbhanāmamahāyanasūtra

'phags pa de bzhin gshegs pa'i snying po zhes bya ba theg pa chen po'i mdo

P924, vol. 36

Ornament Illuminating Exalted Wisdom Sūtra
āryasarvabuddhaviṣayāvatārajñānālokālaṃkāranāmamahāyanasūtra
'phags pa sangs rgyas thams cad kyi yul la 'jug pa'i ye shes snang ba rgyan gyi mdo ces bya ba theg pa chen po'i mdo
P768, vol. 28

Questions of King Dhāraṇīshvara Sūtra / Sūtra Teaching the Great Compassion of a One Gone Thus
āryatathāgatamahākaruṇānirdeśasūtra
de bzhin gshegs pa'i snying rje chen po bstan pa'i mdo / 'phags pa gzungs kyi dbang phyug rgyal pos zhus pa'i mdo
P814, vol. 32

Renunciation Sūtra
mngon par 'byung ba'i mdo
P967, vol. 39

Sūtra on the Ten Grounds
daśabhūmikasūtra
mdo sde sa bcu pa
P761.31, vol. 25
Sanskrit: *Daśabhūmikasūtram.* P. L. Vaidya, ed. Buddhist Sanskrit Texts 7. Darbhanga: Mithila Institute, 1967.
English translation: M. Honda. "An Annotated Translation of the 'Daśabhūmika.'" In D. Sinor, ed, *Studies in South, East and Central Asia,* Śatapitaka Series 74. New Delhi: International Academy of Indian Culture, 1968, 115-276.

Sūtra Unraveling the Thought
saṃdhinirmocanasūtra
dgongs pa nges par 'grel pa'i mdo
P774, vol. 29; Toh 106; Dharma, vol. 18; *The Tog Palace Edition of the Tibetan Kanjur,* vol. 63, 1-160 (Leh: Smanrtsis Shesrig Dpemzod, 1975-1978)
Tibetan text and French translation: Étienne Lamotte. *Saṃdhinirmocanasūtra: L'explication des mystères.* Louvain: Université de Louvain, 1935.
English translation: C. John Powers. *Wisdom of Buddha: Saṁdhinirmocana Sūtra.* Berkeley: Dharma, 1995. Also: Thomas Cleary. *Buddhist Yoga: A Comprehensive Course.* Boston: Shambhala, 1995.

Teachings of Akṣhayamati Sūtra
akṣayamatinirdeśa
blo gros mi zad pas bstan pa
P842, vol. 34

Twenty-five Thousand Stanza Perfection of Wisdom Sūtra
pañcaviṃśatisāhasrikāprajñāpāramitā
shes rab kyi pha rol tu phyin pa stong phrag nyi shu lnga pa
P731, vol. 19
English translation (abridged): Edward Conze. *The Large Sūtra on the Perfection of Wisdom.* Berkeley: University of California Press, 1975.

2. Other Sanskrit and Tibetan Works

A-ku Ḻo-drö-gya-tso / Gung-tang Ḻo-drö-gya-tso (*a khu blo gros rgya mtsho / gung thang blo gros rgya mtsho;* 1851-1930)
Precious Lamp / Commentary on the Difficult Points of (Ḏzong-ka-ḇa's) "Treatise Differentiating Interpretable and the Definitive Meanings, The Essence of Eloquence": A Precious Lamp
drang ba dang nges pa'i don rnam par 'byed pa'i bstan bcos legs bshad snying po'i dka' 'grel rin chen sgron me
Delhi: Kesang Thabkhes, 1982.

Āryadeva (*'phags pa lha,* second to third century C.E.)

Four Hundred / Treatise of Four Hundred Stanzas / Four Hundred Stanzas on the Yogic Deeds of Bodhisattvas

catuḥśatakaśāstrakārikā

bstan bcos bzhi brgya pa zhes bya ba'i tshig le'ur byas pa

P5246, vol. 95

Edited Tibetan and Sanskrit fragments along with English translation: Karen Lang. *Āryadeva's Catuḥśataka: On the Bodhisattva's Cultivation of Merit and Knowledge.* Indiske Studier, 7. Copenhagen: Akademisk Forlag, 1986.

English translation: Geshe Sonam Rinchen and Ruth Sonam. *Yogic Deeds of Bodhisattvas: Gyel-tsap on Āryadeva's Four Hundred.* Ithaca, N.Y.: Snow Lion, 1994.

Italian translation of the last half from the Chinese: Giuseppe Tucci. "Study Mahāyānici: La versione cinese del Catuḥśataka di Āryadeva, confronta col testo sanscrito e la traduzione tibetana." *Rivista degli Studi Orientali* 10 (1925):521-567.

Asaṅga (*thogs med,* fourth century)

Explanation of (Maitreya's) "Sublime Continuum of the Great Vehicle"

mahāynottaratantraśāstravyākhya

theg pa chen po'i rgyud bla ma'i bstan bcos kyi rnam par bshad pa

P5526, vol. 108

Sanskrit: E. H. Johnston (and T. Chowdhury). *The Ratnagotravibhāga Mahāyānottaratantraśāstra.* Patna, India: Bihar Research Society, 1950.

English translation: E. Obermiller. "Sublime Science of the Great Vehicle to Salvation." *Acta Orientalia* 9 (1931):81-306. Also: J. Takasaki. *A Study on the Ratnagotravibhāga.* Rome: Istituto Italiano per il Medio ed Estremo Oriente, 1966.

Five Treatises on the Grounds

1. *Grounds of Yogic Practice*
   yogācārabhūmi
   rnal 'byor spyod pa'i sa
   P5536-5538, vols. 109-110
   Grounds of Bodhisattvas
   bodhisattvabhūmi
   byang chub sems pa'i sa
   P5538, vol. 110
   Sanskrit: Unrai Wogihara. *Bodhisattvabhūmi: A Statement of the Whole Course of the Bodhisattva (Being the Fifteenth Section of Yogācārabhūmi).* Leipzig: 1908; Tokyo: Seigo Kenyūkai, 1930-1936. Also: Nalinaksha Dutt. *Bodhisattvabhumi (Being the XVth Section of Asangapada's Yogacarabhumi).* Tibetan Sanskrit Works Series 7. Patna, India: K. P. Jayaswal Research Institute, 1966.
   English translation of the Chapter on Suchness, the fourth chapter of Part I which is the fifteenth volume of the *Grounds of Yogic Practice:* Janice D. Willis. *On Knowing Reality.* New York: Columbia University Press, 1979; reprint, Delhi: Motilal Banarsidass, 1979.
2. *Compendium of Ascertainments*
   nirṇayasaṃgraha / viniścayasaṃgrahaṇī
   rnam par gtan la dbab pa bsdu ba
   P5539, vols. 110-111
3. *Compendium of Bases*
   vastusaṃgraha
   gzhi bsdu ba
   P5540, vol. 111
4. *Compendium of Enumerations*
   paryāyasaṃgraha
   rnam grang bsdu ba
   P5543, vol. 111

5. *Compendium of Explanations*
vivaraṇasaṃgraha
rnam par bshad pa bsdu ba
P5543, vol. 111

Grounds of Hearers
nyan sa
śrāvakabhūmi
P5537, vol. 110
Sanskrit: Karunesha Shukla. *Śrāvakabhūmi.* Tibetan Sanskrit Works Series 14. Patna, India: K. P. Jayaswal Research Institute, 1973.

Two Summaries

1. *Summary of Manifest Knowledge*
abhidharmasamuccaya
chos mngon pa kun btus
P5550, vol. 112
Sanskrit: Pralhad Pradhan. *Abhidharma Samuccaya of Asaṅga.* Visva-Bharati Series 12. Santiniketan, India: Visva-Bharati (Santiniketan Press), 1950.
French translation: Walpola Rahula. *La compendium de la super-doctrine (philosophie) (Abhidharmasamuccaya) d'Asaṅga.* Paris: École Française d'Extrême-Orient, 1971.

2. *Summary of the Great Vehicle*
mahāyānasaṃgraha
theg pa chen po bsdus pa
P5549, vol. 112
French translation and Chinese and Tibetan texts: Étienne Lamotte. *La somme du grand véhicule d'Asaṅga,* 2 vols. Publications de l'Institute Orientaliste de Louvain 8. Louvain: Université de Louvain, 1938; reprint, 1973.
English translation: John P. Keenan. *The Summary of the Great Vehicle by Bodhisattva Asaṅga: Translated from the Chinese of Paramārtha.* Berkeley, Calif.: Numata Center for Buddhist Translation and Research, 1992.

B̄el-jor-hlün-drup, N̄yel-d̄ön (*dpal 'byor lhun grub, gnyal* [or *gnyan*] *ston,* 1427-1514)

Lamp for the Teaching / Commentary on the Difficult Points of (D̄zong-ka-b̄a's) "The Essence of Eloquence": Lamp for the Teaching
legs bshad snying po'i dka' 'grel bstan pa'i sgron me
Delhi: Rong-tha Mchog-sprul-rnam-pa-gnyis, 1969.

Bhāvaviveka (*legs ldan 'byed,* c. 500-570?)

Blaze of Reasoning / Commentary on the "Heart of the Middle": Blaze of Reasoning
madhyamakahṛdayavṛttitarkajvālā
dbu ma'i snying po'i 'grel pa rtog ge 'bar ba
P5256, vol. 96
Partial English translation (chap. 3, 1-136): Shōtarō Iida. *Reason and Emptiness.* Tokyo: Hokuseido, 1980.

Heart of the Middle
madhyamakahṛdayakārikā
dbu ma'i snying po'i tshig le'ur byas pa
P5255, vol. 96
Partial English translation (chap. 3, stanzas 1-136): Shōtarō Iida. *Reason and Emptiness.* Tokyo: Hokuseido, 1980.

Chandrakīrti (*candrakīrti, zla ba grags pa,* seventh century)

[Auto]commentary on the "Supplement to (Nāgārjuna's) 'Treatise on the Middle'"
madhaymakāvatārabhāṣya
dbu ma la 'jug pa'i bshad pa / dbu ma la 'jug pa'i rang 'grel
P5263, vol. 98. Also: Dharmsala, India: Council of Religious and Cultural Affairs, 1968.
Tibetan: Louis de la Vallée Poussin. *Madhyamakāvatāra par Candrakīrti.* Bibliotheca Buddhica, 9.

Osnabrück, Germany: Biblio Verlag, 1970.

English translation: C. W. Huntington, Jr. *The Emptiness of Emptiness: An Introduction to Early Indian Mādhyamika,* 147-195. Honolulu: University of Hawaii Press, 1989.

French translation (up to chap. 6, stanza 165): Louis de la Vallée Poussin. *Muséon* 8 (1907):249-317; *Muséon* 11 (1910):271-358; *Muséon* 12 (1911):235-328.

German translation (chap. 6, stanzas 166-226): Helmut Tauscher. *Candrakīrti-Madhyamakāvatāraḥ und Madhyamakāvatārabhāṣyam.* Vienna: Wiener Studien zur Tibetologie und Buddhismuskunde, 1981.

Clear Words, Commentary on (Nāgārjuna's) "Treatise on the Middle"

mūlamadhyamakavṛttiprasannapadā

dbu ma rtsa ba'i 'grel pa tshig gsal ba

P5260, vol. 98. Also: Dharmsala, India: Tibetan Cultural Printing Press, 1968.

Sanskrit: Louis de la Vallée Poussin. *Mūlamadhyamakakārikās de Nāgārjuna avec la Prasannapadā commentaire de Candrakīrti.* Bibliotheca Buddhica, 4. Osnabrück, Germany: Biblio Verlag, 1970.

English translation (chap. 1, 25): T. Stcherbatsky. *Conception of Buddhist Nirvāṇa,* 77-222. Leningrad: Office of the Academy of Sciences of the USSR, 1927; rev. reprint, Delhi: Motilal Banarsidass, 1978.

English translation (chap. 2): Jeffrey Hopkins. "Analysis of Coming and Going." Dharmsala, India: Library of Tibetan Works and Archives, 1974.

Partial English translation: Mervyn Sprung. *Lucid Exposition of the Middle Way: The Essential Chapters from the Prasannapadā of Candrakīrti translated from the Sanskrit.* London: Routledge, 1979; Boulder, Colo.: Prajñā Press, 1979.

French translation (chapters 2-4, 6-9, 11, 23, 24, 26, 28): Jacques May. *Prasannapadā Madhyamaka-vṛtti, douze chapitres traduits du sanscrit et du tibétain.* Paris: Adrien-Maisonneuve, 1959.

French translation (chapters 18-22): J. W. de Jong. *Cinq chapitres de la Prasannapadā.* Paris: Geuthner, 1949.

German translation (chap. 5, 12-26): Stanislaw Schayer. *Ausgewählte Kapitel aus der Prasannapadā.* Krakow: Naktadem Polskiej Akademji Umiejetnosci, 1931.

German translation (chap. 10): Stanislaw Schayer. "Feuer und Brennstoff." *Rocznik Orjentalistyczny* 7 (1931):26-52.

Supplement to (Nāgārjuna's) "Treatise on the Middle"

madhyamakāvatāra

dbu ma la 'jug pa

P5261, P5262, vol. 98

Tibetan: Louis de la Vallée Poussin. *Madhyamakāvatāra par Candrakīrti.* Bibliotheca Buddhica, 9. Osnabrück, Germany: Biblio Verlag, 1970.

English translation (chaps. 1-5): Jeffrey Hopkins. *Compassion in Tibetan Buddhism.* London: Rider, 1980; reprint, Ithaca, N.Y.: Snow Lion, 1980.

English translation (chap. 6): Stephen Batchelor. *Echoes of Voidness* by Geshé Rabten, 47-92. London: Wisdom, 1983.

See also references under Chandrakīrti's *[Auto]commentary on the "Supplement."*

Ḏa-drin-rap-ḏen (*rta mgrin rab brtan, tre hor dge bshes,* 1920-1986)

Annotations / Annotations for the Difficult Points of (Ḏzong-ka-ḇa's) "The Essence of Eloquence": Festival for the Unbiased Endowed with Clear Intelligence

drang nges rnam 'byed legs bshad snying po dka' gnad rnams mchan bur bkod pa gzur gnas blo gsal dga' ston

Delhi: Lhun-grub-chos-grags, 1978.

Ḏak-tsang Ṡhay-rap-rin-chen (*stag tshang lo tsā ba shes rab rin chen,* born 1405)

Explanation of "Freedom from Extremes through Understanding All Tenets": Ocean of Eloquence

grub mtha' kun shes nas mtha' bral grub pa zhes bya ba'i bstan bcos rnam par bshad pa legs bshad kyi rgya mtsho

Thimphu, Bhutan: Kun-bzang-stobs rgyal, 1976

Daṃṣhṭasena (*daṃṣṭasena;* attributed so by Dzong-ka-ba; some others identify Vasubandhu as the author)

[Commentary on] the Three Mothers, Conquest over Harm / Extensive Explanation of the Superior One Hundred Thousand Stanza, Twenty-five Thousand Stanza, and Eighteen Thousand Stanza Perfection of Wisdom Sūtras

āryaśatasāhasrikāpañcaviṃśatisāhasrikāṣṭadaśasāhasrikāprajñāpāramitābṛhaṭṭīkā

yum gsum gnod 'joms / 'phags pa shes rab kyi pha rol tu phyin pa 'bum pa dang nyi khri lnga stong pa dang khri brgyad stong pa'i rgya cher bshad pa

P5206, vol. 93

Den-ba-dar-gyay, Ke-drup (*bstan pa dar rgyas, mkhas grub,* 1493-1568)

General Meaning of (Dzong-ka-ba's) "Differentiating the Interpretable and the Definitive": Essence of Eloquence, Garland of White Lotuses

drang nges rnam 'byed kyi spyi don legs par bshad pa'i snying po padma dkar po'i 'phreng ba

Indian ed., n.d. [Photocopy provided by Geshe Lobsang Tharchin]. Also: *Supplementary Texts for the Study of the Perfection of Wisdom at Sera Mey Tibetan Monastic University,* vol. 1, 1-50. Bylakuppe, India: The Computer Center, Sera Mey, 1990.

Decisive Analysis of (Dzong-ka-ba's) "Differentiating the Interpretable and the Definitive"

mkhas grub smra ba'i khyu mchog dge 'dun bstan dar ba chen po'i gsung drang nges rnam 'byed kyi mtha dpyod

Indian ed., n.d. [Photocopy provided by Geshe Lobsang Tharchin]. Also: *Supplementary Texts for the Study of the Perfection of Wisdom at Sera Mey Tibetan Monastic University,* vol. 1, 51-153. Bylakuppe, India: The Computer Center, Sera Mey, 1990.

Dharmakīrti (*chos kyi grags pa,* seventh century)

Seven Treatises on Valid Cognition

1. *Analysis of Relations*
   sambandhaparīkṣā
   'brel pa brtag pa
   P5713, vol. 130
2. *Ascertainment of Prime Cognition*
   pramāṇaviniścaya
   tshad ma rnam par nges pa
   P5710, vol. 130
3. *Commentary on (Dignāga's) "Compilation of Prime Cognition"*
   pramāṇavārttikakārikā
   tshad ma rnam 'grel gyi tshig le'ur byas pa
   P5709, vol. 130. Also: Sarnath, India: Pleasure of Elegant Sayings Press, 1974.
   Sanskrit: Dwarikadas Shastri. *Pramāṇavārttika of Āchārya Dharmakīrtti.* Varanasi, India: Bauddha Bharati, 1968. Also, Yūsho Miyasaka. "Pramāṇavarttika-Kārikā (Sanskrit and Tibetan)," *Acta Indologica* 2 (1971-1972): 1-206. Also, (chap. 1 and autocommentary) Raniero Gnoli. *The Pramāṇavārttikam of Dharmakīrti: The First Chapter with the Autocommentary.* Rome: Istituto Italiano per il Medio ed Estremo Oriente, 1960.
   English translation (chap. 2): Masatoshi Nagatomi. "A Study of Dharmakīrti's Pramāṇavarttika: An English Translation and Annotation of the Pramāṇavarttika, Book I." Ph.D. diss., Harvard University, 1957.
   English translation (chap. 4, stanzas 1-148): Tom J.F. Tillemans. *Dharmakīrti's Pramāṇavārttika: An Annotated Translation of the Fourth Chapter (parārthānumāna),* vol. 1. Vienna: Verlag der Osterreichischen Akademie der Wissenschaften, 2000.
4. *Drop of Reasoning*
   nyāyabinduprakaraṇa
   rigs pa'i thigs pa zhes bya ba'i rab tu byed pa
   P5711, vol. 130
   English translation: Th. Stcherbatsky. *Buddhist Logic.* New York: Dover Publications, 1962.
5. *Drop of Reasons*

hetubindunāmaprakaraṇa
gtan tshigs kyi thigs pa zhes bya ba rab tu byed pa
P5712, vol. 130
6. *Principles of Debate*
vādanyāya
rtsod pa'i rigs pa
P5715, vol. 130
7. *Proof of Other Continuums*
saṃtānāntarasiddhināmaprakaraṇa
rgyud gzhan grub pa zhes bya ba'i rab tu byed pa
P5716, vol. 130

Dignāga (*phyogs kyi glangs po,* sixth century)
Compilation of Prime Cognition
pramāṇasamuccaya
tshad ma kun las btus pa
P5700, vol. 130
English translation (partial): M. Hattori. *Dignāga, On Perception.* Cambridge, Mass.: Harvard University Press, 1968.
Examination of Objects of Observation
ālambanaparīkṣa
dmigs pa brtag pa
P5703, vol. 130
Summary Meanings of the Eight Thousand Stanza Perfection of Wisdom Sūtra
prajñāpāramitāpiṇḍārtha / prajñāpāramitāsaṃgrahakārikā
brgyad stong don bsdus / shes rab kyi pha rol tu phyin ma bsdus pa'i tshig le'ur byas pa
P5207, vol. 94

Dön-drup-gyel-tsen (*don grub rgyal mtshan;* fl. late eighteenth- and early nineteenth centuries)
Four Intertwined Commentaries / Extensive Explanation of (Ḏzong-ka-ḇa's) "Treatise Differentiating the Interpretable and the Definitive, The Essence of Eloquence," Unique to Ge-luk-ḇa: Four Intertwined Commentaries
dge ldan thun mon ma yin pa drang ba dang nges pa'i don rnam par phye ba'i bstan bcos legs bshad snying po'i rgya cher bshad pa drang nges bzhi 'dril
New Delhi: Chophel Legdan, 1975.

Ḏra-ḏi Ge-ṡhay Rin-chen-dön-drup (*rin chen don grub, pra sti dge bshes;* fl. mid-seventeenth century)
Ornament for the Thought / Ornament for the Thought of (Ḏzong-ka-ḇa's) "Interpretable and Definitive: The Essence of Eloquence"
drang nges legs bshad snying po'i dgongs rgyan
Bylakuppe, India: Sera Je Printing Press: 1989.

Ḏzong-ka-ḇa Ḻo-sang-drak-ḇa (*tsong kha pa blo bzang grags pa,* 1357-1419)
Explanation of (Nāgārjuna's) "Treatise on the Middle": Ocean of Reasoning / Great Commentary on (Nāgārjuna's) "Treatise on the Middle"
dbu ma rtsa ba'i tshig le'ur byas pa shes rab ces bya ba'i rnam bshad rigs pa'i rgya mtsho / rtsa shes ṭik chen
P6153, vol. 156. Also: Sarnath, India: Pleasure of Elegant Sayings Printing Press, n.d. Also: *rJe tsong kha pa'i gsung dbu ma'i lta ḇa'i skor,* vols. 1-2. Sarnath, India: Pleasure of Elegant Sayings Press, 1975. Also: Delhi: Ngawang Gelek, 1975. Also: Delhi: Guru Deva, 1979.
English translation (chap. 2): Jeffrey Hopkins. *Ocean of Reasoning.* Dharmsala, India: Library of Tibetan Works and Archives, 1974.
Extensive Commentary on the Difficult Points of the Mind-Basis-of-All and Afflicted Mentality: Ocean of Eloquence
yid dang kun gzhi'i dka' ba'i gnas rgya cher 'grel pa legs par bshad pa'i rgya mtsho
P6149, vol. 154. Also: Delhi: Ngawang Gelek, 1975. Also: Delhi: Guru Deva, 1979.
English translation: Gareth Sparham. *Ocean of Eloquence: Tsong kha pa's Commentary on the*

Yogācāra Doctrine of Mind. Albany, N.Y.: State University of New York Press, 1993.

Extensive Explanation of (Chandrakīrti's) "Supplement to (Nāgārjuna's) 'Treatise on the Middle'": Illumination of the Thought

dbu ma la 'jug pa'i rgya cher bshad pa dgongs pa rab gsal

P6143, vol. 154. Also: Sarnath, India: Pleasure of Elegant Sayings Press, 1973. Also: Delhi: Ngawang Gelek, 1975. Also: Delhi: Guru Deva, 1979.

English translation (chapters 1-5): Jeffrey Hopkins. *Compassion in Tibetan Buddhism,* 93-230. Ithaca, N.Y.: Snow Lion, 1980.

English translation (chap. 6, stanzas 1-7): Jeffrey Hopkins and Anne C. Klein. *Path to the Middle: Madhyamaka Philosophy in Tibet: The Oral Scholarship of Kensur Yeshay Tupden,* by Anne C. Klein, 147-183, 252-271. Albany, N.Y.: State University of New York Press, 1994.

Golden Rosary of Eloquence / Extensive Explanation of (Maitreya's) "Ornament for Clear Realization, Treatise of Quintessential Instructions on the Perfection of Wisdom" as Well as Its Commentaries: Golden Rosary of Eloquence

legs bshad gser 'phreng / shes rab kyi pha rol tu phyin pa'i man ngag gi bstan bcos mngon par rtogs pa'i rgyan 'grel pa dang bcas pa'i rgya cher bshad pa legs bshad gser gyi phreng ba

P6150, vols. 154-155. Also: Delhi: Ngawang Gelek, 1975. Also: Delhi: Guru Deva, 1979.

Great Exposition of Secret Mantra / The Stages of the Path to a Conqueror and Pervasive Master, a Great Vajradhara: Revealing All Secret Topics

sngags rim chen mo / rgyal ba khyab bdag rdo rje 'chang chen po'i lam gyi rim pa gsang ba kun gyi gnad rnam par phye ba

P6210, vol. 161. Also: Delhi: Ngawang Gelek, 1975. Also: Delhi: Guru Deva, 1979.

English translation (chap. 1): H.H. the Dalai Lama, Tsong-ka-pa, and Jeffrey Hopkins. *Tantra in Tibet.* London: George Allen and Unwin, 1977; reprint, with minor corrections, Ithaca, N.Y.: Snow Lion, 1987.

English translation (chaps. 2-3): H.H. the Dalai Lama, Tsong-ka-pa, and Jeffrey Hopkins. *The Yoga of Tibet.* London: George Allen and Unwin, 1981; reprinted as *Deity Yoga.* Ithaca, N.Y.: Snow Lion, 1987.

Great Exposition of the Stages of the Path / Stages of the Path to Enlightenment Thoroughly Teaching All the Stages of Practice of the Three Types of Beings

lam rim chen mo / skyes bu gsum gyi nyams su blang ba'i rim pa thams cad tshang bar ston pa'i byang chub lam gyi rim pa

P6001, vol. 152. Also: Dharmsala, India: Tibetan Cultural Printing Press, 1964. Also: Delhi: Ngawang Gelek, 1975. Also: Delhi: Guru Deva, 1979.

English translation: Tsong-kha-pa, *The Great Treatise on the Stages of the Path to Enlightenment,* vols. 1-3, trans. and ed. Joshua W. C. Cutler and Guy Newland. Ithaca, N.Y.: Snow Lion, 2000-2003.

English translation of the part on the excessively broad object of negation: Elizabeth Napper. *Dependent-Arising and Emptiness,* 153-215. London: Wisdom, 1989.

English translation of the parts on calm abiding and special insight: Alex Wayman. *Calming the Mind and Discerning the Real,* 81-431. New York: Columbia University Press, 1978; reprint, New Delhi: Motilal Banarsidass, 1979.

Medium Exposition of the Stages of the Path / Small Exposition of the Stages of the Path to Enlightenment

lam rim 'bring / lam rim chung ngu / skyes bu gsum gyi nyams su blang ba'i byang chub lam gyi rim pa

P6002, vols. 152-153. Also: Dharmsala, India: Tibetan Cultural Printing Press, 1968. Also: Mundgod, India: dga' ldan shar rtse, n.d. (includes outline of topics by Trijang Rinbochay). Also: Delhi: Ngawang Gelek, 1975. Also: Delhi: Guru Deva, 1979.

English translation of the section on special insight: Robert Thurman. "The Middle Transcendent Insight." *Life and Teachings of Tsong Khapa,* 108-185. Dharmsala, India: Library of Tibetan Works and Archives, 1982.

English translation of the section on special insight: Jeffrey Hopkins. "Special Insight: From Ḏzong-ka-ḇa's *Middling Exposition of the Stages of the Path to Enlightenment Practiced by Persons of Three Capacities,* with supplementary headings by Trijang Rinbochay." Unpublished manuscript.

Praise of Dependent-Arising / Praise of the Supramundane Victor Buddha from the Approach of His Teaching the Profound Dependent-Arising: The Essence of Eloquence

rten 'brel bstod pa / sang rgyas bcom ldan 'das la zab mo rten cing 'brel bar 'byung ba gsung ba'i sgo nas bstod pa legs par bshad pa'i snying po

P6016, vol. 153. Also: Delhi: Ngawang Gelek, 1975. Also: Delhi: Guru Deva, 1979.

English translation: Geshe Wangyal. *The Door of Liberation,* 175-86. New York: Maurice Girodias Associates, 1973; reprint, New York: Lotsawa, 1978; rev. ed., Boston: Wisdom, 1995. Also: Robert Thurman. *Life and Teachings of Tsong Khapa,* 99-107. Dharmsala, India: Library of Tibetan Works and Archives, 1982.

Treatise Differentiating the Interpretable and the Definitive: The Essence of Eloquence

drang ba dang nges pa'i don rnam par phye ba'i bstan bcos legs bshad snying po

Editions: see the preface to my critical edition, *Emptiness in Mind-Only,* 355. Also: Ye shes thabs mkhas. *shar tsong kha pa blo bzang grags pas mdzad pa'i drang ba dang nges pa'i don rnam par phye ba'i bstan bcos legs bshad snying po.* Tā la'i bla ma'i 'phags bod, vol. 22. Varanasi, India: vāṇa dbus bod kyi ches mtho'i gtsug lag slob gnyer khang, 1997.

English translation: Prologue and Mind-Only section translated in this book. Also: Robert A. F. Thurman. *Tsong Khapa's Speech of Gold in the Essence of True Eloquence,* 185-385. Princeton, N.J.: Princeton University Press, 1984.

Chinese translation: Venerable Fa Zun. "Bian Liao Yi Bu Liao Yi Shuo Cang Lun." In *Xi Zang Fo Jiao Jiao Yi Lun Ji,* 2, 159-276. Taipei: Da Sheng Wen Hua Chu Ban She, 1979.

Gen-dün-drup, First Dalai Lama (*dge 'dun grub,* 1391-1474)

Explanation of [Vasubandhu's] "Treasury of Manifest Knowledge": Illuminating the Path to Liberation

dam pa'i chos mngon pa'i mdzod kyi rnam par bshad pa thar lam gsal byed

Collected Works of the First Dalai Lama dge-'dun-grub-pa, vol. 3. Gangtok, Sikkim: Dodrup Lama, 1978-1981. Also: Buxaduor, India: n.p., 1967. Also: Sarnath, India: wa na mtho' slob dge ldan spyi las khang, 1973.

English translation (chapters 1-5): David Patt. *Elucidating the Path to Liberation.* Ann Arbor, Mich.: University Microfilms, 1994.

English translation (chap. 6): Harvey B. Aronson, "The Buddhist Path: A Translation of the Sixth Chapter of the First Dalai Lama's *Path of Liberation.*" *Tibet Journal* 5, no. 3 (1980):29-51; 5, no. 4 (1980):28-47; 12, no. 2 (1987):25-40; 12, no. 3 (1987):41-61.

Great Treatise on Valid Cognition: Adornment of Reasoning

tshad ma'i bstan bcos chen po rigs pa'i rgyan

Collected Works of the First Dalai Lama dge-'dun-grub-pa. Gangtok, Sikkim: Dodrup Lama, 1978-81.

Gen-dün-gya-tso, Second Dalai Lama (*dge 'dun rgya mtsho,* 1476-1542)

Lamp Illuminating the Meaning / Commentary on the Difficult Points of "Differentiating the Interpretable and the Definitive" from the Collected Works of the Foremost Holy Omniscient [Ḏzong-ka-ḇa]: Lamp Thoroughly Illuminating the Meaning of His Thought

rje btsun thams cad mkhyen pa'i gsung 'bum las drang nges rnam 'byed kyi dka' 'grel dgongs pa'i don rab tu gsal bar byed pa'i sgron me

n.d. [blockprint borrowed from the library of H.H. the Dalai Lama and photocopied] volume *'a*

Ḡön-chok-jik-may-w̄ang-ḇo (*dkon mchog 'jigs med dbang po,* 1728-1791)

Precious Garland of Tenets / Presentation of Tenets: A Precious Garland

grub pa'i mtha'i rnam par bzhag pa rin po che'i phreng ba

Tibetan: K. Mimaki. Le Grub mtha' rnam bzhag rin chen phreṅ ba de dkon mchog 'jigs med dbaṅ po (1728-1791), *Zinbun* [The Research Institute for Humanistic Studies, Kyoto University], 14 (1977):55-112. Also, Collected Works of dkon-mchog-'jigs-med-dbaṅ-po, vol. 6, 485-535. New Delhi: Ngawang Gelek Demo, 1972. Also: Xylograph in thirty-two folios from the Lessing collection of the rare book section of the University of Wisconsin Library, which is item 47 in Leonard Zwilling. *Tibetan Blockprints in the Department of Rare Books and Special Collections.*

Madison, Wis.: University of Wisconsin-Madison Libraries, 1984. Also: Mundgod, India: blo gsal gling Press, 1980. Also: Dharmsala, India: Tibetan Cultural Printing Press, 1967. Also: Dharmsala, India: Teaching Training, n.d. Also: A blockprint edition in twenty-eight folios obtained in 1987 from Go-mang College in Hla-s̄a, printed on blocks that predate the Cultural Revolution.

English translation: Geshe Lhundup Sopa and Jeffrey Hopkins. *Practice and Theory of Tibetan Buddhism,* 48-145. New York: Grove, 1976; rev. ed., *Cutting Through Appearances: Practice and Theory of Tibetan Buddhism,* 109-322. Ithaca, N.Y.: Snow Lion, 1989. Also: H. V. Guenther. *Buddhist Philosophy in Theory and Practice.* Baltimore, Md.: Penguin, 1972. Also, the chapters on the Autonomy School and the Consequence School: Shōtarō Iida. *Reason and Emptiness,* 27-51. Tokyo: Hokuseido, 1980.

Gung-ru Chö-jung / Gung-ru Chö-ḡyi-jung-n̄ay (*gung ru chos 'byung / gung ru chos kyi 'byung gnas;* fl. most likely in sixteenth century, since he refutes positions like those of Paṇ-chen S̄ö-nam-drak-b̄a and Jay-d̄zün Chö-ḡyi-gyel-tsen)

Garland of White Lotuses / Decisive Analysis of (D̄zong-ka-b̄a's) "Differentiating the Interpretable and the Definitive, The Essence of Eloquence": Garland of White Lotuses

drang ba dang nges pa'i rnam par 'byed pa legs bshad snying po zhes bya ba'i mtha' dpyod padma dkar po'i phreng ba

sku bum, Tibet: sku bum Monastery, n.d. [blockprint obtained by the author in 1988].

Gung-tang Ḡön-chok-d̄en-b̄ay-drön-may (*gung thang dkon mchog bstan pa'i sgron me,* 1762-1823)

Annotations / Beginnings of Annotations on (D̄zong-ka-b̄a's) "The Essence of Eloquence" on the Topic of Mind-Only: Illumination of a Hundred Mind-Only Texts

bstan bcos legs par bshad pa'i snying po las sems tsam skor gyi mchan 'grel rtsom 'phro rnam rig gzhung brgya'i snang ba

Collected Works of Guṅ-thaṅ Dkon-mchog-bstan-pa'i-sgron-me, vol. 1, 725-876. New Delhi: Ngawang Gelek Demo, 1975. Also: Go-mang, n.d. [ed. printed in India with fixed type].

Difficult Points / Beginnings of a Commentary on the Difficult Points of (D̄zong-ka-b̄a's) "Differentiating the Interpretable and the Definitive": Quintessence of "The Essence of Eloquence"

drang nges rnam 'byed kyi dka' 'grel rtsom 'phro legs bshad snying po'i yang snying

Collected Works of Guṅ-thaṅ Dkon-mchog-bstan-pa'i-sgron-me, vol. 1, 403-723. New Delhi: Ngawang Gelek Demo, 1975. Also: Sarnath, India: Guru Deva, 1965.

Gyel-tsap-dar-ma-rin-chen (*rgyal tshab dar ma rin chen,* 1364-1432)

Commentary on (Maitreya's) "Sublime Continuum of the Great Vehicle" / Commentary on (Maitreya's) "Treatise on the Later Scriptures of the Great Vehicle"

theg pa chen po rgyud bla ma'i ṭīkka

Collected Works of Rgyal-tshab Dar-ma-rin-chen, vol. 2 (entire). Delhi: Guru Deva, 1982. Also: Collected Works of Rgyal-tshab Dar-ma-rin-chen, vol. 2 (entire). Delhi: Ngawang Gelek Demo, 1981. Also: blockprint in the library of H.H. the Dalai Lama, no other data.

Haribhadra (*seng ge bzang po,* late eighth century)

Clear Meaning Commentary / Commentary on (Maitreya's) "Ornament for Clear Realization, Treatise of Quintessential Instructions on the Perfection of Wisdom"

spuṭhārtha / abhisamayālaṃkāranāmaprajñāpāramitopadeśaśāstravṛtti

'grel pa don gsal / shes rab kyi pha rol tu phyin pa'i man ngag gi bstan bcós mngon par rtogs pa'i rgyan ces bya ba'i 'grel pa

P5191, vol. 90

Sanskrit: Unrai Wogihara. *Abhisamayālaṃkārālokā Prajñā-pāramitā-vyākhyā, The Work of Haribhadra.* 7 vols. Tokyo: Toyo Bunko, 1932-1935; reprint, Tokyo: Sankibo Buddhist Book Store, 1973.

Jam-ȳang-shay-b̄a Nga-w̄ang-d̄zön-drü (*'jam dbyangs bzhad pa ngag dbang brtson grus,* 1648-1722)

Brief Decisive Analysis of (D̄zong-ka-b̄a's) "Differentiating the Interpretable and the Definitive"

Collected Works of 'Jam-dbyaṅs-bźad-pa'i-rdo-rje, vol. 12, 473-456. New Delhi: Ngawang Gelek Demo, 1973.

Decisive Analysis of (Maitreya's) "Ornament for Clear Realization" / Decisive Analysis of the Treatise

(Maitreya's) "Ornament for Clear Realization": Precious Lamp Illuminating All of the Meaning of the Perfection of Wisdom

bstan gcos mngon par rtogs pa'i rgyan gyi mtha' dpyod shes rab kyi pha rol tu phyin pa'i don kun gsal ba'i rin chen sgron me

Collected Works of 'Jam-dbyaṅs-bźad-pa'i-rdo-rje, vols. 7-8 (entire). New Delhi: Ngawang Gelek Demo, 1973. Also: Sarnath, India: Guru Deva, 1965.

Great Exposition of the Interpretable and the Definitive / Decisive Analysis of (Dzong-ka-ba's) "Differentiating the Interpretable and the Definitive": Storehouse of White Lapis-Lazuli of Scripture and Reasoning Free from Error: Fulfilling the Hopes of the Fortunate

drang ba dang nges pa'i don rnam par 'byed pa'i mtha' dpyod 'khrul bral lung rigs bai dūr dkar pa'i gan mdzod skal bzang re ba kun skong

Edition cited: Buxaduor: n.d. Also: Collected Works of 'Jam-dbyaṅs-bźad-pa'i-rdo-rje, vol. 11, 3-288. New Delhi: Ngawang Gelek Demo, 1973. Also: dga' ldan pho phrang [blockprint obtained by the author in 1987].

Great Exposition of the Middle / Analysis of (Chandrakīrti's) "Supplement to (Nāgārjuna's) 'Treatise on the Middle'": Treasury of Scripture and Reasoning, Thoroughly Illuminating the Profound Meaning [of Emptiness], Entrance for the Fortunate

dbu ma chen mo / dbu ma la 'jug pa'i mtha' dpyod lung rigs gter mdzod zab don kun gsal skal bzang 'jug ngogs

Edition cited: Buxaduor, India: Go-mang, 1967. Also: Collected Works of 'Jam-dbyaṅs-bźad-pa'i-rdo-rje, vol. 9 (entire). New Delhi: Ngawang Gelek Demo, 1973.

Great Exposition of Tenets / Explanation of "Tenets": Sun of the Land of Samantabhadra Brilliantly Illuminating All of Our Own and Others' Tenets and the Meaning of the Profound [Emptiness], Ocean of Scripture and Reasoning Fulfilling All Hopes of All Beings

grub mtha' chen mo / grub mtha'i rnam bshad rang gzhan grub mtha' kun dang zab don mchog tu gsal ba kun bzang zhing gi nyi ma lung rigs rgya mtsho skye dgu'i re ba kun skong

Edition cited: Musoorie, India: Dalama, 1962. Also: Collected Works of 'Jam-dbyaṅs-bźad-pa'i-rdo-rje, vol. 14 (entire). New Delhi: Ngawang Gelek Demo, 1973. Also: Mundgod, India: Drepung Gomang Library, 1999.

English translation (entire root text and edited portions of the auto-commentary and Nga-w̄ang-b̄el-den's *Annotations*): Jeffrey Hopkins. *Maps of the Profound: Jam-yang-shay-ba's Great Exposition of Buddhist and Non-Buddhist Views on the Nature of Reality.* Ithaca, N.Y.: Snow Lion Publications, 2003.

English translation (beginning of the chapter on the Consequence School): Jeffrey Hopkins. *Meditation on Emptiness,* 581-697. London: Wisdom, 1983; rev. ed., Boston: Wisdom, 1996.

Notes on (Dzong-ka-ba's) "Differentiating the Interpretable and the Definitive"

'jam dbyangs bzhad pa'i rdo rjes mdzad pa'i drang nges rnam 'byed kyi zin bris

Collected Works of 'Jam-dbyaṅs-bźad-pa'i-rdo-rje, vol. 11, 289-331. New Delhi: Ngawang Gelek Demo, 1973.

J̄ang-ḡya Röl-b̄ay-dor-jay (*lcang skya rol pa'i rdo rje,* 1717-1786)

Presentations of Tenets / Clear Exposition of the Presentations of Tenets: Beautiful Ornament for the Meru of the Subduer's Teaching

grub mtha'i rnam bzhag / grub pa'i mtha'i rnam par bzhag pa gsal bar bshad pa thub bstan lhun po'i mdzes rgyan

Edition cited: Varanasi, India: Pleasure of Elegant Sayings Printing Press, 1970. Also: Lokesh Chandra, ed. *Buddhist Philosophical Systems of Lcaṅ-skya Rol-pahi Rdo-rje.* Śata-piṭaka Series (Indo-Asian Literatures), vol. 233. New Delhi: International Academy of Indian Culture, 1977. Also: An edition published by gam car phan bde legs bshad gling grva tshang dang rgyud rnying slar gso tshogs pa, 1982.

English translation of Sautrāntika chapter: Anne C. Klein. *Knowing, Naming, and Negation,* 115-196. Ithaca, N.Y.: Snow Lion, 1988. Commentary on this: Anne C. Klein. *Knowledge and Liberation: A Buddhist Epistemological Analysis in Support of Transformative Religious Experience: Tibetan Interpretations of Dignāga and Dharmakīrti.* Ithaca, N.Y.: Snow Lion, 1986.

English translation of Svātantrika chapter: Donald S. Lopez Jr. *A Study of Svātantrika,* 243-386. Ithaca, N.Y.: Snow Lion, 1986.

English translation of part of Prāsaṅgika chapter: Jeffrey Hopkins. *Emptiness Yoga: The Middle Way Consequence School,* 355-428. Ithaca, N.Y.: Snow Lion, 1983.

Jay-d̄zün Chö-ḡyi-gyel-tsen (*rje btsun chos kyi rgyal mtshan,* 1469-1546)

General-Meaning Commentary / General Meaning of (D̄zong-ka-b̄a's) "Differentiating the Interpretable and the Definitive": Eradicating Bad Disputation: A Precious Garland

drang nges rnam 'byed kyi spyi don rgol ngan tshar gcod rin po che'i phreng ba

Edition cited: Bylakuppe, India: Se-ra Byes Monastery, 1977. Also: Sarnath, India: Guru Deva, 1965. Also: Lhasa, Tibet: par pa dpal ldan, 1987.

Jik-may-dam-chö-gya-tso (*'jigs med dam chos rgya mtsho*); poetic name Mi-pam-ȳang-j̄en-gye-b̄ay-dor-jay (*mi pham dbyangs can dgyes* [or *dges*] *pa'i rdo rje;* 1898-1946)

Port of Entry / Treatise Distinguishing All the Meanings of (D̄zong-ka-b̄a's) "The Essence of Eloquence": Illuminating the Differentiation of the Interpretable and the Definitive: Port of Entry to "The Essence of Eloquence"

drang ba dang nges pa'i don rnam par phye ba gsal bar byed pa legs bshad snying po'i don mtha' dag rnam par 'byed pa'i bstan bcos legs bshad snying po'i 'jug ngogs

bkra shis chos sde, India: 199-?.

Jin-b̄a-dar-gyay, Ga-jang (*sbyin pa dar rgyas, dga' byang*)

Brief Illumination of the Difficult Points of (D̄zong-ka-b̄a's) "Differentiating the Interpretable and the Definitive": Mirror Illuminating Eloquence

drang nges rnam 'byed kyi dka' gnad gsal bar byed pa bsdus don legs bshad gsal ba'i me long

Buxaduor, India: no other data.

Ke-drup-ge-lek-b̄el-sang (*mkhas grub dge legs dpal bzang,* 1385-1438)

Compilation on Emptiness / Opening the Eyes of the Fortunate: Treatise Brilliantly Clarifying the Profound Emptiness

stong thun chen mo / zab mo stong pa nyid rab tu gsal bar byed pa'i bstan bcos skal bzang mig 'byed

Collected Works of the Lord Mkhas-grub rje dge-legs-dpal-bzaṅ-po, vol. 1, 179-702 (edition cited). New Delhi: Guru Deva, 1980. Also: Collected Works of Mkhas-grub dge-legs dpal, vol. 1, 125-482. New Delhi: Ngawang Gelek Demo, 1983. Also: New Delhi: n.p., 1972.

English translation: José Ignacio Cabezón. *A Dose of Emptiness: An Annotated Translation of the* stong thun chen mo *of mKhas grub dGe legs dpal bzang,* 21-388. Albany, N.Y.: State University of New York Press, 1992.

English translation of the chapter on the Mind-Only School: Jeffrey Hopkins. *Ke-drup's "Opening the Eyes of the Fortunate": The Mind-Only School.* Unpublished manuscript.

L̄o-sang-trin-lay-ye-s̄hay (*blo bzang 'phrin las ye shes,* perhaps 1642-1708)

Summarized Meaning of (D̄zong-ka-b̄a's) "Differentiation of the Interpretable and the Definitive: The Essence of Eloquence": Ornament for the Necks of Youths with Clear Intelligence

drang ba dang nges pa'i don rnam par 'byed pa'i bstan bcos legs bshad snying po'i don bsdus blo gsal gzhon nu'i mgul rgyan

Edition cited: Bylakuppe, Mysore: The Computer Center, Sera Mey Monastic University, 1990.

Also: Lhasa: S̄e-ra, 1988. Also: Indian edition, n.d. [photocopy provided by Geshe Lobsang Tharchin]

L̄o-sang-w̄ang-chuk (*blo bzang dbang phyug,* 1901-1979)

Notes on (D̄zong-ka-b̄a's) "Interpretable and Definitive, The Essence of Eloquence": Lamp for the Intelligent

drang nges legs par bshad pa'i snying po'i zin bris blo gsal sgron me: *Notes on the Art of Interpretation: A Lamp to Light the Mind,* being a commentary on Je Tsongkapa's *Essence of Good Explanation*

Bylakuppe, India: Sera Jey Tibetan Monastic University, 1993.

Maitreya (*byams pa*)

Five Doctrines of Maitreya

1. *Sublime Continuum of the Great Vehicle / Treatise on the Later Scriptures of the Great Vehicle*
 mahāyānottaratantraśāstra
 theg pa chen po rgyud bla ma'i bstan bcos
 P5525, vol. 108
 Sanskrit: E. H. Johnston (and T. Chowdhury). *The Ratnagotravibhāga Mahāyānottaratantraśāstra.* Patna, India: Bihar Research Society, 1950.
 English translation: E. Obermiller. "Sublime Science of the Great Vehicle to Salvation." *Acta Orientalia* 9 (1931):81-306. Also: J. Takasaki. *A Study on the Ratnagotravibhāga.* Rome: Istituto Italiano per il Medio ed Estremo Oriente, 1966.
2. *Differentiation of Phenomena and the Final Nature of Phenomena*
 dharmadharmatāvibhaṅga
 chos dang chos nyid rnam par 'byed pa
 P5523, vol. 108
3. *Differentiation of the Middle and the Extremes*
 madhyāntavibhaṅga
 dbus dang mtha' rnam par 'byed pa
 P5522, vol. 108
 Sanskrit: Gadjin M. Nagao. *Madhyāntavibhāga-bhāṣya.* Tokyo: Suzuki Research Foundation, 1964. Also: Ramchandra Pandeya. *Madhyānta-vibhāga-śāstra.* Delhi: Motilal Banarsidass, 1971.
 English translation: Stefan Anacker. *Seven Works of Vasubandhu.* Delhi: Motilal Banarsidass, 1984. Also, of chapter 1: Thomas A. Kochumuttom. *A Buddhist Doctrine of Experience.* Delhi: Motilal Banarsidass, 1982. Also, of chapter 1: F. Th. Stcherbatsky. *Madhyāntavibhāga, Discourse on Discrimination between Middle and Extremes Ascribed to Bodhisattva Maitreya and Commented by Vasubandhu and Sthiramati.* Bibliotheca Buddhica, 30 (1936). Osnabrück, Germany: Biblio Verlag, 1970; reprint, Calcutta: Indian Studies Past and Present, 1971. Also, of chapter 1: David Lasar Friedmann. *Sthiramati, Madhyāntavibhāgaṭīkā: Analysis of the Middle Path and the Extremes.* Utrecht, Netherlands: Rijksuniversiteit te Leiden, 1937.
4. *Ornament for Clear Realization*
 abhisamayālaṃkāra
 mngon par rtogs pa'i rgyan
 P5184, vol. 88
 Sanskrit: Th. Stcherbatsky and E. Obermiller, eds. *Abhisamayālaṃkāra-Prajñāpāramitā-Upadeśa-Śāstra.* Bibliotheca Buddhica, 23. Osnabrück, Germany: Biblio Verlag, 1970.
 English translation: Edward Conze. *Abhisamayālaṃkāra.* Serie Orientale Rome. Rome: Istituto Italiano per il Medio ed Estremo Oriente, 1954.
5. *Ornament for the Great Vehicle Sūtras*
 mahāyānasūtrālaṃkāra
 theg pa chen po'i mdo sde rgyan gyi tshig le'ur byas pa
 P5521, vol. 108
 Sanskrit: Sitansusekhar Bagchi. *Mahāyāna-Sūtrālaṃkāraḥ of Asaṅga* [with Vasubandhu's commentary]. Buddhist Sanskrit Texts, 13. Darbhanga, India: Mithila Institute, 1970.
 Sanskrit text and translation into French: Sylvain Lévi. *Mahāyānasūtrālaṃkāra, exposé de la doctrine du grand véhicule selon le système Yogācāra.* 2 vols. Paris: Bibliothèque de l'École des Hautes Études, 1907, 1911.
 Sanskrit text and translation into English: Surekha Vijay Limaye. *Mahāyānasūtrālaṃkāra by Asaṅga.* Bibliotheca Indo-Buddhica Series, 94. Delhi: Sri Satguru, 1992.

Nāgārjuna (*klu sgrub,* first to second century C.E.)

Six Collections of Reasoning

1. *Precious Garland of Advice for the King*
 rājaparikathāratnāvalī
 rgyal po la gtam bya ba rin po che'i phreng ba

P5658, vol. 129

Sanskrit, Tibetan, and Chinese: Michael Hahn. *Nāgārjuna's Ratnāvalī*, vol. 1. *The Basic Texts (Sanskrit, Tibetan, and Chinese)*. Bonn: Indica et Tibetica Verlag, 1982.

English translation: Jeffrey Hopkins. *Buddhist Advice for Living and Liberation: Nāgārjuna's Precious Garland*, 94-164. Ithaca, N.Y.: Snow Lion, 1998. Supersedes that in: Nāgārjuna and the Seventh Dalai Lama. *The Precious Garland and the Song of the Four Mindfulnesses*, translated by Jeffrey Hopkins, 17-93. London: George Allen and Unwin, 1975; New York: Harper and Row, 1975; reprint, in H.H. the Dalai Lama, Tenzin Gyatso. *The Buddhism of Tibet*. London: George Allen and Unwin, 1983; reprint, Ithaca, N.Y.: Snow Lion, 1987.

English translation: John Dunne and Sara McClintock. *The Precious Garland: An Epistle to a King*. Boston: Wisdom, 1997.

English translation of chap. 1, 1-77: Giuseppe Tucci. "The *Ratnāvalī* of Nāgārjuna." *Journal of the Royal Asiatic Society* (1934):307-324; reprint, Giuseppe Tucci, *Opera Minora*, II. Rome: Giovanni Bardi Editore, 1971, 321-366. Chap. 2, 1-46; chap. 4, 1-100: Giuseppe Tucci. "The *Ratnāvalī* of Nāgārjuna." *Journal of the Royal Asiatic Society* (1936):237-252, 423-435.

Japanese translation: Uryūzu Ryushin. *Butten II, Sekai Koten Bungaku Zenshu*, 7 (July, 1965):349-372. Edited by Nakamura Hajime. Tokyo: Chikuma Shobō. Also: Uryūzu Ryushin. *Daijō Butten* 14 (1974):231-316. *Ryūju Ronshū*. Edited by Kajiyama Yuichi and Uryūzu Ryushin. Tokyo: Chūōkōronsha.

Danish translation: Christian Lindtner. *Nagarjuna, Juvelkaeden og andre skrifter*. Copenhagen: 1980.

2. *Refutation of Objections*
vigrahavyāvartanīkārikā
rtsod pa bzlog pa'i tshig le'ur byas pa
P5228, vol. 95

Edited Tibetan and Sanskrit: Christian Lindtner. *Nagarjuniana*, 70-86. Indiske Studier 4. Copenhagen: Akademisk Forlag, 1982.

Edited Sanskrit and English translation: K. Bhattacharya, E. H. Johnston, and A. Kunst. *The Dialectical Method of Nāgārjuna*. New Delhi: Motilal Banarsidass, 1978.

English translation from the Chinese: G. Tucci. *Pre-Diṅnāga Buddhist Texts on Logic from Chinese Sources*. Gaekwad's Oriental Series 49. Baroda, India: Oriental Institute, 1929.

French translation: S. Yamaguchi. "Traité de Nāgārjuna pour écarter les vaines discussion (Vigrahavyāvartanī) traduit et annoté." *Journal Asiatique* 215 (1929):1-86.

3. *Seventy Stanzas on Emptiness*
śūnyatāsaptatikārikā
stong pa nyid bdun cu pa'i tshig le'ur byas pa
P5227, vol. 95

Edited Tibetan and English translation: Christian Lindtner. *Nagarjuniana*, 34-69. Indiske Studier 4. Copenhagen: Akademisk Forlag, 1982.

English translation: David Ross Komito. *Nāgārjuna's "Seventy Stanzas": A Buddhist Psychology of Emptiness*. Ithaca, N.Y.: Snow Lion, 1987.

4. *Sixty Stanzas of Reasoning*
yuktiṣaṣṭikākārikā
rigs pa drug cu pa'i tshig le'ur byas pa
P5225, vol. 95

Edited Tibetan with Sanskrit fragments and English translation: Christian Lindtner. *Nagarjuniana*, 100-119. Indiske Studier 4. Copenhagen: Akademisk Forlag, 1982.

5. *Treatise Called the Finely Woven*
vaidalyasūtranāma
zhib mo rnam par 'thag pa zhes bya ba'i mdo
P5226, vol. 95

Tibetan text and English translation: Fermando Tola and Carmen Dragonetti. *Nāgārjuna's Refutation of Logic (Nyāya) Vaidalyaprakaraṇa*. Delhi: Motilal Banarsidass, 1995.

6. *Treatise on the Middle / Fundamental Treatise on the Middle, Called "Wisdom"*
madhyamakaśāstra / prajñānāmamūlamadhyamakakārikā
dbu ma'i bstan bcos / dbu ma rtsa ba'i tshig le'ur byas pa shes rab ces bya ba
P5224, vol. 95
Edited Sanskrit: J. W. de Jong. *Nāgārjuna, Mūlamadhyamakakārikāḥ*. Madras, India: Adyar Library and Research Centre, 1977; reprint, Wheaton, Ill.: Theosophical Publishing House, c. 1977. Also: Christian Lindtner. *Nāgārjuna's Filosofiske Vaerker*, 177-215. Indiske Studier 2. Copenhagen: Akademisk Forlag, 1982.
English translation: Frederick Streng. *Emptiness: A Study in Religious Meaning*. Nashville, Tenn.: Abingdon Press, 1967. Also: Kenneth Inada. *Nāgārjuna: A Translation of His Mūlamadhyamakakārikā*. Tokyo: Hokuseido Press, 1970. Also: David J. Kalupahana. *Nāgārjuna: The Philosophy of the Middle Way*. Albany, N.Y.: State University of New York Press, 1986. Also: Jay L. Garfield. *The Fundamental Wisdom of the Middle Way*. New York: Oxford University Press, 1995.
Italian translation: R. Gnoli. *Nāgārjuna: Madhyamaka Kārikā, Le stanze del cammino di mezzo*. Enciclopedia di autori classici 61. Turin, Italy: P. Boringhieri, 1961.
Danish translation: Christian Lindtner. *Nāgārjuna's Filosofiske Vaerker*, 67-135. Indiske Studier 2. Copenhagen: Akademisk Forlag, 1982.

Nga-w̄ang-b̄el-den (*ngag dbang dpal ldan*, b. 1797), also known as B̄el-den-chö-jay (*dpal ldan chos rje*)
Annotations for (Jam-ȳang-shay-b̄a's) "Great Exposition of Tenets": Freeing the Knots of the Difficult Points, Precious Jewel of Clear Thought
grub mtha' chen mo'i mchan 'grel dka' gnad mdud grol blo gsal gces nor
Sarnath, India: Pleasure of Elegant Sayings Press, 1964. Also: Collected Works of Chos-rje ṅag-dbaṅ Dpal-ldan of Urga, vols. 4 (entire)-5, 1-401. Delhi: Guru Deva, 1983.
Explanation of the Conventional and the Ultimate in the Four Systems of Tenets
grub mtha' bzhi'i lugs kyi kun rdzob dang don dam pa'i don rnam par bshad pa legs bshad dpyid kyi dpal mo'i glu dbyangs
New Delhi: Guru Deva, 1972. Also: Collected Works of Chos-rje ṅag-dbaṅ Dpal-ldan of Urga, vol. 1, 3-273. Delhi: Mongolian Lama Gurudeva, 1983.

Pa-bong-ka-b̄a Jam-b̄a-d̄en-dzin-trin-lay-gya-tso (*pha bong kha pa byams pa bstan 'dzin 'phrin las rgya mtsho*, 1878-1941)
Presentation of the Interpretable and the Definitive, Brief Notes on the Occasion of Receiving Profound [Instruction from J̄o-ne Paṇḍita L̄o-sang-gya-tso in 1927] on (D̄zong-ka-b̄a's) "The Essence of Eloquence"
drang ba dang nges pa'i don rnam par bzhag pa legs par bshad pa'i snying po'i zab nos skabs kyi zin bris mdo tsam du bkod pa
Collected Works of Pha-boṅ-kha-pa-bstan-'dzin-'phrin-las-rgya-mtsho, vol. 4, 400-476. New Delhi: Chophel Legdan, 1973.

Paṇ-chen S̄ö-nam-drak-b̄a (*paṇ chen bsod nams grags pa*, 1478-1554)
Distinguishing through Objections and Answers (D̄zong-ka-b̄a's) "Differentiating the Interpretable and Definitive Meanings of All the Scriptures, The Essence of Eloquence": Garland of Blue Lotuses
gsung rab kun gyi drang ba dang nges pa'i don rnam par 'byed pa legs par bshad pa'i snying po brgal lan gyis rnam par 'byed pa utpa la'i phreng ba
Collected Works (gsuṅ 'bum) of Paṇ-chen Bsod-nams-grags-pa, vol. 5. Mundgod, India: Drepung Loseling Library Society, 1982.

Puṇḍarīka, Kalkī (*rigs ldan pad ma dkar po*)
Great Commentary on the "Kālachakra Tantra": Stainless Light
vimālaprabhānāmamūlatantrānusāriṇīdvādaśasāhasrikālaghukālacakratantrarājaṭīkā
bsdus pa'i rgyud kyi rgyal po dus kyi 'khor lo'i 'grel bshad rtsa ba'i rgyud kyi rjes su 'jug pa stong phrag bcu gnyis pa dri ma med pa'i 'od ces bya ba
P2064, vol. 46
English translation of the first section: John Newman. "The Outer Wheel of Time: Vajrayāna Buddhist Cosmology in the Kālachakra Tantra." Ph.D. dissertation, Univ. of Wisconsin, 1987.

Ser-shül Ge-shay Lo-sang-pün-tsok (*blo bzang phun tshogs, ser shul dge bshes;* fl. early twentieth century)
Notes / Notes on (Dzong-ka-ba's) "Differentiating the Interpretable and the Definitive": Lamp Illuminating the Profound Meaning
drang nges rnam 'byed kyi zin bris zab don gsal ba'i sgron me
Delhi: n.p., 1974.

Sha-mar Ge-dün-den-dzin-gya-tso (*zhwa dmar dge 'dun bstan 'dzin rgya mtsho,* 1852-1912)
Notes Concerning Difficult Points in (Dzong-ka-ba's) "Differentiating the Interpretable and the Definitive, The Essence of Eloquence": Victorious Clearing Away Mental Darkness
drang nges legs bshad snying po'i dka gnas las brtsams pa'i zin bris bcom ldan yid kyi mun sel
n.d. [mentioned in Jik-may-dam-chö-gya-tso's *Port of Entry*]

Shay-rap-gyel-tsen, Döl-bo-ba (*shes rab rgyal mtshan, dol po pa,* 1292-1361)
The Mountain Doctrine: Ocean of Definitive Meaning
ri chos nges don rgya mtsho
Gangtok, Sikkim: Dodrup Sangyey Lama, 1976.
Also: 'dzam thang bsam 'grub nor bu'i gling, n.d.
Also: Matthew Kapstein. *The 'Dzam-thang Edition of the Collected Works of Kun-mkhyen Dol-po-pa Shes-rab-rgyal-mtshan: Introduction and Catalogue,* vol. 2, 25-707. Delhi: Shedrup Books, 1992.
Also: Beijing: mi rigs dpe skrun khang, 1998.
Condensed English translation: Jeffrey Hopkins. *The Mountain Doctrine: Ocean of Definitive Meaning.* Unpublished manuscript.

The Great Calculation of the Doctrine, Which Has the Significance of a Fourth Council
bka' bsdu bzhi pa'i don bstan rtsis chen po
Matthew Kapstein. *The 'Dzam-thang Edition of the Collected Works of Kun-mkhyen Dol-po-pa Shes-rab-rgyal-mtshan: Introduction and Catalogue,* vol. 5, 207-252. Delhi: Shedrup Books, 1992.
English translation: Cyrus R. Stearns. *The Buddha from Dol po: A Study of the Life and Thought of the Tibetan Master Dolpopa Sherab Gyaltsen,* 127-173. Albany, N.Y.: State University of New York Press, 1999.

Sthiramati (*blo gros brtan pa,* fl. late fourth century)
Explanation of (Vasubandhu's) "Commentary on (Maitreya's) 'Differentiation of the Middle and the Extremes'"
madhyāntavibhāgaṭīkā
dbus dang mtha' rnam par 'byed pa'i 'grel bshad / dbus mtha'i 'grel bshad
P5334, vol. 109
Sanskrit: Ramchandra Pandeya ed. *Madhyānta-vibhāga-śāstra.* Delhi: Motilal Banarsidass, 1971.
English translation (chap. 1): F. Th. Stcherbatsky. *Madhyāntavibhāga, Discourse on Discrimination between Middle and Extremes Ascribed to Bodhisattva Maitreya and Commented by Vasubandhu and Sthiramati.* Bibliotheca Buddhica, 30 (1936). Osnabrück, Germany: Biblio Verlag, 1970; reprint, Calcutta: Indian Studies Past and Present, 1971.
English translation (chap. 1): David Lasar Friedmann. *Sthiramati, Madhyānta-vibhāgaṭīkā: Analysis of the Middle Path and the Extremes.* Utrecht, Netherlands: Rijksuniversiteit te Leiden, 1937.

Explanation of (Vasubandhu's) "The Thirty"
triṃśikābhāṣya
sum cu pa'i bshad pa
P5565, vol. 113
Sanskrit: Sylvain Lévi. *Vijñaptimātratāsiddhi / Deux traités de Vasubandhu: Viṃśatikā (La Vingtaine) et Triṃsikā (La Trentaine).* Bibliothèque de l'École des Hautes Études, 245. Paris: Libraire Honoré Champion, 1925.
Tibetan: Enga Teramoto. *Sthiramati's Triṃçikābhāṣyaṃ (Sum-cu-paḥi ḥGrel-pa): A Tibetan Text.* Kyoto: Association for Linguistic Study of Sacred Scriptures, 1933.

Explanation of (Vasubandhu's) "Commentary of (Maitreya's) 'Ornament for the Great Vehicle Sūtras'"
sūtrālaṃkārāvṛttibhāṣya
mdo sde'i rgyan gyi 'grel bshad
P5531, vol. 108

Tsay-den-hla-ram-ba (*tshe brtan lha rams pa*); for his three texts, see the footnote on p. 81.

Vasubandhu (*dbyig gnyen*, fl. 360)

Commentary on (Asaṅga's) "Summary of the Great Vehicle"
mahāyānasaṃgrahabhāṣya
theg pa chen po bsdus pa'i 'grel pa
P5551, vol. 112

Commentary on (Maitreya's) "Differentiation of the Middle and the Extremes"
madhyāntavibhāgaṭīkā
dbus dang mtha' rnam par 'byed pa'i 'grel pa / dbus mtha'i 'grel pa
P5528, vol. 108
Sanskrit: Gadjin M. Nagao. *Madhyāntavibhāga-bhāṣya.* Tokyo: Suzuki Research Foundation, 1964. Also: Ramchandra Pandeya. *Madhyānta-vibhāga-śāstra.* Delhi: Motilal Banarsidass, 1971.
English translation: Stefan Anacker. *Seven Works of Vasubandhu.* Delhi: Motilal Banarsidass, 1984. Also: Thomas A. Kochumuttom. *A Buddhist Doctrine of Experience.* Delhi: Motilal Banarsidass, 1982. Also, of chapter 1: F. Th. Stcherbatsky. *Madhyāntavibhāga: Discourse on Discrimination between Middle and Extremes Ascribed to Bodhisattva Maitreya and Commented by Vasubandhu and Sthiramati.* Bibliotheca Buddhica, 30 (1936). Osnabrück, Germany: Biblio Verlag, 1970; reprint, Calcutta: Indian Studies Past and Present, 1971. Also, of chapter 1: David Lasar Friedmann, *Sthiramati, Madhyāntavibhāgaṭīkā: Analysis of the Middle Path and the Extremes.* Utrecht, Netherlands: Rijksuniversiteit te Leiden, 1937.

Explanation of (Maitreya's) "Ornament for the Great Vehicle Sūtras"
sūtrālaṃkārābhāṣya
mdo sde'i rgyan gyi bshad pa
P5527, vol. 108
Sanskrit: S. Bagchi. *Mahāyāna-Sūtrālaṃkāra of Asaṅga* [with Vasubandhu's commentary]. Buddhist Sanskrit Texts 13. Darbhanga, India: Mithila Institute, 1970.
Sanskrit and translation into French: Sylvain Lévi. *Mahāyānasūtrālaṃkāra, exposé de la doctrine du grand véhicule selon le système Yogācāra.* 2 vols. Paris: Libraire Honoré Champion, 1907, 1911.

Treasury of Manifest Knowledge
abhidharmakośakārikā
chos mngon pa'i mdzod kyi tshig le'ur byas pa
P5590, vol. 115
Sanskrit: Swami Dwarikadas Shastri. *Abhidharmakośa & Bhāṣya of Ācārya Vasubandhu with Sphuṭārtha Commentary of Ācārya Yaśomitra.* Bauddha Bharati Series 5. Banaras, India: Bauddha Bharati, 1970. Also: P. Pradhan. *Abhidharmakośabhāṣyam of Vasubandhu.* Patna, India: Jayaswal Research Institute, 1975.
French translation: Louis de la Vallée Poussin. *L'Abhidharmakośa de Vasubandhu.* 6 vols. Brussels: Institut Belge des Hautes Études Chinoises, 1971.
English translation of the French: Leo M. Pruden. *Abhidharmakośabhāṣyam.* 4 vols. Berkeley, Calif.: Asian Humanities Press, 1988.

The Thirty / Treatise on Cognition-Only in Thirty Stanzas
triṃśikākārikā / sarvavijñānamātradeśakatriṃśakakārikā
sum cu pa'i tshig le'ur byas pa / thams cad rnam rig tsam du ston pa sum cu pa'i tshig le'ur byas pa
P5556, vol. 113
Sanskrit: Sylvain Lévi. *Vijñaptimātratāsiddhi / Deux traités de Vasubandhu: Viṃśatikā (La Vingtaine) et Triṃsikā (La Trentaine).* Bibliotheque de l'École des Hautes Études. Paris: Libraire Honoré Champion, 1925. Also: K. N. Chatterjee. *Vijñapti-Mātratā-Siddhi (with Sthiramati's Commentary).* Varanasi, India: Kishor Vidya Niketan, 1980.
English translation: Stefan Anacker. *Seven Works of Vasubandhu.* Delhi: Motilal Banarsidass, 1984. Also: Thomas A. Kochumuttom. *A Buddhist Doctrine of Experience.* Delhi: Motilal Banarsidass, 1982.

The Twenty
viṃśatikā / viṃśikākārikā

nyi shu pa'i tshig le'ur byas pa

P5557, vol. 113

Sanskrit: Sylvain Lévi. *Vijñaptimātratāsiddhi / Deux traités de Vasubandhu: Viṃśatikā (La Vigtaine) et Triṃsikā (La Trentaine).* Bibliotheque de l'École des Hautes Études. Paris: Libraire Honoré Champion, 1925.

English translation: Stefan Anacker. *Seven Works of Vasubandhu.* Delhi: Motilal Banarsidass, 1984. Also: Thomas A. Kochumuttom. *A Buddhist Doctrine of Experience.* Delhi: Motilal Banarsidass, 1982.

English translation (stanzas 1-10): Gregory A. Hillis. *An Introduction and Translation of Vinitadeva's Explanation of the First Ten Stanzas of [Vasubandhu's] Commentary on His "Twenty Stanzas," with Appended Glossary of Technical Terms.* Ann Arbor, Mich.: University Microfilms, 1993.

Vinītadeva (*dul ba'i lha*)

Explanation of (Vasubandhu's) [Auto] Commentary on "The Thirty"

sum cu pa'i 'grel bshad

triṃśikāṭīkā

P5571, vol. 114

W̄el-mang Ḡön-chok-gyel-tsen (*dbal mang dkon mchog rgyal mtshan,* 1764-1853)

Notes on (Ḡön-chok-jik-may-w̄ang-b̄o's) Lectures / Notes on (Ḡön-chok-jik-may-w̄ang-b̄o's) Lectures on (D̄zong-ka-b̄a's) "The Essence of Eloquence": Stream of the Speech of the Omniscient: Offering for Purification

legs bshad snying po'i gsung bshad zin bris su bkod pa kun mkhyen gsung gi chu rgyun dag byed mchod yon

Collected Works of Dbal-maṅ Dkon-mchog-rgyal-mtshan, vol. 2, 376-464. New Delhi: Gyeltan Gelek Namgyal, 1974.

Wonch'uk (Tib. *rdzogs gsal / wen tshig / wen tshegs / wanydzeg,* Chin. *Yüan-ts'e,* 613-696)

Extensive Commentary on the "Sūtra Unraveling the Thought"

'phags pa dgongs pa nges par 'grel pa'i mdo'i rgya cher 'grel pa

P5517, vol. 116

Chinese edition: *Dai-nihon Zokuzōkyō, hsü tsang ching,* 134.d-535.a. Hong Kong Reprint, 1922. Also: *Da Zang Jing,* vol. 34, 581-952, vol. 35, 1-100. Taipei: Xin Wen Fong, 1977. Reconstruction of the first portion of the eighth fascicle and all of the tenth fascicle: Inaba Shōju. *Enjiki Gejinmikkyōsho Sanitsububan no kanbunyaku.* Kyoto: Hōzōkan, 1949.

3. Other Works

Chimpa, Lama, and Alaka Chattopadhyaya. *Tāranātha's History of Buddhism in India.* Simla, India: Indian Institute of Advanced Study, 1970; reprint, Delhi: Motilal Banarsidass, 1990.

Cleary, Thomas. *Buddhist Yoga: A Comprehensive Course.* Boston: Shambhala, 1995.

Conze, E. *The Perfection of Wisdom in Eight Thousand Lines & Its Verse Summary.* Bolinas, Calif.: Four Seasons Foundation, 1973.

Cutler, Joshua W. C. and Guy Newland. *The Great Treatise on the Stages of the Path to Enlightenment.* vols. 1-3. Ithaca, N.Y.: Snow Lion, 2000-2003.

H.H. the Dalai Lama, Tenzin Gyatso. *The Buddhism of Tibet and the Key to the Middle Way.* Translated by Jeffrey Hopkins. London: George Allen and Unwin, 1975. Reprinted in a combined volume, *The Buddhism of Tibet.* London: George Allen and Unwin, 1983; reprint, Ithaca, N.Y.: Snow Lion, 1987.

Hall, Bruce Cameron. "The Meaning of Vijñapti in Vasubandhu's Concept of Mind." *Journal of the International Association of Buddhist Studies* 9, no. 1 (1986):7-23.

Hookham, S. K. *The Buddha Within: Tathāgatagarbha Doctrine according to the Shentong Interpretation of the Ratnagotravibhāga.* Albany, N.Y.: State University of New York Press, 1991.

Hopkins, Jeffrey. *Emptiness in the Mind-Only School of Buddhism.* Berkeley: University of California Press, 1999.

———. *Reflections on Reality: The Three Natures and Non-Natures in the Mind-Only School,* Dynamic Responses to Dzong-ka-ba's *The Essence of Eloquence,* Volume 2. (Berkeley: University of California Press, 2002)

Klein, Anne C. *Knowing, Naming, and Negation.* Ithaca, N.Y.: Snow Lion, 1988.

Lati Rinbochay, Denma Lochö Rinbochay, Leah Zahler, and Jeffrey Hopkins. *Meditative States in Tibetan Buddhism.* London: Wisdom, 1983; rev. ed., Boston: Wisdom, 1997.

La Vallée Poussin, Louis de. *Vijñaptimātratāsiddhi: La Siddhi de Hiuan-Tsang.* Paris: P. Geuthner, 1928-1929.

Nagao, Gadjin M. "What Remains in Śūnyatā? A Yogācāra Interpretation of Emptiness." In *Mahāyāna Buddhist Meditation, Theory and Practice,* edited by Minoru Kiyota, 66-82. Honolulu: University of Hawaii Press, 1978; reprinted in *Mādhyamika and Yogācāra: A Study of Mahāyāna Philosophies,* translated by Leslie S. Kawamura, 51-60. Albany, N.Y.: State University of New York Press, 1991.

Perdue, Daniel E. *Debate in Tibetan Buddhism.* Ithaca, N.Y.: Snow Lion, 1992.

Powers, C. John *The Concept of the Ultimate (don dam pa, paramārtha) in the Saṃdhinirmocana-sūtra: Analysis, Translation and Notes.* Ann Arbor, Mich.: University Microfilms, 1991.

———. *Hermeneutics and Tradition in the Saṃdhinirmocana-sūtra.* Leiden, Netherlands: E. J. Brill, 1993.

———. *The Yogācāra School of Buddhism: A Bibliography.* American Theological Library Association Bibliography Series 27. Metuchen, N.J., and London: American Theological Library Association and Scarecrow Press, 1991.

Roerich, George N. *The Blue Annals.* Delhi: Motilal Banarsidass, 1976.

Ruegg, David Seyfort. *The Literature of the Madhyamaka School of Philosophy in India.* Wiesbaden, Germany: Otto Harrassowitz, 1981.

Smith, E. Gene. *University of Washington Tibetan Catalogue.* 2 vols. Seattle: University of Washington Press, 1969.

Sponberg, Alan. "The Trisvabhāva Doctrine in India and China: A Study of Three Exegetical Models." *Bukkyō Bunka Kenkyū-jo Kiyō* 21 (1982):97-119.

Stearns, Cyrus R. *The Buddha from Dol po: A Study of the Life and Thought of the Tibetan Master Dolpopa Sherab Gyaltsen.* Albany, N.Y.: State University of New York Press, 1999.

———. "Dol-po-pa Shes-rab-rgyal-mtshan and the Genesis of the *gzhan-stong* Position in Tibet." *Asiatische Studien/Études Asiatiques* 59, no. 4 (1995):829-852.

Ueda, Yoshifumi. "Two Main Streams of Thought in Yogācāra Philosophy." *Philosophy East and West* 17 (January-October 1967):155-165.

Wayman, Alex, and H. Wayman. *The Lion's Roar of Queen Śrīmālā.* New York: Columbia University Press, 1974.

Wei Tat. *Ch'eng wei-shih lun, The Doctrine of Mere-Consciousness.* Hong Kong: Ch'eng Wei-Shih Lun Publication Committee, c. 1973.

Willis, Janice D. *On Knowing Reality: The Tattvārtha Chapter of Asaṅga's Bodhisattvabhūmi.* New York: Columbia University Press, 1979; reprint, Delhi: Motilal Banarsidass, 1982.

Wylie, Turrell. "A Standard System of Tibetan Transcription." *Harvard Journal of Asiatic Studies* 22 (1959):261-267.

Index